The Handbook
of Financing
Growth

Founded in 1807, John Wiley & Sons is the oldest independent publishing company in the United States. With offices in North America, Europe, Australia, and Asia, Wiley is globally committed to developing and marketing print and electronic products and services for our customers' professional and personal knowledge and understanding.

The Wiley Finance series contains books written specifically for finance and investment professionals as well as sophisticated individual investors and their financial advisors. Book topics range from portfolio management to e-commerce, risk management, financial engineering, valuation, and financial instrument analysis, as well as much more.

For a list of available titles, visit our Web site at www.WileyFinance.com.

The Handbook of Financing Growth

Strategies and Capital Structure

KENNETH H. MARKS
LARRY E. ROBBINS
GONZALO FERNÁNDEZ
JOHN P. FUNKHOUSER

WILEY

John Wiley & Sons, Inc.

Published by John Wiley & Sons, Inc., Hoboken, New Jersey.
Published simultaneously in Canada.

For general information about our other products and services, please contact our Customer Care Department within the United States at 800-762-2974, outside the United States at 317-572-3993 or fax 317-572-4002.

Designations used by companies to distinguish their products are often claimed by trademarks. In all instances where the author or publisher is aware of a claim, the product names appear in Initial Capital letters. Readers, however, should contact the appropriate companies for more complete information regarding trademarks and registration.

Wiley also publishes its books in a variety of electronic formats. Some content that appears in print may not be available in electronic books.

For more information about Wiley products, visit our web site at www.wiley.com.

Library of Congress Cataloging-in-Publication Data:
The handbook of financing growth : strategies and capital structure /
Kenneth H. Marks . . . [et al.].
    p. cm. — (Wiley finance series)
  Includes bibliographical references and index.
  ISBN 0-471-42957-0 (CLOTH)
  1. Small business—Finance—Handbooks, manuals, etc.   2. Business enterprises—Finance—Handbooks, manuals, etc.   3.
Corporations—Finance—Handbooks, manuals, etc.   I. Marks, Kenneth H.   II. Series.
  HG4027.7.H355 2005
  658.15—dc22
2004024107

Printed in the United States of America.

10   9   8   7   6   5   4   3   2   1

To Kathy, Lauren, Lilly, and Jenna,
in support of doing God's will

Contents

Foreword   **xi**

Preface   **xiii**

Acknowledgments   **xix**

About the Authors   **xxi**

PART ONE

The Financing Process   **1**

CHAPTER 1
Introduction   **3**

CHAPTER 2
Business Performance and Strategy   **6**

The Business Plan and Strategic Initiatives	6
Shareholder Goals and Objectives	8
Current Financial Position	9
Forecasted Performance	10
Scenarios	10
Strategy	11
Updated Forecast	14

CHAPTER 3
Valuation   **15**

Why Value?	15
Approaches to Valuation	16

CHAPTER 4
Capital Structure   **22**

Assimilating the Drivers	26
Developing Liability Limits	40

CHAPTER 5
  Sources of Capital and What to Expect   **44**
    Bootstrapping Sources and Techniques   46
    Individual Investors (Private Placements Not from Angels
      or Institutions)   57
    Angel Investors   58
    Commercial Banks   69
    Asset-Based Lenders   74
    Commercial Finance Companies   86
    Leasing Companies   87
    Private Equity   92
    Venture Capital Funds   94
    Mezzanine Funds   124
    Buyout Funds   128
    Strategic or Industry Investors—Corporate Venture Capital   135
    Merchant Banks   137
    Community Development Initiatives and Government Agencies   138
    Micro-Cap Public Entities   153
    Royalty Financing   155

CHAPTER 6
  Equity and Debt Financings: Documentation and Regulatory
  Compliance with Securities Laws   **161**
    Basic Definition of Debt and Equity   161
    Debt Instruments   164
    Loan Documentation   170
    Equity Instruments   218
    Equity Investment Documentation   222
    Compliance with Securities Laws   251

CHAPTER 7
  Expert Support—The Players and Their Roles   **262**
    Counsel   262
    Board of Directors   264
    Investment Bankers   267
    Accountants   272
    Consultants/Advisers   276
    Summary   277

CHAPTER 8
  Closing the Deal   **279**
    Process Check-in   279
    Final Perspective   286

PART TWO

Case Studies   **287**

Case Study 1: High-Risk Asset-Based Loan/Refinancing   289
Case Study 2: Asset-Based Lender, Assignment for Benefit
of Creditors   292
Case Study 3: Angel Investors   297
Case Study 4: Royalty Financing   300
Case Study 5: Commercial Finance—Trade Financing   302
Case Study 6: Mezzanine Investment   304
Case Study 7: Private Equity—Acquisition to Exit   305
Case Study 8: Private Equity—Restructuring   307
Case Study 9: Private Equity—Acquisition with
Management Participation   309
Case Study 10: Private Equity—Public-to-Private Acquisition   312
Case Study 11: Merchant Bank Implements
Buy-and-Build Strategy   316
Case Study 12: Strategic Investment   319
Case Study 13: Community Development Financing   322
Case Study 14: Debt with Revenue Sharing   326

PART THREE

Financing Source Directory   **329**

Suggested Use of the Directory Section   331

Appendixes

A   Corporate Finance Primer   377
B   Financial Statements   404
C   Discount Rates   415
D   How Fast Can Your Company Afford to Grow?   417
E   Notes about Start-Ups   433

Glossary   **437**

Notes   **467**

Index   **475**

Foreword

Growth consumes cash! It's what I refer to as the "First Law of Entrepreneurial Gravity." You run out of cash and the game is over.

Each year, hundreds of companies fail because of insufficient funding. Others fail to thrive because of a lack of funding. *The Handbook of Financing Growth* will prove invaluable to those CEOs and CFOs searching for the right formula to fund their company's growth. After all, optimal growth isn't possible without the underlying capital structure to support it. The authors have put together a comprehensive sourcebook with a wealth of information on the funding process itself and sources of capital. Far from being simply a textbook, this book is a complete operator's manual on the funding process. I know of few other books on corporate funding that are as comprehensive as this one. Every pertinent subject has been covered here.

The book begins with several chapters that describe the financing process, and then details sources of capital. An entrepreneur unfamiliar with the array of funding options available might at first think of only selling stock (equity), or borrowing from a bank (debt). However, whole spectrums of sources of capital exist and are described in detail in eight chapters and more than a dozen case studies. Not every capital source is right for every growth situation, so the authors are careful to describe the right application for each of these sources. The reader is shown how to develop a funding strategy that is right for his or her opportunity.

Most importantly, the book is full of examples and case studies, giving a practical view to the process. My work at Gazelles and as founder of the Young Entrepreneurs' Organization (YEO) has afforded me the opportunity to meet and work with thousands of entrepreneurs of growing firms. What they need is less theory and more practical applications of the ideas that can help them grow their business. And we learn best from the experiences of others (the very premise of groups like YEO), which is what the authors do best through their well-crafted "live" examples.

The handbook's authors have a wealth of practical experience in the financing arena. Kenneth Marks has been involved as manager, adviser, or board member with more than a dozen emerging growth and middle-market companies ranging from a venture-backed software start-up to a middle-market insurance services provider. Larry E. Robbins is a founding partner of Wyrick Robbins Yates Ponton LLP, a premier law firm located in the Research Triangle Park area of North Carolina. Gonzalo Fernández is a retired vice president and controller of ITT's telecom business in Raleigh, North Carolina. Subsequently he spent 15 years working as a finance executive for emerging growth companies and as an accounting and business consultant to other companies. John P. Funkhouser has been a partner with two venture capital funds and operated as chief executive officer of four companies in a variety of industries.

Growing a business quickly and effectively is perhaps the greatest challenge faced by an entrepreneur. *The Handbook of Financing Growth* is an effective tool for helping meet that challenge. I heartily recommend this handbook to you as a resource for improving the success of your company through effective financing and capital planning.

VERNE HARNISH
Founder, Young Entrepreneurs Organization
and CEO, Gazelles, Inc.

Ashburn, Virginia
March 2005

Preface

We share an enthusiasm and positive outlook for the growth and vitality of America's emerging and middle-market companies. This segment of the economy has unprecedented access to capital and resources relative to any other time in history. Today there is nearly $150 billion of equity capital available, about $90 billion in private equity funds and another $60 billion in venture capital funds—ready to be deployed.[1] These figures do not include the billions of debt capital available from various lenders ranging from commercial banks to specialty finance companies.

Within these pages, we introduce the full spectrum of funding alternatives available to emerging and middle-market companies, and we present practical strategies and techniques as you consider capitalization of your or your client's company.

Our approach to funding a company is process based—driven by the use of funds, the stage and industry of the company, and the investor objectives. We have written this handbook primarily from practical experience and empirical data; and we have included some basic corporate finance theory that is helpful as a foundation in understanding some of the topics discussed within the body of the book.

The focus is on companies with revenues ranging from zero to about $500 million, deemed start-up through middle-market. Representative companies are those in the INC 500 and the Forbes Small Business 100, venture-funded companies, and those many thousands of companies funded with friends' and family money and hard-earned savings and sweat equity.

We find many competent and successful businesspeople commonly misusing terms and having misconceptions about basic aspects of corporate finance. Many times we hear the leader of a company discuss the alternatives for funding the next stage of growth in the business and mentioning venture capital. The fact is that very few companies are a candidate for venture funding and even fewer actually obtain it. Based on anecdotal data, we estimate the funding rate of business plans submitted to venture capitalists to be in the 0.2 percent to 0.5 percent range or 1 out of 200 to 1 out of 500 companies.* Even with such a low funding rate, do not give up! We also hear stories from entrepreneurs who just do not understand why their bank will not lend them the money they need to hire the next round of employees required to support their growth. If only these folks understood the role of the bank or the type of companies that venture capitalists actually invest in; if they only understood the full range of financing alternatives and how to obtain the right type of funds for their needs at the right time. This handbook is meant to address these questions and to provide the basics of corporate finance as well as to provide strategies with which to fund all types of viable operations at the various stages of the company life. In addition, we will drill down into the details to illustrate how to execute a financing plan. We desire to provide the reader a solid foundation and perspective from which to address capital structure questions and the financing needs of the company.

You will note a series of recurring themes with regard to financing. These apply to those who are operating managers reading this handbook and to those advising and supporting the company; it is a bit of motherhood and apple pie, but is central to successful fund-raising:

1. Establish and follow a process.
2. Start raising capital before you need it.
3. It's relatively easy to get an audience with investors compared to getting funding. Be prepared for the tough questions and know your business (get your house in order):
   - Know your market and competition (details).
   - Know your weaknesses and have a solution.
   - Define a clear use of funds (this leads to alternative capital structure and funding sources).
   - Be able to explain your strategy.
   - Identify relationships and levers (this sometimes reveals funding sources and partners).
   - Prepare the management team and rehearse your presentations.
4. Select only a few prospects; otherwise you waste time and get a reputation for shopping the deal.
5. Know what kind of money you need and how it plays into the overall capital structure of the company.

---

*The percentage of business plans funded increases significantly if the basic concept is reasonable and the entrepreneur finds a fundable formula.

6. Sample the market for acceptance and issues; listen to criticism and learn. Go to sources where you have relationships for quick and candid feedback. Look for trends.
7. Be realistic regarding valuation, issues, strengths, weaknesses, and timing.
8. Have alternatives and be creative.
9. Follow the operating principles of "do what you say you are going to do" and "no surprises."

All of this can be summed up into a single word: credibility. There is no substitute for solid operational performance. We believe we saw an infrequent occurrence with the Internet bubble where companies (dot-coms) could raise capital without regard to business execution; those days have passed! There may be some reading this handbook who think they would be lucky to obtain financing of any type; we would challenge you to look at some of these basic issues to determine the root cause of your struggle. Many times the discipline of an institutional investor (equity or debt) forces management to address the hard issues and to better operate the business. If as an operator or leader of a company you can do this prior to obtaining outside financing, you may be in a stronger position to choose your financial backers and to defend a more aggressive valuation. Once again, we are talking about the credibility of management and leaders.

Our target audience is the leaders, managers, investors, and advisers of and to these companies, and those aspiring to one of the many roles in building these firms. More specifically and by its title, this work is a *handbook*, written for entrepreneurs, founders, presidents, CEOs, CFOs, members of a board of advisers and board of directors, lenders, investors, attorneys, accountants, consultants, investment bankers, commercial bankers, controllers, and senior management. In addition, we believe this handbook is a useful resource for students in college and professional education courses focused on entrepreneurial and growth companies. However, unlike either the encyclopedic or the 1-2-3 Home Depot-esque guides that the term *handbook* connotes, this document strives to be far more than that. It's a combination—part reference guide and part repository of practical information and applied research. The contents range from comparative financing vehicle tables charted on the risk-return continuum to detailed capital-instrument definitions to a showcase for real case studies. In our collective opinion, the theoretical without the practical would potentially skew the reader's perspective, or worse, offer incomplete information. To further drive key points home, we have continually tried to pepper the text with comprehensive examples from both successful and unsuccessful companies.

The *financing growth* portion of the title reinforces our focus on the growth aspect of a business, and which financing alternatives are most appropriate. Not only will capital structure differ by industry and by life cycle of a firm, but also by the risk tolerance of the executive team and investors. Peace of mind and security might be more appropriate in the short run than a perfectly optimized mix of debt and equity, or worse, a strategy that leverages assets to their greatest extent possible in order to maximize value. Of course, these same executives must concurrently balance their psychological needs with investors' requirements, internal rates of return, and actual shareholder returns.

Part One of this handbook, "The Financing Process," provides a detailed description of the steps followed in an ideal scenario. We start with an overview of strategy and the importance of defining the objectives of the company and the various stakeholders. Then we transition to a discussion of the use of funds and addressing risk issues. To support this section, we provide a refresher or summary overview of corporate finance in Appendix A. Much of this content is derived from work by Aswath Damodaran in his text *Applied Corporate Finance.*[2]

Aswath Damodaran is an associate professor of finance at New York University's Leonard N. Stern School of Business. He has received several awards, including the NYU Distinguished Teaching Award in 1990, Stern's Outstanding Teacher Award in 1988, and the Professor of the Year Award in 1988, 1991, and 1992. He also offers training programs in corporate finance and valuation at Deutsche Bank, Swiss Bank, Credit Suisse, J. P. Morgan, and Smith Barney. A former instructor at the University of California at Berkeley, he has written several articles for many of the nation's leading financial journals.

We chose not to reinvent the wheel when it comes to the basics, but to use Damodaran's extensive research in this area. We provide a theoretical and practical discussion surrounding capital structure (the design of the balance sheet—i.e., the mix of debt and equity used to fund shareholders' objectives). We place emphasis on the spectrum of funding instruments, sources, and expected rates of return followed by suggestions on the use of third party experts. Lastly we address closing the deal, managing the relationship with the investors/lenders, and exiting or repaying the funds.

Part Two, "Case Studies," provides real examples of transactions with companies in varied stages and industries; this provides the backdrop for a meaningful discussion.

Part Three, "Financing Source Directory," is an extensive list of actual funding sources. It's accompanied by access to our online database.

In Appendix B, we provide a short tutorial regarding financial statements and reporting. Appendix C contains a note about calculating the discount rate used in valuing emerging growth and middle-market privately held companies. Appendix D is a reprint of an article titled "How Fast Can Your Company Afford to Grow?" illustrating how to determine the maximum rate of growth for a particular company based on internally generated cash flow. In Appendix E we present some observations and thoughts about financing start-up companies.

Finally, an extensive Glossary provides a guide to the most common terms used in corporate finance and a practical definition for each.

We want this handbook to be a reference and guide for you as you develop and execute the financing plan for a company. Further, upon completion of reading this handbook, we intend that you will have the basic tools to structure a company's balance sheet to meet its objectives, and the direction to find the required funding.

It is worth noting that where applicable we have adapted content from select writings of specialists in various fields. Though we are knowledgeable in every aspect of the financing process, we want to ensure the reader is receiving information from the most qualified sources with a contemporary perspective. In addition, we have reached out to the investment and lending communities as part of our primary research to capture current data, actual examples, and an industry-based perspective to counter our own experiences and biases.

We are always receptive to questions and comments, so do not hesitate to write us at: khmarks@MarksAndCompany.com, lrobbins@Wyrick.com, gf@MarksAndCompany.com, or jfunk@MarksAndCompany.com.

KENNETH H. MARKS
LARRY E. ROBBINS
GONZALO FERNÁNDEZ
JOHN P. FUNKHOUSER

Raleigh, North Carolina
March 2005

Acknowledgments

We gratefully acknowledge and thank the many contributors and supporters of this work. In particularly we would like to mention Aswath Damodaran, Verne Harnish, Peter Pflasterer, Donald Rudnick, Andy Burch, Tom Holder, Buddy Howard, Chris Mercer, Mark Larson, Ian Cookson, Don Tyson, Dana Callow, Roy Simerly, Ira Edelson, Robert Winter, Matt Emerson, Frank Buckless, David Buttolph, Bruce Kasson, Bob Calcaterra, Linda Knopp, Campbell R. Harvey, and Neil Churchill.

We are most appreciative of the support provided by the Tuck Center for Private Equity and Entrepreneurship of the Tuck School of Business at Dartmouth, and the works and content by Professors Michael Horvath, Colin Blaydon, Fred Wainwright and Andrew Waldeck, Jonathan Olsen, and Salvatore Gagliano; Ross Barrett of VC Experts, Inc.; and Patrick O'Rourke of BizStats.com. Many thanks to the hundreds of industry firms that contributed information to the Financing Source Directory in Part Three.

We are grateful to our case study contributors David MacNaughtan, Robert Newbold, Robert B. Landis, David Warner, Sabine Zindera, Franklin Staley, Vito Russo, Donald Rudnick, George M. Richmond, James Rutherfurd, Leo White, John Hamilton, Valerie Raad, Rick Larson, Mark Wilson, Meg Barnette, and David D. Buttolph.

We appreciate the guidance, confidence, support, and patience of Pamela van Giessen, editorial director, and Jennifer MacDonald, editorial program coordinator, both with our publisher John Wiley & Sons, Inc. Janine Hamlin provided significant support with the creation of graphics. Finally, special thanks to Frank J. Fabozzi for connecting us to Pamela.

About the Authors

Kenneth H. Marks (Raleigh, North Carolina) is the president of JPS Communications, Inc., a fast growth technology subsidary of the Raytheon Company, and he is the principal and managing director of Marks & Company Inc. (www.MarksAndCompany.com), which provides strategic advisory and corporate development services. He has been involved as management, adviser, or board member with more than a dozen emerging growth and middle-market companies ranging from a venture-backed software start-up to a middle-market insurance services provider.

Mr. Marks was a director of a North Carolina–based regional investment bank focused on raising capital for emerging growth companies. Prior to that position, he was the president of a small publicly traded company and president and CEO of an electronics manufacturer he founded and grew to $20 million in revenue.

He is a member of the Young Presidents Organization (YPO); the founding YPO Sponsor of the Young Entrepreneurs Organization (YEO) in the Research Triangle Park, North Carolina, Chapter; a member of the Council for Entrepreneurial Development; and a member of the Association for Corporate Growth.

He created and teaches "Managing Emerging Growth Companies," an MBA elective at the Hult International Business School in Boston (formerly the Arthur D. Little School of Management) in connection with Boston College's Carroll School of Management. He is the author of the publication *Strategic Planning for Emerging Growth Companies: A Guide for Management* (Wyndham Publishing, 1999).

Mr. Marks obtained his MBA from the Kenan-Flagler Business School at the University of North Carolina in Chapel Hill, and his undergraduate studies were in electrical engineering at North Carolina State University.

Larry E. Robbins (Raleigh, North Carolina) is a founding partner of Wyrick Robbins Yates Ponton LLP, a premier law firm located in the Research Triangle Park area of North Carolina. He is a frequent lecturer on the topics of venture capital and corporate finance and serves on the boards of directors of entrepreneurial support organizations, technology trade associations, and charitable and arts organizations. Mr. Robbins received his BA, MBA, and JD from the University of North Carolina at Chapel Hill. He was also a Morehead Scholar at UNC.

Gonzalo Fernández (Raleigh, North Carolina) is a retired vice president and controller of ITT's telecom business in Raleigh, North Carolina. Subsequently he spent 15 years working as a finance executive for emerging growth companies and as an accounting and business consultant to other companies. He is a past president of the Raleigh Chapter of the Institute of Management Accountants. He received his BA in accounting from Havana University, Cuba. He wrote the book *Estados Financieros (Financial Statements)* (UTEHA, México, Third Edition, 1977).

John P. Funkhouser (Raleigh, North Carolina) has been a partner with two venture capital funds, and operated as chief executive officer of four companies in a variety of industries from retail to high technology. In his venture capital capacity, he was a corporate director of more than a dozen companies and headed two venture-backed companies. The most recent company he led from a start-up concept to a public company is a medical diagnostics and devices business. Mr. Funkhouser worked in commercial banking with Chemical Bank of New York, in investment banking with Wheat First Securities, and in venture capital with Hillcrest Group. He has an undergraduate degree from Princeton University and an MBA from the University of Virginia, Darden Graduate School of Business Administration.

The Handbook
of Financing
Growth

The Financing Process

Introduction

For emphasis, we want to point out that there is no silver bullet in funding a company. As much as we would like you to believe that every fund-raising follows the same consistent process, it is just not true. However, what we will do is provide a view that is fairly representative of the key steps that need to be considered and how to navigate the process. In practice you will find that some steps are conducted concurrently with others, and some steps are conducted rather informally. What we have attempted to do is explicitly show the key steps and provide guidance for each. With that said, Figure 1.1 provides an overview of the financing process from the perspective of the issuer and is comprehensive in that it indicates the steps for raising equity; debt placement will be a subset of this process depending on the transaction type. In many instances you will see the word *investor* used interchangeably for either an actual investor or a lender; the line of distinction blurs depending on the characteristics of the deal. We have chosen to segment the process into the following categories for discussion. You'll note that this is also the organization of Part One of this handbook.

- Business Performance and Strategy.
- Valuation.
- Capital Structure.
- Sources of Capital.
- Equity and Debt Financings.
- Expert Support.
- Closing the Deal.

Steps 1 through 3 allow us to obtain a view of the current business and management's plans. In step 1 we review the business plan, strategic initiatives, and shareholder goals and objectives. Step 2 is an analytical

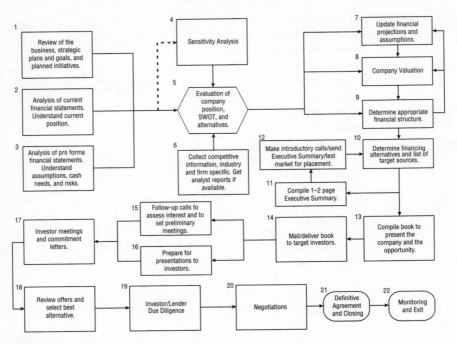

FIGURE 1.1 Financing Process Flow Chart

review of the current financial position of the company. In step 3 we seek to understand the forecasted performance of the company and the underlying assumptions. Combined, we should be able to define and understand:

- The financial position of the company.
- The structure of the current balance sheet.
- The specific use of funds.
- What industry the company operates in.
- The stage of the company.
- The shareholder objectives.
- Management's strengths and weaknesses.
- Management's plans and view of the future.

In many instances shareholder objectives are not well articulated and need clarification, particularly as they relate to funding the business. Given that the focus of this book is start-up through middle-market (revenues up to $500 million) companies, many shareholders are also senior managers of the company. Typical objectives include: (1) addressing personal risk management issues while growing the business and (2) shareholder liquidity. These two topics have significant impact in answering the classic questions "What is the right mix of debt and equity?" and "How do I avoid personally guaranteeing the company's debt?" It is critical to understand these issues early in the process.

Steps 4 through 6 focus on comparing the company to its peers and determining variances. Once base information is collected regarding the industry, the stage is set for a discussion with management about the realism and ranges of potential outcomes, and why they may vary compared to other similar businesses. This discussion should result in the ability to analyze multiple scenarios and determine the variability (risk) in achieving management's forecast. In step 7 we update the assumptions and agree on the financial forecast that we will use in the fund-raising process.

Step 8 helps to determine a range of valuations for the business as an entity. This is critical in bringing alignment of expectations among shareholders, directors, management, and supporting advisers.

In step 9, we assimilate all of the prior steps into a target capital structure and some fallback scenarios. In steps 10 through 12 we test the market as a reality check and determine the likelihood for success given our chosen strategy. The company is looking for an indication of interest on the part of potential investors/lenders. This may be an iterative process, the downside being the risk of the market perceiving that you are shopping the company. There is a careful balance of having alternative sources versus overexposing the company to potential investors/lenders. If this happens, you may not be taken seriously or may be taken seriously by only the less than optimal sources. In Chapter 7 we address the use of experts in the financing process. They can be invaluable in testing the market and potential alternatives, as well as providing an added perspective.

Once the financing strategy has been solidified and initially tested, a so-called book is created to present the company and solicit formal responses; these are steps 13 and 14. In the event that the funding required is solely debt, and depending on the type of debt, an abbreviated amount of information will be required from a traditional book and then some additional financial detail will be added.

Steps 15 through 17 focus on management's presentation of the company during the financing process. Steps 18 through 22, addressed in Chapter 8, are about negotiating, closing the deal, and managing ongoing investor/lender relationships.

CHAPTER 2

Business Performance and Strategy

While this book is not specifically focused on how to analyze a company or how to develop a company strategy, we are providing an overview as it relates to the financing process and to prompt your thinking as you consider the corporate financial plan of your (or your client's) business.

THE BUSINESS PLAN AND STRATEGIC INITIATIVES

Managers seldom have the opportunity to start with a blank balance sheet and assemble the capital structure from scratch. So from a practical perspective we begin to analyze the capital structure for a particular company from its current position. As we begin the process of developing a financing plan to support the growth and progress of a company, we need to understand the business and the major initiatives planned for the foreseeable future. This will lead us to the use of funds.

In the business plan, we are seeking to determine the type of business and what industry it is in, the sources of operating profit, the company's competitors and its relative market position, the trends surrounding the business, and the background of the management team. From management's perspective, this information is probably obvious.

The next step involves developing a list of strategic or key initiatives that management plans to undertake in the one-to-five-year horizon. The details of each initiative needs to be understood. The suggested approach is to develop a schedule of quarterly expenses and investments for the planning period, showing the cash flow required. An example for a single initiative is shown in Table 2.1.

The value in this exercise is to force management to articulate their plan in a time-phased manner. In essence, the team has generated a use of

TABLE 2.1 Sample Worksheet of Strategic Initiative Cash Flow

	Annual Summary		Quarterly Detail							
	Year 1	Year 2	Q1 Y1	Q2 Y1	Q3 Y1	Q4 Y1	Q1 Y2	Q2 Y2	Q3 Y2	Q4 Y2
Staff (loaded costs)	$ 785,500	$1,296,000	$ 45,500	$140,000	$300,000	$300,000	$324,000	$324,000	$324,000	$324,000
MARCOM*	160,000	240,000	10,000	30,000	60,000	60,000	60,000	60,000	60,000	60,000
Software	25,000	10,000	20,000	—	5,000	—	5,000	—	5,000	—
Equipment	574,000	120,000	125,000	329,000	110,000	10,000	—	—	—	120,000
Travel	155,000	210,000	5,000	30,000	60,000	60,000	60,000	50,000	50,000	50,000
Consultants	223,330	267,996	22,333	66,999	66,999	66,999	66,999	66,999	66,999	66,999
Other outside services	250,000	150,000	—	50,000	50,000	150,000	150,000	—	—	—
Facilities	150,000	180,000	15,000	45,000	45,000	45,000	45,000	45,000	45,000	45,000
Maximum	$2,322,830	$2,473,996	$242,833	$690,999	$696,999	$691,999	$710,999	$545,999	$550,999	$665,999
Minimum	1,434,122	1,476,396	102,750	487,374	413,499	430,499	435,099	327,099	327,099	387,099
Probable	1,769,181	1,855,497	209,183	518,249	522,749	518,999	533,249	409,499	413,249	499,499

*Marketing communication.

funds for the project. The projects for a particular company can then be compiled to determine cumulative cash requirements and uses of funds needed to grow the business or meet its needs, including the timing of such funds.

Many times this exercise leads to a new perspective on the actual amount of financing required, the timing, and the alternatives to obtaining the cash flow. The information that is obtained from the compiled version of this is to be synthesized in the steps discussed hereafter. The approach just outlined, coupled with current financial statements and forecasts, provides the view to begin to determine overall capital requirements.

We have examples whereby a company claims it needs more working capital. The follow-on question is, "What is the use of the working capital?": for inventory, to fund customer receivables, to fund new staff to add services. The response directly affects the decision of what funding source(s) to pursue, and the question is partially answered in the process discussed earlier.

Given the approach we are advocating herein, the answer to these questions will become apparent as part of the financial plan. Keep in mind the use of funds as we continue through this handbook—it is a critical component in obtaining the right source of financing.

SHAREHOLDER GOALS AND OBJECTIVES

The structure of a company's balance sheet is directly affected by the type of owners of the business and their goals and objectives with regard to the business. A clear understanding of each owner's (or beneficial owner's) objectives needs to be articulated and agreed upon. Some particular expectations include: holding period, desire to participate in management decisions, expected dividends or disbursements, willingness to risk the capital invested, valuation (current and anticipated), social or community-related expectations, and vision for the future.

In one example, a group of engineers had grown a $10 million technology company from scratch in 10 years. They were near retirement and sought liquidity and less risk. This affected the financing of new equipment, working capital, and the potential recapitalization of the company. Exit was the obvious objective. They hired a professional CEO who was instrumental in successfully selling the company in a short period.

In another example, a growth company with $25 million in revenue is owned by a single majority stockholder who desires to pass the business to his children. This has specific implications as to the types of investors and financing sources he can use to fund the company's continued growth, since the owner's objective will preclude the eventual sale or exit of the business.

As you can begin to see, there are many scenarios and examples that lead to different capital structures.

CURRENT FINANCIAL POSITION

The first step in the financial evaluation of an operating company (versus a non-revenue-generating business in the development stage) is the analysis of balance sheet and cash flow metrics. You need to understand the target company's financial position relative to others in its peer group or industry. What is the average number of days outstanding for its accounts payable, and what should it be relative to the industry? What is the average number of days' sales in accounts receivable, and what should it be based on a comparable group of businesses? How much inventory is the business carrying relative to its peers, and how different is its basic business model insofar as it influences cash flow? The norm or peer group information can be obtained from various data sources such as Dun & Bradstreet, the Risk Management Association (RMA) (formerly Robert Morris Associates), and the Securities and Exchange Commission's EDGAR database for publicly traded entities. In addition, how leveraged is the business (i.e., what is the debt-to-equity ratio)? Who are the current investors and lenders? What is the capital structure of similar businesses?

Other information to obtain in the analysis of the financial statements includes: Is the company current in making payment to existing lenders? Has the company defaulted on debt or payments in the past two to three years? What level of debt has the company been able to service historically? Are there any extraordinary activities or items that have affected historical cash flow or operating income—any windfalls or one-time negative items?

It is important to ensure that the current, historical, and forecasted financial statements are restated to comply with generally accepted accounting principles (GAAP), especially for comparison to other companies and reporting to outside lenders and investors. Compliance to GAAP is a given for public companies, though not the case for many private companies. In addition, owner-related expenses and assets need to be normalized. Common issues surface surrounding owner compensation, whereby the primary stockholder is also an employee and receives compensation that is above or below market value for his or her position; in each case that compensation needs to be adjusted to market value for planning purposes. Other common issues include failure to accrue all the liabilities of a company or to record expenses and revenue in the correct matching and time periods. It often makes sense to have a public accounting firm review or audit the financial statements annually to establish checks and balances on the integrity of the balance sheet data and to provide added credibility for outside parties considering lending to or investing in the company.

Lastly, the financial statements should reflect a company's strategy and operations; they should be a testament to efficient management practices when compared to industry peers. However, mature companies go through transitions where new products are launched and others are deemed to be antiquated. Research and development costs can be cyclical. Early stage companies enter a business life cycle that takes the company through phases of growth with particular concentration on research and development, manufacturing efficiencies, quality systems, sales and marketing, and so on. Financial statements reflect how your company was yesterday and how it is today, and projections or forecasts reflect how the company is expected to perform tomorrow.

FORECASTED PERFORMANCE

Forecasts are a translation of the vision and strategy of the company into financial terms. A common approach is to establish a financial model in a spreadsheet that allows management and investors to analyze the impact on performance based on changing assumptions. For the purposes of fundraising, management should prepare a three-to-five-year plan with balance sheets, income statements, and statements of cash flow, each integrated and supported by detailed schedules and assumptions. These assumptions are going to be tested in due diligence and then adjusted based on the supporting data and particular investors' interpretations—greatly influenced by management's credibility.

There is no need to reinvent the wheel in regard to forecast spreadsheets; there are software programs and spreadsheets commercially available at reasonable prices. We suggest a periodic review and update as the company progresses to ensure assumptions and risks are current.

SCENARIOS

Once we have an understanding from the first three steps in the financing process, we assimilate information about competitors (and their activities) with an analysis of the target company's strengths, weaknesses, opportunities, and threats (SWOT). The intent is to further challenge the assumptions in the forecasted performance and conduct a sensitivity analysis. As an outcome, we expect various scenarios based on varying assumptions; we expect to quantify the alternatives and risks. The result is a better understanding of the financial measures and cash requirements. It allows management to understand the company's capital needs, to act with greater confidence, and to respond to investor questions with clarity.

STRATEGY

Implicit in the discussion about business plans and scenarios is the assumption that there is an underlying business strategy being worked by management supporting a corporate vision and shareholder objectives. The ability to articulate a reasonable and appropriate strategy is critical to a successful financing, especially if equity is involved.

Strategy is about taking a long-term view of what you are trying to accomplish, integrating the dynamics specific to your particular company and to its industry, developing a set of initiatives to achieve a particular future position, and then distilling it down into bite-size activities and actions that in an appropriate sequence allow you to meet your objectives. Strategy is the set of decisions defining the activities that positions your company advantageously relative to your rivals. As stated by Michael Porter,

> *Competitive strategy is about being different. It means deliberately choosing a different set of activities to deliver a unique mix of value. Operational effectiveness is not strategy. Ultimately, all differences between companies in cost or price derive from the hundreds of activities required to create, produce, sell, and deliver their products or services, such as calling on customers, assembling final products, and training employees. Cost is generated by performing activities, and cost advantage arises from performing particular activities more efficiently than competitors. Similarly, differentiation arises from both the choice of activities and how they are performed. Activities, then, are the basic units of competitive advantage. Overall, advantage or disadvantage results from all a company's activities, not only a few.*
>
> *Operational effectiveness (OE) means performing similar activities better than rivals perform them. Operational effectiveness includes but is not limited to efficiency. It refers to any number of practices that allow a company to better utilize its inputs by, for*

*example, reducing defects in products or developing better prod-
ucts faster. In contrast, strategic positioning means performing different activities from rivals' or performing similar activities in
different ways. Strategy is about combining activities.[1]*

Consider some generic strategies to improve a company's position:

- Use the firm's strengths to avoid or reduce the impact of external threats.
- Improve internal weaknesses by taking advantage of external opportunities.
- Use defensive tactics to reduce internal weaknesses and avoid external threats.

Many firms seek strategies that use one of the three tactics previously mentioned to put the company in a position to use its internal strengths to take advantage of external opportunities.

In addition, consider the implications, relative emphasis and importance of the key management factors as illustrated in Figure 2.1. Neil Churchill and Virginia Lewis's research addresses the importance of these factors in growing businesses from start-up through middle-market stages:[2]

- Cash and business resources.
- Matching of business and personal goals of the owner.
- The competency of the owner/manager and his or her ability to delegate.
- The quality and diversity of management.
- Systems and controls (infrastructure).
- Strategic plan.

A strategy need not be brilliant, as long as it is sound, is well conceived, and avoids the obvious errors. The key is not to make the really dumb mistakes. Here is a list of eight common traps in strategic planning to be used as a reality checklist as you contemplate your plan.[3]

1. Failing to recognize and understand events and changing conditions in the competitive environment.
2. Basing strategies on a flawed set of assumptions.
3. Pursuing a one-dimensional strategy that fails to create or sustain a long-term competitive advantage.
4. Diversifying for all the wrong reasons. Ill-considered diversification strategies based on growth for its own sake or portfolio management strategies often create negative synergy and a loss of shareholder value.

5. Failing to structure and implement mechanisms to ensure the coordination and integration of core processes and key functions across organizational boundaries.
6. Setting arbitrary and inflexible goals and implementing a system of controls that fails to achieve a balance among culture, rewards, and boundaries.
7. Failing to anticipate the need to upgrade management skills at the next growth stage by hiring new talents to overcome and bolster in-house weaknesses.
8. Failing to provide the leadership essential to the successful implementation of strategic change.

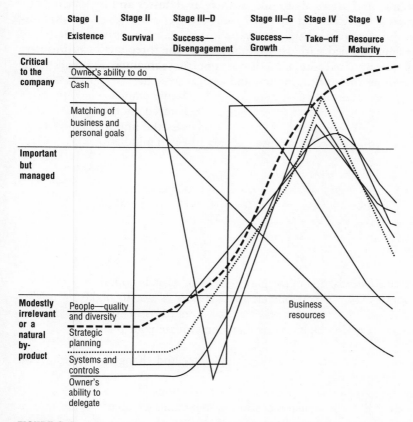

FIGURE 2.1 Management Factors and Stages of Growth
D = Disengage, G = Grow.
Source: Neil C. Churchill and Virginia L. Lewis, "The Five Stages of Small Business Growth," *Harvard Business Review*, May–June 1983, page 7.

A primary issue that surfaces in failed strategy and planning is the lack of fact-based decisions with validated assumptions. Many growth company CEOs have grand plans but fail to realistically determine the source of funds that are required to put the resources and human capital in place, which is a prerequisite to execution and implementation. It is critical that strategies be developed based on data and not on wishful thinking.

UPDATED FORECAST

Following the financing process in Figure 1.1, we now have discussed steps 1 through 6, and are ready to take an objective third party look at the target company forecast and make any changes required based on the outcome of the sensitivity analysis and application of competitive and industry information, coupled with assuring linkage to our clearly defined business strategy. The updated forecast and its supporting schedules and work feeds the discussion for entity valuation and capital structure.

CHAPTER 3

Valuation

A key issue to address early in the financing process is the valuation of the company. In this chapter, we will discuss the core concepts surrounding valuation and how to view the company and its equity. You will find that valuation is expressed as a range of values, not a single data point, based on a buildup of assumptions and different approaches. The valuation of the company in a transaction can be a deal killer if the company and its stockholders do not have realistic expectations. Unrealistic valuation expectations or overemphasis on the same may put off potential investors or buyers; when all else is equal, we argue that valuation is often less of an issue than the terms of deal.

For the purposes of this handbook, we are presenting the basic concepts as they pertain to the financing process—not intending for the reader to become a valuation expert, rather to become conversant in the topic. Valuation is step 8 in our ideal financing process as indicated in Figure 1.1.

In concept, valuation is straightforward, but in practice it can be complex and subjective. We would counsel management and shareholders to obtain objective third party assistance in determining a realistic range of values based on the specific needs and contemplated transaction(s) of the company.

WHY VALUE?

The first step in valuation is determining what you are valuing and why you are doing so. Reasons vary depending on the situation, but typically include: the sale of the company, a capital issuance selling part of the company (to public or private investors), incentive plans, to establish realistic expectations, a merger, litigation, or to establish a benchmark from which to improve operating performance or test a particular strategy.

For clarification, the entity value is equal to the market value of the equity plus the market value of the debt. Occasionally a company may have assets (whether on or off the balance sheet) that can be worth more than the operating value. Such assets are referred to as nonoperating assets. In discussions and negotiations, it is critical to be specific about these terms to avoid confusion over which value (of the equity, the debt, or both) and which assets (whether operating or nonoperating) you are referring to.

APPROACHES TO VALUATION

There are several basic approaches to valuing a business, and subsequently its equity. Valuing a start-up is somewhat unique. We address this in Chapter 5 in the sections regarding angel investors and venture capital. For operating businesses, the three primary and interrelated approaches are:

1. Adjusted book value (net assets).
2. Market value.
3. Discounted cash flow.

Adjusted Book Value Approach (Net Assets)

Adjusted book value is often considered the minimum equity value associated with a company. The shareholders' equity of a company is the difference between the assets and liabilities on its balance sheet as recorded at historical costs (net of depreciation and amortization). This difference is sometimes referred to as the company's book value.

The various assets such as real estate and machinery and equipment can be adjusted to their current market values, and any nonoperating assets or off-balance-sheet assets can be adjusted to their current market values as well. The various liabilities can be similarly adjusted, and any unrecorded liabilities, such as embedded income taxes on appreciated assets, would also be noted.

The difference between assets and liabilities as adjusted to their current market value is referred to as "adjusted book value." Adjusted book value is often a benchmark figure in negotiations over the equity value of a business. There can be a financial and psychological reluctance to selling a company at less than its adjusted book value.

When other valuation methods or negotiations give rise to equity values in excess of book value, intangible assets, sometimes lumped into a single concept called goodwill, are created.

Market Approach

The market approach is based on comparing the value of the target company to those of other companies that have actually traded within a reasonable period of time from when the value is being determined. Comparables are frequently conducted with regard to competitive companies or those in the same industry.

Discounted Cash Flow

Discounted cash flow (DCF) is one of the most common valuation approaches for going concerns and is often used to determine the entity value of a business. This approach presumes that a company's assets and liabilities are assembled for the purpose of creating earnings and cash flow.[1] DCF value is derived by forecasting the expected future performance of the business and determining the amount of cash generated in each future period after making all investments required to continue operating the company (i.e. the cash available to distribute to the owners of the company's debt and equity). These expected future cash flows are discounted to a present value based on the required returns of investors purchasing similar assets, or at the appropriate discount rate for the projected cash flows.

While we will not delve into the financial equations and determinants of DCF, it is helpful to note that the key drivers of this type of valuation are the discount rate applied, the assumptions for the terminal value, and the expected cash flows to be generated by the company. The discount rate is typically determined by a formula called the capital asset pricing model (CAPM), which is influenced by interest rates, the stock market, and company-specific risks. We have provided a summary of the discount rate buildup for emerging growth and lower middle market companies in Appendix C.

Financial investors most often invest based on DCF or net asset values. Strategic and industry investors that have some additional method to gain value from a company may be willing to enter into transactions with values that include some type of synergy or strategic component. This is evidenced by the statistics mentioned in the corporate venture capital section of Chapter 5, whereby corporate venture capitalists sometimes invest at values substantially higher than those offered by traditional venture capitalists.

Earnings before interest, taxes, depreciation, and amortization (EBITDA) times a multiple is often used as a proxy or estimate for DCF valuation. This reference to EBITDA is often used as a rule of thumb in determining a company's initial value. For EBITDA to be relevant for discussion purposes it needs to be normalized for unusual and nonrecurring aspects of performance as well as for excess compensation (above market-based salaries) of owners.

Based on data from the *Daily Deal* (www.thedeal.com) regarding company transactions, historical EBITDA multiples from the past few years for the sale of emerging growth and middle-market companies have ranged from 5.1 to 8.0 on average. From other sources we see many deals that occur lower than 5.1. The data indicates that as a company increases in size, the multiple of EBITDA paid increases.

In most transactions, the investor or buyer will establish the financial value determined by DCF or net assets to use as a baseline for negotiations and benchmarking, even if they eventually propose a higher valuation. In addition to determining a company's net asset value, there are alternate valuation techniques that can be used if the company is operating at a loss, such as options pricing.

The Valuation Process

The major steps in a formal company valuation include:

1. Determine the purpose of the valuation.
2. Assess the current economic environment.
3. Develop a detailed understanding of the:
   - *Industry.* What industry is the company in? What's happening to the industry in general? Trends? How profitable is the industry? Who are the key players? What threatens the industry? How does the target company fit into the marketplace?
   - *Target company's business.* Where does the company add value to its customers? What are the key business processes? What is unique about the company? How strong is management? How is it positioned in its market?
   - *Company's financial performance.* Restated financial statements adjusted for owner-related compensation and perks, related party transactions, and compliance to GAAP.
4. Determine management's outlook and forecasts. Include an assessment of the underlying assumptions in management's forecasts. Do the forecasts account for required capital, staff, and new equipment? Does management have a sales plan? If so, how realistic is it? How does the forecast compare to competitor performance?
5. Analyze similar deals and similar companies (including public company multiples). Include analysis of deals/transactions of like companies, analysis of like company public transactions—most important

for initial public offerings (IPOs)—and analysis of similar company transactions.

6. Evaluate and interpret the results. This will include developing a range of valuations based on projected future cash flow as a stand-alone business, developing valuation scenarios based on the maximum synergy of a strategic buyer or investor, and summarizing the valuation ranges based on type of buyer/investor and type of transaction.

Discounts and Premiums

Another concept to understand is the relationship of discounts and premiums with regard to valuation and investments in a company. Figure 3.1 illustrates the relative relationship of these discounts based on public company multiples. This may help the reader understand why it is generally inappropriate to directly compare public company multiples to those of private companies.

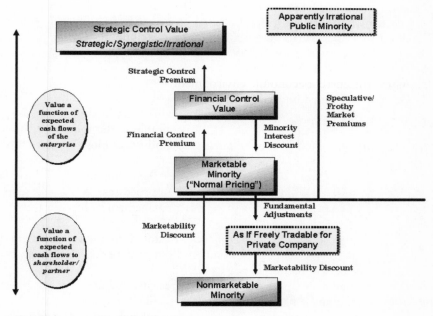

FIGURE 3.1 Relationship of Discounts and Premiums
Source: Chart designed by Z. Christopher Mercer. © Mercer Capital and Z. Christopher Mercer, 2004. www.mercercapital.com. Z. Christopher Mercer, ASA, CFA, *Valuing Enterprise and Shareholder Cash Flow: The Integrated Theory of Business Valuation*, Memphis, TN: Peabody Publishing, LP, 2004, page 363. www.integratedtheory.com.

Public company multiples do not apply to private company transactions for the following reasons:

- Private company equity lacks liquidity.
- Public company multiples are generally stated in terms of after-tax earnings. As mentioned earlier, private company transactions usually consider EBITDA, which is a pretax figure. In addition, many private companies are run for tax efficiency and require restating the income statement for a direct comparison to a public entity.
- Public companies within a specific industry generally maintain capital structures (debt/equity mixes) that are fairly similar. That means the relative price-earnings (P/E) ratios (where earnings include the servicing of debt) are usually comparable. Private companies within the same industry, however, can vary widely in capital structure. The valuation of a privately held business is therefore frequently based on enterprise or entity value, or the predebt value of a business rather than the value of the stock of the business, like public companies. This is another reason why private company multiples are generally based on pretax profits and may not be directly comparable to the price-earnings ratios of public firms.[2]
- Public companies are generally viewed as less risky given their size and access to capital. This is not always true with emerging growth and middle-market businesses.

Other Valuation Factors

Other factors that affect private company valuation include:

- The cyclical nature of the business (less attractive to financial buyers).
- Economic conditions (affects the number of buyers and earnings multiples).
- Convincing buyers/investors that projected cash flows are obtainable. This is a key issue.
- Availability of capital (supply and demand).
- Capital structure of the company (amount of debt vs. equity).

Increasing Company Value

There are two generic approaches to increase the value of a company:

1. Pursue strategies that increase earnings and the return on invested capital (net assets minus non-interest-bearing debt).
2. Pursue strategies that reduce the risk of investment in your company, thus reducing the cost of capital.

Specific actions to increase the return on invested capital include establishing a strong management team, establishing and meeting clear valuation changing milestones, setting or moving industry standards, achieving above industry margins (gross and operating), establishing key alliances/partnerships to provide a competitive advantage, increasing the rate of earnings growth, or increasing cash flow with existing capital.

To reduce the risk of investment in a company, seek to establish a strong management team, reduce the company's dependence on any single individual or key personnel, establish the appropriate capital structure (debt vs. equity), develop recurring sources of income, provide the operating infrastructure to scale the business, and reduce customer concentration.

For additional reading regarding company valuation, we recommend *Valuing Enterprise and Shareholder Cash Flow: The Integrated Theory of Business Valuation* by Z. Christopher Mercer, published in 2004 by Peabody Publishing.

CHAPTER 4

Capital Structure

Development of the capital structure is part of the financing process illustrated in Figure 1.1. Establishing a financing plan and addressing the capital structure is done after management has clearly articulated the company's business plan and can articulate how much funding is required, how it will be deployed, and when it is needed.

Defining the capital structure is a critical decision for any business organization. The capital structure of a company refers to the amount of debt and equity, and the types of debt and equity used to fund the operations of the company. The selection of capitalization alternatives is important not only because of the drive to maximize returns to various organizational constituencies, but also because of the impact such a decision has on an organization's ability to deal with its competitive environment. The prevailing argument, originally developed by Franco Modigliani and Merton Miller ("The Cost of Capital, Corporate Finance, and the Theory of Investment," *American Economic Review*, June 1958), is that an optimal capital structure exists that balances the risk of bankruptcy with the tax savings of debt. In other words, a company should use both equity and debt to fund its operations. Once established, a capital structure comprised of debt and equity should provide greater returns to stockholders than they would receive from an all-equity firm. This strategy is accomplished by reducing the amount of equity and increasing the amount of debt, thereby, in theory, reducing the overall cost of capital.[1] Illustrated in Figure 4.1 is the concept that the cost of capital for a company capitalized entirely with equity is high, and conversely the cost of capital for a company completely leveraged with debt is also high. In between these two extremes, the point designated as the theoretical ideal mix or the low point on the cost of capital curve, a theoretical company has maximized its use of debt and equity to achieve the lowest cost of capital.

In deciding on the right capital structure for a company, shareholders and management must balance the risk of default in repaying debt with the

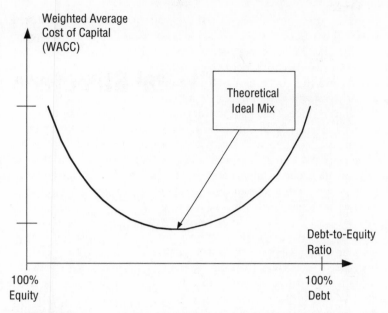

Weighted Average Cost of Capital (WACC)

Theoretical Ideal Mix

Debt-to-Equity Ratio

100% Equity

100% Debt

FIGURE 4.1 Weighted Average Cost of Capital versus Debt-to-Equity Ratio (WACC vs. D/E)

availability of equity capital to pursue growth opportunities. Some emerging growth and middle-market companies may find it easier to obtain debt than equity, making this decision more difficult (when what they really need is equity). If a growth company is too conservative and does not leverage its equity to provide increased capital to invest, it may miss market opportunities and actually erode the overall value of the business by becoming a lesser player in the market—market position and share weighs into company valuation. However, being too aggressive and overleveraging the company may lead to missed financial performance and business failure when things do not go exactly to plan. There is also the issue (which is sometimes perception more than reality) of relinquishing control when issuing new equity. See the discussion later in this chapter.

Despite extensive study and some theoretical appeal, researchers in financial management have not found the optimal capital structure. The best that academics and practitioners have been able to achieve are prescriptions that satisfy short-term goals. In some publications, readers are left with the impression that the use of leverage is one way to improve the performance of an organization. While this can be true in some circumstances, it fails to consider the complexities of the competitive environment, the long-term survival needs of the organization, the discipline of the management of a specific company, or the risk tolerance of the shareholders (particularly as it relates to privately held companies).[2]

Agency costs are the costs incurred or opportunities lost by the shareholders of a company when the interest of management is placed before the interest of the shareholders. The shareholders want managers to operate the firm in ways that maximize the value of their shares, whereas the managers' priority may be, say, to build a business empire through rapid expansion, mergers or acquisitions, which may not increase their firm's share price or value. There is an inherent conflict between management and shareholders in a corporation where management does not have the incentive to optimize performance. There are situations where a major shareholder in a privately held company settles for a suboptimal capital structure so the shareholder can extract greater and disproportionate wealth as a manager through operational actions or other means. An approach to addressing agency costs is to provide increased incentives for management to perform and to weight the capital structure of the company more heavily with debt so that cash flow is significantly tight due to debt service obligations. This debt structure causes the company to operate in a manner designed to meet certain principal and interest payments, in effect focusing management on the return of capital to shareholders disguised as creditors. There is the argument that this use of leverage either to discipline managers or to achieve economic gain is the easy way out, and, in many instances, can lead to the demise of the organization. There are several ways to view the logic behind the capital structure decision based on how one frames the issue. Rather than: "What is an optimal mix of debt and equity that will maximize shareholder wealth?" consider: "Under what circumstances should leverage be used to maximize shareholder wealth? Why?" And for many start-up, emerging growth, and middle-market companies the question is often "What type capital can we obtain—either debt or equity?"[3]

From another perspective, and arguably more appropriate for the readers of this handbook, the capital structure is most likely defined by the stage (and industry) of the company as illustrated in Figure 4.2. In general, equity may be the only alternative capital available to early stage companies, but the pool of financing alternatives grows as the critical mass of the company grows. Small-, medium-, and large-cap publicly traded companies have a broader range of financing alternatives than smaller privately held businesses. Public company capital structures are studied and tracked by analysts based on industry. In contrast to the types of debt and equity in Figure 4.2, we show and discuss the typical funding sources by stage in Chapter 5.

Type of Financing	Start-up $0 to $1.0M	Emerging Growth $1.0M to $10M	Lower Middle-Market $10 to $50M	Middle-Market $50M to $500M
Factoring	Y	Y	Y	Y
Receivables Financing	Y	Y	Y	Y
Inventory Financing	Y	Y	Y	Y
Real Estate Financing/Sale-Leaseback		P	Y	Y
Equipment Lease	Y	P		
Equipment Lease with Warrants	Y	Y	P	
Purchase Order Financing	P	Y	Y	Y
Microloan	Y			
Bridge Loan		Y	Y	Y
Lines of Credit	Y	Y	Y	Y
Revolver		P	Y	Y
Royalty Financing	P	Y	Y	Y
Industrial Revenue Bond		P	Y	Y
Debtor in Possession		P	Y	Y
Term Loan	P	Y	Y	Y
SBA Guaranteed Loan	Y	Y		
Junk Bond			P	Y
Commercial Paper				P/Y
Private Placement Senior Notes and Senior Unsecured Debt				Y
Senior Debt	Y	Y	Y	Y
Junior Debt			P	Y
Subordinated Debt		P	P	Y
Private Equity	Y	Y	Y	P
Public Equity				P/Y

FIGURE 4.2 Types of Debt and Equity by Company Stage
Y = Yes, P = Possible depending on company characteristics and industry.

This chapter provides a detailed approach and perspective to addressing steps 9 and 10 of the financing process as shown in Figure 1.1. Our desire is that management and advisers of start-up, emerging growth, and middle-market companies proactively shape the capital structure of their businesses instead of reacting to the need for cash based on a sequence of events in the corporate life cycle. We encourage readers to establish a baseline showing how their company's capital structure is currently assembled and use the concepts and information within this handbook to determine a capital structure to strive for. In reality there is no one ideal structure for a specific company; there is a range of alternative structures that suffice, some more preferable than others. For the intended readers of this handbook, the desired capital structure will change as the company moves from one business stage to another. Use the resulting information to develop alternate scenarios to achieve the future structure and as a catalyst for action over time to reshape and improve the financial and strategic position of the company. This includes having the right amount and type of capital to grow and meet the needs of the business at the right time. It is a matter of forecasting cash flows to ensure that funding is in place before the cash is needed. The follow-on step is to link the proper financing source with the capital needs of the company. This includes finding the investors, lenders, and institutions that are looking for deals that have the characteristics of yours at the time the company is seeking funds.

ASSIMILATING THE DRIVERS

Figure 4.3 illustrates the elements to be analyzed and considered in making the capital structure decision, particularly as it relates to companies from start-up through middle-market. As you can imagine, there are usually multiple scenarios for a given company depending on its individual situation. There are some generalities that can be made; we address those as this chapter progresses.

Base Assumptions

We begin the process of analyzing the capital structure by establishing assumptions and the underlying premises of the process.

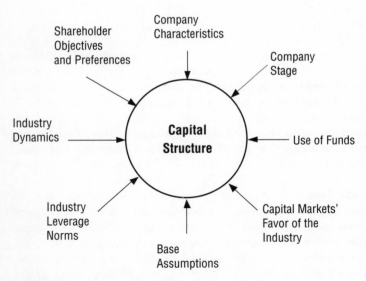

FIGURE 4.3   Factors Shaping Capital Structure

Achieve Shareholder Objectives   The shareholder objective for small-cap through large-cap publicly traded companies is generally accepted as increasing shareholder value. This cannot be generalized for privately held or lifestyle businesses, where in many cases the shareholder objective is to maximize cash distributions to the shareholders. Whatever the objective, it directly affects the capital structure. For example, the capital structures would be significantly different for companies with divergent objectives designed to advance social missions such as creation of employment and meeting certain religious objectives, establishing a legacy for successive generations, or creating cash flow for current shareholder consumption. Along with these objectives come limits and constraints, all of which need to be articulated and understood.

Seek Least Expensive Capital   Within the context of the aforementioned shareholder objectives and supporting the other assumptions herein, we advocate that shareholders and management seek to minimize the cost of their company's capital structure. Well-run companies with solid growth plans, good margins, and experienced management teams can afford the luxury of searching for the better deals. If the company is weak, the capital will not be as cheap, and investors will require a premium for the added risk.

Seek to Optimize the Return on Invested Capital   Within the context of the aforementioned shareholder objectives and supporting the other assumptions herein, we advocate that to optimize return on invested capital (ROIC)[4] shareholders and management operate with proper overall levels of capital and that they efficiently deploy the selected mix of capital.

Shift to a Proactive Mode   Inherent in this handbook is the concept that management and shareholders must be proactive in determining the company's capital structure and preparing for growth. *Key concept: Companies must raise capital when they can, not when they need it.* Highlighting our point we echo the adage that you can borrow capital when you do not need it, but when you really need the capital it is not available.

Match Sources and Uses of Funds   The properly capitalized company will match the individual lives of its assets or investments with the maturity or term of the capital used to acquire the assets or investments. This means funding multiyear investments with capital that remains available for the same term. Likewise, this means funding short-term cash needs with short-lived liabilities—such as lines of credit. Table 4.1 shows examples of matching the source and use of funds.

TABLE 4.1 Example Sources and Uses of Funds

	Use of Funds	Potential Source of Funds	Comment
1	Purchase laptop computers and software	Term debt or lease (capital or operating lease)	If the expected life of the laptops is 24 months, then make the amortization of the loan or lease 24 months. Do not use a short-term line of credit, which may take away from working capital.
2	Procure office furniture and equipment	Term debt or lease (capital or operating lease)	If the expected life of the furniture is five years, then make the amortization of the loan or lease for five years. Do not use a short-term line of credit, which may take away from working capital.
3	Pay operating expenses or routine payroll	Short-term line of credit, accounts receivable financing, factoring	Beyond a base level of permanent working capital, short-term financing can be used to improve cash flow or bridge cash shortfalls.
4	Purchase inventory for resale	Short-term line of credit, inventory financing, extended supplier terms, import financing, or purchase order financing	Financing is tied to the inventory required.
5	Hire engineers to develop a new product line	Term debt or equity	Somewhat dependent on the certainty of success of the new product line and the magnitude of the investment relative to profitability. If there is a high degree of uncertainty, then the company may require additional equity or will want to hedge its risk by obtaining some equity and debt.

TABLE 4.1   *(Continued)*

	Use of Funds	Potential Source of Funds	Comment
6	Build a new facility	Mortgage or rent	Amortization is tied to the useful life of the facility. A common issue with emerging growth and middle-market companies is the distraction of designing and building a new facility. While it may seem fun and creative, designing and managing the construction of a building distracts management from developing their organizations and obtaining new orders to continue a fast rate of growth. The value of the fast growth business may be significantly increased by staying focused on core operations and renting facilities for expansion.
7	Permanent working capital	Term debt or equity	A common error is to rely solely on lines of credit and not establish a base of permanent working capital, thus leaving the company at risk of running short of cash when a weak period occurs.

Use of Funds

The use of funds is a strong determinant in the capital structure of a company. Use of funds is an output of the financial planning process and allows the company to establish not only the amount of capital required, but also a detailed list of assets and resources that will be acquired and when. Table 4.1 provides some examples of sources and uses.

While some of the examples in Table 4.1 may seem like common sense, we often see companies use short-term lines of credit to buy fixed assets, which is a highly inefficient use of capital. For some examples it is easy to directly link the financing source and the funds; in others, the financing may need to consider the level of profitability and the resulting cash flow generated. The balance sheet layout in Figure 4.4 provides a visualization tool for matching maturity of debt and asset life.

Company Stage

For discussion purposes we have divided the company stages into four segments: (1) start-up defined as $0 to $1.0 million in revenue, (2) emerging growth defined as $1.0 million to $10 million in revenue, (3) lower middle-market defined as $10 million to $50 million, and (4) middle-market defined as $50 million to $500 million. Figure 4.2 frames the types of financing vehicles that may be available by stage. "P" is used to indicate types that may be available to a particular stage but are not the norm. Note that in this context "Private Equity" encompasses angel investors, other individual investors, and venture capital.

Company Characteristics

We have assembled a list of drivers that are company specific and that affect the capital structure. These weigh heavily into the process of determining the right mix of debt and equity. The single most influential determinant in raising capital is the quality of management. While not the only determi-

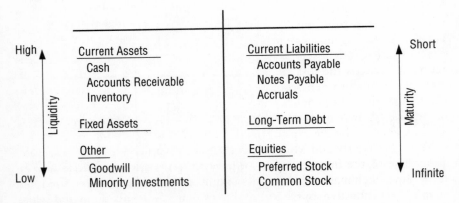

FIGURE 4.4   Balance Sheet Layout

nant, a stronger management team will have greater flexibility in choosing its type and sources of capital than a weaker team that may be forced to take what it can get or get none at all.

- Management strength.
- Stage and progress of the company.
- Ability to generate cash flow.
- Predictability and variability of cash flow.
- Competitive strength.
- Lead time/runway (adequate time to complete a task) to shape the balance sheet.
- Outlook for business performance.
- Current capital structure and ownership.
- Need for financial flexibility to seize unplanned opportunities.
- Strategic initiatives and plans (i.e., acquisitions, alliances, new product lines, etc.).

In addition to these characteristics, the ability of a company to obtain third party credit enhancements will impact the overall capital structure of a company. For example, many early stage companies have no ability to obtain debt financing; however, the company obtains a credit facility based on the strength of a bank guaranty of a shareholder or strategic partner.

Industry Dynamics

From a company's perspective, a higher cost of debt capital may decrease its attractiveness to various stakeholders. Significant external pressure exerted by the pressures of meeting required debt service payments to debt holders may interfere with the company's ability to navigate effectively within its competitive environment. This could cause the company to engage in riskier business activities in order to generate higher returns needed to satisfy current debt service obligations. A common result of an increased return strategy is the loss of a company's ability to respond to a rapidly changing competitive environment. In this respect, the use of excessive levels of debt financing could create an adverse operating environment and could subject managers to both increased discipline and financial constraints imposed by the capital markets on overleveraged companies.

Roy L. Simerly and Mingfang Li conducted research regarding capital structure and the impact of environmental characteristics such as rate of technological change and its diffusion throughout an industry.[5] They refer to environmental dynamism as the rate of environmental change, and the instability created within organizations resulting from that change. Their research indicates in Figure 4.5 that companies in industries characterized as exhibiting high levels of environmental dynamism were more successful if they had relatively low levels of debt. In other words, debt was negatively related to profit in industries experiencing significant technological change. They further examined the relationship between debt and innovation with similar findings. In environmentally dynamic industries, shareholders and management are less likely to risk capital by investing in long-term projects with difficult to forecast profitability.

Across industries there are significant differences in the environmental characteristics impacting firms. Environmental dynamism is a product of several forces operating at one time that includes an increase in the size and number of organizations within an industry.

For stakeholders (including top managers, stockholders, debt holders, and others), as environmental dynamism increases, this phenomenon results in increased inability to assess accurately both the present and future state of the environment. This reduced visibility limits owner and management's ability to determine, with any degree of accuracy, the potential impact of capital structure alternatives on current and future business activities. As levels of environmental dynamism increase and viable alternative capital structures are not pursued, owners and managers experience reduced access to accurate business and financial forecasts needed to make critical decisions.

This research relating to debt of a company is valuable as an input

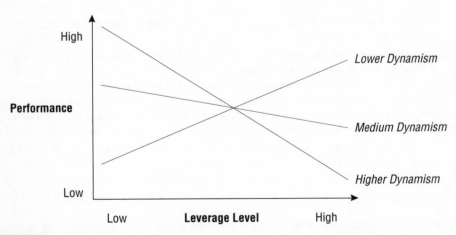

FIGURE 4.5   The Relationship between Economic Performance and Debt across Types of Environments

for consideration as privately held companies consider the balance of debt and equity.

Industry Norms

The classic measure of leverage is the debt-to-equity (D/E) ratio. This ratio compares the total liabilities on a company's balance sheet to the company's equity. Various definitions are used in determining the categories of debt included in the determination of total liabilities; however, most definitions focus on the amount of funded debt owed by a company. Funded debt excludes a company's accounts payable, but includes both short-term debt and long-term debt. Long-term debt is defined as the portion of a loan that has a maturity date greater than 12 months from the date of measurement. Equity is defined by reference to the sum of amounts invested in a company, plus the company's cumulative net earnings after any distributions to shareholders. When the debt-to-equity ratio exceeds 1.0, outside funds provided by lenders exceed the capital provided by investors. It is logical to maintain a balance of debt and equity with a goal being to maintain a D/E ratio similar to the others in the same industry adjusted as discussed herein.

Table 4.2 provides some industry norms based on information derived from tax returns. Lenders and investors will look to published norms as a benchmark to test a company's leverage. The information is national debt-to-equity ratios computed based on data compiled from approximately 4.7 million U.S. corporations filing federal income tax returns. Note that the data includes all corporations, so ratios will be higher for industries (such as service and construction) with a large percentage of cash basis taxpayers since equity for these industries will be lower on a cash basis. Accordingly, these ratios should be viewed in context of the operating and accounting methods predominantly used within the industry.[6]

In the analysis of a company's capital structure, we recommend that the reader obtain additional statistics regarding the details of industry norms for specific assets and liabilities. Potential sources for this type of data are: Risk Management Association (www.rmahq.org), BizStats (www.bizstats.com), BizMiner (www.bizminer.com), and Dun & Bradstreet (www.dnb.com).

Industry Trends

To reinforce the concept we repeat that when a company raises capital is not a function of when it needs it; it is a function of when the capital is available or when the company is positioned to raise it. A compelling argument for

TABLE 4.2 Debt-to-Equity Ratios by Industry

Industry	Debt-to-Equity Ratio
Construction	**2.05**
General building contractors	3.72
Operative builders	1.98
Heavy construction contractors	1.11
Plumbing, heating, and air conditioning	1.90
Electrical work	1.69
Other special trade contractors	1.90
Retail Trade	**2.27**
Building material dealers	1.09
Hardware stores	1.94
Garden supplies and mobile home dealers	2.78
General merchandise stores	1.82
Food stores	2.94
Grocery stores	3.00
Other food stores	2.21
Automotive dealers and service stations	3.64
Motor vehicle dealers	4.35
Gasoline service stations	2.10
Other automotive dealers	2.48
Apparel and accessory stores	1.55
Furniture and home furnishings stores	1.56
Eating and drinking places	2.57
Miscellaneous retail stores	1.58
Drug stores and proprietary stores	0.92
Liquor stores	2.44
Other retail stores	1.84
Wholesale and Retail Trade	**2.26**
Groceries and related products	2.61
Machinery, equipment, and supplies	2.12
Miscellaneous wholesale trade	2.25
Motor vehicles and automotive equipment	4.03
Furniture and home furnishings	2.24
Lumber and construction materials	2.02
Sporting, photographic, toys, and supplies	4.48
Metals and minerals, except petroleum and scrap	1.83
Electrical goods	2.89
Hardware, plumbing, and heating equipment and supplies	1.47
Other durable goods	2.53
Paper and paper products	1.51
Drugs, proprietaries, and druggists' sundries	1.70
Apparel, piece goods, and notions	1.98
Farm-product raw materials	1.99
Chemicals and allied products	2.10
Petroleum and petroleum products	1.25
Alcoholic beverages	1.50
Miscellaneous wholesale trade	2.39

TABLE 4.2 *(Continued)*

Services	2.44
Hotels and other lodging places	2.36
Personal services	1.79
Business services	2.07
Advertising	3.64
Business services, except advertising	1.97
Auto repair and services	3.93
Miscellaneous repair services	1.72
Motion picture production and distribution	1.67
Motion picture theaters	2.43
Amusement and recreation services	1.75
Offices of physicians	4.90
Offices of dentists	2.85
Offices of other health practitioners	2.05
Nursing and personal care facilities	3.40
Hospitals	1.15
Medical laboratories	1.25
Other medical services	2.15
Legal services	3.32
Educational services	2.40
Social services	3.51
Membership organizations	1.05
Architectural and engineering services	2.00
Accounting and auditing services	3.23
Miscellaneous services	1.93
Manufacturing	**1.81**
Food and kindred products	1.38
Meat products	1.30
Dairy products	2.48
Preserved fruits and vegetables	1.61
Grain mill products	1.81
Bakery products	1.94
Sugar and confectionery products	1.10
Malt liquors and malt	2.16
Alcoholic beverages, except malt liquors	0.65
Bottled soft drinks and flavorings	2.22
Other food and kindred products	1.58
Tobacco manufactures	1.08
Textile mill products	1.62
Weaving mills and textile finishings	1.54
Knitting mills	1.45
Other textile mill products	1.72
Apparel and other textile products	2.42
Men's and boys' clothing	2.41
Women's and children's clothing	2.20

(Continued)

TABLE 4.2   *(Continued)*

Other apparel and accessories	3.47
Miscellaneous fabricated textile products	2.25
Lumber and wood products	1.46
Logging, sawmills, and planing mills	1.32
Millwork, plywood, and related products	1.52
Other wood products, including mobile homes	1.71
Furniture and fixtures	1.40
Paper and allied products	1.66
Pulp, paper, and board mills	1.74
Other paper products	1.47
Printing and publishing	1.40
Newspapers	1.25
Periodicals	2.65
Books, greeting cards, and miscellaneous publishing	1.10
Commercial and other printing services	1.99
Chemicals and allied products	1.85
Industrial chemicals, plastics, and synthetics	1.77
Drugs	1.63
Soaps, cleaners, and toilet goods	3.28
Paints and allied products	1.49
Agriculture and other chemical products	1.46
Petroleum including coal products	1.10
Petroleum refining	1.09
Petroleum and coal products—other	2.55
Rubber and miscellaneous plastics products	1.86
Leather and leather products	1.35
Footwear, except rubber	1.14
Leather and leather products—other	1.75
Stone, clay, and glass products	1.83
Glass products	2.35
Cement, hydraulic	1.00
Concrete, gypsum, and plaster products	1.75
Other nonmetallic mineral products	1.65
Primary metal industries	1.60
Miscellaneous primary metal products	2.00
Nonferrous metal industries	1.32
Fabricated metal products	1.36
Metal cans and shipping containers	2.00
Cutlery, hand tools, and hardware	0.82
Plumbing and heating	0.96
Fabricated structural metal products	1.53
Metal forgings and stampings	1.66

TABLE 4.2 *(Continued)*

Coating, engraving, and allied services	1.34
Ordnance and accessories	2.85
Miscellaneous fabricated metal products	1.49
Machinery, except electrical	2.07
Farm machinery	2.57
Construction and related machinery	2.11
Metalworking machinery	1.64
Special industry machinery	1.52
General industrial machinery	1.70
Office, computing, and accounting machines	2.39
Other machinery, except electrical	1.84
Electrical and electronic equipment	2.42
Household appliances	2.45
Radio, television, and communication equipment	1.94
Electronic components and accessories	1.08
Other electrical equipment	4.00
Motor vehicles and equipment	3.88
Aircraft, guided missiles, and parts	3.44
Ship and boat building and repairing	1.82
Other transportation equipment except motor vehicles	1.52
Instruments and related products	1.53
Scientific instruments and measuring devices; watches and clocks	1.48
Optical, medical, and ophthalmic goods	1.09
Photographic equipment and supplies	3.12
Miscellaneous manufacturing	1.54
Transportation and Utilities	**2.40**
Railroad transportation	1.24
Local and interurban passenger transit	4.00
Trucking and warehousing	1.88
Water transportation	1.70
Transportation by air	2.91
Pipelines, except natural gas	4.07
Transportation services—other	2.56
Telephone and other communication services	1.60
Radio and television broadcasting	3.44
Electric services	1.94
Gas production and distribution	1.79
Combination utility services	1.94
Water supply and other sanitary services	2.18

(Continued)

TABLE 4.2 *(Continued)*

Finance, Insurance, and Real Estate	8.07
Banking	7.52
Mutual savings banks	14.92
Bank holding companies	7.25
Banks, except mutual savings banks and holding companies	12.90
Credit agencies other than banks	15.87
Savings and loan associations	40.51
Personal credit institutions	11.29
Business credit institutions	18.57
Other credit agencies; finance not allocable	12.18
Security, commodity brokers and services	17.56
Security brokers, dealers, and flotation companies	21.27
Commodity contracts brokers and dealers	3.52
Life insurance companies	6.54
Mutual property and casualty insurance companies	2.48
Stock property and casualty insurance	1.79
Insurance agents, brokers, and services	1.83
Real estate operators and building lessors	2.61
Lessors of mining, oil, and similar property	0.96
Lessors of railroad and other property	1.21
Condominium and cooperative housing associations	0.98
Subdividers and developers	2.72
Other real estate	2.61
Regulated investment companies	0.03
Real estate investment trusts	0.43
Small business investment companies	1.11
Other holding and investment companies	1.20
Mining	**1.03**
Metal mining	1.13
Copper, lead, and zinc, gold and silver ores	1.14
Other metal mining	1.12
Coal mining	1.04
Oil and gas extraction	0.92
Crude petroleum and natural gas	0.96
Oil and gas field services	0.78
Nonmetallic minerals, except fuels	0.99
Crushed stone, sand, and gravel	0.93
Other nonmetallic minerals	1.26
Agriculture, Forestry, and Fishing	**1.93**
Agricultural production	1.70
Forestry, fishing, hunting, and trapping	2.16

Source: Bizstats.com.

having a financing plan and strategy is so that the company will have fore-casted its future capital needs and be able to take advantage of market oppor-tunities proactively. Certain industry segments go in and out of favor with investors and lenders. Example segments that have gone through recent cycles are telecom (in the late 1990s and early 2000s), biotechnology, nanotechnol-ogy, and outsourcing. The benefits of raising capital when an industry is in fa-vor include greater ease in funding growth and potentially better valuation. For early stage companies, simply being a member of a favored industry may mean the difference between success or failure in the capital raising process.

Related to the investment themes and areas of favor, it is important to understand where in the industry cycle a company is participating and what is the capital structure of comparable companies. Is the industry ex-panding or consolidating? Outlook for overall industry performance (of suppliers and customers and their growth rates and profitability) influences the attractiveness of lending into or investing in companies and how the debt or equity is structured.

Lastly, an overarching factor in evaluating industry trends is the out-look for the general economy and macroeconomic factors, including inter-est rates, inflation, and stability in the oil-producing countries and third world markets.

Shareholder Objectives and Preferences

As mentioned earlier, the objectives and preferences of the shareholder(s) of the company influence and shape a company's capital structure. For exam-ple, if the shareholder of a middle-market company views the business as a personal legacy and desires that it remain in the family for future genera-tions, this begins to limit and define what types of new equity issuance can be appropriate and the deal terms. In another situation, the company may operate as a minority- or woman-owned business enterprise and the owner(s) desire to maintain that status. This imposes limits on the types and terms of equity financings to assure certain regulatory requirements are met.

While it may not seem appropriate for personal preferences to sway the company decision regarding capital structure, that is the reality. In weaker companies and those where their success is closely linked to the participation of shareholder(s) in the business, the willingness to guarantee company liabil-ities directly affects the type of financing that can be obtained. The following is a list of example shareholder preferences or shareholder-specific factors:

- Company importance in the shareholder's overall investment portfolio.
- Shareholder's experience with debt and their philosophical prefer-ence—in effect the shareholder's risk profile.

- Tax preferences of the shareholder(s).
- Shareholder(s) confidence and outlook for the company.

DEVELOPING LIABILITY LIMITS

From a shareholder and company perspective there are limits that can be derived and imposed that will shape the mix and types of debt and equity. In Chapter 5 in the section on commercial banks we present concepts to consider when entering into personal guarantees for the debts of the company. Deciding what liabilities and how much to guarantee provides a natural limit to the amount of debt a company will have. Lenders do not have the insight into operations and the opportunities of the company, yet many have experience with a broad portfolio of businesses. As in the consumer market, businesses can obtain more debt than is healthy for them; so while there are limits inherently imposed by the lenders themselves, these limits in aggregate tend to be an extreme.

Consider a practical limit on the maximum amount of debt available to companies where the primary shareholders will be required to guarantee the debt of their company. This is a typical scenario for emerging growth and middle-market business. The object is to ensure that the shareholder is never required to actually pay a lender from his or her personal accounts. To determine the maximum amount the company can borrow and meet this objective, we can analyze the business using a liquidation balance sheet as shown in Figure 4.6. This provides a worst-case view of the potential liquidation values of the assets of the company and what will be required to be paid. In general, the shareholder should not guarantee any liabilities in excess of the liquidation value of the assets, unless the shareholder is prepared to fulfill any deficiency out of personal assets.

In Figure 4.6 we have presented the balance sheet of a typical product company with $10 million to $15 million in revenue. The liquidation values of the assets and liabilities are shown based on a reasonable scenario. This includes an increase in the liquidation value of other short-term liabilities for the added expenses required to liquidate the assets. We use this example to illustrate a tool that can be used with most businesses and by most shareholders as they contemplate how much they are willing to guarantee.[7] While the initial balance sheet is strong and appears to be more than adequate, in a liquidation scenario it provides just enough collateral coverage to protect the guarantors. Therefore the loan amounts shown provide a debt limit. To increase the debt of the company, it must be accompanied by a matching increase in collateral or an increase in equity. Practically speaking the balance sheet will vary from month to

Assets

Assets	Actual 12/31/2004	Liquidation Value 12/31/2004	
CURRENT ASSETS			
Checking account	198,500	198,500	100%
Accounts receivable	1,625,000	1,300,000	80%
Bad debt reserve	(20,313)	—	0%
Prepaid expenses	7,500	—	0%
Inventory—raw materials	375,587	75,117	20%
Work in progress	703,634	70,363	10%
Inventory—labor	118,913	—	0%
Finished goods	665,214	166,303	25%
Inventory—burden	191,226	—	0%
E&O inventory reserve	—	—	0%
Book to physical reserve	(75,000)	—	0%
TOTAL CURRENT ASSETS	3,737,262	1,810,284	48%
FIXED ASSETS			
Furniture and fixtures	126,952	12,695	10%
Manufacturing equipment	234,956	23,496	10%
Test equipment	61,367	12,273	20%
Office equipment	155,805	10,906	7%
Software	73,409	—	0%
Land	331,821	265,457	80%
Building	1,267,956	887,569	70%
Building fixtures	63,180	—	0%
Accumulated depreciation	(336,001)	—	0%
TOTAL FIXED ASSETS	1,979,445	1,212,396	61%
OTHER ASSETS			
Officers life insurance	21,238	14,867	70%
Other assets	5,000	—	0%
Goodwill (net)	278,000	—	0%
TOTAL OTHER ASSETS	304,238	14,867	5%
TOTAL ASSETS	6,020,946	3,037,547	50%

Liabilities and Equity

Liabilities and Equity	Actual 12/31/2004	Liquidation Value 12/31/2004	
CURRENT LIABILITIES			
Accounts payable	438,021	438,021	100%
Customer deposits and deferred revenue	74,000	74,000	100%
Received not invoiced	105,112	105,112	100%
Bank line of credit	1,000,000	1,000,000	100%
Current portion term loan	84,046	84,046	100%
Current portion capital lease	43,500	43,500	100%
Current portion of building mortgage	55,100	55,100	100%
Payroll taxes payable	41,465	41,465	100%
Accrued salaries and vacation	29,098	29,098	100%
401(k) payable	35,000	35,000	100%
Income taxes payable	128,780	128,780	100%
Other short-term liabilities	134,991	284,991	211%
TOTAL CURRENT LIABILITIES	2,169,113	2,319,113	107%
LONG-TERM LIABILITIES			
Term loan	584,268	915,954	157%
Capital lease	131,500	131,500	100%
Building mortgage	1,147,762	1,147,762	100%
TOTAL LONG-TERM LIABILITIES	1,863,530	2,195,216	118%
TOTAL LIABILITIES	4,032,644	4,514,330	112%
EQUITY			
Capital stock and paid-in capital	100,000	—	0%
Retained earnings	1,164,216	1,160,466	100%
Current earnings	824,086	(2,637,249)	-320%
TOTAL EQUITY	1,988,302	(1,476,783)	-74%
TOTAL LIABILITIES AND EQUITY	6,020,946	3,037,547	50%

Callout (pointing to Other short-term liabilities): Increased to cover costs of liquidating assets

	Actual	Liquidation
Current Ratio	1.72	0.78
D/E Ratio	2.03	(3.06)
ROIC	0.16	n/a
ROE	41.4%	n/a

Secured Debt	Liability
Bank line of credit	1,000,000
Term loan	666,314
Capital lease	175,000
Building mortgage	1,202,862
	~3,046,176

Collateral Liquidation

	Values	Variance	Collateral
Bank line of credit	1,810,284	810,284	Current assets (1st lien)
Term loan	59,371	(608,943)	Fixed assets + 2nd on current assets
Capital lease	23,496	(151,504)	Specific equipment
Building mortgage	1,153,026	(49,837)	Building and land
	3,046,176	0	<< Personal risk to guarantors

FIGURE 4.6 Liquidation Analysis: Lower Middle-Market Company, Inc.

month. Actual use of this technique would be in conjunction with forecasted financial statements in which sensitivity analysis can be performed to determine appropriate limits. We are suggesting that shareholders have a downside plan and assure that management works within the limits initially established by the liquidation scenario.

Though not shown in the example, if the company had issued redeemable preferred stock with a common shareholder guarantee it would be included in the analysis based on the terms of redemption. Redeemable preferred stock will be accounted for as debt, residing on the balance sheet above the equity section and below the debt section. The terms of nonredeemable preferred stock allow it to reside in the equity section of the balance sheet, though upon liquidation, the preferred stock is treated more like subordinated debt in that it is paid after all liabilities are satisfied, but before any distributions to common shareholders. This type of analysis proves to be a useful tool to solve for specific debt-to-equity ratios and other financial measures.

Issues and Combinations

Debt   When structuring debt financings lenders will naturally seek as much collateral as possible to assure the return of their principal. From the company's perspective, it is important to segregate categories of collateral available to each lender to support each individual loan request so as not to inhibit future financings. A simple example: An early stage or emerging growth company seeking to obtain a term loan for permanent working capital might attempt to provide only fixed assets as collateral. While the lender will most likely want a blanket lien on all company assets, reserving accounts receivable and inventory as collateral sources for future loans will provide financing flexibility for the company. In contrast, if the company allows a lien on these assets it will be unable to obtain a future short-term line of credit without renegotiating the term loan; lenders do not like to relinquish collateral. An alternate approach is to negotiate the line of credit and term loan together. The issues are somewhat more complex as the number of debt instruments and lenders increases. Once the discussion begins regarding cross-collateralization, those that may be guarantors are advised to have their personal counsel as part of the negotiations. There are a number of legal subtleties where the best interests of the company may be in conflict with the best interests of the guarantor.

Equity   A common fear for many entrepreneurs is that selling equity in their business will result in loss of control. There are some investors that clearly will control their investments or at least contract for specified control mechanisms; for example, a venture capitalist in an early stage deal may not require absolute percentage control, but will require a variety of control covenants. However, most investors do not invest with nefarious intentions or the desire to operate a business; usually they seek to earn an equitable return on their capital. Conceptually, there is absolute control that is voting control where the majority shareholder (or beneficial majority shareholder) can hire and fire the board and management. Then there is practical control. To address absolute control, the company may consider finding investors that are accustomed to minority investing and are willing to accept a flavor of preferred stock that balances the lack of control with some added incentive; there are a number of creative alternatives. Some of these provide for escalating ownership by the new investors if the company fails to meet certain objectives or performance measures. From a practical perspective, investors invest in management and their ability to do what they say. They know that changing a management team is painful and sometimes detrimental to their potential returns, so it is not a preferred route. From the perspective of the existing shareholders and management, new capital usually means that the business is going through change, and the existing team needs to be open-minded and prepared to adapt to either grow the company to the next level or turn around a difficult situation.

CHAPTER 5

Sources of Capital and What to Expect

This chapter is focused on the funding sources and what to expect from each. In some instances you will find a blurring of terms regarding whether the topic is really a source of capital or a financing instrument. Nonetheless, we have done our best to clarify the differences and provide the information required to understand the alternatives. Figure 5.1 provides a broad overview of the types and sources of funding, and the range of rates of return they target based on their particular business model and risk profile. To support our experiences and assumptions, we solicited the funding sources listed in Part Three of this handbook for their actual data regarding the range of values they use in modeling an investment or loan.

These targeted rates are what you can expect to pay third parties depending on the financial strength of your company, its stage, its industry, the overall credibility of the plan, and risk associated with your business. These annual rates of return are not the realized return on investment of these sources or instruments; these are the modeled or planned returns at the outset of the transaction with your company. The overall actual or realized rates of return for most investors or lenders range from a loss to 25 percent, and the 25 percent is rare over the long term. From time to time there are big winners that make many times their investment—a recent example is Google. The media tends to focus on the high-profile successes and fails to mention the failures, thus leading to the perception that success is the norm rather than the exception. The difference between the planned returns shown in Figure 5.1 and the actual returns indicated in Table 5.1 is a result of the costs and risks associated with the particular portfolio of investments. We are presenting this information to set your expectations and establish a level of realism as you traverse the financing process.

To provide an overview and further set the stage for the detailed discus-

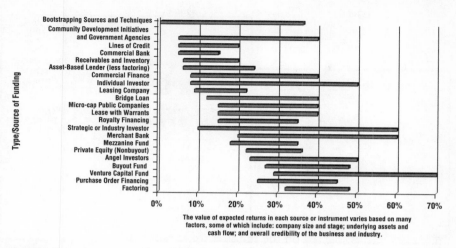

The value of expected returns in each source or instrument varies based on many factors, some of which include: company size and stage; underlying assets and cash flow; and overall credibility of the business and industry.

FIGURE 5.1 Range of Expected Annual Rates of Return Based on Deal Structure As Modeled by the Investor/Lender at the Time of the Transaction

sions to follow, Figure 5.2 highlights the funding sources and the company stages in which they are most likely to invest or lend.

There are usually actions that can be taken on a short-term or on a temporary basis to create cash or funding to bridge to a more permanent solution. It is important to understand and identify what the permanent capital structure is for the stage, size, and industry of your company in evaluating the viability of the interim step. Further, it is important to understand the motivation and business model of the various funding sources, so that you can best position your company to obtain funding

TABLE 5.1 Historical Rates of Return

Source or Benchmark	Long-Term Rates of Return
S&P 500	11.8%
U.S. venture funds	16.3%
U.S. buyout funds	12.6%
U.S. buyout funds—small	24.5%

Source: The venture and buyout data source is Thomson Venture Economics VentureXpert Database; the S&P 500 is based on the prior 10 years ending 6/30/2004.

Funding Source	Start-up $0 to $1.0M	Emerging Growth $1.0M to $10M	Lower Middle-Market $10 to $50M	Middle-Market $50M to $500M
Bootstrapping Sources and Techniques	Y	Y	P	
Individual Investor	Y	Y	P	
Angel Investors	Y	P		
Commercial Bank	P	Y	Y	Y
Asset-Based Lender	P	P	Y	Y
Commercial Finance		Y	Y	Y
Leasing Company	Y	Y	Y	Y
Private Equity (Nonbuyout)		P	Y	Y
Venture Capital Fund	Y	Y	P	
Mezzanine Fund		P	Y	Y
Buyout Fund		P	Y	Y
Strategic or Industry Investor	Y	Y	P	
Merchant Bank		P	P	Y
Micro-cap Public Companies	Y	Y	P	
Community Development Initiatives and Government Agencies	Y	Y	P	
Commercial Paper				P/Y
Private Placement Senior Notes and Senior Unsecured Debt			P	Y
Senior Debt	Y	Y	Y	Y
Junior Debt			P	Y
Subordinated Debt		P	P	Y
Private Equity	Y	Y	Y	P
Public Equity				P/Y
Alliances/Partnering/M&A	Y	Y	Y	Y

Company Stage: <<< Earlier ---- Later >>>

FIGURE 5.2 Funding Sources by Stage
Y = Yes, P = Possible depending on company characteristics and industry.

from these sources as well as negotiate a favorable cost of capital (relative to the norm for that type of source).

We begin our discussion with bootstrapping and then transition to other source alternatives.

BOOTSTRAPPING SOURCES AND TECHNIQUES

Bootstrapping is the term used for nontraditional funding of a company using a series of interim techniques and sources to move from one company stage to another. Bootstrapping somehow implies funding a business when it is not supposed to be funded or in a way that is not expected to work. The technique is routinely used by start-up or early stage businesses that do not have institutional or professional investors, keeping in mind that the great majority of start-up and emerging growth companies do not obtain funding from institutional or professional investors. From the perspective of the entrepreneur or businessperson, bootstrapping may be viewed as a resourceful or creative way to address the financial need of the business for an interim period using the cash flow of the business and minimizing the use of external capital until the cash flow of the business can support ongoing operations. Given that excess funds are rarely available in this situation, bootstrapping may have the benefit of instilling financial discipline in the company's leadership team and processes as they focus on managing cash flow and all of the influencing factors; they grow accustomed to running a tight operation. The downside of bootstrapping is that cash flow decisions can take precedence over business decisions that may be in the long-term best interest of building value. In addition, it takes considerable effort and persistence to implement some of the techniques discussed, so it may distract from the daily management of operations. Lastly, in some industries and markets, it is just not feasible to bootstrap. In reality, bootstrapping can be an effective way to discipline the management team and process, given that excess capital in the hands of inexperienced business people often leads to waste and failure, as we saw in the 1999–2000 Internet bonanza.

Bootstrapping may be a mix of the following techniques, some of which appear to be simply common sense. The cost of bootstrapping is often implicit in the relationship of the participants versus explicit in regard to payment. A key to successful bootstrapping is accurate cash flow management and forecasting. You will see that many of the techniques discussed involve the timing of payments; if you can not accurately and consistently present a realistic cash plan to those supporting the business, you will not have the credibility required to maintain the cash flow juggle inherent in bootstrapping. The result is a failed company in many instances.

Another key to bootstrapping is maintaining a solid credit history and having good credit references. This does not mean that you can not have special arrangements or extended terms. What it does mean is that you make credible commitments and you meet those commitments. If you find your company in the position of missing a commitment, pick up the phone or arrange a meeting with those affected and let them know in advance that you can not do what you said and be prepared to recalibrate their expectations and to provide an updated commitment.

Communication is a very important aspect in managing bootstrapped financing. As we introduce specific techniques and sources, keep in mind the definition of working capital: current liabilities less current assets. Also keep in mind that there is crossover in some of the techniques described and that a combination of these is often deployed.

Friends and Family Loans and Investments

In a start-up, the classic approach to funding a company is to solicit loans and investments from friends, family, and the principal's personal savings. Sometimes successful professionals are willing to invest a portion of their disposable income. These funds are typically provided on the basis of one's relationships and structured in a relatively informal fashion. These dollars usually represent the first ones invested before or around formation of the company and generally range from $1,000 to $250,000 in total from a handful of individuals.

Alternate Revenue

Another common start-up funding technique is for the principals of the start-up company to engage in a business or product line similar to the business they desire to eventually build, using the revenue and income thus produced to fund their existence while they launch the real company. A classic example is when a group of engineers working for a large company desire to start a new product-focused company but do not have the funding to solely develop and market the new product. If the time to market is sufficiently long, the engineers may engage in part-time consulting to fund the base expenses of the company while spending the balance of their time developing the new product. They will work long-hour days in most instances, putting in sweat equity for a shot at launching their company. Though the consulting work is a distraction in the short term, it provides the funding to survive and invest the time and energy in the development stage of a new enterprise.

There is a counterargument that developing an alternate revenue source (or creating a hybrid business model) is less of a distraction than pursuing institutional investors or other alternatives. That was the case for Michael Shinn, founder and CEO of Secure Software Solutions in Chantilly, Virginia. "Raising capital is a tremendous time drain," says Shinn. "I was afraid we would miss the opportunity if we didn't get to market quickly." Rather than take the time to raise capital, Shinn created a hybrid company, offering consulting services while developing his computer systems security product. A blended business model is usually a no-no in most venture capitalists' books, but it worked well for Shinn. Consulting provided an instant source of revenue and proved invaluable to product development. "It let us test our product with real customers, rather than building our technology in an ivory tower, which is what guys tend to do when they get a lot of funding," says Shinn.[1]

Customer Prepayments or Discounting Accounts Receivable

Regardless of the stage of the business, an often-viable source of funds is customer prepayments; we have seen this in start-ups and in Fortune 1000–sized companies. This involves negotiating all or partial payment by the customer in advance of providing the product or service; and may involve staged or progress payments based on completion of certain milestones. In many instances, this is one of the cheapest sources of capital for a company, especially when the customer is a larger business and the amount requested is relatively small. Prepayments are also used to manage credit risks when the customer is a smaller or less established company.

Akin to prepayment is a discount for early payment of an invoice, though much more expensive in theory. Many large companies aggressively pursue accounts receivable discounts. Keep in mind that the buyer that negotiates the price is often not motivated by accounts receivable discounts; so in negotiations do not offer the discount until after the price is set. You may be able to in effect pad the price with the cost of the discount so that you do not impact your margins and you are able to accelerate your cash flow. Typical accounts receivable discounts range from 0.5 percent to 5 percent of the invoice amount for accelerating payment from 30–40 days to 5–10 days. The range of discounts is related to the cost of money at the time of negotiations. During a period with low interest rates discounts are on the lower end of the range.

Supplier/Vendor Financing and Extended Terms

Depending on the type of purchase, many suppliers and vendors will negotiate extended payment terms or special arrangements for some period of time to build loyalty, to facilitate a sale, or to allow the customer to pursue growth. This should translate into improved cash flow.

An example: If the purchase is for a piece of equipment and the intent is to seek long-term financing via a lease or loan, consider asking the supplier to immediately provide the equipment and to provide a period of 60 to 90 days to install the equipment and obtain funding, so that you can implement and begin to use the equipment and generate cash flow, all before having to make any payments. The supplier may request, or you may offer, a small down payment to facilitate this arrangement.

Though many suppliers will not offer permanent extended payment terms, many will work with customers for a period of time by extending payments in exchange for a commitment of ongoing business. The same concept applies if your company is seen as a growth opportunity and the supplier wants your business.

Another strategy borrowed from the manufacturing and retail sectors is that of consignment. This involves a supplier providing inventory at your location for use or resale; however, your company is not invoiced or liable for the inventory until it is actually sold. In other words, title for the inventory does not transfer to you until the instant you sell that inventory. This means that the aging of the invoice due the supplier does not begin until the aging of your receivable from your customer, thus creating the potential for generating revenue with less working capital. Dell, Inc. uses this strategy and actually operates its business on negative working capital because it gets paid by its customer before it is required to pay its suppliers.[2]

Customer and Supplier Barter Arrangements

As mentioned before, understanding the use of funds is critical in determining how to fund a particular need. In some cases, you will find that there is synergy between your company and that of your customers and suppliers that will allow noncash exchanges of goods and services. This noncash exchange, or barter arrangement, can have the effect of reducing the amount of capital that you may need to obtain from cash funding sources, sometimes making it easier to obtain the cash funding.

Revenue and Pricing

The contribution margin from new or incremental revenue is an often-overlooked source of capital, and maybe one of your cheapest sources. A way to analyze this alternative is to determine the selling cycle of your product or service and the required working capital to generate the sale. Couple this with the probability of success in obtaining the new sale if management invested its time and energy to effect the transaction. Compare this scenario and its likelihood of happening to the time, energy, and likelihood of raising new capital. Though it may seem like harder work, and in some instances it is, consider that many management teams have never raised capital and therefore have a better chance of creating their own capital by focusing on new sales than by seeking external funds.

Let us take an example of a media and events company that primarily sells sponsorships to generate revenue. On a period basis, once fixed costs are covered, 50 to 70 percent of any new revenue flows to the bottom line, and customers in this business are accustomed to paying the sponsorship in advance. In effect, this company can raise capital by focusing its efforts on obtaining additional sponsorships instead of pursuing disinterested parties for capital. From a cost of capital perspective, keep in mind that the tax impact of incremental revenue will vary depending on the level of profitability of your particular situation.

New revenue resulting from price elasticity is another overlooked source of growth capital. As a company grows and strengthens its market position, the price decision is sometimes forgotten as the team focuses on obtaining new customers and new orders to meet their monthly and quarterly goals. After analysis of the market and competitive situation of a particular company is conducted, it may be the case that a company can increase its product or service price without any loss in sales volume as customers will continue placing orders at the increased prices. To this extent the price increase is at a percentage level that is acceptable to customers. The contribution margin from the change in price may become a new source of capital to fund investments.

As an example, let us consider a specialty industrial equipment manufacturer with annual sales of $20 million. The newly appointed president met with his sales team in a routine review and asked the question: "How many orders would we lose this year and next if we raise our price 10 percent?" To his surprise, each sales manager responded, "None." The contribution margin from this price increase was nearly 90 percent of the new revenue and generated about $1.8 million before tax of new capital to invest in growing the business during the first year!

Another example: A small communications equipment company with revenues of about $6 million and a strong market position with a niche product line was able to raise its prices 20 percent over a two-year period while dramatically increasing revenue from new orders; the company grew at more than 50 percent a year for several years. With a contribution margin of about 60 percent, this company was able to create more than $1 million in new working capital to support its growth while reducing its bank debt. The move to increase prices was not to take advantage of its customers, but rather to adjust the prices to a fair market value so that the company could reinvest the appropriate capital in the research and development (R&D) of future technologies and products to maintain its market position and build long-term value for its established customers and stakeholders.

Customer and Supplier/Vendor Investments

Depending on the relative market position and competitive nature of the product or service you provide, customers and/or vendors can be valuable sources to fund growth, particularly as it relates to product or service development. There are a number of major corporations that have venture capital or investment funds for start-up and growth companies. These major companies can make hands-off investments or establish partnerships to provide expertise in areas where the start-up or growth company is weak or lacking. Their motivation varies, but typically they have a mission to:[3]

- Provide a window of opportunity by exposing the company to completely new technologies and/or markets (the most common objective).
- Seek opportunities to manufacture and/or market new products.
- Identify companies that might be potentially profitable acquisition targets.
- Seek exposure to new manufacturing or business processes.
- Create or enhance desirable business relationships (such as research contracts or joint marketing initiatives).

Generally, these funds are interested in expanding knowledge, technology, or product lines through their investments. These funds can provide some significant leverage and restrictions on their portfolio companies in a given market. Later in this chapter we have provided a section about strategic investors and corporate venture capital to discuss this topic in more depth.

In addition to those companies with formal venture capital or investment programs, you may seek to engage your customers or suppliers in arrangements that have the same or similar ambitions. The form which such an arrangement takes will vary, but typically can be structured as a strategic relationship such as a joint marketing initiative, distribution agreement, reseller agreement, or teaming agreement. They can also take the form of a joint venture or alliance, but these sometimes require greater scrutiny and oversight and take longer to consummate. Here are some examples.

A small service company focused on telecommuting develops relationships in its market with customers, technology suppliers, and universities as part of its ongoing business. In doing so, it sees the opportunity to develop software that provides a technology to enhance its services to the medical and public safety markets. The company engages with a team from a university to further the development of this software and begins to fund several engineers. As the project progresses, the company raises some initial outside capital from a group of angel investors that have known company management for many years. With a workable product, the company begins to pursue customers and potential contracts; this software operates on several hardware platforms. In the process of bidding on potential contracts, it becomes apparent that the software solution provides value to the hardware manufacturers and that they may benefit from a relationship with this small company to enter these markets. The small company is able to negotiate prepayment of license agreements with the hardware companies and to obtain support hardware and services to finish its development and initial deployments of the software. In effect, this small company has raised a significant amount of capital from partners that view its relationship with them as strategic—all being done through larger company marketing and R&D budgets.

Another example: A growth company with existing products and customers has a new product concept that it wishes to pursue, but needs additional capital to undertake prototyping and development. Management drafts a business plan and determines the timing of the cash flow and potential payback. By examining the use of funds, it is determined that a significant amount of the investment will be used to pay suppliers for tooling, prototyping, advertising, and certifications. A potential funding alternative is to determine how much, if anything, the existing company can invest in this initiative. The next step is approaching a few key suppliers with the business plan seeking terms that allow payment flexibility during the start-up phase and debt relief if the project fails. In return, the suppliers have the opportunity to participate in a royalty stream from the product plus a preferred supplier status as long as they maintain acceptable product quality, delivery, and agreed-upon cost reductions. We have seen this technique used successfully in the electronics, industrial, and pharmaceutical industries.

Deferred Employee Compensation

For many service- and technology-based companies, employee compensation is the single largest use of cash. During start-up or transition periods, some employees may be willing to forgo or reduce their cash compensation in exchange for future payments or other consideration. If an employee is willing to consider this concept, compensation may be deferred as a source of cash. It is recommended that a written agreement be used to clarify expectations and provide for any waivers required by law. As an alternative and if an employee can legitimately meet Internal Revenue Service (IRS) regulations, some employees may be able to become contractors to enhance their ability to be flexible in support of the company's needs. A note of caution: Ensure that the agreement between the employee or contractor and the company provides clear delineation of intellectual property rights and remedies in the event of nonpayment. Without clarity, it will be almost impossible to obtain equity funding if the employee's work product is critical in the valuation of the company.

Let us take the example of a start-up software firm that has identified a team of engineers that it plans to hire upon funding. Most start-ups will find it easier to procure investment dollars if they are actually committed to and implementing their plans versus attempting to sell a concept that they will act on post funding. To break this apparent catch-22, the start-up may consider contracting with those individuals and exchange their deliverables for deferred payment and restricted stock. During the fund-raising process, these individuals may maintain contracts with other sources of income or be employees of nonrelated companies to provide for their personal cash requirements. Upon funding, the company could convert them from contractors to full-time or part-time employees and begin to pay regular salaries. In negotiating the contractor agreement with them, we do not recommend that the expectation be set that they will be paid in full upon the company's receipt of funding. Rather, consider a payment schedule over 6 to 18 months from the date of funding—you will find this much more palatable by the investors.

In the event that your company is an ongoing business versus a start-up, you may find that employees are willing to forgo or reduce their compensation in exchange for equity or deferred bonuses in addition to repayment of the amount forgone. Once again, we recommend you review this with counsel to ensure compliance with applicable laws.

Practically speaking, deferred compensation is a tricky issue. Some employees have the financial resources to defer income, but most live paycheck to paycheck. Asking employees to give up income is the equivalent to asking them to give up their lifestyle, while many are struggling to survive. This option can be of last resort! Management is asking employees to believe management's dream at all costs—and that is not a card that should be played often or lightly. Being up-front with employees is important, and if making payroll is in question, then employees should understand their risk ahead of time, not at the time of decision. Employees will question the integrity of management if faced with deferral or nothing. It is best if deferred income is the employees' idea. A word of advice: Even when things get desperate, always pay the payroll and especially the payroll taxes. The IRS is no fun to battle!

Outsourcing

In many instances, implementation of an outsourcing strategy can result in an increase in working capital coupled with the positive benefit of process scalability while maintaining a variable cost structure. In some situations, outsourcing can increase a company's speed to market. A common theme is to outsource noncore elements of the business; routine processes that are outsourced in growth companies are:

- Payroll and benefits management.
- Product manufacturing.
- Noncritical product and service design.
- Information technology support and maintenance.
- Distribution and selling of products and services.

While outsourcing can increase working capital, this is not always the case. It is critical to understand the motivation of the potential outsourcing partner, and each relationship should be documented with a contract that clearly delineates the terms. The selection of an outsourcing partner is usually given significant consideration and diligence, for it can have such positive and negative impacts on a business. It is critical to understand the entire cost in structuring the relationship, not just a piece-part or transaction cost. You may consider seeking a consultant or adviser who routinely structures outsourcing relationships. One source of information is the Outsourcing Institute (www.outsourcing.com).

Working Capital Management—
Inventory, Accounts Receivable, and Accounts Payable

Though we have mentioned this in prior paragraphs, we deem it important enough to repeat. There is no substitution for solid management of the company's existing working capital to improve cash flow. In most companies, this translates into aggressive and timely collection of accounts receivable, appropriate timing of payment of payables, and carefully balancing inventory to minimize the company's investment while having adequate supplies to meet customer demands.

One concept we have not discussed is collection of past due receivables. Without attempting to write an entire section on accounts receivable collection, we have provided a few notes for your consideration.

Litigation takes a long time and many times does not result in collection of the cash the company needs on a timely basis. Obviously, managing credit risk up front is preferred to collection after the fact, but when a company is confronted with a customer that cannot pay, get creative.

Begin to increase communication with the customer and be willing to accept partial payments. If your company continues to sell to the customer, link delivery of product or service to payments, and get more in receipts than you ship. Lastly, determine if the customer provides a product or service that your company needs; if so, then negotiate to off-set the outstanding balance.

Operating Profit

The obvious and traditional method of financing a company is through the generation of operating profit. We already mentioned this in a prior section when we discussed revenue and pricing. The key to determining the rate of growth that can be sustained through operating profits, or self-funding, is to understand the operating cash flow cycle. Many factors affect the length of a company's operating cash flow cycle: how long the company has to pay suppliers, how long inventory is held, the profit inherent in each dollar of revenue, and the length of time customers use in making payment to your company.[4] From experience, many large organizations will not allow their business units to grow faster than 10 to 15 percent annually, as a baseline measure of their ability to self fund. This is an overall guideline where businesses with higher gross margins may be allowed to grow faster than those with lower gross margins. The concept of self funding through operating profits and cash flow is core to any business, regardless of size.

There are three levers that affect the ability to self fund: cash flow velocity, cost reductions, and price increases. Control of these levers will drive the formula for determining the annual rate of growth that can be funded by internal operating cash flow.[5]

In Appendix D we have provided an excellent *Harvard Business Review* article by Neil C. Churchill and John W. Mullins on determining how fast your or your client's company can grow based on its specific cash flow cycle.

Practically Speaking

Most entrepreneurial ventures are bootstrapped to some extent. Sources of funding come from anywhere the entrepreneur can find it. Much of the funding is through the use of services of other companies who might have an interest in the product or service if fully developed or launched. Entrepreneurs are creative, and how they structure relationships with other companies and obtain services is as varied as their personalities. Venture capitalists give high marks to entrepreneurs capable of developing these relationships. However, the critical issue for the entrepreneur is not to structure deals that could hinder growth or institutional financing in the future. A word of advice: Never lose control of the intellectual property or enter into a relationship that cannot be reshaped into an independent entity capable of demonstrating growth, creating future value, and being financed.

INDIVIDUAL INVESTORS (PRIVATE PLACEMENTS NOT FROM ANGELS OR INSTITUTIONS)

Angel investors typically invest in early stage companies in the seed round of financing. However, there are many individuals who make investments in emerging growth and middle-market companies which are outside the realm of angels. Thus the investors we are discussing in this section.

Some companies will choose to raise capital using a direct private placement soliciting individuals to participate based on a predetermined deal structure. These deals range in size from a few hundred thousand dollars to $5 million based on federal and state securities laws; the structure of these offerings varies. The company will establish a minimum investment amount per investor and seek enough to break escrow. Depending on the type of offering, there will probably be a maximum number of investors accepted (typically 35 nonaccredited). For example: A lower middle-market software company generating $8 million in revenue growing at 25 percent per year needs $900,000 to develop and launch a new product line. Let us assume that the company is not a candidate for institutional venture capital and does not want to increase its leverage. If management has an adequate network to access individual investors, then it may choose to undertake a private placement for the $900,000. There tend to be several types of individual investors.

Types of Investors

- **Unsophisticated emotional investors.** These are the folks that are known to the entrepreneur, but who really should not invest directly in any private placement and do not have the financial capacity to lose their investment; however, they desire to provide support to their friends, family, and community. We suggest that companies do not accept funds from these individuals. They will usually be high maintenance for management—and besides, in many cases, it is the wrong thing to do.
- **Middle- to upper-income individuals (nonaccredited).** There is a segment of the population that does not fit the criteria for being accredited, but has savings and a desire to participate in growth businesses in the community. Be careful with this type of investor, because most of these individuals will be high-maintenance investors for management.

- *Accredited and high net worth individuals.* These are folks who meet the legal requirements for investing and may be reasonably sophisticated (but not necessarily so).
- *Professional investors.* There are ample sophisticated, experienced, high net worth individuals who routinely invest in growing companies. They will usually have a desired deal structure that has worked for them in the past. Some of these may also be angels.

From a positive perspective, individual investors will be less sensitive to price and valuation relative to institutional investors. They seek opportunities to invest in their local communities and to tangentially participate in the growth of successful teams; they are really investing in the people.

However, raising capital with a private placement from individuals is a long and hard process. Post funding, a significant amount of time is required in communicating with the base of investors—keeping them up to speed and aware of the company's activities. In addition, management and the majority stockholder(s) have a fiduciary duty to protect the interest of the minority investors; therefore, taking corporate action may require extra steps and time.

ANGEL INVESTORS*

Angel investors are individuals who use their personal cash to invest in early stage companies. This section describes the fundamentals of angel investing, compares angels with venture capitalists, and offers suggestions for best practices for entrepreneurs.

Angel investors are so named because in the early 1900s wealthy individuals provided capital to help launch new theatrical productions. As patrons of the arts, these investors were considered by theater professionals as "angels." Estimates of the number of active angel investors in the United States vary widely, most being accredited. The SEC Rule 501 states that an "accredited investor" is a person with a net worth of at least $1 million or annual income for the most recent two years of at least $200,000 and a reasonable expectation of $200,000 in annual income for the current year.

---

*The base content of this section is adapted from the "Note on Angel Investing," 2003, by Professors Michael Horvath and Fred Wainwright, Tuck School of Business at Dartmouth College. The authors gratefully acknowledge the support of the Tuck Center for Private Equity and Entrepreneurship. Copyright © 2003 Trustees of Dartmouth College. All rights reserved.

According to Forrester Research, Inc., the number of households in the United States that fit that profile is approximately 630,000.

Angels fill a critical capital gap between friends and family and the venture capitalist (VC). When a start-up requires more than $25,000 but less than about $1.5 million, angels are a viable source of capital. This level of funding is below the radar screen of most VCs, although some will occasionally fund a seed round of as little as $500,000.

During the past few decades, VCs have raised larger and larger pools of capital, and given that the time and expense of reviewing and funding a company are the same regardless of size, it is far more efficient for VCs to fund larger transactions. Though the demarcation line is blurring, angels and VCs rarely compete for the same deals; you will see in Table 5.2 the major differences in their profiles.

Angels Are Varied

Angels can sometimes add significant value to start-up companies. It is important to be aware of the value that is important to your company and its needs as you pursue funding. Keep in mind that angels are subject to their personal idiosyncrasies. One or more of these characterizations may apply to an angel:

Guardian Angel This type of investor has relevant industry expertise and will be actively involved in helping the start-up achieve success. He or she has a strong Rolodex of contacts and has the experience to add substantial value as a board member.

Operational Angel This angel has significant experience as a senior executive in major corporations. For an entrepreneur, this type of investor can add much value because he or she knows what the company needs to do in order to scale up operations. However, be careful because this angel may have no idea of how to operate a small business without the significant management depth found in larger companies. Someone who has been successful in managing by the numbers can be demanding in requests for financial information.

Entrepreneurial Angel An investor that has "been there, done that" may be very valuable to a novice entrepreneur. For example, an entrepreneur can add perspective to the founders on what to expect from investors and how to effectively negotiate financing terms. An entrepreneurial angel with operating experience is ideal!

TABLE 5.2   Angels versus Venture Capitalists

	Angels	VCs
Funding amounts	$25,000 to $1.5 million	$500,000 and above
Motivation to invest	Not just return driven, strong emotional component (bragging rights, psychological benefits of coaching, rush from being involved in fast-paced start-ups)	Mostly return driven with adjustments for relationships with other VCs and reputation among entrepreneurs
Accessibility	Prefer anonymity, reachable via referrals or through angel groups	Highly visible, usually will only look at business plans referred by their network of contacts (attorneys, etc.)
Geographical focus	Regional, within four hours' drive time	Regional, national, or international, depending on the firm
Key reasons to invest	Personal chemistry with entrepreneur, detailed market analysis, sustainable competitive advantages	Nearly developed product, operating history, strong and experienced team, sustainable competitive advantages
Term sheet issuance	Relatively fast (one day to three weeks), terms are somewhat negotiable (more than with VCs)	Can be fast, but usually is at a moderate pace (several weeks); terms fairly standard and not very negotiable
Investment vehicle	Common or preferred stock, occasionally convertible debt (debt convertible to equity shares)	Preferred stock (convertible to common)
Equity percentage	10%–30%	20% or more
Typical postmoney valuation of start-ups	$250,000 to $10 million	$5 million and above
Due diligence	Relatively fast and light	Relatively slow and methodical
Funding process	Lump sum or milestone	Lump sum or milestone
Long-term value added	Operational experience, common sense advice; specific industry expertise	Experience in managing growth, deep pockets, networks of additional sources of capital, Rolodex, experience in managing IPOs and sale exits

TABLE 5.2 *(Continued)*

	Angels	VCs
Reaction to bad news	Roll up the sleeves and help solve the problem, open up Rolodex	Intense communication and coaching; open up Rolodex; help structure joint ventures, new financing rounds, or mergers; fire management
Target exit time	Five to seven years	Three to five years
Target IRR returns	15% to 25%	20% to 40%

Hands-off Angel   A wealthy doctor, attorney, or similar professional must focus on his or her day-to-day career. This type of investor is willing to invest but usually does not have the time or specific expertise to be of much help to the start-up.

Control Freak   Some investors either believe they have all the answers because they have achieved certain wealth or have the personality to convince themselves they know everything. Caveat emptor.

Lemming   Some angel investors will not make a decision unless an informal leader in the angel group invests or makes positive comments about a start-up—success breeds success. Even a term sheet from one or two small investors can allow an entrepreneur to access larger investors, who usually become more interested when they find out that fellow investors have committed. Some lemming investors are particularly astute at leveraging the work of other investors, whereas other lemmings simply trust blindly in the due diligence and term sheets of fellow investors. Generally, these investors are not active in the operating decisions of the company.

Angels Band Together

Angel investors increasingly join one or more informal or formal groups. There are various advantages of working in groups:

- Social bonds and networking.
- Access to prequalified deal flow.
- Leveraging intellectual capital and expertise of individual members.
- Learning from each other regarding deal evaluation skills.
- More extensive due diligence capability.
- Alignment of members' interests.

Angel groups can be structured in various ways:

- Each member owns a portion of the legal entity representing the group.
- Limited liability entities are formed by individuals to invest in specific deals.
- The group is a nonprofit entity, and individual angels invest independently.

Typically an entrepreneur must complete a questionnaire and submit an executive summary or a full business plan. A proactive entrepreneur will understand the angel investing process. Some groups require that a member meet with the entrepreneur and determine if the plan is viable before allowing the entrepreneur to present to the group. Other groups allow the administrative staff and managing director to review the plan and invite the entrepreneur to present without a champion. The questionnaire will typically include the following:

- Name of company.
- Year founded and legal structure (C corporation, S corporation, limited liability company (LLC), etc.).
- Who referred you to this angel group?
- Summary of business (in three sentences or less).
- What problem is your product or service solving?
- What is the size of the market, how much has it grown in the past few years, and what is its projected growth?
- Describe the competition (companies as well as substitute products).
- What are your company's competitive advantages?
- Why will your company succeed in the long run?
- Does the company or its founders have any relevant patents or proprietary technologies (please do not reveal specific proprietary information)?
- What is the relevant experience of each member of the management team? Please enclose a one-page resume of the CEO.
- What is the company's sales and marketing strategy?
- If you have a web site, what is the URL?
- What are the major short-, medium-, and long-range operational milestones you intend to achieve?
- Financial information as shown in Table 5.3.
- Are 50 percent or more of revenues generated from one or two customers?
- What are the three greatest risks of this venture?

TABLE 5.3 Financial Information

	Last Fiscal Year	Projected This Fiscal Year (without Investor Funds)	Projected This Fiscal Year (with Investor Funds)	Projected the Following Fiscal Year (with Investor Funds)
Revenues				
Cost of revenues				
Operating expenses				
Interest expense				
Liabilities				
Number of full-time employees				

- What are the liabilities outstanding other than operational payable and accruals—especially off-balance-sheet items?
- What is your capitalization structure? (How many shares are currently owned by founders and investors? How much capital has been invested so far, and by whom?)
- How much capital are you seeking, and how will this capital be used?
- How many rounds of investment and what amounts do you expect to need in total?
- What is your exit strategy?
- Please list the names and companies of your professional advisers (attorney, CPA, and/or consultant).
- Who is the main contact person at the company? Please provide address, telephone, mobile phone, and fax.

Once the presentation is made (usually in 10 to 30 minutes, including a question-and-answer period) the entrepreneur is asked to leave the room. The angels discuss the opportunity, and if one or more angels are interested, then, depending on the group, either the entrepreneur is invited back at a later date for a more thorough review of the plan or an initial term sheet is developed within a week and presented to the entrepreneur. A list of typical terms is provided in Table 5.4.

Sometimes, if an entrepreneur's presentation is weak but the idea has merits, the entrepreneur will be coached on what to do in order to be able to present in a future meeting. Occasionally, the entrepreneur is matched with an angel who is willing to coach the entrepreneur (informally or for a

TABLE 5.4 Typical Term Sheet Clauses

Clause	Sample Detail
Type of security	Convertible preferred stock (Series A).
Dividend	6% noncumulative.
Conversion	Preferred shares are convertible at any time to common shares at a conversion ratio of 1:1; preferred shares are also convertible at an IPO of at least $15 million.
Dilution protection	Weighted average method. This method minimizes the loss of percentage of ownership of company by an investor due to investments from other investors in future rounds.
Voting rights	One vote per share as if the preferred stock was converted to common stock. A two-thirds vote will be needed to amend the corporate bylaws, issue new stock, incur debt, sell the company, or shut down the company.
Redemption	Stockholder will have the right to force the company to buy back the shares after six years.
Registration rights	If the company completes an IPO, shareholders will be able to register their shares for sale as allowed by law.
Pro rata share offers	Investor can invest in future rounds of financing in order to retain the same percentage ownership in the company.
Board participation	Investor will have representation on the board of directors.
Conditions precedent	Funding will occur only if due diligence is complete, all legal documents are signed, and any special conditions requested by investor are met by company.
Covenants	Company management agrees to provide monthly status reports and make financial records available for inspection at any time. Company agrees to abide by all laws and maintain proper insurance.
Expenses	Company pays for all legal and due diligence expenses regarding this financing round.
Use of proceeds	Hire CFO and sales manager, buy inventory, pay off accounts payable, meet other working capital needs.

fee) in order to raise the quality of the business to fundable status. Some angels specialize in helping entrepreneurs write business plans and develop their strategies.

Angel groups occasionally band together with other angel groups to share due diligence and invest sufficient capital to complete a round of financing.

Evaluation of Business Plans

Companies do not build themselves. People build companies. Ultimately, an angel investor is selecting a management team. A great team can make even a mediocre company achieve reasonable success, whereas a company with the best technology will not be successful with a mediocre management team.

Some of the key factors of a business plan that improve the success potential of a start-up are shown in Table 5.5. While presented in this section, these success factors also apply to traditional venture capital.

Business plans are inherently subject to change. Projections will change. Teams will change. Competitors will surge or fade. Most successful companies make radical changes to their business plans as managers discover the reality of their situation versus their original expectations. Thus the experience

TABLE 5.5 Success Factors

Factor	Description
Management	■ Years of operational experience in a similar industry ■ Start-up experience with a similar business model that led to a successful exit ■ Willing to be coached
Market	■ Addressable market that is fragmented and growing
Technology	■ Patent protected—creates strategically defensible position
Competition	■ Shows that company has some competition, regardless of product or service ■ Clearly summarizes competitors and key threats
Business model	■ Similar to one or more used by successful companies ■ Demonstrates that customers have a real need that product or service addresses ("must have" versus "nice to have")
Exit strategy	■ Identifies target acquirers—shows deal history of acquisitions and IPOs with key financial multiples and ratios
Risks	■ Objectively assesses risks and describes actions to reduce, mitigate, or eliminate them
Financial projections	■ Shows conservative, expected, and targeted figures with assumptions for each ■ Focuses on cash flow and profitability
Capital structure	■ Detailed ■ Preferably shows ownership by founders and only small numbers of unprofessional or inexperienced investors
Investment desired	■ Places an offer on the table—indicates valuation ■ Shows uses of funds in detail ■ Details expected future rounds and uses of funds from each round

of a management team is critical in order to address sudden changes in strategy. Business plans require updates anytime major changes occur. The right angel investor can play a critical role in mentoring management teams and helping prepare them for venture funding.

Valuation Is Highly Negotiable in Early Stage Investing

Valuation is much more of an art than a science, especially for companies with no revenues or profits. In theory, a company is valued based on its ability to generate cash in the future. These future cash flows can be discounted using basic financial formulas in order to estimate the total present value today of all future cash flows.

For companies without positive cash flow but with revenues or net income, comparisons can be made with publicly traded companies in similar industries. For example, if ABC start-up is in the medical software business, and publicly traded companies in the same industry trade for approximately two times annual sales, then it is reasonable to estimate the value of ABC as somewhat less than two times its annual sales. Usually a discount of 20 percent to 40 percent is made for private companies due to the fact that their stock is not publicly traded and the likelihood of matching willing sellers and buyers of private stock is fairly low.

Investors refer to the valuation of a company prior to receiving a round of investment as "premoney." Once funding occurs, at that instant, the value of the company rises by the amount of funding and the "postmoney" value is determined. For example, a company valued at $1 million premoney will be worth $1.2 million postmoney after receiving a round of $200,000 in funding. The investor in that round owns one-sixth of the company ($200,000 is one-sixth of $1.2 million).

If a start-up has no revenues, then valuation is subject to much negotiation and relies more on common practices of angel and venture capital investors. A hot company with patents or competitive advantages and potential for hundreds of millions of dollars in sales will certainly command a larger value than one with only tens of millions in potential sales, but hard rules are difficult to establish in the investing industry. Angels commonly value seed stage, concept-type firms with premoney valuation ranges from $500,000 to $1,000,000, while early stage venture capitalists start with premoney valuations in the $2,000,000 to $3,000,000 range.

Latest Developments in Angel Financing

Angel investor groups have had a difficult time since the stock market debacle in early 2000. Many early stage companies ran out of cash as early stage financing dried up. Of those start-ups that survived, many had to reach out to venture capitalists who insisted on significantly reducing the ownership percentage of previous investors, including founders and angels.

During times of major decreases in start-up valuations from one financing round to the next, the VCs' basic message to earlier investors was, "If you can't invest in the company in this new round of financing to keep it alive, then you don't deserve to own much of it." This is similar to a poker game; those players who are unwilling to up the ante lose everything they placed in the pot in previous betting rounds. Tough, but fair.

Some of the larger angel groups have either formed their own funds or joint ventured with venture capital funds in order to ensure that young companies have the necessary funding in subsequent rounds to support growth. Thus the angels are better able to monitor their investments as the start-ups achieve greater growth.

Tenex Greenhouse, for example, is an angel group in California that has launched a $20 million (target) venture fund using angel and institutional capital to support successful angel-funded start-ups. Tenex Greenhouse also offers intellectual capital, leveraging its members' functional specialties and industry experience to provide support to funded start-ups.

The well-known Band of Angels, started in 1995 in Silicon Valley, now has a $50 million VC fund with capital from institutional investors. From another perspective, Venture Investment Management Company LLC (VIMAC) is a VC fund in Boston that has a network of more than 200 angels who can co-invest on select deals, especially ones that require more advisory work.

One of the results of cross-fertilization of ideas and organizational structures among angels and VCs has been the emergence of typical financing terms (see Table 5.4). Milestone financing is becoming more common. Investors mitigate their risk by setting operational targets for the start-up that need to be met before another portion of funding is made. The pricing and terms of the milestone funding are preset to avoid excessive subsequent negotiations.

Best Practices for Entrepreneurs

As we have mentioned before in this handbook, only a small percentage (0.2 percent to 0.5 percent) of all business plans presented to either angels or VCs receive funding. Entrepreneurs need to read the necessary books and speak to individuals with financing experience or expertise so when the opportunity arises, they are fully prepared to present their concept to investors. Incomplete business plans are unacceptable in today's competitive environment.

Ideas are a dime a dozen. Fundable businesses are those that can demonstrate that they have the products and the people to enter an identifiable market and take significant market share.

Use informal networks to be referred to individual angels and VCs. It vastly increases the chances that your business plan will be reviewed.

Invest capital in your own start-up. Not doing so is a major red flag for investors. Do not refer to angel investors as "dumb money," regardless of who you are speaking with and especially in a public forum. Believe it or not, this has actually been done. These kind of amateur mistakes will haunt you, because investors and VCs are a close-knit group.

During the initial conversations with an angel group and during the presentation to the angels, it behooves the entrepreneur to find out which of the members are the real decision makers. This is difficult to ascertain but can be very valuable information because angels are human and they feel safety in numbers. The entrepreneur should focus on the more experienced angels and the managing directors of the angel group.

If groups of investors are interested, it is far better for the company to have them to invest as a limited liability company (LLC) than as individuals. VCs are weary of complex capitalization structures, and an entrepreneur risks losing access to larger amounts of capital. In addition, company decision making regarding major events can become unwieldy if large numbers of investor-owners need to be consulted. This process can become like herding cats.

Finding an angel investor is like finding a spouse; personal chemistry is critical because it is a long-term relationship. This chemistry may take time to build, so invest quality time in getting to know the angel. If you are dealing with a group of angels, it is the lead angel who will be on your board or who will manage the investment on behalf of others who should be your focus. It is far better in the long run for an entrepreneur to turn down an angel investment because of lack of chemistry and wait for a better match (though this is rarely done if money is made available).

Keep the investor apprised of the company's progress at least monthly if not weekly. If there are problems, alert the investor early about them. Keep investors informed as to possible solutions. If they have the right skills or contacts, involve them in developing the solution or finding the right people to help. Waiting until the last minute before disclosing major issues risks losing the confidence of the company's investor group.

Practically Speaking

Entrepreneurs owe a tremendous debt of gratitude to angel investors. Angels are the backbone of our capitalist system; they allow ideas to flourish, and allow managers to become heads of companies and jobs to be created. Generally, angels are successful entrepreneurs or investors who want to share in the energy of a new idea and the potential growth of its development. Typically, they require less return for the risk assumed, because generally they are believers, willing to invest at inception. This does not mean they are not savvy. All money is hard to raise. Most of the time angels will be your best investors because they are as committed as the entrepreneur to developing the idea. Institutional interest is in realizing profits and getting there as fast as possible. Angels are more patient, probably because they are in early and are part of developing the idea for commercialization. They are probably more emotionally attached.

COMMERCIAL BANKS

Commercial banks are widely known as a source of debt financing for businesses. They generally provide lines of credit, term loans, and revolving loans. Traditionally, commercial banks are cash flow lenders and view collateral as a secondary source of repayment; from experience, bankers' actions do not always evidence this thinking. Focus is placed on lending to borrowers that have durability and predictability of cash flows. To assure liquidity and stability for the public, banks are highly regulated by state banking commissions or similar bodies, the Federal Deposit Insurance Corporation (FDIC), and by the Office of the Comptroller of the Currency (OCC). Banks are scrutinized for base capital, profitability, liquidity, credit quality, and management, and are required to monitor and rate each loan with quality codes or risk ratings. These codes are established by the bank and relate to, among other things, the type collateral, loan-to-asset value, cash flow coverage, and guarantees. Combined, these impact the price charged a borrower, or cost of capital or interest rate, and the status of the loan in the bank's portfolio.[6] Bank regulators can force a bank to place a loan in nonaccrual or write down a fully performing loan if some factor is of concern to them. This regulatory control is a large determinant of what might be deemed an acceptable risk.[7] This mode of operation coupled with the commodity nature of the banking business translates into a relatively conservative posture inherent in the culture and mind-set of bankers in relation to growth companies—especially given that most growth companies consume cash, not generate it. For start-up companies, collateral becomes more important given that most fail within the first five years.[8]

Most loans are made based on historical financial performance and minimum asset collateral values. The decision to lend is based on the 3 C's of credit: character, collateral, and capacity, where capacity is the ability and willingness to pay.[9]

The bank is not an investor, nor do the bank's returns justify accepting significant risk. Banks are essentially the lowest-risk lenders. You will find that most banks will not lend to a company with a debt-to-equity ratio greater than 2.0 to 3.0 without some additional guarantee or collateral.

This is the converse of asset-based lenders (ABLs), which primarily make their lending decisions based on the quality of the underlying assets and secondarily on cash flow. There are many specialty lenders and commercial finance companies that provide various forms of debt; these lenders tend to understand a specific form of debt exceptionally well and have the business processes in place to manage their risk, or they have expertise in a specific industry and have adjusted their lending program and structure to accommodate the nuances of that business.

It is important to note that many larger regional and national banks now have asset-based lending divisions as well as capital market groups that provide private equity. A key in selecting a financing source is the inherent culture and the actual people that you will interface with and those that make the decisions affecting your relationship with them. We recommend that you determine the work experience and background of the lending team assigned to your company. Most commercial bankers turned asset-based lenders do fine in a relationship until the client's business has difficulties or goes sideways. Then they revert to their instincts, which may be much more conservative. This is not necessarily bad, except that a knee-jerk reaction may be to push your company to take action that is not in its best interest; the bank may call your line of credit and force you into a reactionary mode.

Now the converse argument: Many of the major banks have acquired strong and credible asset-based lending firms and have allowed them to maintain their autonomy. These lenders bring the expertise, temperament, and monitoring processes as true asset-based sources of finance. We advocate knowing your lender and what his or her true disposition is relative to what your business is likely to need with regard to its size, stage, and industry.

Confidence in a company and management is developed from a variety of sources. Many times it begins with referrals from known professionals such as attorneys and accountants, and is coupled with the quality of financial data; over time it is a function of doing what you say. As with many other sources of capital, banks tend to look at the background and depth of management, management's focus on the customer, the type customers and the company's value to them, why customers buy from the company, and a thoughtfully developed and viable business plan. Lastly, banks look for management that is willing to "work through the tough times."[10] For many lenders, their greatest fear is how management will act when the business goes sideways or in the ditch.

Financial covenants should be more important to company management than the interest rate or up-front fees charged in establishing a credit facility with a bank. The financial covenants need to be structured in a manner that will provide the least constraint given a company's business and operations. It is difficult to foresee the future and foretell a problem that does not exist today but could be one tomorrow. Covenants have often forced companies to take action that was not good business in order to avoid defaulting on the loans; you want to avoid this.

The next logical topic surrounds the use of personal guarantees. Our collective experience shows that banks will request, and many times require, personal guarantees from the principals and management of emerging growth and middle-market client companies. These guarantees usually include spousal guarantees where the bank is looking to personal assets as backup collateral. Guarantees are usually intended to assure that management does not walk away or abdicate their responsibility to the bank when trouble occurs within the company. A principal's personal guarantee gives the lender comfort that when the going gets difficult, the principal will remain committed to corrective actions or an orderly liquidation.[11]

Strategies for Structuring Personal Guarantees

Developing an effective strategy for structuring and managing the personal guarantee begins with understanding your lender's objectives and perspective. Secondly, it is important to understand your company's current and forecasted financial position relative to liquidation under federal bankruptcy laws.

A philosophy we promote is that of isolating the risk of your business from personal assets, even when personal guarantees are involved. This requires personal and business financial planning. If you are a significant shareholder and manager of an emerging growth or middle-market company, and anticipate you will be required to sign a personal guarantee, you may consider engaging counsel that fully understands personal and corporate bankruptcy. As an individual, this counsel should not be counsel to your company to prevent the conflict of interest inherent in the discussions. Conversely, we recommend the same from a company perspective; that you have experienced bankruptcy counsel review your debt strategy. We discuss the concept of a liquidation balance sheet in more detail in Chapter 4, "Capital Structure."

Here are six proposed actions to consider when negotiating the terms of debt with the bank and other lenders with the general objective of committing to as little as required when signing a guarantee:

1. Pursue a written agreement specifying that certain terms of the guarantee will change based on improved financial performance of the company. An example: If your company will have a debt-to-equity ratio of 3:1 post financing, agree to reduce or limit your guarantee when the company's debt-to-equity ratio falls below 2:1. Also consider having the guarantee become less onerous over time, based on the bank's continued relationship with your company.
2. Seek to limit the guarantee by not having your spouse sign, so that it is based solely on your personal guarantee. Be prepared to provide a financial statement showing only your individually owned assets and liabilities. In most states this limits the risk to only assets held solely in your name, not joint assets or those of your spouse.
3. Seek quantified limits on the amount of the guarantee either in relative terms or absolute terms. For example: You may have a line of credit with $2 million total availability. You may seek to limit your exposure to 20 percent of the outstanding balance or a maximum of $200,000. This is particularly appropriate with multiple owners whereby you may seek to limit your exposure based on your percentage ownership.
4. Seek to exclude any assignment or lien on a personal asset or real estate such as a house or property.
5. Seek to limit any risk unless you commit a fraud in managing the business; this is sometimes referred to as a fiduciary guarantee.
6. Assure that the lender must exhaust all remedies against the collateral underlying the loan before the lender can seek recovery from the guarantor. Blanket guarantees usually allow the lender to go directly to the guarantor and ignore the collateral—they will go to the quickest source of liquidation.[12]

Practically Speaking

Unless the banker feels very comfortable with the operations and their security, the bank will ask for a guarantee. And as a borrower, you have a choice not to sign but the bank knows that it is not likely. At this stage, the bank clearly has the advantage in negotiations. Unless there has been a trust violated, banks generally do not like to go after personal assets, particularly homes or belongings. They want your attention and your best efforts to make the company successful. One of the common phrases in banking regarding guarantees is "Who has whom?" In most cases, the loans far exceed the value of the guarantor's personal net worth and often with high net worth individuals their equity is not liquid; it is in real estate or equity in private companies. If things go badly, generally it is in both parties' interest to negotiate a mutually acceptable plan to rescue or protect the bank and company. If you have signed a guarantee and it is for a small portion of your net worth, then it is meaningful. If it is more a multiple of your net worth, then you and the bank need to work together (and generally the guarantee will be waived over time), which is what the bank wants anyway. For the bank to be repaid, it needs management's expertise to resolve the operating issues.

Banking Business

Companies want to develop a good working relationship with a bank and have an advocate for the company within the bank. We suggest that you develop a working relationship with more than one bank—not to play one bank against another, but to mitigate the risk of bank policy changes and to assure that your company has alternatives when your needs may not suit an existing relationship. Banking is built on personal relationships, and you cannot build a relationship quick enough when difficult situations or needs arise. In addition, bank officers have a high turnover rate and it is difficult to predict when turnover will occur. So you do not want to be caught in the early stage of building a new relationship and have a crisis occur.

Sometimes banks get in trouble when bank management leads its lenders to increase the number of loans on their books at a rapid rate. This is generally done because their existing loan portfolio cannot earn enough to fulfill industry earnings expectations. So why do we care? If your company's loan is one of those that is really marginal in the bank's normal mode operation, once the wave of rapid loan-making is over, your loan may very well be deemed a problem credit—even if you make all the payments on time. This may lead to pressure by the bank for you to repay the loan or for you to improve your financial position at a rate that was not expected. In a worst case, the bank may call the loan and demand repayment.

There are other instances in the life of a bank and other macroeconomic issues that sometimes cause the bank to change its disposition relative to credit risk. Though you cannot control these, they may affect you and your company.

Lastly, the size of the asset base of the bank matters as you consider which banking relationship to establish. Each bank has a loan lending limit per risk (that is you or your company). If you choose a smaller bank as your lender, look ahead several years and determine if their borrowing limit is adequate to support your company's foreseeable borrowing needs.

Keep in mind that most loan documentation provides demand for repayment features if the bank feels insecure, regardless of the term of the loan. This is a very subjective covenant and leaves the company at risk if it does not have alternatives at hand. Thus we are back to the recommendation of having more than one banking relationship established.

ASSET-BASED LENDERS

Asset-based lenders encompass a broad category of firms that provide debt financing by lending against the assets of a company. As we have seen in other areas of finance, there is a lack of standardization with the use of terms among firms; we will, however, attempt to provide a reasonable level of differentiation. Typically, ABLs are unregulated nonbank lenders (though they may be owned by a bank) that have the flexibility to make more highly leveraged loans based on the situation and collateral specific to their client's business. A true asset-based loan will be repaid from the liquidation of the collateral regardless of the state of the business. It is more important for the collateral to perform than for the company to perform. An ABL's key concerns are the liquidation value of its loan's underlying assets and potential management fraud. These concerns lead to control and close monitoring of their collateral.[13]

The larger ABLs tend to have specific financing programs based on industry, company stage, or type of financing. The broad categories of asset-based lending are discussed hereafter. Keep in mind that we are discussing the generic version of these financings, and that there are hybrid versions that may contain a mix of terms or features from several.

To balance the subsequent discussion of asset-based loans and some potential negative attributes, we highlight four benefits of asset-based financing:

1. The entire cost of an asset-based loan is paid with pretax dollars, unlike most equity costs.
2. ABLs do not seek a seat on the board or any control of the company, just a risk-adjusted and fair return on their money.
3. ABL relationships can usually be terminated by paying off the balance of outstanding debt to the ABL and any accrued interest and fees. Equity and other sources can be much more difficult to exit.

4. Asset-based loans are evergreen in nature, with no set amortization or payment schedule. They can grow as the business grows, unlike many other forms of financing.

Documents required to begin meaningful discussions with an ABL usually include: prior year and most recent interim financial statements; the previous month-end's accounts receivable and accounts payable agings; personal financial statements from the primary stockholder(s) with Social Security number(s); and the potential client company tax identification number.

Accounts Receivable Financing

In accounts receivables financing (A/R financing), the lender, which may be an asset-based lender, commercial finance company, or commercial bank, advances funds to the client's bank account against a line of credit (LOC) based on a percentage of the eligible outstanding receivables. Prior to an advance, the client company usually submits a report that shows the calculated availability and the requested draw against the LOC. This allows the lender to closely monitor the collateral supporting the LOC. The lender has a bank lockbox in which payments from the client company's customers are received and credited against the outstanding balance of the LOC. If the lender is a bank, the formal monitoring process just described may be somewhat relaxed; a lockbox may not be used and reporting may only be required monthly. This dynamic exists because the financially stronger firms probably have supporting cash flow and other risk-mitigating characteristics. Unlike in factoring, the client company retains legal ownership of its invoices throughout the process and has the risk of collection. Figure 5.3 illustrates this process.

Example Availability   Following is a simplified analysis (neither fees nor interest taken into consideration) of the available funds for an accounts receivable LOC where the company has $1 million of receivables outstanding and has already drawn $400,000 in a prior period:

Outstanding accounts receivable balance	$1,000,000
Less A/R > 90 days past due (ineligibles)	(75,000)
Total eligible A/R	925,000
Available to borrow (80% of eligible)	740,000
Less the outstanding LOC balance	(400,000)
Available to borrow	$ 340,000

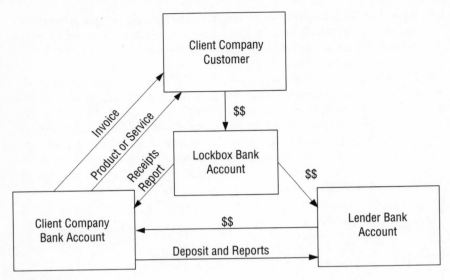

FIGURE 5.3 Accounts Receivable Financing Process

Terms and Conditions The various terms and conditions are subject to negotiation at the time of establishing the LOC. Following is a typical list of terms contained in an ABL term sheet, with some editorial comments as appropriate:

- *Borrower.* Establishes what entity is being lent to.
- *Guarantor(s).* Who is required to guarantee the LOC. This may be individuals or another corporation.
- *Credit line or amount.* Establishes the maximum amount the lender is willing to advance.
- *Purpose.* Defines the use of proceeds of the LOC.
- *Sublimits.* May limit advances to a single customer or against a specific collateral.
- *Advance formula.* Outlines the specific formula to be used in calculating the LOC availability. Typical advance rates range from 70 percent to 85 percent of eligible receivables. Defines the phaseout of eligibility of past due receivables, which is sometimes gradual versus binary.
- *Interest rate.* Typically based on the prime rate or LIBOR. Ranges from prime to prime plus 10 percent for very difficult situations. The higher interest rate covers the commercial interest rate plus added in-

terest for the additional risk. A subparameter to this term is the number of days in which interest is charged after receipt of payment of an invoice, which is typically one to five days. Also will include a default rate and possibly an overadvance rate.

- *Fees:*
  - *Closing commitment fee.* This is a one-time origination fee, and ranges from 0.25 percent to 2 percent.
  - *Facility fee.* Charged for providing the credit facility; ranges from 0 percent to 2 percent and sometimes payable in multiple years.
  - *Minimum loan fee.* Provides a minimum interest payment to the lender if the outstanding loan balance drops below a predetermined amount.
  - *Early termination fee.* Provides a fee for early termination by the client company.
  - *Collateral monitoring fee or service charge.* In some instances, the lender will charge a monthly fee to support the staff required to monitor the LOC. Typical monthly amounts range from $1,000 to $8,000.
- *Collateral.* Specifies the collateral that is securing the LOC and what lien position is required. In some cases, this term will prohibit other liens or loans. It is important to anticipate future financings and make provisions early on if other debt is expected.
- *Term.* Provides for the length of time that the LOC is committed by the lender.
- *Conditions.* Usually provides for such items as: required agreements, material adverse change clauses, lockbox and bank account requirements, reporting and audit requirements, key man insurance, and special terms specific to the client company.
- *Expenses.* A company can expect to pay for costs and fees related to periodic audits and visits by the lender. In addition, defines party responsible for payment of expenses related to closing.
- **Deposits.** Usually required at the time of acceptance by the client company of the lender's term sheet as a show of good faith. Refundable or credited against the LOC at some future time.

Cash Flow When a company's sales are increasing, A/R financing creates positive cash flow by accelerating the cash cycle by the number of days for payment granted to the client company's customers. Warning! If a company is using A/R financing and sales begin to slow, causing negative cash flow and reduced borrowing availability, at that time cash receipts will be going to pay off the LOC, not for operating purposes.

Total Cost   In comparing the cost of various financing alternatives, the total cost including all fees needs to be considered, not just the interest rate. While A/R financing can be comparable in cost to a traditional bank LOC, this is typically true only for companies with very strong balance sheets and solid credit history. Typically, A/R financing is somewhat more expensive than a traditional bank LOC; however, it offers more flexibility and may be available to companies that are not bankable. There are lenders that routinely provide A/R financing to troubled companies and for turnaround situations. The total cost of A/R financing is based on the various factors, many of which are defined by the terms listed before, including the actual utilization of the LOC. These total costs range from prime plus a few tenths of a percent to prime plus 10 to 12 percent.

Factoring

Factoring is expensive, but it is a valuable form of financing. Factoring is an agreement between the lender (factor) and your company (client company) in which the factor purchases the accounts receivable generated by the company's product or services. As such, a company with a weak balance sheet and/or losses can fund new sales more easily—however, with a higher cost than conventional bank financing. The reasons for factoring as a source of working capital include taking advantage of supplier discounts for early payments and cash discounts, fewer lending covenants than a standard bank line of credit, and not losing business to better financed competitors. A factoring relationship can often be established in one to two weeks. With factoring there may be no credit limit placed on your company; the credit constraints are based on the creditworthiness of the client company customers. For factoring to be a viable financing alternative, the company factoring its receivables needs to have either a significant gross margin, low overhead costs, and/or enough price elasticity to be able to pass the cost of factoring to the buyer to absorb the cost. In working capital crisis situations such as rapid sales growth or turnaround, the cost is often worth the speed, flexibility, and funding availability to solve the cash need.

Factoring Terminology

■ *Nonrecourse and full recourse factoring* pertains to the financial obligation of the company in the event of nonpayment by the end customer of the purchased accounts receivable. With nonrecourse factoring, the factor buys the receivable and assumes the risk of customer payment. The factor, in effect, guarantees against customer payment loss, unlike a secured lending facility. The factor will also provide the end customer credit check, undertake collection, and manage the bookkeeping functions relating to accounts receivable.[14]

Recourse factoring is far more prevalent in the current economy. With recourse factoring, the factor accepts assignment of the receivable but does not assume the credit risk; the company retains responsibility for managing the receivable. Generally, the lender will finance invoices up to 90 days from delivery of goods or services, then charge them back to the company if not paid by the end customer.[15]

- *Notification* refers to the practice of providing notice to the end customer that a particular invoice has been factored. Some factors charge an additional fee for not notifying the end customer. This is done in cases where the company assesses a risk of loss of business from a potential show of financial weakness for having to factor (which is historically seldom the case).
- *Advance rate* is the amount of money provided immediately to the company factoring its accounts receivable, expressed as a percentage (usually from 75 percent to 90 percent) of the total invoice.
- *Discount rate* is the fee charged to the company factoring its accounts receivable.
- *Factor* refers to the company that purchases accounts receivable.
- *Reserve for holdback* is the amount of money that is not immediately provided to the company factoring its accounts receivable, expressed as a percentage of the total invoice amount. That is, Advance Rate + Reserve = 100% of Total Invoice Amount. This money, minus the discount rate, is paid to the factor's client company once payment is received by the factor.[16]

Factoring Process   The major steps involved in the factoring process are shown in Figure 5.4. They include: delivery of the product or service to the buyer, buyer acceptance, merchant submission of invoice to the factor, and discounted payment to the merchant.

- *Client company customer credit approval.* The factor establishes preapproved credit lines for its client's customers.
- *Product or service delivery.* The client delivers its product or service for approved orders to its customers and bills them. Proof is then provided to the factor. In the case of notification factoring, the invoice indicates that payment is due to the factor.
- *Collection.* Payment from the end customer to the factor is typically via a secured lockbox. When received, the factor credits the client

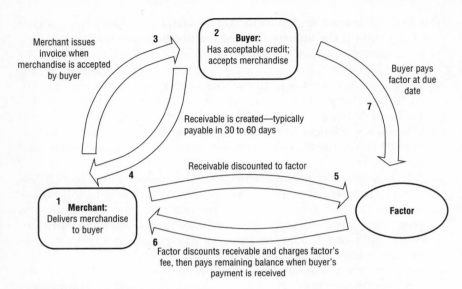

FIGURE 5.4   Factoring Process
Source: IIG Capital LLC.

company's account. In nonrecourse factoring, the factor fully manages
the receivables including the lockbox, cash application, and collection of past dues. Customer deductions or disputes over delivery
terms or product/service are immediately reported to the client company. The factor maintains the accounts receivable ledgers and provides this information either by paper reports or electronically to the
client company.

- *Default.* In the event an end customer defaults, the amount in question
  is charged to the client company's factoring account by the factor. The
  client company repays the default by submitting new sales that will not
  have advances or the factor retains the reserve for holdback. The client
  has incentive to expedite the collection effort.

- *Funding.* As needed, the factor will provide the client company with
  cash advances prior to the maturity date of the invoices. This allows
  the client company to be paid upon delivery of the product/service
  while actually offering credit terms to its customers. Typical advance
  rates are up to 90 percent of the value of the invoice. These advances
  are subsequently liquidated by collection proceeds from their
  customers.

Total Cost   There are several methods that factors use singly or in combination: discounts, the interest charged on advances against receivables, a factoring commission, and a monthly administration fee.

- The discount is a set fee amount that is charged on each invoice. The range in many cases varies significantly from 0.5 percent to 3 percent.
- The interest charged on the face value of invoice or actual funds outstanding may range from prime or a base rate plus 2 percent to 4 percent.
- The factoring fee/commission is quoted in 5- or 10-day increments: 0.5 percent per 10 days (which is .25 percent/5 days) to 1 percent per 10 days (0.5 percent/5 days). The standard range is 0.6 percent to 1.0 percent per 10 days. A staggered cost such as 3 percent for the first month and 0.6 percent per 10-day period thereafter may be made available.
- The monthly fee may be a fixed dollar amount or a percent of funds used or invoices outstanding (a subtle but potentially significant cost difference). This may be included as a loan covenant known as monthly minimum fee for anticipated volume of factored accounts.

This potentially complex pricing matrix needs to be understood. The teaser rate of prime plus 2 percent (which is near a bank rate if that were all to be charged) is routinely combined with the discount and/or monthly fee. When all of those costs are combined, this cost is in excess of a standalone 0.6 to 1.0 percent per 10-day fee despite its enticing introduction. If the client company understands its collection cycle and aberrations it can negotiate more favorable pricing.[17] In total, factoring can easily cost 20 to 40 percent annually.

Factoring versus Credit Insurance   Credit or A/R indemnity insurance can be purchased to protect your company in the event of default in payment by a customer. To some degree, factoring provides the same effect as credit insurance coupled with collection services. Unlike factoring, credit insurance does not improve cash flow unless your company has a claim. Generally, factoring is more expensive.

Inventory Financing

The financing of inventory is typically combined with A/R financing. The terms discussed in the prior section regarding A/R financing apply. Terms that will be added or modified to the list discussed in the A/R financing section include:

- *Sublimit* will be modified to include an inventory limit.
- *Advance rate* will be specified for the inventory. These rates are typically low relative to the A/R limit, ranging from 10 to 50 percent of the inventory liquidation value. There may be staggered advance rates for raw materials work in process and finished goods. The advance is determined by marketability of the inventory in the event the lender must sell it.
- *Fees* typically are expressed as prime rate plus a percentage. In addition, there may be a monthly analysis fee. Inventory appraisals may be required preloan to provide the "expert" assessment of marketability to assist in establishing the advance rate. The more complex the inventory, the higher the cost of appraisal. Quarterly audits by the asset-based lender are at the client company's cost in most cases.
- *Collateral* will be expanded to include inventory.
- *Reporting* will be expanded to include inventory. Detailed monthly reports on raw materials and finished goods typically from a perpetual inventory system are required.

Adding inventory to an A/R LOC usually increases total LOC availability. In most cases the inventory loan does not exceed the accounts receivable line of credit or factoring.

Purchase Order Financing

Purchase order (PO) financing can be used to finance the purchase or manufacture of specific goods that have already been sold. It can used for payments to third party suppliers for goods, for issuing letters of credit, and for making payments for direct labor, raw materials, and other directly related expenses.[18] PO financing tends to work well for importers and exporters of finished goods; outsourced manufacturing; and wholesalers, assemblers, and distributors.

Firms that provide PO financing seek client companies with strong management expertise in their particular field/industry; client company suppliers and subcontractors who have a proven track record—reliable sourcing; valid purchase orders issued by creditworthy customers; and verifiable repayment from a factor, bank, another asset-based lender, letter of credit, or the ultimate customer.[19]

PO Financing Process A simplified PO financing process includes the following steps:[20]

1. The end customer purchase order is verified.
2. The client company provides a budget showing the cost to produce the final product.
3. Funds are disbursed to support fulfillment of the order.
4. The production cycle is monitored and inspected.
5. When the final product is delivered to the end customer, the lender factors that invoice; part of those factoring proceeds are used to repay the purchase order financing.

Term Loans

Term loans are typically provided for the financing of fixed assets such as computers, machinery, equipment, leasehold improvements, and real estate. These loans vary in length from several years for computers to 10 to 40 years for real estate based on the expected life of the asset. Equipment loan-to-value rates are based on a percentage of the orderly or forced liquidation appraisal of the asset, and real estate loans are based on a percentage of a fair market value (FMV) appraisal. Rates charged are based on the creditworthiness of the client company and the marketability of the asset(s).

Key facets of a term loan include:

- *Amount*, which may be based on a percent of the underlying assets.
- *Type of amortization*—full or partial amortization.
- *Length of amortization.*
- *Interest rate.*

Term loans are also used to provide permanent working capital. Given the relative financial strength and stage of the borrowing company, some lenders will seek a guarantee from the Small Business Administration (SBA) to reduce the risk of the loan to them (see the section later in this chapter on the types of SBA loans).

Other Types of Asset-Backed Lender Financing

Among the other types of ABL financing, we list a few:

- Capital expense (capex) lines of credit assist capital-intensive companies with preapproved financing for equipment purchases.

- Import financing provides cash to secure inventory when the end buyer has acceptable credit and/or the underlying commodity is exchange-traded or has a large liquid market.[21] Figure 5.5 provides a typical example of the import financing process.
- Debtor-in-possession financing supports bankruptcy reorganizations.
- Sales leaseback arrangements provide a method to refinance existing fixed assets and owner-occupied real estate. See additional content on this topic later in the chapter under the "Leasing Companies" section.
- Venture banking or trade tranche is a concept similar to trade finance. Transcap Trade Finance in Northbrook, Illinois, provides what it terms a "global trade tranche." Transcap acts on behalf of a client company to purchase finished goods inventory for a fee, primarily from non-U.S. suppliers. Then Transcap supports order fulfillment from the purchasing of the inventory through delivery to the client's customer by monitoring the transactions logistics. The funding is provided almost without regard to the current financial condition of the client. What must be clear is Transcap's exit. This type of transaction is usually completed in 30 to 120 days at a fee of 1 to 3 percent of the inventory cost per month. The funding can even work for a start-up if it can convince Transcap that the overall opportunity is significant. On

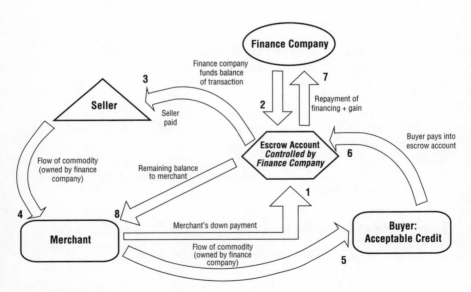

FIGURE 5.5 Import Financing
Source: IIG Capital LLC.

the other end of the spectrum, it is appropriate for $500 million and larger companies with cash flow issues. The value for the client company is access to goods, global purchasing expertise and logistics, improved cash flow, and nonimpairment of existing working capital. It does not work for the purchase of services or intellectual property.[22]

- Transactional Equity (a trademark of IIG Capital LLC) consists of cofinancing the down payment required by banks as part of credit or other financing. This is an attractive structure for merchants whose transactions backlogs exceed available capital because it allows them to add incremental profit to their bottom line.[23] Figure 5.6 illustrates a typical transaction.

- Warehouse financing involves the use of securely stored goods as financing collateral. It allows companies operating in the soft commodities as well as in the mining, metals, and petroleum industries to deposit their inventory in a secure warehouse operated by an independent party. The warehouse operator provides a receipt certifying the deposit of goods of a particular quantity, quality, or grade. A company can use the receipt, usually by transferring title, to obtain financing. From a financier's point of view the credit risk of certain companies may be unacceptable. But the potential client may have a

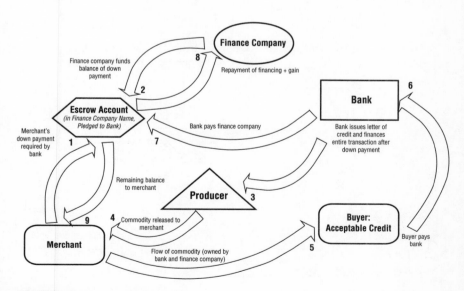

FIGURE 5.6 Transactional Equity
Source: IIG Capital LLC. Transactional Equity is a trademark of IIG Capital LLC.

viable business. If the client has an inventory of commodities, waiting to be delivered to buyers, the financier can shift the credit risks away from the client by financing the commodity and not the commodities firm. Through the use of warehouse financing, the financier utilizes the services of an independent, bonded collateral manager to control the underlying goods, thereby mitigating the credit risks of the commodity processor, trader, or intermediary. In case of bankruptcy or payment delays the financier can liquidate the goods in order to make itself whole.[24] Figure 5.7 illustrates the process.

COMMERCIAL FINANCE COMPANIES

Commercial finance companies are sometimes asset-based lenders that have a narrower niche (specialty finance) or a broader scope of services and credit facilities. In some cases they provide financing only of those items listed here under "Offerings" or a subset thereof. For example: There are companies that solely provide purchase order financing and factoring, and they classify themselves as commercial finance companies. There are also very large finance organizations with a broad spectrum of lending and investing activities that deem themselves commercial finance companies. Once again, there is not industry consistency in the use of the term. For examples of actual companies, see the Financing Source Directory in Part Three.

Here is a list of offerings that we have found regarding commercial finance companies that are in addition to the ones listed in the section discussing ABLs.

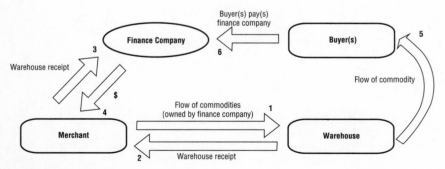

FIGURE 5.7 Warehouse Financing
Source: IIG Capital LLC.

Offerings

- *Senior debt* broadly defines lending with a first lien position against a company's assets. It includes letters of credit, revolving lines of credit, term loans, bridge loans and short-term credit lines.
  - A *revolver or revolving credit line* is a debt facility made available up to a specified amount, without a fixed repayment schedule, that the borrower may draw on and repay as needed. It is usually secured by a first lien position on the current assets of the company. Banks and commercial finance companies offer these with certain financial and operational covenants.
  - A *senior term loan* is an amortizing or partially amortizing term loan that is secured with a first lien position on the assets of a company. The term is usually three to five years. Partially amortizing term loans may include a warrant position to offset some of the risk of repayment. This type of loan is sometimes referred to as a senior stretch term loan.
  - *Bridge loans* provide interim financing with the provision to roll over to a longer-term financing vehicle.
- *Junior debt* is either unsecured or has a lower priority than that of another debt claim on the same asset or property. It is also called subordinated debt or mezzanine debt. See the "Private Equity" section of this chapter.
- *Equity co-investments with senior debt* occur in certain cases when a lender will agree to take a relatively small equity position in a transaction in conjunction with making available a senior debt facility. The equity portion is usually under the same terms and coincides with a private equity investment.
- *Mortgage debt financing.*
- *Cash flow collateralized debt obligation and other structured finance.*
- *Leases.* See the next section, "Leasing Companies."

Figure 5.8 provides a summary view of the characteristics of the various types of term loans.

LEASING COMPANIES

When a company leases equipment, it benefits from the asset's use, not its ownership. As a result, the company does not consume capital that can be used for expansion, growth, or other resource acquisition. Leases are made based on the value of the asset and the credit quality of the borrower.[25]

Characteristic	Senior Term Loan	Senior Subordinated or Senior Stretch Loan	Junior Subordinated	Senior Real Estate Loan
			Type	
Advance				
Dependent on Cash Flow and Assets	X	X		
Dependent on Cash Flow			X	
Up to 100%				X
Structure				
5+-Year Term, Flexible Amortization	X	X	X	
5+-Year Term, 20-Year Amortization				X
Interest Rate	~P	~P+	~P++	~P
Collateral				
First Lien on Assets	X			
Second Lien on Assets		X	?	
First Lien on Real Estate; Second Lien on Other Assets of the Business				X
Equity Participation				
None	X			X
Usually None, Dependent on Situation		X		
Typically Required			X	

FIGURE 5.8 Term Loan Characteristics
P = Prime rate as a baseline.
? = Depends on the situation.

Leasing companies can be independent finance businesses or units of banks. They provide capital by procuring equipment for their clients in exchange for a commitment of a series of payments. Some leasing companies focus on specific industries and have special programs tailored for certain types of equipment, while others are broad-based in scope. Those with industry specialization sometimes have the ability to be more aggressive in pricing given their understanding of the equipment values and paths to liquidation or resale. In some cases and depending on the amount of the lease, leases are easier to obtain and less sensitive to the customer's creditworthiness, particularly when the equipment being leased is ordinary.

When considering leasing as a financing alternative, ask the following questions:[26]

- How long will your company need to use the equipment?
- What does your company intend to do with the equipment at the end of the lease?
- What is the tax impact of a lease given the company's tax situation?
- How will the lease impact your tax situation?
- What are the company's expected future needs, and how does the lease fit into a total financing plan?

Types of Leases

For financial reporting purposes, leases can be divided into two categories: capital leases and operating leases. An operating lease is a short-term lease or usage agreement that allows the company (lessee) to acquire use of an asset for a fraction of the asset's useful life. This type of lease is accounted for by the lessee without showing the asset or liability (for the lease payment obligations) on the balance sheet. The lessee accounts for rental payments as an operating expense on the income statement.[27] For example, a company may enter an operating lease to rent a computer system for a year. Operating leases should appear as a note to the balance sheet to disclose the annual amount of minimum rental payments for which the company is obligated, the general terms of the lease, and any other relevant information. The benefits of an operating lease include the reduced risk of asset obsolescence (for technology equipment) and off-balance-sheet financing, allowing a company to effectively borrow additional long-term capital without negatively impacting its debt-to-equity ratio.

An operating lease must possess all of the following elements to meet Financial Accounting Standards Board (FASB) rules:

- Lease term is less than 75 percent of estimated economic life of the equipment.
- Present value of lease payments is less than 90 percent of the equipment's fair market value.
- Lease cannot contain a bargain purchase option (i.e., less than the fair market value).
- Title does not pass automatically to the lessee at the end of the lease term.

A capital lease is a direct substitute for the purchase of an asset with a term loan. It is a noncancelable contract to make a series of payments in return for use of an asset for a specified period of time. It transfers substantially all the benefits and risks inherent in the ownership of the property to the lessee. Typical terms transfer the asset to the company at the end of the lease or allow the company to purchase the asset for a minimal price. Interest and depreciation are expensed as payments are made against the capital lease. A capital lease tends to generate expenses sooner than an equivalent operating lease.

In both operating and capital leases, there is usually some type of deposit required. It is sometimes in the form of prepayment of the first and last payments.

Venture Leasing

Venture leasing companies generally provide equipment for start-up and emerging growth companies. There tend to be two types of venture leasing:

1. The first type is offered by traditional leasing companies that have targeted venture capital–backed businesses and have tailored their marketing and product structure. In this case they do not seek an equity position in the lessee. These firms usually require a minimum level of venture funding be invested and full financial disclosure. The transaction is usually structured as an operating or true lease for 18 to 36 months, and is for equipment that is essential to the operations of the business.
2. The second type is offered by a venture leasing company that seeks an equity stake in the lessee, typically in the form of warrants or options. The lessee has generally received venture investment and is

evaluated based on its growth potential. Typically there is no deposit required with regard to the lease transaction, and it is structured for a three-to-four-year term. As in the prior paragraph, full financial disclosure is required.

When negotiating with a venture leasing firm, the concept is to seek a lower interest rate and lower payments in exchange for warrants, given that the strike price of the warrants is appropriate. In an ideal situation, the warrants will be at or above the current equity valuation. Venture leasing can be a less dilutive financing alternative than raising additional venture funds.

Sale Leaseback

A company can unlock or reallocate existing capital by selling existing assets to a leasing or finance company with an agreement to lease those same assets over time; this is referred to as a sale leaseback arrangement. This technique is useful for companies that have already invested in certain fixed assets and need to shift the use of that capital. It is also a viable technique for companies that have equity in real estate. There are tax implications, so we counsel a company to evaluate that impact.

Some venture leasing firms will do a sale leaseback arrangement with early stage companies that have already invested in fixed assets. This may be an alternative for asset-intensive venture-backed companies that are between rounds and need additional capital to meet their next milestones, yet do not want to further dilute the founders' shares by accepting a premature round.

What Can Be Leased

- Agricultural, forestry, fishing equipment.
- Amusement games and machines.
- Banking equipment.
- Computer hardware and software.
- Construction equipment.
- Electrical equipment.
- Industrial and manufacturing equipment.
- Materials-handling equipment.
- Medical equipment.
- Mining, oil, and gas extraction equipment.
- Office equipment.
- Printing/publishing equipment.

- Restaurant equipment.
- Telecommunications equipment.
- Transportation equipment and vehicles.
- Vending equipment.

PRIVATE EQUITY

Private equity is a term used to broadly group funds and investment companies that provide capital on a negotiated basis generally to private businesses. This category of firms is a superset that includes venture capital, buyout—also called leveraged buyout (LBO)—and mezzanine and expansion funds. The industry expertise, amount invested, transaction structure preference, and return expectations vary according to the mission of each. Additional information about the fund types mentioned is provided hereafter in this handbook.

Over the past decade, private equity has developed into a major asset class, providing significant risk/reward benefits to institutional investors' portfolios. During the 1980s, the industry was still considered a niche sector, with less than $10 billion in capital invested annually. However, since 1990 over $730 billion has been committed to private equity funds, with over $340 billion committed in the past three years alone. Top-quartile managers have realized a net internal rate of return (IRR) in excess of 17 percent over the past 12-year period of economic cycles.[28]

Private equity is an alternative asset in which many institutional investors in the United States allocate on average 7.5 percent of their total portfolios.[29] About 50 percent of the private equity in the United States is provided by public and private pension funds, with the balance from endowments, foundations, insurance companies, banks, individuals, and other entities who seek to diversify their portfolios with this investment class.[30]

Private equity firms act as the intermediary between institutional investors and the entrepreneurial and portfolio companies (issuers). In addition, there are publicly traded investment companies that play the same role between public investors and the same issuer market. Their investments are sometimes augmented by angel and corporate investors. Issuers include the following types of companies:

- New ventures (early and later stage).
- Middle-market private companies:
  - Expansion.
  - Change in capital structure (recapitalization).
  - Change in ownership.

- Public companies:
  - Going private.
  - Leveraged buyouts.
  - Financial distress.
  - Special situations.
  - Private investment in public equities (PIPE).

Figure 5.9 provides a perspective of the private equity landscape and the players.

You will find that the types of firms and the types of investments they make are not clearly delineated. Some venture funds invest in the same rounds of financing alongside buyout funds that provide expansion and growth capital. It seems a bit confusing because the terms in the private equity business are not used consistently among firms. Some firms will only take a controlling interest while others will make minority investments. The actual deal structure varies greatly based on the experience and preferences of the general partners of each of these types of firms.

In some instances, private equity firms take a controlling interest in the target investment, with minority stakes left to management and prior company stockholders, some of whom may have been involved in creating the company or developing the company to the stage where the acquisition or investment became attractive.

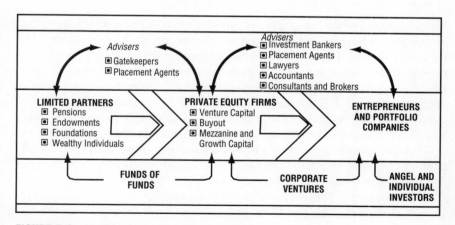

FIGURE 5.9 Private Equity Landscape Chart
Source: Tuck Center for Private Equity and Entrepreneurship, Tuck School of Business at Dartmouth, http://mba.tuck.dartmouth.edu/pecenter/about/index.html.

In other situations the private equity firms leverage their buyouts by pooling bank and other financial institution debt in a financial package that could include convertible subordinate debt and tranches of unsecured financing.

Some private equity firms deal only in a specific business field where they have a strong expertise, while others seek opportunities in diverse industries.

Many private equity firms have staffs with strong management skills, although they seldom take a day-to-day operating role in the firms they acquire or in which they invest. Their staffs are accustomed to consulting and guiding company executives in how to achieve growth and profitability that will increase firm value during the holding period. The support staff could be organized as a management consulting arm of the firm, and it may charge fees to portfolio companies.

In the past, private equity firms typically purchased a private company, spruced it up, and then took it public or sold it to another operating company, hopefully at a profit. Today, more private equity firms are passing portfolio companies among themselves. Such deals, where investment firms are on both sides of a transaction, used to be relatively rare. In 2001, for instance, there were only $2.5 billion worth of such deals, according to Dealogic, which tracks merger-and-acquisition activity. In contrast, there were almost $41 billion worth in the first seven months of 2004.[31]

VENTURE CAPITAL FUNDS

Venture capital (VC) is probably one of the most misused financing terms, attempting to lump many perceived private investors and investment types into one category. In reality, very few companies receive funding from venture capitalists—not because they do not have good companies, but primarily because they do not fit the funding model. One venture capitalist commented that his firm received hundreds of business plans a month, reviewing only a few of them and investing in maybe one, and this was a large fund. This ratio of plan acceptance to plans submitted is common.

Venture capital is primarily invested in young companies with significant growth potential. Industry focus is usually technology or life sciences, though large investments have been made in recent years in e-businesses and certain types of service companies such as outsourcing. Investments tracked by the MoneyTree Survey[32] are grouped into the following segments:

- Software.
- Biotechnology.

- Telecommunications.
- Networking and equipment.
- Medical devices and equipment.
- Semiconductors.
- Computers and peripherals.
- Information technology services.
- Financial services.
- Industrial/energy.
- Business products and services.
- Consumer products and services.
- Media and entertainment.
- Electronics/instrumentation.
- Retailing/distribution.
- Health-care services.
- Other.

Industry Overview*

This section is intended to provide an overview and current perspective of the VC industry, and to set the stage for the balance of the discussion surrounding venture capital.

The steady upward trend in venture capital continued in the second quarter of 2004 with investments of $5.6 billion going into 761 companies. (See Table 5.6.) This compares to $5.0 billion invested in the first quarter of 2004 and $5.4 billion in the fourth quarter of 2003. Over the past two years, quarterly investing has drifted upward at a deliberate pace, ranging from $4.3 billion to this quarter's high of $5.6 billion.

The life sciences sector (biotechnology and medical devices together) continued to dominate other industries as it has for the past eight consecutive quarters. Investments in the sector totaled $1.4 billion, or 25 percent of all venture capital. Proportionately, life sciences investing remained near historical highs.

The software industry held on to the top slot in the second quarter of 2004 as the largest industry category. Software companies garnered $1.2

---

*Data and information in this section is current as of July 27, 2004, and provided by PricewaterhouseCoopers, Thomson Venture Economics, and the National Venture Capital Association MoneyTree Survey. None of the parties can warrant the ultimate validity of the data. Results are updated periodically. All data is subject to change at any time.

TABLE 5.6 Venture Capital Investments by Industry, Q2 2004, Q1 2004, Q2 2003 (dollar amounts in millions)

Industry	Q2 2004		Q1 2004		Q2 2003	
	# of Deals	Amount Invested	# of Deals	Amount Invested	# of Deals	Amount Invested
Software	212	$1,204.2	182	$1,042.0	204	$ 982.7
Biotechnology	85	$ 922.8	77	$ 968.1	71	$ 712.9
Telecommunications	59	$ 518.1	63	$ 546.5	67	$ 640.6
Medical Devices and Equipment	70	$ 485.3	56	$ 344.8	54	$ 424.0
Networking and Equipment	44	$ 458.8	44	$ 397.2	45	$ 415.1
Semiconductors	53	$ 437.4	46	$ 373.6	44	$ 351.7
Media and Entertainment	36	$ 345.9	30	$ 147.0	45	$ 191.9
Computers and Peripherals	35	$ 227.2	32	$ 254.6	21	$ 150.3
Information Technology Services	35	$ 185.3	38	$ 254.4	37	$ 168.3
Health-Care Services	19	$ 176.8	11	$ 45.5	15	$ 38.8
Business Products and Services	28	$ 165.7	23	$ 104.5	21	$ 134.3
Industrial/Energy	33	$ 147.6	37	$ 206.5	36	$ 266.4
Electronics/Instrumentation	21	$ 144.6	10	$ 49.1	20	$ 104.5
Financial Services	16	$ 104.8	14	$ 157.0	20	$ 114.2
Retailing/Distribution	9	$ 52.5	9	$ 35.8	10	$ 35.0
Consumer Products and Services	5	$ 4.0	13	$ 34.7	13	$ 34.7
Other	1	$ 1.6	1	$ 0.3	4	$ 7.5
Grand Total	761	$5,582.6	686	$5,048.6	727	$4,772.9

Source: PricewaterhouseCoopers/Thomson Venture Economics/National Venture Capital Association MoneyTree Survey.

billion going into 212 companies; both figures were comfortably above the prior quarter. The decline abated in the networking industry with 44 companies getting $459 million in mostly follow-on rounds. The telecommunications industry did not fare as well, with a decline from Q1 2004 to $518 million going to 59 companies in Q2 2004, again mostly in follow-on rounds.

As shown in Table 5.7, a total of 229 companies in the early stage of development were funded in Q2 2004, the highest number since Q2 2002. Proportionately, they accounted for 30 percent of all companies, the highest percentage since Q1 2001. And early stage companies captured $1.2 billion or 21 percent of all venture capital in the period, well above recent quarters. Average funding per company of $5.1 million exceeded the $4.6 million average over the prior four quarters.

Expansion stage companies, which typically account for the largest total dollars and number of deals, increased slightly as well. Expansion stage funding was $2.8 billion in Q2 2004, or 50 percent of all investing, compared to $2.6 billion and 51 percent in Q1 2004. Average funding per company at $8.1 million exceeded the $7.5 million average over the prior four quarters. Later stage funding was flat. Investments in Q2 2004 were $1.6 billion, or 28 percent of all investing versus $1.6 billion and 31 percent of all investing last quarter.

Companies receiving their first round of venture capital rebounded in Q2 2004 to their highest level in two years. (See Table 5.8.) A total of $1.2 billion or 21 percent of all venture capital went to these companies, compared to $981 million and 19 percent of fundings in Q1 2004. In terms of number of companies, 208 first-timers accounted for 27 percent of all companies receiving financings in the second quarter, up from 172 and 25 percent of all companies in the previous quarter. Average funding per company was essentially flat at $5.6 million, reflecting continued emphasis on capital efficiency.

Additionally, companies receiving their second/third-time investments also charted an upward course with a 13.8 percent uptick in deals and 19.9 percent more dollars invested in the second quarter than in the first quarter.

The most active venture investors in the United States closed five or more deals each in Q2 2004. (See Table 5.9.) Of the more than 2,100 transactions reported in Q2 2004, the most active firms accounted for 744, or 35 percent of all investments. The top 13 firms accounted for almost 8 percent of the deals completed in the quarter. New Enterprise Associates topped the list with a total of 24 deals, while U.S. Venture Partners came in second having made 16 investments during the quarter. Morgenthaler Ventures, Draper Fisher Jurvetson, and Polaris Venture Partners were also

TABLE 5.7 Venture Capital Investments by Stage of Development, Q2 2004, Q1 2004, Q2 2003 (dollar amounts in millions)

Stage of Development	Q2 2004		Q1 2004		Q2 2003	
	# of Deals	Amount Invested	# of Deals	Amount Invested	# of Deals	Amount Invested
Start-up/seed	51	$ 82.8	39	$ 80.4	54	$ 95.2
Early stage	229	$1,169.2	193	$ 852.5	207	$ 957.5
Expansion	342	$2,766.0	315	$2,563.1	336	$2,529.7
Later stage	139	$1,564.6	139	$1,552.6	130	$1,190.6
Total	761	$5,582.6	686	$5,048.6	727	$4,772.9

Source: PricewaterhouseCoopers/Thomson Venture Economics/National Venture Capital Association MoneyTree Survey.

TABLE 5.8 Venture Capital Investments by Sequence of Financing, Q2 2004, Q1 2004, Q2 2003 (dollar amounts in millions)

Sequence of Financing	Q2 2004		Q1 2004		Q2 2003	
	# of Deals	Amount Invested	# of Deals	Amount Invested	# of Deals	Amount Invested
First	208	$1,154.8	172	$ 981.2	177	$ 985.4
Second and third	272	$2,102.9	239	$1,753.9	276	$1,672.8
Fourth, fifth, and sixth	225	$1,857.6	207	$1,973.1	204	$1,754.2
Seventh and beyond	56	$ 467.3	68	$ 340.3	70	$ 360.5
Total	761	$5,582.6	686	$5,048.6	727	$4,772.9

Source: PricewaterhouseCoopers/Thomson Venture Economics/National Venture Capital Association MoneyTree Survey.

TABLE 5.9 Most Active Venture Capital Investors, Q2 2004

Company	City	State	Number of Deals
New Enterprise Associates	Baltimore	MD	24
U.S. Venture Partners	Menlo Park	CA	16
Morgenthaler Ventures	Menlo Park	CA	15
Draper Fisher Jurvetson	Menlo Park	CA	14
Polaris Venture Partners	Waltham	MA	14
Alta Partners	San Francisco	CA	13
Austin Ventures	Austin	TX	12
Village Ventures	Williamstown	MA	12
Bessemer Venture Partners	Larchmont	NY	11
Canaan Partners	Rowayton	CT	11
Sutter Hill Ventures	Palo Alto	CA	11
Foundation Capital	Menlo Park	CA	11
Intel Capital	Santa Clara	CA	11
Advanced Technology Ventures	Waltham	MA	10
Pequot Capital Management	Westport	CT	10
Menlo Ventures	Menlo Park	CA	10
Charles River Ventures	Waltham	MA	10
MPM Capital	Boston	MA	10
Carlyle Group, The	Washington	DC	10
Mayfield Fund	Menlo Park	CA	10
Battery Ventures, L.P.	Wellesley	MA	9
Versant Ventures	Menlo Park	CA	9
Venrock Associates	New York	NY	9
Frazier Healthcare and Technology Ventures	Seattle	WA	9
Rho Ventures	New York	NY	9
Sierra Ventures	Menlo Park	CA	9
TL Ventures	Wayne	PA	9
Mobius Venture Capital	Palo Alto	CA	9
ARCH Venture Partners	Chicago	IL	8
Benchmark Capital	Menlo Park	CA	8
VantagePoint Venture Partners	San Bruno	CA	8
Trident Capital	Palo Alto	CA	8
St. Paul Venture Capital, Inc.	Eden Prairie	MN	8
Oak Investment Partners	Westport	CT	8
Mellon Ventures, Inc.	Pittsburgh	PA	8
Maryland Department of Business and Economic Development	Baltimore	MD	8
Crosslink Capital	San Francisco	CA	8
Blue Chip Venture Company	Cincinnati	OH	8

(Continued)

TABLE 5.9 *(Continued)*

Company	City	State	Number of Deals
Asset Management Company Venture Capital	Palo Alto	CA	7
General Catalyst Partners	Cambridge	MA	7
Redpoint Ventures	Menlo Park	CA	7
Three Arch Partners	Portola Valley	CA	7
Sofinnova Ventures	San Francisco	CA	7
Sequoia Capital	Menlo Park	CA	7
Portage Venture Partners	Northfield	IL	7
Kleiner Perkins Caufield & Byers	Menlo Park	CA	7
Kodiak Venture Partners	Waltham	MA	7
InterWest Partners	Menlo Park	CA	7
Essex Woodlands Health Ventures	Chicago	IL	7
De Novo Ventures	Menlo Park	CA	7

Source: PricewaterhouseCoopers/Thomson Venture Economics/National Venture Capital Association MoneyTree Survey.

among the most active investors in the second quarter, reporting 14 or more deals each.

Finally, as shown in Table 5.10, Silicon Valley and the Northeast areas continue to see the majority of the venture investment in terms of deals and dollars.

Value-Added Investors*

VCs have two very powerful mechanisms to effect change in a portfolio company. VCs can replace management (with board approval) or force the sale of a company (by refusing to invest additional capital). Both of these measures, while effective, are quite drastic. There are a number of other ways that VCs impact the operations of portfolio companies.

---

*The base content of this section is adapted from "Note on Venture Capital Portfolio Management," 2003, by Professors Colin Blaydon and Fred Wainwright, Tuck School of Business at Dartmouth, and Andrew Waldeck. The authors gratefully acknowledge the support of the Tuck Center for Private Equity and Entrepreneurship. Copyright © Trustees of Dartmouth College. All rights reserved.

TABLE 5.10 Venture Capital Investments by Region, Q2 2004, Q1 2004, Q2 2003 (dollar amounts in millions)

Region	Q2 2004		Q1 2004		Q2 2003	
	# of Deals	Amount Invested	# of Deals	Amount Invested	# of Deals	Amount Invested
Silicon Valley	230	$2,133.1	193	$1,594.7	205	$1,602.6
New England	103	$ 916.7	93	$ 793.1	89	$ 541.0
New York Metro	57	$ 327.0	44	$ 285.9	59	$ 387.0
Northwest	44	$ 325.8	33	$ 236.5	24	$ 95.2
Texas	38	$ 300.9	36	$ 228.9	40	$ 274.8
Los Angeles/Orange County	37	$ 264.8	38	$ 185.1	39	$ 394.3
Southeast	43	$ 260.4	59	$ 381.0	67	$ 231.9
San Diego	26	$ 239.0	30	$ 287.0	28	$ 211.8
Midwest	48	$ 168.9	35	$ 240.6	38	$ 183.7
Philadelphia Metro	34	$ 140.9	21	$ 260.8	25	$ 215.4
DC/Metroplex	43	$ 132.4	42	$ 244.3	42	$ 175.4
SouthWest	13	$ 117.5	12	$ 41.6	10	$ 35.6
Colorado	13	$ 84.5	19	$ 93.4	24	$ 243.3
North Central	16	$ 81.0	17	$ 151.0	21	$ 106.5
Upstate New York	7	$ 40.9	9	$ 12.0	4	$ 33.0
Sacramento/Northern California	3	$ 25.0	1	$ 5.3	3	$ 5.4
Alaska/Hawaii/Puerto Rico	2	$ 15.1	1	$ 2.7	3	$ 7.7
South Central	4	$ 8.9	3	$ 4.7	5	$ 18.6
Undisclosed/other	0	$ 0.0	0	$ 0.0	1	$ 9.4
Total	761	$ 5,583	686	$ 5,049	727	$4,772.9

Source: PricewaterhouseCoopers/Thomson Venture Economics/National Venture Capital Association MoneyTree Survey.

Generally all VC firms will provide the following assistance to portfolio companies:

Financing or Exit Transactions   VC firms by nature have unique insight into the current trends in the private equity markets. In addition to providing market insight, VC firms will often make introductions for portfolio companies to other VC firms when looking for a lead investor for another round of financing. Most venture firms also have relationships with commercial banks which can be used when portfolio companies require debt financing. Finally, venture firms also have strong relationships with leading investment banks and are highly active in the selection of the banking syndicate and throughout the IPO process.

Strategic Advice   All firms can utilize their extensive experience as investors in, and in some cases operators of, similar businesses to provide strategic advice to growing companies.

Team Building/Recruiting   Most firms take some role in helping to recruit and build out the senior management team. Many firms focus a great deal of their energy on evaluating management teams and making additions or changes where appropriate—including recruiting and interviewing prospective new hires. Some firms, such as Bessemer, have even expanded to include formal executive search and recruitment departments, focused solely on placing world-class talent into their portfolio companies.

Leveraging Contacts   All VCs have extensive contacts within their respective industry segments. VCs leverage these contacts for a number of purposes, including negotiating transactions on behalf of portfolio companies or sourcing exit transactions. Portfolio companies can also leverage these contacts directly to assist in new business development, sales support, and gathering market intelligence. In addition, leveraging contacts also includes resource sharing within the portfolio. Accell Partners, Battery Ventures, Crosspoint Venture Partners, and many others as well actively encourage interaction among portfolio company management teams.

Crisis Management   Start-ups from time to time may experience times of crisis, such as the loss of a major customer or senior member of management, a cash crunch, or a major design or development issue. During these times, VCs will utilize any and all available resources, in rare cases acting as interim management, in order to protect or save their investment.

Venture Funding Process

Referring to our baseline financing process flow chart in Figure 1.1, the process to obtain venture funding encompasses steps 1 through 9. Key to raising venture capital is matching your deal to investor criteria. Secondly, there needs to be a compelling story for a company that solves a real problem, addressing a "painkiller to a painful area" versus "vitamins to make you feel better."[33] Said in another way, there must be a market need for a "must have" versus a "nice to have" product, service, or solution. The following list cites criteria that the target business and team need to possess to be a candidate for venture funding.[34] Obviously not all businesses fit every item, but most are required:

- Quality management for the stage of the venture. Show how you are building a qualified team, advisory board, and board of directors.
- Product addresses a key aspect of the customer's business.
- Customer is targetable and accessible.
- There is a market beyond early adopters. The literal majority of entrepreneurs perform inadequate market research. Instead they try one of the following two approaches: (1) "The market is there!" (I guess that means "Take our word for it." We won't.) or (2) "We're part of the $220 billion electronics industry. If we get just 0.01 percent of it, we'll be a $22 million company." While the arithmetic may seem sound, this argument is so intellectually offensive that it leads to the immediate conclusion that the team's whole fabric is shallow and rhetorical. Scientific market research is almost never easy, but almost always possible. VCs look for a team that has segmented the overall market to isolate their specific opportunity, anchors their claims to solid, third party observations, and can focus on the specific target.[35] Know the size of the markets and who are the largest players, their share of market, growth trends of industry versus players, what are the biggest issues facing the industry. How does your company fit? Be prepared to address concerns about the industry.
- Customer is willing to change with defined purchasing processes.
- Understand the selling process. Who are the decision makers? Are other parties critical to the decision process? What is the lead time to sell? Will it be a relationship or commodity sale? Be able to articulate a detailed benefits analysis to the customer.
- Can understand/leverage corporate partners.
- Can understand and articulate necessary milestones in the go-forward plan.

- Have a workable business model with above-average margins. Explain the detailed financial model.
- Have a clear understanding of competitive/alternative landscape and trends. A cavalier dismissal of this threat, manifested in the oft-heard phrase "We have no competition," is a near-certain predictor of performance shellshock later on. Many VCs insist that the business plans seriously reviewed contain a competitive matrix—for instance, a comparison by relevant features of the product/service versus all other logical purchase alternatives.[36]
- Have exclusive access to defined products, processes, or intellectual property.
- Have an investment/funding strategy (including an exit strategy).
- Have an unfair competitive advantage.
- Foreseeable that the investment can have a 10 times return in 5 to 10 years.
- Use a model for strategic planning; the model should reflect vision and market execution. The strategic plan must have milestones and metrics to measure those milestones. Outline the risks to your plan and explain why you can navigate.

An alternate view is to define what criteria will get the target company removed from or filtered out of the process quickly. We highlight a few issues:[37]

- Lack of alignment of values with partner.
- Management clearly lacks the background (for instance, no one has prior related success).
- Me-too business (for instance, "only needs 1 percent market share").
- Large capital requirement/too long to market.
- Business plan and business model are lacking.
- The plan is for a product, not a business.
- Unrealistic funding/investment strategy.
- Underestimating the competitive response.
- Does not understand the selling process for the product/service.
- Lacks ring of truth.

Following is a list of additional elements that venture capitalists mention as key investment criteria, shown in descending order of importance.[38] Couple the two preceding lists and these key elements, and you have a solid filter or test for determining the probability of obtaining venture funding:

- Management capable of a sustained intense effort.
- Management thoroughly familiar with the market.

- Management with demonstrated leadership.
- Management that can evaluate and react to risk well.
- Investment exit exists.
- Significant market growth.
- Management with a track record relevant to the venture.
- Management that can articulate the venture well (can tell the "compelling story").

Be Prepared!

Assuming that you are able to pass the criteria described and prepared to address the topics mentioned, you can expect to engage in a process with a venture fund that resembles the one shown in the diagram in Figure 5.10. Given the significant number of unsolicited business plans submitted to venture capitalists, most firms are best accessed through their network of trusted advisers and resources. This network includes lawyers, accountants, venture partners, investment bankers, and consultants who are routinely engaged by the target venture firm. If these are not the same advisers to your company, you may need to be prepared to switch. Whether or not in writing, there is usually an implied agreement that if they introduce you and help you obtain financing then you will begin to use their services.

As you may have observed, raising venture capital is not a scientific process. In fact it is fairly subjective. VCs like to travel in packs. It has often been said that if you can attract one VC with serious interest, others follow. The way to attract a crowd is to have the interested VC firm set up meetings with other VC firms after declaring its interest. The company is building the syndicate for the lead VC firm. VCs prefer not to invest alone; they desire the deep pockets of a partner and they want the assurance of another investor's eyes and brains.

If you have approached a number of firms and everyone is turning you down or dragging their feet, you have to assess whether the deal is

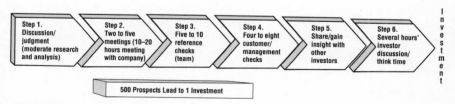

| Step 1.
Discussion/
judgment
(moderate research
and analysis) | Step 2.
Two to five
meetings (10–20
hours meeting
with company) | Step 3.
Five to 10
reference
checks
(team) | Step 4.
Four to eight
customer/
management
checks | Step 5.
Share/gain
insight with
other
investors | Step 6.
Several hours'
investor
discussion/
think time | Investment |

500 Prospects Lead to 1 Investment

FIGURE 5.10 Venture Funding Steps
Source: Robert S. Winter, "Venture Funding Process and Valuation," 1997, Slide 10.

financeable in its present form. A deal can get shopworn; investors often talk among themselves and can kill interest in a deal if there is any structural flaw in management or the business plan. So you have to ask yourself constantly, "Do I have the proper management? Is the team deep enough?" Remember VCs do not fall in love with technology or products but rather management. Founders and technical inventors are not generally suitable to be CEOs.

The fund-raising process can be frustrating and time-consuming. In fact, it slows corporate progress while management seeks financing. The most debilitating aspect is that the VC decision-making process is a prolonged event. If you get a quick no, it is because you do not fit their investment criteria. Rarely is there a quick yes. If there is initial interest, the partner will begin the investment process of performing exhaustive due diligence on the proposed management team and business model. There will be many meetings with industry leaders, friends of the firm, and your team. Management must simultaneously keep pushing forward with planned activities to build the business. Responding to due diligence requests makes you better at explaining the deal and answering concerns. Over the financing process, you will become more articulate, better focused, and armed to answer real or perceived concerns.

Be persistent. Give short- and long-term milestones. Tell the VCs when you make those milestones even if they were lukewarm on the investment; maintain a flow of communication. How an investment is perceived changes as circumstances change. Certain events can lead to financings—technology breakthrough, scientific community sponsorship, a reputable angel investor, a large sale, industry partners, and changes in the conditions affecting public markets. Entrepreneurs receive accolades from VCs for persistence. There is nothing wrong with repackaging the deal with answers to old concerns.

When a venture fund rejects your company for funding, it is not the end. You need to capitalize on the reasons for turning down the investment, and assess whether the concerns are valid and whether the issues can be addressed. Shopping puts your deal in front of more eyes and "beauty is in the eye of the beholder." Thus it is critical to shop but be aware of how the investors are viewing your deal. Are you hearing the same objections? Are you changing your presentation to address concerns from earlier meetings?

The Meetings

As mentioned, there will be a series of meetings with you and your team to position the company and to provide investors with support for your claims, the experiences and perspective of management, the chemistry among the team, and the underlying assumptions being made. These meetings should be two-way communications in which you are also able to better understand and assess your potential partners. In steps 3 and 4 there are a number of reference, customer, and management checks to validate backgrounds and test assumptions. As the process nears the point where a decision is made to invest, a case for or against is going to emerge, such as:

1. Strong technical team.   BUT   1. Doubtful CEO.
2. Chance to lead the market.   2. Big chance for slippage.
3. High upside.   3. Too much capital required.
                                            4. Weak investor group. . . .[39]

The more introspective you and your team can be, and develop real alternatives or solutions to the "BUT" side of this equation, the greater chance you will have for passing through the filter and obtaining the investment sought. More importantly, you will likely have a stronger company and will have increased the chances for success.

As mentioned, having a realistic and clear funding strategy is important. Understanding the typical venture model will help determine if you are a candidate and have the appetite for venture capital investors. Funds are usually deployed in various stages, typically named: "seed, series A through series D," and so on. The stages are also referred to as "first round," "second round," and so on. Follow-on funding may be characterized as mezzanine or bridge round, usually completed 6 to 12 months prior to an initial public offering. Each stage is intended to take place at a point in the life of the company where the value has significantly increased with a target step-up in valuation over the prior round valuation. Following the burst of the Internet bubble, many companies have seen follow-on round valuations decrease; this is referred to as a down round. When a down round occurs, prior investments are usually significantly diluted.

Figure 5.11 illustrates the building of value through milestones with staged investments. Generally, the amount of money invested in a round increases as the stages progress. Seed investments range from a nominal investment to about a million dollars. Preseed investment is typically monies provided by friends, family, founders, and an angel investor; occasionally a venture fund will provide the seed round. Depending on the size of this start-up capital, some companies skip the seed round and accept an initial investment from a venture capitalist (or a syndicate of venture capitalists) as their A round, which varies in size from $1 million to $5 million. In the biotechnology and semiconductor industries, the initial rounds may be

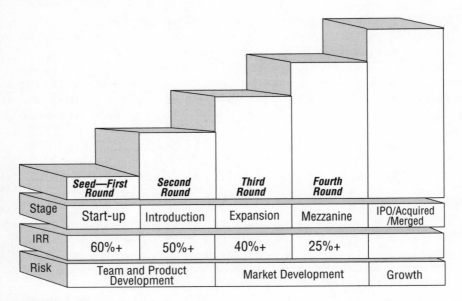

	Seed—First Round	Second Round	Third Round	Fourth Round	
Stage	Start-up	Introduction	Expansion	Mezzanine	IPO/Acquired /Merged
IRR	60%+	50%+	40%+	25%+	
Risk	Team and Product Development		Market Development		Growth

FIGURE 5.11 Value Buildup
Source: Robert S. Winter, "Venture Funding Process and Valuation," 1997, Slide 9.

much larger. Obviously, there are exceptions to all of these generalizations. Average investments by round are illustrated in Figure 5.12.

The exit strategies are reasonably direct: Either take the company public or sell to a strategic acquirer. As a fallback, a company may be merged with another and better positioned for one of the prior exits mentioned. Other potentially less favorable exit alternatives include sale of the portfolio company to another investment firm, sale back to management, or liquidation.

Selecting a Venture Capitalist

Just as the quality of management in the target is important, so is the quality of the venture investor important to the success of the target company. We encourage you to explore and understand the background of the venture investors that you choose. If you choose to pursue venture funding, consider that the partners in the venture firm will become co-workers.

Table 5.11 compares the pros and cons of venture investment partners.

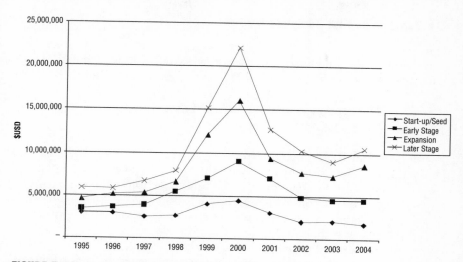

FIGURE 5.12 Average Venture Capital Investment by Stage
Source: PricewaterhouseCoopers/Thomson Venture Economics/National Venture Capital Association MoneyTree Survey.

TABLE 5.11 Investor Comparison

Investor Type	Pros	Cons
Venture capitalist	■ Deep pockets ■ Must invest ■ Rich network of resources ■ Active partner	■ Expensive ■ Desires exit strategy ■ Usually has contractual negative control
Private investor	■ Less expensive ■ More total money available ■ Can be flexible on exit ■ Willing to take more risk ■ Less onerous terms ■ May be willing to take a noncontrol position	■ Has more alternatives ■ Hard to find ■ Less money per investor ■ Requires more investors ■ Time consuming
Corporate VC	■ Can strengthen focus ■ Can add strategic leverage (i.e., marketing, technology, manufacturing, and support) ■ Instant credibility	■ Unclear motive ■ Must align to their company ■ May limit market potential

Source: Robert S. Winter, "Venture Funding Process and Valuation," 1997, Slide 14.

The Venture Capital Business Model

Understanding the business model and economics behind the venture firm may help you better understand the motives and actions of the VCs you partner with. We highlight some of the key facets of the VC model:

- Young VCs tend to look at markets and data.
- Experienced VCs tend to look at people.
- A typical fund:
    - Invests in 10 to 15 companies.
    - Expects one company to "return the fund" or generate enough gains to repay the entire amount of the fund back to the limited partners.
    - Expects one to four companies to fail.
    - Expects the rest of the companies to have minimal to reasonable returns.
    - Has a life of 10 years.
    - Leverages expertise in certain areas by investing in a portfolio of companies in an industry.
    - Invests in stages, based on milestone completion.
- VC investments:
    - Are structured to return 10 times their investment in five years.
    - Hold for three to seven years; average is about four years.
    - Expected returns depend on stage of the company; vary from 25 to 70 percent annually.
    - Must have a minimum projected portfolio company market cap of $100 million.
    - Historically have achieved overall multiples of 7× for an IPO, 2× for a sale, and .1 to .2× for a liquidation.

Valuation*

At the core of every venture capital financing is a mutually accepted valuation of the company by investor and entrepreneur. A valuation reflects both the entrepreneur's determination of the acceptable amount of ownership that may be given in return for the venture firm's capital and expertise, and the venture investor's determination of the risks and rewards of the investment. This dynamic is often misunderstood—and with harmful

---

*The content is this section is largely based on "Understanding Valuation: A Venture Investor's Perspective," by A. Dana Callow Jr., managing general partner, and Michael Larsen, senior associate, life sciences, both of Boston Millennia Partners.

consequences. Understanding valuation from the venture investor's perspective is crucial. Realizing how valuations are determined and adjusted throughout the life of the company is critical to the investor-entrepreneur relationship and the ultimate success of the company.

Valuation methodologies differ by the stage of investment and the availability of quantitative and qualitative data. However, the basic language and components of venture capital valuation are universal, simple, and should be well understood before you engage in a discussion of valuation with a venture capital investor. We will explain how venture investors consider, construct, and justify valuations of early stage companies, and will offer perspective on the dynamic role of valuation throughout the life of a company.

The Basic Math

Any private equity deal will focus on the premoney valuation of the company. This is the estimated or notional value of the company as it stands prior to any purchase of equity. Determining the premoney valuation of the company, combined with the amount of capital accepted by the company, determines the amount of equity ownership sold in exchange for capital. The resulting valuation after the investment of capital is called the postmoney valuation. For example, in a company with a premoney value of $5 million, a $5 million investment would buy a 50 percent ownership stake in the company.

$$\text{Premoney Valuation} + \text{Invested Capital} = \text{Postmoney Valuation}$$
$$\text{Price per Share} = \text{Premoney Valuation/Premoney Shares}$$

It is important not to focus just on the valuation negotiation. Just as important as the negotiation of the premoney valuation is the entrepreneur's decision as to the amount of capital to accept, which is predicated on how efficiently the company will use capital.

Methodology—Differentiating Data

Early stage investing is far from an exact science. Early stage companies are often comprised of little more than an entrepreneur with an idea. Valuations at the seed stage are generally driven by factors that by their nature are subjective. These include appraisals of the CEO and management team, novelty of the value proposition, evaluation of intellectual property, expected time to market, expected path to profitability, estimated capital needs and burn rate, syndicate risk, sector volatility, and deal structure. In postseed investing, intermediate data points such as events demonstrating proof of principle and product validation will factor strongly in valuation determinations. As a company matures to a revenue stage, more quantifiable data is produced in the form of operating statistics and performance indicators. Actual results allow investors to more accurately model quarterly and annual revenue, EBITDA, cash burn, pipeline close rates, backlog, bookings, and enterprise valuation.

Table 5.12 may be oversimplified (and should not be considered as a guide to minimum valuation levels) but it does indicate the valuation trend line of a typical investment as the company matures. Risk varies inversely with the quality and quantity of data. The high degree of uncertainty inherent in seed and early stage investments translates into low premoney valuations. Failure rates of start-up companies are high, so investors must be compensated for placing their capital at such risk. Conversely, late stage and mezzanine investors have the benefit of predictive financial models that help to mitigate risk. They pay for the reduced risk with higher premoney valuations, allowing for less upside.

Venture investors see hundreds, if not thousands, of business plans each year. Every plan includes an attractive budget and aggressive growth plan. Forecasts, as illustrated in Figure 5.13, claim to be predicated on conservative assumptions including minimal market penetration, product pricing, and gross margin. Regardless of how they are constructed, these forecasts are almost always overly optimistic in their assumptions. A venture investor will "scrub the numbers," rationalize assumptions, and run sensitivities based on varying degrees of execution, competitive pricing pressure, seasonality, and the like. The resulting rationalized forecast may

TABLE 5.12 Valuation by Stage

Financing	Company Stage	Data	Risk/ Uncertainty	Value* (MM)
Seed	Incorporation; early development	Soft data; value proposition, etc.	Extremely high	$1+
Series A	Development	Validation, time to market	Very high	$3+
Series B	Shipping product	Preliminary revenue	High	$7.5+
Series C+	Shipping product	Predictive revenue	Moderate	$10+
Later-stage/ mezzanine	Shipping product, profitable	Hard data; EBITDA, net income	Lower	$20–50+

*Based on 2003 market information.

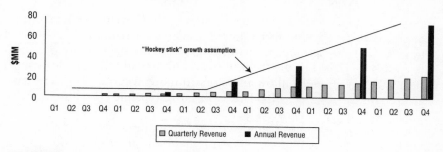

FIGURE 5.13   Company Growth Forecast

represent only a fraction of the original plan. Figure 5.14 illustrates a ratio-nalized forecast.

Discounting from the original forecast may reveal significantly greater capital requirements than first expected. As an entrepreneur, it is in your best interest to understand the short- and long-term capital requirements of your company. These capital requirements will provide the underpinning of your company's long-term financing strategy. How much must be raised now? When will the next financing be needed? What significant milestones will be accomplished during that time? An understanding of the long-term financing strategy is crucial. A seasoned entrepreneur works with investors to develop a financing strategy based on building value from one financing to the next and understanding how value will be measured.

FIGURE 5.14   Rationalized Forecast

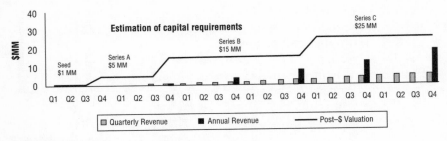

FIGURE 5.15   Long-Term Financing Strategy

Figure 5.15 illustrates a staged financing strategy. Building a company requires time and cash.

- *Seed financing.* The seed financing will provide the capital needed to support salaries for founders/management, R&D, technology proof-of-concept, prototype development and testing, and so on. Sources of capital may include personal funds, friends, family, and angel investors. Capital raised is limited due to its diluting impact at minimal valuations. The goal here is to assemble a talented team, achieve development milestones, proof of concept, and anything else that will enable you to attract investors for your next financing.
- *Series A financing.* Typically the series A is the company's first institutional financing—led by one or more venture investors. Valuation of this round will reflect progress made with seed capital, the quality of the management team, and other qualitative components. Generally, a series A financing will purchase a 25 percent to 50 percent ownership stake. Typical goals of this financing are to finalize product development for information technology companies, hire top talent, achieve value-creating milestones, further validate product, expand business development efforts, and attract investor interest in the next financing (at an increased valuation).
- *Series B financing.* The series B is usually a larger financing than the series A. At this point, we can assume for information technology companies that development is complete and technology risk removed. Early revenue streams may be taking shape. Valuation is gauged on a blend of subjective and objective data—human capital, technical assets, intellectual property, milestones achieved thus far, comparable company valuations, rationalized revenue forecasts.

Goals of this financing may include operational development, scale-up, further product development, revenue traction and value creation for the next round of financing.

- *Series C financing.* The series C may be a later stage financing designed to strengthen the balance sheet, provide operating capital to expand the company operations, finance an acquisition, develop further products, or prepare the company for exit via IPO or acquisition. The company often has predictable revenue, backlog, and EBITDA at this point, providing outside investors with a breadth of hard data points to justify valuation. Valuation metrics, such as multiples of revenue and EBITDA, from comparable public companies can be compiled and discounted to approximate value.

Figure 5.16 demonstrates the typical relationship between the post-money valuation as determined in a venture investment and the intrinsic market valuation of the enterprise that might be realized in a sale of the company. The implied premoney valuations of the seed and series A investments exceed the market valuations at the time of those investments. This early value premium is the result of qualitative data employed in the early stage valuation methodology. The venture investor is valuing the intangibles of the idea and human capital. Moving forward to the series B financing, premoney valuations fall in relation to market value. Interim valuations are generally below market value; this affords investors a risk premium in valuation to compensate for the illiquid nature of private equity.

Applying Perspective

The preceding example illustrates the stepped function of valuation. Each financing is designed to provide capital for value-creating objectives. Assuming

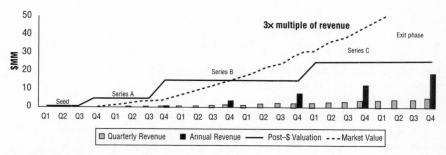

FIGURE 5.16 Building Enterprise Value

objectives are accomplished and value is created, financing continues at a higher valuation commensurate with the progress made and risk mitigated. However, problems can and will arise during this time that may adversely affect valuation. When a financing cannot be raised at a step-up in valuation, investors may structure a flat round or a down round in which valuation is reduced. A down round can result from premature capital shortages from overspending, failure to achieve value-creating milestones, or suboptimal operating performance. Overpricing of a prior financing or softening capital markets may also play a role. Down rounds are undesirable—they undermine management and investor confidence. They also bring unwanted write-downs to venture investors' portfolios. However, many companies have built success stories despite going through a down round.

The valuation of a company at a discrete point in time is subject to a certain range of interpretation. Most seasoned venture investors will value a company within a 10 to 15 percent range of comparably staged portfolio companies if they have exhausted all quantitative and qualitative data available. Given the consistency that is generally seen in the market, the key factor in choosing one VC over another should rarely be based in valuation.

In the long term, interim valuations will factor only modestly in the realization and distribution of proceeds upon exit. Investors will keep management incentivized. Remember to take the long view. Avoid arbitrary step-ups in valuation. Plan for the next financing and make sure there is ample justification for a step-up in valuation if milestones are achieved. In the end, the minutiae of valuation will matter very little. Valuation can make a good investment more attractive, but it will not salvage a poor one. A company will usually receive several financings before an exit is realized. Building value is the shared objective of entrepreneur and investor. A mutual understanding between investor and entrepreneur of the risks and rewards driving a valuation is crucial to starting a relationship on equal ground.

Other Contributing Factors in Valuation

Outside of the milestone-based measures, other factors contribute to the price paid by the VC for new shares:[40]

- Condition of public and private financial markets.
- Strength of management for the milestone stage.
- Terms and conditions of the round.
- Trends in the venture market.
- Strategic significance of the company's product.

Many times, the terms and conditions of the investment are far more important than the actual price agreed upon. The investment should be evaluated based on a combination of elements of the deal structure[41]—broadly, valuation, terms and conditions, and the planned exit:

- Valuation.
- Amount and timing of the investment.
- Form of the investment.
- Board compensation.
- Vesting of management's ownership.
- Additional management members.
- Conversion rights.
- Preemptive rights of the investors.
- Employment agreements.
- Proprietary rights of the company.
- Exit strategy.
- Lockup rights.

Partner Interaction with Portfolio Companies*

As the founders or management of a venture-backed company, you can expect the partner of the lead venture capital firm to interact in a number of ways to provide input and collect information to monitor their investment.

Board Representation When venture firms invest in a private company, most receive one and sometimes two seats on the company's board of directors. Board members have a fiduciary responsibility to ensure that the company is being managed in the best interests of all of its shareholders. Board members receive regular updates on how the business is performing and the key strategic issues that it faces. Members are expected to attend regular board meetings, which can occur monthly for early stage companies or quarterly for later stage companies. Prior to each board meeting, each member receives a detailed board package, which is a collection of materials intended to be an all-inclusive update and review of the business. In addition to current financials, board packages typically contain a written update on progress in the business as well as a detailed explanation of

---

*The base content of the section is adapted from "Note on Venture Capital Portfolio Management," 2003, by Professors Colin Blaydon and Fred Wainwright, Tuck School of Business at Dartmouth, and Andrew Waldeck. The authors gratefully acknowledge the support of the Tuck Center for Private Equity and Entrepreneurship. Copyright © Trustees of Dartmouth College. All rights reserved.

the key issues being discussed at that particular board meeting (such as compensation plans, hiring of key managers, etc.).

Investor Information Provisions   VCs and all other investors have information rights that are detailed in the shareholders' rights agreement, which is agreed to prior to the closing of a financing. Through these information provisions, investors typically are entitled to receive interim financial statements (which can be either monthly or quarterly), annual budgets or forecasts, and completed audited financial statements. Many VCs will request additional information to be included along with these interim financial statements, which help track the company's progress in achieving certain agreed-to milestones (such as number of customers or number of employees). In an effort to keep all investors better informed, private companies are now also including written business summaries with interim financial statements. These updates would cover any important business developments, such as additions to the management team, major new customer wins, or loss of a key customer. Using the last as an example, a realistic assessment should be presented indicating how to acquire customers to offset the sales volume loss. If no near-term offsetting sales gains are achievable, then management would present a fallback alternative downsizing plan showing commensurate expense reductions. Other alternatives would need to be prepared and presented with a recommendation for board discussion and approval.

Additional Informal Communication   VCs will regularly call, e-mail, and visit many of their respective CEOs and other senior managers. Some VCs expect to communicate with 80 percent to 90 percent of their portfolio companies at least once a week. Investors use these opportunities to ask additional questions or to receive additional management insights. In addition, these situations also present management with a chance to ask questions, seek guidance, and get feedback from investors as well. Many investors believe casual and informal communication with management often provides the most meaningful insights into business or management performance.

Company Performance Monitoring*

In general, the information venture firms choose to focus on to monitor their performance is largely determined by the stage and sector of each

---

*The base content of this section is adapted from "Note on Venture Capital Portfolio Management," 2003, developed by Andy Waldeck (Tuck 2004) under the supervision of Adjunct Professor Fred Wainwright and Professor Colin Blaydon of the Tuck School of Business at Dartmouth College, Center for Private Equity and Entrepreneurship.

company. For example, for a prerevenue biotech investment, a VC will want to track expenses and be updated on the status of the regulatory approval process. An investor in that same company at a later stage may track the sales pipeline (i.e., future revenue), expenses, and progress on future R&D efforts. Listed in Table 5.13 are examples of the type of information that VCs would focus on depending on stage.

Managing a Venture-Dominated Board

Caution: The following section may get you excited, especially if you are a VC. These paragraphs are not intended to criticize, but to provide the reader a perspective from entrepreneurs.

Leading or managing the board of a venture-backed company has dynamics that are not found in other companies. In discussing this topic, company management may benefit from understanding the psyche of a venture capitalist. We believe that the following four quotes from venture capitalists provide insight into how they may view the world. As with any generalization, there are exceptions.

Quote #1: "We cannot pick our winners." Imagine playing a game each year at the Christmas party where each venture partner tries to pick their most successful companies (meaning those that will be successfully exited) in the coming year, and they discover after years of play they cannot. Companies that may appear to being doing well from an operations or a technology development viewpoint today may encounter significant

TABLE 5.13 Staged-Based Measurement

	Early Stage (Prerevenue)	Early Revenue	Close to Profitable/ Profitable
Financial metrics	■ Operating expenses ■ Cash burn	■ Operating expenses ■ Cash burn ■ Revenue	■ Revenue ■ Gross margin ■ Operating expenses ■ Cash
Business milestones	■ Product development ■ Additions to the team	■ Product development ■ Customer input on product features ■ Team ■ Sales pipeline	■ Sales pipeline ■ Bookings ■ Team ■ Marketing plan

problems later in the corporate development process. This reality creates a healthy amount of skepticism and self-doubt. We believe every venture capitalist has a nagging fear the investment will not prove out and that he or she will be held responsible for poor judgment by his or her partners. Notwithstanding, the VC wants to believe the investment will prove successful for all the reasons that justified the investment. This is the root of the paranoia: "I believe in this investment but I'm not sure." As we will discuss, upon being presented with unforeseen or uncontrollable variables, some venture capitalists have a tendency to react emotionally and protectively, which can result in biased decisions.

Quote #2: "My experience is that often winners are decided by the stars and moon aligning." What this means is there is a bit of luck associated with determining a winner. Several venture portfolios lived and died exclusively on the dot-com industry. Successful venture firms exited early and initiated option strategies to protect fluctuating stock prices and lock in profits. It is all about market timing. You have to ask where those successful companies are today. Many have been liquidated because they were built without credible operating strategies. Were the successful VCs smart or lucky? Think of biotech companies. When do you know you have a winner? It could take as much as a 10-year development cycle with results really concrete only after conducting blind phase III trials. Great science and management teams have fallen to a drug candidate's unexpected side effects, the inability to prove statistically significant end points and, in certain cases, regulatory politics. Were the venture capitalists in successful biotechs smart, or did they invest in a portfolio of companies that yielded successes?

To give further examples, think of the long adoption curve for the telephone, television, and computer. Great products and solutions are often slow to be adopted, particularly if there is a perceived satisfactory existing method or product. People are not change friendly; most people resist learning new things until they have to. For venture capitalists and management, it generally takes longer for investments to mature than is anticipated. Patience requires a strong belief in management and products.

The other big unknown is the stock market. For years, it seemed the IPO market got hot for companies within specific industries and drove valuations up significantly. Market timing for a specific industry is unpredictable, but what is predictable is that when the market rotates to a particular industry sector there is a window to successfully finance, exit, or consolidate. Management has to have the company ready to take advantage of such market opportunities; finance, merge, exit when the market is available because that is where the highest valuation will occur. Venture-backed companies that are not ready may never see another up cycle. Venture-backed management fails when it believes there will be greater value later and does nothing to exit during a bull market.

Quote #3: "For us, it is all about putting the right fannies in the right seats to build a team. If any entrepreneur asks me what to do, I know I'm in the wrong investment." If there is an element of luck, or certain uncontrollable industry or market variables, to building corporate value and successfully exit, then there has to be an emphasis on hiring management and, more specifically, building a team. Venture capitalists usually do not operate and they need managers who can navigate through icebergs. In the back of a venture capitalist's mind, he or she is always assessing the management because it is all about building confidence. Most companies, to use a NASCAR phrase, will "hit the wall" (encounter difficult obstacles) at some point and there is potential for serious damage to investment returns. This is particularly true with technology development companies, early stage companies, or novel technologies trying to develop new markets. Consequently, there will be a crossroad where VC investors will doubt their management decisions. Precisely when the going gets tough, less experienced venture capital firms will be the first to complain, raise doubts about strategy and direction, and ask unanswerable questions requiring soothsaying managerial talents. From a manager's perspective, it is incumbent to build a team to instill calm through managerial confidence in a shared strategic vision.

Make sure your team has consistent interaction with the VCs at board meetings, present well-rehearsed presentations on their areas of expertise, and relay a consistent strategy. VCs should not look to a manager, but rather to a team of managers and gain confidence in the team as a whole versus the individual. Never ask a venture capitalist to develop strategy; the VC's inquisitive, and sometimes aggressive, questioning is often to test management's commitment and confidence in their own strategy. Is the team considering known and unforeseen variables? Imagine if the venture capitalist always knew when the entrepreneur was steering through icebergs!

Quote #4: "Returns come from diversifying risk through a portfolio of companies. You have to place multiple bets to find winners." When an entrepreneur reads and understands these four quotes, we believe he or she will better understand the venture capital perspective. "One venture board member used to arrive for meetings and immediately ask to find an earlier flight back. The first priority was always telling us how busy he was and his travel itinerary." Many investors see an investment as just part of a larger portfolio and view board meetings as quarterly updates. They want the big picture: "Are we on plan? What has changed? How are we adjusting to the changes? What effect does this have on our short-term and long-term plans/results?"

Board meetings must be controlled and informative, provide full disclosure, contain the right amount of detail to demonstrate strong knowledge, and end with strong optimism and assurance to investors of the possibility of strong returns. Meetings should generally not last more than two to two and a half hours.

We emphasize the need for full disclosure and integrity; investors have to be aware of all the downside possibilities, and you must immediately notify them of any material problems. With that said, however, your primary focus must be on the upside. We believe that companies can succeed because they are willed to succeed by management but only if they have the time to succeed. Time is associated with investment and investor confidence. Pessimistic leaders fall by the wayside because they do not provide vision, and thus provide no leadership. When encountering adversity, use creativity to reach your goal a different way. Markets will change, and you have to adapt your strategy accordingly. That is why they back you. Come off the wall, assess the damage, and get back in the race. VCs want gamers; they know obstacles will arise.

As mentioned, understanding the venture capitalist's viewpoint is critical to managing the board. Remember the venture capitalist is sitting on numerous boards and reviewing multiple deals, and gleans lots of knowledge tidbits from many sources. He may have or had investments in your industry and like to recite their experiences. Be sensitive to those experiences even if not relevant to your company. This represents his point of reference and he does not want to repeat a mistake.

A problem for many entrepreneurs is that venture capitalists are generalists, and are not operational. They do not want to make your decisions but they will be inquisitive about everything. I have found that entrepreneurs often fall into the trap of trying to discuss and decide corporate strategy with their venture partners. Mistakenly, they assume the venture capitalist actually wants to be a part of the decision process. What the venture capitalist seeks is the comfort that you believe in your strategy and can support your position when cross-examined. If the entrepreneur actually asks for advice, venture capitalists immediately assume they may have the wrong person. Venture capitalists are like a large lake on a windy day when no whitecaps appear. It is because the water's not deep. Venture capitalists cannot take deep dives. Entrepreneurs must.

VCs sit on at least three boards. Coupled with ongoing investment diligence, it is difficult to give any one company but so much mind share. Thus, start off each meeting with your strategic goals and how you are progressing toward them. Do not assume your venture board remembers the problems from a quarter ago; do not assume they read your board package! Review issues in light of the larger strategy. Talk about issues and potential solutions, and always relate them to the investment opportunity, a profitable exit. Each meeting, begin with the vision, deal straightforwardly with issues and obstacles, address how to solve these concerns, and end with selling the vision again.

Entrepreneurs will be judged on their ability to build teams, handle problems, and stay focused on attaining corporate goals. Remember everything takes longer than projected or expected. Venture capitalists are prepared for this. In today's environment, they are prepared to put two to four times their initial investment into a deal that is progressing and demonstrating results. As an entrepreneur CEO, never let the company become cash constrained; start initiating fund-raising months before conservative projections show cash shortfalls. Never, never, never surprise venture investors with calls for capital! This is why we were so adamant previously when we stated that entrepreneurs had to take advantage of bull markets for financing purposes. Rarely has anyone ever written articles about being overcapitalized.

Here are six keys for success in VC-backed company board meetings:

1. Instill investor confidence in the management team.
2. Communicate belief in the corporate vision in the face of adversity.
3. Stay focused on the big picture and progressing toward goals and exits.
4. Understand that venture capitalists do not want to be a part of the operating decision process.
5. Understand that a company is just another investment requiring returns.
6. Surround yourself with people smarter than you are.

Trends

In today's environment VCs are seeking proven managers who have already grown a company and shown their prowess. This makes it difficult for the entrepreneur with ideas but little experience to raise venture capital. VCs are looking at expansion and later stage deals with favor. In general they would rather back a more mature deal where they can exit in two to three years than a start-up with a more traditional funding cycle.[42] The implications are that early stage deals are tough to get done, and this increases the need and demand for quality angel investors.

Lastly, VCs are seeking the efficient use and deployment of invested funds. This concept of capital efficiency is in the vein of returning to industry basics as seen in the early 1990s. Unlike the period during the Internet bubble, today VCs prefer to invest more traditional amounts in tranches that will cap the total investment in a company at $20 million to

$30 million. This means that a company can foreseeably go from seed round through its final VC round using no more than $20 million to $30 million and be a viable ongoing business; obviously there are exceptions such as the biotechnology industry. VCs who invest in technology companies that create software are seeking offshore suppliers and partners to stretch their investment dollars.

MEZZANINE FUNDS*

Mezzanine funds are typically subordinated debt lenders and seek businesses that have high potential for growth and earnings but are currently unable to obtain from a bank all of the funds necessary to achieve their goals. This may be because of a lack of collateral, higher balance sheet leverage, shorter operating history, or a variety of other, transitional reasons. As risk lenders, mezzanine investors consider investment opportunities outside conventional commercial bank parameters. Ideally, mezzanine investors prefer companies that, in a three-to-five-year period, can exit mezzanine financing through additional debt from a senior lender, an initial public offering, or an acquisition. In addition to these financial criteria, a critical consideration is the quality of the people involved. Strong management is important, and mezzanine investors look closely at an entrepreneur's hands-on operating achievements and proven management ability. The track record of a company's management team is a valuable indicator of its ability to achieve future success.

The typical borrowing profile of a company funded by a mezzanine fund is:

- Strong management.
- Strong cash flow.
- Insufficient senior financing.
- Insufficient collateral.
- High leverage.

Mezzanine funds typically provide financing for:

- Acquisitions and management buyouts.
- Business expansion.

---

*The base content of this section is adapted from "Mezzanine Capital Financing for Small and Midsize Businesses," written by Donald Tyson, PNC Bank.

- Recapitalizations.
- New product launches and diversification.
- Long-term working capital to support growth.
- Equipment and owner-occupied real estate purchases.
- Dividends.

Businesses and situations usually *not* of interest to mezzanine investors include:

- Start-ups.
- Seed capital.
- Prerevenue or development stage companies.
- Non-owner-occupied real estate investment.
- Any business unable to support additional debt service from its cash flow.
- Turnaround situations.

An interested company should contact a mezzanine investor for a preliminary screening to determine whether mezzanine financing is appropriate for its situation. The company then works closely with its bank and the mezzanine investor to structure a complete financing package. Alternatively, a bank unable to fully satisfy the financing needs of a growing company may suggest a mezzanine investor.

Mezzanine Financing/Subordinated Debt

Mezzanine is a term used to describe financing that fits on the balance sheet between commercial bank debt and traditional shareholder's equity. While this type of financing is a form of debt (typically a subordinated loan), it is often referred to as an investment.

Mezzanine financing is not generally used by firms to cover day-to-day operations; rather, it is used during transitional periods in the life of a company when extra financing is required. Mezzanine loans are used for long-term or permanent working capital, equipment purchases, management buyouts, strategic acquisitions, recapitalizations, acquisitions of commercial real estate, and other worthwhile business purposes. Typically, a business will be in a situation where its commercial bank is unable to fully meet its credit needs. In these situations, the business owners have two options: (1) raise additional capital through the sale of equity in the business, or (2) raise additional debt by borrowing from a mezzanine lender. If you have a successful company and need a substantial investment, but do not want to give up large amounts of equity or control, mezzanine financing may be for you.

Equity versus Mezzanine Debt

Equity investment may be attractive to some businesses because it does not require interest payments or principal amortization. However, equity financing may also involve higher long-term costs, the inability to exit, and management control issues. An equity investor will look to earn, at a minimum, a 25 percent to 35 percent return on the investment as compensation for the risks taken. Equity investors want to have some input into the management of the business in order to protect their investments, and have to be bought out to terminate the relationship.

By contrast, mezzanine financing may offer the advantages of a lower cost, no management control, and a predefined exit arrangement. Mezzanine investors usually seek a 15 percent to 30 percent return on investment, some of which can be generated through fees or stock warrants. When the mezzanine investor earns much of its return through fees tied directly to the performance of the company (instead of through stock ownership), the investor participates in the success *or* failure of the company, and these fees are limited to the life of the financing arrangement. In this way, mezzanine financing can eliminate the outside ownership and management control issues that often concern entrepreneurs, and it does not dilute the equity of the shareholders.

Loan Structure

Mezzanine loans are structured to accommodate the financing needs of growing companies. The mezzanine investor predicates the investment decision on the firm's cash flow and projected growth rather than on collateral. Typically, mezzanine loans are unsecured; the mezzanine investor presumes that there will be little or no recovery of principal from a liquidation, and the investment is priced accordingly. However, the investor may require a subordinate claim on corporate assets, second to the senior lender. The terms of a mezzanine deal are usually flexible, generally involving five-to-seven-year maturities with no amortization. Repayment of principal is usually due at maturity or deferred until later in the loan term and is scheduled to fit the borrower's needs and cash flow projections. Creativity in structuring loans is a strength of the mezzanine investor.

Loan Size

Mezzanine investors fill a niche in the financing market, and some provide funding for smaller businesses and in smaller amounts than most other investors. While mezzanine investments are available in all amounts, the smallest investments ranging from $100,000 to $750,000, most deals today are $1,000,000 plus in size. Larger investments are made by many mezzanine funds with loans that range from $10 million to $50 million, or more.

Price

Mezzanine financing presents a greater degree of risk to the investor, so it is considerably more expensive for the business than borrowing from a bank. The price of mezzanine debt typically includes a base interest or coupon rate on the loan with an additional pricing vehicle to ensure that the investor participates in the success (or failure) of the business. This vehicle can take the form of a stock warrant or a royalty, often called a success fee or revenue participation fee, that is based on the growth of the business. The pricing is structured to fit the unique characteristics of the business and the deal. In some instances, a success fee will have variable terms to protect the lender from nonperformance of the company; you may hear the term *ratchet* used in this context. Typically, mezzanine investors seek overall returns of 15 percent to 20 percent or more on investments. In addition, expect to pay an application fee of 0.5 percent to 2 percent plus a commitment fee of 1 percent to 3 percent, both amounts as a percent of the total transaction value.

The portion of the pricing that rewards the investor based on the firm's success should be carefully considered. A warrant or any other financial vehicle that ties into the equity of the company may have disadvantages and costs similar to those of a straight equity investment. Mezzanine investors that do not use these types of vehicles usually have a lower cost, no management control, and an easier exit strategy. Instead of using an equity-based vehicle, these investors base a portion of the pricing on the firm's measurable financial success during the loan term, using a fee based on a formula tied to the firm's income statement. The simplest of these success fees works much like a royalty: The firm pays the investor a periodic fee equal to a small percentage of that period's gross revenues. Therefore, as sales increase or decrease, so goes the return to the mezzanine investor.

If the company wishes to exit the mezzanine investment prematurely, there may be some costs to doing so. These costs may include a prepayment penalty or a yield maintenance calculation to ensure that the investor is guaranteed a minimum return on the investment. These costs should be defined up front to ensure a smooth exit strategy.

Pricing questions to ask a mezzanine investor include:

- What is the interest or coupon rate of the loan?
- What are the other pricing components?

- Is there an equity component to the price?
- What are the costs to exit the relationship and pay off the loan?

Prepayment or Early Exit   Usually subordinated debt can be prepaid; however, there are terms in the transaction documents (negotiable) that will provide what is in effect a prepayment fee. A couple of examples are the sum of the average remaining success fees or the discounted NPV of the remaining success fees. Alternatively, the firm may continue to pay the remaining success fees through the original maturity date of the loan.

Practically Speaking

Mezzanine financing is typically not available to early stage or venture capital–backed companies until the business has demonstrated significant commercial success and consistent growth. While mezzanine players may not have significant collateral positions as required by commercial banks, they are debt players and typically have restrictive financial covenants to protect their debt. Mezzanine players are often found in leveraged management buyouts where the company's cash flow justifies greater leverage than the company's asset coverage. The companies financed by mezzanine lenders generally have a proven financial history and cash flows that justify additional leverage.

Remember that lenders in liquidation must be repaid before the equity holders; thus if events cause the company to go sideways or take a turn downward, the company's management may not be able to change course without the lender's permission because of restrictive covenants. This often leads to raising additional equity to pay off debt at precisely the wrong time to price the new stock. Thus, significant shareholder dilution can result. If all goes well, dilution is avoided and everyone wins.

BUYOUT FUNDS*

A leveraged buyout (LBO) is an acquisition of a company or division of another company financed with a substantial portion of borrowed funds. In

---

*The base content of this section is adapted from "Note on Leveraged Buyouts," 2003, by Professors Colin Blaydon and Fred Wainwright, Tuck School of Business at Dartmouth; Jonathan Olsen; and Salvatore Gagliano. The authors gratefully acknowledge the support of the Tuck Center for Private Equity and Entrepreneurship. Copyright © Trustees of Dartmouth College. All rights reserved.

the 1980s, LBO firms and their professionals were the focus of considerable attention, not all of it favorable. LBO activity accelerated throughout the 1980s, starting from a basis of four deals with an aggregate value of $1.7 billion in 1980 and reaching its peak in 1988, when 410 buyouts were completed with an aggregate value of $188 billion.

The perception was the deals were less risky. LBO targets were established companies with histories of profitability, defined market niches, and proven management teams. Significant leverage was generally available through mezzanine lenders who augmented traditional lenders. At the time this was primarily the hunting ground of mezzanine lenders. Management was often attracted because they had little equity in their companies and could obtain significant positions in the buyout. Until the industry demanded more equity in the deals, the management teams often faced the insurmountable task of repaying debt at the sacrifice of growth and internal investment. Thus it was difficult to adapt to market changes. With greater equity investments, management has the ability to balance the computing uses of cash.

In the years since 1988, downturns in the business cycle, the near-collapse of the junk bond market, and diminished structural advantages all contributed to dramatic changes in the LBO market. In addition, LBO fund raising has accelerated dramatically. From 1980 to 1988 LBO funds raised approximately $46 billion; from 1988 to 2000, LBO funds raised over $385 billion. As increasing amounts of capital competed for the same number of deals, it became increasingly difficult for LBO firms to acquire businesses at attractive prices. In addition, senior lenders have become increasingly wary of highly levered transactions, forcing LBO firms to contribute higher levels of equity. In 1988 the average equity contribution to leveraged buyouts was 9 to 17 percent. In 2000 the average equity contribution to leveraged buyouts was almost 38 percent, and for the first three quarters of 2001 average equity contributions were above 40 percent. From the data we have in 2004, the contributions have begun to trend downward and are in the 35 percent range.

These developments have made generating target returns (usually 25 to 30 percent) much more difficult for LBO firms. Where once they could rely on leverage to generate returns, LBO firms today are seeking to build value in acquired companies by improving profitability, pursuing growth including roll-up strategies (in which an acquired company serves as a platform for additional acquisitions of related businesses to achieve critical mass and generate economies of scale), and improving corporate governance to better align management incentives with those of shareholders. Fund returns are now a result of operational improvements (50 percent), leverage (20 percent), and multiple expansion (30 percent), whereas during the Internet bubble returns were driven by multiple expansion (55 percent), operational improvements (15 percent), and leverage (30 percent).

In the context of this handbook, you will find the terms *buyout* and *leveraged buyout* used with the same intended meaning. These firms provide a potential funding alternative that may allow shareholder liquidity and growth capital combined into one transaction.

History of the LBO

While it is unclear when the first leveraged buyout was carried out, it is generally agreed that early leveraged buyouts were carried out in the years following World War II. Prior to the 1980s, the leveraged buyout (previously known as a bootstrap acquisition) was for years little more than an obscure financing technique.

In the postwar years, the Great Depression was still relatively fresh in the minds of America's corporate leaders, who considered it wise to keep corporate debt ratios low. As a result, for the first three decades following World War II, very few American companies relied on debt as a significant source of funding. At the same time, American businesses became caught up in a wave of conglomerate building that began in the early 1960s. Executives filled boards of directors with subordinates and friendly outsiders and engaged in rampant empire building. The ranks of middle management swelled, and corporate profitability began to slide. It was in this environment that the modern LBO was born.

In the late 1970s and early 1980s, newly formed firms such as Kohlberg Kravis Roberts and Thomas H. Lee Company saw an opportunity to profit from inefficient and undervalued corporate assets. Many public companies were trading at a discount to net asset value, and many early leveraged buyouts were motivated by profits available from buying entire companies, breaking them up, and selling off the pieces. This bust-up approach was largely responsible for the eventual media backlash against the greed of so-called corporate raiders, illustrated by books such as *The Rain on Macy's Parade* by Jeffrey A. Trachtenberg (Times Business, 1996) and films such as *Wall Street* and *Barbarians at the Gate*, the latter based on the book by Bryan Burrough and John Helyar (Harper & Row, 1990).

As a new generation of managers began to take over American companies in the late 1970s, many were willing to consider debt financing as a viable alternative for financing operations. Soon LBO firms' constant pitching began to convince some managers of the merits of debt-financed buyouts of their businesses. From a manager's perspective, leveraged buyouts had a number of appealing characteristics:

- Tax advantages associated with debt financing.
- Freedom from the scrutiny of being a public company or a captive division of a larger parent.
- The ability for founders to take advantage of a liquidity event without ceding operational influence or sacrificing continued day-to-day involvement.
- The opportunity for managers to become owners of a significant percentage of a firm's equity.

Theory of the Leveraged Buyout

While every leveraged buyout is unique with respect to its specific capital structure, the one common element of a leveraged buyout is the use of financial leverage to complete the acquisition of a target company. In an LBO, the private equity firm acquiring the target company will finance the acquisition with a combination of debt and equity, much like an individual buying a house with a mortgage. Just as a mortgage is secured by the value of the house being purchased, some portion of the debt incurred in an LBO is secured by the assets of the acquired business. Unlike a house, however, the bought-out business generates cash flows that are used to service the debt incurred in its buyout. In essence, the acquired company helps pay for itself (hence the term *bootstrap acquisition*).

The use of significant amounts of debt to finance the acquisition of a company has a number of advantages, as well as risks. The most obvious risk associated with a leveraged buyout is that of financial distress. Unforeseen events such as recession, litigation, or changes in the regulatory environment can lead to difficulties meeting scheduled interest payments, technical default (the violation of the terms of a debt covenant), or outright liquidation. Weak management at the target company or misalignment of incentives between management and shareholders can also pose threats to the ultimate success of an LBO.

There are a number of advantages to the use of leverage in acquisitions. Large interest and principal payments can force management to improve performance and operating efficiency. This "discipline of debt" can force management to focus on certain initiatives such as divesting noncore businesses, downsizing, cost cutting, or investing in technological upgrades that might otherwise be postponed or rejected outright. In this manner, the use of debt serves not just as a financing technique, but also as a tool to force changes in managerial behavior.

Another characteristic of the leverage in LBO financing is that, as the debt ratio increases, the equity portion of the acquisition financing shrinks to a level at which a private equity firm can acquire a company by putting up anywhere from 20 to 40 percent of the total purchase price. Private equity firms typically invest alongside management, encouraging (if not requiring) top executives to commit a significant portion of their personal net worth to the deal. By requiring the target's management team to invest in the acquisition, the private equity firm guarantees that management's incentives will be aligned with its own.

To better understand the basics, here are the key terms and concepts regarding LBOs:

- *Transaction fee amortization.* This reflects the capitalization and amortization of financing, legal, and accounting fees associated with the transaction. Transaction fee amortization, like depreciation, is a tax-deductible noncash expense. In most cases the allowable amortization period for such fees is five to seven years (although in some cases LBO firms may choose to expense all such fees in year 1 so as to present the cleanest set of numbers possible going forward).

- *Interest expense.* For simplicity, interest expense for each tranche of debt financing is calculated based on the yearly beginning balance of each tranche. In reality, interest payments are often made quarterly, so interest expense in the case of the target LBO may be slightly overstated.

- *Capitalization.* Most leveraged buyouts make use of multiple tranches of debt to finance the transaction. A simple transaction may have only two tranches of debt, senior and junior. A large leveraged buyout will likely be financed with multiple tranches of debt that could include (in decreasing order of seniority) some or all of the following:

  - *Revolving credit facility (revolver).* This is a source of funds that the bought-out firm can draw upon as its working capital needs dictate. A revolving credit facility is designed to offer the bought-out firm some flexibility with respect to its capital needs; it serves as a line of credit that allows the firm to make certain capital investments, deal with unforeseen costs, or cover increases in working capital without having to seek additional debt or equity financing.

  - *Bank debt.* Often secured by the assets of the bought-out firm, this is the most senior claim against the cash flows of the business. As such, bank debt is repaid first, with its interest and principal payments taking precedence over other, junior sources of debt financing.

  - *Mezzanine debt.* Mezzanine debt is so named because it exists in the middle of the capital structure and is junior to the bank debt incurred in financing the leveraged buyout. As a result, mezzanine debt (like each succeeding level of junior debt) is compensated for its lower priority with a higher interest rate.

- **Subordinated or high-yield notes.** Commonly referred to as junk bonds and usually sold to the public, these notes are the most junior source of debt financing and as such command the highest interest rates to compensate holders for their increased risk exposure.

Each tranche of debt financing will likely have different maturities and repayment terms. For example, some sources of financing require mandatory amortization of principal in addition to scheduled interest payments. Some lenders may receive warrants, which allow lenders to participate in the equity upside in the event the deal is highly successful. There are a number of ways private equity firms can adjust the target's capital structure. The ability to be creative in structuring and financing a leveraged buyout allows private equity firms to adjust to changing market conditions.

In addition to the debt financing component of an LBO, there is also an equity component. Private equity firms typically invest alongside management to ensure the alignment of management and shareholder interests. In large LBOs, private equity firms will sometimes team up to create a consortium of buyers, thereby reducing the amount of capital exposed to any one investment. As a general rule, private equity firms will own 70 to 90 percent of the common equity of the bought-out firm, with the remainder held by management and former shareholders.

Another potential source of financing for leveraged buyouts is preferred equity. Preferred equity is often attractive because its dividend interest payments represent a minimum return on investment while its equity ownership component allows holders to participate in any equity upside. Preferred interest is often structured as pay-in-kind (PIK) dividends, which means any interest is paid in the form of additional shares of preferred stock. LBO firms will often structure their equity investment in the form of preferred stock, with management and employees receiving common stock.

- **Cash sweep.** A cash sweep is a provision of certain debt covenants that stipulates that any excess cash (namely free cash flow available after mandatory amortization payments have been made) generated by the bought-out business will be used to pay down principal. For those tranches of debt with provisions for a cash sweep, excess cash is used to pay down debt in the order of seniority. For example, in the case of the target the cash sweep does not begin to pay down junior debt until year 4.

- *Exit scenario.* As a general rule, leveraged buyout firms seek to exit their investments in five to seven years. An exit usually involves either a sale of the portfolio company, an IPO, or a recapitalization (effectively an acquisition and relevering of the company by another LBO firm).

Buyout Firm Structure and Organization

The equity that LBO firms invest in an acquisition comes from a fund of committed capital that has been raised from a pool of qualified investors. These funds are structured as limited partnerships, with the firm's principals acting as general partner, and investors in the firm (usually investment funds, insurance companies, pension funds, and wealthy individuals) acting as limited partners. The general partner is responsible for making all investment decisions relating to the fund, with the limited partners responsible for transferring committed capital to the fund upon notice of the general partner.

As a general rule, funds raised by private equity firms have a number of fairly standard provisions:

- *Minimum commitment.* Prospective limited partners are required to commit a minimum amount of equity. Limited partners make a capital commitment, which is then drawn down (a takedown or capital call) by the general partner in order to make investments with the fund's equity.
- *Investment or commitment period.* During the term of the commitment period, limited partners are obligated to meet capital calls upon notice by the general partner by transferring capital to the fund within an agreed-upon period of time (often 10 days). The term of the commitment period usually lasts for either five or six years after the closing of the fund or until 75 to 100 percent of the fund's capital has been invested, whichever comes first.
- *Term.* The term of the partnership formed during the fund-raising process is usually 10 to 12 years, the first half of which represents the commitment period (defined above), the second half of which is reserved for managing and exiting investments made during the commitment period.
- *Diversification.* Most funds' partnership agreements stipulate that the partnership may not invest more than 25 percent of the fund's equity in any single investment.

The LBO firm generates revenue in three ways:

1. *Carried interest.* Carried interest is a share of any profits generated by acquisitions made by the fund. Once all the partners have received an

amount equal to their contributed capital any remaining profits are split between the general partner and the limited partners. Typically, the general partner's carried interest is 20 percent of any profits remaining once all the partners' capital has been returned, although some funds guarantee the limited partners a priority return of 8 percent on their committed capital before the general partner's carried interest begins to accrue.

2. *Management fees.* LBO firms charge a management fee to cover overhead and expenses associated with identifying, evaluating, and executing acquisitions by the fund. The management fee is intended to cover legal, accounting, and consulting fees associated with conducting due diligence on potential targets, as well as general overhead. Earlier fees, such as lenders' fees and investment banking fees, are generally charged to the acquired company after the closing of a transaction. Management fees range from 0.75 percent to 3 percent of committed capital, although 2 percent is common. Management fees are often reduced after the end of the commitment period to reflect the lower costs of monitoring and harvesting investments.

3. *Co-investment.* Executives and employees of the leveraged buyout firm may co-invest along with the partnership on any acquisition made by the fund, provided the terms of the investment are equal to those afforded to the partnership.

STRATEGIC OR INDUSTRY INVESTORS— CORPORATE VENTURE CAPITAL

A strategic investor is one that can benefit from an investment in ways other than just a direct financial return. These investors are typically companies or holding companies that either invest directly into a portfolio business or have established an investment subsidiary to do the same. Some of these subsidiaries are formalized as corporate venture capital (CVC) arms of the business while others are less formal and reside under a business development or corporate development function. There is a distinction between companies that have formal venture investing businesses or programs that systematically seek out and routinely invest as part of an ongoing strategy of growth and innovation, and the ones that opportunistically invest or do so only to meet a certain strategic goal. From the perspective of the management of a potential portfolio company, the former will probably have a clearly defined process and criteria for target company analysis.

CVC Investments

In 2003, $1.1 billion was invested in growth oriented companies by corporate venturing groups, representing 6 percent of all venture capital investment. The amount invested by CVCs has tracked similarly to the trends of the overall venture capital industry. The 2003 figures were close to the activity seen in the last prebubble year, 1997, when corporate venturing groups invested $957 million, also representing 6 percent of total venture capital invested in that year.[43]

According to Ernst & Young's Corporate Venture Capital Report,[44] a majority of the CVC groups make their investment decisions based on the investment opportunity providing a clear strategic advantage to the parent company. A smaller percentage pursue only financial objectives, and a minor portion of the CVC groups pursue both strategic and financial goals. The number one strategic objective cited in the report was to create a window into technology development outside their company.

These venture funds usually invest in companies that are in development stages or have begun shipping product. Sometimes they are the lead investor, but more often they will be one in a syndicate of investors. This correlates with the data indicating that the majority of their investments are in second round or later stage opportunities, though some investments are made in first rounds. CVCs typically do not invest in start-ups or early stage rounds.[45]

CVC Value Add

An interesting observation is that the valuation of a deal with a strategic investor tends to be more than double that of the same stage transaction without a CVC. In addition to potentially providing cheaper capital, the CVC can pull expertise and resources from the parent company to help accelerate the growth of the portfolio business. The brand of the parent and market validation provided by having the parent invest often lends significant credibility to the emerging company. Among other potential synergies are the availability of technologies from the parent and potential operations support and resources in the United States or overseas, when multinational corporations participate.

Potential Downside

The drawback of having a CVC involved is the potential for the portfolio company to begin to shape its activities based on the influence of the CVC, and not listen to the market in whole. In addition, some potential customers of the portfolio company may not materialize if they are competitors of the CVC's parent, thus limiting the market size of the company. Strategic investors generally increase the valuation of the company and provide capital on more favorable terms, and may provide an exit for early investors if they choose to eventually purchase the company, but they can also prevent the company from realizing its ultimate potential.

The CEO of a software start-up in discussions with several CVCs noted:

> *In working with a couple of these groups there is not necessarily commonality of objectives in trying to get venture funding. While it is true that they are seeking "deals" that would enhance their market position and/or revenues, how they get there can cause debate. In one case, our software model did not fit the direction of their strategic marketing group. We do not know exactly why, but we suspect it had to do with our promotion of open standards. In the other case, it was probably that the internal product groups were having difficulty agreeing on what was their product approach; this was probably because of the natural competition between these groups. So I guess my caution is that there is a lot of money available in the CVC groups . . . [but] getting to the end game (funding) is perhaps more tedious than traditional VC funding.*[46]

How Do CVCs Get Deals?

Unlike traditional venture capital firms, only a small portion of their deal flow comes from professional service providers like accountants and attorneys. A significant portion of CVC deal flow is directly from entrepreneurs, traditional venture capitalists, parent company employees, and opportunities that the CVC identified itself.[47]

Non-CVC Strategic Investments

See the first section of this chapter on bootstrapping and customer and supplier/vendor investments.

MERCHANT BANKS

A merchant bank is a firm that provides investment banking services and makes direct investments, typically private equity or mezzanine financing. As an investment bank, it acts as an agent for the client company, while as an investor it takes the role of principal. This business model came from the nineteenth-century merchant banks founded by businessmen like Baring, Warburg, Grenfell, and the Brown brothers.[48] In our research we obtained information from 18 firms that made a range of investments from $500 thousand to more than $100 million in support of an ongoing relationship with their portfolio companies. Some of these firms had industry expertise and extensive analysis and research support in a particular area.

Some of the merchant banks provide investment banking services and accept payment of their fees in the form of equity in the transaction (i.e., investing in the deal). Others co-invest with a buyer or investor in their client's transaction to maintain the relationship seeking longer-term financial gains. In some instances, the merchant bank has funds to invest to facilitate a transaction.

We did find some instances where a merchant bank had multiple funds such as a venture fund, a mezzanine fund, and a buyout fund. Most expressed interest in public and private companies.

When establishing a relationship with a merchant bank, it is important to quickly assess what role they are working from, as an agent or as a principal. For additional information on both, see the appropriate section in this handbook.

COMMUNITY DEVELOPMENT INITIATIVES AND GOVERNMENT AGENCIES

Many resources providing services and funding for the start-up of companies exist, most having an economic or social development thrust. Here we provide an overview of some of these.

Incubators*

To help navigate the process of starting and growing a company, some entrepreneurs turn to business incubators, which provide start-up firms with an array of customized business support services, such as mentoring, flexible leases, and access to office space, research facilities, and manufacturing equipment. In addition to services, about one-third of the incubators in North America provide microloans and revolving credit to

---

*The base content of this section is adapted from work provided by the National Business Incubation Association, www.nbia.org.

assist in financing the business, and many others have indicated interest in providing funds.

And no, incubators did not die during the dot-com bust. Business incubators, which trace their roots back to the 1950s, continue to nurture emerging companies toward business success worldwide. More than 900 of these programs are in operation in the United States alone, the majority of which are nonprofit programs that aim to create jobs, diversify economies, revitalize neighborhoods, or commercialize new technologies.

So, how can you determine if an incubator is right for your business? And how can you decide which incubation program is right for you?

"The bottom line for entrepreneurs is whether their goals are compatible with a prospective incubator's mission and whether a particular incubator is the right tool for helping them achieve success," said Dinah Adkins, president and CEO of the National Business Incubation Association (NBIA), an international membership organization serving incubator professionals; university, government, and economic development officials; consultants; and others. For instance, some incubators have as their mission to serve biotechnology companies, while others focus on serving minority-owned firms. An entrepreneur must consider whether an incubator's mission and array of available services make sense for his or her business.

A 1997 study by the University of Michigan et al. revealed that approximately 87 percent of graduates from the nation's mature incubation programs were still in business. At the time of the study, most of those firms had been in business at least five years, and many considerably longer.

Not all start-up assistance programs that call themselves incubators meet the criteria that experts have found to be key to successful incubation, however. Prospective incubator clients should look for a program that offers customized business assistance services, flexible space and leases to meet changing needs, and programs that facilitate networking among colleagues and mentors.

Some people think of business incubators as a place where entrepreneurs can find inexpensive rent. However, although a facility with appropriate amenities may be a component of a successful incubator, the hallmark of these programs is the array of business support services they provide entrepreneurial clients. "Business incubators are service programs, not buildings," Adkins said. "No building can grow companies, provide mentoring and handholding, and assist an emerging company in meeting the benchmarks necessary for growth." In fact, many incubators charge higher-than-market rental rates because clients receive so much more than just space.

While an incubator's services can be beneficial to many start-up companies, not all emerging ventures are suited to an incubation program. So, who makes a good incubator client?

For starters, many incubator managers agree that entrepreneurs must do their homework before approaching an incubator. The ideal incubator client is an entrepreneur who has a well-developed business idea, a viable market, a business plan, a desire to learn, and a strong entrepreneurial drive. Only then can incubator staff help an entrepreneur develop the business and the skills necessary to make it succeed.

Adele Lyons, executive director of the Gulf Coast Business Technology Center in Biloxi, Mississippi, noted that an entrepreneur also must be willing to roll up his or her sleeves and invest time and energy in the new venture. "An entrepreneur really has to be willing to get in there and do the hard work," she said. "They need to be ready to be the worker bee of the business and realize they are not going to draw a big salary immediately."

An entrepreneur's commitment to his or her business is important, but Lisa Ison, president of the New Century Venture Center in Roanoke, Virginia, said she also looks for clients who are open to suggestions from staff and other entrepreneurs. "We look at not only whether an entrepreneur has a viable idea, but whether he or she is someone who recognizes that they need help to grow their business," Ison said. "An incubator isn't just a place to hang your hat. We encourage our clients to network and interact with each other to learn from the experiences of others."

The benefits to the business can be significant, even for those with a business background. "Being a part of the incubator and working with an advisory team taught me a lot about basic business processes, such as human resources, finance, and customer relations," said Jay Foster, president of SoftSolutions, Inc., a Roanoke, Virginia, information technology company and a recent graduate of the New Century Venture Center. "Even though I had formal training in business [Foster has an MBA] and previous business experience as an independent consultant, I still had much to learn."

That is where an incubator can help. Many business incubation programs offer clients educational seminars covering a variety of business topics, networking events to bring together clients and community leaders, and access to advisory teams comprising business people from a variety of backgrounds. These experts help clients with everything from creating a business plan to troubleshooting technologies to securing patents.

For instance, staff at the incubation program affiliated with Springfield Technical Community College (STCC) in Massachusetts help clients make contacts with potential funders who might be able to assist in the development of their firms. Incubator clients then practice company pitches with the staff to perfect their presentation skills before making their pitches.

"The incubator environment is focused on sharpening the skills needed to acquire resources," said Fred Andrews, CEO of Fred Andrews Consulting Services and former executive director of the STCC program. Being associated with a successful incubation program sometimes gives clients a leg up on their competition, too. "Local bank presidents have said they are very interested in any of STCC incubator clients because they know they are much more 'bankable' than other small businesses," Andrews said.

Business incubators provide entrepreneurs with many of the tools they need to make their ventures successful, but both incubator managers and clients agree that entrepreneurs must be committed to the process to get the most out of the incubator experience.

"Be a sponge," Andrews advised potential incubator clients. "Keep your eye on what you want to do and seek out mentors within the incubator environment who can help you do it. Network with other entrepreneurs; network with visitors to the incubator. Network, network, network. Incubator managers are constantly looking for ways to create opportunities for their clients, so make sure you're aware of all the opportunities available to you and take them."

Types of Incubators

Incubation programs come in various shapes and sizes and serve a variety of communities and markets. Most North American business incubators (about 90 percent) are nonprofit organizations focused on economic development. About 10 percent of North American incubators are for-profit entities usually set up to obtain returns on shareholders' investments.

- Forty-seven percent are mixed use, assisting a range of early stage companies.
- Thirty-seven percent focus on technology businesses.
- Seven percent serve manufacturing firms.
- Six percent focus on service businesses.
- Three percent concentrate on community revitalization projects or serve niche markets.

Today, there are about 1,000 business incubators in North America, up from only 12 in 1980. There are about 4,000 business incubators worldwide. The incubation model has been adapted to meet a variety of needs, from fostering commercialization of university technologies to increasing employment in economically distressed communities to serving as investment vehicles.

Incubator sponsors—organizations or individuals who support an incubation program financially—may serve as the incubator's parent or host organization or may simply make financial contributions to the incubator. About 25 percent of North American business incubators are sponsored by academic institutions, 16 percent are sponsored by government entities, 15 percent are sponsored by economic development organizations, 10 percent are sponsored by for-profit entities, and 10 percent are sponsored by other types of organizations. About 5 percent of business incubators are hybrids with more than one sponsor, and 19 percent of incubators have no sponsor or host organization.

Selecting an Incubator

Just as incubators screen prospective clients, so too should entrepreneurs screen prospective incubators. Here are some questions to ask when considering entering an incubation program:

Track Record
- How well is the program performing?
- How long has the program been operating?
- Does it have any successful graduate companies, and if so, how long have they been in business independent from the incubator?
- What do other clients and graduates think of the program?

Graduation Policy
- What is the program's graduation policy—that is, what are the incubator's exit criteria?
- How flexible is the policy?
- How long, on average, have clients remained in the program? (Incubators typically graduate companies within three years.)

Qualifications of Manager and Staff
- How long has the current staff been with the program?
- How much time does the staff spend on-site?
- Have they had any entrepreneurial successes of their own?
- Do they actively engage in professional development activities or are they a member of a professional/trade association to keep them up to date on the latest in incubation best practices?

Does the Incubation Program Offer the Services and Contacts You Need?
What services do you need to make your venture successful? Business plan development, legal and accounting advice, marketing, Internet access, manufacturing facilities? Is access to a particular market critical? Then consider finding an incubator that specializes in that market. Special focus incubators are programs that work with companies within a particular niche, such as gourmet foods, biotechnology, the arts, and software. Be sure the program offers what you need or can connect you to service providers who can meet those needs.

Do You Meet the Incubator's Criteria? Find out the incubator's qualifications for accepting clients before applying. For example, some incubators expect prospective clients to have fully developed business plans, whereas others require a less developed idea and offer business plan development assistance.

Is the Program's Fee Structure Right for You? Most for-profit incubators exchange space and services for an equity share in their client companies, whereas most nonprofits charge fees for space and services. If a large cash infusion and speed to market are essential for your business success, then giving up equity in your company in order to secure quick cash may be right for you. But if you believe you have the skills to raise your own funding (with some assistance), don't want to give up any equity in your venture, and are willing to build your company more slowly, then paying fees for services and space may be a better choice.

Terms and Conditions

The working relationship between the entrepreneurial company and the incubator are typically documented within several agreements. Here is a list of the type agreements that may be entered into, and comments where appropriate:[49]

- *Services agreement.* The agreement establishes the overall understanding between the parties. It addresses the specific programs and services that the incubator will provide, and rates where applicable. It defines the required reporting and expected meetings, as well as providing for the customary legal protections for each party.
- *Lease agreement.* This is a typical facilities lease agreement providing for periodic rent payments and the customary tenant/landlord terms and conditions.

- *Stock option agreement or member interest purchase agreement.* These agreements provide the right to purchase a portion of the equity or ownership of the company based on certain terms, conditions, and events.

Community Development Financial Institutions

Community development financial institutions (CDFIs) are financial institutions that have community development as their primary mission and that develop a range of strategies to address that mission.[50]

There are five generally recognized CDFI types:

Community Development Banks These banks provide capital to rebuild economically distressed communities through targeted lending and investment.

Community Development Credit Unions These credit unions promote ownership of assets and savings and provide affordable credit and retail financial services to low-income people with special outreach to minority communities.

Community Development Loan Funds These loan funds aggregate capital from individual and institutional social investors at below-market rates and lend this money primarily to nonprofit housing and business developers in economically distressed urban and rural communities.

Community Development Venture Capital Funds Community development venture capital (CDVC) funds make equity investments in businesses in economically distressed areas in the United States and around the world. They invest in companies in a variety of industries and at different stages of development, from seed to expansion. Utilizing a number of legal structures, from for-profit corporations to not-for-profits to limited liability companies, CDVC funds are mission-driven organizations that benefit low-wealth people and communities while working to earn solid financial returns. Most CDVC funds invest in a focused geographic area.[51]

Similar to other institutional investors, CDVC funds are looking to invest in companies with strong management, good ideas, impressive growth potential, and the promise of high financial returns. They also focus on the number and quality of jobs that will be created and the impact their investments will have on low-income communities. Each fund has its own investment criteria and process for submitting business plans.[52]

Microenterprise Development Loan Funds   These loan funds foster social and business development through loans and technical assistance to low-income people who are involved in very small business or self-employed and unable to access conventional credit.

Small Business Administration*

The U.S. Small Business Administration (SBA) is an independent agency of the executive branch of the federal government. It is charged with the responsibility of providing four primary areas of assistance to American small businesses. These are: advocacy, management, procurement, and financial assistance. Financial assistance is delivered primarily through the SBA's business loan programs, investment programs, disaster loan programs, and bonding for contractors. Here we provide an overview of the programs that relate to the funding of emerging growth and middle-market companies. The SBA offers numerous loan programs to assist small businesses. It is important to note, however, that the SBA is primarily a guarantor of loans made by private and other institutions.

SBA's Business Loan Programs   The SBA administers three separate, but equally important, loan programs. The SBA sets the guidelines for the loans, while its partners (lenders, community development organizations, and microlending institutions) make the loans to small businesses. The SBA backs those loans with a guarantee that will eliminate some of the risk to the lending partners. The agency's loan guarantee requirements and practices can change, however, as the government alters its fiscal policy and priorities to meet current economic conditions. Therefore, past policy cannot always be relied upon when seeking assistance in today's market.

Federal appropriations are available to the SBA to provide guarantees on loans structured under the agency's requirements. With a loan guarantee, the actual funds are provided by independent lenders who receive the full faith and credit backing of the federal government on a portion of the loan they make to small business.

The loan guarantee that SBA provides transfers the risk of borrower nonpayment, up to the amount of the guarantee, from the lender to the SBA. Therefore, when a business applies for an SBA loan, it is actually applying for a commercial loan, structured according to SBA requirements, which receives an SBA guarantee.

---

*This section is a compilation of content about the Small Business Administration from its web site at www.sba.gov, annotated with the authors' comments.

In a variation of this concept, community development organizations can get the government's full backing on their loan to finance a portion of the overall financing needs of an applicant small business.

SBA's Investment Programs   In 1958 Congress created the Small Business Investment Company (SBIC) program. SBICs, licensed by the Small Business Administration, are privately owned and managed investment firms. They are participants in a vital partnership between government and the private sector economy. With their own capital and with funds borrowed at favorable rates through the federal government, SBICs provide venture capital to small independent businesses, both new and already established. SBICs act as other venture capital firms, however with a different source of funding, which places some restrictions on structure.

All SBICs are profit-motivated businesses. A major incentive for SBICs to invest in small businesses is the chance to share in the success of the small business if it grows and prospers.

SBA's Bonding Programs   The Surety Bond Guarantee (SBG) Program was developed to provide small and minority contractors with contracting opportunities for which they would not otherwise bid. The SBA can guarantee bonds for contracts up to $2 million, covering bid, performance, and payment bonds for small and emerging contractors who cannot obtain surety bonds through regular commercial channels.

SBA's guarantee gives sureties an incentive to provide bonding for eligible contractors, and thereby strengthens a contractor's ability to obtain bonding and greater access to contracting opportunities. A surety guarantee, an agreement between a surety and the SBA, provides that the SBA will assume a predetermined percentage of loss in the event the contractor should breach the terms of the contract.

The New Markets Venture Capital (NMVC) Program is a developmental venture capital program designed to promote economic development and the creation of wealth and job opportunities in low-income geographic areas and among individuals living in such areas.

Basic 7(a) Loan Guarantee   The 7(a) Loan Guarantee Program serves as the SBA's primary business loan program to help qualified small businesses obtain financing when they might not be eligible for business loans through normal lending channels. It is also the agency's most flexible business loan program, since financing under this program can be guaranteed for a variety of general business purposes.

Loan proceeds can be used for most sound business purposes including working capital, machinery and equipment, furniture and fixtures, land and building (including purchase, renovation, and new construction), leasehold improvements, and debt refinancing (under special conditions). Loan maturity is up to 10 years for working capital and generally up to 25 years for fixed assets. More information can be obtained at www.sba.gov/financing/sbaloan/7a.htm.

Certified Development Company (CDC), a 504 Loan Program   The 504 Loan Program provides long-term, fixed-rate financing to small businesses to acquire real estate or machinery or equipment for expansion or modernization. Typically a 504 project includes a loan secured from a private-sector lender with a senior lien, a loan secured from a CDC (funded by a 100 percent SBA-guaranteed debenture) with a junior lien covering up to 40 percent of the total cost, and a contribution of at least 10 percent equity from the borrower. The maximum SBA debenture generally is $1 million (and up to $1.3 million in some cases).

The maximum SBA debenture is $1,000,000 for meeting the job creation criteria or a community development goal. Generally, a business must create or retain one job for every $50,000 provided by the SBA. The maximum SBA debenture is $1.3 million for meeting a public policy goal. The public policy goals are:

- Business district revitalization.
- Expansion of exports.
- Expansion of minority business development.
- Rural development.
- Enhanced economic competition.
- Restructuring because of federally mandated standards or policies.
- Changes necessitated by federal budget cutbacks.
- Expansion of small business concerns owned and controlled by veterans.
- Expansion of small business concerns owned and controlled by women.

Proceeds from 504 loans must be used for fixed-asset projects such as: purchasing land and improvements, including existing buildings, grading, street improvements, utilities, parking lots, and landscaping; construction of new facilities or modernizing, renovating, or converting existing facilities; or purchasing long-term machinery and equipment. The 504 Program cannot be used for working capital or inventory, consolidating or repaying debt, or refinancing.

Interest rates on 504 loans are pegged to an increment above the current market rate for 5-year and 10-year U.S. Treasury issues. Maturities of 10 and 20 years are available. Fees total approximately 3 percent of the debenture and may be financed with the loan. Generally, the project assets being financed are used as collateral. Personal guaranties of the principal owners are also required. To be eligible, the business must be operated for profit and fall within the size standards set by the SBA. Under the 504 Program, the business qualifies as small if it does not have a tangible net worth in excess of $7 million and does not have an average net income in excess of $2.5 million after taxes for the preceding two years. Loans cannot be made to businesses engaged in speculation or investment in rental real estate. Additional information can be obtained at: www.sba.gov/financing/sbaloan/cdc504.htm.

Microloan, a 7(m) Loan Program   The Microloan Program provides short-term loans of up to $35,000 to small businesses and not-for-profit child-care centers for working capital or the purchase of inventory, supplies, furniture, fixtures, machinery, and/or equipment. Proceeds cannot be used to pay existing debts or to purchase real estate. The SBA makes or guarantees a loan to an intermediary, who in turn, makes the microloan to the applicant. These organizations also provide management and technical assistance. The microloans themselves are not guaranteed by the SBA. The microloan program is available in selected locations in most states. This program is delivered through specially designated intermediary lenders (nonprofit organizations with experience in lending and in technical assistance). Additional information can be obtained at www.sba.gov/financing/sbaloan/microloans.htm.

Loan Prequalification   The SBA provides a loan prequalification program that allows business applicants to have their loan applications for $250,000 or less analyzed and potentially sanctioned by the SBA before they are taken to lenders for consideration. The program focuses on the applicant's character, credit, experience, and reliability rather than assets. An SBA-designated intermediary works with the business owner to review and strengthen the loan application. The review is based on key financial ratios, credit and business history, and the loan-request terms. The program is administered by the SBA's Office of Field Operations and SBA district offices. This program is delivered through nonprofit intermediaries such as small business development centers and certified development companies operating in specific geographic areas. Additional information can be obtained at: www.sba.govfinancing/sbaloan/prequalification.htm.

Export Working Capital   The Export Working Capital Program (EWCP) was designed to provide short-term working capital to exporters. The EWCP supports export financing to small businesses when that financing is not otherwise available on reasonable terms. The program encourages lenders to offer export working capital loans by guaranteeing repayment of up to $1.5 million or 90 percent of a loan amount, whichever is less. A loan can support a single transaction or multiple sales on a revolving basis.

Designed to provide short-term working capital to exporters, the EWCP is a combined effort of the SBA and the Export-Import Bank (Ex-Im). Ex-Im could assume country risks the private sector is unable or unwilling to accept. The two agencies have joined their working capital programs to offer a unified approach to the government's support of export financing. The EWCP uses a one-page application form and streamlined documentation with turnaround usually 10 days or less. A letter of prequalification is also available from the SBA.

In addition to the eligibility standards listed later, an applicant must be in business for a full year (not necessarily in exporting) at the time of application. SBA may waive this requirement if the applicant has sufficient export trade experience. Export management companies or export-trading companies may use this program; however, title must be taken in the goods being exported to be eligible.

Most small businesses are eligible for SBA loans; some types of businesses are ineligible and a case-by-case determination must be made by the agency. Eligibility is generally determined by business type, use of proceeds, size of business, and availability of funds from other sources.

The proceeds of an EWCP loan must be used to finance the working capital needs associated with a single or multiple transactions of the exporter.

Proceeds may not be used to finance professional export marketing advice or services, foreign business travel, participation in trade shows, or staffing U.S. support in overseas operations, except to the extent such expenses relate directly to the transaction being financed. In addition, proceeds may not be used to make payments to owners, to pay delinquent withholding taxes, or to pay existing debt.

The applicant must establish that the loan will significantly expand or develop an export market, it is currently adversely affected by import competition, will upgrade equipment or facilities to improve competitive position, or is able to provide a business plan that reasonably projects export sales sufficient to cover the loan.

SBA guarantees the short-term working capital loans made by participating lenders to exporters. An export loan can be for a single or for multiple transactions. If the loan is for a single transaction, the maturity should correspond to the length of the transaction cycle with a maximum maturity of 18 months. If the loan is for a revolving line of credit, the maturity is typically 12 months, with annual reissuances allowed two times, for a maximum maturity of three years.

There are four unique requirements of the EWCP loan:

1. An applicant must submit cash flow projections to support the need for the loan and the ability to repay.
2. After the loan is made, the loan recipient must submit continual progress reports.
3. SBA does not prescribe the lender's fees.
4. SBA does not prescribe the interest rate for the EWCP.

For those applicants that meet the SBA's credit and eligibility standards, the agency can guarantee up to 90 percent of loans (generally up to a maximum guarantee amount of $1.5 million). A borrower must give the SBA a first security interest equal to 100 percent of the EWCP guarantee amount. Collateral must be located in the United States.

International Trade Loans   If your business is preparing to engage in or is already engaged in international trade, or is adversely affected by competition from imports, the International Trade Loan Program may be available for your company.

The applicant must establish that the loan will significantly expand or develop an export market, and that the applicant is currently adversely affected by import competition, will upgrade equipment or facilities to improve competitive position, or is able to provide a business plan that reasonably projects export sales sufficient to cover the loan. Although most small businesses are eligible for SBA loans, some types of businesses are ineligible and a case-by-case determination must be made by the agency.

The proceeds of an SBA international trade loan may be used to acquire, construct, renovate, modernize, improve, or expand facilities and equipment to be used in the United States to produce goods or services involved in international trade, and to develop and penetrate foreign markets. Proceeds of this type of loan cannot be used for debt payment.

Loans for facilities or equipment can have maturities of up to 25 years. For the international trade loan, the SBA can guarantee up to 85 percent of loans of $150,000 and less, and up to 75 percent of loans above $150,000. The maximum guaranteed amount is $1,250,000. Only collateral located in the United States and its territories and possessions is acceptable as collateral under this program. The lender must take a first lien position (or first mortgage) on items financed under an international trade loan. Additional collateral may be required, including personal guarantees, subordinate liens, or items that are not financed by the loan proceeds.

Defense Economic Transition Assistance The SBA's Defense Economic Transition Assistance (DETA) Program is designed to help eligible small business contractors to make the transition from defense to civilian markets.

A small business is eligible if it has been detrimentally impacted by the closure (or substantial reduction) of a Department of Defense installation, or the termination (or substantial reduction) of a Department of Defense program on which the small business was a prime contractor, subcontractor, or supplier at any tier. In addition, a business can be deemed eligible if it is located in a community that has been detrimentally impacted by these same actions.

The DETA program provides financial and technical assistance to defense-dependent small businesses that have been adversely affected by defense reductions. The goal of the program is to assist these businesses to diversify into the commercial market while remaining part of the defense industrial base. Complete information on eligibility and other rules is available from each SBA district office.

This program can be used in conjunction with both SBA's 7(a) and 504 loan programs and generally follows the provisions of each program. In order to be eligible for this program, small businesses must derive at least 25 percent of their revenues from Department of Defense or defense-related Department of Energy contracts or subcontracts in support of defense prime contracts in any one of five prior operating years.

Small businesses interested in utilizing this program must also meet at least one of the program's policy objectives:

- Job retention—retains defense employees.
- Job creation—creates job opportunities and new economic activities in impacted communities.
- Plant retooling and expansion—modernizes or expands the plant and enables it to remain available to the Department of Defense.

U.S. Community Adjustment and Investment Program (CAIP) CAIP is a program established to assist U.S. companies that are doing business in areas of the country that have been negatively affected by the North American Free Trade Agreement (NAFTA). Funds administered by the U.S. Department of the Treasury allow for the payment of fees on eligible loans. These fees include the 7(a) Program guarantee fee (and subsidy), the 504 Program guarantee, CDC fees, and lender fees. Depending on the loan size, the fees can be sizable.

The CAIP works with the SBA in both their 7(a) Loan Guarantee Program and 504 Loan Program to reduce borrower costs and increase the availability of these proven business assistance programs. CAIP can be used with both the 7(a) and 504 loan programs.

To be eligible, certain criteria must be met; for example, the business must reside in a county noted as being negatively affected by NAFTA, based on job losses and the unemployment rate of the county; this was recently expanded to allow for granting eligibility to defined areas within a county (which will allow SBA to react quickly in offering to provide assistance when, for example, a plant closes).

In addition, there is a job creation component. For 7(a) loans, one job has to be created for every $70,000 that SBA guarantees. For 504 loans, one job has to be created for every $50,000 that SBA guarantees. Currently, more than 230 counties in 29 states are designated as eligible.

Pollution Control Loan Program   Pollution Control Loans are 7(a) loans with a special purpose of pollution control. The program is designed to provide financing to eligible small businesses for the planning, design, or installation of a pollution control facility, including recycling. This facility must prevent, reduce, abate, or control any form of pollution.

This program follows the 7(a) guidelines with the following exception: Use of proceeds must be for fixed assets only.

CAPLines Loan Program   CAPLines is the umbrella program under which the SBA helps small businesses meet their short-term and cyclical working capital needs. A CAPLines loan, except the Small Asset-Based Line, can be for any dollar amount that does not exceed SBA's limit. (See the 7(a) Loan Guarantee Program for more information on the SBA's basic requirements.)

There are five short-term working capital loan programs (lines of credit) for small businesses under the CAPLines umbrella:

1. *Seasonal Line.* This line is an advance against anticipated inventory and accounts receivable help during peak seasons when businesses experience seasonal sales fluctuations. Can be revolving or nonrevolving.
2. *Contract Line.*This line finances the direct labor and material cost associated with performing assignable contract(s). Can be revolving or nonrevolving.
3. *Builders Line.* If you are a small general contractor or builder constructing or renovating commercial or residential buildings, this can finance direct labor and material costs. The building project serves as the collateral, and loans can be revolving or nonrevolving.
4. *Standard Asset-Based Line.* This is an asset-based revolving line of credit for businesses unable to meet credit standards associated with

long-term credit. It provides financing for cyclical growth, recurring, and/or short-term needs. Repayment comes from converting short-term assets into cash, which is remitted to the lender. Businesses continually draw from this line of credit, based on existing assets, and repay as their cash cycle dictates. This line generally is used by businesses that provide credit to other businesses. Because these loans require continual servicing and monitoring of collateral, additional fees may be charged by the lender.

5. *Small Asset-Based Line.* This is an asset-based revolving line of credit of up to $200,000. It operates like a standard asset-based line except that some of the stricter servicing requirements are waived, provided that the business can consistently show repayment ability from cash flow for the full amount.

Except for the Small Asset-Based Line, CAPLine loans follow the SBA's maximum loan amounts. The Small Asset-Based Line has a maximum loan amount of $200,000. Although most small businesses are eligible for SBA loans, some types of businesses are ineligible, and a case-by-case determination must be made by the agency. Eligibility is generally determined by type of business, size, and use of proceeds.

Each of the five lines of credit has a maturity of up to five years; however, because each is tailored to an individual business's needs, a shorter initial maturity may be established. CAPLines funds can be used as needed throughout the term of the loan to purchase assets, as long as sufficient time is allowed to convert the assets into cash at maturity.

Holders of at least 20 percent ownership in the business are generally required to guarantee the loan. Although inadequate collateral will not be the sole reason for denial of a loan request, the nature and value of that collateral does factor into the credit decision.

MICRO-CAP PUBLIC ENTITIES*

In some market cycles, including that of the Internet bubble of the late 1990s, the interest in high-tech issues is so robust that concept or resume initial public offerings (concept IPOs) are feasible. Feeding frenzies in the

---

*The base content of this section is adapted from the articles "Concept IPO's" and "Shell Corporations" provided by www.VCExperts.com. Written permission requested and granted specifically for this publication. All rights reserved, VC Experts, Inc.

public market spotlight certain underwriters who are prepared, on a best-efforts basis, to agree to promote a public offering of securities in a company that has no sales or earnings—only a concept and/or the impressive resumes of its officers and directors. The prospectus of a concept offering will, to be sure, contain Draconian warnings that the offering is "speculative" and involves a "high degree of risk." In the appropriate market environment, however, those warnings often attract rather than repel investors. There are international variations on the theme. Some auction markets— the British Unlisted and the Vancouver Stock Exchange, for example—admit to trading shares of development stage companies. Despite the occasional success stories, few if any experienced professionals recommend the premature public offering as a desired strategy, since the burdens of public registration are so significant and the risks of failure are magnified in the public arena; there are fewer excuses and little forgiveness for losses and poor performance.

Another occasionally used technique for raising money is to gain control of a small public entity. The concept is to organize a shell corporation—no assets, no business—and take it public. Because of the unfortunate connotations of the term *shell* in the financial arena, sponsors have developed the alternate label of acquisition company or specified purpose acquisition company (SPAC). The sole purpose of a shell/SPAC offering is to raise a relatively modest amount of money, and more importantly, to get a number of shares outstanding in the hands of the public. Usually the shares are sold in units—for example, one share of common plus warrants at the current offering price. The sponsors of the shell corporation then find an operating company with which to merge. The merged companies then start reporting the results of operations; if and when those results are promising, the existing stockholders exercise their warrants, injecting needed capital into the enterprise. The object of this exercise is to go public first and then find a business operation afterward; in that sense it is like a concept offering. But the concept is pure, unsullied by even a business description except to find companies after the IPO with which to merge; warrants (purportedly, at least) supply an evergreen source of financing at attractive prices for the original investors.

Another method, a variation on the shell strategy, involves the identification of an existing shell or inactive public company (IPC) as a candidate for a reverse acquisition. A typical example is a company recently emerging from bankruptcy, stripped of its assets other than a modest amount of cash, the assets having been disposed of and the creditors paid in a reorganization proceeding usually labeled a liquidating Chapter 11. The principal asset of the IPC (other than the cash, if any) is its public registration (although the shares are not then trading on a national market system) and a roster of shareholders.

Transaction expenses are reportedly lower in a reverse acquisition, even after adding in significant postclosing expenses necessary to acquaint the financial community with the business of the newly public firm. Indeed, in the end, the ownership remaining with the shareholders of the target is not supposed to be dramatically different than if an IPO were successful. The latter, however, is supposed to offer speed, greater certainty of completion, less burdensome filing requirements, and independence from general market conditions. The company's fund-raising effort starts, in fact, after the acquisition closes and the shares are listed. Thus, a bridge loan, a private placement, and/or an offshore offering under Regulation S often accompany the acquisition.

In the case of both SPACs and IPCs, a certain amount of heightened SEC scrutiny can be expected, especially as the impact of Sarbanes-Oxley is vetted.

Lastly, there are cases whereby a very small publicly traded company exists with solid financial fundamentals, a respectable balance sheet, reasonable earnings and cash flow, and some level of routine trading. However, the company needs new products, services, or technologies to grow. A merger or acquisition by one of these companies with a privately held growth company seeking capital sometimes makes a compelling story and provides an opportunity to meet both companies' needs.

ROYALTY FINANCING

Royalty financing is an advance against future product or service sales. The advance is repaid by diverting a percentage of the product or service revenues to the investor who issued the advance. This approach to financing works for established companies that have a product or service, or emerging companies about to launch a product with high gross and net margins.[53] Traditional uses of royalty financing are for businesses in mining, energy, and life science markets. However, we have found some applications for technology companies.

Royalty financing may be applicable to companies involved in life sciences, such as specialty pharmaceuticals and biotechnology firms. These companies may gain considerable advantage by selling current royalty entitlements or future royalties to create nondilutive sources of capital. Some royalty finance companies will purchase all or part of a company's entitlement and may structure transactions to include upside participation via sales thresholds to minimize the cost of capital. In some instances, the royalty financing may be structured with a fixed monthly principal payment and royalty payments that return a multiple of the initial investment, plus stock warrants.[54]

Technology Example #1—A Software Company

This example is from Peter Moore, founder of Banking Dynamics, a consulting firm in Portland, Maine.[55]

Moore structured a financing to help a software company grow its sales. He approached the Greater Portland Building Fund and Coastal Enterprises Inc., quasi-public economic development organizations charged with developing business in the state. He sought an advance of $200,000 against its future sales. If the advance was made, each investor would get 3 percent of the software company's sales for 10 years, or until they received payments totaling $600,000. This $600,000 would represent the original $200,000 investment plus $400,000. For the investors to receive the agreed-upon $600,000 within the maximum allowable time frame, the software company would have to generate total sales of $20 million over 10 years. Although the software company had less than $1 million in sales at the time, it had over the course of its three-year life doubled sales each year. "This was a big selling point," Moore says. Moreover, investors were comforted by the fact that the firm's software program, which helps companies manage hazardous-waste streams, meant there were 300,000 potential customers, he points out.

The transaction was structured so that the time frame was flexible—up to 10 years to make repayment; however the return, $600,000, was not. Because of this, the return the investors could earn was variable as well, and ranged from marginal to exceptional. Specifically, if the software company repaid the advance in 10 years, the investors would earn a compound annual return of 11.6 percent on their investment. If, however, the company's sales mushroomed and $600,000 was paid to the investors in five years, their compound annual return also mushroomed to 24.5 percent.

It took Moore and his client about four months to negotiate the deal. One of the key terms was for a delay in the commencement of royalty payments. Specifically, royalties did not accrue until 90 days after the deal closed. In addition, the actual royalty payments did not have to be paid until 60 days after the revenues were recognized. "All in all, it was five months from the time the company received the financing until the first payment was due," Moore says. "This gave the owners the time they needed to put the capital to work and start producing sales."

This example is atypical because the investors were willing to take a below-market return for an early stage deal with an unproven market record. This illustrates that angel investing is as varied as the personalities and experience of the individual investors. Typically, more sophisticated investors would have required some form of equity participation in the form of warrants, preferred stock, or common stock.

Technology Example #2—Applied Intelligent Systems

In another example,[56] Jim Anderson didn't have the luxury of mulling over a range of options when he was looking for capital for Applied Intelligent Systems Inc. (AISI), a $4 million maker of machine vision systems in Ann Arbor, Michigan. Once the darling of venture capitalists, his industry had become poison to investors after dozens of machine vision companies performed poorly or failed altogether. AISI had been able to obtain several infusions of venture capital, but by the time Anderson went hunting for money to launch the company's third product "it was career suicide for a venture capitalist to throw money into our industry," says Anderson.

AISI was able to convince a development fund to enter into a nontraditional financing technique that could foster growth without handicapping a company's ability to retain earnings and without diluting its ownership. The fund made an investment that entitles it to a portion of a company's revenue stream. Over time, those slices of revenue—royalties—allowed the fund to recoup its investment. There were three components of AISI's royalty financing:

The Investment The fund provided a $700,000 investment in thirds, after AISI met certain preset conditions. To obtain the first $233,333, AISI had to turn the prototype product into a preproduction model that demonstrably worked. The second sum would be collected when AISI began production, and the final disbursement arrived when the company began shipping the new product. At every stage, AISI had to account for all its expenditures and was subject to audits by the fund. Although the fund didn't have a seat on AISI's board, Anderson found it easiest to include fund management in board and other company meetings. In all, the investment period took about six months.

Paying Royalties AISI arranged to pay the fund for the life of the product. AISI paid the royalty—of about 5 percent—on a quarterly basis. The fund had negotiated its royalty on the basis of a number of factors. Key among them: the 25 percent rate of return that the fund required, the expected five-year life span of the product, and the sales projections for the product—more than $30 million over that five-year period. AISI would, of course, pay the royalty beyond the five-year period if the product's sales continued. In case AISI needed to extricate itself from the arrangement, Anderson also negotiated an exit clause. AISI could buy out the fund at any time for $1 million.

The Conversion As time passed sales related to the new product grew much faster than overall sales at the company, and it was foreseeable that this would continue beyond its five-year life span. With this outlook, it became apparent that the royalty payout would be significantly greater than expected. AISI desired to stop the royalty payments, but didn't have the $1 million to buy out the fund. Instead of borrowing the money to pay off the fund, Anderson elected to pay with equity in AISI—an option that a more possessive business owner might have eschewed. Using the valuation of AISI's stock during the company's most recent round of equity financing, Anderson translated the $1 million into a 10 percent stake for the fund.

There were two key ingredients that made royalty financing workable for AISI. The first was the timing of the repayment. It is rare that the people you owe money to will wait until you have it in hand. However, it is not necessarily the best solution, unless you have the second ingredient: pricing flexibility. A royalty is going to erode your profit margin unless you are able to raise the price you charge for your product by at least as much as the royalty fee.

Fund management points out that this kind of structure can make some difficult-to-finance companies, such as service operations or medium-growth businesses, more attractive to investors. Further, royalty financing does not require that a company have significant assets as collateral nor does it require enormous sales growth before an investor can achieve a reasonable return.

Royalty financing is essentially the provision of capital in exchange for a percentage of a revenue stream. The actual royalty percentage, the term, and the exit clause are all negotiable. In this case, these are some of the advantages that this structure had over a conventional equity investment or loan:[57]

- *No dilution.* The ownership of the company remains the same unless you decide you want to create a conversion feature and sell the revenue stream for equity or attach stock warrants to the agreement.
- *Great timing.* Payments to investors are not required until you start making sales.
- *Invisibility.* No liability shows up on the balance sheet.
- *Flexibility.* You can use this structure to finance a specific product or your entire company.

Intellectual Property Royalty Financing

Intellectual property (IP) royalty financing is a viable alternative for some companies. IP royalty financing is nonrecourse debt financing. A licensor of IP can take the future cash flow expected from a license agreement and receive a cash payment up front, representing the present value of the future cash flows. This allows the owner of the IP to leverage today what the owner expects to get in the future, and thus add another tool for IP exploitation. Often faced with limited options and funds, financing a royalty stream can provide much-needed capital to research institutions, small and mid-cap companies, and individual inventors. This type of financing is not particular to any specific type of IP. It includes patents, copyrights, trademarks, and trade secrets. Unlike other types of financing, IP royalty financing allows the owner of the IP to retain all of the upside in asset value. IP royalty financing is a unique source of capital collateralized by IP royalties. This may be an attractive vehicle for companies with robust royalty streams and a need for capital.[58]

Royalty Financing for Mining

Funding for advanced exploration, feasibility studies, mine development, and mine site capital improvements or production expansion is often a major problem for many small and midsize mining companies. Traditional methods of financing these projects have been through personal loans from friends and relatives, bank loans, joint ventures, and attempting to take the company public. Often, none of these financing methods are available or suitable for small and midsize miners. Traditional financing methods may not be economically suitable because of drains on capital or operating income or problems associated with losing operating control or sacrificing the owner's equity. Mineral product, lending, and investment market conditions may also prevent miners from relying on typical capital funding methods at times when money is most needed. There are royalty-based financing techniques that mining companies can obtain to fund their operation and growth.

Royalty-based financing for mining is a specialized technical and financial niche in the mining industry that provides custom-tailored methods for mining companies to acquire mine development and production expansion capital. Royalty companies and investment groups can provide the miner with capital for improvement, expansion, or purchase while also providing the necessary return on investment to both the miner and the royalty group. One of the main benefits of royalty-based financing is that a production royalty allows the miner to maintain 100 percent ownership in the mine. For many mining operations, capital funding can be obtained without any payback obligation except the creation of a royalty based only on mineral production and sales.[59]

Life Science Applications of Royalty Financing

Though we have illustrated some creative concepts, royalty deals are less common outside the biotech industry. Smaller biotech companies that have spent years developing a compound often take royalties in exchange for distribution rights from a larger pharmaceutical partner. In these cases, the royalties can be from 5 to 20 percent, depending on how far the compound has progressed through the regulatory process and how large the market is for the compound. The biotech company typically has no distribution capability and needs royalties as a source of revenue to fund future compound development. As a compound completes various phases of trial review by the Food and Drug Administration (FDA), pharmaceutical distribution interest increases because the compound's market and advantages over existing compounds become more quantifiable.

Royalty deals are generally used when a product has a proven track record or a quantifiable market; there needs to be a concrete way to estimate potential revenue streams. Another common use of royalties occurs where a larger company wants to discontinue distributing a product line and sells it for an up-front fee and royalty.

Usually, royalties are exchanged for rights to intellectual property where inventors or owners do not have the capability to manufacture or distribute a commercial product. Inventors often find themselves with a royalty prepayment and future royalties in exchange for the IP rights. Many of these deals are not very satisfactory because the products often do not get commercialized or do not get the proper marketing support and attention. Priorities and management change inside larger companies, and it is difficult to protect the inventor and ensure the product will be successful.

Equity and Debt Financings: Documentation and Regulatory Compliance with Securities Laws

Understanding basic definitions and characteristics of debt and equity is fundamental to the financing process and fund-raising activities. Recognition of securities regulatory compliance goes hand in hand with an understanding of the underlying debt and equity components of a company's capital structure. This chapter provides detailed guidance into the principal drivers behind the negotiation and structuring of the terms and conditions of debt and equity instruments, as well as an overview of certain securities regulations and their impact on the issuance of debt and equity in connection with the capitalization of a company.

These guidelines can be used as a checklist for entering into equity and debt financing transactions. A solid understanding of these issues will enhance your negotiating, but is not a substitute for legal counsel and other advisers who should be hired in accordance with your specific situation.

Though there is some redundancy in the content of Chapter 6 and that of Chapter 5, the authors feel that the presentation of each is important to provide a complete understanding of the financing process and potential issues. In addition, each of these chapters can be used as a reference without reading the other.

BASIC DEFINITION OF DEBT AND EQUITY

Management has two basic choices that relate to the type of capital chosen to finance their company. The two choices are commonly known as debt and equity, although there are many combinations and permutations of each category. Equity is typically defined as an ownership interest in an entity that permits a holder of the equity instrument to participate in the growth and success of the entity. This participation is normally represented by the right of the equity holder to claim a proportional interest in a company's assets and profits. In most cases there is no fixed obligation for a company to repay an equity holder the amount of the holder's investment at any fixed point in time. An individual equity holder's proportional interest in a company is determined by taking the total number of shares of equity owned by the individual and dividing that number by the total number of shares of equity of the entire company that are outstanding and held by all equity holders. A primary advantage of issuing equity is the characteristic that most equity carries with its issuance no fixed obligation on the part of a company to repay the amount of equity invested. The primary disadvantage of issuing equity is that the issuance dilutes the ownership interest of existing equity holders in the future growth of the company.

Within the definition of equity, there are two primary categories that describe ownership opportunities available to an equity holder. These categories of equity are typically referred to as common stock and preferred stock.

The attributes of common stock are normally determined by reference to the corporate statutes and case law of the jurisdiction in which the company is incorporated. A fundamental right of a holder of common stock is the right to elect directors of the entity. The directors in turn elect or appoint the officers of a company. In contrast, preferred stock is governed by the same statutes and case law as common stock, but in many cases the holder of preferred stock is not entitled to vote. Common stock is acquired in many cases pursuant to the terms of a subscription agreement in which the purchaser of the common stock makes certain representations to a company, but the purchaser receives few or no rights other than those conferred by statute or case law.

Preferred stock, in contrast, is normally acquired under the terms of a stock purchase agreement. A stock purchase agreement is a contract between a company and the purchaser of the preferred stock, and as such, the contract contains a variety of agreements between the company and the purchaser that exceed the minimal rights granted by statute or case law to a common stockholder. Preferred stock is entitled to priority over common stock in the payment of dividends and distributions made by a company. Other rights typically granted to the holder of preferred stock are examined more closely later in this chapter.

Debt is normally described as a liability or obligation of a company that is evidenced by a note or written obligation of the company to repay the debt with interest at some future point in time, on a specified schedule or by a specified maturity date. In contrast with the rights of an equity holder, a debt holder normally has no right to vote on the affairs of a company, and no right to participate in the growth of a company's assets or profits, except to receive scheduled principal and interest payments. The rights to payment of principal and interest are, however, senior in priority to the rights of equity holders to receive dividends and distributions of a company, and the rights of a holder of debt may be secured by a pledge of a security interest in the assets or the cash flows of the company.

There are several advantages to issuing debt, including the fact that debt holders have no right to participate in the growth and appreciation of a company, and therefore, existing equity holders are not diluted. In addition, debt instruments contain specified repayment schedules and as a result management has the ability to plan for the repayment of the debt instrument. Disadvantages related to the issuance of debt include the diversion of cash away from the operations and growth of the business resulting from scheduled repayments of principal and interest. Other disadvantages include limitations on the freedom of management to operate a company. These limitations are described in restrictive covenants normally contained in loan documents, and they may adversely impact the ability of a borrower to enter into certain types of transactions such as mergers and acquisitions, to exceed certain levels of additional debt, or to hold capital expenditures to specified levels.

The distinction between debt and equity blurs when each of these types of securities is granted hybrid rights. For example, preferred stock may bear a dividend payable on a regular basis that looks similar to an interest payment. In addition, a preferred stock purchase agreement may contain provisions requiring a company to redeem or pay back consideration paid for the preferred stock at a specified time in the future. In each case, the distinction between debt and equity begins to blur. In contrast, companies may issue debt with features that permit the holder to convert the debt to equity based on an agreed-upon per share price or formula that references the market value of a company's common stock. When a debt instrument contains a provision that permits the holder to pay interest by issuing additional notes, the effect is to cause the debt instrument to closely resemble a preferred stock with a redemption feature. Because a company can design debt or equity instruments with a variety of features intended to provide the entity with flexibility in determining its capital structure, the underlying documentation takes on added significance in that care must be taken to match the provisions of the documentation with the expectation of the executives designing an entity's financial model.

Compliance with Securities Laws

An issuer of debt or equity must comply with local, state, and federal securities laws when the type of debt or equity to be issued falls within the definition of a security. In most cases, conventional corporate debt and equity fall within the federal definition of a security, with a general exception for debt that is borrowed from a traditional bank for short-term working capital purposes. An interpretation of what is covered by the federal definition of security generally includes the issuance of any instrument in which the purchaser of the instrument expects to earn a profit solely from the efforts of another. In this context, the expectation generally associated with equity—an expectation of participation in the assets and profits of a company—causes equity in virtually all cases to be a security. With regard to debt, federal statutes have interpreted the return of principal and interest under instruments with terms of nine months or more to be included within the definition of a security.

Once included within the definition of a security, a company must either register the security with the applicable agency—the U.S. Securities and Exchange Commission, for example—or find an exemption from the registration requirements of the applicable agency. While public offerings of securities receive a great deal of attention, by far the most frequent type of transaction covering debt or equity is exempt from the registration process. A detailed discussion of transactional securities exemptions is included later in this chapter, together with an overview of the federal registration process.

DEBT INSTRUMENTS

Debt instruments may be categorized into two broad categories of either secured debt or unsecured debt. Secured debt is a loan extended to a borrowed based primarily on the ability of the borrower to repay the loan from the cash flows of its business operations. The basic loan transaction is coupled with a grant by the borrower of a security interest in the assets or cash flows of the borrower. In the event that the borrower is unable to repay the loan out of the cash flows of its business, the lender may take title to the assets pledged as security and then sell the assets. The sale of assets is normally performed pursuant to rules that are found in the Uniform Commercial Code of the state in which the lender is located. The lender may then apply the proceeds of the sale of the pledged assets to repay the secured debt. In the event that the proceeds of the sale of assets are insufficient to repay the principal, accrued but unpaid interest, and fees associated with the loan default, a lender then has a claim against the general assets of the borrower. In many cases a loan will be guaranteed by an officer, director, or shareholder of the borrower. A lender may also proceed to collect any unpaid amounts from a guarantor or from the proceeds of the sale of any assets that a guarantor may have pledged to support the original loan request.

An unsecured loan is made by a lender when the borrower is able to convince the lender that the general credit of the borrower is sufficient to insure repayment of the requested loan. When an unsecured loan is extended by a lender to a borrower, the borrower is typically well established and has a history of successfully retiring credit extended by secured and unsecured lenders. If a borrower enters into secured debt transactions at the same time as unsecured debt is borrowed, the unsecured debt holder is junior to the secured debt in terms of repayment. In the event that two classes of debt exist within a company—secured and unsecured—upon the occurrence of an event of default in the credit facilities, the unsecured lender waits until the secured lender is satisfied and paid in full before being able to perfect any claims on the assets of the borrower. Because of the priority of payments to secured lenders first and then to unsecured lenders, unsecured loans are generally considered more risky and therefore carry a higher interest rate than secured loans.

Securing the Commitment

In order to convince a lender to expend the time and resources necessary to evaluate a borrower's loan request, the borrower must be able to articulate a rational purpose for the loan request together with a financial plan that supports repayment of the requested loan. The traditional method for starting the loan request process is the preparation of a business plan for the borrower that includes information regarding the borrower's historical business and performance, together with a forecast of the future performance of the company. The forecast includes a clear description of the use of proceeds of the loan together with a narrative and financials that illustrate the application of the loan proceeds and the borrower's ability to repay the loan.

If the use of proceeds relates to an acquisition, the business plan and financial forecasts typically illustrate a variety of assumptions made in connection with the borrower's decision to pursue the acquisition, including any assumptions relating to economies of scale available to the combined entities. The lender will also be provided with information relating to the acquisition, which may include an offering memorandum prepared by the target company, a letter of intent where the parties have negotiated the basic terms of a transaction, or a definitive agreement where the transaction terms and conditions have been fully negotiated. Where the use of proceeds relates to the acquisition of specified assets, the business plan would include quotes from vendors of the designated assets as well as a description of the operating and financial benefit to the company of the designated equipment. For loan requests that involve borrowing to support operations, a borrower would provide forecasts of the levels of assets used to secure the loan, such as levels of accounts receivable and levels of inventory.

In evaluating the financial forecasts, a lender will make its own determination as to whether a borrower's assumption relating to financial performance, combined efficiencies, invoice amounts, or assumptions relating to levels of assets are reasonable. In smaller loans, the bank and its internal underwriters and credit officers will make the determination. In larger syndicated loans, the bank may rely on outside industry experts to validate the borrower's assumptions. In any event, the lender must be presented with a detailed set of assumptions and the basic modules used by the borrower in building its financial model. Without access to these underlying assumptions, the lender will not be positioned to evaluate a borrower's assumptions, and the approval process will either be delayed or terminated by the lender due to a lack of confidence in the financial sophistication of the borrower.

Fundamental to the success of any loan request is an understanding of the nature and character of loans made by specific lending institutions. Due diligence by a borrower can reduce or eliminate false starts related to making loan requests to lenders that are not involved in the type of loan requested. Most financial institutions have web sites that describe in detail the types of loans being made by the institution. Reviewing web sites and marshalling information from attorneys and accountants serving a borrowing will enhance the loan request process.

Commitment Letter

After a lender finishes its evaluation and review of a borrower's loan request and business plan and evaluates the results of any studies performed by outside consultants, if the review is favorable, the lender will issue a commitment letter. The purpose of a commitment letter is to provide a borrower with an outline of the fundamental terms and conditions relating to the lender's willingness to enter into a loan transaction, as well as to ensure that the lender issuing the commitment is the sole and exclusive manager selected by the borrower. The outline can vary from a one-page summary to a complex, multipage letter setting forth in detail the various components of the loan package. With a detailed description of the lender's proposal in hand, a borrower may then use the commitment letter to serve a variety of purposes, including providing third parties with confidence that the borrower is capable of consummating a transaction, particularly in the mergers and acquisitions arena.

In order to clarify the scope and purpose of the proposed loan, the lender will typically restate in its own words its understanding of the transactions underlying the loan request. In connection with an acquisition, for example, the commitment letter will state the various components of the transaction, including amounts of debt and equity required in order to consummate the transaction. In most cases the fees associated with committing to make the loan and the fees associated with originating the loan will be stated in the commitment letter. In larger syndicated loans or in commitments to borrowers who are publicly traded and who may be required to disclose certain fundamental terms of the commitment, fees required to be paid by the borrower will be segregated from the basic loan terms and set forth in a separate fee letter. In these larger loans the borrower will not normally be permitted to disclose to third parties or in securities filings the amount of fees to be charged by the lender, in order to maintain confidentiality of the lender's fee schedule.

If the loan requested by the borrower is in excess of the amount of loan desired to be advanced by the lender, the commitment letter would normally describe a syndication process. While the committing lender stands behind the commitment to fund the entire loan in this situation, the commitment letter would normally name the committing lender as the administrative agent for arranging a syndicate of lenders who will participate in making the overall loan. Placing a company's loan request in front of lenders who may participate in a loan syndication requires that the administrative agent have confidence in the information supplied by the borrower in support of the loan. The commitment letter will state that not only must the borrower cooperate with the administrative agent in placing the loan participations, but that the borrower represents that information provided to the administrative agent is complete and correct in all material respects.

When a commitment letter is issued, there will normally be some period of time that lapses between the issuance of the letter and the closing of the loan described in the commitment letter. In addition, in many cases, the borrower has requested a time line for the issuance of a commitment letter that does not permit the lender to finalize all of its due diligence. In both of these instances, a lender will typically include a variety of conditions to the lender's obligation to fund the loan in the commitment letter. Some conditions will be broadly stated and relate generally to the lender completing due diligence, while other conditions will be phrased in terms of market conditions remaining stable throughout the period leading up to the closing date. When the objective of a borrower is to provide comfort to a third party that financing will be available to complete a transaction with the third party, minimizing conditions contained in the commitment letter is imperative, particularly general conditions related to continuing due diligence.

Commitment Letter Summary of Terms and Conditions

As the size of a proposed transaction increases, lenders will typically generate a commitment letter that contains general terms and conditions relating to the obligation of the lender to make the loan. A summary of specific terms and conditions of the loan will, however, be contained in a separate document. Terms contained in the summary include the specific name of the borrower, any guarantors, the name of the lender, a description of the size and nature of the committed facility or facilities, interest rate alternatives, pricing grids, maturity dates of the facility, security for the loan, intercreditor arrangements, amortization schedules, prepayment terms, detailed conditions to closing, financial covenants, affirmative and negative covenants, representations and warranties, events of default, and indemnification of the lender. The summary provides a road map for a financial officer to review in order to determine whether the requirements of the lender can be met prior to negotiation of final terms or prior to the drafting of definitive loan agreements.

Where the commitment letter contains an obligation on the part of a lender to provide several different types of facilities to one borrower, the lender may reserve the right to change the pricing and yield allocation between differing facilities. For example, a lender making a commitment including a senior secured facility, a junior secured facility, and an unsecured facility will make certain assumptions about market conditions, and the assumptions will serve as the basis for allocating amounts of the loans included in each facility type. Where the lender determines that the assumptions regarding market conditions or the financial performance of the borrower have changed, the lender will want to reserve some flexibility to change the relative size of the facilities that have been committed. This feature is known as market flex rights. In exercising market flex, a lender would keep the overall size of a commitment stable, but could increase the size of the senior debt facility while reducing by a like amount the size of a junior component of the facility. Changing the size of the components of the commitment would not give rise to a claim by a borrower that the lender had failed to meet its commitment. In most cases, while the overall cost of capital or interest rate may change, the flexibility to make the changes rather than terminate a commitment is beneficial to the borrower and to the lender.

Fee Letter

Where a lender separates information regarding fees from the base commitment letter, the normal reasons stated for the structure will relate to the lender's desire to maintain the confidentiality of the fees quoted as being payable in connection with the loan. Fees that may be required in connection with the commitment, closing, or maintenance of a loan include fees that may be described as commitment fees, underwriting fees, structuring fees, financial advisory fees, ticking fees, expense reimbursements, and administrative fees.

Commitment, structuring, or underwriting fees are generally payable when a lender issues a commitment letter. At the time a lender issues a commitment, the loan proceeds are factored into the lender's loan base, and consequently reduce the amount of loans that could otherwise be originated by the lender. Lenders will continue significant efforts to underwrite the loan during the documentation process. Because the lender's opportunity to make additional loans is restricted by the size of the commitment, and as a result of the expenses associated with underwriting a loan, a lender will charge a fee to reflect the opportunity cost of extending the commitment and the lender's operating costs related to underwriting the loan. Although the commitment or underwriting fees may be paid at delivery of a commitment or at closing, depending on the practice of the lender, the fees are earned by the lender at the time the commitment is made and are payable even if the borrower does not close the loan.

The size of a commitment fee normally varies by the risk associated with the type of loan being made. For senior secured credit facilities, it is not uncommon for structuring and commitment fees to range in the aggregate up to 2 percent of the loan amount. For junior or subordinated loans, a commitment fee up to 2.5 percent of the loan amount would not be unusual.

Ticking fees are similar to payments required by lenders for unused borrowing capacity. Ticking fees are charged when a commitment is expected to extend over a protracted period of time, and where a closing is anticipated to take place at some distant time in the future. In mergers and acquisition transactions that must meet regulatory or other approvals, significant periods of time can lapse between commitment and closing. Many lenders will charge the borrower for maintaining the facility open during this extended period of time. A ticking fee may start at the time of the commitment or after the lapse of a stated period of time if the loan has not closed. One-half of 1 percent of the committed loan amount is a typical ticking fee.

A fee letter will generally provide that out of pocket expenses incurred by a lending in connection with the underwriting or closing of a loan must be reimbursed by the borrower. This category of expenses would normally include legal fees, consultant's fees, and credit reports that are incurred by the lender.

For syndicated loans as well as loans where the lender or agent for the lending group must perform tasks throughout the life of the loan related to matters such as calculation of financial covenants or determination of borrowing base amounts, an annual administrative fee is paid to the lender. The amount of the fee varies but is determined by the lender taking into account the intensity of the ongoing administration that must be performed in connection with the type of loan being made to the borrower. For syndicated loans to middle-market companies, fees charged range from $25,000 to $150,000 annually.

LOAN DOCUMENTATION

Loan documentation can be as simple as a lender's standard promissory note with blanks filled in describing the loan amount, interest rate, and payment schedule. For larger more complicated loans, a loan documentation package might include a credit agreement, note, security agreement, guarantee agreement, collateral assignment agreement, pledge agreement, intercreditor agreement, subordination agreement, and financing statements.

Credit Agreement

A typical credit agreement will contain five or six primary sections. These sections include a description of the size and type of the credit facility, applicable interest rates, a covenants section, a section dealing with representations and warranties, a section describing events of default, and a section indicating the conditions that must be satisfied in order for the lender to make the loan. Although different lenders will organize their documentation in a variety of formats, the sections just mentioned will cover virtually all fundamental issues addressed in a credit facility agreement.

Type of Credit Facility

Credit facilities fall into two primary categories of loans. These loans are normally labeled either term loans or revolving loans. Each type of loan has certain general characteristics that are normally found in any lender's loan documentation.

Term Loans   A term loan is a fixed amount of money advanced by a lender to a borrower where the borrower is expected to repay the loan amount plus interest over a specified period of time. The repayment terms are negotiated based on the ability of the borrower to repay the loan based on financial projections provided by the borrower and agreed to by the lender. A term loan may be repaid in a lump sum at the end of a fixed period or amortized and paid in specified periodic payments during the term of the loan. Where the use of proceeds of the loan relates to the acquisition of a specific asset or business, the repayment terms may be varied during the life of the loan. For example, it would not be unusual for a term loan to require interest only for an initial period of time, followed by gradually increasing requirements to pay down principal over the life of the loan. Where the loan is used to acquire an asset that generates even cash flows or returns during the life of the asset, amortization of the loan will normally be required in equal payments of principal and interest over the useful life of the asset. The typical life of a term loan will in many cases match the life of the asset acquired with the proceeds of the loan. The term of a loan used to acquire computer equipment would be much shorter than the term of a loan used to acquire real property or a business. Lenders price loans and determine interest rates by assessing risks related to repayment of the loan. As the term of a loan increases, risks increase that internal or external factors may alter the ability of a business to repay a loan, and therefore interest rates are normally higher with longer-term loans.

Many term loans will have prepayment requirements based upon a borrower's excess cash flow or in connection with the sale of borrower assets. These prepayments are in addition to the scheduled amortization of a loan. Where a borrower makes a voluntary prepayment, a lender may assess a penalty under certain circumstances that relate to the interest rate associated with the loan. For loans bearing a fixed interest rate, a prepayment fee may be assessed against a borrower in connection with a partial or full payoff of a loan. The fee is normally not greater than 3 percent and is not normally assessed beyond the third year of the term of the loan. With respect to London Interbank Offered Rate (LIBOR) loans, a LIBOR breakage fee or a reimbursement of any funding losses is assessed against the borrower in all cases where a borrower makes a prepayment prior to the end of a LIBOR interest period. Funding losses are calculated by comparing interest rates at the time of the full or partial repayment with the interest rate applicable to the LIBOR interest period selected by a borrower. LIBOR interest periods are relatively short with most borrowers selecting periods with durations of one month, three months, or six months.

Revolving Loans   Revolving loans, also known as revolvers or revolving credit facilities, are loans with stated maximum loan amounts, but variable amounts that can actually be drawn down by a borrower that are determined periodically by reference to certain levels of borrower assets. Assets used to determine a borrower's available loan amount normally include accounts receivable and inventory. As a borrower's level of accounts receivable and inventory increases, the borrower's loan capacity increases up to a predetermined maximum loan amount. In order to determine the actual loan capacity of a borrower at any given time, a lender will review what is called the borrowing base. In determining the amount of borrowing base, a lender will give a borrower credit for a percentage of accounts receivable, generally up to 80 percent, and a percentage of inventory, generally up to 50 percent. Before applying percentages to a borrowing base to determine credit availability, a lender will make a calculation, set forth in the loan documentation, as to which accounts receivable and which portions of inventory are eligible to be included in the base. Accounts receivable may be excluded from eligibility on the basis of aging, relationship to bad credit history with payments to the borrower, or based on the type of entity owing the account receivable. Governmental agencies are types of entities that may be excluded from the calculation of the aggregate amount of borrowing base available to a borrower due to governmental restrictions on the pledge of its accounts payable. Inventory may be excluded if stale, out of date, unpackaged, or opened.

It is customary for a borrower to pay down a revolving loan with the collection of its accounts receivable such that the availability under a loan package increases with collections applied to the loan and decreases as amounts are redrawn. Drawdowns under a revolving credit facility may continue so long as the borrower is not in default under any of the terms or conditions of the loan agreement; however, the ability to draw down under a revolving credit facility is terminated upon the occurrence of an event of default under the loan agreement. This ongoing increase and decrease in availability distinguishes the revolving credit facility from a term loan, because as a term loan is paid down, availability is permanently decreased. Even though the revolving credit facility amounts outstanding will fluctuate during the term of the loan, there is stated or fixed amortization of a revolver under normal circumstances. The maturity date or term of a revolver may be as short as one year and as long as seven years, with the full amount outstanding under the loan due and payable on the maturity date.

Revolving credit facilities in many cases will also permit a company to use availability to provide suppliers or customers with letters of credit. When the borrower requests a letter of credit under a revolving credit facility, the issuance of the letter of credit will reduce overall availability of the credit facility as long as the letter of credit is outstanding. Fees associated with the issuance of a letter of credit are in addition to commitment or underwriting fees assessed in connection with the origination of a revolving credit facility. These fees range from an annual fee of 1 percent of the amount of the letter of credit, payable monthly for the period that the letter of credit is outstanding, to a fee equal to the base interest rate margin percentage. If a borrower's interest rate is stated as LIBOR plus 6.5 percent, the interest rate margin percentage is 6.5 percent and the annual fee charged in connection with the issuance off a letter of credit would be 6.5 percent of the face amount of the letter of credit.

Interest Rate and Pricing Alternatives   For the average borrower, interest rate alternatives are relatively simple. The borrower makes a loan request and the lender inquires as to whether the borrower would prefer a fixed rate or a variable rate. Depending on the risk profile of the borrower, and to a certain extent on the lending guidelines of the lender, the borrower will make a selection that satisfies one of two primary considerations. In this respect a borrower who desires a predictable payment stream will select a fixed interest rate and equal periodic payments of principal and interest over the life of the loan. In economic climates where interest rates appear to be rising, the fixed interest rate alternative may be chosen because it looks to be the least expensive alternative over the estimated life of the loan. In contrast, a borrower may elect a variable rate of interest because in the short term the loan payments are significantly less than a fixed rate alternative. More importantly, when the borrower believes that interest rates will fall, selecting a variable rate preserves the borrower's flexibility to move down in the absolute rate of interest being paid without having to refinance the loan.

In this segment of the marketplace, where the borrower is dealing primarily with its local commercial banker, the pricing of the interest rate where the variable rate option is selected is based off of the bank's prime rate, the Eurodollar bid rate, or the LIBOR rate. In most cases a financially healthy local business can expect to receive pricing at prime plus 1 percent per annum, or LIBOR plus 200 to 300 basis points per annum. These loans may be priced slightly lower or slightly higher based on the trends in performance of the borrower. It is assumed in most of these cases that the loans are secured by the assets of the borrower, or by a guarantee of the owners of the business.

For a loan extended by a local commercial or community bank, the relationship between the banker and the borrower makes documentation of these types of loans quite simple. The bank will use a standard promissory note, standard loan agreement, standard security agreement, and standard guarantee. The documentation is sufficient to protect the lender, but simple and easy to use for the parties to close the loan and for the lender to advance the funds. The commercial or community banker is relying as much on a belief in the owners of the business and their integrity for repayment as the banker is relying on the loan documentation. As a result, local lifestyle businesses and professional firms constitute a significant portion of the loans extended within most communities. The nature of the loan process should also provide guidance for a local business owner or professional as to the profile of the business that must be established within a community in order to increase the probability of success in obtaining credit from local commercial and community bank lenders.

In securing credit for local real estate development and construction, local builders and developers will rely heavily on their commercial and community bankers for credit necessary to develop and construct smaller office buildings, single-family and multifamily developments, apartments, strip shopping centers, and industrial complexes. In order to move from construction and development loans to permanent long-term credit facilities, these local developers will, for larger projects, work with commercial mortgage brokers to place loans with national lending institutions. While development and construction loans are almost always based on variable interest rates, most developers are comfortable with the risks associated with variable loans due to the short-term nature of construction and development loans. Most of these loans will be repaid within three years. In contrast, loans secured to provide take out or permanent financing for these larger real property projects are in most cases fixed rate loans. The loans are secured for periods normally not shorter than 7 years and not longer than 15 years.

Given market fluctuations that builders have historically experienced over periods extending this long, most of these borrowers will attempt to reduce their upside interest rate risk by selecting a fixed rate even though the periodic payment obligations are larger in the short term than a variable rate. National lenders in these larger loan categories will normally raise capital by going either directly or indirectly to the public capital markets where interest rates are normally tied to U.S. Treasury securities of the same maturity. For example, a builder requesting a 10-year fixed rate mortgage from a national lender would pay an interest rate tied to 10-year constant-maturity Treasuries. The national lender will be able to borrow in the public markets at a rate slightly higher than the current 10-year Treasury rate, and in turn will pass on to the builder a fixed rate that is one to two percentage points per annum higher than its cost to borrow the funds in the marketplace.

As the size of a borrower's loan request increases, the credit quality of the borrower begins to play a significantly increasing importance in determining the interest rate that a borrower will have to pay. At the high end of the credit quality scale, corporations with credit ratings in the top two or three levels or grades assigned by Standard & Poor's or Moody's go directly to the public markets and borrow funds by issuing commercial paper. The process for qualified borrowers is quick and relatively inexpensive. The funds borrowed mature within 30, 60, or 90 days and the borrower goes back into the market to the extent that funds are not available from operations or long-term loan agreements to repay the short-term commercial paper borrowings. Companies with credit ratings that permit them to access the commercial paper markets are normally very large regional, national, or globally recognized companies.

When the credit facility size requested is large, and the borrower's credit is not rated at the top of the credit pile by Standard & Poor's or Moody's Investors Service, interest rate pricing increases in direct proportion to the amount of leverage that the loan request creates for the borrower. These larger credit facilities may be requested in order to support market or product expansions, for business line or company acquisitions, or simply to refinance existing credit lines that may lack flexibility needed by the borrower due to market conditions (or the existing facilities may be unwieldy due to the fact that they were structured during better financial times for the borrower). These loans typically are accompanied by complex commercial loan documentation and for the most part have little if anything to do with the quality of the relationship between the lender and the management of the borrower. Where the primary owners of the borrower are either private equity sponsors or management with a track record of success with the lender, relationships may come into play. In these cases, the relationship normally gets the attention of the lender, but the intensity of the loan documentation is not diminished.

Interest rates charged for larger loans within leveraged companies are a function in most cases of two variables. One variable is the credit rating of the borrower assigned by Standard & Poor's or by Moody's. The other significant variable is the amount of leverage, or the debt-to-equity and debt-to-cash-flow ratios of the borrower. As the leverage ratios increase, the absolute rate of interest charged also increases.

In these larger, leveraged facilities, there may be several different tranches of loans requested. For example, there may be a senior secured facility that is comprised of a revolver and a term loan. In many cases the term loan is divided into two segments. One segment of the term loan is expected to be amortized during the term of the loan, and the other segment has modest or no principal amortization. These secured loans may be coupled with mezzanine financings that are unsecured. Recently, a significant portion of mezzanine debt has been displaced by junior secured debt coupled with a borrower's placement of unsecured high yield debt. Although unusual, where the absolute leverage ratios do not exceed certain levels established by lenders as part of their underwriting criteria, some of these loan requests, particularly for leveraged acquisitions by existing companies, may be made with no equity contributed to support the acquisition. As interest rates rise from the current historical lows, the potential for consummating transactions not supported by equity will diminish or disappear, but this is a normal occurrence in the interest rate cycle.

In facilities that are structured to finance leveraged or in many cases distressed companies, the interest rate charged will be established by reference to a base rate plus a margin. A borrower is generally given the choice of selecting either a LIBOR base rate or the lender's prime rate. The final interest rate will be determined by adding the margin to the base rate selected by the borrower. In reviewing applicable margins, it will come as no surprise that the margin applicable to senior secured loans will be less than the margin added to mezzanine or junior secured loans. While high yield loans based on the sale of bonds by a borrower are normally fixed over the life of the loan, these instruments are also unsecured and carry interest rates slightly less than those charged by mezzanine lenders due to the fact that the purchaser of the note has the ability to buy and sell the notes in open market purchases. This liquidity is desirable for purchasers of these instruments and the liquidity normally translates into slightly lower fixed interest rates even though the instruments are unsecured.

Whether the loan is secured or unsecured, the applicable margin typically varies by reference to the overall leverage of the borrower. For example, a borrower may be charged prime plus 8 percent where its overall leverage is greater than 6 to 1, with the 8 percent margin reducing pro rata as the leverage ratio falls below 6 or 5 or 4 to 1, and conversely the interest rate margin increases as leverage moves up.

Representations and Warranties

Representations and warranties are important to lenders for a variety of reasons. The initial give-and-take of negotiating representations and warranties provides in-depth information to a lender about the business of the borrower. This information-gathering exercise assists in underwriting the loan and in confirming data that has previously been presented to the lender in the borrower's business plan. As the loan agreement is negotiated, a lender and borrower will spar over the intensity of a loan agreement's representations and warranties. The intensity is, in most cases, a discussion of the modifiers that a borrower may make to the various pieces of information requested by the lender. These modifiers relate typically to the knowledge of the borrower and to materiality. Although the lender wins most of these discussions, introduction of modifiers can be important not only at the initial drawdown of a loan, but during the life of a loan, particularly a revolver, as the representations and warranties must be true and accurate at the time of each draw under the revolver. Where a borrower and lender cannot agree upon a knowledge or materiality modifier, a borrower must provide information to the lender specifically identifying why the borrower cannot state a representation or warranty in the absolute. Specific information modifying the intensity of a representation or warranty is normally contained on a schedule of exceptions. An exception disclosed on a schedule to the loan agreement permits a borrower to comply with a lender's request for information without breaching a provision of the loan agreement by making a false statement. After taking into account a borrower's schedule of exceptions, if the borrower cannot certify that the representations and warranties are true and correct, the loan will not be made at all, and as such, accuracy of the representations and warranties, as modified by the schedule of exceptions, will be a condition to the obligation of a lender to fund a loan.

In short-form standard preprinted loan agreements for typically smaller loans, the number of representations and warranties is limited. In larger loans and in all syndicated loans, the borrower will be required to make representations in 20 to 30 different categories of information requested by a lender. These categories of information may be divided into as few as three general categories relating to the business of a borrower. Most of the information falls into a category relating to either the borrower's organizational structure, the borrower's financial statements, or the borrower's operations.

Borrower's Organizational Structure   Basic information such as the borrower's state of incorporation and capital structure are normally required as part of the information included in the representations and warranties. Where a borrower is part of a complex corporate organization, a lender will require detailed information regarding subsidiaries and affiliates in order to protect the lender's access to the cash flows or assets that have been used to support the loan request. A lender will also request information regarding a borrower's physical locations in order to determine where to make filings that relate to perfecting the lender's security interest in any collateral pledged by a borrower. Standard bylaws of virtually any corporation will require that a borrower have board approval to enter into a loan agreement, and a lender will require certification that the appropriate board action has been taken, that authorized officers have signed the loan documentation, and that no restrictions are contained in the company's articles of incorporation, bylaws, or board action that would prevent the lender from enforcing the loan agreements against the borrower. A borrower will also certify that closing the loan will not result in the violation or breach of any contract or agreement to which the borrower is a party. In regulated industries, if a borrower fails to maintain appropriate regulatory approvals to operate, the business will close, operations will cease, and cash flow will terminate. As a result, lenders require that a borrower certify that all regulatory approvals for continued operation of the entity are in place, and that the closing of the loan will not violate any statute or regulation applicable to the borrower or any of the borrower's licenses.

Borrower's Financial Statements   Lenders rely heavily on a borrower's financial strength in underwriting a loan request. A borrower's financial statements are utilized by a lender to determine whether the loan request can be satisfied by the borrower from its operations. In addition, the lender and borrower will negotiate financial covenants that must be achieved in order for a loan to be advanced, and during the life of a loan, the financial covenants must be maintained in order to avoid having a lender require that the loan be paid in full prior to the end of its expected term. It should be remembered that in the event that a borrower fails to achieve the negotiated financial covenants, a lender can demand to be paid in full prior to the expected date of maturity even when the borrower has met its obligations for payment of principal and interest. So in negotiating the financial covenants, there is a natural tension between the lender and the borrower that should be obvious here.

In order to secure a loan, the borrower must place an optimistic set of financials in front of the lender. The financials must not only be strong from a historical numbers standpoint, but the financials must also be strong on a going forward basis. If the borrower is optimistic in its forecasts, the lender will set the loan's financial covenants in a manner that matches the forecasts. If the forecasts are unrealistic, the borrower will end up in default under the financial covenants early in the loan. If the forecasts are conservative, the borrower may not receive approval from the lender for funds sufficient to accomplish the objectives of the initial loan request. As a result, a borrower must present realistic forecasts or suffer the potential for an event of default early in the loan term. It should be noted that forecasting is by its nature an inexact science and where lenders are apprised by a borrower of unusual trends or unexpected obligations that do not threaten the real ability of a borrower to repay a loan in a manner that is consistent with the original terms, lenders will work with borrowers to reset financial covenants to the newly determined forecasted results of the borrower.

Naturally, it is imperative that a lender receive a strong affirmation from a borrower that the financial information submitted to a lender is accurate, true, and correct. The representations and warranties relating to financial statements are normally made in absolute terms without knowledge or materiality modifiers, including a statement that the borrower made its disclosures in a manner that eliminates the potential for undisclosed liabilities being discovered in the future. The numbers submitted by a borrower are either correct or not as far as a lender is concerned, and if a lender determines that the financials are not correct, the loan will not be advanced or if the loan is in place the loan will be terminated. Outside auditors will provide comfort to a lender that a borrower's financial statements are representative of the operations of the borrower. This comfort comes in three formats: a compilation, a review, or an audit. A compilation is the lowest form of comfort, and an audit is the highest level of comfort provided by outside auditors. For smaller borrowers and transactions, a lender may not require an audit; however, for larger loans and all syndicated loans, audits are standard requirements of a lender. Because most audits are performed once a year, there is normally a gap between the date of a borrower's last audit and the date of a loan closing. Lenders will accept unaudited financial statements for the gap period, but require a certification by the borrower that the financial statements have been prepared in accordance with generally accepted accounting principles (GAAP). Statements that have not been audited are submitted to the lender and contain modifiers that clarify that the statements are prepared in accordance with GAAP, but that they are subject to normal year-end audit adjustments, none of which will be material.

Where a borrower intends to use the proceeds of a loan for an acquisition, a lender will require that the borrower provide projections for the combined operations of the borrower and the acquisition target. The projections serve to guide a lender as to the aggregate amount of debt that the combined operations can support. In many larger acquisitions, a buyer assumes economies of scale will be achieved in the combined companies. These assumptions relate for the most part to cost savings, and in order for a lender to give a borrower credit for the forecasted savings, outside consultants are usually required to confirm the borrower's assumptions. The consultants vary, but range from nationally recognized accounting firms to specialized consulting groups serving specific industry segments. In addition to forecasts of operations, a leveraged lender requires the borrower to present pro forma balance sheets of the combined entities. The pro forma statements are presented based on an assumption that the acquisition has closed and the lender has advanced the proceeds of the loan to the borrower. At this point, the lender will test the balance sheet against the financial covenants negotiated in connection with the origination of the loan. If the combined entities meet or exceed the threshold financial covenants, the loan closing will take place. Otherwise, the lender will either refuse to close, or more likely, will require the borrower to bring additional equity to the closing in order to bring the required financial covenants into compliance with the ratios that have been negotiated.

In addition to the representations and warranties related to the financial statements, a borrower will also certify that the financial information on its tax returns is accurate, that all taxes that are due have been paid, and that there are no Internal Revenue Service audits of the borrower currently taking place. A borrower will also make a representation and warranty that all other taxes such as sales and use taxes and employment and excise taxes have been paid in full. Lenders are especially careful to obtain detailed representations about taxes due to the priority of the claims that can be made and the severe actions that can be taken by the Internal Revenue Service if back taxes are owed.

Borrower's Operations The largest number of individual representations and warranties made by a borrower relate to the borrower's ongoing operations. A lender carefully examines disclosures made in connection with the operating representations and warranties, because in many cases, these disclosures provide a forecast of the future success of a business. For example, if a borrower discloses a significant number of pieces of litigation, a lender will be wary of making a loan if the borrower is being sued on a regular basis. Also, where a borrower is bringing a significant number of claims related to its accounts receivable, a lender will evaluate the claims carefully for indications that the borrower lacks sophistication in performing credit checks on its customers, thus potentially making the statement of revenues included in the financial statements suspect.

Environmental representations and warranties are examined with extreme care, particularly when a borrower is securing a loan with real property. Where a borrower's property is contaminated with hazardous wastes, a lender will generally decline to take the property as collateral in order to avoid the potential for getting in the property's chain of title and as a result becoming responsible for cleaning up the hazardous waste.

General representations and warranties related to whether the borrower has good and valid title to its property provide comfort to a lender that if there is an event of default, the lender can take possession of the borrower's property and liquidate the property to pay off the borrower's loan without fighting over which party should be entitled to the proceeds of any such liquidation. A borrower will certify also that it is not in default under any material loan or contract as a way of giving a lender comfort that no contingencies in the operation of the borrower's business will arise unexpectedly. Most borrowers have 401(k) plans, profit sharing plans, or pension plans with varying levels of obligations to fund these programs. A borrower must provide guidance to its lender as to its compliance with the ERISA laws that govern these retirement programs. In the absence of compliance, particularly with respect to plans that are unfunded or underfunded, material liabilities can arise that disrupt the cash flows and ability of the borrower to repay the lender. These disruptions can undermine the financial vitality of even the most sophisticated types of businesses.

Lenders will request confirmation to be provided by a borrower that immediately before and immediately after a loan closes, the borrower will be solvent. Where the borrower is struggling to make its payments or to meet financial covenants contained in a loan agreement, the prospect of insolvency of course will severely affect the ability of a company to borrow funds. Where a loan is made in connection with a weak borrower, a lender will require a solvency opinion in order to maintain its liens and priority of liens in the event that the borrower is unable to meet its obligations as they come due and as a consequence files for protection under the bankruptcy statutes. If creditors are successful in challenging the solvency opinion, a lender may lose its secured position and significantly disadvantage itself with respect to its normal senior position in relation to unsecured creditors.

Loan Covenants

Covenants contained in loan documentation are agreements between the lender and the borrower. Affirmative covenants relate to actions that are permitted or required to be taken by a borrower. Negative covenants are actions that a borrower is prohibited from taking. Financial covenants include requirements that a borrower maintain specified financial ratios relating to the borrower's operations and balance sheet during the loan term. Borrowers are required to make prepayments of principal amounts of their loans in connection with events such as the sale of equity, the sale of assets, or the sale or issuance of debt, and also out of excess cash flow.

While actions included in the negative covenant section of the loan agreement may in certain circumstances be waived by a lender, these waivers are normally granted or denied in the sole discretion of the lender, without any discussion as to the reasonableness of the grant or denial. Similar to warranties and representations, a borrower must be in compliance with each of the loan covenants not only at the time the loan proceeds are advanced to the borrower, but at all times during the life of a loan. If a borrower fails to maintain compliance with loan covenants, a lender may declare the loan in default and accelerate the maturity date of the loan to match the date of default.

Affirmative Covenants   A borrower must comply with the lender's requirement to take certain actions and to provide certain information during the term of a loan. These actions are referred to as affirmative covenants. Lenders expect that a borrower will continue to conduct its business in the manner in which the business was operated leading up to the loan. Operational aspects of a business that must be maintained include the maintenance of accurate books and records, payment of insurance premiums, the payment of taxes, the payment of debts and obligations as they come due, and the maintenance of cash management systems designed to ensure that the lender is in control of the cash flows of the borrower. Access to ongoing financial information is important to lenders in order to constantly monitor the financial strength of the borrower. As a result, borrowers will be obligated to provide weekly, monthly, quarterly, and annual financial statements as well as all financial information generated by a borrower that is to be included in the budgeting process.

Compliance with all laws is a typical affirmative covenant, particularly where the borrower is involved in a regulated industry. A borrower is also required to provide its lender with ongoing, updated disclosures related to the business and specifically focused on ensuring that the borrower's representations and warranties are current, complete, and correct. While the activities of a large company might require weekly updates of disclosures to maintain their accuracy, it is customary for disclosure updates to be made in connection with either loan drawdowns or in connection with the delivery of quarterly and annual financial statements. Exceptions to the general rule are made for material changes in the borrower's business, which must be disclosed to the lender promptly.

Negative Covenants In order to underwrite a company's loan request, a lender will spend a great deal of time understanding the borrower's business. Time spent in this regard is reflected in the amount of effort expended by a lender in the loan agreement negotiations defining the nature and extent of activities that are prohibited during the loan term. The objective of these negotiations is to ensure that the borrower will continue its existing business and operate the business in a manner that is consistent with the borrower's business plan and the supplemental information and materials presented by the borrower in the course of the loan application process.

Breach of a negative covenant results in the same remedy that results from a breach of an affirmative covenant or a breach of a representation or warranty—the borrower's loan is accelerated and the borrower must immediately repay the lender in full. Although violation of a negative covenant will result in loan acceleration, certain negative covenants are not absolute prohibitions but rather limitations on the level of specific activities.

In order to establish limitations on borrower activities, a lender will define in the loan agreement specified expenditures or actions that will be restricted. For example, a borrower may be prohibited from (1) making capital expenditures in excess of an agreed-upon amount, (2) making dividends or distributions in excess of certain levels, (3) making investments, loans, or advances in excess of specified amounts, (4) incurring additional indebtedness in excess of agreed-upon levels, (5) creating additional liens, (6) selling assets, (7) canceling loans owed to the borrower, and (8) entering into leases for terms longer than a specified maximum term and in excess of specified maximum lease payment amounts. The lender will establish the minimums and maximums based upon the business plan and forecasted financial statements presented to the lender in connection with the origination of the loan. Once the parameters of the restrictions have been determined, the lender and borrower will negotiate buffers around the parameters drawn from the borrower's business plan in order to provide the borrower with cushions in each of the restricted categories in order to take into account the inevitable variances that the borrower will experience in its actual performance compared to its business plan.

In addition to features of the loan agreement that are intended to deal with day-to-day operations and the establishment of limitations on certain operational aspects of the business, lenders will also impose limitations that impact a borrower on the macro level. These limitations are expressed for the most part in the context of a change of control or in limitations on acquisitions of new businesses by the borrower.

While loans are not extended to a borrower based strictly on the persons or entities that happen to be the owners of the business, lenders are critically aware of the attitude of owners toward a business and the business owner's reputation within a community or within an industry. As a result, where the controlling interest in a business changes hands or control of the company changes as a result of the sale of equity by the borrower, a lender will require that the loan be repaid in connection with the closing that has triggered the change of control. Although this change of control feature is found in virtually all smaller loans, the provision is also found in larger syndicated loans, even where the owners of the borrower have not guaranteed the loan. Many larger syndicated loans are facilitated by equity sponsors whom lenders recognize as being in the position of providing incremental capital in the event that the business falters. If the equity sponsors sell out, it is rare that an existing lender stays in the loan. Moreover, when the transaction generating the change of control is a leveraged buyout, the existing lender will either be taken out completely or recapitalized as a result of the new owner's need to gain unencumbered access to the company's assets to secure the acquisition loan and to support the leverage applied to the transaction.

Prepayment Covenants   Fundamental changes in the capital structure of a business, sales or other types of liquidations of assets, destruction of insured assets, and financial performance over and above that projected by a borrower in its loan request are all events that may trigger an obligation on the part of a borrower to prepay some or all of an outstanding loan. Where the borrower has a term loan and a revolver in place, proceeds associated with a prepayment are generally applied first to the term loan and the amount of the term loan is permanently reduced. Thereafter, any remaining prepayment proceeds are used to pay down the borrower's revolver.

The issuance of equity is a primary target for early loan retirement. Sales of equity, if not carved out as prepayment events, provide a lender with the opportunity to mitigate risk of repayment, particularly in long-term loans. Where carve-outs have been negotiated, the sale of equity may still trigger prepayments, but only to the extent required to bring the borrower within certain financial covenant ratios. Additional carve-outs might require a borrower to apply proceeds of an equity financing that are in excess of certain minimal amounts.

The proceeds of additional debt issuances, to the extent permitted at all, will be used to pay down existing debt so that the overall financial ratios do not change or at least to the extent that the financial ratios are not impaired by the additional debt.

Lenders are quick to claim operating cash generated in amounts typically called excess cash flow. Excess cash flow is defined by reference to the specific industry segment of the borrower, but the concept generally can be defined in terms of the excess of revenues over all expenditures for a particular period, regardless of whether the expenditures are operating or capital in nature. Where the borrower is heavily leveraged, a lender may require 100 percent of excess cash flow to be used to prepay outstanding loan balances. As a borrower's total leverage declines, the percentage of excess cash flow required to be prepaid on loan amounts declines. A typical excess cash flow percentage for a non–highly leveraged borrower would be a requirement to prepay the outstanding loan amounts down in an amount equal to 25 to 50 percent of the borrower's excess cash flow. For borrowers with low aggregate debt amounts, a lender may forgo an excess cash flow prepayment obligation completely.

Financial Covenants   Financial covenants are structured by lenders to measure the performance of a borrower against the borrower's business plan and against specific financial parameters that the lender applies in connection with the underwriting of each loan in its loan portfolio. Measurement techniques vary by industry segment, but for the most part, the techniques are all designed to provide a lender with detailed information regarding the ability of the borrower to repay the loan amounts during the life of the loan. Where a borrower fails to achieve specified financial covenants, a lender must decide whether to require a payoff of the loan or whether to grant the borrower a waiver from compliance with the financial covenants. Waivers are routinely provided where the borrower is financially sound, making its payments of principal and interest, but where the borrower has missed achieving financial results forecasted in its business plan.

Financial covenants are generally stated as numerical or financial ratios applied to specified operating and balance sheet categories of information. In some cases, however, financial covenants are stated in terms of absolute numbers. For example, where a borrower's business plan includes annual assumptions regarding its assumed level of capital expenditures, a lender will in many cases include a financial covenant, based on the information contained in the borrower's business plan, that limits the amount of capital expenditures the lender will permit in any given year or measurement period. In addition, where a borrower's business plan makes certain assumptions regarding its ability to generate cash flow to support the aggregate size of the loan request, a lender may include a financial covenant that is based on achieving minimum levels of cash flow during a measurement period. Other categories of absolute amounts stated as financial covenants include minimum revenue and minimum cash. As the financial health of a borrower declines, the number of financial covenants stated as absolute minimums or maximums increases in order to give a lender several different ways to measure the borrower's performance against its business plan and forecasts.

In negotiating financial covenants, an important factor is the determination of when the financial covenants will be measured. For stable companies, financial covenants may be measured annually at the time that a borrower provides audited financial statements to the lender. Moreover, most lenders will evaluate financial covenants at all times relevant to the life of the loan compared to the business plan of the borrower. This analysis leads to financial covenants that change during the life of a loan. In the early measurement periods, overall leverage ratios will be high, but as the loan is paid down, the permitted leverage ratio will track down with the reduction in lender debt. Conversely, ratios measuring the cash flow of a company compared to the annual debt service of a company will generally increase over the life of a loan to reflect growth assumed in the borrower's business plan and reduction in the outstanding loan balances over the life of the loan.

In connection with an evaluation of the timing of financial covenants, borrowers subjected to measurement at periods less than a year or at times outside of the presentation of audited statements should factor in the accounting methods used to state financial performance in the measurement period. While interim period statements will be prepared in accordance with GAAP, and the financial covenants will be measured assuming compliance with GAAP, many calculations included in the interim statements will be estimates of the actual amounts received or expended during the period. In contrast, a borrower's financial covenants will be calculated based on the audited financial statements. As a result, when negotiating interim period financial covenants, assumptions about the interim period adjustments must be taken into account.

In most cases the borrower will calculate the ratios to determine its compliance with the loan agreement financial covenants, and the lender will review and evaluate the borrower's calculations. In distressed cases, the lender will also require a borrower's outside auditors to perform the ratio analysis and sign off on the calculation submitted to the lender. Where the financial covenants are being calculated in a distressed situation or for a struggling borrower, a lender may want more up-to-date information than an annual calculation. In these distressed types of situations, a borrower may be required to perform quarterly calculations of the financial covenants contained in the loan agreement. It is in these frequent measurement instances that a borrower must be extremely careful to negotiate the calculation of financial covenants based on the company's historical periodic performance, taking into account any seasonality or business cycle trends in its financials. Simply taking a borrower's annual statements and assuming equal performance that will be measured throughout a year will normally yield covenant violations on a regular basis, unless the calculations include results of operations for a trailing 12-month period, rather than for just one quarter. Retailers are prime examples of borrowers who must adjust financials for seasonality, as many retailers achieve 40 percent of their sales in the final two months of each year.

Market analysts normally use four or five categories of financial ratios to evaluate the economic health of a company. Among the most important of these categories of ratios are leverage ratios, liquidity ratios, operating ratios, and profitability ratios. While operating and profitability ratios are important in evaluating the performance of a company, lenders focus on the liquidity and leverage ratios to supplement the financial covenants imposed on a borrower that are based on absolute minimum or maximum calculations applied to specific financial information.

Liquidity Ratios Liquidity ratios measure a borrower's ability to meet its obligations in the near term. The current ratio, quick ratio, and net working capital ratio are included in the liquidity category. The current ratio compares a borrower's current assets to current liabilities. For most lenders and as applied to most industry segments, this ratio must stay at a 1 to 1 ratio or more at all times during the life of a loan. A borrower's cash plus accounts receivable compared to its current liabilities is known as the quick ratio. This ratio excludes inventory, but otherwise is similar to the current ratio in that it measures the ability of a borrower to survive in the short term. Lenders look for a ratio in the neighborhood of 1 to 1 in structuring a financial covenant for a typical healthy borrower. Net working capital is a measure of the excess of current assets over current liabilities compared to a borrower's total assets. An acceptable ratio varies significantly from industry to industry, and as such the ratio does not see widespread use or applicability.

Leverage Ratios Leverage ratios measure not only the extent that debt comprises a component of a borrower's capital structure and whether a borrower can safely take on additional debt, but also the ability of a borrower to meet its debt payments as they come due. The most common leverage ratio is measured by comparing the borrower's debt to the borrower's equity. For smaller loans, the debt-to-equity ratio will be stated as a 1 to 1, or perhaps as much as a 2 to 1 ratio. Although many smaller companies will have outstanding debt owed to their owners, the debt may more closely resemble equity in that the business owner has total control over how, when, and where the owner loan will be repaid. If a business owner is willing to subordinate the owner loans to bank debt, then the lender will normally include the owner loans in equity and exclude them from debt. This practice is consistent with the philosophy behind the debt-to-equity calculation being a measure of funds borrowed from third party sources compared to funds provided to the business by its owners.

As the size of the loan transaction grows, it is not uncommon for the aggregate amount of debt funded by lenders to dwarf the amount of equity capital provided by the business owners or equity sponsors. In these leveraged transactions, there are at least three categories of financial covenants that are included in the loan agreements and measured on a quarterly or annual basis. These categories are assigned various names by different lenders, but generally the financial covenants can be labeled (1) minimum debt service coverage ratio, (2) minimum fixed charge coverage ratio, and (3) maximum total leverage ratio.

An analysis of loan documentation from the typical leveraged lender will reveal two variations of the minimum debt service coverage ratio. The first alternative is a calculation where a borrower's earnings before interest, taxes, depreciation, and amortization (EBITDA) is measured against the borrower's interest payment obligations owed during the measurement period. A second alternative measures a borrower's EBITDA against its principal and interest payments owed for the measurement period. In each case, the lender is evaluating the borrower's ability to repay the amount of the loan requested. Ratios negotiated for minimum debt service coverage rarely fall below 1.25 to 1, because a lower ratio would mean that a borrower would expend virtually all of its cash flow to service debt, leaving the borrower with little if any cash flow to pay for unexpected or unbudgeted items.

Calculation of a borrower's minimum fixed charge coverage ratio compares the borrower's EBITDA to the borrower's fixed charges. Fixed charges include a borrower's principal and interest payments on all debt, amounts paid for capital expenditures and amounts paid for taxes, or amounts distributed to owners of the borrower to pay for taxes resulting from the flow-through of income from operations of the borrower. Adding the concept of fixed charges to a financial covenant calculation permits a lender to evaluate the ability of a borrower to make payments not only for debt service, but to make ongoing, ordinary course of business and tax payments required to maintain the health and competitive strength of the borrower.

The maximum total leverage ratio calculation can be defined as the measurement of a borrower's debt compared to the borrower's EBITDA. This calculation is formulated in two primary covenants that differ slightly. One covenant found in most if not all leveraged loan documents measures a borrower's total debt to EBITDA. The other covenant, almost always coupled with the total debt covenant and rarely standing alone, measures senior debt to EBITDA. Market conditions and individual lender underwriting guidelines cause total leverage ratios to vary from time to time; however, recent market conditions have caused lenders to loosen each of these ratios. Current transactions are being completed in certain industries with maximum total leverage ratios between 6 to 1 and 7 to 1. While senior debt coverage ratios are more conservative, recent trends have pushed these leverage calculations to exceed a 4 to 1 ratio.

When loan requests have been made in connection with a proposed leveraged acquisition, financial covenants will be developed based on the combined balance sheet and combined forecasted operating performance of the borrower and its target. In order to move forward in the acquisition process, a borrower seeking to consummate the acquisition without an independent ability to satisfy the purchase price must present a commitment from a lender sufficient to support the acquisition. Because there may be significant time gaps between the commitment and the actual funding of the loan, financial covenants are used as a condition to the obligation of a lender to make a loan. In the terms of a commitment letter and also included in the definitive loan agreement documentation, a lender will require that a borrower provide, at the time of a proposed closing, calculations of all financial covenants on a pro forma basis, assuming that the transaction has closed and that the acquisition loan is in place. If the pro forma calculations do not meet the negotiated financial covenant minimums, the lender will either refuse to close, or in most cases, the borrower must reduce the size of the loan requested by raising additional equity capital to support the loan.

Events of Default

Loan agreement documentation may contain a primary action or event that triggers an event of default such as the failure of the borrower to pay principal or interest in a timely fashion. As the size of a loan increases, lenders expand the list of events of default. The categories of events of default in larger loans will normally follow the major sections of a loan agreement, such as the failure to pay principal and interest, the breach of a representation or warranty, or the failure to abide by the terms of the loan agreement section dealing with affirmative or negative covenants. Where the breach relates to a failure to pay principal and interest, lenders are reluctant to provide borrowers with more than a short-term ability to cure the default, and in many cases, no time to cure a payment default. Lenders acknowledge, however, that many representations and warranties and many covenants can be breached without generating a significant amount of risk that a loan will not be repaid. Where the breach or default is not material to the overall health of the borrower, a lender will permit a borrower to cure the default within a specified period of time. If the borrower is able to effect a cure, the loan remains in place with no changes. If the default is not cured, then a borrower must either negotiate a waiver for the default or pay off the loan. Where the default relates to a financial covenant, the lender and borrower may simply renegotiate the financial covenants to reflect the borrower's current operating performance. A renegotiation is normally documented in writing as an amendment to the loan agreement. Financial covenants are routinely renegotiated in situations where the lender determines that the borrower is capable of making principal and interest payments not only in the short term, but also in the long term. Where a loan requires increasing payments of principal during the life of the loan or a large lump sum payment at the end of the loan term, lenders are challenged by the task of determining the potential for a borrower to continue performance under the loan terms and market conditions that will affect the ability of the borrower to obtain financing to take out the lender at the time a lump sum payment is due.

Events of default may be structured to cover significant events that have been assumed in the borrower's business plan, such as obtaining or maintaining regulatory approvals and licenses, securing additional equity, or entering into and closing specified contracts. Where existing contracts or relationships are material to a borrower's ability to meet forecasts contained in its business plan, a lender may describe an event of default in terms of a material breach of the specified contracts or relationships. Significant events that are not normally assumed in a business plan, such as the sale of the borrower or a change in control of the borrower, also serve as events that trigger an ability on the part of a lender to accelerate the maturity date of a loan.

Termination of a line of business or reduction of a significant amount of revenues related to a line of business that is material to the future earnings potential of a borrower will be events of default described in many leveraged asset-based and cash flow–based loans. These events of default precede in most cases a payment default, but they are for the most part accurate predictors of a borrower's ability to repay a loan in the long term. Although it may be difficult for a lender to accelerate the maturity date of a loan that is current in relation to all payments of principal and interest, most lenders will reserve this right because it gives the lender and the borrower time to finalize a refinancing strategy before the full impact of the lost revenue affects the borrower's ability to seek alternatives outside of formal insolvency proceedings.

Miscellaneous events of default under the terms and conditions of a borrower's loan agreement might include failure to pay an outstanding judgment, an uninsured loss, or the occurrence of an event of default under any other loan agreement to which the borrower is a party. Events of default that reference other agreements or loans are generally known as cross defaults.

Events of default related to solvency are contained in smaller loan documentation and in complex, large loan agreements. These events of default include situations where other creditors of the borrower have seized assets, where the borrower has filed for protection under the bankruptcy laws, and where a borrower's creditors have instituted involuntary bankruptcy proceedings for the borrower.

Remedies Available upon an Event of Default   When an event of default occurs, the first action taken by most lenders is to elect to increase the applicable rate of interest under the loan documents to the default rate stated in the loan documentation. Default rates of interest are normally stated in terms of a fixed additional annual rate of interest on top of the current rate applicable to the borrower. Additional interest or the default rate of interest may be as much as four percentage points higher than the current interest rate, although a standard default rate used by many lenders is 2 percent.

In addition to a default rate of interest, a lender may terminate the loan and declare any and all amounts outstanding under the loan to be due and payable. At this time, any obligation of a lender to make advances under a revolving credit facility will also terminate. This action by a lender typically cripples a borrower in default and forces serious consideration of filing a formal insolvency proceeding, so the actions are taken by a lender normally only after careful consideration of all of the alternatives to the termination of the revolving credit facility.

A borrower may be required under the loan documentation to marshall all of its assets and bring them to a centralized location where the lender will liquidate the assets to satisfy the outstanding balance of the loan. While this is an obligation that simplifies the life of a lender, the fact that a borrower is in default or, even worse, insolvent in many cases makes the obligation illusory, particularly where the loan has not been guaranteed by an owner or third party.

It should also be noted that in connection with a loan agreement where a lender has exercised its rights to accelerate the maturity date of a loan in default, the lender may take parallel tracks and pursue any guarantors of the loan agreement simultaneously with its actions against the borrower.

The Promissory Note

The basic provisions of a promissory note issued in connection with smaller loans include the name of the borrower, the name of the lender, the amount of the loan, the interest rate payable, the payment schedule that the borrower is expected to meet, default interest rates, and terms of the loan that are enacted in connection with a loan default. As the size of the loan increases, the length of the promissory note becomes shorter as most of the basic provisions relating to the loan are included in the loan documentation and the promissory note simply references the loan agreement and any related loan documentation such as security agreements and incorporates the terms of the related agreements into the promissory note by the reference. Promissory notes are for the most part negotiable instruments. A negotiable instrument is defined as an agreement that may be bought and sold in the marketplace, with the underlying terms and conditions of the negotiable instrument enforceable against the party obligated under the negotiable instrument. The party entitled to enforce the terms and conditions of the negotiable instrument is the entity that has physical possession of the negotiable instrument, assuming that the party has acquired the instrument for value and in good faith.

With regard to the great majority of loans for middle-market companies, the promissory note is held to maturity by the originating lender. As the size of the loan increases, the probability increases that the loan will be resold in the marketplace, or syndicated and resold in pieces to the marketplace with the originating or committing lender maintaining or keeping a specified portion of the loan amount and recruiting other lenders to join in the loan by purchasing portions of the committing lender's obligation to advance funds. In a loan syndication, even though the committing lender is responsible for selling the loan participations, it is rare that a committing lender will not include safety nets or market outs (a market out permits a lender to terminate its commitment) that will eliminate any obligation to fund a committed loan based on adverse market conditions. In addition as the size of a loan increases, the probability increases that once a participation has been negotiated with a member of the loan syndicate, the holder of the participation will during the life of the loan resell the loan in the marketplace. Reasons that members of a syndicate sell loan participations vary from the performance of the borrower to internal decisions regarding loans to specified industry segments to bank consolidations where the acquiring lender is not involved in the specified industry segment or type of loan made by the syndicate.

As the size of a loan increases and the probability of a borrower's loan being syndicated increases, borrowers are increasingly careful to negotiate syndicate provisions that give the borrower some voice in selecting or approving members of the syndicate. In contrast to where a borrower is funded by a single lender and the relationship between the lender and the borrower determines the outcome of all elective provisions of the loan and all amendments and waivers granted under the loan, when a loan is syndicated, all of these decisions are determined by reference to a majority of votes by the members of the syndicate based on the pro rata amount of the syndicated loan held by each syndicate member. Under these circumstances, admitting a lender to the syndicate who has a reputation for hard-nosed tactics or a reputation for being difficult with respect to obtaining reasonably requested loan covenant waivers or loan amendments can place a significant amount of pressure on the borrower when its performance does not meet pro forma or forecasted levels. As a result, borrowers should attempt to retain some limited controls over the selection of members of a syndicate that may be recruited by the agent for the loan's syndication.

As the size and complexity of a loan increases, the potential for a borrower to be confronted with several differing groups of lenders also increases. For example, in connection with leveraged acquisition financing, committing lenders may include three or four categories of loans in any given commitment. The categories of loans might include a senior credit facility comprised of a revolver, a term loan that requires amortization of principal, and a term loan that is essentially interest only for the life of the loan. These loans may be coupled with mezzanine loans or more recently with junior secured loans, and these junior loans may then again be coupled with an obligation on the part of the committing lender to raise capital in the high yield loan markets. Where the commitment package contains loans with the significant variety of characteristics as are contained in senior secured, junior secured, and high yield unsecured loans, a borrower must be equipped to handle the reporting requirements and ongoing management of lenders with significantly differing agendas. These types of commitments form only a small portion of the loans made to middle-market companies, but when they apply, management must be sophisticated and ready to deal with the complexities associated with understanding the drivers related to each category of lender involved in the commitment.

The Security Agreement

In many respects a security agreement contains the same types or categories of information as a loan agreement. The borrower will make representations, warranties, and covenants, and the agreement will contain provisions relating to events of default similar to those contained in the loan agreement. Although the loan agreement and the security agreement serve two discrete purposes, the agreements work hand in hand with each other. If there is an event of default under the loan agreement, there is automatically an event of default under the security agreement. The converse also holds true.

Where a security agreement diverges from the basic provisions of a loan agreement relates for the most part to the grant of a lien or security interest in a borrower's assets, and in the description of what actions a lender is entitled to take in connection with a loan default.

In reviewing the section of the security agreement dealing with the grant of a lien or encumbrance on the assets of a borrower, a lender is particularly careful in describing the assets subject to the lien. If assets are not specifically described, then the courts have held that the assets are not covered by a lender's security interest and in the event of a default or insolvency, the lender moves over to the unsecured creditor category and in most cases will be significantly disadvantaged.

Under the application of general principles of common law, the grant of a security interest in assets of a borrower creates an equitable interest in the assets. Under certain circumstances, the holder of an equitable interest in a borrower's assets would be subject to legal obligations to fulfill the terms and conditions of obligations relating to the assets, particularly where the assets are contracts of the borrower with unfulfilled obligations. As a result, most security agreements contain provisions specifying the relationship of the lender and the borrower and indicating that the lender is acting as the agent for the borrower in all cases and that the lender is not assuming any obligations under any contract or with respect to any asset of the borrower simply by taking a security interest from the borrower. For the most part, however, these legal obligations do not arise, with respect to contracts or to specified property of a borrower, particularly real property, until a lender forecloses on its security interest and takes title to the contract or real property. At such time, a lender must determine whether it is willing to assume the obligations related to the asset.

In addition to the grant of the security interest, a lender is most interested in determining whether the lender has a first priority security interest in the assets of a borrower. To make this determination, a lender will require a representation and warranty from a borrower and the representation and warranty must be supported by a search of the appropriate regulatory agency for each state in which the borrower operates. The search is performed by attorneys for the lender in most cases, as well as supported by a search performed by attorneys for the borrower. If the search turns up either notices of existing liens or liens that were previously incurred and subsequently paid off but not removed from the public records, the liens must be paid off or terminated on the public record prior to closing the loan.

In connection with the representations and warranties made by a borrower to a lender in a security agreement, the number and intensity of the representations and warranties is less than in the loan agreement. The representations and warranties are focused, however, on ensuring that the assets pledged as collateral for the loan are in fact owned by the borrower, that no other pledges of liens exist with respect to the assets, that the appropriate corporate actions have been taken to grant the lien, that the location of all of the assets is correctly stated, and where specialized assets are involved, that appropriate actions have been taken to ensure that the lien granted to the lender is in fact valid. Specialized assets would include intellectual property and licenses to operate granted by state or federal agencies. Intellectual property such as patents can of course be pledged as collateral to support a loan request; however, in order for a lender to protect its security interest, the public must be placed on notice that the lien exists. This notice may only be given by a specified method that requires a filing in the federal patent and trademark office. Where a state or federal agency has granted a license or permission to operate, the granting of a security interest in the license is a complicated process and may in fact be prohibited. In this respect, various licenses or permissions to operate are granted in the sole and exclusive discretion of various state and federal agencies, and as a result, even though a borrower may desire to pledge its license to operate, which is normally quite valuable, as security for a loan, lenders are not guaranteed the opportunity to take over the operating license by merely taking a security interest in the license. In contrast, a lender may be required to work its way through a complicated process prior to being granted a license, and the risks associated with this process are normally stated with a great deal of particularity in the security agreement.

Every state has adopted some form of what is commonly known as the Uniform Commercial Code. Each state's version of the Uniform Commercial Code varies slightly from the remaining states' versions of the code, but the general principles applicable to the code may be applied across the board. It is Article 9 of the Uniform Commercial Code that deals with the relationship of lender to borrower in secured transactions. This article deals not only with the creation of a security interest, but also its perfection—or the manner in which the remainder of the world knows that a lender has an interest in the property of a borrower—and the manner in which the parties operate upon the occurrence of an event of default. Virtually all security agreements refer to a particular state's version of the Uniform Commercial Code as governing the terms and conditions of the security agreement and particularly the events surrounding the grant of a security interest and the rights of a lender in connection with an event of default under the loan or security agreement.

Perfecting a security interest is defined as the act that is performed by a lender that informs the rest of the world that the lender has taken a security interest in certain specified assets of the borrower. This act or notice of this act, under the terms of the applicable Uniform Commercial Code, ensures that in an event of default by the borrower, when the proceeds of the sale of assets subject to the security interest are sold, the lender with the perfected security interest will receive the proceeds of the sale in priority to any other creditors of the borrower. It should be noted that the perfection process is normally affected by a lender filing what is known as a financing statement in the places required by the Uniform Commercial Code or other applicable statute. Most recently, the filing requirements have been simplified such that a lender will normally file with the secretary of state in the state of incorporation of the borrower as well as with any secretary of state located in any state in which the borrower has operations or where collateral is located. The primary exception to this rule relates to intellectual property and negotiable instruments. Security interests in intellectual property, such as patents, trademarks, and service marks, are perfected by filing a financing statement with the United States Patent and Trademark Office, while security interests in negotiable instruments are perfected by obtaining possession of the negotiable instrument.

As noted earlier, where the asset to be used to secure the loan is a license issued by a state or federal agency, such as a license to engage in banking, or a license issued by the Federal Communications Commission (FCC) for operation of a telecommunications carrier, a radio station operator, or a television station operator, there may be no way to perfect a lender's security interest in the absolute. That is, in the event that a lender forecloses on the operator, and the lender sells the license to the station at auction, before the purchaser may own and operate the station, the FCC must approve the new owner. In these cases, the lender will solicit the good faith efforts of the existing owner to cooperate in facilitating the transfer of a license to either the lender or more likely to a third party purchaser who is successful in bidding for the license in the event that the borrower has defaulted under the loan documentation.

Collateral Assignment Where a borrower has a contract that contains valuable rights to receive revenue or where the contract secures rights for the borrower to operate a division or segment of its business under the terms of the contract, an agreement separate from the security agreement may be entered into with the lender. Under the terms of this separate agreement, known generally as a collateral assignment agreement, the borrower will transfer to its lender an equitable right to take advantage of the contract and either continue to receive designated revenue or continue to operate a division or segment of the borrower's business after the occurrence of an event of default.

In order to ensure that the lender receives the benefit of the collateral assignment, the lender will secure a consent on the part of the borrower and any other party to the contract that is subject to the collateral assignment. The consent will preclude the borrower from changing any terms of the contract, and require that any party to the contract will, prior to terminating the contract, provide the lender with notice and a reasonable opportunity to cure any default in the terms and conditions of the contract that the borrower has failed to cure after notice of default. The lender will also secure the agreement of each party to the collaterally assigned contract to recognize the lender as the successor in interest to the borrower after any borrower event of default where the lender takes over the contract. In the event that the lender succeeds to the interest of the borrower, the contracting party will also agree that no event of default will be declared by virtue of the lender taking over the contract.

The Intercreditor Agreement

When a borrower owes obligations to two or more lenders, the relative rights of the lenders may be difficult to determine unless all of the parties enter into an agreement that describes the relationship of each of the loans. While on the surface, this issue may seem reasonably easy to evaluate and set up rules that protect each of the lenders, the actual implementation is in many respects quite difficult. For example, where a borrower has a revolving credit facility with one lender and a secured term loan with another lender, as long as the borrower is in compliance with the loan agreements there is no problem. However, when a borrower becomes financially troubled and begins to sell off assets to survive, complications arise in the lending relationships. A classic example of this situation is where the borrower sells assets securing the term loan and deposits the proceeds of the sale in its bank account. Invariably a lender extending a revolving credit facility will impose a cash management system, including a lockbox arrangement, on the borrower. If the borrower enters a formal insolvency proceeding after its sale of assets but before paying down the term loan with the proceeds of the asset sale, there will be a fight with the revolving credit holder over who is entitled to the cash from the sale. The revolver lender typically negotiates a security interest in the accounts receivable, proceeds of the accounts receivable, and the borrower's bank accounts. If the asset sale proceeds are deposited in the borrower's bank account prior to filing, the revolving lender will use the proceeds to pay down its revolving credit facility, and the term loan lender may be out of luck unless there is an intercreditor agreement in place to trace the cash flows within the company.

In contrast with the situation where two lenders have different sets of collateral to secure their loans, a typical circumstance involving an intercreditor agreement involves multiple lenders making one loan in the aggregate to the borrower. These loans may be described as syndications or participations, but in each case, a group of lenders will be looking to one pool of cash to divide among the lending group. This traditional intercreditor situation obligates each member of the lending syndicate to maintain its pro rata percentage of the borrower's loan under all circumstances. The prototype case is where one member of the syndicate serves as the bank of record for the borrower. In this capacity the bank will normally have access to all of the bank accounts of the borrower, its cash management system, and all of its negotiable instruments or investment securities. In the absence of an intercreditor agreement, the bank of record would be in a superior position if the borrower were to default on the syndicated loan, in that it could sweep all of the borrower's accounts and apply the proceeds to the outstanding loan amount in which the lender had participated. The intercreditor agreement would supercede or override the ability of the bank of record to gain an advantage simply because the lender was closest to the borrower's money. Under the terms of the intercreditor agreement, the bank of record would be obligated to return to the borrower's bank agent any of the monies captured that were in excess of the lender's pro rata amount of the aggregate loan, plus its pro rata portion of any expenses incurred by the bank syndicate in pursuing collections efforts.

Subordination Agreement   A close relative of the intercreditor agreement is the subordination agreement. In a subordination agreement, instead of agreeing how to split proceeds associated with the liquidation of assets to pay off a loan, the parties agree as to the priority of payments among the lenders. Subordination agreements vary in intensity based on the degree to which the subordinated lenders agree to abstain from taking actions to collect payment on loans in default.

In subordination agreements where the parties have relatively equal bargaining power, but the loans are clearly ranked in order of priority of repayment, a subordinated lender may agree not to take any actions against a borrower for a fixed period of time. This period is known as a standstill period. These periods of time vary, depending on the type of loan, from 30 days to as much as 180 days. At the end of the standstill period, even though a subordinated lender may begin collection activities, the subordination agreement will typically require the subordinated lender to pay all proceeds of sales of collateral to the senior lender until the senior lender is paid in full, and all of the senior lender's expenses incurred in connection with the borrower's default have been reimbursed. Only then may the subordinated lender begin to apply the proceeds of any asset sales toward repayment of its loan.

Where the bargaining power of the lenders is not equal, a senior lender may require an absolute standstill. Where an absolute standstill is required, the senior lender will extract a variety of covenants from the subordinated lender. These covenants include agreements not to accept any payments from the borrower until the senior debt has been paid in full, and agreements not to amend or transfer the subordinated debt instruments or enter into any transaction that would in any way alter the relative priority of payments to the two lenders.

A normal carve-out from the prohibition against payments on subordinated debt includes an ability on the part of the borrower to pay interest, but not principal, on the subordinated debt as long as the borrower is not in default under any of its obligations under the senior debt or the subordinated debt. This carve-out terminates simultaneously with the occurrence of an event of default under any of the borrower's loan agreements. From the moment of default forward, any payments made by the borrower to the subordinated lender must be returned to the senior lender. In addition, even after an event of default occurs with respect to the subordinated lender, no action may be taken by the subordinated lender that would result in an execution on a judgment or similar claim against the borrower until the senior lender is paid in full. It is also customary in subordination agreements for the subordinated lender to grant a power of attorney to the senior lender to take any and all actions that would otherwise be available to a subordinated lender to protect its rights related to the obligation owed to it by the borrower.

Guarantees

There are two basic kinds of guarantees with dramatically different opportunities for recourse by the holder of the guarantee. The guarantee most often used by lenders is known as a guarantee of payment and performance. The differentiating characteristic of a guarantee of payment and performance is an ability of the lender to make a claim directly against the guarantor notwithstanding the fact that the lender actually loaned funds to an entity different than the guarantor. In this case, the guarantor has received some benefit or consideration, either direct or indirect, as a result of the lender extending credit to the borrower. Traditional relationships include an owner of a business who guarantees business debt, a parent corporation that guarantees the debt of a subsidiary, or a family member who guarantees the debt of another member of the family. Although some guarantees are obtained from investors with little or no relationship to the business other than the compensation received in exchange for a guarantee, this type of financial relationship has waned in recent years as high net worth individuals have become increasingly sophisticated in the compensation and equity negotiated in exchange for investments in the nature of a guarantee.

In contrast with a guarantee of payment and performance, a much less often used guarantee is known as a guarantee of collection. In this type of guarantee, a lender must exhaust all of its remedies against the borrower before proceeding against the guarantor. As might be expected, commercial lenders can rarely be convinced to use this type of guarantee, and when requested, the typical response is that the lender will gladly give up its rights to collateral upon payment in full so that the guarantor may proceed directly against the borrower. It is customary also for a lender to take the position that by virtue of the relationship between the borrower and the guarantor, it is the guarantor who is in the best position to maximize value out of the proceeds of the sale of borrower assets.

In the process of negotiating a guarantee, a lender will clarify the type of guarantee being given by the guarantor as a preliminary condition of the guarantee. That is, the lender will make it abundantly clear in the loan guarantee that upon the occurrence of an event of default, the lender may proceed directly against the guarantor and the proceeding may begin immediately upon the default. After the clarification, the lender and guarantor establish ground rules relating to the ongoing relationship between the borrower and the lender. In this regard, the lender will retain the right to enforce the guarantee even if the loan agreement is amended as to its term, and the collateral covered is changed, to the extent that any collateral is released as security for the loan, changes resulting from any adverse impacts on the financial position of the borrower. The guarantee will not be changed with respect to any individual guarantor to the extent that other guarantors are released from their guarantees, with or without the permission of the borrower or the remaining guarantors.

It should be noted that with respect to individual guarantees, most lenders will require both husband and wife to sign the guarantee. This joint guarantee permits the lender to gain access to property owned jointly by the guarantors. In contrast, if only one spouse signs the guarantee, then property held in the name of the husband and wife may not be accessed by the lender in any attempt to collect on the guarantee.

In the context of guarantees granted by more than one individual, the nature of the guarantee is significant. If the guarantee is joint and several, this means that a lender may proceed against any of the guarantors that the lender believes is best positioned to satisfy the amount of the defaulted loan. As a result, fierce negotiations take place in the context of guarantees granted by several guarantors where the ability to repay the amounts guaranteed vary significantly from guarantor to guarantor. For example, where two individuals guarantee a business loan, and both individuals are owners of the business, if one of the owners has a net worth significantly in excess of the other owner, the wealthier owner will attempt to negotiate out of a joint and several guarantee. In these cases of unequal repayment power, the fight between the lender and the guarantors is to reduce the amount of the guarantee to an amount equal to the guarantors' percentage ownership of the borrower in most cases.

If the guarantors are unable to negotiate several guarantees, or guarantees related to some fixed percentage of the borrowed amounts, rather than the entire loan, sophisticated guarantors will require all owners of the borrower or all guarantors to enter into an agreement that obligates the various owners to reimburse the wealthiest guarantor for amounts paid in satisfaction of the guarantee. This agreement protects a high net worth guarantor in the event that a lender determines to proceed solely against the guarantor having the highest probability of satisfying the defaulted loan amount. In many cases the high net worth guarantor will simply pay the guaranteed amount rather than suffer through litigation that is in most cases a futile effort at slowing the lender down or an effort to defer the guarantee payment while the borrower attempts to recover from its financial crisis.

In many guarantees, particularly where all of the guarantors are owners of a business rather than high net worth sponsors, the agreement will divide the ultimate liability for the loan default into amounts that equal the pro rata ownership of the guarantors. It should be noted that these agreements do not bind a lender, and the lender will remain free to collect the entire defaulted obligation from the guarantor most financially able to satisfy the obligation. It will then be the obligation of the paying guarantor to collect from the remaining owners their pro rata portion of the defaulted loan, if possible.

In the negotiation of the guarantee agreement, lenders will in many cases request that the owners of a business sign a guarantee unlimited as to amount so that the borrower can increase its borrowing capacity without having to get guarantees signed each time a loan amount increases. This unlimited guarantee should not be signed by a guarantor for obvious reasons, and the guarantee that is signed should have a stated amount as the maximum liability assumed by the guarantor. Careful evaluation of most commercial and community bank guarantees will reveal that the guarantee normally does have a stated guaranteed amount, but that contained in the covenants section of the guarantee is an agreement that a guarantor will also pay the lender's cost of collection and attorney's fees. Attorney's fees typically will be stated as a percentage of the loan amount—routinely 15 percent is used—and a guarantor will be responsible for these costs in addition to the guaranteed loan amount unless the guarantor is able to negotiate the collection costs and attorney's fees out of the maximum amount of the guarantee.

Categories of Debt Instruments

For the typical borrower, the alternative loan types available can be described in two broad categories. These categories are generally known as secured and unsecured loans. Within each category of loan is a multiple of choices for a potential borrower. Depending on the type of entity that will be the borrower, loan alternatives will quickly be focused on a few choices.

For large companies with excellent credit, national lenders will compete for their business with aggressive loan proposals where the lender is secured by the general creditworthiness of the borrower. These loans are extended in most cases without security being pledged as collateral for the loan. In contrast, most loans to lower-middle-market companies are made by commercial or community banks, and the loans are secured either by the assets or cash flow of the borrower or by the guarantee of the owners of the business. These secured loans are straightforward instruments, with fixed repayment schedules where the use of loan proceeds will fund borrower expenditures for equipment purchases, working capital, or small acquisitions.

Secured Loans

Secured loans can generally be described as loans tailored to match the fixed assets or cash flows of a company. The amount of a secured loan is tied to either the level or amount of assets or the amount of cash flows of the borrower. These two general categories of loans are referred to as either asset-based financings or cash flow–based financings. In either case, the loans are secured by a pledge of the assets of a company.

Asset-Based Financings   The traditional definition of asset-based financing refers to a loan extended to a borrower in the form of a revolving credit facility or term loan. In many cases a borrower will combine a revolving credit facility with a term loan.

An asset-based loan in the form of a revolving credit facility focuses on the level of current assets of a company. A loan amount is negotiated up front and the amount of the loan that a lender funds will be a function of the levels of assets generated or held by the borrower. Typical revolving credit facilities apply a negotiated percentage to the level of accounts receivable and the level of inventory in order to determine the variable levels of borrowing capacity available to a borrower during the life of a loan. While negotiated availability depends on the percentage applied to each category of assets, acceptable percentage levels for accounts receivable hover around 80 percent, and for inventory, around 50 percent. As the credit quality and history of a borrower with a lender start to provide a lender with a stable view of the financial performance of a borrower, the percentages applicable to inventory and to accounts receivable will increase in each category.

Before applying an applicable percentage to the borrower's assets, a lender will require a borrower to prepare a borrowing base certificate. In the borrowing base certificate, the lender will specify the types of inventory and accounts receivable that do not qualify for inclusion in the calculation of borrowing availability. This concept of qualification is known as eligibility. When eligibility is applied to accounts receivable, aging and credit quality are two important factors. A lender will exclude from eligibility any accounts owed to the borrower that are older than a specified aging. This aging process may exclude accounts as early as 90 to 120 days from the date of invoice. In addition, where an account is related to payments due from a specified customer or affiliate of a specified customer, and if the customer has other accounts outstanding that exceed the aging limits, the current amounts will also be excluded from eligibility even though they may be 30, 60, or 90 days old. Where an account receivable relates to a governmental agency, the account receivable is excluded from eligibility unless the agency has given permission to the lender to collect the account in an event of default under the loan agreement. Eligibility applied to inventory normally is a function of the last period of time since the category of inventory has been used or sold. Inventory that is slow moving, stale, out of date, or damaged in some respect will not be included in the eligibility calculation. Time periods used to determine whether inventory is slow moving vary by industry, but in most cases the period of time that inventory can sit and still be counted would not extend beyond one year.

Another form of accounts receivable lending is known as factoring. Factoring is slightly different in the legal relationship between the lender and the borrower in that the lender is actually purchasing the account receivable instead of lending against it. While the factor purchases the account receivable, the result to most borrowers is transparent because cash is advanced and all collections from the account must be used to satisfy the advance. The economic consequences of a factoring transaction are in most cases twofold. First a higher interest rate to the borrower is charged than in a traditional asset-based loan. Second, the factor typically advances a lower percentage of the account receivable up front in order to ensure that when all accounts are settled, the accounts receivable that are uncollectible will not exceed the amounts advanced to the borrower, since the factor has purchased legal title to the accounts.

Purchase order financing is also included in the category of asset-based lending. Lenders making advances based on purchase orders will typically charge higher rates of interest than traditional asset-based lenders. In order to underwrite purchase order financing, a lender must understand not only the creditworthiness of the borrower, but also the creditworthiness of the customer. In addition, a lender must be positioned to evaluate the probability that the borrower has access to materials and labor or inventory to support the purchase order. As a result, this type of lending is people intensive for a lender and since the pricing of a loan must take into account the costs of a lender managing the loan process, the pricing to a borrower is higher here than in traditional lending situations.

Real property loans are normally stand-alone transactions for most borrowers in the lower middle markets. The loan for an average borrower is typically used to purchase office space, warehouse space, retail location, or other property associated with the operation of a local business. Given the aggregate purchase price of most real property, the loan term must be much longer than the typical loan term for an asset-based loan, and as a result, real estate loans are separated from the day-to-day or operations financing activities of a company. Typical loan terms for real property transactions are a minimum of seven years, and depending on the lender and market conditions, may extend to 30 years. Preferred pricing for these loans is a fixed interest rate for what is known as the permanent loan. A permanent loan is placed on a parcel of real property when construction is complete. Most construction loans are for shorter periods of time, normally three years or less. Due to the shorter terms, most construction loans are variable interest rate loans. The interest rates typically have a base rate of the lender's prime rate or LIBOR, coupled with a margin of plus 1 percent for a prime base rate and plus 200 basis points for a LIBOR base rate. Currently, where a commercial or community bank has access to LIBOR funds, a borrower will choose LIBOR because the rate is approximately two percentage points less than prime.

Secured lending instruments have exploded in structure and alternatives over the past 10 years with various types of asset pools being used to secure the issuance of publicly traded debt by a variety of public and private entities. These securitized public offerings are not available directly to smaller companies, but the smaller companies participate by transferring locally originated loans to entities that aggregate the loans and in turn sell securities backed by the streams of income collected from the individual loans. The earliest of these loan aggregations involved pooling of home mortgages. Known generally as collateralized mortgage obligations, this security class spread to automobile loans and various other consumer-based credit. The concept underlying each of these facilities is a security based on a widely aggregated base of payors that spreads the risks of default into tiny pieces. This risk profile makes the security aggregating the loans relatively safe as an investment, and as a result this class of security has flourished in the public markets. For smaller businesses, the opportunity here is to be the local originator of the home loan or consumer loan and then to sell the loan to the entity aggregating the loans. A mortgage broker or automobile loan broker may enter this market with much lower levels of capital than those required to start a community bank.

Cash Flow–Based Financings   Cash flow–based loans are considered when a borrower generates significant cash flows from an asset base that is relatively small. Typical borrowers meeting this definition will be licensed or regulated by state or federal agencies, or companies with significant intangible assets based on intellectual property discoveries controlled by the company. Although the borrower's loan amounts are based on the calculation of its cash flows, the lender will normally take a security interest in all of the company's assets in order to control the asset base that is generating the cash flows in the event of a default under the loan agreement.

In companies having strong cash flows, lenders calculate the amount of borrowing capacity by placing a multiple on the agreed-upon cash flows of the borrower. As a starting point, the borrower will provide its EBITDA to the lender as part of the loan request. In connection with underwriting the loan, a lender will make certain adjustments to the borrower's calculation of EBITDA in order to normalize the calculation and better understand the stability of the borrower's cash flows. For example, if a borrower exhibits tendencies that indicate recurring requirements for capital expenditures such that cash will be routinely required to support the identified purchases, the lender will add back amounts to the depreciation calculation, in effect reducing EBITDA.

After the borrower and lender agree upon a stabilized calculation of EBITDA, the lender will apply its specific underwriting guidelines to the calculation to determine the amount of the loan and the schedule of amortization applicable to the loan. Interest rates are normally within a tight band for lenders falling into similar categories. That is, the interest rate that a borrower is quoted from a commercial or community bank will not vary significantly among all similar lenders; however, rates may vary dramatically when comparing a local commercial lender with a national asset-based lender. In addition, the amount of leverage that each of these lenders will permit in connection with their underwriting guidelines varies significantly. As the lender permits more leverage, the interest rates or pricing of the loans will escalate as well.

Within any specific group of lenders, interest rates or pricing and loan costs and fees will vary depending on the loan portfolio strategy of the lender. Lenders desiring to grow loan portfolios, particularly where a lender is attempting to gain access to a new industry segment, may be significantly more aggressive in pricing, costs, and fees than under their normal underwriting guidelines. Borrowers should perform due diligence on the local lending environment in order to determine whether any of these characteristics apply.

In connection with determining loan size, a lender will test the borrower's financial statement presentation against its underwriting guidelines. A minimum and a maximum financial ratio are tested first, and these ratios are normally supplemented by ratios determined by the lender to be important to understanding the financial health of the borrower. The two primary ratios are minimum debt service coverage and maximum leverage.

Minimum debt service coverage compares a borrower's cash flow available to pay debt with the expected repayment schedule of the lender. A typical minimum debt service coverage ratio would be 1.25 to 1 in order to provide for a cushion between the amount of debt service expected and the cash flow generated by the borrower. Where the business plan of the borrower assumes revenue growth over time or economies of scale related to an acquisition, the lender and borrower will negotiate graduated payments of principal in addition to regularly scheduled interest payments. These scaled amortization schedules might start with no principal amortized in year one of the loan, and during the life of a seven-year loan, start with 5 or 10 percent amortization of the loan in the early years and back-end load the amortization schedule to permit the borrower's growth or economies of scale to mature. Minimum debt service coverage is a ratio that does not move significantly with market trends to either increase or decrease the amount of leverage that is acceptable for a borrower at any given moment.

Maximum leverage ratio is a concept that does fluctuate with market conditions. As the capital markets ease general credit availability, lenders will increase the amount of leverage permitted in connection with a loan request. In today's environment, capital providers are bullish on the economy and as a result, maximum leverage ratios have moved up and are consistently seen in the 5.5 to 6.0 to 1 range. The ratio measures a company's total debt, including senior and junior debt, to the company's EBITDA. Although there is no direct relationship between the absolute amount of debt that a company can carry as there is in the calculation of the minimum debt service coverage ratio, the indirect relationship and parameters have developed over time and are normally recognized by virtually all lenders. In addition to the calculation of maximum debt service coverage ratio, all senior secured lenders will measure the amount of senior debt extended to a borrower in relation to the borrower's EBITDA. This ratio is generally recognized by all senior lenders and these lenders' proposals will fall within industry guidelines of 3 to 4 to 1 range. The ratio will vary with market conditions and, as is applicable with maximum leverage, the factors underlying lender willingness to move up or down relate to the general strength of the economy and the current interest rate environment. In other words, when interest rates are low, debt service is reduced and leverage multiples should be higher than when interest rates are high and debt service levels, accordingly, will also be higher.

Junior Secured Loans For larger leveraged transactions, the supply of capital has increased significantly in the previous two years. As returns on investments in venture capital, private equity, and public securities have fallen, entities that aggregate capital have increasingly looked to the debt markets for stability of returns and also increased returns. This desire has accelerated with public market performance and the increased volatility associated with investments in all but the macro-cap (enterprise value greater than $1 billion) companies. Junior secured loans are now being placed by private investors, by hedge funds, by specialized lending funds, and increasingly by mezzanine funds.

A junior secured loan is underwritten by a lender by examining the portion of a borrower's assets, cash flow, or enterprise value that is not used to support a senior secured loan. For example, if a senior lender makes advances based on 80 percent of accounts receivable and 50 percent of inventory, then in theory there should be room for a loan based on the probability of collecting the proceeds of assets sold or collected that are excluded from the senior secured borrowing base. Where a lender is considering a loan without including accounts receivable or inventory as support for the loan, the lender will underwrite the junior secured loan based on the lender's evaluation of the enterprise value of the borrower. In evaluating enterprise value, the lender will consider the liquidation or sale or residual value of the borrower's goodwill, trademarks, patents, licenses, or franchises. In effect, a junior secured loan permits a borrower to fully utilize its borrowing base and residual intangible value.

Junior secured loans initially were limited to transactions in which the borrower desired to make an acquisition or in a distressed recapitalization, but increasingly these loans have gained favor as an instrumental part of an ongoing borrower's capital structure, and increasingly are giving mezzanine lenders significant competition for funds required by a borrower to close the gap between senior secured facilities and available equity. Junior secured lenders have priced their loans slightly lower than mezzanine lenders and typically do not require equity kickers as part of their loan package requirements. In this respect, particularly for private equity funds and companies backed by private equity funds, the borrower is able to increase leverage and reduce equity required to support a leveraged transaction, effectively increasing the size of the private equity fund by the amount of incremental leverage available for use in connection with the acquisition of target companies.

Unsecured Loans

An unsecured loan is extended by a lender where the borrower has either a long history of loan compliance with a lender or an extremely strong balance sheet. Commercial and community bank lenders make unsecured loans on a frequent basis to borrowers that have track records of success within their communities. These loans normally take the form of a line of credit made available to the borrower when needed or a term loan where the amount requested is more than the borrower wants to expend at any one given time in order to preserve liquidity in the short term. The lender will still underwrite the loan request in a manner that is similar to a secured loan; however, the lender in these cases relies on the strength of the general creditworthiness of the borrower to support the loan request.

Unsecured loans are documented by a loan agreement setting forth the terms of the loan and any financial covenants or other underwriting guidelines determined by the lender to be important measures of the borrower's ongoing financial strength. In many cases the financial covenants are not related to levels of debt that can be serviced, because most companies that qualify for unsecured loans have low leverage ratios. It is more likely that the financial covenants used to measure the performance of the borrower, if any are required, will relate to profitability, net worth, or perhaps revenue of the borrower, and the measurements are in many cases performed only annually.

Pricing of unsecured loans in the context of a relationship transaction between a local commercial lender or community bank and a local borrower will normally be slightly higher than the pricing of a comparable asset-based loan. Although the amount of risk between the two loans may be negligible for a local business with excellent credit, the capital markets and underwriters assess the risk as being higher and as a result the interest rate will be higher.

As the size of the borrower increases and the size of the loan increases, the opportunity for obtaining unsecured loans is reduced in most cases. There are always exceptions to the rule, and in this case the exceptions are sizable. For example, nationally recognized and financially stable companies included in the Fortune 500, with high credit ratings, have access to the commercial paper market. As stated earlier, companies with access to this market issue debt in one-, two-, and three-month terms at the best interest rates available. These large commercial transactions are completed quickly and efficiently in the U.S. capital markets, but access to these markets is limited to only a few financially strong companies.

High Yield Debt In contrast to the commercial paper markets, where excellent credit is a prerequisite to borrowing funds, the capital markets have always been receptive to unsecured borrowings known as high yield debt, and from time to time also called junk bonds. Although the market window for high yield debt opens and closes on a regular basis, investment bankers have raised billions of dollars recently in the form of high yield debt transactions.

The anatomy of a high yield transaction involves a borrower intending to make an acquisition or to borrow funds to permit the borrower to make capital expenditures in advance of generating revenue from the newly acquired assets. With its business plan in hand, a potential high yield candidate would make a presentation to its investment bankers that couples its senior debt, junior debt, and equity with the proceeds of the high yield offering in order to fully fund its business plan or acquisition.

Recent successful high yield offerings have taken place in the telecommunications industry where switching equipment, fiber, routers, and related communications capital expenditures were made in order to permit the company to provide service to customers. These business plans supported an enormous appetite for capital in the telecommunications industry, especially following the initial deregulation of the industry, in the hopes that capital deployed for infrastructure could be paid for by an infinite demand on the part of consumers for data and voice telecommunications services. Although the initial offerings were successful, the anticipated levels of usage and customers never materialized and much of the debt was never repaid, and as a result, huge losses were taken in this market segment by the initial high yield investors and equity sponsors.

The lure of high yield debt continues for investors today, but the target markets have contracted significantly. Now, instead of funding expenditures designed to provide a channel to incremental customers, the high yield market is focused on providing a component of the capital structure of an acquiring company in connection with leveraged acquisitions. As a result, high yield loans in today's market are being underwritten by existing and well-defined cash flow streams, or underwritten by confirmation and analysis of cost savings in leveraged transactions for industry segments where growth cannot be assumed.

High yield debt is attractive because it is unsecured debt and it is available at relatively attractive pricing. Current high yield transactions are being priced in the 10 to 12 percent annual interest rate range for companies with excellent but not top tier credit, and in the 14 to 16 percent range for companies that can obtain credit ratings, even though the rating is at the lowest recognized level for the rating agencies. In addition to its attractive pricing, attractive that is in relation to the cost of equity which would be priced much higher in terms of expected return, high yield debt is serviced with interest only during the life of the debt and upon maturity a lump sum of the principal outstanding is due and payable. Because of the time and effort associated with the placement of high yield debt, one of its less desirable features is the lack of an ability to pay off the loan prior to some stated passage of time. In many cases, high yield debt is noncallable for a period of three years and thereafter callable only upon payment of a prepayment penalty of 1 to 3 percent of the aggregate amount of debt. In times where interest rates are falling, this noncallable feature delays the advantages that a borrower may receive in connection with reduced debt service associated with refinancing its debt.

Borrowers find that accessing the capital markets for high yield debt is faster than going public. Investment bankers assessing a privately held borrower's ability to raise funds in the high yield market will propose a time line that is significantly shorter than that associated with raising equity. The reason for the expedited time frame is that high yield debt is raised in a private placement. Most offerings are made under Rule 144A promulgated by the Securities and Exchange Commission (SEC). Rule 144A is available to issuers of high yield debt who only approach institutional investors meeting extremely high financial strength requirements. Individual investors may not participate even if they quality as high net worth candidates. In connection with a Rule 144A offering, a borrower's investment bankers will normally have investors ready, willing, and able to fund large loan amounts that range from a low of $50 million to amounts exceeding $1 billion. These transactions are closed in a matter of weeks in many cases.

In connection with high yield debt offerings, the borrower will agree to register the debt securities with the SEC. The registration process must be completed within a fixed time frame or penalties may be assessed by the holders of the high yield debt. Registration of the debt securities provides market liquidity for the purchasers of the high yield debt, and as a result, the borrower is issuing a security with desirable market characteristics.

Mezzanine Financings   In attempting to describe the characteristics of mezzanine finance, the parameters are so divergent that it is difficult to describe with specificity all of the elements that might be included in the definition of mezzanine debt. As a result, most writers attempting to define mezzanine debt would simply state that it resides in the capital structure of a company between senior debt and equity, and maintains some elements of debt and equity.

Mezzanine finance is used primarily to bridge the gap between equity and debt in acquisitions and recapitalizations. Mezzanine lenders rarely take control of a company. Even though a mezzanine lender may take equity in connection with a mezzanine loan, the equity is not designed to provide the lender with an ownership position in the borrower. Rather, the so-called equity kicker is used as a tool to provide an overall higher return on its investment than just the interest rate charged. The form of equity taken is normally a warrant to purchase shares in the borrower. The purchase price of the warrant is nominal, and the aggregate amount of shares subject to be purchased under the warrant is determined by estimating an amount of money to be paid at the end of the loan term that, coupled with current and deferred interest under the mezzanine debt, will yield an overall internal rate of return to the mezzanine lender that satisfies its target or hurdle return rate. The value of the warrants is interpolated by reference to the borrower's business plan, taking an assumed industry multiple and the borrower's forecasted EBITDA for the period in which the mezzanine loan comes due, and using these assumed financial markers to determine the value of the borrower at the time the measurement is made. The warrants will be required to be purchased by the borrower from the lender at the end of the term of the loan, and the proceeds of the purchase will be included in the lender's overall internal rate of return calculation.

Mezzanine lenders concentrate their initial underwriting efforts much like an equity investor. That is, these lenders generally will extend credit only to seasoned, mature, and experienced management teams with track records of success in the target industry. Management must have a meaningful opportunity to participate in the upside of the entity through equity ownership, and the equity ownership is under the best of circumstances, offered by well-known and successful private equity sponsors. Sponsorship is important in leveraged transactions given the narrow opportunity for miscues in these deals. In the event of a shortfall in operations, mezzanine lenders may bring additional capital to a borrower, but these lenders want to partner with substantial private equity sponsors that have access to their own capital to participate in any shortfalls.

Only after a mezzanine lender is satisfied with management and with the equity sponsors will the lender evaluate the cash flow of a borrower in order to determine whether to extend mezzanine debt. Normally mezzanine debt is unsecured debt and subordinated to senior secured debt. The subordination feature of mezzanine debt is traditionally a full standstill. That is, while a mezzanine debt holder may receive interest during the life of the senior debt loan, no principal amortization may take place. In addition, upon the occurrence of an event of default under the borrower's senior secured credit facility, the mezzanine lender may take no action to recover its loan until the senior secured facility, including the senior secured lender's fees and expenses, has been paid in full. The subordination provisions also include a requirement that a mezzanine lender return to the senior secured lender any payments received from the borrower after an event of default, including any interest payments.

Although historically unsecured, mezzanine debt is being given a run for its money as capital being made available by junior secured lenders has increased geometrically over the past three years, primarily as a result of hedge funds entering this asset category. The entry of junior secured lenders has squeezed the pricing for mezzanine debt with overall returns being capped in many cases in the high teens, and with no equity component. Senior lenders have gradually embraced the junior secured lender and in today's environment are typically indifferent among junior secured debt, mezzanine debt, and equity, as long as each category is fully subordinated to the rights of the senior lender. Moreover, as the cost of junior secured debt stabilizes, it appears that the overall cost will be less not only in overall cost to the borrower, but in the amount of current interest payments, placing less strain on the senior facility and as a result gaining favor with secured lenders.

Mezzanine lenders' participation and importance grow in sync with growth in multiples paid for corporate acquisition targets. For example, when capital markets price companies in terms of multiples of EBITDA, as the pricing multiples grow from three to five times EBITDA to five to seven times EBITDA, there is a spreading gap between the amount of capital that senior lenders are willing to lend to a company and the amount of equity that equity sponsors are willing to invest in a company.

Historically, the gap has been filled by mezzanine lenders taking positions with creative repayment structures or overall investment return characteristics. These creative structures include dividing the mezzanine interest payments between a currently due and payable rate of interest and coupling the current pay with an accrued interest amount payable in kind over the life of the loan. The payable interest coupon together with the accrued interest payment are then added to the estimated value of equity negotiated by the lender as part of its overall compensation. The aggregate cost of capital including all three components ranges from 18 percent to 25 percent internal rate of return (IRR), required by the mezzanine lender depending on the industry and the overall leverage of the borrower.

When the mezzanine debt includes a deferred interest rate, a borrower is deemed to be paying the deferred interest rate during the life of the loan by issuing periodic notes to the lender equal to the deferred interest rate amount. This deferred payment is called the payable-in-kind (PIK) portion of the interest rate charged by a mezzanine lender. PIK payments are not due until the maturity of the debt instrument. In addition, mezzanine debt holders may permit borrowers to elect to make PIK payments during the life of the loan in lieu of the debt instrument's currently payable interest rate. PIK features may be elected by a borrower to fund capital expenditures that may not otherwise be afforded, or in some cases to avoid having to make payments that could place the borrower into default with its senior lender.

In negotiating mezzanine debt loan agreements, the components of the loan agreement will look quite similar to those contained in senior secured loan documentation, although security documents appear in a relatively small percentage of these deals. The main differences in the two instruments include the interest rate and the manner in which it is paid, no amortization of loan principal during the life of the senior loan, full subordination to the senior credit facility, and financial covenants that are less restrictive than those contained in the senior facility. Mezzanine loans have terms of five to seven years, always structured so that maturity falls after the maturity date of the borrower's senior credit facility. Loan terms are negotiated also to coincide with exit strategies articulated by management of the borrower in any business plan presented to the mezzanine lender in connection with its solicitation of the lender. The exit strategies include the normal business plan alternatives of sale, recapitalization, or initial public offering.

Convertible Debt and Convertible Preferred Stock Convertible debt or preferred stock is issued by a borrower when a lower interest rate or dividend is desired and the borrower is willing to suffer the potential dilution of the lender converting the instrument into common equity of the borrower. Interest or dividend rates on convertible instruments have historically been pegged at a fraction of the normal cost of capital for a borrower, because the investor is betting that the value of the underlying shares of stock, into which the debt will convert, will grow in an amount that exceeds a market rate of return for the instrument.

Pricing strategies for not only the interest or dividend rate, but the share conversion price vary by the strength of the borrower. In public transactions, most of which are structured as convertible preferred stock securities, dividend or interest rates may be 3 to 4 percent below the rate otherwise available to the borrower. For financially healthy companies, the share conversion price may be set at a premium over its current market price in an amount that may be as much as 40 percent. In other words, the company's share price must increase by 40 percent before the holder of the security would be motivated to convert the instrument into equity of the issuer.

In private companies, the instrument is typically structured as debt with an agreed-upon process used to determine the fair market value of the issuer's stock during the life of the debt instrument. In established companies with stable cash flows, the purchaser of the debt instrument will require the issuer to buy the instrument back at fair market value at designated times during the life of the loan based on the then current company appraisal. In growth companies, the purchaser normally takes the shares and waits for a traditional exit in the form of a company sale, recapitalization, or initial public offering.

Bridge Loans   Bridge loans can be described in a manner that fits the name by which they are called. That is, a loan is advanced by a private or commercial lender that assists the borrower in bridging the time gap between its need for cash and some well-defined liquidity event. Bridge loans are normally fixed amount term loans due within 12 months of issuance. While these loans may be secured or unsecured the majority of bridge loans are unsecured, generally with no payments of either principal or interest due until the maturity date of the loan for bridge loans with 30- to 90-day maturities and for longer-term bridge loans made in the context of venture capital investments. Interest rates charged for bridge loans vary by industry and strength of the borrower, but a typical rate would be 8 to 10 percent in today's interest rate environment for an early stage company. For more mature companies, and perhaps counterintuitive to normal pricing models, the interest rate would be higher.

Where a bridge loan is made in order to provide a growth or technology-based company time to finalize a debt or equity financing, the bridge loan is typically coupled with one of two equity-flavored attributes. In addition to the stated interest rate on the bridge loan principal outstanding, the investor extending a bridge loan may require warrants as an equity kicker, or the investor may require that the loan be convertible into specified equity of the borrower at the option of the investor, or both. The amount of warrants issued in connection with a bridge loan is known as warrant coverage. In order to determine the number of warrants to be issued, an investor will state a required percentage of warrant coverage that is needed in order to induce the investor to make the bridge loan. The stated warrant coverage percentage is then applied to the aggregate loan amount, and the product of the percentage and the loan amount is divided by an assumed value per share of the borrower. The quotient yields the number of shares included in the warrant. In early stage investments, the strike price for acquiring the shares subject to the warrant is a nominal amount. As the financial stability of the borrower increases, its bargaining power increases to negotiate a strike price that more closely resembles the fair market value of the company's equity securities.

Specialized Lending

Various categories of specialized lenders and loans have been described in other sections of this book. These lenders and loan types include structures and are based on loan documentation that have previously been described in this chapter. Lenders in this category include the commercial bankers and specialized lenders participating in the Small Business Administration (SBA) loan programs. Loans extended under the auspices of the SBA serve the lower end of middle-market companies, but this segment is where the great majority of middle-market companies reside. SBA loan programs are favored by local commercial lenders and community banks because of the guarantees provided in connection with qualifying loans. Consequently, in the event that an SBA borrower defaults, the local bank is only partially at risk for the potential loan loss. This backup guarantee has increased the appetite of commercial lenders, and for the 2004 calendar year more SBA loans were initiated than at any other time in the life of the SBA loan program, and the record was broken only eight months into the year. With this record pace of lending, the SBA program is currently under stress for gaining access to additional funds to support its guarantees and loan participations, and the program has been temporarily suspended due to its huge success in 2004. Although the SBA program is intended to provide small business with incremental access to capital that might not otherwise be available, many small borrowers are excluded from the benefits of the program due to its significant underwriting and collateral requirements. Most start-up businesses have little if any equity in the business, and as a result if they want to participate in the SBA programs they must pledge personal assets, most frequently in the form of second mortgages on their homes or pledges of their investment securities. If the business owner does not own real property or possess liquid securities, the borrower must secure a high net worth individual to guarantee the SBA loan. In the absence of business assets, personal assets, or outside guarantees, a small business owner will not qualify for the SBA program. Although the program provides capital to many small businesses, it is ironic that the owners who most need the capital do not qualify for any of it.

Another form of specialized lending is the industrial revenue bond. For companies desiring to expand their offices, factories, and warehouses in a local community, there is normally a local governmental authority that provides a mechanism for issuing debt at very low interest rates. Virtually all of these loans are used to buy and develop real property projects. Lenders are in many cases incentivized to purchase this debt as part of their obligations to support the local community development efforts. Most of these loans are tax free to the investors and provide lower borrowing rates to the companies borrowing the funds, and the loans will be made only to the extent that the borrower promises that in connection with the development of the facility the company will generate incremental jobs for the local community.

Related to industrial revenue financing is low-income housing finance. Instead of tax benefits at the state level, low-income housing regulations are promulgated at the federal Department of Housing and Urban Development (HUD) level and the tax attributes are embedded in the Internal Revenue Code. In exchange for agreeing to fixed levels of rent that may be charged over the life of a project, a low-income housing developer will obtain favored financing if the project meets all of the HUD requirements. These attributes are based primarily on tax credits available to the real estate developer and its investors. The credits may under certain circumstances be bought and sold, and as such, provide unique incentives for obtaining equity investor support for the projects.

One final type of specialized lending relates to the distressed financial condition borrower considering filing for a formal insolvency. While this type of loan is limited to the insolvency arena, the structure and characteristics of the loan are similar to the characteristics described in this chapter. Generally known as debtor in possession (DIP) lending, this type of loan is negotiated in most cases immediately prior to a borrower filing bankruptcy. Immediately upon filing, the borrower will request that the bankruptcy court approve the loan and grant priority of the DIP lender's security interest over all of the borrower's other creditors. The motion is generally granted; however, this type of loan is normally reserved for distressed borrowers that can make the case for continued revenue streams notwithstanding the insolvency filing. Large retailers and established manufacturers are candidates for this type of loan. Start-up companies and early stage technology companies do not fit the profile for obtaining this type of credit.

Credit Rating and Reporting Agencies

In many of the types of loans discussed in this chapter, access to the described loan is not available unless the borrower has been rated by one of the two main credit rating agencies. These agencies are Standard & Poor's and Moody's. In order to be rated, a borrower will make a presentation to each of the agencies, and depending on the industry, the company's historical financial performance, the leverage of the company, and various other financial measurement indicators and financial ratios, the agency will assign a rating to the company's debt. The designation of rating for each of the companies varies, but the rule applicable to each system is that the higher the credit rating, the lower the interest rate that the borrower will have to pay for debt raised in the public markets.

Each ratings system assigns a grade and a risk associated with a company's debt. The grading falls into two general categories—investment grade and junk grade. High yield debt is issued by companies whose rating is in the junk grade category. Each grade is coupled with a risk factor labeling the borrower as either a higher or lower grade risk within its category.

In addition to the rating agencies, Dun & Bradstreet is a reporting agency that assembles information regarding the payment history and debt levels of a company. In exchange for membership in the reporting agency, a participating member may request and receive credit reports on any company within the Dun & Bradstreet system. Suppliers and vendors participate in the system, and before opening accounts they will normally perform a credit check on the potential customer in order to determine the credit terms that will be extended to the customer.

EQUITY INSTRUMENTS

The capital stock of a company is represented by shares of either common stock or preferred stock. A company can be capitalized with only common stock, but preferred stock is normally issued in addition to common stock and not as a stand-alone equity. Preferred stock and common stock are each entitled to receive dividends, but where a company has outstanding preferred and common stock, the holders of preferred stock are entitled to receive dividends in priority to the holders of common stock.

Common stock can be structured as voting or nonvoting shares. Common stock always represents an ownership interest in a company, and the holder of a voting common stock interest in a company is entitled to vote to elect directors, and to vote on fundamental corporate activities such as mergers and acquisitions. In the context of a sale of the stock of a company capitalized with only common shares, the holders of common stock are entitled to receive their pro rata share of the proceeds of the stock sale, based on the number of shares each shareholder owns over the aggregate number of shares owned by all shareholders. In the context of a corporate liquidation, the holders of common shares are entitled to receive the residual portion of the assets of the company only after all creditors have been paid in full.

Preferred stock can be structured as a traditional straight preferred, convertible preferred, or participating preferred. Traditional preferred stock represents an ownership interest in a company, but in most cases, the preferred has no voting rights. The characteristics of a traditional preferred stock included a fixed dividend and the right to receive the face value of the preferred stock and any dividends prior to the distribution of any assets to the holders of common stock. Straight preferred looks more like debt than equity in many respects because it is paid prior to common stock but after all debt, and it does not share in the capital appreciation of the company. Dividends could be structured as cumulative or noncumulative. That is, if a company were unable to pay a dividend on a noncumulative preferred stock, there would never be an obligation to pay the missed dividend. Conversely, if the company missed a cumulative dividend payment, the dividend would be owed to the preferred stockholders and must be paid in full prior to any distributions, including dividends, to the common stockholders.

Convertible preferred stock is an equity instrument that in many cases would include voting rights based on the number of shares of common stock into which the preferred stock could be converted. In contrast to straight preferred stock, convertible preferred is based on the premise that at any given moment, a greater return may be ascribed to either the face value of the preferred or the fair market value of the common stock into which the preferred may be converted. As a result, the holder of convertible preferred has the luxury of waiting until the time of an exit and then deciding whether to demand repayment of the face value of the preferred stock, plus any accrued or cumulative but unpaid dividends, or to convert the preferred into common shares. The election made by the holder will depend on which alternative results in a higher return or greater proceeds. For example, if a company is being sold for $1,000,000 and a preferred holder owns $100,000 of convertible preferred that can be converted into 20 percent of the company, the holder would elect to convert into common and receive $200,000 or 20 percent of the sale proceeds.

Participating preferred is perhaps the best of all worlds for an investor in that the holder takes priority over the common shareholders in terms of proceeds of a sale or liquidation, and in addition, after receiving the face value of the preferred plus any accrued or cumulative but unpaid dividends, the holder is entitled to receive a pro rata portion of any remaining assets or proceeds. The pro rata portion of proceeds that a participating preferred holder is entitled to receive is based on the number of shares of common stock into which the preferred could be converted divided by the aggregate number of common shares. Using the same company example as before, the holder of participating preferred would be paid $100,000 first and in priority over all common shares, plus 20 percent of the remaining $900,000 or $180,000. The total proceeds to the holder of participating preferred would be $280,000, making participating preferred the choice of sophisticated investors evaluating early stage or emerging growth companies that are candidates for institutional venture capital investment.

Securing the Equity Investment

In many respects, preparing the materials required to support a request for an equity investment is similar to the exercise performed by companies looking for debt. A company making the request for equity must be able to articulate a reasonable financial plan describing the use of proceeds of the investment. However, instead of preparing financials that are focused on generating cash flow to repay the money invested over a fixed period of time, the company will demonstrate the potential for capital appreciation in the investment through its financial forecasts. Most equity requests are coupled with an analysis of the potential for capital appreciation in connection with specified events. These events are typically known as exit strategies. Historically, companies seeking equity investments have described three general exit strategies as being available to equity investors. These strategies have a variety of combinations and permutations that may be attached to each category, but the basic alternatives include a merger or acquisition taking the form of a sale of the company's stock, an initial public offering of the company's equity securities, or a recapitalization in which the investor's equity position is purchased or redeemed by the company.

Preparing for an equity investment involves a significant amount of time and attention dedicated to generating a business, strategic, and financial plan for the company. The business plan will describe the company's financial plan for using the proceeds of the equity offering in a detailed budget showing inflows of capital and expected outflows. In connection with the financial plan, a company expecting to raise capital will expend a significant amount of time and energy in developing a business plan. The business plan generally is thought of as a road map for a potential investor to follow the thought process of the company as it determines its own rationale for securing the investment.

Business plans take many shapes and forms, but the best plans are those that are succinct yet demonstrate that management has a full understanding of its target market. The plan must also provide an investor with comfort that management has paid attention to the smallest of details.

Great business plans start with an executive summary that concisely states the premises underlying the request for investment. The executive summary is followed by what is commonly known as the setup—in other words, a description of either the problem that the company intends to solve or the market opportunity that the company intends to attack. Once the setup is stated, the business plan must contain a clear statement of the company's objective, which is the company's solution to the problem or unique value proposition that permits the company to attack the market more aggressively than its competitors. While a great solution or unique value proposition will generate interest in many investors, it is the strategy section that sophisticated investors will examine under a microscope. This section includes the company's strategy for accomplishing its objective or solving the problem articulated by the company.

Of significant interest to the potential investor is the financial section supporting the company's strategy. And while revenue forecasted by the company will be tested and examined, a significant investor focus will be on the company's cost structure. The cost structure must line up with the requested equity investment or the offering will inevitably fail.

There are a couple of strategies used by companies in connection with developing cost structures in support of equity requests. The first and perhaps most desirable alternative is known as a fully funded business plan. In this alternative, the company requests capital that will, under its assumed financial model, be the only capital required to achieve its objective. The capital may be a combination of debt and equity. Fully funded business plans are expected when the proposal relates to the acquisition of a target company.

In contrast, where a company's objective is long-term in nature, such as a biotechnology company, the business plan must be designed to match up with significant milestones, since fully funding a budget designed to discover, develop, and market a start-up company's proposed drug candidate is not feasible. In this respect, the company will identify specific milestones that have been recognized by the investment community as demonstrating acceptable progress in the drug discovery or development process. Upon achievement of the specified milestone, and assuming that the company correctly forecasted the costs to achieve the designated milestone, the company would normally expect to go back to the investment community to obtain financing sufficient to achieve its next series of milestones.

In either a fully funded case or a milestone case, the investor will conduct significant due diligence in an effort to confirm the reasonableness of the cost estimates. In addition, where the plan is not fully funded, the investor will carefully evaluate the company's assumptions relating to value created by achieving designated milestones. If the cost structure proposed by the company does not match an investor's analysis, in most cases the investor will pass and not make the investment. Where the analysis relates to value created by milestones, if there is a difference of opinion between the company and the investor as to whether the proposed budget permits the company to realistically claim value appreciation upon achieving certain milestones, the investor may remain engaged in discussions with the company, but only to the extent that the two parties come to an agreement on revised budgets or milestones.

If the investor and company agree on budgets and the ability of management to accomplish the objectives of the business plan, the investor and the company must agree on company valuation in order to determine the amount of equity that will be issued in exchange for the proposed investment. In setting valuation for start-up companies, the process is as much an art as it is a science. Investors look to comparably positioned companies in similar industries as a starting point. Exclusive control over products or potential products with large addressable markets will add value to an investor's initial valuation discussion. Early adoption of the start-up's technology or services by customers willing to pay premium prices for the products or services will also add value. But what is most important to the sophisticated investor is the quality of management involved with the business. Quality in this respect means seasoned, mature, and experienced managers with a track record of success in raising capital, commercializing products, and generating financially rewarding exits for prior investors. A business plan that is not supported by a management team with these characteristics has little probability of successfully raising equity capital in today's financial environment at any valuation for the company.

Where the equity investment is requested in connection with a proposed acquisition or by a company with existing revenue and earnings, the valuation process follows the traditional valuation metrics. These metrics include the discounted cash flow analysis valuation method, the comparable company valuation method focusing on earnings or EBITDA multiples, and the replacement cost method.

EQUITY INVESTMENT DOCUMENTATION

When negotiations between a company and an investor or group of investors begin to stabilize, the parties will initiate the documentation process. Because definitive documentation and final due diligence on the part of an investor is time-consuming and in many cases expensive, the company, but more frequently the investor, will propose a term sheet containing fundamental terms and conditions before definitive documentation is prepared. In the term sheet, the company and the investor will attempt to create an investment structure acceptable to each of the parties. The term sheet that is finally agreed upon will describe the securities that the investor will purchase, and the terms and conditions that must be satisfied prior to closing the transaction. While the actual closing of a transaction may include many documents, the term sheet normally describes the fundamental provisions of four main agreements—the stock purchase agreement, the certificate of incorporation, the investors' rights agreement, and the shareholder agreement.

Equity Investment Term Sheet

In many respects the term sheet is where the most action occurs in the investment process. As the parties negotiate the terms of the deal, valuation of the company and the role of existing management in the ongoing entity will be carefully documented. Several concepts relating to valuation of the company are important to understand in the negotiating process. The impact of slight nuances in the words used to finalize the term sheet can have dramatic impacts on the amount of equity retained by the owners.

Premoney and Postmoney Valuation   The first two concepts relate to understanding the significance of premoney and postmoney valuation, and the factors that impact ownership percentages retained by existing shareholders. While relatively straightforward in concept, understanding premoney valuation also requires an understanding of the terms that are superimposed on the concept. In its most understandable form, premoney valuation simply means the value of a company before an investment is made. When the premoney valuation of a company is added to the amount of investment, the two components are added together to obtain the postmoney valuation. For example:

Premoney valuation	$1,000,000
Investment amount	$1,000,000
Postmoney valuation	$2,000,000

Implicit in the example is an assumption that the owners of the company and the investors will each own 50 percent of the company immediately after the investment is consummated. The calculation of actual percentage will depend on the application of variables that are included in most investment term sheets. These variables include the size of the company's option pool and whether it is calculated on a premoney or postmoney valuation, the type of security being purchased—common stock, preferred stock, or participating preferred—the existence of any outstanding convertible securities, and whether the investor is requiring a multiple return prior to sharing proceeds of an exit event with the remaining common shareholders.

Not understanding the implications of any of these variables can result in severe surprises to management and to the owners of a business raising capital. In evaluating the impact of a term sheet condition requiring a 25 percent option pool, the difference to the current owners between the option pool percentage being applied to the premoney valuation as opposed to the postmoney valuation is dramatic. The difference can be illustrated as follows:

Twenty-Five Percent Option Pool Calculated on a Premoney Valuation Basis

Premoney valuation	$1,000,000	
Premoney capitalization		
Existing owners		750,000 shares
Option pool		250,000 shares
Investment amount	$1,000,000	
Investor shares		1,000,000 shares
Postmoney valuation	$2,000,000	
Fully diluted capitalization		2,000,000 shares

Understanding the impact of the option pool in this example becomes apparent when the shares owned by current shareholders is compared to the shares owned by investors immediately after the investment is consummated. While the example looks like a 50–50 split based on the investment amount, the investors own 1,000,000 shares and the owners own 750,000 at the time the money is invested. In order to understand this dynamic, management and the owners must understand the manner in which investors define the fully diluted capitalization of a company. In the example, the fully diluted capitalization is 2,000,000 shares even though only 1,750,000 shares are issued and outstanding. A sophisticated investor always counts the option pool as being outstanding whether or not the options have been granted and whether or not the options granted have been exercised or even have a reasonable chance of being exercised. So the unwary owner, agreeing to create an option pool without considering the consequences or impact on the company's fully diluted capitalization, will end up with a significant surprise at closing.

To contrast the impact of determining the size of the option pool based on a postmoney calculation, the following example is illustrative:

Twenty-Five Percent Option Pool Calculated on a Postmoney Valuation Basis

Premoney valuation	$1,000,000	
Premoney capitalization		
Existing owners		750,000 shares
Investment amount	$1,000,000	
Investor shares		1,500,000 shares
Option pool		750,000 shares
Postmoney valuation	$2,000,000	
Fully diluted capitalization		3,000,000 shares

The resulting equity ownership retained by the owners in these examples is dramatically different. In the case where no option pool is required, the amount of shares issued to the investor is equal to the amount held by the owners, and each group owns 50 percent of the company. Where the option pool size is determined on a premoney valuation basis, the owners hold approximately 42.85 percent of the company immediately after the investment is closed and the investors hold the remaining 57.15 percent of the outstanding shares. As options are granted and exercised, the owners and the investors will be diluted until the option pool is exhausted and the final capitalization will be owners 37.5 percent, option pool grantees 12.5 percent, and investors will end up with their bargained-for 50 percent. The most dramatic consequences are illustrated in the postmoney example where the owners start at 33.3 percent and the investors start at 66.7 percent. After the grant and exercise of the entire option pool, the final capitalization is dramatically different with the negotiated structure yielding 25 percent for the owners, 25 percent for the option pool grantees, and the investors ending up with the originally agreed-upon 50 percent ownership interest in the company.

In each of these examples, the basic valuation discussion is exactly the same. The company's premoney valuation is $1,000,000 and the investment amount is $1,000,000. The impact of superimposing an option pool on the premoney valuation changes the share dynamics significantly, but the most dramatic impact is when the option pool is discussed with the percentage being applied to the postmoney valuation.

Liquidation Preference   A liquidation preference is discussed in the context of a preferred stock offering of equity. The liquidation preferences can be stated in terms of what is known as straight preferred stock, convertible preferred stock, or participating preferred stock.

Straight preferred stock is essentially equivalent to debt. This type of preferred stock is not commonly used in today's private investment climate, but it still has significance in the public markets. Straight preferred is sold to investors for a face amount, normally coupled with a fixed stated dividend. The dividend may be cumulative or noncumulative, current cash pay, deferred, or payment in kind. Noncumulative dividends must be declared in order for the holder of the preferred to receive the dividend payment amount, while cumulative dividends accrue whether or not the board declares a dividend, and any accrued but unpaid dividends must be paid prior to payment of any dividends on a company's common stock.

A dividend with a current cash payment requirement is normally associated with either investments in public companies or investments made by private equity investors in leveraged acquisitions. In these cases, the company forecasts cash flow sufficient to satisfy the dividend obligation, with most of these investments being associated with larger companies enjoying relatively stable and existing cash flows.

Where the dividend is a current cash payment obligation of a company, in many cases, particularly in connection with leveraged buyouts, the company may under certain circumstances satisfy its dividend obligation by issuing a note for any dividend payment that the company is unable to make. This payment in kind may be required either for cash flow reasons or as the result of applying financial covenants to its balance sheet on a pro forma basis and determining that the dividend could not be paid without violating the financial covenants imposed on the company by a senior lender. In connection with mezzanine financings where the investment is structured as preferred stock, an investor may determine its overall return requirements are too high for the company to support out of cash flow, but the return that is required could be met by deferring a portion of the dividend, or interest payment when structured as subordinated debt, until the end of the investment period.

Convertible preferred stock is structured to permit an investor to hold its investment until a liquidity event or exit, and at the time of the exit, choose between a return of the face amount of the preferred stock plus accrued but unpaid dividends, or to convert the investment into common stock and take its pro rata shares of the proceeds of the liquidity event. The following example assumes that an investment of $1,000,000 was made for convertible preferred stock that equaled 50 percent of the company.

Proceeds of the sale of company stock	$10,000,000
Return of original investment plus accrued but unpaid dividends	$ 1,250,000
Pro rata percentage of sale proceeds	$ 5,000,000

In this example, the holder of convertible stock would elect to convert into common stock and receive $5,000,000 instead of $1,250,000 based on the original investment plus accrued but unpaid dividends.

Conversely, and using the same transaction assumptions, if the sale proceeds had only generated $1,500,000, the holder of the preferred stock would have elected to take $1,250,000 instead of the $750,000 amount calculated by reference to 50 percent of the sale proceeds. In making an election to take the face amount of the investment plus accrued but unpaid dividends, the investment looks more like debt than equity.

The liquidation preference associated with participating preferred stock can take many shapes and forms. The basic participating preferred stock investment returns an investor's original investment, plus accrued but unpaid dividends, and then permits the investor to receive a pro rata share of any remaining assets calculated on the assumption that the preferred stock holders had converted their shares into common stock. The following example assumes that an investment of $1,000,000 was made in exchange for participating preferred stock representing 50 percent of the equity of the company.

Proceeds of the sale of company stock	$10,000,000
Return of original investment plus accrued but unpaid dividends	$ 1,250,000
Net proceeds available for distribution to remaining shareholders	$ 8,750,000
Pro rata percentage of sale proceeds	$ 4,375,000
Total return to participating preferred	$ 5,600,000

In this example, even though the holders of participating preferred stock own 50 percent of the company, the overall percentage of proceeds received in connection with the transaction is 56 percent. Calculating the impact of the participation feature on various sale proceeds scenarios would show that as the total return increases, the percentage of the overall proceeds retained by the holders of participating preferred stock goes down, with the residual percentage approaching the nominal or stated 50 percent rate in the preceding example when the returns are significant.

In addition to the basic participation rights illustrated, in the current investment climate, there are two variations on the basic theme that are at least discussed in many term sheet negotiations. One of the variations is company friendly and one of the variations is favorable to investors.

A company favorable variation includes a preferred stock structure where the investor is subject to a cap on the negotiated participation rights. For example, the participating preferred stock might be structured such that an investor would receive the original investment and then a maximum of three times the amount of the original investment in participation rights. The effect of a cap on participation requires an investor to convert its shares of preferred stock to common stock in order to receive an amount in excess of the cap. By converting, the investor forgoes the participation right. The election to convert to common stock essentially makes the investment a convertible preferred where the returns exceed the cap. In other words, if the return to the holder of preferred stock is capped, the holder converts into the pro rata share of the company in order to receive a larger share of the proceeds. For lower return amounts, the participation feature is protected. Using the example previously assumed where a $1,000,000 investment is made in a company with a $1,000,000 premoney valuation, the alternatives can be illustrated as follows:

Proceeds of the sale of company stock	$10,000,000
Return of original investment plus accrued but unpaid dividends	$ 1,250,000
Net proceeds available for distribution to remaining shareholders	$ 8,750,000
Pro rata percentage of sale proceeds	$ 4,375,000
Total return to participating preferred	$ 5,600,000
Cap on participation (3× investment)	$ 3,000,000
Election to convert to pro rata percentage	$ 5,000,000
Amount to participating preferred	$ 5,000,000

In this example, the impact of the cap resulted in the investor not receiving the full benefit of the participation feature. Because the negotiation of a cap adversely impacts the return available to an investor, only the strongest of companies with the best bargaining positions will be able to achieve or to negotiate this limiting feature.

In contrast to the company favorable variation, an investor favorable variation is negotiated where the company is financially weak or distressed, very early stage where the risk of failure is high, or where the company has raised several rounds of investment, but has yet to achieve significant milestones or revenue. In this variation, the participating preferred will negotiate a multiple return of the original investment, after which the holder of the preferred stock will participate to the extent of the negotiated pro rata percentage of the company. In this example, the preferred stock investment is $1,000,000 and the percentage ownership of the company is 50 percent. Instead of a traditional 1× return of original investment, the investor has negotiated a 2× return.

Proceeds of the sale of company stock	$10,000,000
Return of 2× original investment plus accrued but unpaid dividends	$ 2,250,000
Net proceeds available for distribution to remaining shareholders	$ 7,750,000
Pro rata percentage of sale proceeds	$ 3,875,000
Total return to participating preferred	$ 6,125,000

In this example, which is based on an example of a very early stage company with no prior preferred investments, even though the holders of the participating preferred stock own 50 percent of the equity in the company, the multiple liquidation preference generates an absolute return of 61 percent of the sale proceeds.

Multiple liquidation preferences are common also in situations where a company has been successful in raising capital, but less successful in achieving milestones or significant revenue. In these types of cases, the company's fair market value may be significantly less than the sum of the liquidation preferences for prior investments made in the company. This type of financing structure is known as a restart or cram-down financing. For example, the company characteristics would include several series of preferred stock financings, such as series A, B, C, D, and E rounds where each round involved an investment of $1,000,000. The aggregate liquidation preferences would therefore be $5,000,000. In the absence of an agreement to the contrary, an investor considering a new series F round would either share proceeds pro rata with the prior rounds and then with all the shareholders, or the series F investor would receive its investment first, then the remaining series A through E investors would receive their investments, followed by all shareholders participating in any residual proceeds. In this example, we will assume that the company has not achieved significant milestones as forecasted, that the fair market value of the company is $1,000,000, and that the series F investment amount is $1,000,000, with a 2× multiple. The investment results in a 50 percent ownership of the company for the series F investor.

Proceeds of the sale of company stock	$10,000,000
Return of 2× original investment plus accrued but unpaid dividends	$ 2,250,000
Net proceeds available for distribution to remaining preferred shareholders	$ 7,750,000
Return of series A through series E preferred stock preferences, exclusive of accrued but unpaid dividends	$ 5,000,000
Net proceeds available for distribution to remaining shareholders	$ 2,750,000
Pro rata percentage of sale proceeds	$ 1,375,000
Total return to series F preferred	$ 3,625,000

In this example, even with a 2× multiple applied to the series F investment, the holders of series F participating preferred stock would only receive 36.25 percent of the proceeds of the sale. As a result, in negotiating its up-front terms and conditions, the series F investor would need to negotiate a multiple greater than 4× its original investment amount in order to receive a return equal to 50 percent of the proceeds in the example.

While the application of significant multiples to later stage cram-down investments is required in order to achieve desired financial return results, in some cases required returns can never be achieved under the company's assumed financial forecasts. In these cases, a later stage investor will require all prior preferred stockholders to convert their preferred stock to common stock immediately prior to the closing of the new series F investment. Under a forced conversion scenario, the series F investor in the preceding example would participate in the remaining proceeds of sale immediately after being repaid its original investment plus accrued but unpaid dividends. In this instance, the series F investor would not need to negotiate a multiple liquidation preference as the anticipated return would be equal to $5,600,000 in the example, with the results being the same as in the basic participating preferred example.

Voting Rights In the privately held company context, almost all preferred stock investments include the right to vote shares based on the number of shares of common stock into which the investor may convert the preferred stock. These rights are typically manifested in a right to vote side by side or together with the common stock, on an as converted basis, and not as a separate class. In addition to the general right to vote, holders of preferred stock may be granted specific voting rights with respect to the election of directors and with respect to any negotiated negative covenants. For example, the holders of a designated class of preferred stock may be entitled to elect a specific number of directors for the board of directors and the company may not merge with or acquire another company without the approval of a specified percentage of the holders of the preferred stock. The specified percentage varies based on the actual negative covenant in question, but at a minimum would require a majority vote and in most cases would not exceed a requirement to obtain more than 80 percent of the vote of the holders of the preferred. The percentage is not 100 percent in most cases, because the requirement of a unanimous vote could give the holder of a small percentage of the preferred stock a block on fundamental or important actions of the company even where a majority of all other shareholders are in favor of the action.

Protective Provisions   An owner of preferred stock holds shares issued in connection with the negotiation of a contract between the company and the investor. These contract rights include covenants that are generally referred to as protective provisions. Without a specified vote by the holders of preferred stock, the company is contractually prohibited from taking certain actions. These actions usually involve items fundamental to the ownership of the preferred shares, and the protective provisions are embodied in these contractual covenants, because the typical holder of preferred shares does not own a majority of the stock of the company. Included in the list of protective provisions are prohibitions on the following actions unless the specified percentage of preferred shareholders agree with the action: liquidation of the company, amendment of the charter or bylaws in a manner that would adversely affect the preferred stock, creation of a class of stock senior to the preferred stock, redemption of shares, payment of dividends, borrowing money in excess of an agreed-upon maximum, or changing the size of the board of directors.

Antidilution Provisions   Antidilution provisions focus on issuances of shares at a per share price less than the price paid by the investor for the investor's preferred stock. Issuances above the investor's per share price do in fact dilute the ownership interest of the investor, but only in rare cases do higher priced issuances trigger antidilution provisions included in a company's charter documents. Two types of antidilution protection form the basis for most investors. These protections are known as either weighted average–based or ratchet-based antidilution.

Weighted average–based antidilution is company friendly. In order to calculate the actual protection, an understanding of one of the fundamental provisions of preferred stock is required. The provision relates to the manner in which the number of shares of preferred stock is converted into common stock. For example, assuming an investment of $1,000,000 by a preferred stock investor, if the per share initial conversion price (ICP) is $1, the investor would be entitled to convert the investment into 1,000,000 shares of common stock. Applying weighted average antidilution protection to this assumed investment would generate the following calculation based on the associated assumptions of a dilutive investment to determine a new conversion price (NCP).

New investment	1,000,000 shares
New investment price	$.50 per share
Total shares outstanding	2,000,000 before new investment

$$NCP = ICP \times (A + B)/(A + C)$$
$$= \$1.00 \times (2,000,000 + 500,000)/(2,000,000 + 1,000,000)$$
$$= \$1.00 \times 2,500,000/3,000,000$$
$$= \$1.00 \times 0.8333$$
$$= \$.8333$$

where   ICP = $1.00
            A = number of shares outstanding before new issue
            B = number of shares that new consideration would purchase at the conversion price in effect prior to the new issue
            C = number of new shares issued

Predilutive investment conversion shares	1,000,000 shares
Postdilutive investment conversion shares	1,000,000/.8333 = 1,200,048 shares

In the weighted average–based antidilution calculation, the absolute percentage of shares held by the original investor goes down, but the investor's ownership in relation to the original owner's goes up because the investor is now entitled to 1,200,048 shares and the original owner's shares remain static at 1,000,000.

Full ratchet antidilution protection is dramatically different in its consequences to existing shareholders. Under full ratchet antidilution, an investor's conversion price moves down to the exact level of the new investment. Using the previous assumptions, the investor would be entitled to convert the preferred stock into 2,000,000 shares of common stock immediately after the issuance. The calculation is performed by changing the preferred holders' $1.00 conversion price to the new per share price of $.50 and dividing the investment amount of $1,000,000 by $.50 instead of $1.00.

Although the basic full ratchet calculation is unpleasant for existing common shareholders, when a new investor's percentage of ownership is stated as a percentage of the company assuming the investment has already been made, companies subject to full ratchet antidilution protection must perform multiple calculations to determine the new conversion price. For example, using the previous assumptions where the initial investment calculation would transfer one-third of the company to the new investors, if a full ratchet applies, the old investors would, by virtue of the new investment, increase the number of assumed existing shares from 2,000,000 to 3,000,000. By making this adjustment, the $.50 per share assumed conversion price no longer generates a number of shares equal to one-third of the company, but rather only one-fourth of the company or 1,000,000 out of 4,000,000. In order to place the investor in position to convert the preferred stock to one-third of the company the new investor must receive not 1,000,000 shares, but 1,500,000 in order for the assumed one-third ownership position to be accurate. By increasing the number of shares that the preferred stock investor must receive, and at the same time maintaining the assumed investment amount at $500,000, the per share conversion price must be reduced from $.50 per share to $.33 per share. However, issuing shares at $.33 per share again triggers the full ratchet antidilution protection, and the existing preferred stockholders now will be entitled to receive 3,000,000 shares instead of 2,000,000 shares. By making this adjustment the new investors must receive 2,000,000 shares instead of 1,500,000 shares resulting in a conversion price of $.25 instead of $.33. This adjustment now requires another round of calculations and the adjustments continue until the shares subject to the full ratchet antidilution protection stabilize at the new conversion price. This death spiral in conversion price forces many companies into a restart where early stage investors are crammed down into a nominal equity position. In order to retain management, new investors must provide for revised equity incentive compensation based on creative new series of equity that are permitted to participate in liquidity event proceeds after the new investors but before all existing investors.

Redemption   As part of the planning for an exit strategy, investors negotiate provisions relating to a liquidity event as part of the term sheet. In addition to the traditional exit strategies of initial public offerings, mergers and acquisitions, and recapitalizations, investors will also negotiate the right to require the company to purchase or redeem their shares after a negotiated period of time if no liquidity event has occurred. A typical time period of five years is established, and at any time after the passage of five years, the investor may require the company to purchase the investor's preferred stock for a price equal to the greater of the fair market value of the underlying common stock into which the preferred may be converted or the original purchase price plus accrued but unpaid dividends. The redemption may be triggered by the vote of a majority of the holders of preferred shares. In order to permit the orderly liquidation of the shares, most redemption features contain provisions that permit the company to make installment payments over three years.

The redemption feature is subject to statutory limitations imposed on companies that preclude redemptions unless the company is able to make the purchase out of its capital surplus. Capital surplus is generally an amount equal to the equity invested in a company less cumulative operating losses. If the statute precludes redemption, investors may negotiate for board control in order to manage the ability of the company to effect the redemption or to cause the company to enter into serious negotiations for additional equity investments or the sale of the company. An investor will elect the redemption feature where the company is not making progress towards a liquidity event. The feature in many cases is of little real benefit to the investor due to the fact that if the company is not performing, there will be few if any funds to satisfy the redemption obligation.

Registration Rights   With most investments in privately held companies, and in connection with private placements in publicly traded entities, investors negotiate registration rights to facilitate liquidity events. The standard registration rights granted to an investor in a privately held company include demand registration rights, short-form registration rights, and piggyback or incidental registration rights.

Demand registration rights are triggered by the passage of time following the initial investment date, or by the passage of time following the initial public offering of securities by the company. The initial passage of time is normally not less than five years. At the five-year time frame, if the company has not registered its securities, the investors are granted the right to demand that their shares be registered. The registration process is time-consuming and expensive, and normally not an effective right of the investor unless the company is able to attract an investment banker to underwrite the offering. Nevertheless, the negotiation of a demand registration right is a fundamental right obtained by investors.

A more effective right is the right of investors to demand registration after the initial public offering of securities by the company. Investors negotiate one or two demand registration opportunities for the holders of preferred stock. In this case, the company has gone through a significant amount of due diligence with investment bankers and successfully offered securities to the public. With an established public market, investors have a realistic chance of liquidity. While the investors have, at this time, normally met minimum holding requirements to sell securities to the public in Rule 144 transactions, the aggregate amount of securities held by investors typically serves as an obstacle to selling all of their shares. Under Rule 144, the amount of unregistered stock that investors can sell in any given 90-day period in a private placement is limited to 1 percent of the issued and outstanding shares of the company. In contrast, if the investor is selling shares registered with the SEC by the company, the investors can liquidate their entire holdings in one sale. It is in the interests of the company and its shareholders in many cases to facilitate a registered sale, because a prolonged sale of blocks of investor shares every 90 days has a depressing effect on a company's share price. Once the company is public, its filings with the SEC will chronicle all shareholders with registration rights. With access to this knowledge, the market may depress the share price simply by virtue of the shares that can come to market at any given time. This effect is called overhang.

In addition to demand registration rights, investors negotiate short-form registration rights. After a company has been public for a year, and if the company is current with all of its required filings, companies meeting certain minimum valuation levels may take advantage of Form S-3. This form provides a mechanism for companies to register shares using an abbreviated SEC filing that is not as expensive or as time-consuming as Form S-1, the form companies use in connection with initial public offerings. Investors negotiate an unlimited number of short-form registration opportunities; however, the company is not normally required to effect more than two such registrations in any given year, and the amount of securities to be registered must meet minimum size requirements. The minimum size of a short form offering ranges from $1 million to $5 million in aggregate value of securities offered.

Piggyback or incidental registration rights permit investors to add their securities to any offering that is being registered by the company. Piggyback rights are unlimited in number, but subject to restrictions that may be imposed by the company's investment bankers. For example, in connection with a traditional initial public offering of securities by a company, investment bankers would normally restrict the investors from selling shares under the assumption that most initial public offerings are intended to provide the company and not investors with liquidity to accomplish the company's business plan. Recent offerings, however, have turned this traditional mentality upside down, with private equity investors, but not venture capital investors, having the opportunity to sell significant company stakes in the initial public offering. These offerings typically involve mature companies, with stable and significant cash flows, where the offering is used to refinance existing debt and in effect replace the private equity investors with public investors.

In connection with an initial public offering of securities, investors who have received registration rights are required to enter into lockup agreements. These agreements preclude investors from selling shares of the company's stock for a period of 180 days following the effective date of a company's public offering. Lockup agreements are required by a company's investment bankers in order to manage the offering process and avoid shareholders selling blocks of shares in the 180-day period. This restriction is designed to permit the company and its investment bankers to stabilize the company's share price immediately following the offering by avoiding significant price swings that may be caused by sales of shares into a thinly traded market for company shares.

Board Composition   Although most venture capital preferred stock investors take a minority investment percentage in their portfolio companies, control of the board, or at least assurance that the board will act independently, is a significant negotiating term. Composition of a venture backed company's board may be negotiated to reflect this independence by naming an equal number of existing owners and investors to the board with one independent board member being selected by the consent of the investors and the existing owners. In this respect, fundamental operation of the company is placed to a large extent in the hands of the independent board member, whose vote will break any deadlocks between the investors and the existing owners. The strategy behind this negotiation includes a recognition on the part of the investors that they must gain the confidence of existing owners in the decision making process. By taking less than a majority on the board, management obtains comfort that the investors cannot force the company to take a specific action without the vote of the independent director. Conversely, if management and the existing owners can convince the independent director that an action is proper, they can take the action, subject only to any contractual negative covenants that the company concedes in the negotiation process. The negative covenants are, therefore, known by all parties prior to consummation of the preferred stock investment.

Employee Stock Options   As previously illustrated, an important negotiation term is the size of the employee stock option pool. By negotiating the size up front, existing owners and investors know the boundaries of dilution that will be imposed on shareholders, and the dilution cannot be changed in the absence of an agreement by existing owners and investors. It should be noted from the examples dealing with antidilution protection that the percentage of a company that an investor bargains for is based on the assumption that all options have been granted. The effect of this assumption is that in the early stages of an investment, investors own a higher percentage of the company than their investment would purchase, but as options are granted, the percentage decreases until the option pool is exhausted and the investors reach their agreed-upon residual company equity percentage.

Most employee option pools are designed as qualified option pools, which means that options up to the aggregate size of the pool can be granted, but the options must be granted at the then current fair market value of the company's shares as determined by the board of directors. Options normally vest over time, with vesting schedules generally extending over three or four years following the date of the option grant.

Founder Share Vesting   A term sheet feature that is perhaps the most contested term, other than valuation, is the requirement by investors that the equity held by founders of an early stage company vest over time. This feature is based on the premise that much of the valuation attributed to early stage companies will only be realized to the extent that the founders stay with the company and fulfill the objectives of their business plan. If a founder determines not to continue with the company, investors or the company will be granted the right to repurchase some or all of the founders' shares. The purchase price for vested shares is normally fair market value, determined by an independent third party if the founder and the company are unable to agree on price. In contrast, the purchase price for unvested shares is generally a nominal amount or an amount equal to the price paid by the founders where an actual cash investment has been made. In negotiating this purchase right, investors are attempting to ensure that the value anticipated at the time of investment will be achieved by the ongoing efforts of the founders, and if not, that controlling the shares will permit the company to recruit replacement management without diluting the remaining shareholders.

In determining vesting periods, the maturity of the company is taken into account. In this respect, companies with customers and revenues may permit founders to retain an initial percentage of their shares that are subject to no vesting. The residual shares will then vest over a three-to-four-year period. Vesting schedules vary from pro rata vesting on a monthly basis over the full vesting term to a combination of cliff vesting at the end of one year with the balance of the shares vesting ratably on a monthly basis over the balance of the vesting period.

Miscellaneous Term Sheet Provisions   It is rare that an investor will have completed its due diligence investigation of a target company at the time of negotiation of a term sheet. As a result, term sheets are nonbinding indications of interest, with the opportunity for either party to terminate negotiations. Termination provisions are crafted to provide investors with a defined period of time to complete their due diligence, and it is customary for the company to provide investors with a period of exclusivity during which the company will not negotiate with any other investors. At the end of the exclusivity period, either party is free to terminate the negotiations or seek alternative investors.

The term sheet will also include a list of negative and affirmative covenants that the company must observe as long as the investors maintain a significant investment in the company. Affirmative covenants include obligations on the part of the company to provide investors with monthly and quarterly unaudited financial statements, an annual audited statement, and a proposed annual budget thirty days before the start of each fiscal year.

Investors will also jealously guard the right to purchase ongoing sales of securities by the company. Most companies have eliminated preemptive rights to purchase shares that otherwise are available under some state corporate law statutes. As a result, without a contractual right to purchase shares, an investor could fund the important start-up phase of a company and then be excluded from participating in company offerings as the company matures. Although the right to participate in future offerings negotiated in the term sheet is most often used in connection with additional purchases at higher valuations, the right also protects investors by giving them the right to maintain their percentage ownership in the event of subsequent issuances at lower or nominal valuations.

Where the target company value is based on intangibles or intellectual property, investors will negotiate term sheet provisions requiring all employees, contractors, and consultants to enter into nondisclosure and development agreements. The development agreement portion of the requirement is designed to insure that the covered parties agree that any proprietary rights developed during employment or as a consultant belong to the company. Where key individuals have the ability to replicate the business plan of the company, and therefore the value of the investors' investment, designated individuals will be required to execute noncompetition and nonsolicitation agreements.

The Stock Purchase Agreement

The stock purchase agreement frames the parameters of the economics of the investment transaction; provides specific baselines for the representations and warranties of the company, the founders, and the investors; and designates the ancillary agreements that must be obtained and the actions that must be taken by the company in order to close the transaction.

Basic Investment Transaction   The stock purchase agreement opens with a section describing the basic structure of the securities acquisition. It is in this section that the parties establish the obligation of the purchasers to purchase and the company to issue the securities that have been designated in the company's term sheet. The amount and price of the securities designated in the purchase agreement have been determined based on the pre-money valuation of the company negotiated in the term sheet.

In staged or phased stock purchases, the opening section will describe the timing of subsequent stock purchases and any milestones that must be achieved as conditions to the obligation of the purchasers to make the additional purchases.

Representations and Warranties   While investors will have completed a substantial amount of due diligence prior to negotiation of the stock purchase agreement, in most investment cases, the representations and warranties section provides investors with supplemental information either confirming the investor's prior due diligence or identifying issues that need further examination. The due diligence is confirmed either by the company making an absolute and unqualified representation and warranty about a specific area, or where the company cannot make an unqualified statement, detailed information regarding the qualification is chronicled on the company's disclosure schedule and compared by the investor to information the investor was provided in connection with initial due diligence.

In addition, where an investor intends to negotiate definitive documentation first and finalize due diligence after signing the purchase agreement, the representations and warranties section serves to provide an opportunity to decline to make an investment to the extent that the investor determines in the follow-on due diligence that the representations and warranties are inaccurate or untrue. In some transactions, investors will include indemnification provisions in the stock purchase agreement, and in these instances, the representations and warranties serve as a baseline of information used by an investor to determine whether information supplied by the company in connection with the investment was inaccurate. If information is in fact inaccurate, investors look to the false representation or warranty as the basis for indemnification to the extent that the false or inaccurate information can be tied to damages suffered by the investor.

Stock purchase agreements negotiated in connection with early stage investments may dedicate a separate section of warranties and representations relating to the founders of the company. This section is not normally found in later stage investments. In a founder's representation and warranty section, the investor attempts to determine whether the founder is subject to any contracts that could conflict with the business plan presented to the investors. The potential conflicts that concern investors generally arise in connection with noncompetition agreements, nonsolicitation agreements, or confidentiality agreements. The examination extends to determine whether the founder is involved in any litigation. Also of concern to investors is the question of whether the founder has any other arrangements with other investors to sell founder stock or to vote in a predetermined manner.

Investors are asked to make representations and warranties in a stock purchase agreement that relate to their authority to make the purchase, as well as the circumstances surrounding their investment. Investors will confirm their financial status and whether they meet the minimum requirements for accredited investor status under Rule 501 of Regulation D. In this regard, the company will rely on the investor's representations and warranties to ensure compliance with the applicable private placement exemption claimed by the company. Importantly, the investors will in this section confirm their understanding the stock is being purchased in a private placement, and that there is no public market for the company's securities. Coupled with this affirmation is a representation and warranty by the investor that the shares are being purchased for investment, with no view toward distributing the shares, and that the shares must be held for an indefinite period of time in the absence of a public offering.

In order to evaluate the list of representations and warranties made by the company, it simplifies the analysis if the long list of representations and warranties is organized into three broad categories. The categories are corporate organization, financial statement presentation, and company operations.

Corporate Organization   An investor pays close attention to the corporate organization section. It is in this section that the company confirms that it has the right, power, and authority to issue the securities. In addition, the company confirms that the board of directors has authorized the securities to be issued and all other required actions in connection with the issuance have been taken. Where a company has issued securities to a large group of shareholders, the investor will require assurances that the company has complied with all securities laws for each sale of securities undertaken by the company. If the company has not complied with securities laws, there may be a significant repurchase obligation on the part of the company for any shares issued outside of compliance with these laws.

A significant representation and warranty made by the company relates to the capitalization of the company. The number of shares of stock issuable to an investor is based on an accurate understanding of all securities issued by a company, including all warrants, rights to purchase, options, and instruments that may be convertible into the company's securities. If the capitalization section is inaccurate or incomplete, an investor will have a basis for demanding an adjustment in the number of shares issued in connection with the stock purchase agreement.

Typically, the capitalization section will contain not only an analysis of the company's capital structure immediately before the investment is made, but also a capitalization table for the company on a pro forma basis assuming the investment has been consummated. In the pro forma capitalization table, investors will confirm their due diligence relating to any outstanding securities that have been granted antidilution protection. If the price paid in the current round triggers the antidilution protection, the impact of the protection must be illustrated in the pro forma capitalization table.

Financial Statement Presentation   The importance of the company's financial statements increases as the maturity of the company increases. That is not to say that early stage financials are disregarded by investors. To the contrary, the statements are scoured for outstanding liabilities that must be paid or satisfied out of the proceeds of an investor's investment. But in early stage deals, many companies have little or no revenues, so the emphasis is on historical costs and outstanding liabilities. Where early stage founders have accumulated salaries during the start-up phase of a company, it is common for investors to force the forgiveness or conversion of these debts to equity prior to closing the investment.

The financial statements also contain provisions relating to contingent liabilities of a company. Investors focus on these disclosures, particularly where the contingency relates to litigation or where the financial statement reflects significant future obligations owed in connection with material contracts, particularly real property leases.

Financial statement presentation required in connection with private placements is typically an audit for the two most recently completed fiscal years, and unaudited statements for the months lapsing between the last audit and the closing date. The financial statements required include a balance sheet, income statement, and statement of cash flows for each of the periods. All financial statements must be presented in a form that has been prepared in accordance with generally accepted accounting principles (GAAP), applied on a consistent basis throughout the periods covered.

The financial statements will be coupled with a narrative representation and warranty that the company has no liabilities or obligations, contingent or otherwise, except for those set forth in the financial statements or disclosed in the company's disclosure schedule. In addition, the company will indicate whether any of its assets are encumbered by mortgages, deeds of trust, liens, loans, or other encumbrances.

Where there is a gap between the date of the last financial statements and the date of closing, investors require financial representations and warranties from a company that bring down the financial statements to the date of closing. This bring-down representation and warranty contains a variety of separate statements, all relating to the financial performance and incurrence of obligations between the most recent financial statements and the date of closing.

Company Operations   The examination of company operations by a potential investor focuses on discrete segments of the operations of the company depending on the stage and maturity of the company. For later stage companies, the focus is on existing material contracts, recurring revenue sources, proprietary assets, outstanding obligations, and contingent liabilities that could significantly alter the forecasted performance of the company. In earlier stage companies, an investor will perform significant due diligence on the proprietary assets of the company, including analysis of patent filings and intellectual property controlled by the company. In addition, material contracts that either grant or in-license (obtain rights to intellectual property from a third party) intellectual property are examined under the microscope as part of the examination of operations by an investor. The issues of importance to investors include an understanding of whether the company has exclusive control over the intellectual property, whether the company has long-term commitments requiring significant cash obligations, and whether the company has the ability to terminate contracts that may have been entered into when the company needed cash flow to survive.

Most investors prefer to examine all exceptions to any warranty or representation in lieu of permitting a company to modify representations and warranties with materiality or knowledge. The disclosures made by a company are of significant importance to the investor and under normal circumstances, the investor prefers to decide what disclosures are material. As a result, in connection with early stage investments, it is rare to find materiality modifiers in the purchase documentation, because investors want to investigate all obligations of the company. As the maturity of a target company increases, the ability to list all exceptions to a warranty or representation becomes a burden to the disclosing company and investors become more willing to establish materiality limits to the disclosure schedule, unless the disclosure relates to a core asset or intellectual property.

Conditions to Closing In connection with the finalization of documentation relating to a stock purchase agreement, the parties will describe all deliveries and actions that must be provided or taken by the company and by the investors in order for the closing to be consummated. All ancillary agreements required of shareholders or required to be filed by the company will be described, and these action items and agreements must be fulfilled prior to closing. Where an investor negotiates a definitive agreement prior to completion of all due diligence, the investor's due diligence must be completed prior to closing in addition to completion of the designated action items and execution of designated agreements.

Although most investors will negotiate conditions to closing as part of the stock purchase agreement, the primary route to closing involves a signing and simultaneous closing. In this case, the conditions to closing constitute a closing checklist for the company and the investor. As a checklist for closing, the investor is entitled to receive ongoing assurances that the representations and warranties made by the company are in fact accurate as of the date of closing. Because the stock purchase agreement may have been negotiated over 30 to 90 days, the company will continue to update its disclosure schedule until the actual date of closing and an investor will be diligent in evaluating the disclosures up until the actual moment of closing.

Certificate of Incorporation

Although some private placements involve the sale of common stock, many investments by sophisticated investors involve the purchase of preferred stock. The terms and conditions, and the rights and preferences related to preferred stock are found in a company's certificate of incorporation. It is common for companies to establish provisions in their original certificate of incorporation that permit the board of directors to negotiate preferred stock terms and then simply file the negotiated terms. This alternative is known as blank check preferred.

When a company does not have blank check preferred stock available, the company will negotiate the terms and conditions of the preferred stock security that it desires to issue, and then submit the proposed terms and conditions to the shareholders of the company. Submitting the terms and conditions to shareholders is required in order to amend the certificate of incorporation of a company that does not have blank check preferred. Most privately held companies have not made this election at the time of their incorporation, and as a result, this alternative is not available to them at the time of their investment closing.

In addition to traditional terms and conditions found in a company's certificate of incorporation, when an investor finalizes a preferred stock investment, the terms and conditions of the preferred stock will be included in a company's certificate of incorporation. There are several fundamental rights and privileges granted to the holders of preferred stock and these rights and privileges are described in detail in the certificate of incorporation. The rights and privileges include the following categories: dividends, liquidation preference, voting, conversion (including adjustments to the conversion price or antidilution protection), and redemption.

Dividends   The dividends section of the certificate of incorporation may include provisions indicating that no dividends are contemplated to be paid, that dividends will be paid at a specified rate when and only when declared by the board of directors, or that dividends will accrue on the preferred stock at a specified rate whether or not declared by the board of directors. Dividends that accrue whether or not paid are known as cumulative dividends.

Where preferred stock is created with alternative dividend payment terms, a description of the alternative is contained in the certificate of incorporation. Alternative terms may involve dividend structures that permit the company to make dividend payments in kind (PIK payments). PIK payments ease the cash flow demands of a company and may be elected by a company under the terms of the certificate of incorporation. The contrast between a PIK dividend and a cumulative dividend is that in the PIK alternative, the company issues a note or share of stock based on the fair market value of the company's stock. If the issuer is public, the dividend recipient can then sell the security and receive liquidity for the dividend payment that is not available if the dividend is cumulative.

Liquidation Preference   Preferred stock receives its senior financial attributes in the liquidation preference section. It is in this section that the preferred stock is designated straight preferred, convertible preferred, or participating preferred. In today's financial environment, a very high percentage of investments in early stage companies include participating preferred features. As the strength and maturity of a company increases, the percentage reduces and the primary vehicle for investment is convertible preferred.

Attributes of straight preferred are focused primarily on the holder receiving the original amount of the preferred plus accrued but unpaid dividends prior to the receipt of any return.

Although the section is labeled liquidation, the certificate of incorporation contains a section that obligates a company to treat mergers and acquisitions, and the sale or lease of all or substantially all of the assets of the company as a liquidation. In the event that the holders of preferred stock determine that liquidation treatment is not in their best interests, they can elect out of the treatment.

Convertible preferred permits an investor to view a liquidity event and to evaluate the investor's potential return under alternative financial scenarios. The alternatives permit the investor to compare returns generated by taking the original amount of investment plus accrued but unpaid dividends, and comparing this amount with the investor's pro rata amount of proceeds of the liquidity event assuming conversion of the preferred stock to common stock.

Participating preferred generates the highest return to an investor in that the investor takes both of the alternatives available to the holder of convertible preferred. These returns include an amount equal to the original investment plus accrued but unpaid interest, and an amount equal to the holder's pro rata share of proceeds on an as converted to common stock basis.

Voting   Preferred stock is granted voting rights in most early stage, venture capital, and private equity investments. In later stage companies, especially publicly traded companies, preferred stock voting rights are not granted.

The number of votes that a holder of preferred stock is entitled to cast is equal to the number of shares of common stock into which the preferred stock may be converted. The preferred stock may be granted separate rights to elect a designated number of directors to the board of directors of the company. These rights are negotiated frequently where the investor takes a minority position in the company. In the absence of a special certificate of incorporation provision, the investor would not be able to elect any director. After electing any designated board member, the preferred stock may vote with the remaining common stockholders for the election of the balance of the board of directors.

The voting section also contains a description of the protective provisions that the investor negotiated as part of the term sheet. These protective provisions are included in the certificate of incorporation to place the rest of the world on notice that the company may not take certain actions without the approval of the holders of preferred stock. The actions requiring preferred shareholder approval include: no liquidation of the business, no amendment to the articles of incorporation, no creation of a class of securities senior to the preferred stock, no redemption of shares, no dividends on shares, no borrowing in excess of specified amounts, and no increase or decrease in the size of the board of directors. The list of prohibited items is longer in some cases, but the actions just described are considered so fundamental to the financial interests of the preferred shareholder that they are almost always included in some form.

Conversion Conversion rights are normally divided into two categories—voluntary and mandatory conversion. Voluntary conversion may be elected by the holder of preferred stock at any time. Mandatory conversion is triggered by two primary actions—either a company's initial public offering (IPO) or a vote of the majority of the holders of preferred stock to convert. An IPO triggers mandatory conversion because investment bankers taking the company public do not want the company's capital structure complicated by the rights negotiated by the holders of preferred. These rights are viewed by public shareholders and institutions as concentrating too much power in too few hands. Consequently, access to the public markets and their liquidity is normally sufficient to convince preferred stock investors that mandatory conversion at the time of an IPO is consideration commensurate with the loss of preferred stock rights.

Conversion is the process by which an investor moves from the debtlike preferred instrument into the common stock category in order to take advantage of the participating features of common stock. The factor that determines the number of shares that an investor is entitled to receive is called the conversion price. The calculation of common shares is simple arithmetic. The aggregate investment amount is divided by the conversion price to determine the number of common shares to be received by the preferred stockholder. In the calculation, one variable that can dramatically change the calculation is the manner in which accrued but unpaid dividends are treated. In early stage or venture capital–backed deals, although the dividends are stated as being cumulative, they are hardly ever declared. As such, the typical early stage conversion section would take the original purchase price and divide by the conversion price with no other adjustments. As companies mature and the investor groups begin to include private equity investors or the companies are publicly traded, the calculation of the number of common shares does include accrued but unpaid dividends. Where the preferred stock has been outstanding for several years, the initial percentage ownership of the preferred stock holders creeps up quickly.

In most instances involving privately held companies, the conversion price is fixed and it is only adjusted in the event that the company issues shares at a price less than the price paid for the preferred stock. If the company does issue shares at a lower price, then an adjustment mechanism is triggered and the number of shares into which the preferred stock may be converted is increased. There are two basic mechanisms for adjusting the conversion price—weighted average–based and ratchet-based antidilution. These mechanisms are illustrated previously in the section describing the negotiation of the term sheet.

When a small-cap public company issues preferred stock in a private placement, the conversion price in many cases is not fixed. These equity issuances, otherwise known as private investment in public equities (PIPE) investments, have conversion prices that float based on the price of the company's registered shares on the date that an investor converts. For companies with undercapitalized balance sheets, the attraction of a PIPE investment is significant. The funds may be raised quickly, and there are thousands of investors with funds willing to make an investment in large or bulk purchases where the investment can be liquidated quickly. In order for the investment to be liquidated, the underlying shares of common stock must be registered; this is normally a process that must be initiated by the company immediately after the investment is finalized, and the registration process must be completed within a limited period of time in order to avoid penalties.

In the context of a public company, a situation arises frequently that is known as the death spiral. In this situation, the preferred stock is issued and in unrelated transactions, investors begin to short the public shares. The shorting process places significant downward pressure on the company's share price and as the price falls, the number of shares into which the preferred stock may be converted increases directly in proportion to the fall in share price. As the number of shares that could potentially be outstanding in connection with the conversion of the preferred stock increases, the market responds by reducing the value of each share. Now with downward general market forces applying downward pressure in connection with the shorting process, the share price spirals downward. In order to reverse the spiral, the issuing company must be able to use the proceeds of the preferred stock offering to bolster sales and revenue; however, in most cases, the investment proceeds for these smaller companies is used to satisfy existing obligations and not for growth opportunities. As a result, the companies are permanently relegated to penny stock status, and due to the reduced share price are unable to raise additional capital. The only solution for many of these small-cap stocks is a formal insolvency.

Redemption   Redemption provisions provide moderate protection for investors involved in investments that are going sideways. These provisions are included in the certificate of incorporation in order to provide investors with a potential exit strategy where the company is not qualified for an IPO, and the performance of the company precludes a merger or acquisition at an attractive price. Pricing of the redemption is based on either the original investment plus accrued but unpaid dividends, or an amount equal to the fair market value of the common stock into which the preferred stock may be converted. The investor selects which valuation method to use, and the company is obligated to purchase the stock in cash if available, or if not, in installments over typically a three-year period.

Investors' Rights Agreement

The investors' rights agreement covers four primary rights granted to investors in connection with preferred stock investments. These rights may not be amended or reduced without the approval of a majority of the preferred stockholders. The primary rights include securities registration rights, information rights, preemptive rights to acquire new securities issued by the company, and a grouping of affirmative and negative covenants to which the company must adhere.

Registration Rights   The registration rights section of the investors' rights agreement includes three types of rights granted to investors. These rights include demand registration rights, incidental or piggyback registration rights, and short-form registration rights. Shares covered by these registration rights are known as registrable shares. Investor expenses incurred in connection with these offerings are paid for by the company, but any underwriting discounts or commissions are deducted from the proceeds otherwise payable to the investor. The company agrees to maintain all of its SEC filings and reports at any time that it is publicly traded and there are registrable shares held by investors.

Demand registration rights are granted to investors at the time of purchase of the preferred stock, but the rights do not vest until the earlier one of two specified periods of time have lapsed. It is customary for an investor to receive two such demand rights. The vesting periods are stated as either a fixed amount of time such as five years, or the passage of 180 days after the effective date of a company's initial public offering. Both rights are coupled with minimum dollar amounts of shares that must be offered for sale in order to trigger the registration right, and most minimums are at least $5,000,000, with $10,000,000 being a typical trigger in early stage venture financings. Demand rights generally terminate in the event that the investor can sell all remaining shares within one 90-day period under Rule 144 without restriction.

Each of the terms *incidental, piggyback*, or *company registration* describes the same right granted to investors under the investors' rights agreement. This right permits a holder of registrable shares to add shares to any offering of securities for cash that is proposed by the company, with certain exceptions. Generally excluded from this right are registrations for company combinations in connection with mergers and acquisitions under SEC Rule 145 transactions and registrations related to securities underlying convertible debt instruments. The company is obligated to give the holder of registrable securities advance notice of any company registration, and the holder a reasonable amount of time to decide whether to participate in the offering. If the holder decides to register shares, the shares will be liquidated in connection with the offering. Investors are typically granted an unlimited number of company registration rights.

Short-form registrations provide an opportunity for investors to take advantage of SEC rules permitting streamlined registration guidelines on the use of SEC Form S-3 for companies that have been public for more than a year. Because the restrictions on the use of Form S-3 other than the one year requirement and timely filing of all periodic reports are related to issuances by the company, using SEC Form S-3 for registration of investor shares is efficient and available for many smaller companies. Investors will normally be subjected to aggregate dollar minimums of $1,000,000 to $5,000,000 per filing and a maximum of one or two registrations per year.

Conditions applicable to an IPO registration include so-called lockup agreements, in which investors agree not to sell stock within 180 days of the effective date of an offering. With respect to company registrations and short-form registrations, all investor rights are subject to blackout periods during which the company may suspend a registration statement if the board of directors determines in good faith that it would be detrimental to the company to continue with the registration. This option is exercised when a company believes that a material event may occur during the registration period, and the company determines that it is not ready to disclose the event because disclosure could jeopardize the event such as an acquisition or because the disclosure is premature and there is a reasonable business purpose served by maintaining the confidentiality of the information in the short term.

Information Rights   Because many investors take a minority position in their portfolio companies, they do not have the voting power or board power to force a company to provide them with ongoing information unless the obligation is negotiated in connection with the closing of the investment. Information rights fall within this category of rights, and included within this negotiated right will be an obligation on the part of the company to provide monthly and quarterly unaudited financials, annual audited financial statements, and annual budgets delivered 30 days before the beginning of any fiscal year. All statements are required to be prepared in accordance with GAAP, applied on a consistent basis throughout all periods covered, with the only exception being that the monthly and quarterly statements may be subject to normal year-end adjustments and the statements may not contain all footnotes otherwise required to comply with GAAP.

Preemptive Rights   Investors' rights agreements normally contain provisions that provide an investor with the right to protect the investor's pro rata percentage ownership of the company. The right is called by a variety of names including first right of refusal, right of first offer, option to purchase, or preemptive right. In each case, the company must provide notice to an investor of any issuance of securities. The investor has a predetermined number of days to elect to purchase the offered securities. If the offer is declined, a company may then sell the offered securities to a third party on the same terms within a set period of time, normally not more than 90 days. If the proposed sale has not been consummated within the designated time period, or in the event that the company changes the terms of the proposed sale, then the company must again permit the investor an opportunity to purchase the securities offered. Standard exceptions to the right include issuances under a preapproved option plan, shares issued in connection with an IPO, and securities issued in connection with mergers and acquisitions.

Covenants   Affirmative covenants negotiated by an investor include an obligation on the part of the company to obtain standard confidentiality, noncompete, and nonsolicitation agreements from all employees. In addition, the company normally agrees that it will not grant employee options unless the grants have predetermined vesting schedules.

Negative covenants typically require the approval of a majority of the holders of preferred stock before the company can engage in specified activities. The activities include prohibitions on loans to third parties, guarantees of third party debt, investments in third parties, borrowings in excess of agreed-upon and budgeted amounts, transactions with affiliates, setting or changing compensation to senior executive officers, or selling, transferring, or encumbering the intellectual property of the company.

Shareholders' Agreement

The shareholders' agreement contains two categories of agreements. The first agreement grants investors and the company the right to purchase shares of stock that owners desire to sell. In addition, this agreement covers the situation where owners have identified purchasers for their shares, and in this case, the owners are obligated to permit the investors to sell shares to an identified purchaser on a pro rata basis.

The second type of agreement relates to voting matters. In a voting agreement, all of the owners and investors will agree to vote their shares in accordance with the terms of the agreement. These terms include voting for a specified board size and specified board members, as well as a requirement on the part of owners to vote with investors in the event of an acquisition approved by a majority of the shareholders of the company. This vote requirement that is associated with an acquisition is known as a drag-along right. Investors negotiate a drag-along right in order to avoid conflicts with minority owners who may not want to sell the company at this time or on the terms as negotiated. The drag-along right precludes minority shareholders from exercising dissenters' rights. Dissenters' rights provide minority shareholders a mechanism for challenging the value of an acquisition through a third party valuation. Signing a drag-along right eliminates this dispute resolution mechanism, because if exercised, dissenters' rights proceedings are disruptive to the closing of a transaction.

COMPLIANCE WITH SECURITIES LAWS

Raising capital requires knowledge of not only the financial markets but the securities markets. A company must comply not only with federal securities laws, but also with the securities laws of each state in which the issuer sells a security. The overview of securities regulation contained in this section of the chapter deals only with federal securities regulation.

Private Placements

Virtually all fund-raising by privately held companies involves the sale of a security. While much has been written about companies attempting to raise capital by using instruments designed to avoid compliance with the securities laws, few of the schemes have succeeded. As a consequence, management should assume that the issuance of debt or equity to an investor is the sale of a security. Based on this assumption, companies must be aware of the regulatory requirements applicable to the sale of securities. Generally, it may be stated with some degree of accuracy that absent an exemption, the sale of securities requires registration of the securities with the SEC and compliance with the SEC's antifraud provisions. While this statement may be intimidating to a manager or owner of a company, the range of exemptions from registration covers most securities sales, but all sales of securities are subject to the application of the antifraud provisions of the SEC.

Privately held companies rely on two primary transactional exemptions from registration under federal securities laws. The first exemption from registration is provided by Section 4(2) of the 1933 Securities Act. This section provides an exemption for sales of securities by an issuer that does not involve a public offering. Privately held companies have relied on the so-called 4(2) exemption for the private placement of securities, but the exemption is not a defined set of rules. Consequently, issuers were forced to interpret and rely on federal case law that interpreted the legislation, but the cases evolved over time so issuers were always struggling to determine the most recent interpretation of the statute.

In contrast, the second exemption from registration is provided by a set of rules promulgated by the SEC and known as Regulation D. If an issuer follows the rules set forth in Regulation D, the issuer is afforded a safe harbor from registration for the securities issuance. It should be noted that transactional exemptions afforded by Section 4(2) and Regulation D are still subject to the SEC's antifraud provisions.

Companies raising private capital will in most cases attempt to comply with the provisions of Regulation D, since the rules are straightforward and easy to understand. Regulation D contains three specific transactional exemptions. The most commonly used exemption is contained in Rule 506 of Regulation D. Under this rule, if the issuer complies with the safe harbor rules, an unlimited amount of capital can be raised by the company.

Within Regulation D, there are several basic rules that apply to issuers attempting to comply with the safe harbor. The first rule relates to the number of investors that may participate. Under Regulation D, an issuer can sell securities to an unlimited number of accredited investors and no more than 35 nonaccredited investors. When evaluating the status of an investor, individuals qualify for accredited status if they have either a net worth of $1 million or income of $200,000 for the past two years and a reasonable expectation of the same amount of income for the current year. Corporations qualify for accredited investor status if they have more than $5 million in assets, or if all of the owners of the corporation are accredited investors.

In connection with Rule 506 Regulation D private placements, there are no specific rules for the information that must be supplied to accredited investors. If the offering will be made to a nonaccredited investor, Rule 502 of Regulation D contains detailed guidelines as to the type and intensity of financial and nonfinancial information to be supplied to the nonaccredited investors. While the intensity of the information required to be delivered to nonaccredited investors varies by the size of the offering, the general disclosure requirements follow the guidelines for small public offerings on SEC Form SB-1 or SEC Form SB-2. In any event, an issuer would be wise to follow the outlines provided in these forms as they are comprehensive checklists of information relating to all material aspects of a business, including its financial position. The document that normally is used in connection with disclosures is known as either an offering memorandum or a private placement memorandum. Companies desiring to issue securities should have a formal business plan prepared as a starting point for complying with any required disclosures. Appropriate risk factors will be developed and added to a business plan, and together the materials form the basis for compliance with any applicable Regulation D disclosure requirements.

Rule 506 of Regulation D is generically referred to as a private placement, and as such, Regulation D prohibits general solicitation and advertising. These rules apply not only to the company, but to anyone acting on behalf of the company.

In connection with the sale of securities under Rule 506, issuers are required to make a determination that the purchasers are buying the securities for their own account and without a view toward distributing or immediately reselling the securities to a third party. The issuer will take reasonable steps to ensure compliance with this provision of Rule 506 by placing a legend on the issued securities indicating that the securities are restricted and that they may not be resold without either being registered or being transferred pursuant to a valid transactional exemption.

Companies are entitled to pay commissions in connection with the sale of securities under Rule 506; however, most states impose restrictions on the payment of commissions to registered broker-dealers.

Public Offerings

In the limited circumstances where a company desires to issue securities and the company cannot qualify for a transactional exemption, or where the company desires to access the public markets, the registration process is required. While this chapter is not designed to present a comprehensive overview of the going public process, an overview of the general tasks and time lines may be instructive for management of companies considering an offering.

Prior to beginning the registration process, a company must prepare a detailed business plan with comprehensive historical and forecasted financial statements. With these materials in hand a company begins the process of attempting to convince investment bankers that the company is qualified to operate as a public company.

Once the investment banking team is selected, a working group is assembled. The working group typically meets in what is known as an all-hands meeting. Attending this meeting will be a lead investment banking team, supporting investment bankers from additional investment banks, accountants, attorneys for the company and the investment bankers, and management. In the all-hands meeting the lead investment banker provides a time line for completing the offering.

The time frames associated with completing a public offering include the following segments:

- Approximately 60 days to complete the company's presentation of its business and its finances in what is called the registration statement or prospectus.
- Filing with the SEC, after which approximately 30 days elapse prior to receipt of detailed comments from the SEC on the contents of the prospectus.
- Approximately 60 days during which the company and the SEC correspond and the company files amendments to the prospectus.
- After the prospectus is cleared by the SEC, the company prints the prospectus, circulates the prospectus to participating investment

banks, and completes approximately two weeks on the road making presentations to institutional investors, also known as the road show. At the end of the road show, the company and the bankers hold a pricing session in which the demand generated during the road show will determine whether the company consummates the offering and at what price.

- After pricing, the company will within a day direct the investment bankers to begin sales of the securities being issued, either on an exchange such as the New York Stock Exchange, or over the counter on Nasdaq. At this time, the company will have completed the going public process. The elapsed time for completion of this process is, for most initial public offerings, approximately six months.

Other forms of offering for companies that are already public include offerings on Form S-3, otherwise known as a short-form offering. Form S-3 can only be used by companies that have been public for at least one year and have filed all of their SEC required filings in a timely fashion, and for company offerings, by companies with $75 million in securities owned by the public and not by insiders.

Form S-4 is used by public companies to register shares issued in connection with business combinations. Transactions covered by this form include most mergers and acquisitions. Included in Form S-4 is an analysis of each company and a description of the operations of the combined companies.

Form S-8 is the form used to register shares issued in connection with a public company's employee plans. For example, publicly traded companies register incentive option plans under Form S-8. When a company has shares registered under this form, the employees receiving option grants may exercise an option grant and sell the shares simultaneously. Public companies typically have arrangements with investment banks that permit the simultaneous sale with minimal paperwork. Upon completion of the sale, the underwriter forwards the proceeds of the sale to the company for the option strike price, and to the employee for the difference between the strike price and the fair market value sale price of the shares sold.

Deal Structures and Specialized Offerings

As companies search for new and creative financing techniques, the alternatives available are increasingly unique and focused on the capital needs of the company. As investment bankers, accountants, and attorneys examine the needs of their constituent companies, alternative financing structures are generated to fulfill these needs. While these alternatives seem unlimited, a few of the basic transaction structures used to obtain capital or liquidity that are utilized by public and private companies fall within a limited number of general categories. These categories of specialized deal structures and finance structures include private investments in public equities (PIPEs), high yield offerings, reverse mergers into public shells, fairness hearings, and shelf registrations.

Private Investment in Public Equities   PIPEs are being increasingly used by public companies as a fast and inexpensive method of raising capital. In a traditional PIPE transaction, a company will select an investment banker with experience in the company's core business segment. The bankers typically are familiar with not only the company's operations, but the types of investors willing to invest in the company's industry. Because companies using this type of financing technique are already public, there is a significant amount of information available in the public domain relating to the company.

As the company begins the PIPE investment process, the investment bank will assist in the preparation of a private placement memorandum. The memorandum contains virtually all of the information required to be disclosed in connection with a public offering. After the investment bank has scouted the pool of potential investors, management of the company will generate a presentation to be used in private meetings with investors. The meetings will be conducted in a manner similar to the road show conducted in connection with a public offering. If the meetings generate sufficient interest, the investment bankers will begin to compile a book of potential purchasers. If investors indicate sufficient interest at an acceptable price for the company, a closing will take place. The closing is typically a private placement meeting the transactional exemption afforded by Rule 506 of Regulation D. Securities purchased in a PIPE transaction may be common or convertible preferred stock. In the perfect case, the entire fund-raising process may take as little as 30 days.

In connection with the private placement, the company will covenant to register the common stock, or the common stock into which the preferred stock may be converted. The covenant is typically two-staged. The first stage is an agreement to file for registration of the covered securities with the SEC within 30 to 90 days of the closing of the transaction. The second trigger is a covenant that the registration statement will be declared effective within six months of the closing. In the event that the company does not meet either deadline, a penalty is assessed. The penalty is normally stated as a cash payment due to the investors, and the amount of the penalty varies but is generally in the range of 1 percent of the offering for each month that a deadline is not achieved.

For the company, a PIPE provides access to institutional investors for the most part. As opposed to an initial public offering where 30 to 40 percent of the offering will be sold to individual or retail investors, a PIPE is typically sold exclusively to institutions.

High Yield Offerings   Public or private companies may desire to raise capital through the high yield offering process. If the issuing company is public, the process may be expedited because the materials prepared for prior public offerings may be referred to in the process of generating disclosure documents. Where the company is private, the process may take as long as an initial public offering of equity securities, because the issuance of the high yield notes will subject the company to the ongoing filing requirements of the 1934 Securities and Exchange Act. In addition, with recent legislation, companies with publicly traded high yield debt are subject to the Sarbanes-Oxley requirements for independent directors and audit committees.

A high yield offering is similar to a PIPE in that the initial issuance of securities is limited to certain institutional investors. Private placements of this nature qualify under Rule 144A. Participating qualified institutions are willing to invest in private companies, but they require an issuer to register the high yield notes within six months of the closing of the high yield transaction. Once the company has registered the notes, it becomes subject to the reporting requirements of a public company.

In structuring high yield transactions, the investment bankers will determine whether the company has the ability to pay interest on the notes prior to their maturity. High yield notes are generally structured as interest only during the life of the note. In addition, the notes may not generally be repaid or redeemed for a minimum period of time. The minimum time during which prepayment is precluded varies from deal to deal, but is normally not less than three years. After the three-year period ends, most high yield offerings have some type of prepayment penalty associated with an early payoff.

Virtually all high yield offerings are established as unsecured loans. In order to facilitate this type of offering, most high yield transactions are structured as loans to a holding company. In this respect, the issuer can place secured debt at its operating company level. Placing secured debt at the operating company level insures that senior lenders have their loans located where the issuer's assets are located.

High yield offerings are debt offerings so the investment banking expenses are lower than in equity offerings. Although the initial transaction is structured as a private placement, and therefore the company may receive the proceeds of the offering more quickly than in an IPO, investor requirements to register the high yield notes cause the transaction to be essentially equivalent to a public offering in terms of legal, accounting, and printing expenses.

Reverse Mergers into Publicly Traded Shells   Private companies face a daunting task in convincing an investment banker to dedicate the time and attention that it takes to evaluate a company. Assuming that the time is invested to evaluate a company, it is even a greater risk for an investment banker to devote a team of professionals to run the going public gauntlet. Not only must market conditions be right in general, but the company industry segment must be in favor in order to achieve a successful initial public offering. Throughout the evaluation period and the public registration process, management must juggle the demands of registration with maintaining the operations of the business in a manner that is consistent with the forecasts that the investment bankers relied upon to make their initial investment decision. If operations falter in the midst of the registration process, or if market conditions suffer an adverse change, the probability of a successful offering is diminished significantly. With all of these risks encircling a company and standing between the company and going public, it is not a surprise that many companies have searched diligently for an alternative process.

Merging a private company with a publicly traded shell accomplishes this objective. Publicly traded shell corporations exist as a result of two primary plans. Either the company sold or liquidated its business, leaving the shell, or the sponsors of the company devoted the resources to getting the company public with a long-term plan of leveraging the public registration into a significant ownership interest in a private company desiring to enter the public markets on an expedited basis.

Structuring the transaction results in the public company issuing shares to the private company in a transaction that normally qualifies for transactional exemption treatment under Rule 506 of Regulation D. The combination of the two companies is accomplished by the public company creating a wholly owned new subsidiary. The private company is then combined with and into the subsidiary in a manner that results in the private company becoming a wholly owned subsidiary of the public company. This transaction structure is known as a reverse triangular merger.

Although the private company shareholders receive restricted stock and cannot immediately sell the shares, liquidity can be achieved by either negotiating registration rights or by holding the shares for a year and then selling under the guidelines of SEC Rule 144. Rule 144 permits the sale of 1 percent of the outstanding shares of a company by an investor every 90 days.

While a reverse triangular merger avoids the time, expense, and risk associated with the going public process, unless the publicly traded shell has retained capital or raised capital in its initial registration process, the resulting value to a private company is minimal. That is to say that the private company owners have been diluted in the combination by an amount equal to the percentage of ownership that is ceded to the public shareholders, and now in a diluted state, the combined companies must go back to the market if additional capital is needed. It is rare that a combination of a public shell and a private company would not immediately need to access the markets for capital.

Although for the reverse merger strategy the cost is high to the owners of the private company, by merging with the public company they gain access to a much larger body of potential investors. This body of investors requires the liquidity afforded by the public registration process and serves as a pool of investors for the newly combined company. The cost of capital is high in this arena, but the capital serves a legitimate need and these investors have provided much needed cash to many companies that would not be in existence today without the start-up cash.

Fairness Hearings   In contrast with large corporate mergers where securities issued by a public company in connection with a merger are registered on SEC Form S-4, issuers look for private placement exemptions in smaller transactions due to the cost and time required in connection with the Form S-4 registration process. While some transactions clearly qualify for a transactional exemption under Rule 506 of Regulation D, where the target company has a large number of shareholders, complying with the limit of 35 or less nonaccredited investors may be impossible. Section 3(a)(10) of the Securities Act provides a solution in many cases involving an exchange of securities in connection with a merger or acquisition.

Section 3(a)(10) describes a process by which securities can be issued in connection with a merger or acquisition and qualify for an exemption from registration. Unlike Rule 506 of Regulation D, however, a shareholder in the target does not receive restricted securities, and if the acquiring company is publicly traded, the target shareholders may immediately sell shares received in the transaction, subject to certain volume limitations imposed on affiliates. In effect, the exemption is essentially equivalent to a registration of the securities for nonaffiliates in that they receive freely tradable shares.

In order to qualify for the transactional exemption, (1) the securities must be received in an exchange, (2) a state governmental entity must have authority to approve the fairness of the transaction, (3) there must be a hearing in which the governmental agency approves the fairness of the transaction, and (4) the hearing must be open to the public. If these criteria are met, the fairness hearing procedure provides an effective method for complying with securities regulations and providing target shareholders with an opportunity for immediate liquidity without navigating the time-consuming and expensive SEC registration process.

Shelf Registrations   SEC Rule 415 covers matters relating to shelf registrations. A shelf registration is a registration statement filed by an issuer where the issuer is preparing for an offering of securities, but cannot specifically identify the transaction structure at the time of the initial registration. The SEC permits this type of registration in order to provide companies with an opportunity to access the public markets when the timing for a transaction has been identified. In this respect, the normal process would require the company to identify its transaction and begin the registration process with the SEC. Although large issuers might finish the process in a relatively short period of time, smaller issuers are in many cases subject to review, which can cause the registration process to take 60 to 90 days.

Where a company needs to act quickly, either to consummate a transaction or to raise capital, the shelf registration process affords a solution. The issuing company, having completed the registration process, simply files an update to the shelf registration statement, and the securities can be issued. This technique is used to permit companies to more accurately time access to the capital markets when the so-called market windows are open, and to issue shares in connection with mergers and acquisitions. The issuance of shares in connection with mergers and acquisitions is especially useful in the context of a public company's roll-up strategy. In a roll-up scenario, the public company makes a series of acquisitions over a short period of time. In lieu of registering shares for each deal, the company simply pulls down from its shelf registration an amount of shares sufficient to close each deal, thereby avoiding the cost and time that would otherwise be required to register each transaction.

Shelf registrations permit a company a great deal of flexibility in that they permit the company to dispose of the registered shares over a two-year period. In addition, a company may file what is known as an unallocated shelf registration statement. Unallocated registration statements permit a company to wait to see market conditions, and only later at the time of closing the transaction determine the amount of securities to be offered and whether the offering should be debt or equity or a combination of both. This financing flexibility has gained increasing importance for companies operating in capital-intensive industries.

CHAPTER 7

Expert Support—
The Players and Their Roles

In addition to the management team, there are a number of people who are critical to developing and executing the financing plan and therefore are essential elements to a successful company. These people include counsel (i.e., lawyers), directors, investment bankers, accountants, and consultants/advisers. Understanding the roles of these people and what should be expected from them is the topic of this chapter.

COUNSEL

Counsel is a critical member of your strategic and financial planning team. As management considers its financing alternatives and potential actions, it needs to understand the issues and ramifications. Counsel should be an expert in transaction structuring and in compliance with securities law issues. There are many issues that arise out of various corporate financing actions that will not be contemplated by management until counsel makes management aware of the consequences. Counsel cannot prepare the best structure without a comprehensive understanding of the company and its strategic focus; facilitating this awareness is the role of the CEO.

Counsel has to be a confidant, someone with whom management can discuss ideas, issues, and strategies before taking a proposal to the board. Counsel needs to be well respected and experienced. In many cases, he or she will be your advocate in negotiations with counsel for third parties. It is important to have a lawyer who is a "deal doer" as opposed to a "deal killer." Deal doers have the best interest of the company in mind and are focused on completing deals and finding ways to make transactions close. In all deals, there are obstacles and emotions that arise even after the business principals have agreed on the major terms.

Be apprehensive if the party that you are dealing with engages special counsel or changes counsel. From experience, the goal of that new firm will be to impress its new client by demonstrating the firm's technical capability and knowledge of the law. Generally, these firms want to renegotiate the major deal terms to prove they are a value-added partner. These deals will take longer, be more expensive, and be more contentious.

As mentioned before, counsel (and your other advisers) needs to have the right experience and background for the task at hand. Though you may have a long and successful relationship with personal counsel that may be strong in real estate, estate planning, or some other discipline, that lawyer is probably not the right counsel for corporate financings and transactions. In our experience, these folks will focus on the wrong issues and spend much time getting up to speed, the end result being either a poorly done deal or a failed transaction. If you find yourself in the situation of having the wrong counsel, ask your existing counsel to help you find and evaluate new counsel with the right skills; do this before you begin the financing or transaction process, not afterward. Having counsel that is known for doing deals and for expertise in transactions and finance will be invaluable in the financing process and lend credibility to your initiative.

Some attorneys are also excellent businesspeople. It is critical to have counsel who can, without having all of the situational information, balance their role as legal and business adviser without unduly influencing their clients to make certain decisions. This is true of most third party advisers. Usually the CEO is in a unique position and must balance the advice and perspective of counsel with his or her own industry knowledge and experience. Some firms have partners that cross over from counsel to an informal investment banker. This is not bad if they have the marketing skills, deal instincts, experience, and available staff time; but it can be problematic if their role is not well understood and defined.

Regarding fees, negotiate the terms of engagement with your counsel before beginning the process. You may consider sharing the risk of success of the deal by having discounted front-end rates and a back-end bonus based on completion of the transaction—especially where you can differentiate between strictly legal services and business advice. We recommend having an overall budget established for each adviser's fees and having an agreement to check in upon reaching a certain percentage use of that amount, allowing you to manage the cost of the transaction and make course corrections if required.

BOARD OF DIRECTORS

The authors of this handbook have cumulatively served on several dozen boards of both entrepreneurial and public companies, and can offer opinion based on experiences. We believe CEOs not only control the composition of the board but also set the tone for how it functions. How a board is composed and what the CEO expects of the board is important. We have been on boards where CEOs load the board with friends and discuss company issues at the surface level. In these situations, we have found the board well compensated but rarely challenging or constructive. These CEOs tend to avoid criticism and advice. Generally, these CEOs want feel-good accolades from others. Notwithstanding, the boards appear independent and have members with influential titles; but the members are not fully engaged from a business perspective. However, with Sarbanes-Oxley legislating board independence, audit committees, and management/director accountability, this type of board will not be the norm in the future. CEOs will have to take a serious view to composing and managing their boards.

How should a CEO compose a board, and what should be expected from the board? The board should be composed of individuals who can help the company through a rich network of potential customers, investors, vendors, and partners. It is very helpful to have a truly independent board made up of experienced industry managers who are willing to discuss issues frankly and openly. Many boards meet quarterly to review corporate performance, but these meetings do not normally focus on specific operating issues concerning the company. Members will focus on issues that arise at the board meeting and freely discuss these issues, but we have found a lot of the advice to be more generic and strategic in nature than specific to our situation. What you want from your board has to be thought out in advance in order to ensure that the board members address issues relating to their particular areas of expertise.

For instance, one author was involved in a medical device business. As CEO, he wanted to bring certain skill sets in a number of areas to the board. He desired a customer, a hospital administrator, another device CEO who had more experience than he had, a pharmaceutical CEO because the device monitored therapeutics, a senior executive from his distribution partner, a senior partner from one of our largest institutional investors, and a former investment banker. Later, he added a former accountant to act as financial expert to comply with Sarbanes-Oxley requirements for a head of the audit committee. The combination of these various skills was most helpful and allowed members to assume roles of expertise. In discussing sales concerns, there was a board member customer who could discuss technical issues or concerns from the hospital perspective. His distribution partner was from a large organization, and having the divisional head on the board gave her and him a unique perspective into both organizations and allowed for better communication and planning. The pharmaceutical CEO brought the selling partner's marketing perspective and a Rolodex of contacts. The device CEO provided a wealth of knowledge regarding potential operational pitfalls associated with various stages of product development and growth. For entrepreneurial companies there is always great concern about financings and new funding sources. Having an investment banker and an institutional investor on the board greatly enhanced discussions surrounding new investment timing, pricing, and sources.

He was pleased with the board and its composition because the board was highly experienced and independent, and each member had an area of expertise that was recognized by the others. As a consequence, the board had almost no turnover in seven years and worked together well. Interestingly, none of the directors had previously worked with the others before coming on the board. In fact, he only had known two of the directors casually before asking them to serve. The concern was finding the best people with the greatest experience in their areas of expertise. The board's composition strategy dictated the type of expertise required in the search.

We offer our experience as an example, but obviously each board should be reflective of the necessary skills to confront the issues facing or that will face the management. Spending significant time developing the strategy about board composition is critical to company success and board effectiveness. Our experience is that CEOs often put people on the board that do not have significant industry experience nor expertise that can help a company. This is a mistake because the CEO cannot count on the advice of his board, nor does he or she have experts to call upon. No one person has all the answers, and while consultants are often used in larger companies to complement corporate skills, the board is an entrepreneurial company's collection of experts to sharpen strategic thinking.

Here are a few dos and don'ts that we believe CEOs should consider:

- The board establishes parameters for acceptable corporate performance, and management works for the board. They are not buddies, and it is imperative to maintain a professional relationship with each member. Never forget they are being paid to manage CEO performance and assess the managerial skills required to lead the company. We have seen CEOs display feelings of betrayal when directors have questioned their skills or ability to build teams. Building the confidence of the board in management is critical to CEO success. If the CEO uses individual members as confidants, they are aware of his mortality, periods of indecision, and personal motivations that may conflict with corporate needs. CEOs often cast the seeds of their own demise despite reasonable performance.

■ Do not overwhelm directors with day-to-day details. Board meetings are not the time to display vast technical knowledge of the business or the product. Remember the board establishes operating performance and strategic issues. Do not discuss leaves, branches, or individual trees; the board should establish policy. Within this context, details are important in discussion of how they could affect the whole and what strategies are required to assure the well-being of the whole. Engineers and other leaders with technical backgrounds have to work conscientiously to ensure their presentations reflect a strategic focus or a need to refocus strategy.

■ State clearly what is needed from the board before each meeting and gear the meeting appropriately. Board packages should take on a format that is consistent, states corporate and departmental objectives, and gives the right level of detail and tools to establish and evaluate corporate objectives. Provide information that supported prior strategic decisions, as well as historical financial information, in checking your budget. Each department presentation should reflect the managers' work and assessment. Presentations should be practiced and critiqued to ensure essential content and clarity. Working on presentations as a team allows management to have a consistent strategic view and offer potential solutions.

■ Compensate fairly. Good people want to be helpful, but it's important not to take advantage of them. When compensated fairly, the board will feel an obligation to work in your interest and to think about the issues. Provide equity incentives as well as current remuneration when possible.

■ Anything sent to the board should be preapproved by the CEO. This is essential to ensuring consistency and not being surprised by a board member's own interpretation of what someone else has said.

If a CEO wants an independent board with great expertise applicable to the business, the CEO must develop a plan and actively work to bring on the best talent available. Remember, the sign of a good manager is the ability to delegate to subordinate managers and to rely upon directors' knowledge and experience complementary to the CEO's. Utilize the expertise and develop roles for your directors to better assure compatibility. Be professional in all interactions with directors.

In the venture capital section of Chapter 5, we discuss venture capitalist board participation.

INVESTMENT BANKERS

Investment banks are financial intermediaries (not investors) that act as an underwriter or agent for corporations raising capital or seeking strategic transactions. Many maintain broker/dealer operations, maintain markets for previously issued securities, provide market analysis, and offer advisory services to investors. Investment banks generally provide advisory services relating to mergers and acquisitions, private equity placements, and corporate restructuring. Some investment banks offer a subset of the services mentioned, particularly the small and niche boutiques.

There are several tiers or levels of investment banks. The largest are global and often referred to as the "bulge bracket" firms and include the likes of Lehman Brothers, Credit Suisse First Boston, Merrill Lynch, Citigroup (Smith Barney), Morgan Stanley Dean Witter, J. P. Morgan Chase, and Goldman Sachs, as well as the less recognized firm UBS.[1] The second tier firms are usually regional in nature and have focused operations in a geographic area or in an area of specialty. The third tier firms are referred to as boutique firms and specialize in a particular market niche.

For the purposes of this handbook, most emerging growth and middle-market businesses will be served by second and third tier investment banks until their revenue exceeds $50 million to $100 million. In fact, most start-up and emerging growth companies will only be able to attract the attention of the third tier firms and placement agents, because of the small size of the potential transaction and the limited fees involved.

Investment bankers are the corporate finance and mergers and acquisitions professionals and the analysts and underwriting specialists who will work with a client company. In small firms, a handful of individuals may play various investment banking roles in the relationship with a client company. In larger firms, there are multiple individuals who fill each role mentioned.

Path to an IPO

By the time the company can hire a first or second tier investment bank, it has created substantial market value. While the dot-com era was the exception, most companies seeking investment banking assistance have created a proven product, demonstrated significant revenue and earnings growth, and are seeking additional capital to grow and/or they are seeking an exit for their original investors through an initial public offering. Another corporate growth and financing strategy is through merger or acquisition. Investment bankers are usually well versed in both acquisitions and financings. The investment bankers are the company's avenue to access public investors and funds.

It has been said that a venture capitalist's best friend is an investment banker. Once the venture fund has developed the company to the point of having strong revenues, earnings, and leadership along with a developed product or service in growth markets with a defensible niche, then the fund can consider selling the company's equity in the public market and potentially exiting its investment. For the venture capitalist, an initial public offering (IPO) represents a potential payday. Six months after an IPO, the venture capital managers can distribute shares to their limited partners, who can then sell the shares and hopefully realize a good return. During this six-month lockup period, the venture capitalist is completely at risk for market conditions, unless the venture capitalist hedges its position. In a hedge situation, the venture capitalist will normally place a collar around the top and bottom acceptable pricing positions of the portfolio company. While the upside is capped in this scenario, so is the downside. Recently, venture capitalists and private equity firms have been able to sell larger and larger positions in an IPO. These situations involve companies with strong and stable cash flows such as rural telecommunications companies and yellow pages publishers.

From company management's perspective, going public involves significant benefits and risks, and must be studied and weighed carefully. Raising public capital comes with significant fiduciary responsibilities and reporting requirements. The company begins to operate in a glass house; all important transactions, events, and quarterly financials are publicly announced. The company has to provide financial guidance to investors and meet expectations created. Operating as a public entity is very different from operating as a private company where the board generally represents the vast majority of ownership and decisions are kept quiet. To go public, management accepts a lot of responsibility. While it may appear that management has little say in the decision to go public, few companies have achieved public status where the management team was not integrally involved in the going public decision. Venture capital investors seeking liquidity may decide that an IPO is not a viable alternative due to market or other conditions and may pursue a merger or acquisition exit strategy. Managers who see strong growth potential may not want to sell in the short term, so going public is often a more attractive alternative in order to provide the company's investors with a liquidity event.

For the management team, going public means selling new investors on the future prospects of the business. While it can be a great day for investors when a company goes public, it is also a weighty proposition for management. After the investment bankers have a closing dinner they move on to another deal. Early investors hope the company can sustain its performance for a period of time that permits them to liquidate their investment and count their shekels. But management and in many respects early investors are locked into their positions long after the IPO, and as such they must share the risks related to the incremental costs of being a public company, such as the costs associated with legal reporting and auditing requirements. These obligations add significant costs to the operating budgets of companies accessing the public markets. Recently the level of costs applicable to middle-market public companies has geometrically increased due to the burden of compliance with Sarbanes-Oxley rules.

In thinking about the corporate maturation process, investment bankers play a pivotal role in a company's development. It is important to know the investment firms and which ones have analysts covering your industry. If your company is an IPO candidate and investment bankers concur, making fast friends with your banker is easy. The world has moved to transaction-based investment houses, though bankers will still attempt to sell you on their relationship. Until the 1990s, investment banks operated on a reputation for bringing good deals to investors, so the investors often purchased securities based on the quality of the investment bank as opposed to an understanding of the transaction. Companies cherished their relationships with investment banks because those houses had the ability to maximize value and market their client companies to investors through their analysts. This was a win-win approach, with both sides benefiting from the relationship. Companies were often associated with a particular investment bank. Some banks served middle-market companies, others just the Fortune 500, and yet others sold riskier deals. There was a pecking order, and through the 1980s and part of the 1990s most technology companies wanted one of the "four horsemen" to take them public. It was a mark of a good company to have a horseman leading the deal.

With the end of the Glass-Steagall Act (i.e., commercial banks are no longer restricted from owning investment banks), many of the highly reputable investment banks were bought and with that relationships were destroyed. Investment bankers in partnership structures got rich and retired, while others were left to work within the new rules imposed by their commercial bank brethren. The industry changed significantly, and many investment bankers left the industry or started new houses. This is obviously a simplified history, but the point we are making is that a long-term relationship between companies and their investment banks is no longer the rule. Because personnel changed and investment banks were sold and consolidated, the industry became more transaction oriented. The investment banks housed inside commercial banking operations were expected to serve larger clients with large financings and thus greater profit potential. Although investment houses built reputations with specific industries and specific market segments, they were asked to serve new and larger markets. Thus a void has developed in the lower middle markets.

Notwithstanding, the important decision factors for selecting an investment bank are the same as they were years ago:

- Does the investment bank serve my market and my industry?
- Is there a well-respected industry analyst who will follow my company and write on its progress given the new rules affecting the relationship between banker and analysts operating under the umbrella of the same company?
- Does the firm have strong institutional investor relationships, and is the firm's opinion respected?
- Does the firm have a strong retail distribution network?

The process is one based on trust. The investment bank is selling its reputation to investors by backing the company. The company is selling itself to new investors and the investment bank is, in essence, confirming the story through its analyst's due diligence. As an investor, the more one trusts the industry analyst and his or her work, the more receptive the investor is to a company supported by that analyst. Once a company is selected by an investment banker, or vice versa, completes the SEC registration process, and begins the IPO road show (a one-to-two-week selling trip across the country to meet with institutional investors), the company has little say in the process. The investment bank arranges the interviews, seeks interest, and hopefully completes the transaction within the pricing range negotiated. If all goes well, the financing takes place and the investment bank will receive industry standard commissions for completing the transaction. Public equity deals generally pay 7 percent of the offering proceeds to the underwriting group, while private deals are normally set at 5 percent of the amount raised. Debt transactions are priced in the range of 2 percent of the amount of debt raised.

The Boutique Investment Bank

The services of the boutique or niche investment bank are similar to those in the first tier:

- Mergers and acquisitions.
- Valuation analysis and fairness opinions.

- Private equity and/or debt placements.
- Public equity offerings.
- Reverse mergers.
- Short-term bridge financing.
- Strategic consulting.

The smaller firms tend to focus on a particular set of services and target industries, such as software companies. Many of these smaller firms focus solely on private debt and equity placements along with mergers and acquisitions advisory functions. These firms are positioned to support the financing needs and services of the emerging growth and lower-middle-market companies. Some of these firms have strong reputations for conducting due diligence and bringing solid client companies to investors and buyers; these firms are valuable to the client company and provide initial validation of the company's credibility to the investment community. There are other small investment banks that are simply matchmakers, providing no filter or credibility to the company seeking financing. The function performed by a matchmaker is sometimes referred to as that of a placement agent.

Fees for investment banking services typically include a retainer, which may be one-time or monthly, and a success fee contingent upon successful completion of the transaction. In some instances, you will find smaller firms that will operate solely on a contingency fee. It is important to utilize a fee structure that aligns the investment bank's incentive with your company's objectives. Most larger firms have moved to a monthly retainer plus a contingency or success fee payable only upon a successful closing of a transaction.

Important decision factors for selecting a small or niche investment bank include:

- The reputation and credibility of the principals of the firm.
- The background and experience of the banker working with your company.
- Does the firm have a positive track record for doing what it says? (This is usually not questioned in the tier one and two investment banks.) Generally, investment banking engagements are structured as "best efforts" arrangements; there is no guaranteed success unless they are able to fund the project.
- Does the firm have the resources to allocate to your project in the time frame required to meet your company's objectives?
- Is the firm willing to commit to a time line for completion of your project?

Role of the Investment Banker
in the Financing Process

The investment banker typically manages the financing process and assists in preparing the company to be presented to potential investors. The value of an investment bank is its relationships and credibility with investors, its understanding of the market and its dynamics, and the ability to lead and drive the financing process to closure. Because investment banks are intermediaries and generally not providers of capital, some executives elect to execute transactions without them in order to avoid the fees. However, an experienced, quality investment bank adds significant value to a transaction and can pay for its fee many times over while improving the chances of closing the deal.

For all functions except sales and trading, the services should go well beyond simply making introductions or brokering a transaction. Depending on the size of your company and the bank involved, projects may include detailed industry and financial analysis; preparation of relevant documentation such as an offering memorandum or presentation to the board of directors; assistance with due diligence; providing a fairness opinion; negotiating the terms of the transaction; coordinating legal, accounting, and other advisers; and generally assisting in all phases of the project to ensure successful completion.[2]

ACCOUNTANTS

Like other professions, there are tiers or levels of certified public accountant (CPA) firms that focus their practices on specific market segments and customer needs. The Big Four accounting firms are Deloitte & Touche, Ernst & Young, KPMG, and PricewaterhouseCoopers; each has offices globally. In addition, firms like Grant Thornton, BDO Siedman, and McGladrey & Pullen have large U.S. presence and international offices. There are many regional and local firms.

Though it may be obvious, accountants perform various distinct types of services—auditing, financial reporting, and tax consulting; there are many sublevels of specialization. From the audit perspective, the historical role of accountants has been to give investors confidence in the company's financial statements and to provide an independent confirmation of its financial position.

Role of Accountants[3]

As part of the relationship with start-up and early stage companies, accountants provide services as part of a formal engagement, and advice and guidance informally. These informal services are really an investment in hopes of securing a longer-term relationship. The traditional services include a compilation, review, or audit of the financial statements of the company and preparation of tax returns. Informally, the partners and senior members of their staff review business plans and provide feedback and insights. Many times they can assist with the content and form of the financial plan that supports the business plan and provide a critical eye regarding the financial projections and business model. They see many financial plans and can make recommendations on how to best present the company and improve credibility, saving headaches and potential embarrassment. Experienced accountants can be strategic advisers and play significant roles in developing operating plans.

From a tax perspective, accountants can provide critical guidance to the company and its founders with tax planning issues such as:

- Preserving net operating losses (NOLs).
- Establishing and retaining research and development (R&D) tax credits.
- Making important tax elections to protect the founders' and company's interests.
- Structuring, accounting, and analyzing the tax ramifications of compensation, stock options, phantom stock, restricted stock, or stock appreciation rights so that an adverse situation with regard to personal and corporate income is not created.
- Assuring the company is established to meet the qualified business venture (QBV) status for certain tax credits. QBV requires ongoing audits or reviews to maintain the status.

In addition, accountants assist and advise on establishing accounting and control policies. Examples would include guidelines for revenue recognition, validating revenue models for new business types, and month-end closing procedures. This is critical in early stage companies that may have creative or new business models that might give rise to accounting complexities. This is particularly true if the company has outside investors or plans to pursue a public offering. The financial statements will need to comply with generally accepted accounting principles (GAAP) and potentially meet the Securities and Exchange Commission's variants thereof. Some accounting firms provide the service that bridges the resource and intellectual capital gaps between in-house bookkeeping and appropriately closing the books to reconcile accounts and to generate financial statements and schedules. This involves augmenting the in-house accounting team's capabilities with one or more staff accountants.

Many accounting firms are well connected in their business communities and have a network of clients and others in the marketplace. This network typically includes potential investors and partners that can help the company accelerate its growth and be successful.

For middle-market companies (depending on company internal competencies and staffing) accounting firms provide traditional audits, prepare tax returns, advise on tax treatment of transactions, and augment internal analysis requirements. With the advent of Sarbanes-Oxley legislation, the consulting services they can provide are limited. When not in conflict with Sarbanes-Oxley rules, other potential consulting services that many accounting firms provide include: due diligence support for transactions; valuation work; forensic audit assignments; development of disaster recovery plans; risk assessment projects; and evaluating, recommending, and implementing information technology systems. With many of these projects it is important to distinguish between audit and nonaudit client role to eliminate conflicts of interest.

In summary, having a plan that demonstrates financial expertise, controls, and accountability is required to raise capital. Having the right accounting firm and partner-level support will enhance a company's ability to be successful with its financing process. While young companies often argue against audits and opt for reviews to save money, it is our experience that in order to package a company for future financings, investors want to see audited historical statements. Too many unanswered questions can arise without a formal audit, which result in fighting unnecessary battles and distract from the financing process. Get audited annually.

Selecting an Accounting Firm

If your company is publicly traded, you will need to engage one of the firms allowed to perform pubic audits. Recent Sarbanes-Oxley legislation requires that the auditors of publicly held companies be registered with the Public Company Accounting Oversight Board. As of July 2004 there were about a thousand such firms registered.[4]

A key element in selecting an accounting firm is the chemistry with the assigned partner and securing access to the partner. Partner-level interaction and attention are vital for the leadership of young and emerging companies; most of the value in the relationship is the informal guidance and services mentioned earlier.[5] If the partner does not have the mind share to contribute to your business, you will not get the value required. Before selecting a firm, ask to meet the team that will be supporting your company.

A second important determinant: Does the firm have past experiences in the areas and stages of the business that your company requires? Prior experience can be invaluable to managers in developing business and strategic plans to meet current market conditions and current competitive trends.

Other questions:

- Does the firm have the industry experience and know the nuances that affect financial reporting so that your company's financial statements are comparable to others in similar businesses?
- Does the firm have expertise and experience with the type of investors or lenders that will most likely fund your growth, and do they understand the accounting and tax issues given the likely deal structures of the likely financings?
- Does the firm have staff in physical proximity to where the business operation(s) are located?
- What firm or partner does your counsel recommend?
- What firm has the relationships with potential investors and lenders?
- Is the firm expanding and seeking new clients? Is the firm overloaded?

Managing the Relationship

As with other advisory relationships, the accounting advice you obtain will be only as good as the information and detail you share. Share the vision, the business plan, management's aspirations, exit strategies and thoughts, and shareholder objectives—full disclosure. As with your counsel, accountants can be of value in preventing issues proactively if they know about them. They can also help you clean up mistakes after the fact, but that is usually more painful. The timing of communication is critical in maintaining confidence, credibility, and integrity with those professionals who support the business.

Seek to establish a relationship where you feel comfortable calling as required. Establish an understanding up front regarding the billing procedures of each service provider. Most accountants and lawyers will actually assist the client company in establishing and managing a budget if asked. If you have trouble with the issues described, you may have the wrong firm.

Lastly, your company can get fired from the accounting relationship for not being honest, for not telling the whole truth, for lacking concern for doing what is right, for having conflicting engagements, or for causing concern due to any sense of impropriety. Ethical behavior of the board and management team is critical! If an accounting firm fires you, your reputation in the investor community is hurt. These situations create credibility issues for third parties related to the company, and could represent a major setback to the company plans. Getting management's credibility back on track will take time and expensive efforts. And sometimes the CPA withdrawal of services will precipitate removal of the CEO or CFO, or both.

CONSULTANTS/ADVISERS

Depending on the size and stage of your company, and the particular skills within the leadership team, consultants and advisers can augment and support management as they pursue growth strategies and seek funding. We provide an overview of the major types of firms and their services as they relate to the financing process.

Management consulting firms provide many of the same corporate finance services as investment banks but tend to focus less on the transaction aspect. In many instances they provide their services based on time and materials versus transaction success. Their efforts typically emphasize the operating and marketing strategies to position the company for success followed by transaction support services. They do not underwrite offerings, provide analyst coverage of traded stocks, or have trading desks. The range of services tends to be broader than that of investment banks. They offer advice and support earlier in the financing process and after closing, whereas most investment banks focus on the financing transaction itself. You will find some firms offer corporate development advisory services, an integrated approach to consulting and investment banking services focused on value-creation activities and issues. A key for most readers of this handbook will be finding the right size firm with appropriate industry or stage skills to undertake an engagement. Like investment banks, management consulting firms have several tiers of players that focus on certain types and stages of companies. Assessing the skills, background, and reputation of the partner that will work with your organization is one of the top priorities in selecting a management consulting firm.

The consulting groups of major accounting firms provide advisory services that compete with investment banks. Some of them, like Grant Thornton, differentiate themselves by providing fully integrated corporate finance services (acquisitions, divestitures, and financing) to middle-market companies on a global basis. Their transactions are generally below the target size for global investment banks. The smaller regional banks, brokers, and boutiques (with whom they do not compete) generally do not operate on a global basis and are not able to integrate a full-service offering. These integrated services include accounting, consulting, and tax advice, which enables them to add further value and resolve transaction issues that inevitably arise. Their strategy is to improve the probability of closing the deal below the radar of the major investment banks. Additionally, their global network of offices and contacts enables them to identify overseas buyers and resolve transaction issues, again with the aim of having a higher percentage of transactions with overseas buyers, who are frequently willing to pay a higher price and are favored by management for leaving the existing structures in place.[6] The size financing that these firms will undertake depends on their particular niche and area of expertise. There are many smaller firms that will undertake assignments ranging from writing business plans for start-ups and pursuing venture funding for them to niche financial service providers that offer the same services as the boutique investment banks but on a time and materials basis only. Again, the key to success with any of these is the credibility and network of the partner assigned to your company.

There are other professional services firms that combined unique expertise with various aspects of the financing process to deliver integrated services. An example is valuation firms, which have core expertise in business and asset valuation. Inherently they provide valuation and advisory services to companies contemplating strategic alternatives. Some of these firms have coupled investment banking operations to deliver a broad array of corporate finance services. The same concept holds true with certain firms that provide interim executives. In general, you will find that many of these firms have strengths and expertise in a particular industry, company stage, or type of transaction. If it is a smaller firm, the background and experience of the firm's principals will drive their credibility. Hiring larger consulting firms might not be practical for smaller companies. But there are experienced local and regional consultants and advisers that can be used at a reasonable cost that provide exceptional service and value.

SUMMARY

All companies need a team of qualified and credible advisers to support leadership's vision and ambitions. We suggest that you carefully interview and assemble a group of professionals that have the focus, expertise, network, and mind share to enable company management to make sure-footed, solid decisions as they contemplate and execute on the financing process. They are not all needed at once. Prioritize, and be aware of the cost and benefits of the engagements and timing of support. The mix of these professionals and their firms is a function of the credibility of the company's management, size of the company checkbook, stage and industry of the company, and the realistic growth opportunity of the business.

CHAPTER 8

Closing the Deal

PROCESS CHECK-IN

In Chapter 1 we outlined the overall financing process and provided a flow chart (in Figure 1.1) to highlight the fundamental elements of capital formation and to provide a framework for discussion and analysis. We addressed the need to understand the current financial and strategic position of the company, the business plan, industry comparable performance, and the forecast and a go-forward strategy. Without a clear strategic vision and a disciplined business plan, companies seeking capital will be comparatively disadvantaged in their search, operating in a reactive rather than proactive mode. In Chapter 3 we presented the basic concepts used to establish the business valuation, and we emphasized the importance of securing buy-in among the stakeholders with respect to realistic valuations. Without a realistic sense of valuation, stockholders may cause management to expend significant time and organizational resources only to have a potential transaction fall apart in midstream. In Chapter 4 we presented a framework to view the capital structure of start-ups, emerging growth companies, and middle-market companies. We highlighted the concept that raising capital is driven by "when a company can raise money" and not by "when it needs funds." We provided a lookup table (Figure 4.2) indicating the major types of financing by company stage. Chapters 5 and 6 provided an overview of the many funding sources and the mechanics of debt and equity instruments. And then in Chapter 7 we introduced our perspective of the roles of the key professionals that will support management and the stockholders as they navigate the financing process. In the pages to follow, we will provide an overview of the last phase of the process.

The Team

In the ideal situation, management will be able to recruit a team of advisers or interim talent to focus on discrete parts of the financing and to provide support in their areas of expertise. Drawing upon outside resources for specialized expertise allows company leadership to focus on a macro strategy encompassing the entire business and strategic plan. In many cases, management starts with existing relationships and incrementally adds to its network of resources until the transaction team has sufficient knowledge and experience to close the transaction. In start-up and early stage companies, management is intimately involved in almost every step of the financing process.

Table 8.1 presents the members of the team most likely to be involved in the financing process based on the stage of the company. Team composition is subject to significant variation based on the actual circumstances and roles of the individuals involved, on the company's industry segment, and on the nature of the capital being raised. The financing team table is presented to cause the reader to consciously think about who should be involved in closing a capital formation transaction.

Testing the Market

Once the target capital structure is defined and/or the desired funding identified, the financing team will extract an executive summary from its business plan that provides an overview of the company and the amount and description of the funding it seeks (for relatively small debt transactions this step may be omitted or potential lenders may simply have an application form). The executive summary is a two- or three-page narrative that includes a brief statement of the company's market opportunity; key management's background; the company's products, services, or solutions; summary financial information; and a description of the use of proceeds of the financing.

The executive summary is then sent to a target list of potential lenders or investors seeking indications of interest. If the company has an investment bank, consultant, or adviser involved in the financing process, the summary would customarily be selectively forwarded to targeted financial sources from them versus directly from management. Advisers play a key role in the success of most transactions. In many cases, the target financial source may have conducted business with the adviser previously, and as such, prior successes with the target enhance the company's profile or at least increase the probability that the target will even bother to read the executive summary.

The Book

A disclosure document (the book) with relevant information is compiled to present the opportunity and the company. Depending on the type of capital sought and the potential audience, the book will vary from an informal business plan to a detailed, legal offering memorandum, filled with risk

TABLE 8.1 Typical Financing Team

Team Member	Start-up $0 to $10 Million Revenue	Emerging Growth $1 Million to $10 Million Revenue	Lower Middle-Market $10 Million to $50 Million Revenue	Middle-Market $50 Million to $500 Million Revenue
Lead stockholder(s)	Yes	Yes	Sometimes	Sometimes
Lead board member(s)	Yes	Yes	Yes	Sometimes
Company president	Yes	Yes	Yes	Yes
Chief financial officer	Usually there is not one	Yes or Controller	Yes	Yes
Other key managers*	Yes	Yes	Yes	Sometimes
Legal counsel	Yes	Yes	Yes	Yes
Accountant	Yes	Yes	Yes	Yes
Investment banker	Usually not	Sometimes	Sometimes	Yes
Consultant/adviser	Sometimes	Sometimes	Sometimes	Sometimes
Interim leadership	Sometimes	Sometimes	Sometimes	Sometimes

*May include a technical founder, chief technical officer, head of sales, head of marketing, or operations lead (or a combination thereof), depending on the nature of the business and how important that team member is to the future success and performance of the business.

factors and securities regulation disclaimers. We recommend that management, company advisers, and company counsel be involved in all aspects of the preparation of the book. There is a balance to be struck between marketing the company and its prospects and complying with the legal requirements of full and fair securities regulation disclosure rules that apply to companies whether they are seeking equity or debt.

Preparing the Team

Because there will invariably be meetings with potential investors and lenders, full preparation for these discussions is essential. Socialization of the financing strategy among the team increases input and buy-in, as well as creating an opportunity for management to rehearse the presentation of the plan and company story to a friendly audience in preparation for calls and formal meetings. Roles need to be clearly defined so that responses to questions can be crisp and succinct. It is helpful to create a written summary of the financing plan in conjunction with the business plan and to discuss the plan with operating managers in advance of any calls or meetings. It is important that the team speak with a consistent message.

If the company does not have in-house talent to drive the process or cannot afford the allocation of company human resources required to be dedicated to the project, management should contract with an adviser or consultant to lead the process. Experience is a key element to ensuring a smooth process and the maximization of the results on behalf of the stockholders. Having the right team to augment and support management can make the difference between success and failure in the capital formation process.

Timing

Most deals and transactions have a natural pace and time line. It is a function of the people involved, their firms' needs and their personal needs, the overall supply of opportunities, and the relative competitive environment surrounding the situation. Once a company understands its probable types of investors and lenders, it can establish a financing process and time line to better control the outcome. There are times when transactions stall, and at some point the company must make a decision to move on. An overriding theme that we espouse is to continue to do what is required to grow the company regardless of hopeful or promised transactions or deals. Companies and managers that find and create ways to act on their plans despite resource shortfalls are generally in a better position to control their destinies and the outcome of the financing process versus those with good ideas who wait for perfect timing and the action of others.

By testing the market and understanding various parties' interests, the company can take control of the process and create momentum, especially when there are real logical drivers that can establish the need to close the transaction. One of those logical drivers that will not work in the company's favor is running out of cash; that may signal the wrong message and potentially drive away investors or lenders. An example of a positive driver: the launch of a new product line to enter a certain market at a certain time driven by industry dynamics, where meeting a certain window of opportunity may give the company a significant advantage in the market. Another example may be an opportunistic acquisition where the timing is controlled by the selling company or in which your company may be able to buy the business before it goes to auction. Other less important drivers can be meeting year-end objectives of the company, investor, or lender. If the investor or lender is a strategic (versus financial) partner, they may have certain internal drivers that can play to your company's advantage. These can be ascertained by gaining insight into their plans.

Sometimes there is a tendency by management to lock onto a single potential investor or lender at the exclusion of others. Investors and lenders expect competition. Entering discussions with a single party one at a time reduces the competitive dynamics and sometimes leaves the company without the required capital if the deal falls apart. A better alternative is to test the market and determine a short list of preferred investors or lenders and drive the process as a selective auction.

Due Diligence

Due diligence is the investigatory process performed by investors or lenders considering a transaction with the company. Due diligence is conducted to evaluate the business and its finances. In connection with the sale of a company due diligence may be more rigorous than that of a traditional bank loan; however, it is subject to the perceived risk and stage of the company coupled with the type of transaction contemplated and the preferences of the parties involved. Depending on the type and size of transaction, the due diligence could take several months. However, there are investors and lenders that can respond very quickly and are willing to close transactions in weeks versus months.

The level of due diligence is sometimes a point of negotiation. In larger transactions, where lenders or investors are not part of a competitive process, the nature and extent of due diligence is not negotiable. For instance: Selling a middle-market company to a large corporation will probably follow a pattern established by the large corporation. Larger companies usually have defined processes and have extensive due diligence requirements. These larger companies typically use a combination of outside consultants and advisers with specialized areas of expertise that converge on the target company from various locations. Management of a relatively small target company can quickly become overwhelmed and in many cases is significantly outnumbered. The smaller company can mitigate the potential negative effects of this situation with planning, through control of the on-site process, and by limiting the number of visitors at any one time.

From the perspective of the investor or lender, due diligence is conducted to validate the assumptions they made when drafting the term sheet or commitment letter. Undisclosed liabilities, including tax exposure, environmental noncompliance risks, product warranty issues, and many other areas are thoroughly evaluated to prevent surprises after the deal is closed. Critical or showstopping issues that will be revealed during due diligence need to be determined early in the financing process and corrective action plans implemented.

Regarding logistics, the company may prepare an office, conference room, or off-site location as the data room so that any document required by the investor or lender is presented and held there for review and analysis. It is recommended that there be a point person for controlling the documents being reviewed and responding to particular questions. When responding to questions the point person should stick to the question subject matter. There is a tendency to expand the answer into other areas not pertaining to the question. This results from an eagerness to please and to be nice to the other party. It is the objective of any due diligence team to establish a rapport with target management in order to obtain as much unfiltered information regarding the target as possible. The point person may inadvertently be drawn into a discussion in which he or she is not prepared, sharing inaccurate or partial information or drawing attention to a topic that might otherwise not have been highlighted. It is best to stay focused on the original question and address only what was requested.

Counsel should be involved in determining the nature and extent of materials to be included in the data room. In many cases data room materials will relate to legal or financial issues that should be addressed only by counsel or the company's financial officers. Counsel or the company's financial officers should answer questions relating to the data room because the questions will be prepared by the lender's or investor's counsel.

Negotiations

This section summarizes the concepts management should consider when preparing for and engaging in financing transaction negotiations. There are many well-written books on the topic of negotiations, deals, and alternative deal structures. You may consider reading *Dealmaker: All the Negotiating Skills and Secrets You Need* by R.L. Kuhn (Nightingale Conant, 1992).

Early in the formation of the financing team, determine who on the team will represent the company and negotiate the transaction. Discuss and document the principles that will guide key decisions and assure that ground rules are established. Once the type transaction is determined, minimum goals need to be agreed upon so that the team understands its walkaway point. These are the minimum terms, conditions, and values that must be met for the transaction to be acceptable to the company. An understanding of these concepts by board and shareholders prior to entering negotiations is essential, because these two groups will be required to approve any negotiated transaction.

For many types of financings, the lender or investor will present the company with a term sheet or commitment letter. In either case, it will outline the broad terms and conditions in which they are willing to invest in or lend to the business. In some cases, a financing team will choose to accept a broad, general term sheet and then negotiate the specific terms as part of the final transaction documentation, also known as the definitive agreements. Where speed to closing is essential, the parties may go directly to definitive documentation. This practice is more prevalent in the equity and mergers and acquisitions as opposed to debt financing.

From a practical perspective, most start-up and emerging growth companies have no ability to negotiate from a position of strength. Moreover, these early stage companies typically start the search for capital too late to close the transaction before the company finds itself in a financial bind. The relative position of a late-starting company can be improved by preparation and creativity in negotiating the material terms of the transaction. Keep in mind that the premise of this handbook is to shift the company from a reactive and disadvantaged negotiating position to a proactive and relatively strengthened position.

Managing Investor and Lender Relationships

While closing is the culmination of the capital formation process, it is only the start of an ongoing relationship between the company and its financial partner.

Fundamental to the relationship between a company and its financial partner is an ongoing reporting obligation. In many cases, institutional lenders and investors structure the reporting requirements to satisfy obligations that they have to their partners or stockholders, to the financial markets, or to regulatory agencies. In addition, they may negotiate visitation rights to attend board of directors meetings, actually participate on the board of directors, or appoint one or more board members. Regardless of the formal rights provided, periodic communication is important using the concept of "no surprises." This means that the company keeps its investors and lenders abreast of progress even if it is bad news. Negative performance surprises erode management credibility and may force management into a reactive or defensive position with its investors. When material adverse events occur, management must promptly inform investors and lenders and present an action plan that is reasonable, that can be implemented, and that is responsive to the adverse event.

FINAL PERSPECTIVE

Establishing a proper and preferred capital structure is an iterative process for virtually every company of every size. There are many details that management must address and many variables that can change in midstream. the manner in which the capital formation process is addressed. No management team should underestimate the fact that raising money can be difficult and time-consuming. Nonetheless, a company's chances to obtain funding to grow the business can be enhanced with planning, credibility, and persistence.

As we presented earlier in this handbook, having a solid business plan and realistic vision for the company is fundamental to understanding the mix of capital required to fund a company's growth. Coupling this plan with strong management is a formula for success in the capital formation process. Clear vision and strong management will not lead to success unless it is matched with the ability of the company to report performance according to plan to lenders and investors. Meeting revenue and expense budgets builds credibility over time, and with credibility comes success in the financial markets. Even when there are variances, as we all know there will be at some point in time, providing prompt information regarding a miss and management's plan for correcting the issue or event is critical in maintaining the confidence of an investor or lender group.

Investors and lenders are in business to deploy capital to obtain a respectable return based on reasonable and appropriate risk. In today's market, the supply of capital far exceeds the number of quality companies. Those companies that have a clear vision, strong management, and predictable results will find a receptive audience. Remember, quick successes are the exception. Persistence and focus are required to successfully shape the capital structure and navigate the financing process to closure.

Two

Case Studies

In this part,* we are providing a sampling of actual investment and loan transactions by some firms listed in Part Three's Financing Source Directory that follows. We have applied a uniform format for consistency of presentation and obtained content from the funding source, and in some cases, from their portfolio company; the case is written from the lender's/investor's voice unless otherwise indicated. There are 14 case studies in all. When the information was available we have provided a profile of the investor/lender, a profile of the case, insight into the investor or lender's strategy and analysis, summary financial information, transaction details, posttransaction issues, lessons learned, and background about the contributor. The following table provides a cross-reference for the cases to allow you to focus on your particular area of interest.

---

*These cases are presented only for information purposes in support of related explanations contained in this book. No representation is made that other firms or companies will or are likely to receive funding. Some information may have been modified. Nothing contained herein constitutes an offer to sell or a solicitation of an offer to buy securities. Such an offer or solicitation may be made only by a properly authorized offering document.

Case Cross-Reference

Case No.	Firm Type*	Firm	Case Description	Case	Business Description
1	AB	Greenfield Commercial	High-risk ABL	$4MM loan	Manufacturer/assembler
2	AB	Greenfield Commercial	Assignment for benefit of creditors (financing a distressed company)	$0.9MM loan, management purchase	Packing material
3	AI	New Mexico Private Investors	Initial funding and sale of company	MESO	Fuel cells
4	CF	Drug Royalty	Royalty asset-based	AVANIR - operational liquidity	Pharmaceutical
5	CF	IIG—International Investment Group	Trade financing	Factoring, import financing, inventory and warehouse financing, and transaction equity	Manufacturing, metal, alloy, coffee, and pig iron
6	PE	Brookside Capital Partners	Mezzanine investment	McKenzie $7.25M subdebt	Sports products
7	PE	Graham Partners	Acquisition through exit	Eldorado	Architectural stone
8	PE	Meriturn Partners	Restructuring	Dunn $10MM preferred equity; subdebt	Specialty paper
9	PE	Meriturn Partners	Acquisition with management participation	Johnston Textiles—asset acquisition from Chapter 11	Tech and decorative
10	PE	The Riverside Company	Public to private transaction	Dwyer, with family and management	Franchises
11	MB	Veronis Suhler Stevenson	Buy and build strategy	Hanley Wood investment	Construction industry media
12	SI	Siemens	Siemens and three other investors	MontaVista funding	Systems software
13	VC	SJF Ventures	Community development finance	Ryla $2MM series B	B2B teleservices
14	VC	Vested for Growth	Debt with revenue participation	Bortech $500k	Welding equipment

*Note: Key at beginning of Part Three.

CASE STUDY 1: High-Risk Asset-Based Loan/Refinancing

FIRM'S PROFILE

Greenfield Commercial Credit (GCC) is a high-business-risk asset-based lender/factor that provides loans to storied companies in bank refinancing (kick-outs), debtor in possession (Chapter 11 reorganization), high growth, and highly (10 percent down) leveraged buyouts. Client companies routinely have consequential losses, negative net worth, tax problems, and significantly past due accounts payable and cannot find conventional financing from banks, other niche lenders, or venture capital. Working capital in a crisis is needed for the troubled company to fund sales growth, cost cutting activities, new market entry, or a combination of necessary changes for survival. The source of this funding is derived from leveraging various assets in combination such as accounts receivable, inventory, equipment, and/or real estate and purchase order financing.

GCC was created by a former senior banker and a successful entrepreneur to fill the small to middle-market commercial financing void between banks and venture capital. The company, now in its tenth year, hired experienced credit personnel for key sales positions and credit administration personnel with sales skills. All key personnel have significant experience in lending to and/or operating small to midsize companies defined as under $50 million in annual sales. A critical item for loan approval is the collateral and having an understanding of potential collectibility risks. This analysis, for example, may include knowing the cost(s) of finishing work in process in the case of a manufacturer as well as any specific market conditions. The company must have an understandable financial history (reasons for current difficulties), a workable plan to return to profitability, good accounting controls, and, if necessary, strong consulting support. The turnaround is usually accomplished by increasing sales and improving productivity (reducing costs). The distressed company uses higher-cost money to buy time to cure problems. The typical interest rate that GCC charges to compensate for the higher business risk that banks will not accept is prime rate plus 8 percent. Invariably, the existing lending relationship is acrimonious, which further complicates the creation of solutions. This makes GCC a viable financing source option. GCC is a lender, not an investor, taking neither dividends nor success fees. Rapid GCC field decisions on loan structure and collateral value coupled with prompt action by headquarters translates into a timely comprehensive response for their clients' financial needs.

Many GCC clients return to conventional lending or sell at a nondistressed price within two years of funding. In response to continued erratic behavior by the banking community in making and retaining small to midsize commercial loans, several clients now with positive net worth and profits have chosen to remain with GCC. The reasons often cited for not returning to a banking relationship are the aggressive collateral advance rates and proven ability to respond in a crisis. Please refer to Part Three's Financing Source Directory for additional information.

CASE PROFILE

GCC funded a $4,000,000 loan in the spring of 2004. The lending facility included accounts receivable and inventory with a $1,000,000 term loan on equipment. Purchase order financing has been made available as needed for growing raw material requirements to fill the sales backlog. Procedurally, it is a revolving loan with monthly interest payments and a five-year amortization on the term loan.

The company had negative cash flow due to losses. This was the primary reason why many other lenders would not make the needed term loan. The high collateral advance rates of 85 percent on accounts receivable and 40 percent on inventory were needed to pay off the existing lender in full. Greenfield used a 67 percent advance rate on the liquidation value of equipment. The bank was unwilling to accept any loan principal write-off or delay any portion of its repayment, so an unsecured or subordinated note was not an option. The additional working capital provided by the term loan was essential for the company's future. GCC enabled the company to pay the bank, reduce account payables, address a tax problem, and fund sales growth.

The company is a manufacturer/assembler of subassemblies of a major consumer product in a mature market. The market had been depressed for several years and began rebounding in early 2003. Further issues arose with the increasing cost and decreasing availability of raw materials. The bank had capped the line of credit and increasing sales was not financially possible. The inability to buy material on open terms and the growing tendency of their customers stretching payment terms exacerbated the working capital issues. The history of the manufacture of quality products and timely delivery was in jeopardy.

From Greenfield's perspective, the company has the following strengths:

- An essential manufacturing niche not easily replaceable by overseas manufacturers due to the very demanding just-in-time production needs of its clientele.
- The ultimate product, while routinely changed, will not become obsolete anytime soon.
- A single owner of 15 years who delegated authority. The company also has management strength at key positions in accounting, manufacturing, and material procurement.
- The 24 months of losses suffered were typical for the industry at the time.
- Rapid response (in a historical perspective) in making painful but essential personnel cuts and other cost reductions. The cash flow breakeven had been reduced by over 20 percent, so each additional sale had a more positive impact.
- Historically being proactive in addressing its past-due accounts payable issues.

As a result of Greenfield's funding, the company can now make better decisions by having a stable funding source as part of the business turnaround plan. The results of the predictable aggressive funding had a near immediate impact on sales and profitability. In addition, the company was able to eliminate the legal fees associated with continuous short-term loan renewals and supplier lawsuits. The company is now able to produce the higher-margin but cash-intensive sales when the improper financing kept them from it. Greenfield expects this company to return to conventional bank financing in two years.

GREENFIELD DEAL SOURCE AND PROCEDURES

The deal source for the loan discussed was from the prior lender itself who knew our record of funding distressed companies. The company first contacted Greenfield in

December 2003. Within 48 hours of the regional manager receiving a detailed loan request package, a detailed written expression of interest was issued. This expression of interest included a detailed loan structure complete with collateral advance rates and workable cost/benefit analysis. All critical issues that had caused the eventual turndown by the other prospective lenders were discussed with and approved by Greenfield management prior to issuance of that letter. The company had the typical hesitancy to act due to the Greenfield pricing model. As other funding options disappeared, the existing lender became increasingly restrictive until April 2004 when the company chose to move forward with the Greenfield financing plan. After an audit of collateral and financial records, the loan was funded one week later. Greenfield has closed asset-based loan transactions in as few as 10 days and factoring transactions in as few as five days from the start of the audit.

REPORTING REQUIREMENTS

All asset-based lenders have collateral and financial reporting requirements. These are essential in funding the distressed transaction based on collateral:

- Ongoing weekly borrowing-base certificates that detail current sales and collections from a secured bank lockbox.
- Monthly accounts receivable and accounts payable aging, inventory reports, and financial statements.
- Quarterly collateral audits.
- Periodic visits by Greenfield staff.
- Updated cash flow projections as needed.

These reports also help Greenfield be proactive in anticipating the ever-changing client working capital requirements.

ABOUT THE CONTRIBUTOR

Donald M. Rudnik is regional manager, Greenfield Commercial Credit (drudnik@greenfield credit.com). He has 28 years of experience in direct lending to small and midsize businesses and significant experience in numerous operations of distressed companies. He has also assisted in operating and selling the assets of two failed savings and loans for the Resolution Trust Corporation (federal agency). He has written several articles on lending to distressed companies and has spoken nationally on various topics to bankers, consultants, and entrepreneurs.

CASE STUDY 2: Asset-Based Lender, Assignment for Benefit of Creditors

FIRM'S PROFILE

Greenfield Commercial Credit (GCC) is a high-business-risk asset-based lender/factor that provides loans to storied companies in bank refinancing (kick-outs), debtor in possession (Chapter 11 reorganization), high growth, and highly (10 percent down) leveraged buyouts. Client companies routinely have consequential losses, negative net worth, tax problems, and significantly past due accounts payable and cannot find conventional financing from banks, other niche lenders, or venture capital. Working capital in a crisis is needed for the troubled company to fund sales growth, cost cutting activities, new market entry, or a combination of necessary changes for survival. The source of this funding is derived from leveraging various assets in combination such as accounts receivable, inventory, equipment, and/or real estate and purchase order financing.

GCC was created by a former senior banker and a successful entrepreneur to fill the small to middle-market commercial financing void between banks and venture capital. The company, now in its tenth year, hired experienced credit personnel for key sales positions and credit administration personnel with sales skills. All key personnel have significant experience in lending to and/or operating small to midsize companies defined as under $50 million in annual sales. A critical item for loan approval is the collateral and having an understanding of potential collectibility risks. This analysis, for example, may include knowing the cost(s) of finishing work in process in the case of a manufacturer as well as any specific market conditions. The company must have an understandable financial history (reasons for current difficulties), a workable plan to return to profitability, good accounting controls, and, if necessary, strong consulting support. The turnaround is usually accomplished by increasing sales and improving productivity (reducing costs). The distressed company uses higher-cost money to buy time to cure problems. The typical interest rate that GCC charges to compensate for the higher business risk that banks will not accept is prime rate plus 8 percent. Invariably, the existing lending relationship is acrimonious, which further complicates the creation of solutions. This makes GCC a viable financing source option. GCC is a lender, not an investor, taking neither dividends nor success fees. Rapid GCC field decisions on loan structure and collateral value coupled with prompt action by headquarters translates into a timely comprehensive response for clients' financial needs.

Many GCC clients return to conventional lending or sell at a nondistressed price within two years of funding. In response to continued erratic behavior by the banking community in making and retaining small to midsize commercial loans, several clients now with positive net worth and profits have chosen to remain with GCC. The reasons often cited for not returning to a banking relationship are the aggressive collateral advance rates and proven ability to respond in a crisis. Please refer to Part Three's Financing Source Directory for additional information.

CASE PROFILE

The company is a manufacturer and distributor of packing materials and was created in the mid-1990s; it is privately held by hands-on owners. The industry is mature and the product mix is roughly half in commodity sales and half in specialty production (value-added) creation of new packaging configurations with just-in-time production. The company grew during the technology boom with many new products coming to market. By outservicing their competition, the company grew to mid-seven-figure revenue annually. However, during this time, its primary customer failed and filed Chapter 11. The company risked losing much of its net worth and a third of its sales. The failed customer was 750 miles away and did have access to other markets. The decision was made to buy the customer and hopefully add 33 percent to 50 percent in new business. The acquisition was funded by the existing lender, a small business lending section of a large bank; the loans were cross collateralized. The annual sales of the combined company became approximately $10 million.

Within two years after the purchase, the technology bubble burst. Fewer new products came to market (reducing sales and the higher gross margin items) and the overall economy began to weaken. The 9/11/01 attack on the United States occurred and new products were delayed. As with many companies in financial distress and in retrospect, cost cutting was slow. Despite the problems, suppliers were cooperative with the struggling business. The proactive nature of the owners in honoring limited payment promises was explained as a reason for the continued support. The company unsuccessfully sought an investor. The outlook was bleak.

Bank Response to Deteriorating Situation

The existing bank was aware of the various problems. The losses in both locations caused the loan classification change from "satisfactory" to "watch" to "loss." In the highly regulated banking industry, many companies, especially the small to midsize on the watch list, seldom leave it and remain at the same bank. Nonetheless, and despite all efforts, no new bank or niche lender was forthcoming.

The bank began to take the standard steps to exit the troubled loan. These steps included declining requests for a higher line of credit, beginning to reduce the existing line amount, raising the interest rates (several times), eliminating any overdraft privileges, and issuing several (over the months) quarterly loan forbearance agreements, with fees and ensuing legal costs. The bank's goal was unmistakable. The owners were (unlike many in the same situation) not in denial about the situation. They had approached the bank about a modest write-off to permit refinance by Greenfield. As a high-business-risk lender, we cannot stretch too far past realistic collateral parameters. The need for a loan write-off or subordination was required to fund. The bank was unwilling to accept either. With the subordination the bank retains lien rights behind the new lender (Greenfield) who is to make weekly or monthly payments based on a small percent of sales. This should have been sufficient incentive for bank cooperation to solve its problem as it might just have collected the entire loan if the company survived.

During this negotiation, the loan was transferred from the originating small business department to special asset management. The special asset department of any bank is not there for loan retention and there was no improvement in the bank relationship as the efforts by Greenfield failed to obtain the bank's cooperation. The company still provided current data to GCC while it planned its next action. The bank finally agreed to a write-off, but the collateral fell too low to support the new amount required and to provide working capital for the company's survival.

The time left to take action was limited. Chapter 11 was not feasible due to anticipated legal costs and would not have solved the problems with the level of debt and accounts payable issues. A less costly form of restructure was chosen in the form of an assignment for benefit of creditors (ABC). In this situation, if a bid on the assets with a new lender was successful, current ownership would have been retained by management with removal of the liabilities. There would be a better chance for survival.

FINANCING OF ASSIGNMENT FOR BENEFIT OF CREDITORS

Greenfield provided a factoring facility in purchasing the accounts receivable (less than 90 days from invoice date). Approximately $500,000 was made available using accounts receivable as an asset. A term loan of $400,000 was provided using a lien against personal assets on an interest-only basis. The use of funds included the legal and administration fees of approximately $50,000, bank payoff at $500,000, and 25 percent of the total accounts payable.

The cost of this high-risk financing is broken down by factoring and the term loan. The cost for factored (purchased) accounts receivable was 1 percent per each 10-day period outstanding. As the collection period was normally 40 days, the cost was estimated at 4 percent. There were no other line fees or discounts. The 85 percent advance rate on new sales would provide working capital. The term loan was at prime plus 8 percent. The loans were cross collateralized. The monthly term interest payment came from the proceeds from factoring.

REPORTING REQUIREMENTS

The reporting requirements were minimal. GCC required customary documents for a factoring arrangement and an interest-only term loan:

- Copies of invoices to be factored and proof of delivery when funds are needed.
- Monthly accounts payable aging, proof of tax payments, and financial statements.

ROLE OF CONSULTANT AND COUNSEL

Rally Capital Services, LLC is a financial consulting firm that specializes in providing financial, administrative, and operational management services to underperforming and distressed companies in or out of bankruptcy. Rally offers these companies a clear definition of its operational needs with a realistic assessment of available alternatives to bankruptcy, including, in Illinois, the common law assignment for benefit of creditors, to facilitate a buyer's acquisition of a troubled business or its assets.

The case profile set forth represents an appropriate factual situation that combined the professional resources of GCC and Rally in the acquisition and financing of a troubled business by a third party purchaser.

PURCHASE OF FINANCIALLY DISTRESSED COMPANY BY MANAGEMENT

In reorganizing a financially distressed company, there are several available options, including the filing for protection in bankruptcy. Another option is the sale of the assets of the company to an unrelated third party; this could include management or other outside groups that did not have a prior ownership interest in the company. This sale could be accomplished in bankruptcy, through a foreclosure and sale, or through the use of a common law assignment for benefit of creditors in Illinois.

DEFINITION OF ASSIGNMENT FOR BENEFIT OF CREDITORS

The majority of the definitional information herein was supplied by the Chicago-based consulting firm Rally. A principal of Rally also served as the assignee in the above-referenced case study.

In many situations, the ABC can be used to accomplish a more cost-efficient liquidation of assets of a distressed company or as a reorganization technique. For the purposes of this short example, the use of the ABC as a reorganization technique is described:

- A voluntary transfer of assets to a third party (assignee) for the purpose of liquidating a debt and paying at the assignor's creditors. The company signs a document known as the "Trust Agreement and Assignment for Benefit of Creditors" conveying the assets of the assignor to an independent third party for the sole purpose of converting the assets to cash through a liquidation or other form of sale.
- The role of the assignee is to take charge of the company and its assets to begin liquidation. The assignee is required to provide notice to creditors to prevent further attempts by the creditors to obtain payment out of trust.

ASSIGNEE'S RETURNS OF BIDS SALE

Name of Company

Address

Sales of Assets

Date—Name of Assignee (not individually but solely as Assignee) will accept a bid for the purchase of his right, title, and interest over certain assets of (Company) including but not limited to (list of assets) located at (address).

For a cash price of $ (mid six figures), which includes $ (low to mid five figures) $XX, and $XXX of administrative fees. The assignee reserves right to solicit higher bids and that the next bid is required to be $ (mid five figures) stated amount more than the aggregate consideration.

Terms and Conditions

Date and location and time of bid.

Usually the stated in aggregate and "As Is" "Where Is" statement that the next competitive bid must be in certified or cashier's check for (typically) 20 percent, with the remainder due in 24 hours, forfeiture of deposit conditions, and other noteworthy legal verbiage.

Assignee	*Attorney for Assignee*
Name, address, etc.	Name, address, etc.

LEGAL NOTICE

A public notice acceptable in common law assignments in Illinois is usually published two successive times within a short period. The purpose of publishing notice of the sale is to maximize exposure and generate the interest of the public at large in order to secure the highest and best price for the assets in a commercially reasonable transaction.

The states with laws governing ABC all have some differences. This is intentionally a guideline, *not* an expression of any legal opinion or advice by Greenfield or Rally Capital.

The advantages that an ABC provided in this transaction were the following:

- The company chose the assignee who was well respected and who was represented by experienced counsel, enabling the preservation of the debtor's business as a going concern.
- There was less court supervision and thus a faster process with lower costs.
- The public notice and detailed affidavit of claim issued by the assignee had a proactive argument for commercial reasonableness.
- The lender liens were eliminated by the agreement with the partial payment as funded by GCC.

One of the potential negatives is that the creditors that disagreed with the proposed settlements may still file an involuntary bankruptcy petition. The few but consequential creditors worked together and thus that potential unraveling of the transaction did not occur.

SUMMARY

A profitable company was caught in the technology bust recession. The 9/11/01 attack complicated the situation. The company suffered losses and the bank looked to exit the loan. The best way to retain ownership and have a realistic chance for corporate survival was an assignment of benefit of creditors instead of Chapter 11. The company was sold to existing management. Other bids never materialized. The bank as secured lender could have risked liquidation and a further loss.

The high costs in time and legal fees for Chapter 11 may well lead to more restructures using this method. Liquidity and the ability to raise working capital are hypercritical in any reorganization. The cooperation for the company's suppliers was needed and, with a proactive history of management, was received. A highly competent assignee and other representatives were able to guide the company through this difficult situation.

The economy has begun to rebound, and the company has grown with the addition of new products. Recovery of sales and profits was quicker than anticipated. The company made full payments to its suppliers even though legally not required to do so. A new lender saw the company's potential as well as improved balance sheet and income statement, paying off Greenfield Commercial Credit in full.

The company took necessary legal action to protect the business and undertook the ABC. The right transitional lender for funding a distressed company was found, and it returned to profitability. This is not a textbook case but is nonetheless reality.

ABOUT THE CONTRIBUTOR

Donald M. Rudnik is regional manager, Greenfield Commercial Credit (drudnik@greenfield credit.com). He has 28 years of experience in direct lending to small and midsize businesses and significant experience in numerous operations of distressed companies. He has also assisted in operating and selling the assets of two failed savings and loans for the Resolution Trust Corporation (federal agency). He has written several articles on lending to distressed companies and has spoken nationally on various topics to bankers, consultants, and entrepreneurs.

CASE STUDY 3: Angel Investors

FIRM'S PROFILE

New Mexico Private Investors, Inc. (NMPI, www.nmprivateinvestors.com) is an affiliation of accredited private investors and venture capital companies working together to invest in businesses with world-class potential from technology based on patented/proprietary products or processes. Ideally, the valuation of such companies will have the potential to exceed $100 million in five years.

NMPI is similar in structure to the Band of Angels in Silicon Valley. There are also similarities with the Tech Coast Angels, which operates in Los Angeles, Orange County, and San Diego. NMPI has a network with other angel groups in the Southwest to facilitate providing the first round of funding prior to strategic corporate or venture capital investments in subsequent financings. Please refer to Part Three's Financing Source Directory for additional information.

CASE PROFILE

Meso Fuel, Inc. (MFI) is an Albuquerque, New Mexico–based company that was created by a spin-out from Meso Systems, Inc. (MSI), also headquartered in New Mexico. In this case, MFI was acquired by Intelligent Energy, Ltd. (IE), based in London. IE is planning a public offering on the AIM market (a public stock market similar to Nasdaq but operated by the London Stock Exchange). It is anticipated that this public offering will provide a successful liquidity event for the MFI investors within a two-year period from the date of the spin-off.

Chuck Call, Ph.D., founded MSI at Pacific Northwest Labs in Washington State in 1998. The company's technology captures particles in the air and conducts an analysis for possible bioterrorism substances, then rapidly reports the findings to handheld devices. MSI has been successful with this and related technologies in addition to work with hydrogen generators that are used with fuel cells. Given that the analysis of airborne particles and hydrogen generators are distinctly different technologies, MSI created MFI as a wholly owned subsidiary; this arrangement was adequate for a short period. Without adequate revenues and cash flow to fund growth, MSI spun off a part of MFI in the fall of 2002 to focus on raising capital for itself.

Ned Godshall, Ph.D., then with Sandia National Labs and on leave from the lab in 1992, became one of New Mexico's serial entrepreneurs. Call recruited Godshall to join and lead MFI. His training at Stanford in materials sciences, coupled with an incredible work ethic, was important in accelerating the company's growth.

While MSI had financed the early growth of MFI, as a spin-off MFI had to pursue its own operating capital. Early funding was from a local venture capital firm that provided less than $1 million as a convertible note. Additional funds were obtained through a Small Business Innovation Research (SBIR) and other research grants. A series A venture capital round provided the remainder of the capital. The convertible notes were converted at a discount in the series A round.

Godshall and several of the early investors were members of New Mexico Private Investors. After a presentation to the NMPI and with the help of a few other angels, MFI was launched. Blake Ridgeway, who has a variety of business experience including new business and entrepreneurial activities at Public Service of New Mexico, joined to strengthen the management team. MFI strategy was to team with fuel cell companies in a number of vertical markets (excluding handheld, cell phone, and automotive). There were about 75 target fuel cell companies to vet.

In early 2003 the business was on track and making progress in establishing relationships with several dozen fuel cell companies. It was actually working with about a dozen. Research contracts were in process and reasonably on target, but commercial revenues and prototypes were somewhat behind. The company had plans to raise additional capital in the fall of 2003. It was targeting another round of several million dollars. With the capital markets still soft, it was difficult to find investors willing to fund a B round. Nonetheless, management pushed ahead on several fronts. They were confronted with the classic catch-22: Should they first find the right fuel cell partners and then raise the capital, or the other way around?

By late 2003, MFI had begun discussions with IE, a company with a strong intellectual property position in fuel cells. IE also possessed a creative approach to marketing fuel cells. The two companies, both with unique technologies in their respective areas of expertise, formed a potentially strong team. IE, with perhaps a stronger management team and a greater knowledge of the true nearer-term potential of fuel cells, proposed a business combination.

The MFI team believed there was significant merit to the IE proposal, acted quickly, and reached an agreement in principle with IE. There was risk for MFI if it spent too much time working the merger with IE and it failed; this would distract from their work to advance the fuel generation technology and prevent them from seeking other sources of capital.

As MFI worked through due diligence they reviewed a myriad of documents, maintained communication with existing investors, and kept a low profile to avoid any media or public disclosure. MFI investors sought liquidity. IE had recognized a positive change in the alternate investment market (AIM). Independently of MFI, IE was preparing a filing of its own to offer securities on the AIM. The pressure was on both IE and MFI to complete (or not complete) the deal. The planned offering was in June 2004. MFI would bolster the IE offering; however, both sides had some work to do on the terms, as well as investor information meetings and the all-important legal details to comply with both U.K. and U.S. laws.

Suffice it to say the merger of MFI into IE was completed, and IE is still planning its initial public offering. MFI investors' issues included:

- What is the transaction value of the pound/dollar?
- How long would the lockup period be?

- How does one sell stock in the United Kingdom?
- Or will IE register American depositary receipts (ADRs) on a U.S. market?

MFI investors appear to be in a good position to exit their investment as part of IE. Their actual returns will vary depending on when shares are actually sold, though a good return on investment is expected.

LESSONS LEARNED/EXPERIENCE APPLIED DURING TRANSACTION PROCESS

Note that the deal was not planned for, but when the opportunity was offered, MFI management decided it made the best sense for the investors.

ABOUT THE CONTRIBUTOR

George M. Richmond is a founder of New Mexico Private Investors, Inc., based in Albuquerque, New Mexico, an affiliation of angel investors and partners with venture capital firms that make investments in early stage, high technology companies. His e-mail is geomrich1@comcast.net and you can contact him by telephone at (505) 856-0245.

George M. Richmond began his investment career in 1967, when he joined the New York Stock Exchange firm of J. R. Timmins & Co. as an investment analyst. He has continued to work in the investments community to the present.

His professional affiliations have included the New York Society of Security Analysts and professional associations in Philadelphia, Chicago, and Detroit. In 1974, he became a Chartered Financial Analyst (CFA). Reflecting his current activities in private investments, he resigned his CFA charter in 1999.

Richmond joined the Northern Trust Company of Chicago in 1978 and subsequently was named director of investment research in the Trust Department. While in that position, he was asked to review venture capital investments, both partnerships and individual company investments for certain family clients of the bank. Several years later he moved to the Capital Market Department to develop the venture capital activities for the bank. Among his responsibilities were forming a Small Business Investment Company, Northern Capital Corporation, as well as soliciting, reviewing, and making venture capital investments on behalf of Northern Capital Corporation.

Richmond subsequently formed his own investment company, Richmond Corporate Services, where he provides business and professional services to private companies and entrepreneurs and makes investments in private high technology companies. Richmond has seen, reviewed, prepared, and analyzed business plans of private companies for more than 15 years.

He earned an AB in economics from Lafayette College, Easton, Pennsylvania, and did graduate studies in finance and investments at the Baruch School of Business, City University of New York. He is on the board of directors of T/J Technologies, Inc., an Ann Arbor, Michigan–based company developing fuel cells, batteries, and ultracapacitors, as well as the Physical Science Institute (PSI) of New Mexico State University. The mission of PSI is to commercialize the technologies developed in the university's colleges.

Additionally, he has been a guest lecturer at business schools at Wayne State University, Eastern Michigan University, and the University of New Mexico.

CASE STUDY 4: Royalty Financing

FIRM'S PROFILE

Drug Royalty offers innovative sources of royalty-based financing to inventors, institutions, and life sciences companies who develop pharmaceutical products, diagnostics, or medical devices. Drug Royalty provides royalty financing through one of two models:

1. Acquisition of existing royalty streams from licensors.
2. Creation of new royalty contracts by providing capital in return for a percentage of product revenues.

A versatile and responsive company with a flexible approach to doing business, Drug Royalty boasts unique depth and breadth of expertise in science and technology, valuation and financing, pharmaceutical marketing, and clinical development. Please refer to Part Three's Financing Source Directory for additional information.

CASE PROFILE

Avanir Pharmaceuticals (AVN) is a publicly held California corporation. It was formed in 1988 and has been publicly traded on the American Stock Exchange since 1990.

Avanir is a drug discovery and development company focused on novel treatments for chronic diseases. The company's most advanced product candidate, Neurodex, is in phase III clinical development for pseudobulbar affect, and in phase II clinical development for neuropathic pain. The company's first commercialized product, Abreva, is marketed in North America by GlaxoSmithKline Consumer Healthcare and is the leading over-the-counter product for the treatment of cold sores.

Avanir sought additional capital to fund the clinical development of its pipeline product Neurodex. At a time when equity markets were particularly unwelcoming to technology stocks, Avanir elected to monetize part of its royalty entitlement on the sales of Abreva.

Avanir ended up selling a portion of its future royalty stream on North American sales of Abreva to Drug Royalty USA for $24.1 million. Avanir retains rights to all current and future royalties from product sales in the rest of the world. Avanir also retains the rights to other potential product indications, such as HSV2 and herpes zoster.

The terms of the license purchase agreement with Drug Royalty provided for an initial payment of $20.5 million that was received on December 24, 2002. Avanir retains rights to 50 percent of royalties earned on sales of Abreva in excess of $62 million a year. On May 1, 2003, Avanir received an additional $3.6 million from Drug Royalty upon approval of the extension of one of Avanir's key patents.

This investment opportunity was a private asset sale between the parties and involved no intermediaries.

STRATEGY AND ANALYSIS FOR INVESTMENT/LENDING OPPORTUNITY

To guard against bankruptcy risks, Drug Royalty typically seeks the consent of the licensee to such transactions, including the rights to direct payment and the audit and intellectual property (IP) rights in the underlying license agreement. In addition, Drug Royalty typically receives a security interest on the underlying IP.

Expected internal rate of return (IRR) for this transaction is in the range of 15 to 25 percent.

FUNDING

To date, Drug Royalty has purchased more than 25 separate royalty streams from a wide range of clients, including inventors, academic institutions, research institutions, biotechnology companies, and pharmaceutical companies.

Funds for the Avanir transaction were sourced from internally generated cash flows, as well as through an operating line of credit provided by two global financial institutions.

POSTTRANSACTION ISSUES

Royalty financing is nondilutive and typically noncontrolling, resulting in no change to management structures or corporate governance. As an asset purchase, the monetization of Abreva royalties left Avanir's stock ownership unchanged.

Monetization of royalties on commercialized IP provides immediate cash flows upon closing, minimizing exit concerns. Further exit strategies include the securitization of a portfolio of royalty interests.

LESSONS LEARNED/EXPERIENCE APPLIED DURING TRANSACTION PROCESS

As a publicly traded biotechnology company, Avanir Pharmaceuticals had a number of means of raising capital available to it at the time of the transaction. Electing to monetize a royalty stream provided it with nondilutive capital that could be reinvested in promising development projects. The effect on Avanir's stock price immediately following the announcement of the transaction, which was effectively an asset sale at fair market value, was positive. Furthermore, twice in the 18 months following the transaction, Avanir has been able to raise equity capital at prices in excess of those prevailing at the time, thereby minimizing the dilution to existing stockholders.

ABOUT THE CONTRIBUTOR

David MacNaughtan is senior vice president, business development with Drug Royalty.

MacNaughtan joined Drug Royalty in October 2002, after serving as vice president, business development with Paladin Labs Inc., where he successfully completed a series of licensing transactions. Prior to Paladin, he was an investment manager with Royal Bank Capital Corporation, where he was responsible for venture capital investing and served as a director or ex officio observer on the boards of a number of life sciences companies. MacNaughtan began his career as a process development engineer with Hemosol Inc., a Canadian biotechnology firm. He holds a master's degree in chemical engineering from Queen's University and an MBA from the University of Toronto.

CASE STUDY 5: Commercial Finance—Trade Financing

FIRM'S PROFILE

Headquartered in New York City with representatives hroughout the world, IIG Capital LLC is a nonbank lender that provides financing for global movement of goods and services. IIG Capital focuses on providing middle-market and smaller companies with alternative forms of short-term financing for qualified trade and commercial finance transactions in both domestic and international markets. IIG Capital's innovative financing solutions can be employed on a stand-alone basis, particularly when more traditional financing may not be available, as well as in conjunction with or to supplement traditional bank financing and capital raising. Through hands-on experience in the marketplace, the firm possesses the requisite knowledge and expertise to develop customized financing solutions covering a wide range of objectives and requirements. IIG Capital has deployed over $2 billion of capital in trade finance transactions since its inception in 1997.

Refer to Part Three's Financing Source Directory for additional information.

IIG Capital's Approach to Trade Finance

- **Global expertise.** IIG Capital's *international financing specialists* have hands-on experience in a vast array of global market sectors.
- **Relationship orientation.** IIG Capital is *focused on its customers' needs*. Its team works one-on-one with clients to understand their business, developing financing solutions to assist in facilitating their ability to meet their transactional goals and achieve their short-term and long-term strategic objectives.
- **Transactional focus.** IIG Capital is *transaction-oriented*, focusing on financing the transaction and its underlying assets. While the credit risk of the borrower may not necessarily be acceptable on a stand-alone basis, the business can be viable.
- **Flexibility.** *Thinking outside the box*, IIG Capital is able to accommodate diverse market sectors and financing structures to which banks and other lenders may not be accustomed.
- **Seamlessness.** IGG Capital can structure credit facilities to cover customers' financing needs throughout the entire trade process from inception on, covering manufacturing purchase orders, shipping, inventory, and sales.

The following represent only some of the structures utilized as the foundation in the design of customized financing solutions to meet the diverse needs of middle-market and smaller companies:

- **Asset-based lending.** IIG Capital can structure a financing program that leverages the customer's assets in support of its business objectives.
- **Receivables financing and factoring.** Utilizing a company's own accounts receivable, IIG can provide financing to companies by securing the financing with or factoring the receivables from qualifying customers. May also include purchase order financing.
- **Import/export financing.** When a potential transaction does not meet the minimum size required to qualify for bank financing, IIG can provide financing as lender to the transaction.

- **Warehouse and inventory financing.** For qualifying goods, IIG Capital will structure flexible warehouse and inventory financing facilities to accommodate transaction flows.
- **Transactional Equity.** IIG Capital can provide additional equity that a transaction requires to qualify for bank financing. Because its products complement, rather than being in competition with, traditional banking products, companies can greatly increase their financing capabilities by using the two sources in combination. Transactional Equity is a trademark of IIG Capital LLC.
- **Participations.** When finance companies have limited capital or are limited by internal exposure guidelines, IIG can provide the additional capital needed to fund viable transactions.

Target Client Profile

- Middle-market and smaller companies, including start-ups.
- Markets across the globe, particularly in developing and emerging market countries.
- Varied industries, from high-tech to manufacturing to commodity.
- Strong management.
- Facilities starting at $2.5 million, up to $40 million.
- Accounts receivable: typically a broad base of account debtors, may include purchase order financing.
- Inventory: supported by strong controls and inventory systems.
- Special situations: working capital financing needs to assist clients in capitalizing upon market opportunities, including bulk purchases, liquidations, or vendor discounts.

RECENTLY COMPLETED TRANSACTIONS

Transactional Equity Deal

A Colorado-based privately held company was able to complement its existing bank credit facility with a $10 million Transactional Equity line from IIG Capital. As a result, its senior lender was able to increase its existing line by approximately $30 million.

Advantages of IIG Capital's Financing

- Provided client with an additional source of investment capital.
- Enabled bank to maintain its client despite bank's inability to provide the additional capital the client was requesting.
- Developed business relationships among client, bank, and IIG Capital that have proved to be highly lucrative for all parties.

Inventory Finance Deal

An Argentine fruit processor was able to use its firm purchase orders to obtain a $3 million line from IIG Capital.

Transaction Structure

- Financing was provided against a firm purchase order from a U.S. buyer whose creditworthiness was preapproved by IIG Capital.

- When the order is complete, the client makes arrangements in conjunction with the collateral manager to deliver the product to the shipping company, and warrants are exchanged for shipping documents.

Export Finance Deal

A Panamanian holding company with banana plantations in Colombia and Costa Rica obtained a $10 million export finance loan from IIG Capital.

Transaction Structure

- Financing was provided by discounting a supply and purchase contract from a well-known, creditworthy multinational company.
- There are weekly shipments of product, with payment made the following week.
- Once per month IIG Capital applies installments due based on a predetermined repayment schedule and returns excess funds to its client.

ABOUT THE CONTRIBUTORS

Martin Silver, Managing Partner, and David Hu, Managing Partner, both with IIG Capital LLC.

CASE STUDY 6: Mezzanine Investment

FIRM'S PROFILE

Brookside Capital Partners provides mezzanine capital to U.S.-based small and midsize companies, with annual revenues of at least $15 million and EBITDA of at least $3 million. Brookside Capital Partners does not target specific industries but does prefer manufacturing and service businesses. Target companies typically have the following attributes:

- History of profitable and predictable financial performance.
- Defensible market positions or proprietary technology.
- Sustainable growth.
- Superior management.

Brookside Capital generally provides junior capital to finance the following needs:

- Strategic acquisitions of existing businesses.
- Buyouts by internal or external management teams.
- Growth capital.
- Leveraged recapitalization to provide shareholder liquidity or intergenerational wealth transfer.

Please refer to Part Three's Financing Source Directory for additional information.

INVESTMENT STRUCTURE AND CAPABILITIES

A typical Brookside Capital Partners financing is between $3 million and $7.5 million, although larger transactions can be accommodated through a co-investment partnership with an affiliate. The investment will generally be structured as subordinated debt with interest paid on a current basis plus warrants to purchase capital stock.

CASE PROFILE

Brookside Capital Partners invested subordinated debt in McKenzie Sports Products, Inc. (Granite Quarry, North Carolina), the leading designer and manufacturer of taxidermy forms and supplies used by hunters and fishermen to mount trophies. McKenzie is also the leading designer, manufacturer, and distributor of lifelike three-dimensional foam targets used by archers in both practice and competition.

FUNDING

On October 7, 2003, Brookside Capital Partners, in conjunction with its affiliate, invested $7.25 million in subordinated debt with warrants to support the acquisition of McKenzie Sports Products, Inc. by RFE Investment Partners.

ABOUT THE CONTRIBUTOR

David D. Buttolph is managing director of Brookside Capital Partners. Prior to joining Brookside Capital he was a partner of two mezzanine investment funds at Canterbury Capital Partners, totaling in excess of $400 million. While at Canterbury he served on the boards of numerous portfolio companies. Prior to joining Canterbury, Buttolph was a senior vice president at LaSalle Business Credit, Inc., for five years. He was also a district manager/vice president of Barclays Business Credit, Inc. He is a 1979 graduate of Boston University and received his master's in business administration from Suffolk University in 1980. He has served as an adjunct lecturer on mergers, acquisitions, and buyouts at the Fordham University Graduate School of Business.

CASE STUDY 7: Private Equity—Acquisition to Exit

FIRM'S PROFILE

Graham Partners is a private equity firm based in suburban Philadelphia that focuses on acquiring and investing in privately held middle-market manufacturing companies. Since the firm's founding in 1988, Graham Partners has closed over $3 billion in acquisitions, joint ventures, financings, and divestitures and has had firsthand involvement in the operations of companies in numerous different manufacturing sectors. Graham Partners currently manages a private equity fund with 16 investment professionals and a total staff of 26 including accounting and administrative professionals.

Graham Partners possesses a unique combination of financial and operating resources, and has a heritage of working within the context of a family industrial concern. As such, the firm has the ability to develop meaningful partnerships with management teams and family owner/operators for the purpose of creating considerable company value appreciation over a four-to-seven-year period. While primarily focused on domestic manufacturing businesses with revenues between $20 million and $250 million, Graham's access to substantial capital resources and its longstanding relationships with customers, suppliers, industrial peers, and affiliated investors provide the firm with the flexibility to pursue a wide variety of investment opportunities.

Graham Partners is sponsored by the Graham Group, a privately held concern founded in 1960 that is comprised of industrial and investment businesses. Graham's industrial businesses operate out of roughly 60 locations worldwide and are involved in manufacturing consumer and industrial products for a wide range of end market applications. Please refer to Part Three's Financing Source Directory for additional information.

CASE PROFILE

Eldorado Stone, headquartered in San Marcos, California, is a rapidly growing producer of architectural stone veneer for residential and commercial siding applications. With a reputation for outstanding product quality and exceptional customer service, Eldorado has attained a leading market position in its industry niche. Eldorado's products are manufactured at multiple facilities strategically located within the United States, and are sold to a customer base extending throughout the world. Graham Partners acquired Eldorado in February 2001. During Graham's roughly three-year ownership of the company, the private equity firm worked with management to nationalize Eldorado's product offering, consolidate its outstanding base of franchisees, and increase sales by over 300 percent.

STRATEGY AND ANALYSIS FOR INVESTMENT

Eldorado was one of 10 portfolio companies in Graham Partners' vintage 1999 fund. Graham's strategy is to acquire businesses, like Eldorado, that are benefiting from product substitution or raw materials conversion trends in their industries, where Graham Partners can utilize its extensive operating resources, contacts, and expertise to add value during its holding period. In Eldorado's case, the company is the beneficiary of the ongoing shift to manufactured stone from traditional siding materials, such as natural stone, brick, stucco, and vinyl.

EXIT

Eldorado Stone was sold on June 2, 2004, in an all-cash transaction to a strategic acquirer for an enterprise value of over $202 million, plus an excess working capital adjustment of approximately $8 million. As a result of the sale, Graham Partners distributed to its investors roughly half of the capital it had invested to date from its vintage 1999 leveraged buyout fund. The Eldorado sale yielded Graham roughly a 4.4× gross return on equity invested and a gross IRR of 57 percent.

CASE STUDY 8: Private Equity—Restructuring

FIRM'S PROFILE

Meriturn Partners is an investor and adviser for middle-market restructurings and turn-arounds. As an investor, Meriturn manages the Meriturn Fund, LP, which invests up to $10 million per transaction in middle-market restructuring and turnaround opportunities. As an adviser, Meriturn works with lenders, shareholders, and management teams to enhance the survivability and growth of companies experiencing operational or financial difficulties.

Meriturn's professionals have dedicated their careers to developing solutions to dynamic and complex corporate problems, and have overseen more than 100 restructurings, turnarounds, transactions, and strategic assignments worth over $10 billion.

Meriturn is deeply involved in every stage of the restructuring and turnaround process. It represents investors and clients as if the business was its own, and offers the unique synergies of an investment group combined with an advisory services firm. This benefits clients and portfolio companies by enabling access to a greater pool of restructuring experience, industry knowledge, resources, relationships, and capital to develop solutions to complex situations.

Meriturn has offices in San Francisco and Raleigh-Durham. Refer to Part Three's Financing Source Directory for additional information.

CASE PROFILE

Dunn Paper, Inc. is a leading North American producer of specialty coated and machine-glazed papers serving flexible packaging companies, gift-wrap producers, bag manufacturers, labelers, and food-service companies. The company is based in Port Huron, Michigan, and was founded in 1924. Dunn's web site is at www.dunnpaper.com.

Transaction Date: October 9, 2003

Meriturn was contacted by Fleet Capital, senior lender to the former parent company, Curtis Papers. Curtis Papers was for sale, but after reviewing the business, Meriturn chose to focus on only the mill in Port Huron.

Meriturn had been an early bidder for the company but had lost out on price. Meriturn was brought back into the process after the initial bidder failed to close the transaction and after the mill had been shut down for two weeks. The largest hurdle was closing the deal fast enough to (1) prevent an asset liquidation by the former lender and creditor committee and (2) restart the mill to avoid losing customers and hurting the future viability of the business. The mill had a negative EBITDA of $2.5 million in the 12 months before the transaction.

Meriturn was the sole equity sponsor for the transaction, which included co-investments from several members of Dunn's management.

STRATEGY AND ANALYSIS FOR INVESTMENT

Meriturn worked with management under an extremely tight schedule to complete due diligence, structure the financing, and close the transaction within a 15-day time frame. Over

$10 million of preferred equity, convertible subordinated debt, and two tranches of bank debt were structured by Meriturn to complete the acquisition and to provide capital for growth. Citizens First, Inc. (Nasdaq: CTZN) provided the bank financing with certain guarantees provided by the U.S. Department of Agriculture.

Significant Turnaround Actions

- Reduced cost structure by $4.5 million through head count reductions, machine rationalization, and power contract, property tax, and supplier price negotiations.
- Reduced volume by 25 percent and refocused the mill on only its highest-margin and most efficient production.
- Renegotiated union contract to improve work rule flexibility and discipline.
- Began long-overdue programs of cost-reducing upgrades and maintenance.
- Initiated a company-wide incentive compensation program that provided benefits to all employees.

POSTINVESTMENT ISSUES

In the first two quarters after the transaction closed, pulp and energy prices reached historical high points, depressing margins and delaying the financial turnaround. However, the company's lower cost structure insulated it from the dramatic losses experienced throughout the rest of the paper industry, and Dunn continued to make money throughout this time period.

Meriturn made no changes in the management team after the acquisition.

MERITURN PARTNERS' CONTROL ROLE AND DUNN'S REPORTING RELATIONSHIP

Meriturn Partners controls more than 70 percent of the company and has three of the four board seats, with a Meriturn partner serving as chairman. Meriturn maintains a close reporting relationship, with monthly board meetings held telephonically, and quarterly meetings on location. Additionally, Meriturn receives management reports covering items such as efficiency of operations, sales by product, working capital, and debt balances and availability.

HOLDING/EXITING OBJECTIVE

Meriturn Partners is a relatively long-term buyer in the turnaround field. Meriturn works to stabilize operations, turn companies around, then run and grow them profitably for three to five years before selling them.

LESSONS LEARNED/EXPERIENCE APPLIED DURING ACQUISITION PROCESS

Meriturn has five rules for restructurings:

1. Turnarounds tend to take more time and money than planned.
2. Renewed growth never comes as fast or in as much volume as one projects.
3. You need to invest based on your downside case—let the upside be just that.
4. When change is required it should be rapid and decisive—indecision is the enemy.
5. Outcomes must be measurable.

ABOUT THE CONTRIBUTOR

Franklin Staley is a director for Meriturn Partners in its San Francisco, California, office and focuses on both investment and advisory work for the firm. He can be reached at franklin@meriturn.com. Prior to Meriturn Partners, Staley spent 10 years in finance, strategy, and management positions. Most recently he was the vice president for strategy for Axcellis, Inc., a service provider to the security alarm and systems integration industries. At Axcellis, he was responsible for all fund-raising, financial management, and strategic partnerships. Prior to joining Axcellis, he managed KKS Inc. (a vertically integrated health and wellness company), where he executed a corporate turnaround that increased company revenues by 75 percent within nine months. As part of this restructuring, his team focused the company's development efforts on higher-margin services, longer-term sales contracts with a national purchaser, and higher-volume sales, rather than its "box" retail operations. In addition, he overhauled the billing, financial, and marketing operations of an affiliated business of KKS. Prior to joining KKS, he was an associate for SG Cowen Securities in its Technology Group, where he focused on IPOs, follow-on transactions, private placements, and mergers and acquisitions for small and mid-cap clients. He was previously a financial analyst for Lehman Brothers in its Leveraged Finance and Restructuring Groups, and a credit analyst for Chase Manhattan. Staley serves as a board director for the Allen P. and Josephine B. Green Foundation. He earned a BA degree in economics from Kenyon College and an MBA from the Amos Tuck School at Dartmouth College.

CASE STUDY 9: Private Equity—Acquisition with Management Participation

FIRM'S PROFILE

Meriturn Partners is an investor and adviser for middle-market restructurings and turnarounds. As an investor, Meriturn manages the Meriturn Fund, LP, which invests up to $10 million per transaction in middle-market restructuring and turnaround opportunities. As an adviser, Meriturn works with lenders, shareholders, and management teams to enhance the survivability and growth of companies experiencing operational or financial difficulties.

Meriturn's professionals have dedicated their careers to developing solutions to dynamic and complex corporate problems, and have overseen more than 100 restructurings, turnarounds, transactions, and strategic assignments worth over $10 billion.

Meriturn is deeply involved in every stage of the restructuring and turnaround process. It represents investors and clients as if the business was its own, and offers the unique synergies of an investment group combined with an advisory services firm. This benefits clients and portfolio companies by enabling access to a greater pool of restructuring experience, industry knowledge, resources, relationships, and capital to develop solutions to complex situations.

Meriturn has offices in San Francisco and Raleigh-Durham. Refer to Part Three's Financing Source Directory for additional information.

CASE PROFILE

Johnston Textiles is a leading manufacturer of technical and specialty textiles. The company produces a wide range of industry-recognized products sold into industrial, furnishings, and hospitality markets worldwide, such as 100 percent spun polyester fabrics for napery and work wear markets; bedding and top-of-the-bed products; fire-retardant fabrics; upholstery fabrics; fabrics for use in rubber, automotive, and abrasive products; and Jacquard and dobby woven decorative fabrics. The company's products have significant brand awareness under brands such as Wellington Sears, Interweave, Duration, Caress, and Chef Check. Johnston is headquartered in Phenix City, Alabama, and operates three modern textile manufacturing facilities in Phenix City, Valley, and Opp, Alabama. The company also has a sales, marketing, and design center in Valley, Alabama, and operates an ISO-certified textile testing facility (TexTest) in Valley.

For more information on Johnston Textiles, the web site is at www.johnstontextiles.com.

Transaction Date: December 5, 2003

The opportunity resulted from Meriturn's relationship with Congress Financial's workout group. Congress was the lead creditor for Johnston Industries (the former company).

Meriturn Partners was the sole equity sponsor for the transaction, which included co-investment from several members of Johnston's management. The entity name was changed to Johnston Textiles, Inc. at the time of the acquisition.

Some significant issues were overcome during negotiations in regard to pension, health care, and other legacy liabilities remaining with the bankruptcy estate. In addition, operational changes needed to occur (incentive plans, access to key suppliers, plant closures, etc.).

STRATEGY AND ANALYSIS FOR INVESTMENT

Johnston Industries, Inc. filed for Chapter 11 bankruptcy protection on January 31, 2003, as a result of an inflated cost structure, overseas competition for its commodity products, high debt load, and pension liabilities. The company initiated a corporate restructuring, but its lenders chose to force a 363 bankruptcy sale of its main business divisions (Fabrics, Fiber, and Composites) in order to liquidate their holdings.

In October 2003 Meriturn bid on the assets of the Fabrics Division and was selected as the "stalking horse" bidder. The Fabrics Division had a negative EBITDA of $6.8 million in 2003.

Meriturn worked through the 363 bankruptcy sale process and completed the acquisition on December 5, 2003. Meriturn structured over $31 million of preferred equity and bank debt for the transaction, with Fleet Capital providing acquisition and working capital debt for growth.

During the reorganization process, the management team:

- Rationalized product lines and eliminated commodity businesses.
- Closed two high-cost commodity manufacturing facilities.
- Improved quality and service.
- Initiated a company-wide incentive compensation program that provided benefits to all employees.

- Increased prices.
- Renewed product development for growth.

With the infusion of capital from Meriturn, the new company has a strong balance sheet, a leaner cost structure, and the financial resources to remain a world-class designer, manufacturer, and supplier of technical and specialty textile products.

POSTINVESTMENT ISSUES

The need for better information on a timely basis to make more disciplined management decisions led to the undertaking of certain information systems (IS) projects. There were also head count reductions at various levels of management to create a flatter organization and reduce expenses.

MERITURN PARTNERS' CONTROL ROLE AND JOHNSTON TEXTILES' REPORTING RELATIONSHIP

Meriturn Partners controls more than 70 percent of the stock and has three of the four board seats, with a Meriturn partner serving as chairman. Meriturn maintains a close reporting relationship, with monthly board meetings held telephonically, and quarterly meetings on location. Additionally, Meriturn receives management reports covering items such as efficiency of operations, sales by product, working capital, and debt balances and availability.

HOLDING/EXITING OBJECTIVE

Meriturn Partners is a relatively long-term buyer in the turnaround field. Meriturn works to stabilize operations, turn companies around, then run and grow them profitably for three to five years before selling them.

LESSONS LEARNED/EXPERIENCE APPLIED IN THIS CASE

Meriturn has five rules for restructurings:

1. Turnarounds tend to take more time and money than planned.
2. Renewed growth never comes as fast or in as much volume as one projects.
3. You need to invest based on your downside case—let the upside be just that.
4. When change is required it should be rapid and decisive—indecision is the enemy.
5. Outcomes must be measurable.

ABOUT THE CONTRIBUTOR

Vito Russo is a director for Meriturn Partners in its Raleigh, North Carolina, office and focuses on both investment and advisory work for the firm. He can be reached at vito@meriturn.com. Prior to Meriturn Partners, Russo spent 13 years in management, corporate recovery, and accounting positions. Most recently, he was the general manager of a software business unit at Nortel Networks (NYSE: NT). As a general manager at Nortel, he was responsible for all business operations for software products targeted at the telecom service provider market (for example, Sprint and Verizon). In this capacity, he managed product development, marketing, sales, and customer service. While he managed the business, revenue grew 50 percent and EBIT doubled. At Nortel, he also managed a team that developed and maintained the strategic plan for a new product line with over $500 million in R&D expenses, was a member of the team that introduced and launched the Spectrum Peripheral Module (a product with $1 billion of first-year sales), and developed and implemented a plan to improve the manufacturing of wireless PCS radios, doubling weekly throughput. Prior to joining Nortel, Russo worked in the Los Angeles office of Price Waterhouse, now PricewaterhouseCoopers (PWC). While with PWC, he consulted on bankruptcies, accountant malpractice cases, and various middle-market business engagements. Russo is a certified public accountant (CPA) licensed in both California and North Carolina. He earned a BA in economics-business from the University of California at Los Angeles and an MBA from the Owen Graduate School of Management at Vanderbilt University.

CASE STUDY 10: Private Equity—Public-to-Private Acquisition

FIRM'S PROFILE

The Riverside Company, with offices in New York, Cleveland, Dallas, and San Francisco, is the leading private equity firm investing in premier companies at the smaller end of the middle market. Riverside has more than $1 billion of capital under management and has earned its investors realized gains of nearly four times their original cash investments on exited transactions. In addition to four pre-1995 acquisitions, the firm has brought to market the Riverside Capital Appreciation Funds of 1995, 1998, 2000, and 2003, attracting investors from pension funds, endowments, funds of funds, insurance companies, and banks. Since its inception in 1988, Riverside has invested in more than 85 acquisitions across a variety of industries. Please refer to Part Three's Financing Source Directory for additional information.

CASE PROFILE

The Dwyer Group, Inc. provides a diverse array of specialty services internationally through its service-based, brand-name franchise businesses. These businesses provide high-quality residential and light commercial services. Specialty services is one of the fastest-growing franchise categories.

The Dwyer Group, Inc. currently owns six businesses: Rainbow International, Mr. Rooter, Mr. Electric, Mr. Appliance, Glass Doctor, and Aire Serv. Dwyer provides services to approximately 750 franchisees located in the United States and Canada. The company's international master licensees service approximately 240 franchisees in 14 other countries. The Dwyer Group, Inc. also provides services to an associate company, DreamMaker Bath & Kitchen, which includes 134 franchisees in the United States and 129 franchises through its master licensees in 12 other countries.

For more information regarding The Dwyer Group, Inc. or its franchise concepts, visit the company's web site at www.dwyergroup.com.

Company's Analysis and Market

Dwyer is a leader in the multiconcept franchise world. Few franchisors have been as successful in managing multiple brands under one umbrella. In each of the sectors where Dwyer competes, it has one of the most recognized brand names and has significant market share relative to the competition.

Dwyer has an outstanding corporate culture led by a superb management team, which enjoys an excellent reputation in the industry and has the creative focus and enthusiasm to build the core business. Dwyer possesses strong franchise system fundamentals; franchisees are happy, revenue is growing systemwide and per franchise, and renewal rates are very good.

Dwyer's product lines are not cyclical, and much of the financial performance has come from existing franchisees who are successfully building their businesses.

Strategy and Analysis for Investment Opportunity

Until the acquisition by Riverside in October 2003, the Dwyer Group was a publicly held company that traded on Nasdaq under the symbol "DWYR." Its franchisees service more than two million homes and businesses per year and generate over $400 million in annual retail sales. Over the past five years, Dwyer's revenues have grown by a compounded annual rate of 19 percent.

"We've been eyeing small public companies for some time as a possible source of attractive acquisitions," commented Stewart Kohl, managing general partner. "We hope that The Dwyer Group is the first of a number of take-private opportunities for Riverside."

During negotiations for the deal, the parties faced the following issues:

- **Valuation of Dwyer.** Riverside based valuation on the company's current and projected earnings. Dwyer was represented by a special, independent committee appointed from its board of directors, as well as by its investment bank. Through several meetings, this group and Riverside reached a mutually agreeable consensus.
- **Rollover investment by certain Dwyer stockholders and senior management.** Typically, Riverside seeks management teams that are willing to roll over a portion of the proceeds of the sale into the new transaction. Such investments underscore the partnership that has been forged between Riverside and the management team and—importantly—aligns their interests.
- **Management options.** These are a customary and key component of all Riverside leveraged buyout transactions. Riverside works with its management teams to develop a schedule and structure of performance-based options, which function as a vital incentive and clear reward for excellent teams such as Dwyer's.

When appraising a leveraged buyout, Riverside seeks to strike a balance between a superior return and a reasonable risk. The firm aims to deliver to its investors a gross internal rate of return (IRR) of at least 20 percent, not including add-on acquisitions or the multiple arbitrage realized by increasing a company's EBITDA to a higher level. (See transaction details table.)

Transaction Details ($ Million)

	Preinvestment	Postinvestment	Characteristics/Terms/Type
Annual revenue	$27.4		
Annual EBITDA	$7.4		
Short-term debt	$0.4	$3.4	
Long-term debt	$2.1	$25.2	Senior revolver and term loans and subordinated debt
Total liabilities	$6.1	$36.9	
Preferred	$0.0	$0.0	None
Common	$22.1	$30.9	Riverside, Dwyer family, and management
Total assets	$28.2	$67.8	
Options/warrants	$3.0/$1.1	15.0%/3.0%	Preinvestment: realized value of options and warrants at closing on 10/30/03. Postinvestment: performance-based options and warrants on subordinated debt as a percentage of funded equity

Transaction Date: October 30, 2003

The acquisition of The Dwyer Group, Inc. was Riverside's 11th transaction of 2003.

Dwyer was founded in 1981 by Don Dwyer, who envisioned it as an opportunity to help others develop and realize their entrepreneurial dreams. The Dwyer Group has been a success because of its focus, a nurturing environment in which it teaches franchisees to run their own businesses, and its unique corporate culture. In January 1999, Don's daughter Dina took over as CEO of the company.

In 1993, The Dwyer Group went public. Ten years later, the company became privately owned by Riverside and other stockholders, including members of the Dwyer family and The Dwyer Group's senior management. Riverside paid $6.75 per share to Dwyer's public stockholders who were not participating in the management buyout, which represented a premium of approximately 59 percent over the $4.25 closing price on May 9, 2003, the last trading day before the announcement of the transaction.

"Dwyer has an industry-leading management team that has been remarkably successful in developing a sound franchise system in which the franchisees consistently grow their businesses year-over-year," explained Loren Schlachet, a Riverside principal based in the firm's San Francisco office. "Over the next several years we expect that consumers will continue to place increasing emphasis on branding and a dependable, professional service offering by providers, and Dwyer is perfectly positioned to capitalize on this trend. We will continue to support Dwyer's organic growth through investment in people, as well as consider acquisitions that either are complementary to the existing brands or that target home services."

"The Dwyer Group has always strived to align itself with winners, and this is no exception," said Dina Dwyer-Owens, president and CEO of The Dwyer Group. "Having the support of The Riverside Company is a huge affirmation of the strength of our brands within the franchising and trade services industries. This not only complements the team that we have in place, but it also allows us to aggressively go after substantial growth in all areas of our business. Franchise owners will benefit by an accelerated rate of expansion of our brands, and we will continue to stay focused on providing them with the support they need to grow their businesses. The Dwyer Group's success is directly proportional to their success. An investment in The Dwyer Group is also an investment in our entire network."

POSTINVESTMENT ISSUES

Riverside/Dwyer Relationship

In each of its transactions, Riverside's goal is to partner with management to build a company during the firm's ownership period. Since many management teams, including Dwyer's, invest alongside Riverside, interests are aligned and strategic objectives are agreed upon to add value to the company. Riverside's investment management philosophy is based on collaboration, aligned objectives, autonomy (that is, letting a strong management team continue to do its job well), and providing operating resources when helpful.

As the majority shareholder of Dwyer, Riverside holds sway on the board of directors, which also includes Dina Dwyer-Owens. Riverside is currently working with Ms. Dwyer-Owens to appoint two additional outside board members who will provide strategic value to the company through experience in the franchise industry or related businesses.

Riverside will help Dwyer continue its growth by providing additional capital as well as operating resources in the form of experienced operating partners or outside consultants.

Issues Since Acquisition

One of the best ways Riverside helps its portfolio companies grow is through identifying and closing complementary, or add-on, acquisitions. In January 2004, Riverside and Dwyer acquired the company's first add-on, Harmon Glass Company, to combine with Dwyer's existing glass franchise business, Glass Doctor.

Harmon, which operates as both an auto glass retailer and third party administrator for the insurance industry, generated $186 million of net revenues in 2003 and was the third largest player in the auto glass replacement industry. Glass Doctor's strategy for the Harmon transaction is to convert the majority of Harmon's company-owned glass shops into Glass Doctor franchises, creating the second largest automotive glass replacement company in the United States.

In addition to this transaction and the evaluation of additional add-on acquisition opportunities, Riverside has worked with Dwyer's management to identify organic growth initiatives for Dwyer's other franchise concepts.

Holding/Exit Objective

Riverside's objective is to make its portfolio companies bigger and better during the firm's period of ownership. This often equates to closing one, two, or three add-ons, and generating organic growth to double or triple the portfolio companies' sizes. This is most often accomplished five to seven years after acquisition, at which point the company is sold to a buyer who can continue its level of growth.

LESSONS LEARNED/EXPERIENCE APPLIED DURING ACQUISITION PROCESS

Riverside reinforced its belief in aligning objectives with an exemplary management team, which is the fuel necessary to empower significant growth and to create value for all shareholders.

What did Riverside learn during the acquisition of Dwyer?

- An understanding of and commitment to the franchise business model as the most successful approach for local businesses in Dwyer's lines of business.
- The necessity of sharing common values and cultures between a buyer and a seller. Dwyer lives by its "Code of Values," and Riverside emphasizes its "Principled Partners" approach to leveraged buyouts in order to create excellent references.
- The value of identifying and completing add-on acquisitions in order to supplement Dwyer's strong organic growth.
- Dwyer's vow to support its franchisees by providing value-added services and the ability to achieve their dreams.

ABOUT THE CONTRIBUTOR

Robert B. Landis joined Riverside in 2002. He has more than 22 years of commercial and investment banking experience gained at Deutsche Banc Alex. Brown and its predecessors, and at Citibank. At Deutsche, he developed industry expertise in the consumer, industrial, transportation, aerospace, and telecommunications sectors and headed the firm's North American corporate finance group as it made a transition to an investment bank. At Citibank, he was vice president of the Multi-National Group. Prior to that, he was a major in the U.S. Army, commanding distribution operations in Bavaria and managing a staff of 170.

He holds a BS from the University of Colorado and an MBA in international management from the American Graduate School of International Management.

CASE STUDY 11: Merchant Bank Implements Buy-and-Build Strategy

FIRM'S PROFILE

Veronis Suhler Stevenson (VSS) is a leading merchant bank specializing in the media, communications, and information industries. Since its inception in 1981, VSS has completed more than 630 transactions. The firm has acted as a financial adviser across the full spectrum of media industry segments including business magazines and trade shows; consumer magazines; broadcast TV; cable and radio; newspapers; business information services; consumer, professional, and educational books; specialty media and marketing services; entertainment; and the Internet. Veronis Suhler Stevenson provides a full range of services to media owners including advisory services on a variety of M&A and corporate finance transactions, private equity financing, mezzanine debt, as well as in-depth research on the communications industry. Veronis Suhler Stevenson's senior professionals have decades of experience leading media firms as owners and senior executives, managing acquisition strategies, and advising media companies as investment bankers.

VSS Fund Management LLC has managed four private capital funds since 1987 totaling approximately $1.5 billion with more than 33 portfolio companies and 153 add-on acquisitions in the media, communications, and information industries. Veronis Suhler Stevenson's third private equity fund, VS&A Communications Partners III, LP, capitalized at over $1 billion, is one of the largest private equity funds devoted exclusively to investments in the media. Together with Fund III's predecessor buyout funds and VSS Mezzanine Partners, LP, the realized and unrealized enterprise value of these investments totals approximately $7 billion.

VSS was founded by operating executives from the media industry, not by bankers. About half of its staff is from the media business and the other half from Wall Street media groups. In VSS, expertise drives everything. The focus is on building businesses and growing companies first and foremost, then on transactions. This is contrary to most investment banks and illustrates the difference between an investment banking mind-set and that of a merchant bank.

Refer to Part Three's Financing Source Directory for additional information.

CASE PROFILE

Hanley Wood, LLC is the premier business-to-business media network serving North America's residential and commercial construction industries. Through five operating divisions, the company produces award-winning magazines and web sites, marquee trade shows and events, rich data, and custom marketing solutions. The company also is North America's leading provider of home plans. Founded in 1976, Hanley Wood is a $200 million company owned by VS&A Communications Partners III, LP, the private-equity affiliate of media industry merchant bank Veronis Suhler Stevenson.

After 20 years of growing the company, one of the founding partners of Hanley Wood, Inc. decided to retire in 1999. The shareholder group determined that an outright sale was the most desirable way to monetize his ownership position, despite their willingness and wish to remain with the company. An investment bank was hired to conduct the auction, and invited VSS to participate in the bidding process. While VSS typically generates investment opportunities through direct calling and relationships, this case was special because VSS had known the company and its management team for more than 15 years. Consequently, VSS was able to move quickly and forcefully to win the auction. At the time of the sale of Hanley Wood in 1999, the company had revenues of about $100 million with solid cash flow.

Since the investment by VSS, Hanley Wood has completed 21 synergistic acquisitions, largely consolidating the market, broadening product portfolio, and increasing market share. Revenues have more than doubled, and EBITDA has tripled in the past five years, despite a severe media recession and the events of September 11, 2001. In 2002, VSS structured and placed a tranche of mezzanine financing in order to allow the company to continue buying and launching new product lines in a difficult financing market.

STRATEGY AND ANALYSIS FOR INVESTMENT

Hanley Wood fit VSS's model for investing in the media industry as a company that had significant market presence and strong management, and would be the platform for future growth and acquisitions (a buy-and-build approach). The transaction was structured so that management and prior owners hold about 13 percent of the business and VSS, along with its LP co-investors, holds the balance.

VSS saw the opportunity to assist Hanley Wood by working with management to determine objectives, develop a strategic plan, identify acquisitions, and structure and finance transactions. VSS views itself as a partner with management. Given its operating and financial expertise, VSS shares with Hanley Wood management a common perspective on how value is created through improving operating performance and targeting strategic acquisition opportunities.

POSTINVESTMENT ISSUES

Post closing, one owner retired and the other stayed with a significant incentive based on company performance. As Hanley Wood has grown, it has bolstered its already strong management team with several key additions.

LESSONS LEARNED/EXPERIENCE APPLIED DURING GROWTH PROCESS

The major lesson learned during the investment period is that it is critical to avoid allowing an acquisition program, and the associated cost cuts that facilitate it, to interfere with the pursuit and launch of organic growth initiatives. Hanley Wood management was an experienced acquirer prior to the VSS buyout, and had an established track record of making acquisitions work. Partnered with VSS, the volume of the program was greatly enhanced, and required significant debt capital to support it. When financing is tight and buying opportunities abound, it is all too easy to delay or cancel new products and brand extensions, in order to maximize the bottom line. After two years of successful acquisitions in 2000 and 2001, Jeffrey Stevenson, president and co-CEO of VSS, challenged management to redouble its focus on organic growth, while maintaining the pace of the acquisition effort. The results have been dramatic, in that over $10 million of profitable revenue streams were created in the following three years. These new revenue streams not only helped to support the acquisition program with additional earnings, but helped to lay the foundation for future growth—a critical component for what is expected to be a high exit multiple when the company is sold.

ABOUT THE CONTRIBUTORS

Eric Van Ert, CFA, is director of private equity at VSS. Since joining VSS in 2001, Van Ert's responsibilities have included sourcing new investment opportunities, structuring investments, valuation and financial analysis, due diligence, and monitoring of portfolio companies. He is on the board of directors of Hanley Wood and GoldenState Towers. Prior to joining Veronis Suhler Stevenson in 2001, Van Ert was director of corporate development at Hanley Wood, and financial analyst for Lockheed Martin. He earned an MBA from American University and a BS with honors from Saint Michael's College, and is a CFA charterholder.

James P. Rutherfurd is executive vice president and managing director, private equity, Limited Partners Communications. Since joining VSS in January 1999, he has been involved with both the firm's investment banking business as head of the VSS investment bank and its private equity business as a senior principal in VS&A Communications Partners III. He has worked on approximately $3 billion of transactions while at VSS across several media sectors, including newspapers, broadcasting, consumer magazines, and marketing services. He is also one of the firm's NASD supervisors. Prior to joining VSS he served as a managing director in the Mergers & Acquisitions Group and co-head of J. P. Morgan's Media Group. He was previously a director in the First Boston Corporation's Media Group and a corporate lawyer at Rogers & Wells. Rutherfurd has closed more than $28 billion in media industry transactions including advisory engagements, equity and debt underwritings, equity swaps, and syndicated bank loans. His clients have ranged across many segments of the media industry, including newspapers, television, cable, magazines, radio, information services, Internet services, and entertainment.

Rutherfurd holds a JD from the University of Virginia School of Law and a BA from Princeton University.

CASE STUDY 12: Strategic Investment

FIRM'S PROFILE

Siemens Venture Capital GmbH (SVC), a subsidiary of Siemens AG, is the 700 million euro corporate venture organization for all of Siemens' businesses worldwide, playing a key role in the Siemens global network of innovation. With offices in Munich, San Jose (CA), Boston (MA), and through Siemens Israel, Ltd. in Rosh Ha'ayin near Tel Aviv, SVC focuses on emerging technologies and services with the potential to expand the scope of Siemens' core businesses.

Siemens AG, based in Munich, Germany, is a multinational corporation with a balanced business portfolio of activities predominantly in the field of electronics and electrical engineering. The company conducts business in seven groups: Information and Communications, Automation and Control, Power, Transportation, Medical, Lighting, and Financing and Real Estate. Siemens AG's most recent worldwide revenues were around $89 billion.

SVC currently has investments in more than 70 start-up companies and 30 venture capital funds focusing primarily in areas such as information and communications, automation and control, medical solutions, transportation systems, power, and security technologies.

The Siemens Venture Capital team takes a hands-on approach to its investments. In addition to financial support, SVC plays an active role in the growth of portfolio companies by providing strategic management guidance and access to Siemens' global network of internal and external resources.

SVC investment partners are committed to building strong relationships with portfolio companies. They have developed a collaborative culture in which they work closely with their senior management teams to gauge a start-up's progress and determine how best to achieve quality and sustainable growth.

By leveraging the global power and resources of Siemens, SVC enables entrepreneurs to increase their visibility in the marketplace and gain credibility, ultimately creating greater access to worldwide sales and service channels. Please refer to Part Three's Financing Source Directory for additional information.

CASE PROFILE

MontaVista Software Inc. is a leading global supplier of systems software and development tools for intelligent connected devices and the associated infrastructure. MontaVista provides a commercial-grade Linux-based operating system (OS) and universal development platform. MontaVista's products address software developer needs encompassing applications ranging from communications infrastructure to consumer electronics. Headquartered in Sunnyvale, California, MontaVista is a privately held company funded by several corporate investors.

In April 2004 MontaVista announced four new investors: Siemens Venture Capital, which led the funding, as well as Samsung Ventures America, Infineon Ventures, and China Development Industrial Bank in Taiwan. The total investment in MontaVista since it was founded is now $72 million.

TRANSACTION LEAD

The investment resulted from Siemens Venture Capital investigating a number of emerging Linux vendors. In close collaboration with Siemens' Corporate Technology group, Siemens Venture Capital had identified that Linux was an emerging technology that held significant potential benefits for Siemens. Siemens Venture Capital's research found MontaVista's business strategies to be well aligned with Siemens' needs and engaged a number of Siemens groups in evaluating MontaVista.

MontaVista had also recognized the strategic importance of Siemens both as a customer and as a potential investor. The company had contacted Siemens Venture Capital a number of times over several years, but in earlier contacts MontaVista and the Linux market had not advanced sufficiently to generate sufficient interest within Siemens.

By early 2004, the timing was right, precipitated by the confluence of market trends and MontaVista's growing strength.

KEY ISSUES THAT WERE OVERCOME DURING NEGOTIATIONS

When Siemens Venture Capital began investment discussions with MontaVista, MontaVista was pleased to have the dialogue. However, prior to the investment, MontaVista was already well capitalized, which led the company and its investors to closely scrutinize the potential investment. At the same time Siemens Venture Capital was price sensitive. What drove the successful outcome to the negotiations was Siemens Venture Capital's compelling strategic value. (See transaction details table.)

Transaction Details

	Preinvestment	Postinvestment	Characteristics/Terms/Type
Annual revenue	~ $20 million		
Annual EBIT	Loss		
Short-term debt	None	None	
Long-term debt	None	None	
Total liabilities	Small	Small	Primary liability was deferred revenue due to MontaVista's subscription-based pricing model
Options/warrants	No warrants	No warrants	The company has an employee stock option plan

STRATEGY AND ANALYSIS FOR INVESTMENT

In August 2003, Gartner Inc. reported that the embedded software tools total available market was close to $1 billion. In 2003, Venture Development Corporation (VDC) placed MontaVista Software as the number one commercial embedded Linux company worldwide, based on market share. In June 2004, in an updated report, VDC gave MontaVista a dominant market share in the embedded Linux market (just under 50 percent).

"MontaVista Software provides a robust and quality product, for which there is real demand, especially in Taiwan and China, where Linux is already the fastest-growing embedded OS," said Irene Shih, assistant vice president, China Development Industrial Bank Inc. "We expect the demand for embedded Linux will continue to increase at a rapid rate, and believe MontaVista Software has a management team that can successfully execute on this opportunity."

POSTINVESTMENT ISSUES

Since the investment MontaVista has continued to grow. MontaVista's role within Siemens has grown significantly. At least one business unit within Siemens is achieving the benefits identified by Siemens Venture Capital and Corporate Technology. A number of others have begun to engage with MontaVista. Siemens Venture Capital's work with MontaVista has contributed to MontaVista's growth both through building relationships within Siemens and through providing expertise and strategic guidance in multiple market areas.

Siemens Venture Capital's objectives with its investment in MontaVista are twofold. As MontaVista's products and services are increasingly relied upon within Siemens, a primary objective is to help MontaVista grow from a well-capitalized early stage company to a well-capitalized, profitable larger company. Siemens Venture Capital also expects a healthy financial return for its investment.

Lessons Learned/Experience Applied during Transaction Process

So far this investment appears to be a success from the perspectives of both the growth of the company and Siemens' leveraging of the company's products and services. The timing from Siemens' perspective demonstrated that in this case there needed to be significant interest from at least one operating unit within Siemens before exploring investment discussions with Siemens Venture Capital. The timing from MontaVista's perspective demonstrated that there are significant business benefits to adding strategic investors even when the company is already well capitalized.

About the Contributors

Sabine Zindera is the vice president of marketing communications for Siemens Venture Capital. Dave Warner is the chief financial officer of MontaVista Software.

CASE STUDY 13: Community Development Financing

Firm's Profile

SJF Ventures, formerly Sustainable Jobs Fund, was founded by David Kirkpatrick and Rick Defieux in 1999. At its inception, its founders ensured that the firm would qualify as a community development financial institution (CDFI).

One of the fundamental goals of community development venture capital (CDVC) was the creation and retention of quality, high-paying jobs for low-income people. The Community Development Venture Capital Alliance (CDVCA), the trade group of the CDVC industry, defined its mission as promoting "the use of the tools of venture capital to create jobs, entrepreneurial capacity, and wealth to advance the livelihoods of low-income people and the economies of distressed communities."

By 2003, SJF had two operating entities: SJF Ventures I, LP, the for-profit equity investment arm, and SJF Advisory Services, an allied not-for-profit that provided portfolio companies with technical assistance in workforce development, environmental sustainability, and asset development for low-income workers. By this time, SJF had invested in 14 companies, having chosen from total deal flow of close to 2,000, with 24 institutional co-investors. Nine of its 14 portfolio companies had achieved breakeven or better on a net income basis, compared to their net loss position when SJF invested.

In addition, these investments had fulfilled SJF's mission. They provided over 1,500 jobs, with a net gain in excess of 750. All but one of the companies provided employer-paid health insurance of some sort, and many provided training, 401(k)s, and profit sharing or employee stock options. Three-quarters of the portfolio company employees were entry-level or semiskilled, and 77 percent of the company sites and 64 percent of the employee residences were located in economically distressed areas.

In 2003, with its available capital nearly fully invested (including amounts set aside for reserves), SJF was prepared to start efforts to raise funds for SJF Ventures II, LP, with a target between $25 million and $50 million. As in the previous fund, SJF Ventures II would invest in preferred equity and subordinated debt positions with warrants (the right to purchase shares of the company's stock in the future at a prearranged price).

SJF's efforts to raise its second fund did not begin in earnest until the second quarter of 2004. It appeared that some of the major banks that had invested in the first fund were facing disappointing results from their private equity portfolio, and this contributed to a wait and see attitude on their part about reinvesting with SJF. Understandably, they wanted to see if SJF could achieve exits from its investments, and the fund, just over four years old, was still several years away from harvesting a significant number of exits. In April 2004, SJF I recorded its first premium exit (a 3× 70 percent IRR return in two years), and distributed more than $1 million to its limited partners, representing 10 percent of invested capital. The fund used this good news to launch its fund-raising for SJF II; still, the message from would-be investors continued to be that exits (and, in the absence of those, evidence of increased portfolio value, such as would be generated by an outside investment in a portfolio company at a higher valuation) remain a critical factor in their reinvestment decision. Please refer to Part Three's Financing Source Directory for additional information.

CASE PROFILE

Ryla Teleservices was founded in 2001 by Mark Wilson and his wife Evelyn (Shelly). Ryla is a business-to-business teleservices center.

- Mark Wilson engaged Elpis Group to assist with raising capital soon after Ryla's start-up, as it was clear that he would not be able to self-fund the operations. Elpis's Najah Ade-Drakes referred Ryla to Rick Larson, a managing director of SJF whom she had met at a venture fair in Atlanta.

- Starting pay would be $8.50 per hour, there would be options for commissions on all sales, and all permanent staff would have 80 percent of their health insurance paid. While the operation would be located in Woodstock, Georgia, a relatively prosperous community north of Atlanta, its employees would likely come from lower-income areas further north of the city.

- In 2002 and early 2003, SJF invested a total of $700,000 to fund Ryla's operations. In August 2002, SJF invested $500,000 in series A participating preferred stock, at a $1.25 million premoney valuation. In February 2003, SJF invested an additional $200,000 in a series A-1 round, at a $2.1 million premoney valuation, a 10 percent increase in the share price. Following the series A-1 investment, SJF's ownership in the company was 36 percent, while Wilson's share was 55 percent. (Nine percent was reserved for an option pool.)

- In the summer of 2003, Rick Larson was pleased with Ryla's performance. Not only was it doing well, but it was creating high-quality entry-level jobs. Due to its growing workforce, Ryla was able to increase to 100 percent the portion of health insurance premiums it paid for permanent workers, and provided a 401(k) plan, extensive training opportunities, and a number of other benefits. In an industry prone to high turnover, Ryla's workforce was stable, enthusiastic, involved, and productive.

- Ryla had three major clients and a workforce of more than 100, and it had reached cash-flow breakeven in June 2003. One of its current clients wanted to double the business it sent to Ryla, and the business development executive recently hired by Mark Wilson had already generated interest from some major Atlanta area corporations. To handle the business, the company was planning to raise a $2 million B round, mostly as subordinated debt. The use of sub debt was an option that would allow the Wilsons to maintain 51 percent ownership and continue to qualify for MBE certification. Mark Wilson believed the MBE certification along with being a domestic corporation would give Ryla a competitive advantage with bids in the public sector and with private sector firms with diversity programs.

COMPANY'S ANALYSIS AND MARKETS

Teleservice firms (also called call centers) create a large number of low-skilled jobs. The top four teleservice firms, West Corporation, Convergys, SITEL, and Teletech, employed a total of 123,800 people in 2002 and generated revenue of almost $5 billion in that year. Estimates placed U.S. call center employment in 2002 between 1.9 million and 7 million, including companies' internal call centers, whose employment is difficult to determine. The global market for outsourced call center services, in which an operation contracted with another firm to handle its customer contact activities, was estimated at $35 billion in 2001, and was expected to grow by 21 percent annually to $90 billion by 2006.

The immediate image of teleservices as the disrupter of countless dinners across America covered only a small fraction of the industry, which included everything from customer care for high-tech firms and automobile manufacturers through business-to-business financial record updating and bill collection.

Ryla Teleservices is a niche player in the call center market. Mark Wilson had started as a call center associate for Dun & Bradstreet (D&B) (NYSE: DNB), and worked his way up to vice president, managing call centers. In 2000, D&B decided to outsource a portion of its call center operations. Wilson said, "I suggested that, rather than outsource to someone else who didn't know the D&B culture and business model, they should outsource the work to me." D&B agreed and became Ryla's first customer.

SJF I has reserves set aside for follow-on investment, and would willingly invest alongside a new outside investor that could establish a new share price. (The SJF valuation policy only allows markups of the value of investments when an investment in the company is made by an investor new to the company.) SJF I might reinvest in Ryla on a solo basis for compelling business reasons (either positive or defensive).

HOLDING/EXITING OBJECTIVE OF SJF VENTURES I

With regard to its investment in Ryla, SJF's preferred stock purchase agreement contains a five-year put provision, in keeping with the fund's goal of exiting its investments within five years. Likely exit scenarios for its investment in Ryla include: acquisition by a larger player in the call center space, refinancing by a mezzanine private equity fund, or a management buyback/buyout of SJF's stake. Creating an employee stock ownership plan (ESOP) that could purchase SJF's shares is also a possibility in a company like Ryla that has an engaged workforce, revenues above $5 million, and the prospects for solid profitability.

LESSONS LEARNED/EXPERIENCE APPLIED DURING FINANCING PROCESS

SJF and Ryla presented the company to nearly 20 venture firms and mezzanine investors in searching for the $2 million in series B funding. While one Atlanta area venture firm expressed interest in Ryla, its main question for Wilson was, "What could you do with $5 million?," and it agreed to stay in touch with the company and serve as an informal adviser. One mezzanine fund (sub debt with warrants) contacted early in 2004 continues to express interest in the company, but has not conducted aggressive due diligence. Several factors appear to have worked against Ryla's efforts to raise the series B funding:

1. The small size and structure of the round. Venture funds generally seek to put larger amounts of capital to work, and most do not invest via the sub debt with warrants structure. Mezzanine lenders tend to look for companies that have more free cash flow than does Ryla, which is operating just above breakeven.
2. Ryla's age and industry sector. The company is still recording its first profitable year and is on a rapid growth trajectory, which has dampened EBITDA and depressed its margins below industry benchmarks. Since an investment in the company at this point would likely be valued as a multiple of EBITDA (rather than as a multiple of revenue, which was the case in SJF's investment in Ryla when it was not yet profitable), the company might not command as high a valuation as management or SJF might like.
3. The furor over offshore outsourcing and the early 2004 introduction of the National Do Not Call Registry have raised questions among investors about the call center industry. While Ryla's B2B focus is not affected by the Do Not Call issue, its commitment to a highly paid domestic workforce (relative to wage rates offshore) is contrarian in an industry where profitability has traditionally been driven primarily by low labor costs.
4. The slow progress raising the series B allowed the company to grow out of its need for capital. It has been forced to find ways to generate cash internally, by managing accounts payable and seeking more favorable receivables terms. In addition, it has been able to use its larger size to renegotiate some of its expensive receivables factoring, in part by seeking other bids for this financing.

As of September 2004 SJF remains actively involved with the company. Through SJF Advisory Services, the fund helped the company adopt a broad-based stock option plan in August 2004. Through his board role, Rick Larson remains active in advising Wilson on a range of strategic and operational issues, in addition to providing promotional and networking opportunities for the company. The company continues to grow and field interest from private equity firms. Its status as a domestic, high-quality minority-owned call center has led to strategic relationships with major call center industry players, who view a partnership with Ryla as a way to win contracts with government agencies (that cannot be sourced offshore) and Fortune 100 companies (under supplier diversity initiatives). Ryla's management and board are increasingly focused on pursuing more value-added work that can result in higher gross margins and net income for the company. By August 2004, the company's valuation had grown to $4,750,000 based on the same valuation formula used for the series A-1 preferred investment.

SOURCE

This case draws heavily on *SJF Ventures and Ryla Teleservices: 2003* by Ann Leamon (with the assistance of Rick Larson, Mark Wilson, and Meg Barnette), a case study commissioned by the CDVCA. Readers interested in a better understanding of this case may want to obtain a copy for reference. To order copies call 1-212-594-6747; write Community Development Venture Capital Alliance, 330 Seventh Avenue, 19th Floor, New York, NY 10001; or go to www.cdvca.org. SJF and Ryla executives have provided updated information.

CASE STUDY 14: Debt with Revenue Sharing

FIRM'S PROFILE

Vested for Growth (VfG) is a source of growth capital in New Hampshire offered through the nonprofit New Hampshire Community Loan Fund (NHCLF). Over the past 20 years, NHCLF has lent more than $60 million to provide quality housing and jobs and promote economic opportunity for New Hampshire families. VfG supports entrepreneurs with long-term perspective and a commitment to growth by sharing responsibility for running the company and sharing profits with the employees. To achieve this goal, VfG provides two tools: (1) capital investments (debt or equity) up to $500,000 and (2) peer learning groups to help CEOs successfully apply this business philosophy as a way to grow their companies.

VfG aims to widen the economic winners' circle for employees of its portfolio companies, including those without post–high school education. The two areas of focus are to find new ways to engage employees that boost performance and to develop quality systems that result in continued improvement. To encourage meeting these objectives, the entrepreneur establishes annual mission goals and, if met, is able to reduce the cost of the VfG capital. This provides a "good driver" incentive discount.

VfG invests only in New Hampshire–based companies that share the VfG business philosophy, offer a strong growth proposition, and offer a range of jobs, including positions for individuals who do not have post–high school education. VfG invests mainly in early stage companies, during a growth or succession phase. The preferred investment vehicle is debt with revenue participation, but the full range, from debt to straight equity, is eligible depending on the nature of the investment. Investments range from approximately $200,000 to $500,000. Please refer to Part Three's Financing Source Directory for additional information.

CASE PROFILE

After founding Bortech, Inc. in 1989 and running it for 10 years, Rees Acheson and Tedd Benson were ready to pursue other interests. But they wanted to find a buyer who would take Bortech to the next level of success while also keeping the company's jobs in New Hampshire and investing in and sharing the profits and decision making of the company with its employees. Bortech's current CEO, Leo White, was the perfect fit.

Bortech manufactures a patented bore welder utilizing a new welding technique that cuts the repair time of bores from several hours to under an hour. Bores are holes into which pins are inserted to allow parts of machines to pivot or rotate. Over time, the pins wear the holes thin and so the bore walls must then be built up, either by welding the inside of the hole or by inserting a bushing into it. The bore welder's portability allows the machine to repair equipment in the field rather than in repair shops, and its automated process allows it to get to bores that hands could not access to create consistency in the welding that was not achievable before.

Recognizing the strength of Bortech's technology, White began looking for a bank loan to finance the acquisition. Bortech's physical assets, however, were small—primarily consisting of its patented bore welders—compared to the company's asking price, and many banks were concerned about collateral for a loan. Bortech seemed to be caught in a funding gap—too risky for debt, but too small for venture capital. Fortunately for Bortech, Vested for Growth, a program of the New Hampshire Community Loan Fund that provides risk capital of up to $500,000 to small businesses in New Hampshire, was designed to fill that gap. Leo White was referred to VfG by a member of its advisory committee.

Recognizing Bortech's growth potential as well as White's past business experience and commitment to outstanding employment practices, VfG provided $500,000 in the form of debt with revenue participation ($500,000 at 9 percent over 10 years plus 1.44 percent of gross sales). With this financing, White took over Bortech in November of 2002. Since then the company has outperformed its peers. While machine and tool industry sales for 2003 declined by 18 percent, Bortech came within 5 percent of matching a 10-year sales record and halfway through 2004, it was now 35 percent ahead of those sales. Consequently, the annual participation payment was on target with VfG's pricing projections giving VfG a 14.3 percent IRR after one year with a trajectory to achieve a 20 percent IRR at the end of 10 years.

VfG's "good driver" incentive discount is tied to mission progress relating to new initiatives that engage employees. Bortech put a profit sharing plan in place, conducted financial training for all employees so that they can understand how their jobs connect to the company's bottom line, used a democratic process to write an employee handbook, and instituted a formal quality control process. Accordingly, the company earned the $3,500 good driver discount for its first year, and it has chosen to add it to their profit sharing pool. In addition, the company added two new assembly and technical support positions that allowed them to hire two people whose formal education ended in high school, along with one business development manager. Bortech also added short-term disability benefits, a 401(k) program, and term life insurance to all employee benefits. Bortech is having a solid first two years in both social and financial returns.

STRATEGY AND ANALYSIS FOR INVESTMENT

Bortech was a solid first transaction for VfG. The company has a patented product, dominated its market, and possessed a 10-year track record. While Leo White had never owned a company, his business experience was strong and his values were aligned with those that VfG seeks—including sharing the success of the business with its employees with a profit sharing plan.

POSTINVESTMENT ISSUES

This year Bortech is 35 percent ahead of last year's sales and its growth prospects look good. The company has hired a new salesperson and is on track to meet its objectives. Leo White has made significant progress and has gained additional credibility in a short period.

VfG obtains monthly financial statements from Bortech and conducts site visits periodically. John Hamilton, director of enterprise development for VfG, is part of the board of advisers of Bortech; they meet every other month.

Lessons Learned from the Process

For future deals, VfG will seek ways to reduce up-front legal fees; this transaction involved three parties and three law firms. In addition, VfG will attempt to structure royalty payments due monthly or quarterly, not annually.

About the Contributors

The case profile has been adapted from the article "Bortech, Inc., a Vested for Growth Portfolio Company" by Leo White, CEO of Bortech, Keene, New Hampshire, and John Hamilton, director of enterprise development, Vested for Growth (jhamilton@vestedforgrowth.com).

Three

Financing
Source Directory

In this part, we provide a number of cross-reference tables and listings of actual firms involved in providing capital for emerging growth and middle-market companies. Our desire is to link the concepts and strategies previously presented with real firms and provide a valuable resource listing for your use once you have determined your or your client's needs.

This directory section provides only a partial list of the sources available—there are literally thousands. We developed our list and database by reaching out to a long list of potential participants and inviting them to provide information about their firms specifically for this book; about 400 companies responded. We view this as an ongoing effort that will evolve over time. Accordingly, we have established an online database for your use that is located at www.HandbookOfFinancingGrowth.com. To access the database from this site, you will need the following reader code: "HOFG_Reader." A detailed listing of each source in this book can be viewed online. In addition, we have provided advanced search capabilities to allow you to sort the data in ways that we may not present in our cross-reference tables in this book. In addition, we will endeavor to grow the database over time and to keep the listings current.*

The firms discussed or referenced in this section are the ones that actually write the checks versus those that may lead you to the ones that write the checks. We make this distinction because it is a significant one that you should be aware of in your pursuit of capital. In Chapter 7, "Expert Support—The Players and Their Roles," we have a full discussion about the roles of the professionals that you need to consider to support the funding process.

While we have segmented the type investor or lender into major groups, keep in mind that there is crossover among firms given that some span multiple categories. For more detail on the nuances and subcategories, please refer to Part One of this book where we discuss sources of capital. The major categories provided for in this section and the online database are:

AB	Asset-based lender
AI	Angel investor
BN	Commercial bank
CF	Commercial finance
GOV	Government agency
IN	Individual investor
LC	Leasing company
MB	Merchant bank
PE	Private equity fund
SI	Strategic or industry investor
VC	Venture capital fund

---

*We are providing the information about funding sources based on the information provided to us. We do not guarantee the accuracy or completeness, nor do we provide any type of warranty, including one of fitness for use. Our mention of keeping the database current is based on reasonable efforts and only to the extent we continue to support this book project and web site, of which there are no guarantees we will do; however, most likely we will do so for two to three years from the publication date of this book. Further, we can provide no assurances that you will obtain funding from any source regardless of your or your company's situation. Financing Source Directory (firms' directory listing), firms' and companies' profiles, and cases are presented to enhance the book information with actual business data and are not intended to serve as endorsements, and/or representations of preferred management solutions by and from the authors or contributors. Case, profile, and firm directory data are the sole responsibility of the firms that have provided the information and have authorized the authors' use of it as reference material. Participant firms have chosen to disguise some data to protect confidentiality as deemed necessary by them.

The database ID in the charts refers to the record ID in the online database at the link provided earlier.

SUGGESTED USE OF THE DIRECTORY SECTION

The first grouping of tables is organized so that the user can visually search by type of funding source and then by size of investment or loan required based on the minimum funding provided by each source. Once a number of potential sources are identified, you can seek contact and supporting information about those firms from the second grouping of charts; those are provided in alphabetical order by firm name. (See below for a listing of the tables.) Alternatively, you may choose to access the online database as mentioned earlier in this section.

Table Name	Page No.
Angel Investors by Minimum Funding	332
Individual Investors by Minimum Funding	332
Commercial Banks by Minimum Funding	332
Asset-Based Lenders by Minimum Funding	333
Commercial Finance Companies by Minimum Funding	334
Leasing Companies by Minimum Funding	334
Venture Capital Funds by Minimum Funding	335
Private Equity Funds by Minimum Funding	338
Merchant Banks by Minimum Funding	343
Strategic or Industry Investors by Minimum Funding	343
Government Agencies by Minimum Funding	343
Master List by Firm with Location Information	344
Master List by Firm with Contact Information	355
Master List by Firm with Summary Criteria	366

Angel Investors by Minimum Funding

($ millions)

Firm	Database ID	Type	State	Geographic Preference	Minimum Revenue	Typical Deal Size	Minimum Funding	Maximum Funding
Great Lakes Angels, Inc.	509	AI		Midwest		0.25	0.05	6.00
CL Fund	362	AI	PA	Western Pennsylvania	1.00	0.30	0.10	0.50
First Advisors, Inc.	383	AI	TX	Texas		0.50	0.10	1.00
Sand Hill Angels, LLC	311	AI	CA	West Coast		0.25	0.15	0.50
Tri-State Investment Group	312	AI	NC	Carolinas and Virginia	—	0.50	0.20	0.35
Desert Angels	329	AI	AZ	Southwest	—	0.50	0.25	0.70
Private Investors Forum	313	AI		Mid-Atlantic, Northeast		.25–.5	0.25	1.00
Robin Hood Ventures	352	AI	PA	Mid-Atlantic		0.50	0.25	0.50
Tech Coast Angels	500	AI		West Coast		.5–1.0	0.25	1.50
Tri-State Private Investors Network	439	AI	NY	North America	—			2.00
Bi-State Investment Group	519	AI	KA	Kansas City region				
Northern Illinois Angels LLC	314	AI	IL	Midwest				

Individual Investors by Minimum Funding

($ millions)

Firm	Database ID	Type	State	Geographic Preference	Minimum Revenue	Typical Deal Size	Minimum Funding	Maximum Funding
TechStock	446	IN	CA	Asia, USA				10.00
ArcHelion Capital Partners	345	IN	FL	Northeast, Florida		1.00	1.00	2.00
Meriwether Capital, L.L.C.	433	IN	NY	Mid-Atlantic, Northeast				

Commercial Banks by Minimum Funding

($ millions)

Firm	Database ID	Type	State	Geographic Preference	Minimum Revenue	Typical Deal Size	Minimum Funding	Maximum Funding
Washington Mutual Equipment Finance	251	BN	CO	USA	10.00	.75–2.5	0.25	15.00
Charter One Bank, N.A.	241	BN	MI	Midwest, Northeast	5.00	5.00	1.00	25.00
Bank of the West	472	BN	CA	West Coast		10.00	2.00	50.00
M&I Bank	341	BN	MN	Southwest, Midwest		10–15	5.00	30.00
Comerica Bank, Technology & Life Sciences Division	350	BN	VA	Mid-Atlantic	5.00	3.00		
Crescent State Bank	270	BN	NC	Mid-Atlantic				

Asset-Based Lenders by Minimum Funding

| | | | | | | ($ millions) | | |
Firm	Database ID	Type	State	Geographic Preference	Minimum Revenue	Typical Deal Size	Minimum Funding	Maximum Funding
BFI Business Finance, Inc.	363	AB	CA	West Coast		2.00	—	4.00
Friend Capital Funding, LLC	112	AB		USA, global		0.15	0.01	10.00
Hartsko Financial Services, LLC	489	AB	IL	Asia, Europe, USA		0.50	0.05	4.00
King Trade Capital	508	AB	TX	Other, USA, Canada			0.05	
Yale Capital, Inc.	111	AB	NY	NY, NJ, & CT only			0.05	5.00
Greenfield Commercial Credit	188	AB	IL	USA	1.00		0.05	5.00
Platinum Funding Corp	167	AB	NY	USA	1.00		0.10	6.50
Business Alliance Capital Corp.	553	AB	NC	USA	2.0	1–12	0.10	15.00
RAI Group	526	AB	NJ	USA		3.0	0.3	7.5
State Bank	504	AB	TX	USA		2–5	0.50	50.00
Transcap Trade Finance	113	AB	NY	Southeast		1.50	0.50	5.00
Capital TempFunds, Inc.	503	AB	FL	North America		3.00	0.50	10.00
Royal Bank Asset Based Finance	144	AB	ON	USA	1.00	1.00	1.00	10.00
Standard Federal Bank	507	AB	MI	Mid-Atlantic, Southeast, Canada	5.00	2–25	1.00	50.00
Wells Fargo Business Credit, Inc.	242	AB	GA	Midwest,USA	8.00	3.00	1.00	100.00
Siemens Financial Services, Inc.	265	AB	NC	USA,Canada	10.00	<10	2.00	25.00
Hilco Capital LP	227	AB	IL	USA			3.00	25.00
GE Corporate Financial Services	217	AB	NY	USA		10.00	4.00	50.00
Healthcare Finance Group, Inc.	502	AB	NY	USA			5.00	30+
Maple Commercial Finance Group	405	AB	NJ	North America, Europe, USA, Australia	25.00	25.00	5.00	150.00
PNC Business Credit	255	AB	WA	West Coast		10–20	5.00	100.00
STAG Capital Partners	552	AB	MA	USA	20.00	20.00	5.00	25.00
U.S. Bank Business Credit	237	AB	OR	North America		10.0	5.0	25.0
Callidus Capital Corporation	140	AB	ON	Northeast, Canada		15.00	5.00	150.00
Paragon Financial Group, Inc.	214	AB	FL	USA				
United Capital Funding Corp.	484	AB	FL	North America, Europe, USA		0.25		1.00
Westgate Financial Corp.	235	AB	NJ	North America		0.10		2.00

Commercial Finance Companies by Minimum Funding

						($ millions)		
Firm	Database ID	Type	State	Geographic Preference	Minimum Revenue	Typical Deal Size	Minimum Funding	Maximum Funding
J D Factors	505	CF	CA	North America		.10	0.005	2.00
Enterprise Corporation of the Delta	335	CF	MS	Southeast		0.20	0.05	1.50
Rockland Credit Finance LLC	506	CF	MD		1.00	3.00	0.10	7.00
Four J Funding	528	CF	NJ			2-20	0.50	100.00
Chatham Capital	322	CF	GA	USA		5.00	1.50	25.00
Cardinal Capital Partners	320	CF	TX	Europe, USA	10.00	25.00	2.00	1,000.00
IIG Capital LLC	394	CF	NY	Europe, USA, worldwide but OECD country risk	6-12	7-10	2.00	30.00
RAI Group—Private Label Credit Cards	527	CF	NJ	USA		2-5	2.00	100.00
CapitalSource Finance LLC	191	CF	MD	USA		20-30	5.00	50.00
CSG Investments, Inc.	347	CF	TX	North America, USA, South America	10.00	50.00	5.00	200.00
W. P. Carey & Co. LLC	513	CF	NY	North America, Europe, USA		50.00	5.00	500.00
GE Commercial Finance	282	CF	NY	Europe, USA		35.00	10.00	1,000.00
Antares Capital Corporation	258	CF	IL	USA		75.00	15.00	200.00
J&D Financial Corporation	542	CF	FL	North America, Europe, USA	30.00	.1/mnth	.01/mnth	4/mnth

Leasing Companies by Minimum Funding

						($ millions)		
Firm	Database ID	Type	State	Geographic Preference	Minimum Revenue	Typical Deal Size	Minimum Funding	Maximum Funding
Capital Equipment Leasing	253	LC	CA	USA		0.25	0.01	10.00
CapitalWerks, LLC	267	LC	CA	USA		0.5-1.0	0.03	25.00
Complete Leasing Corporation	465	LC	VA	USA		2.00	0.10	10.00
Orix Financial	154	LC	NH	USA	10.00	1-2.5	0.50	5.00
Baxter Capital Corporation	125	LC	IL	USA	2.10	1.50	1.00	5.00

Venture Capital Funds by Minimum Funding

($ millions)

Firm	Database ID	Type	State	Geographic Preference	Minimum Revenue	Typical Deal Size	Minimum Funding	Maximum Funding
Wisconsin Rural Enterprise Fund, LLC	364	VC	WI	Midwest		0.10	0.02	0.20
The Aurora Funds	109	VC	NC	Southeast, USA			0.05	2.00
CrossBridge Venture Partners	464	VC	CA	Asia, USA		0.50	0.10	1.00
Highland Capital Partners	336	VC	MA	Europe, USA			0.10	50.00
Mofet Venture Capital Fund	412	VC	Israel	West Coast, North America, Northeast, USA		5.00	0.10	2.00
Murex Investments I, L.P.	444	VC	PA	Mid-Atlantic	0.40	0.50	0.10	1.00
Synetro Capital—Synetro Ventures (early stage)	142	VC	IL	Midwest			0.10	1.00
Acorn Campus	131	VC	CA	West Coast, greater China		1.50	0.20	3.00
Charlotte Angel Partners	330	VC	NC	Carolinas		0.40	0.20	0.50
Research Triangle Ventures	296	VC	NC	Southeast		1–3	0.20	0.60
ARCH Development Partners	493	VC	IL	Midwest		0.50	0.25	2.00
CEI Community Ventures	307	VC	ME	ME, NH, VT, MA		0.35	0.25	0.25
Limburg Ventures BV	414	VC	Neth	Europe, Meuse Rhine Euro region	—	1.00	0.25	2.00
Mentor Capital Partners Ltd	187	VC	PA	Mid-Atlantic, Northeast			0.25	1.00
Mohr Davidow Ventures	243	VC	CA	West Coast, Mid-Atlantic, USA		3–5	0.25	10.00
New York City Investment Fund	365	VC	NY	New York City only		.75–1.0	0.25	4.00
Pacific Horizon Ventures	201	VC	WA	West Coast, Pacific Northwest region		.25–10	0.25	2.50
Southern Appalachian Management Company, LLC	372	VC	TN	Southeast, Southern Appalachia	0.10	1.00	0.25	0.75
Giza Venture Capital	366	VC		Israel-related		3.00	0.30	7.00
BP Marsh Private Equity	381	VC		North America, Europe, USA		1.00	0.40	5.00
A. M. Pappas & Associates, LLC	316	VC	NC	USA			0.50	5.00
Access Venture Partners	252	VC	CA	West Coast, Southwest, Midwest		2–5	0.50	5.00
Alloy Ventures	260	VC	CA	West Coast		4.00	0.50	7.50
Antares Capital Corporation	127	VC	FL	Southeast, Texas	2.00	1.00	0.50	2.00
BayTech Venture Capital	387	VC	Germany	Europe			0.50	5.00
Biofrontier Partners USA	459	VC	CA	West Coast, Asia, Northeast		3.00	0.50	6.00
Deutsche Effecten- und Wechsel-Beteiligungsgesellschaft AG	437	VC	Germany	Europe			0.50	5.00
Diamondhead Ventures	315	VC	CA	USA		3.00	0.50	5.00
EonTech Ventures SA	380	VC		Europe		1.50	0.50	3.00
gcp gamma capital partners	386	VC		Europe		1.50	0.50	3.00
Generics Asset Management Ltd	541	VC	UK	Europe, USA	10.00	1.00	0.50	5.00
Genesis Campus	547	VC	TX	USA		2.00	0.50	3.00
GrowthWorks Capital Ltd.	434	VC	BC	Canada		3.00	0.50	10.00
Guide Ventures, LLC	176	VC	WA	West Coast		1.50	0.50	10.00
Leo Capital Holdings, LLC	426	VC	IL	USA		1.50	0.50	10.00
Monumental Venture Partners, LLC	462	VC	VA	Mid-Atlantic			0.50	3.00
Mountaineer Capital	397	VC	WV	Mid-Atlantic, Midwest, Southeast, West Virginia	10.00	1.00	0.50	2.00
Novo A/S	199	VC	Denmark	North America, Europe, USA		0.5–10	0.50	10.00
Outlook Ventures	326	VC	CA	West Coast		2.00	0.50	5.00
Scope	411	VC		Europe		2.00	0.50	3.00

(Continued)

Venture Capital Funds by Minimum Funding (Continued)

($ millions)

Firm	Database ID	Type	State	Geographic Preference	Minimum Revenue	Typical Deal Size	Minimum Funding	Maximum Funding
SJF Ventures	124	VC	NC	Mid-Atlantic, Midwest, Southeast, Northeast	0.50	0.75	0.50	1.70
SOFINNOVA Partners	264	VC		Europe			0.50	15.00
Tech Capital Partners Inc.	429	VC	ON	Southwestern Ontario		1.50	0.50	4.50
Yaletown Venture Partners Inc.	393	VC	BC	West Coast		1.00	0.50	2.50
Salem Capital Partners, LP	333	VC	NC	Mid-Atlantic, Southeast, Northeast	3.00	1.50	0.75	3.00
Scottish Equity Partners	306	VC	UK	UK & Ireland			0.90	8.80
@Ventures	389	VC	MA	USA			1.00	7.50
Abingworth Management	223	VC		Europe, USA		5.00	1.00	20.00
Allegiance Capital Limited Partnership	415	VC	MD	Mid-Atlantic	10.00	15.00	1.00	3.00
Brook Venture Fund	328	VC	MA	Northeast	0.50	2.00	1.00	4.00
Concord Ventures	490	VC	Israel	Israel		2.50	1.00	10.00
Edelson Technology Partners	130	VC	NJ			3.00	1.00	3.00
Frontier Capital	123	VC	NC	Mid-Atlantic, Southeast	2.00	1.50	1.00	3.00
Funk Ventures	171	VC	CA	West Coast, USA		2.50	1.00	5.00
Geneva Venture Partners	170	VC	CA	West Coast, Europe		2.00	1.00	5.00
GrandBanks Capital	219	VC	MA	Mid-Atlantic, Southeast, Northeast, Europe, Canada		5.00	1.00	12.00
Harbert Management Corporation —Venture Partners	309	VC	AL	Mid-Atlantic, Southeast		2.00	1.00	7.50
Hopewell Ventures	398	VC	IL	Midwest		2.50	1.00	5+
Horizon Ventures	331	VC	CA	CA, AZ		3.00	1.00	5.00
IDG Ventures Europe	169	VC		Europe		3.00	1.00	8.00
Infineon Ventures GmbH	497	VC	Germany			2.50	1.00	5.00
LogiSpring	378	VC		North America, Europe		5.00	1.00	10.00
Mayfield	122	VC	CA	West Coast		3.50	1.00	10.00
River Cities Capital Funds	277	VC	NC	Midwest, Southeast	1.00	3.00	1.00	6.00
SpaceVest	355	VC	VA	USA		15.00	1.00	10.00
Telos Venture Partners	516	VC	CA	West Coast		5.00	1.00	3.00
Thomas Weisel Venture Partners	359	VC	CA	West Coast, Northeast	—	2-10	1.00	15.00
Three Arch Partners	276	VC	CA	USA		5.00	1.00	20.00
Zon Capital Partners LP	518	VC	NJ	Mid-Atlantic			1.00	2.00
Baird Venture Partners	278	VC	WI	Midwest, Southeast	—	5-15	2.00	5.00
Lighthouse Venture Partners, LLC	521	VC		Southeast	—	2.50	2.00	5.00
MTI Partners Limited	469	VC		Europe		5.00	2.00	15.00
Net Partners	263	VC	Italy	West Coast, Europe		4.00	2.00	6.00
Salix Ventures	334	VC	MA	USA	2.00	3.00	2.00	4.00
StarVest Partners, L.P.	494	VC	NY	North America, USA			2.00	20.00
Thomas, McNerney & Partners	463	VC	MN	USA			2.00	
Edison Venture Fund	107	VC	NJ	Mid-Atlantic	4.50	3.50	2.50	8.00
FA Technology Ventures	551	VC	NY	Northeast		4.0	3.0	8.0
Global Catalyst Partners	467	VC	CA				3.00	10.00

Company	No.	Type	State	Region					
Key Venture Partners	120	VC	MA	USA	3.00	5.00	3.00	10.00
North Atlantic Capital	452	VC	ME	Mid-Atlantic, Northeast	3.00	3.00	3.00	10.00
Sierra Ventures	369	VC	CA	USA	2.00	5.00	3.00	25.00
Cross Atlantic Partners, Inc.	385	VC	NY	USA		5.00	3.50	7.00
Advent International	203	VC	MA	USA		8.00	5.00	20.00
Essex Woodlands Health Ventures	129	VC	IL	USA		10.00	5.00	15.00
Primus Venture Partners, Inc.	175	VC	OH	USA		10.00	5.00	15.00
QuestMark Partners	420	VC	MD	USA	4–5	30.00	5.00	15+
Wales Fund Managers Limited	419	VC	UK	Wales, UK		£.275	£.05	£1
Arcturus Capital	455	VC	CA	West Coast				
Capital Investments	116	VC	TX	Southwest, North America				
Eastern Technology Fund	440	VC	PA	Mid-Atlantic				
Falcon Fund	529	VC	CA	Southwest	—			
InnovationsKapital	371	VC	NC	Europe, Nordic area				
Intersouth Partners	106	VC	NC	Mid-Atlantic, Southeast		0.5–5		
SBV Venture Partners	435	VC	CA	West Coast				
SCP Private Equity Partners	344	VC	PA	USA		5–10		
Security Technlogy Ventures, LLC	138	VC	CA	USA				
Triton Ventures	229	VC	TX	Southwest				
Vencon Management Inc.	146	VC	NY	Europe, USA, West Asia				
Ventures West Management Inc.	275	VC	BC	Canada				
Walker Ventures	226	VC	MD	Mid-Atlantic				

Private Equity Funds by Minimum Funding

($ millions)

Firm	Database ID	Type	State	Geographic Preference	Minimum Revenue	Typical Deal Size	Minimum Funding	Maximum Funding
New Mexico Private Investors, Inc	325	PE	NM	Southwest		0.50	0.10	1.00
FirstFloor Capital	391	PE	WP	Asia, Southeast Asia focus		1.00	0.25	2.50
Meritage Private Equity Funds	200	PE	CO	USA		7.00	0.25	10.00
Southwest Value Acquisitions LLC	533	PE	AZ	West Coast, Southwest	2.00	5 Rev*	0.25	5.00
Agrarian Capital, LLC	319	PE	IL	North America		1.50	0.50	5.00
Austin Capital Partners, L.P.	153	PE	OH	Midwest	8.00	1–3	0.50	4.00
Cherry Tree Investments, Inc.	447	PE	MN	Midwest		1.50	0.50	2.00
Exeter Capital Partners	374	PE	NY	USA		3.00	0.50	5.00
H. Katz Capital Group	481	PE	PA	Europe, USA	5.00		0.50	10.00
Infocomm Investments Pte Ltd	520	PE		Asia, USA			0.50	5.00
Longmeadow Capital, LLC	353	PE	MA	Northeast		2.00	0.50	5.00
Metapoint Partners	408	PE	MA	Mid-Atlantic, Midwest, Southeast, Northeast	8.00	10.00	0.50	5.00
NewWest Mezzanine Fund LP	189	PE	CO	Rocky Mountain region	5.00	2.00	0.50	3.00
SouthPointe Ventures, LLC	273	PE	GA	Mid-Atlantic, Southeast	5.00	6.00	0.50	1.00
Autumn Hill Capital Group, LLC	236	PE	PA	Europe, USA	3.00	5–25	0.75	20.00
AP Capital Partners	250	PE	FL	Mid-Atlantic, Asia, Southeast, Northeast, USA	10.00		1.00	10.00
Argosy Partners	349	PE	PA	Mid-Atlantic, Southeast, Northeast	10.00	2–4	1.00	5.00
Artisan Capital	156	PE	CA	USA	10.00	5.00	1.00	50.00
Baring Private Equity Partners	523	PE		Europe			1.00	15.00
Birchmere Capital LP	268	PE	PA	Mid-Atlantic		1.5–3.0	1.00	4.00
Boston Millennia Partners	115	PE	MA	USA	1.00	5.00	1.00	30.00
Centerfield Capital Partners	346	PE	IN	Midwest	5.00	2–3	1.00	4.00
Convergent Capital Partners	249	PE	MN	USA	10.00	3.50	1.00	7.00
Davis, Tuttle Venture Partners, LP	323	PE	TX	West Coast, Southwest, Midwest		5–20	1.00	12.00
GMB Mezzanine Capital	301	PE	MN	USA			1.00	10.00
High Street Capital	475	PE	IL	USA	10.00		1.00	10.00
L&L Capital Partners	135	PE	CT	North America		3.00	1.00	4.00
Marquette Capital Partners, Inc.	327	PE	MN	Midwest, USA	10.00	2–5	1.00	10.00
PRIVEQ Capital Partners	234	PE	ON	Other, USA, Canada	5.00	2–3	1.00	4.00
Prudent Capital	479	PE	DC	Mid-Atlantic, Northeast	5.00	3.00	1.00	10.00
PS Capital Partners, LLC	197	PE	WI	Midwest	5.00	10.00	1.00	5.00
River Associates Investments, LLC	536	PE	TN	North America	10.00	10–15	1.00	10.00
RockWood Equity Partners, LLC	151	PE	NY	USA	10.00	15.00	1.00	5.00
Synetro Capital — Synetro Capital Partners	143	PE	IL	Midwest	8.00		1.00	5.00
Transpac Capital	424	PE		Asia		8.00	1.00	60.00
TRF Private Equity	538	PE	PA	Mid-Atlantic	2.50	2.50	1.00	4.00
Trident Growth Fund, LP	321	PE	TX	Southwest, Southeast	5.00	1.50	1.00	2.00
Venture Capital Solutions, LP	110	PE	NC	Southeast	3.00	1.50	1.00	2.00
Zenith Capital Partners LLC	211	PE	CA	North America, USA	10.00	50.00	1.00	50.00

*Revenue.

Firm	No.	Type	State	Region				
Caledonian Private Equity Partners, LLC	375	PE	CA	Europe, USA	10.00	30.00	1.50	25.00
Kachi Partners	161	PE	CO	Southwest, Midwest, Rocky Mountain states			1.50	3.00
BB&T Capital Partners	132	PE	NC	Mid-Atlantic, Midwest, Southeast, Northeast	10.00	10.00	2.00	12.00
Blue Sage Capital	160	PE	TX	Southwest	5.00		2.00	12.00
C3 Capital Partners	196	PE	MO	Midwest		4.00	2.00	8.00
CID Equity Partners	238	PE	IN	USA	20.00	6.00	2.00	10.00
DeltaPoint Capital Management, LLC	403	PE	NY	New York State	5.00	20.00	2.00	6.00
Emigrant Capital Corporation	286	PE	NY	USA	15.00	20.00	2.00	20.00
Hamilton Robinson LLC	478	PE	CT	Mid-Atlantic, Midwest, Southeast, Northeast, USA	10.00		2.00	20.00
Hammond Kennedy Whitney & Co., Inc.	147	PE	IN	USA	20.00		2.00	10.00
Hastings Equity Partners	317	PE	MA	USA	3.00	10.00	2.00	5.00
HSBC Capital	517	PE	NY	USA	10.00		2.00	15.00
Main Street Capital Holdings LLC	340	PE	PA	Mid-Atlantic, Midwest, Southeast, Northeast	15.00	5–50	2.00	10.00
Main Street Mezzanine Fund, LP	510	PE	TX	USA			2.00	15.00
MCM Capital Partners, L.P.	134	PE	OH	USA	20.00	40.00	2.00	10.00
Merion Investment Partners	178	PE	PA	Mid-Atlantic, Southeast, Northeast	10.00	4–5	2.00	5.00
Najeti Ventures LLC	501	PE	CT	Mid-Atlantic, Midwest, Southeast, Northeast			2.00	7.00
Navigator Equity Partners	357	PE	NJ	Mid-Atlantic, Northeast	10.00		2.00	5.00
NewCastle Partners LLC	240	PE	CT	USA			2.00	10.00
Northwood Ventures	432	PE	NY	Europe, USA	—	4.00	2.00	5.00
Norvest Capital Partners Inc.	473	PE	ON	Canada	20.00	4.00	2.00	10.00
Oxford Investment Group	186	PE	MI	Asia, Europe, USA	10.00		2.00	20.00
Peterson Partners	498	PE	UT	West Coast, Midwest	8.00	20.00	2.00	10.00
Prism Mezzanine Fund SBIC, L.P.	522	PE	IL	Midwest	10.00	5.00	2.00	8.00
Summer Street Capital Partners LLC	159	PE	NY	Mid-Atlantic, Midwest, Southeast, Northeast	20.00	4.00	2.00	10.00
Summit Partners	486	PE	MA	North America, Europe, USA		41.00	2.00	250.00
Warwick Group, Inc.	193	PE	CT	USA		10–50	2.00	20.00
Agio Capital Partners I, L.P.	449	PE	MN	Midwest, Southeast	100.00	5.00	2.50	8.00
Bridge Street Capital Partners, LLC	348	PE	MI	Midwest			2.50	7.50
Invest Mezzanine Capital Management GmbH	149	PE		Europe	12.00	3.30	2.50	6.30
Riverlake Partners	284	PE	OR	West Coast, Asia, Midwest, Western Canada			2.50	10.00
Brookside Capital Partners	152	PE	CT	USA	20.00	5.00	3.00	7.50
Brookstone Partners	274	PE	NY	Mid-Atlantic, Midwest, Southeast, Northeast	10.00	5–10	3.00	15.00
Calvert Street Capital Partners	118	PE	MD	USA	20.00	30.00	3.00	25.00
CHB Capital Partners	395	PE	CO	USA	15.00		3.00	15.00
Dorset Capital Management	423	PE	CA	USA	20.00		3.00	10.00
E*Capital Corporation	133	PE	CA	West Coast, USA		5.00	3.00	7.00
Eureka Growth Capital	269	PE	PA	Mid-Atlantic, Midwest, Southeast, Northeast	10.00	5.00	3.00	8.00
Florida Capital Partners, Inc.	163	PE	FL	USA	10.00	20.00	3.00	15.00

(Continued)

339

Private Equity Funds by Minimum Funding (Continued)

Firm	Database ID	Type	State	Geographic Preference	Minimum Revenue	Typical Deal Size	Minimum Funding	Maximum Funding
Franklin Street Equity Partners, Inc.	390	PE	IL	North America	25.00	40.00	3.00	25.00
Greyrock Capital Group	166	PE	CA	USA	10.00	7.00	3.00	10.00
Harbert Management Corporation— Mezzanine Capital	299	PE	AL	USA	10.00	5.00	3.00	12.00
Kline Hawkes & Co	450	PE	CA	West Coast, Northeast, USA	5.00	5.00	3.00	15.00
National City Equity Partners, LLC	483	PE	OH	North America		10.00	3.00	20.00
Navis Capital Partners Limited	410	PE	WP	Asia	20.00	15.00	3.00	30.00
Pine Creek Partners	474	PE	DC	Mid-Atlantic, Northeast, Eastern U.S.	10.00	10.00	3.00	15.00
Prometheus V, LLC	358	PE	GA	USA		15.00	3.00	7.00
River Capital	342	PE	GA	Southwest, Mid-Atlantic, Midwest, Southeast	10.00	25.00	3.00	10.00
Rocky Mountain Capital Partners	257	PE	CO	USA	10.00	5.00	3.00	100.00
Steel Capital Corp.	210	PE	CT	North America, Asia, Europe		50.00	3.00	12.00
Thrive Capital Partners	172	PE	MT	West Coast	6.00	7.00	3.00	25.00
TriWest Capital Management Corp	396	PE	Alberta	West Coast, Midwest, Canada		8.00	3.00	60.00
American Capital	220	PE	MD	North America, Asia, Europe, USA	20.00		4.00	20.00
AsiaVest Partners, TCW/YFY	400	PE		Asia, USA		5.00	4.00	25.00
Golub Associates Incorporated	294	PE	NY	USA	5.00	8.00	4.00	20.00
Huron Capital Partners, LLC	453	PE	MI	North America, USA		30.00	4.00	25.00
Wynnchurch Capital	318	PE	IL	North America, USA		7.50	4.00	30.00
Caltius Mezzanine Partners	468	PE	CA	USA	10.00	10.00	5.00	20.00
Cambridge Capital Partners LLC	233	PE	IL	USA	30.00	30.00	5.00	30.00
Canterbury Capital Partners	173	PE	NY	West Coast	20.00	15.00	5.00	15.00
Century Park Capital Partners, LP	207	PE	CA	North America	15.00	40.00	5.00	25.00
Dubin Clark & Company, Inc.	126	PE	CT	North America		15.00	5.00	30.00
Gleacher Mezzanine LLC	168	PE	NY	North America, Europe, USA	20.00	75.00	5.00	30.00
Graham Partners, Inc.	182	PE	PA	North America, Europe	20.00	20.00	5.00	20.00
Grey Mountain Partners, LLC	228	PE	NY	USA		15–25	5.00	30.00
Halyard Capital Fund	119	PE	NY	North America, Europe, USA		10.00	5.00	40.00
HBM BioVentures Ltd.	471	PE		North America, Europe			5.00	15.00
Hunt Special Situations Group, L.P.	300	PE	TX	USA	20.00		5.00	25.00
Key Principal Partners	117	PE	OH	USA	25.00	10–15	5.00	75.00
Lincolnshire Management	164	PE	MA	North America, USA	30.00	125.00	5.00	40.00
Lombard Investments, Inc.	288	PE	CA	North America, Asia		25.00	5.00	50.00
Merisel, Inc.	209	PE	IL	USA		25.00	5.00	15.00
Midwest Mezzanine Funds	287	PE	IL	USA	20.00	8.00	5.00	15.00
Peachtree Equity Partners	487	PE	GA	Mid-Atlantic, Midwest, Southeast, USA	20.00	8.00	5.00	15.00
Pouschine Cook Capital Management, LLC	456	PE	NY	USA	15.00	30.00	5.00	15.00
Riordan, Lewis & Haden	485	PE	CA	West Coast	15.00		5.00	15.00
RoundTable Healthcare Partners	431	PE	IL	North America, Europe, USA		30–50	5.00	70.00
Seaport Capital	185	PE	NY	USA	7.00	15.00	5.00	40.00

Sterling Venture Partners	441	PE	MD	Mid-Atlantic, Midwest, USA			5.00	15.00
StoneCreek Capital	285	PE	CA	West Coast, USA		35.00	5.00	50.00
Trivest Partners, L.P.	192	PE	FL	USA		30–250	5.00	45.00
Tuckerman Capital	302	PE	NH	USA	5.00	10.00	5.00	25.00
Wafra Partners LLC	179	PE	NY	North America, USA, Caribbean		40.00	5.00	40.00
Wingate Partners	180	PE	TX	USA	40.00	50.00	5.00	20.00
Dunedin Capital Partners Limited	404	PE		UK		15.00	6.00	40.00
Linsalata Capital Partners	279	PE	OH	North America			7.00	40.00
McKenna Gale Capital Inc.	460	PE	ON	Canada		30.00	7.00	75.00
The Riverside Company	212	PE	NY	North America, Europe	20.00	45.00	7.00	70.00
Albion Alliance LLC	231	PE	NY	North America, Europe	10.00	15.00	8.00	30.00
Sovereign Capital Limited	368	PE	UK	UK only		36.40	9.10	27.30
American Industrial Partners	244	PE	CA	North America, potential global reach	30.00	100.00	10.00	50.00
Arsenal Capital Partners	292	PE	NY	USA		75–125	10.00	100.00
Astorg Partners	224	PE		Europe		100.00	10.00	60.00
Baring Private Equity Partners Asia	409	PE	CA	Asia	40.00	15.00	10.00	25.00
Blue Point Capital Partners	266	PE	OH	North America	50.00	75.00	10.00	60.00
Castanea Partners	550	PE	MA	USA, Canada	25.00		10.00	20.00+
Centre Partners Management LLC	399	PE	NY	North America		150.00	10.00	70.00
Harbour Group	491	PE	MO	North America		125.00	10.00	100.00
Kirtland Capital Partners	150	PE	OH	Mid-Atlantic, Midwest, Southeast, Northeast	25.00	50.00	10.00	75.00
Lineage Capital	289	PE	MA	North America, USA	20.00		10.00	40.00
Long Point Capital, Inc.	451	PE	MI	USA	25.00	75.00	10.00	30.00
MedEquity Capital, LLC	337	PE	MA	USA	10.00	15–20	10.00	50.00
Merit Capital Partners, LLC	194	PE	IL	USA	20.00	20.00	10.00	85.00
Morgenthaler	272	PE	OH	North America	25.00	80.00	10.00	85.00
Pacific Corporate Group LLC	225	PE	CA	North America	75.00	50.00	10.00	200.00
Saw Mill Capital	216	PE	NY	North America, Europe, USA			10.00	100.00
Thoma Cressey Equity Partners	181	PE	IL	North America	25.00	30.00	10.00	60.00
Thompson Street Capital Partners	202	PE	MO	North America		50.00	10.00	30.00
Windjammer Capital Investors	297	PE	CA	North America, USA	50.00	20.00	10.00	60.00
York Street Capital Partners	158	PE	NJ	USA		10–20	15.00	100.00
BA Capital Partners Europe	422	PE		Europe		25.00	15.00	75.00
Charlesbank Capital Partners, LLC	343	PE	MA	USA, Canada		50.00	15.00	75.00
CIVC Partners	208	PE	IL	North America, USA	40.00	50.00	15.00	125.00
FdG Associates	361	PE	NY	North America		60–100	15.00	50.00
Roark Capital Group	512	PE	GA	USA		50.00	15.00	75.00
The CapStreet Group, LLC	293	PE	TX	Southwest, Southeast	50.00	100.00	15.00	50.00
Englefield Capital LLP	254	PE		Europe		50.00	20.00	100.00
Parthenon Capital	190	PE	MA	North America	75.00	30–50	20.00	100.00

(Continued)

341

Private Equity Funds by Minimum Funding *(Continued)*

						($ millions)		
Firm	Database ID	Type	State	Geographic Preference	Minimum Revenue	Typical Deal Size	Minimum Funding	Maximum Funding
The Shansby Group	476	PE	CA	USA	20.00	30–40	20.00	60.00
Behrman Capital	425	PE	NY	North America, USA	40.00	200.00	25.00	100.00
Code Hennessy & Simmons LLC	384	PE	IL	USA		200.00	25.00	100.00
Nautic Partners, LLC	174	PE	RI	North America, Europe, USA	50.00	40.00	25.00	75.00
Tailwind Capital Partners	213	PE	NY	USA		50.00	25.00	125.00
Berkshire Partners LLC	184	PE	MA	North America, Europe, USA	50.00		30.00	250.00
Candover Investments Plc	421	PE	UK	Europe		150.00	30.00	500.00
Crescent Capital Investments, Inc.	367	PE	GA	Europe, USA	20.00	120.00	30.00	110.00
Aerostar Capital LLC	373	PE	WY	North America, Europe	50.00		50.00	250.00
New Mountain Capital	141	PE	NY	North America	50.00	100.00	50.00	200.00
Terra Firma Capital Partners Ltd	290	PE	UK	Europe		400.00	150.00	500.00
Triton Pacific Capital Partners, LLC	406	PE	CA	USA	5.00		2–10 equity	10 equity
Meritum Partners, LLC	303	PE	CA	North America	25.00	6 equity	3 equity	
Gresham Private Equity Limited	524	PE	NSW	Australia, New Zealand			A20	A60
Alpine Investors, LP	525	PE	CA	USA	10.00	5–15		
Appian Holdings	139	PE	IL	North America	5.00	20.00		75.00
Avocet Ventures, LLC	114	PE	NC	West Coast, Midwest, Southeast	10.00			
Champlain Capital	530	PE	CA	USA	5.00			
Cornerstone Capital Advisors, Ltd.	283	PE	PA	Midwest, Northeast				
DW Healthcare Partners	454	PE	UT	USA				
Founders Equity Inc.	145	PE	NY	USA				
FSN Capital Partners AS	379	PE	Norway	Europe, Scandinavia				
H.I.G. Capital, LLC	332	PE	CA	USA				
HLHZ Investments, LLC	543	PE	CA	North America, Europe		25		10
Kasten Group, LLC	511	PE	IL	USA	5.00			
KRG Capital Partners	388	PE	CO	USA	25.00			
Linx Partners, LLC	165	PE	GA	Mid-Atlantic, Southeast, Northeast	20.00			
Mankwitz Kurtz Investments, LLC	198	PE	CO	Mid-Atlantic, Midwest	12.00	45.00		500.00
Pfingsten Partners, L.L.C.	488	PE	IL	Europe, USA	25.00	150.00		
Quad-C Management	531	PE	NY	North America, Midwest, Southeast, Europe				
SilkRoad Equity, Inc.	261	PE	NC	Midwest, Europe, USA	10.00			
Talisman Capital Fund I, LLC	248	PE	OH	North America	10.00			
The Oxford Investment Group	246	PE	MI	Midwest, Europe, Southeast, Europe				
Torquest Partners	281	PE	ON	North America	10.00			
Venturis	232	PE		Europe, Netherlands				
Westar Capital	514	PE	CA	North America	10.00			
ZS Fund L.P.	245	PE	NY	North America				

Merchant Banks by Minimum Funding

Firm	Database ID	Type	State	Geographic Preference	Minimum Revenue	Typical Deal Size	Minimum Funding	Maximum Funding
Agawam Partners LLC	376	MB	NY	USA	5.00	20.00	1.00	5.00
Milestone Merchant Partners, LLC	121	MB	DC	Mid-Atlantic, Southeast, Northeast, USA	20.00		1.00	20.00
Tech Strategies	221	MB	MA	North America	5.00	5.00	1.00	60.00
Roynat Capital	470	MB	NC	North America	20.00	5.00	2.50	10.00
Gladstone Capital Corporation	256	MB	VA	USA	10.00	10.00	3.00	15.00
Thomas Weisel Healthcare Venture Partners	495	MB	CA	North America, USA	—	5–6	3.00	8.00
Baird Capital Partners	280	MB	WI	Midwest, Southeast	15.00	20–60	5.00	25.00
Caymus Partners LLC	492	MB	GA	USA		25.00	5.00	100.00
Clairvest Group Inc.	239	MB	ON	North America	20.00	15.00	10.00	20.00
Goense Bounds & Partners	148	MB	IL	USA		75.00	10.00	40.00
Imperial Capital Corporation	324	MB	ON	North America, USA	50.00	50.00	10.00	
Newhaven Corporate Finance Limited	370	MB		North America	20.00	25.00	10.00	50.00
Veronis Suhler Stevenson	230	MB	NY	North America, Europe, USA		<500M	25.00	
Edgeview Partners	436	MB	NC	USA		70.00		
Global Strategy & Capital Group	407	MB	CA	North America, Europe, USA, South America		25–250		
Hyde Park Capital Partners, LLC	108	MB	FL	USA		40.00		
Olive Capital LLC	204	MB	NV	North America, Europe, USA, Middle East		25–250		
The Legacy Equity Group, LLC	136	MB		USA				

Strategic or Industry Investors by Minimum Funding

Firm	Database ID	Type	State	Geographic Preference	Minimum Revenue	Typical Deal Size	Minimum Funding	Maximum Funding
Sustainable Development Fund	537	SI	PA	Pennsylvania			0.10	5.00
Vested for Growth	308	SI	NH	NH		0.35	0.10	0.50
ITF Global Partners	177	SI	NY	USA			4.00	
Drug Royalty Corporation Inc.	128	SI	ON	North America, Asia, Europe		20.00	5.00	50.00
Siemens Venture Capital GmbH	382	SI	Germany	North America, Europe, Israel			.5 euro	.5 euro
Next Step Advisors	482	SI	AZ	West Coast, Southwest	0.10			

Government Agencies by Minimum Funding

Firm	Database ID	Type	State	Geographic Preference	Minimum Revenue	Typical Deal Size	Minimum Funding	Maximum Funding
Overseas Private Investment Corporation	295	GOV	DC	New and emerging markets			0.10	250.00

Master List by Firm with Location Information

Firm	Database ID	Type	City	State	Web site
@Ventures	389	VC	Andover	MA	www.ventures.com
A. M. Pappas & Associates, LLC	316	VC	Research Triangle Park	NC	www.ampappas.com
Abingworth Management	223	VC	London		www.abingworth.co.uk
Access Venture Partners	252	VC	San Francisco	CA	www.accessventurepartners.com
Acorn Campus	131	VC	Cupertino	CA	www.acorncampus.com
Advent International	203	VC	Boston	MA	www.adventinternational.com
Aerostar Capital LLC	373	PE	Wilson	WY	www.aerostarcapital.com
Agawam Partners LLC	376	MB	New York	NY	www.agawampartners.com
Agio Capital Partners I, L.P.	449	PE	Edina	MN	www.agio-capital.com
Agrarian Capital, LLC	319	PE	Champaign	IL	www.agrariancapital.com
Albion Alliance LLC	231	PE	New York	NY	www.albionalliance.com
Allegiance Capital Limited Partnership	415	VC	Baltimore	MD	www.allcapital.com
Alloy Ventures	260	VC	Palo Alto	CA	www.alloyventures.com
Alpine Investors, LP	525	PE	San Francisco	CA	www.alpine-investors.com
American Capital	220	PE	Bethesda	MD	www.americancapital.com
American Industrial Partners	244	PE	San Francisco	CA	www.aipartners.com
Antares Capital Corporation	127	VC	Miami Lakes	FL	www.antarescapital.com
Antares Capital Corporation	258	CF	Chicago	IL	www.antareslev.com
AP Capital Partners	250	PE	Orlando	FL	www.apcpartners.com
Appian Holdings	139	PE	Naperville	IL	www.appianholdings.com
ARCH Development Partners	493	VC	Chicago	IL	www.archdevelopmentpartners.com
ArcHelion Capital Partners	345	IN	North Palm Beach	FL	www.archelion.com
Arcturus Capital	455	VC	Los Angeles	CA	www.arcturusvc.com
Argosy Partners	349	PE	Wayne	PA	www.argosycapital.com
Arsenal Capital Partners	292	PE	NY	NY	www.arsenalcapital.com
Artisan Capital	156	PE	San Diego	CA	www.articap.com
AsiaVest Partners, TCW/YFY	400	VC	Singapore		www.asiavest.com
Astorg Partners	224	PE	Paris		www.astorg-partners.com
Austin Capital Partners, L.P.	153	PE	Cleveland	OH	www.austincapitalpartners.com
Autumn Hill Capital Group, LLC	236	PE	Cranberry Township	PA	www.autumnhillcapital.com
Avocet Ventures, LLC	114	PE	Raleigh	NC	www.avocetventures.com
BA Capital Partners Europe	422	PE	London		www.bacpeurope.com
Baird Capital Partners	280	MB	Milwaukee	WI	www.bairdcapitalpartners.com
Baird Venture Partners	278	VC	Milwaukee	WI	www.bairdventurepartners.com
Bank of the West	472	BN	San Francisco	CA	www.bankofthewest.com
Baring Private Equity Partners	523	PE	London		www.bpep.com
Baring Private Equity Partners Asia	409	PE	Foster City	CA	www.bpepasia.com

Company	Number	Type	City	State	Website
Baxter Capital Corporation	125	LC	Deerfield	IL	www.baxtercapital.com
BayTech Venture Capital	387	VC	Munich	GERM	www.baytechventure.com
BB&T Capital Partners	132	PE	Winston Salem	NC	www.bbandt.com/capitalpartners
Behrman Capital	425	PE	New York	NY	www.behrmancap.com
Berkshire Partners LLC	184	PE	Boston	MA	www.berkshirepartners.com
BFI Business Finance, Inc.	363	AB	San Francisco	CA	www.bfifinance.com
Biofrontier Partners USA	459	VC	San Diego	CA	www.biofrontier.co.jp
Birchmere Capital LP	268	PE	Wexford	PA	
Bi-State Investment Group	519	AI	Lenexa	KA	www.kcbig.com
Blue Point Capital Partners	266	PE	Cleveland	OH	www.bluepointcapital.com
Blue Sage Capital	160	PE	Austin	TX	www.bluesage.com
Boston Millennia Partners	115	PE	Boston	MA	www.millenniapartners.com
BP Marsh Private Equity	381	VC	London		www.bpmarsh.co.uk
Bridge Street Capital Partners, LLC	348	PE	Grand Rapids	MI	www.bridgestreet.com
Brook Venture Fund	328	VC	Wakefield	MA	www.brookventure.com
Brookside Capital Partners	152	PE	Greenwich	CT	www.brooksidecapitalpartners.com
Brookstone Partners	274	PE	New York	NY	www.brookstonepartners.com
Business Alliance Capital Corp.	553	AB	Mooresboro	NC	www.baccorp.com
C3 Capital Partners	196	PE	Kansas City	MO	www.c3cap.com
Caledonian Private Equity Partners, LLC	375	PE	La Jolla	CA	www.caledonianprivateequity.com
Callidus Capital Corporation	140	AB	Toronto	ON	www.calliduscapital.ca
Caltius Mezzanine Partners	468	PE	Los Angeles	CA	www.caltius.com
Calvert Street Capital Partners	118	PE	Baltimore	MD	www.calvertstreetcapital.com
Cambridge Capital Partners LLC	233	PE	Chicago	IL	www.cambridgecapital.com
Candover Investments Plc	421	PE	London	UK	www.candover.com
Canterbury Capital Partners	173	PE	New York	NY	www.canterburycp.com
Capital Equipment Leasing	253	LC	La Jolla	CA	www.celeasing.com
Capital Investments	116	VC	McKinney	TX	www.capitalinvestments.cc
Capital TempFunds, Inc.	503	AB	Fort Lauderdale	FL	www.capitalfactors.com
CapitalSource Finance LLC	191	CF	Chevy Chase	MD	www.capitalsource.com
CapitalWerks, LLC	267	LC	Santa Ana	CA	www.capitalwerks.com
Cardinal Capital Partners	320	CF	Dallas	TX	www.cardinalcapital.com
Castanea Partners	550	PE	Newton	MA	www.castaneapartners.com
Caymus Partners LLC	492	MB	Atlanta	GA	www.caymuspartners.com
CEI Community Ventures	307	VC	Portland	ME	www.ceicommunityventures.com
Centerfield Capital Partners	346	PE	Indianapolis	IN	www.centerfieldcapital.com
Centre Partners Management LLC	399	PE	New York	NY	www.centrepartners.com
Century Park Capital Partners, LP	207	PE	San Francisco	CA	www.centuryparkcapital.com
Champlain Capital	530	PE	San Francisco	CA	www.champlaincapital.com
Charlesbank Capital Partners, LLC	343	PE	Boston	MA	www.charlesbank.com

Master List by Firm with Location Information (Continued)

Firm	Database ID	Type	City	State	Web site
Charlotte Angel Partners	330	VC	Charlotte	NC	www.capnc.com
Charter One Bank, N.A.	241	BN	Troy	MI	www.charteronebank.com
Chatham Capital	322	CF	Atlanta	GA	www.chathamcapital.com
CHB Capital Partners	395	PE	Denver	CO	www.chbcapital.com
Cherry Tree Investments, Inc.	447	PE	Minnetonka	MN	www.cherrytree.com
CID Equity Partners	238	PE	Indianapolis	IN	www.cidequity.com
CIVC Partners	208	PE	Chicago	IL	www.civc.com
CL Fund	362	AI	Pittsburgh	PA	www.clfund.com
Clairvest Group Inc.	239	MB	Toronto	ON	www.clairvest.com
Code Hennessy & Simmons LLC	384	PE	Chicago	IL	www.chsonline.com
Comerica Bank, Technology & Life Sciences Division	350	BN	Reston	VA	www.comerica.com
Complete Leasing Corporation	465	LC	Middleburg	VA	www.completeleasingcorp.com
Concord Ventures	490	VC	Herzelia	Israel	www.concordventures.com
Convergent Capital Partners	249	PE	Minneapolis	MN	www.cvcap.com
Cornerstone Capital Advisors, Ltd.	283	PE	Pittsburgh	PA	www.cstone-ltd.com
Crescent Capital Investments, Inc.	367	PE	Atlanta	GA	www.crescentcapital.com
Crescent State Bank	270	BN	Cary	NC	www.crescentstatebank.com
Cross Atlantic Partners, Inc.	385	VC	New York	NY	www.crossatlanticpartners.com
CrossBridge Venture Partners	464	VC	San Bruno	CA	www.crossbridgevp.com
CSG Investments, Inc.	347	CF	Plano	TX	www.csginvestments.com
Davis, Tuttle Venture Partners, LP	323	PE	Houston	TX	www.davistuttle.com
DeltaPoint Capital Management, LLC	403	PE	Rochester	NY	www.deltapointcapital.com
Desert Angels	329	AI	Tucson	AZ	www.edesertangels.com
Deutsche Effecten- und Wechsel-Beteiligungsgesellschaft AG	437	VC	Jena	Germany	www.dewb-vc.com
Diamondhead Ventures	315	VC	Menlo Park	CA	www.dhven.com
Dorset Capital Management	423	PE	San Francisco	CA	www.dorsetcapital.com
Drug Royalty Corporation Inc.	128	SI	Toronto	ON	www.drugroyalty.com
Dubin Clark & Company, Inc.	126	PE	Greenwich	CT	www.dubinclark.com
Dunedin Capital Partners Limited	404	PE	Edinburgh		www.dunedin.com
DW Healthcare Partners	454	PE	Salt Lake City	UT	www.dwhp.com
E*Capital Corporation	133	PE	Los Angeles	CA	www.e-cap.com
Eastern Technology Fund	440	VC	King of Prussia	PA	www.easterntechnologyfund.com
Edelson Technology Partners	130	VC	Woodcliff Lake	NJ	www.edelsontech.com
Edgeview Partners	436	MB	Charlotte	NC	www.edgeviewpartners.com
Edison Venture Fund	107	VC	Lawrenceville	NJ	www.edisonventure.com
Emigrant Capital Corporation	286	PE	New York	NY	www.emigrantcapital.com

Company	No.	Type	City	State	Website
Englefield Capital LLP	254	PE	London		www.englefieldcapital.com
Enterprise Corporation of the Delta	335	CF	Jackson	MS	www.ecd.org
EonTech Ventures SA	380	VC	Luxembourg		www.eontechventures.com
Essex Woodlands Health Ventures	129	VC	Chicago	IL	www.essexwoodlands.com
Eureka Growth Capital	269	PE	Philadelphia	PA	www.eurekagrowth.com
Exeter Capital Partners	374	PE	New York	NY	www.exeterfunds.com
FA Technology Ventures	551	VC	Albany	NY	www.fatechventures.com
Falcon Fund	529	VC	West Covina	CA	www.falconfund.com
FdG Associates	361	PE	New York	NY	www.fdgassociates.com
First Advisors, Inc.	383	AI	Austin	TX	www.firstadvisors-inc.com
FirstFloor Capital	391	PE	Kuala Lumpur	WP	www.firstfloorcapital.com
Florida Capital Partners, Inc.	163	PE	Tampa	FL	www.fcpinvestors.com
Founders Equity Inc.	145	PE	New York	NY	www.fequity.com
Four J Funding	528	CF	Hackensack	NJ	www.raigroup.com
Franklin Street Equity Partners, Inc.	390	PE	Chicago	IL	www.ablumbrown.com
Friend Capital Funding, LLC	112	AB			www.friendfunding.com
Frontier Capital	123	VC	Charlotte	NC	www.frontierfunds.com
FSN Capital Partners AS	379	PE		Norway	www.fsncapital.no
Funk Ventures	171	VC	Canoga Park	CA	www.funkventures.com
gcp gamma capital partners	386	VC	Vienna		www.gamma-capital.com
GE Commercial Finance	282	CF	New York	NY	www.gecapital.com
GE Corporate Financial Services	217	AB	New York	NY	www.gelending.com
Generics Asset Management Ltd.	541	VC	Cambridge	UK	www.genericsgroup.co.uk
Genesis Campus	547	VC	Dallas	TX	www.genesiscampus.com
Geneva Venture Partners	170	VC	San Francisco	CA	www.genevavc.com
Giza Venture Capital	366	VC	Tel Aviv		www.gizavc.com
Gladstone Capital Corporation	256	MB	McLean	VA	www.gladstonecapital.com
Gleacher Mezzanine LLC	168	PE	New York	NY	www.gleacher.com
Global Catalyst Partners	467	VC	Redwood Shores	CA	www.gc-partners.com
Global Strategy & Capital Group	407	MB		CA	www.gsgroup.net
GMB Mezzanine Capital	301	PE	Minneapolis	MN	
Goense Bounds & Partners	148	MB	Lake Forest	IL	www.goensebounds.com
Golub Associates Incorporated	294	PE	New York	NY	www.golubassoc.com
Graham Partners, Inc.	182	PE	Newtown Square	PA	www.grahampartners.net
GrandBanks Capital	219	VC	Newton Center	MA	www.grandbankcapital.com
Great Lakes Angels, Inc.	509	AI	Chicago		www.glangels.org
Greenfield Commercial Credit	188	AB	Chicago	IL	
Gresham Private Equity Limited	524	PE	Sydney	NSW	www.gresham.com.au
Grey Mountain Partners, LLC	228	PE	New York City	NY	www.greymountain.com
Greyrock Capital Group	166	PE	San Francisco	CA	www.greyrockcapitalgroup.com

(Continued)

Master List by Firm with Location Information *(Continued)*

Firm	Database ID	Type	City	State	Web site
GrowthWorks Capital Ltd.	434	VC	Vancouver	BC	www.growthworks.ca
Guide Ventures, LLC	176	VC	Seattle	WA	www.guideventures.com/
H. Katz Capital Group	481	PE	Southampton	PA	www.katzgroup.com
H.I.G. Capital, LLC	332	PE	San Francisco	CA	www.higcapital.com/
Halyard Capital Fund	119	PE	New York	NY	www.halyardcapital.com
Hamilton Robinson LLC	478	PE	Stamford	CT	www.hrco.com
Hammond Kennedy Whitney & Co., Inc.	147	PE	Indianapolis	IN	www.hkwinc.com
Harbert Management Corporation— Mezzanine Capital	299	PE	Birmingham	AL	www.harbert.net
Harbert Management Corporation—Venture Partners	309	VC	Birmingham	AL	www.harbert.net
Harbour Group	491	PE	St. Louis	MO	www.harbourgroup.com
Hartsko Financial Services, LLC	489	AB	Deerfield	IL	www.hartsko.com
Hastings Equity Partners	317	PE	Framingham	MA	www.hastingsequity.com
HBM BioVentures Ltd.	471	PE	Baar	Switzerland	www.hbmbioventures.com
Healthcare Finance Group, Inc.	502	AB	New York	NY	www.hfgusa.com
High Street Capital	475	PE	Chicago	IL	www.highstr.com
Highland Capital Partners	336	VC	Lexington	MA	www.hcp.com
Hilco Capital LP	227	AB	Northbrook	IL	www.hilcocapital.com
HLHZ Investments, LLC	543	PE	Los Angeles	CA	www.hlhz.com
Hopewell Ventures	398	VC	Chicago	IL	www.hopewellventures.com
Horizon Ventures	331	VC	Los Altos	CA	www.horizonvc.com
HSBC Capital	517	PE	New York	NY	
Hunt Special Situations Group, L.P.	300	PE	Dallas	TX	www.huntssg.com
Huron Capital Partners, LLC	453	PE	Detroit	MI	www.huroncapital.com
Hyde Park Capital Partners, LLC	108	MB	Tampa	FL	www.hydeparkcapital.com
IDG Ventures Europe	169	VC	London		www.idgve.com
IIG Capital LLC	394	CF	New York	NY	www.iigcapital.com
Imperial Capital Corporation	324	MB	Toronto	ON	www.imperialcap.com
Infineon Ventures GmbH	497	VC	Munich	Germany	www.infineonventures.com
Infocomm Investments Pte Ltd	520	PE	Singapore		
InnovationsKapital	371	VC	Gothenburg		www.innkap.se
Intersouth Partners	106	VC	Durham	NC	www.intersouth.com
Invest Mezzanine Capital Management GmbH	149	PE			www.investmezzanin.at
ITF Global Partners	177	SI	New York	NY	www.itfgp.com
J D Factors	505	CF	Redondo Beach	CA	www.jdfactors.com
J&D Financial Corporation	542	CF	North Miami	FL	www.jdfinancial.com

Company	No.	Type	City	State	Website
Kachi Partners	161	PE	Boulder	CO	www.kastengroup.com
Kasten Group, LLC	511	PE	O'Fallon	IL	www.keyprincipalpartners.com
Key Principal Partners	117	PE	Cleveland	OH	www.key.com/keyprincipalpartners/venturecapital.html
Key Venture Partners	120	VC	Waltham	MA	www.kingtradecapital.com
King Trade Capital	508	AB	Dallas	TX	www.kirtlandcapital.com
Kirtland Capital Partners	150	PE	Willoughby Hills	OH	www.klinehawkes.com
Kline Hawkes & Co	450	PE	Los Angeles	CA	www.krgcapital.com
KRG Capital Partners	388	PE	Denver	CO	www.llcapitalpartners.com
L&L Capital Partners	135	PE	Westport	CT	www.leocapholdings.com
Leo Capital Holdings, LLC	426	VC	Northbrook	IL	
Lighthouse Venture Partners, LLC	521	VC			
Limburg Ventures BV	414	VC	Maastricht	Netherlands	www.limburgventures.com
Lincolnshire Management	164	PE	Boston	MA	www.lincolnshiremgmt.com
Lineage Capital	289	PE	Boston	MA	www.lineagecap.com
Linsalata Capital Partners	279	PE	Mayfield Heights	OH	www.linsalatacapital.com
Linx Partners, LLC	165	PE	Atlanta	GA	www.linxpartners.com
LogiSpring	378	VC	Geneva		www.logispring.com
Lombard Investments, Inc.	288	PE	San Francisco	CA	www.lombardinvestments.com
Long Point Capital, Inc.	451	PE	Royal Oak	MI	www.longpointcapital.com
Longmeadow Capital, LLC	353	PE	Longmeadow	MA	www.longmeadowcapital.com
M&I Bank	341	BN	Minneapolis	MN	
Main Street Capital Holdings LLC	340	PE	Canonsburg	PA	www.mainstcap.com
Main Street Mezzanine Fund, LP	510	PE	Houston	TX	www.mainstreethouston.com
Mankwitz Kurtz Investments, LLC	198	PE	Greenwood Village	CO	www.mkinvestmentsllc.com
Maple Commercial Finance Group	405	AB	Jersey City	NJ	www.maplesecurities.com
Marquette Capital Partners, Inc.	327	PE	Minneapolis	MN	www.marquettecapitalpartners.com
Mayfield	122	VC	Menlo Park	CA	www.mayfield.com
McKenna Gale Capital Inc.	460	PE	Toronto	ON	www.mckennagale.com
MCM Capital Partners, L.P.	134	PE	Cleveland	OH	www.mcmcapital.com
MedEquity Capital, LLC	337	PE	Wellesley Hills	MA	www.medequity.com
Mentor Capital Partners Ltd	187	VC	Yardley	PA	www.mentorcapitalpartners.com
Merion Investment Partners	178	PE	King of Prussia	PA	www.merionpartners.com
Merisel, Inc.	209	PE			
Merit Capital Partners, LLC	194	PE	Chicago	IL	www.meritagefunds.com
Meritage Private Equity Funds	200	PE	Denver	CO	www.meritum.com
Meritum Partners, LLC	303	PE	San Francisco	CA	www.meriwethercapital.net
Meriwether Capital, L.L.C.	433	IN	New York	NY	www.metapoint.com
Metapoint Partners	408	PE	Peabody	MA	

(Continued)

Master List by Firm with Location Information (*Continued*)

Firm	Database ID	Type	City	State	Web site
Midwest Mezzanine Funds	287	PE	Chicago	IL	www.midwestmezzanine.com
Milestone Merchant Partners, LLC	121	MB	Washington	DC	www.milestonecap.com
Mofet Venture Capital Fund	412	VC	Herzliya	Israel	www.mofet.co.il
Mohr Davidow Ventures	243	VC	Menlo Park	CA	www.mdv.com
Monumental Venture Partners, LLC	462	VC	Vienna	VA	www.mvpfunds.com
Morgenthaler	272	PE	Cleveland	OH	www.morgenthaler.com
Mountaineer Capital	397	VC	Charleston	WV	www.mtncap.com
MTI Partners Limited	469	VC	Watford		www.mtifirms.com
Murex Investments I, L.P.	444	VC	Philadelphia	PA	www.murexinvests.com
Najeti Ventures LLC	501	PE	Southbury	CT	www.najeti.com/
National City Equity Partners, LLC	483	PE	Cleveland	OH	www.ncepi.com
Nautic Partners, LLC	174	PE	Providence	RI	www.nauticpartners.com
Navigator Equity Partners	357	PE	Summit	NJ	www.navigatorequity.com
Navis Capital Partners Limited	410	PE	Kuala Lumpur	WP	www.navis.com.my
Net Partners	263	VC	Milan	Italy	www.net-partners.com
New Mexico Private Investors, Inc	325	PE	Albuquerque	NM	www.nmprivateinvestors.com
New Mountain Capital	141	PE	New York	NY	www.newmountaincapital.com
New York City Investment Fund	365	VC	New York	NY	www.nycif.org
NewCastle Partners LLC	240	PE	Greenwich	CT	www.newcastle-partners.com
Newhaven Corporate Finance Limited	370	MB			www.newhavencorp.com
NewWest Mezzanine Fund LP	189	PE	Denver	CO	www.mezzcap.com
Next Step Advisors	482	SI	Scottsdale	AZ	www.nextstepadvisors.com
North Atlantic Capital	452	VC	Portland	ME	www.northatlanticcapital.com
Northern Illinois Angels LLC	314	AI	Naperville	IL	www.northernillinoisangels.com
Northwood Ventures	432	PE	Syosset	NY	www.northwoodventures.com
Norvest Capital Partners Inc.	473	PE	Toronto	Ontario	www.norvestcapital.com
Novo A/S	199	VC	Bagsvaerd	Denmark	www.novo.dk
Olive Capital LLC	204	MB	Las Vegas	NV	www.olivecapital.com
Orix Financial	154	LC	Rye	NH	www.orixfinancialservices.com
Outlook Ventures	326	VC	San Francisco	CA	www.outlookventures.com
Overseas Private Investment Corporation	295	GOV	Washington	DC	www.opic.gov
Oxford Investment Group	186	PE	Bloomfield Hills	MI	www.oxfordinvestmentgroup.com
Pacific Corporate Group LLC	225	PE	La Jolla	CA	www.pcgfunds.com
Pacific Horizon Ventures	201	VC	Seattle	WA	www.pacifichorizon.com
Paragon Financial Group, Inc.	214	AB	Boca Raton	FL	www.paragonfinancial.net
Parthenon Capital	190	PE	Boston	MA	www.parthenoncapital.com
Peachtree Equity Partners	487	PE	Atlanta	GA	www.peachtreeequity.com
Peterson Partners	498	PE	SLC	UT	www.petersonpartnerslp.com

Pfingsten Partners, L.L.C.	488	PE	Deerfield	IL	www.pfingstenpartners.com
Pine Creek Partners	474	PE	Washington	DC	www.pinecreekpartners.com
Platinum Funding Corp	167	AB	NY	NY	www.platinumfundingcorp.com
PNC Business Credit	255	AB	Seattle	WA	www.pncbusinesscredit.com
Pouschine Cook Capital Management, LLC	456	PE	New York	NY	www.pouschinecook.com
Primus Venture Partners, Inc.	175	VC	Cleveland	OH	www.primusventure.com
Prism Mezzanine Fund SBIC, L.P.	522	PE	Chicago	IL	www.prismfund.com
Private Investors Forum	313	AI			www.privateinvestorsforum.com
PRIVEQ Capital Partners	234	PE	Toronto	ON	www.priveq.ca
Prometheus V, LLC	358	PE	Atlanta	GA	www.prometheuspartners.com
Prudent Capital	479	PE	Washington	DC	www.prudentcapital.com
PS Capital Partners, LLC	197	PE	Milwaukee	WI	
Quad-C Management	531	PE	New York	NY	www.quadcmanagement.com
QuestMark Partners	420	VC	Baltimore	MD	www.questmarkpartners.com
RAI Group	526	AB	Hackensack	NJ	www.raigroup.com
RAI Group—Private Label Credit Cards	527	CF	Hackensack	NJ	www.raigroup.com
Research Triangle Ventures	296	VC	Raleigh	NC	www.rtventures.com
Riordan, Lewis & Haden	485	PE	Los Angeles	CA	www.rlhinvestors.com
River Associates Investments, LLC	536	PE	Chattanooga	TN	www.riverassociatesllc.com
River Capital	342	PE	Atlanta	GA	www.river-capital.com
River Cities Capital Funds	277	VC	Raleigh	NC	www.rccf.com
Riverlake Partners	284	PE	Portland	OR	www.riverlakepartners.com
Roark Capital Group	512	PE	Atlanta	GA	www.wroarkcapital.com
Robin Hood Ventures	352	AI	Wayne	PA	www.robinhoodventures.com
Rockland Credit Finance LLC	506	CF	Owings Mills	MD	www.rocklandcredit.com
RockWood Equity Partners LLC	151	PE	New York	NY	www.rockwoodequity.com
Rocky Mountain Capital Partners	257	PE	Denver	CO	www.rockymountaincapital.com
RoundTable Healthcare Partners	431	PE	Lake Forest	IL	www.roundtablehp.com
Royal Bank Asset Based Finance	144	AB	Toronto	ON	www.rbc.com
Roynat Capital	470	MB	Charlotte	NC	www.roynat.com
Salem Capital Partners, LP	333	VC	Winston-Salem	NC	www.salemcapital.com
Salix Ventures	334	VC	Andover	MA	www.salixventures.com
Sand Hill Angels, LLC	311	AI	Los Altos	CA	www.sandhillangels.com
Saw Mill Capital	216	PE	Briarcliff Manor	NY	www.sawmillcapital.com
SBV Venture Partners	435	VC	San Mateo	CA	www.sbvpartners.com
Scope	411	VC	Stockholm		www.scope.se
Scottish Equity Partners	306	VC	Glasgow	UK	www.sep.co.uk

(Continued)

Master List by Firm with Location Information (*Continued*)

Firm	Database ID	Type	City	State	Web site
SCP Private Equity Partners	344	VC	Wayne	PA	www.scppartners.com
Seaport Capital	185	PE	New York	NY	www.seaportcapital.com
Security Technlogy Ventures, LLC	138	VC	Campbell	CA	www.stvc1.com
Siemens Financial Services, Inc.	265	AB	Charlotte	NC	www.siemensfinancial.com
Siemens Venture Capital GmbH	382	SI	Munich	Germany	www.siemensventurecapital.com
Sierra Ventures	369	VC	Menlo Park	CA	www.sierraventures.com
SilkRoad Equity, Inc.	261	PE	Winston-Salem	NC	www.silkroadequity.com
SJF Ventures	124	VC	Durham	NC	www.sjfund.com
SOFINNOVA Partners	264	VC	Paris		www.sofinnova.fr
Southern Appalachian Management Company, LLC	372	VC	Oak Ridge	TN	www.southappfund.com
SouthPointe Ventures, LLC	273	PE	Atlanta	GA	www.southpointeventures.com
Southwest Value Acquisitions LLC	533	PE	Scottsdale	AZ	www.valueacquisitions.com
Sovereign Capital Limited	368	PE	London	UK	www.sovereigncapital.co.uk
SpaceVest	355	VC	Reston	VA	www.spacevest.com
STAG Capital Partners	552	AB	Boston	MA	www.stagcapital.com
Standard Federal Bank	507	AB	Troy	MI	www.standardfederalbank.com
StarVest Partners, L.P.	494	VC	New York	NY	www.starvestpartners.com
State Bank	504	AB	Austin	TX	www.statebanktx.com
Steel Capital Corp.	210	PE	Greenwich	CT	www.steelcapital.com
Sterling Venture Partners	441	PE	Baltimore	MD	www.sterlingpartners.us
StoneCreek Capital	285	PE	Irvine	CA	www.stonecreekcapital.com
Summer Street Capital Partners LLC	159	PE	Buffalo	NY	www.summerstreetcapital.com
Summit Partners	486	PE	Boston	MA	www.summitpartners.com
Sustainable Development Fund	537	SI	Philadelphia	PA	www.trfund.com
Synetro Capital—Synetro Capital Partners	143	PE	Chicago	IL	www.synetrocapital.com
Synetro Capital—Synetro Ventures (early stage)	142	VC	Chicago	IL	www.synetrocapital.com
Tailwind Capital Partners	213	PE	New York	NY	www.tailwindcapital.com
Talisman Capital Fund I, LLC	248	PE	Dublin	OH	www.talcappart.com/index.html
Tech Capital Partners Inc.	429	VC	Waterloo	ON	www.techcapital.com
Tech Coast Angels	500	AI			www.techcoastangels.com
Tech Strategies	221	MB	Needham	MA	www.techstrategies.org
TechStock	446	IN	San Jose	CA	www.techstockventure.com
Telos Venture Partners	516	VC	Palo Alto	CA	www.telosvp.com
Terra Firma Capital Partners Ltd	290	PE	London	UK	www.terrafirma.com
The Aurora Funds	109	VC	Durham	NC	www.aurorafunds.com
The CapStreet Group, LLC	293	PE	Houston	TX	www.capstreetgroup.com
The Legacy Equity Group, LLC	136	MB			www.legacyequitygroup.com

352

Company	No.	Type	City	State	Website
The Oxford Investment Group	246	PE	Bloomfield Hills	MI	www.oxfordinvestmentgroup.com
The Riverside Company	212	PE	New York	NY	www.riversidecompany.com
The Shansby Group	476	PE	San Francisco	CA	www.shansbygroup.com
Thoma Cressey Equity Partners	181	PE	Chicago	IL	www.thomacressey.com
Thomas Weisel Healthcare Venture Partners	495	MB	San Francisco	CA	www.tweisel.com
Thomas Weisel Venture Partners	359	VC	Menlo Park	CA	www.twvp.com
Thomas, McNerney & Partners	463	VC	Minneapolis	MN	www.tm-partners.com
Thompson Street Capital Partners	202	PE	Saint Louis	MO	www.thompsonstreet.net
Three Arch Partners	276	VC	Portola Valley	CA	www.threearchpartners.com
Thrive Capital Partners	172	PE	Bozeman	MT	www.thrivecapital.com
Torquest Partners	281	PE	Toronto	ON	www.torquest.com
Transcap Trade Finance	113	AB	New York	NY	www.transcaptrade.com
Transpac Capital	424	PE			
TRF Private Equity	538	PE	Philadelphia	PA	www.trfund.com
Trident Growth Fund, LP	321	PE	Houston	TX	www.tridentgrowthfund.com
Tri-State Investment Group	312	AI	Chapel Hill	NC	www.tignc.com
Tri-State Private Investors Network	439	AI	New York	NY	www.angelinvestorfunding.com
Triton Pacific Capital Partners, LLC.	406	PE			
Triton Ventures	229	VC	Austin	TX	www.tritonventures.com
Trivest Partners, L.P.	192	PE	Miami	FL	www.trivest.com
TriWest Capital Management Corp	396	PE	Calgary	Alberta	www.triwest.ca
Tuckerman Capital	302	PE	Hanover	NH	www.tuckermancapital.com
U.S. Bank Business Credit	237	AB	Portland	OR	www.usbank.com
United Capital Funding Corp.	484	AB	Saint Petersburg	FL	www.ucfunding.com
Vencon Management Inc.	146	VC	New York	NY	www.venconinc.com
Venture Capital Solutions, LP	110	PE	Winston-Salem	NC	www.vcslp.com
Ventures West Management Inc.	275	VC	Vancouver	BC	www.ventureswest.com
Venturis	232	PE			www.venturis.nl
Veronis Suhler Stevenson	230	MB	New York	NY	www.vss.com
Vested for Growth	308	SI	Concord	NH	www.vestedforgrowth.com
W. P. Carey & Co. LLC	513	CF	New York	NY	www.wpcarey.com
Wafra Partners LLC	179	PE	New York	NY	www.wafrapartners.com
Wales Fund Managers Limited	419	VC	Cardiff	UK	www.wfml.co.uk
Walker Ventures	226	VC	Glenwood	MD	www.walkerventures.com
Warwick Group, Inc.	193	PE	New Canaan	CT	www.warwickgroup.com
Washington Mutual Equipment Finance	251	BN	Denver	CO	www.wamu.com
Wells Fargo Business Credit, Inc.	242	AB	Atlanta	GA	www.wellsfargo.com/com/bus_finance/wfbci.jhtml

Master List by Firm with Location Information *(Continued)*

Firm	Database ID	Type	City	State	Web site
Westar Capital	514	PE	Costa Mesa	CA	www.westarcapital.com
Westgate Financial Corp.	235	AB	Hoboken	NJ	www.westgatefinancial.com
Windjammer Capital Investors	297	PE	Newport Beach	CA	www.windjammercapital.com
Wingate Partners	180	PE	Dallas	TX	www.wingatepartners.com
Wisconsin Rural Enterprise Fund, LLC	364	VC	Spooner	WI	
Wynnchurch Capital	318	PE	Lake Forest	IL	www.wynnchurch.com
Yale Capital, Inc.	111	AB	New York	NY	www.yalecapital.com
Yaletown Venture Partners Inc.	393	VC	Vancouver (Canada)	BC	www.yaletown.com
York Street Capital Partners	158	PE	Bedminster	NJ	www.yorkstreetcapital.com
Zenith Capital Partners LLC	211	PE	San Mateo	CA	www.zenith-partners.com
Zon Capital Partners LP	518	VC	Princeton	NJ	www.zoncapital.com
ZS Fund L.P.	245	PE	New York	NY	www.zsfundlp.com

Master List by Firm with Contact Information

Firm	Database ID	Type	Contact	Title	E-mail	Phone
@Ventures	389	VC	Brent Faduski		bfaduski@ventures.com	(978) 684-7500
A. M. Pappas & Associates, LLC	316	VC	Ford S. Worthy	Partner	info@ampappas.com	(919) 998-3300
Abingworth Management	223	VC	Victoria Stewart	Analyst	stewart@abingworth.co.uk	+44 (0)207 534 1500
Access Venture Partners	252	VC	Bob Rees	Managing Director	bob@accessventurepartners.com	(415) 586-0132
Acorn Campus	131	VC	T. Chester Wang	General Partner	tcwang@acomcampus.com	(408) 777-8090
Advent International	203	VC	Mike Pehl	Partner	mpehl@adventinternational.com	(617) 951-9400
Aerostar Capital LLC	373	PE	Robert Paulson	President	aerostarcapital@cs.com	(888) 280-5666
Agawam Partners LLC	376	MB	Francis L'Esperance	President	fal@agawampartners.com	(212) 717-2541
Agio Capital Partners I, L.P.	449	PE	Kenneth F. Gudorf	President	ken@agio-capital.com	(952) 938-1427
Agrarian Capital, LLC	319	PE	Dennis D. Spice	Managing Director	dspice@agrariancapital.com	(217) 351-7000
Albion Alliance LLC	231	PE	Alastair Tedford	Principal	atedford@albionalliance.com	(212) 969-6650
Allegiance Capital Limited Partnership	415	PE	W. Gary Dorsch	General Partner	gdorsch@allcapital.com	(410) 662-6314
Alloy Ventures	260	VC	Craig Taylor	Managing Partner	craig@alloyventures.com	(650) 687-5000
Alpine Investors, LP	525	PE	Collin Hathaway		chathaway@alpine-investors.com	(415) 309-9100
American Capital	220	PE	Mark Opel	Principal & Sr. VP	mark.opel@americancapital.com	(301) 951-6122
American Industrial Partners	244	PE	William I. Morris	Vice President	will@aipartners.com	(415) 788-7354
Antares Capital Corporation	127	VC	Jonathan I. Kislak	General Partner	jkislak@antarescapital.com	(305) 894-2888
Antares Capital Corporation	258	CF	David M. Brackett	Managing Director	dbrackett@antareslev.com	(312) 697-3999
AP Capital Partners	250	PE	Richard M. Powell	Managing Partner	rpowell@apcpartners.com	(407) 210-6534
Appian Holdings	139	PE	Subhash Bedi	Partner	sbedi@appianholdings.com	(630) 301-0757
ARCH Development Partners	493	VC	Tom Churchwell	Managing Partner	tlc@archdp.com	(312) 828-9970
ArcHelion Capital Partners	345	IN	Jeff Broadhead		jeffbroadhead@archelion.com	(561) 694-3566
Arcturus Capital	455	VC	Stephen Watkins	General Partner	businessplan@arcturusvc.com	(213) 473-1800
Argosy Partners	349	PE	Knute C. Albrecht	General Partner	knute@argosycapital.com	(610) 971-9685
Arsenal Capital Partners	292	PE	Paul Cabral	Admin	pcabral@arsenalcapital.com	(212) 771-1717
Artisan Capital	156	PE	Sanjay Datta	Director	sanjay@articap.com	(858) 755-9600
AsiaVest Partners, TCW/YFY	400	PE	Irwin Lim	Director	irwin.lim@asiavest.com	(656) 236-9570
Astorg Partners	224	PE	Thierry Timsit	Partner	ttimsit@astorg-partners.com	+331 53054050
Austin Capital Partners, L.P.	153	PE	Darrell W. Austin	Managing Partner	dwaustin@dwaustin.com	(216) 574-2284
Autumn Hill Capital Group, LLC	236	PE	James Brown	Principal	jbrown@autumnhillcapital.com	(724) 473-9479
Avocet Ventures, LLC	114	PE	William J. Mercer	President	wjmercer@avocetventures.com	(919) 573-1865
BA Capital Partners Europe	422	PE	William Obenshain	Managing Director	louise.j.aston@bankofamerica.com	020 7174 5985
Baird Capital Partners	280	MB	Paul J. Carbone	Managing Partner	pcarbone@rwbaird.com	(888) 761-9641
Baird Venture Partners	278	VC	Paul J. Carbone	Managing Director	pcarbone@rwbaird.com	(888) 761-9641
Bank of the West	472	BN	Jack Bertges	Vice President	jbertges@bankofthewest.com	(415) 399-7270
Baring Private Equity Partners	523	PE	Lyndal Howison		mail@bpep.com	+44 20 7290 5000
Baring Private Equity Partners Asia	409	PE	Jack Hennessy	Partner	jh@bpepasia.com	(650) 378-1150

(Continued)

Master List by Firm with Contact Information (Continued)

Firm	Database ID	Type	Contact	Title	E-mail	Phone
Baxter Capital Corporation	125	LC	Vito Giustino	Director	vito_giustino@baxter.com	(847) 948-2538
BayTech Venture Capital	387	VC	Dr. Rolf Schneider-Guenther	Managing General Partner	info@baytechventure.com	+49 89 2171 26120
BB&T Capital Partners	132	PE	David Townsend	Managing Partner	dgtownsend@bbandt.com	(336) 733-2420
Behrman Capital	425	PE	Tom Perlmutter	Principal	tperlmutter@behrmancap.com	(212) 980-6500
Berkshire Partners LLC	184	PE	Jeanine H. Neumann	Director	jneumann@berkshirepartners.com	(617) 227-0050
BFI Business Finance, Inc.	363	AB	Gretchen Wile	Vice President	gwile@bfifinance.com	(415) 641-5475
Biofrontier Partners USA	459	VC	Hinako Schroeter Ohtaki	President	hinako@biofrontier.co.jp	(619) 531-1100
Birchmere Capital LP	268	PE	Richard L. Stover	Managing Director	rstover@birchmere.net	(724) 940-2300
Bi-State Investment Group	519	AI	Joe Kessinger		jkessinger@ecjc.com	
Blue Point Capital Partners	266	PE	James P. Marra	Principal	jmarra@bluepointcapital.com	(216) 5354700
Blue Sage Capital	160	PE	Peter Huff	Principal	peter.huff@bluesage.com	(512) 5361900
Boston Millennia Partners	115	PE	Dana Callow	Managing General Partner	dana@millenniapartners.com	(617) 428-5150
BP Marsh Private Equity	381	VC	Rupert Marsh	General Partner	marshr@bpmarsh.co.uk	+44 207 730 2626
Bridge Street Capital Partners, LLC	348	PE	John J. Meilner	Managing Partner	john@bridgestreetcapital.com	(616) 732-1051
Brook Venture Fund	328	VC	Andrew D. Clapp	Partner	argila@yahoo.com	(781) 295-4000
Brookside Capital Partners	152	PE	David D Buttolph	Managing Director	dbuttolph@brooksideintl.com	(203) 618-0202
Brookstone Partners	274	PE	Dan Cohn-Sfetcu	Principal	cohnsfetcud@brookstonepartners.com	(212) 302-7007
Business Alliance Capital Corp.	553	AB	Barry D. Yelton	Sr. Vice President	yeltonbacc@bellsouth.net	(828) 657-0030
C3 Capital Partners	196	PE	Steven Swartzman	Principal	sswartzman@c3cap.com	(816) 756-2225
Caledonian Private Equity Partners, LLC	375	PE	Darryl L. Iaws, Ph.D.	General Partner	dll@cscvgroup.com	(858) 456-5542
Callidus Capital Corporation	140	AB	Sam Fleiser	President	sfleiser@calliduscapital.ca	(416) 572-2008
Caltius Mezzanine Partners	468	PE	Don Jamieson	Associate	djamieson@caltius.com	(310) 996-9575
Calvert Street Capital Partners	118	PE	Barry L. Johnson	Managing Director	bjohnson@cscp.com	(443) 573-3712
Cambridge Capital Partners LLC	233	PE	David Posner	Managing Partner	info@cambridgecapital.com	(312) 425-3600
Candover Investments Plc	421	PE	Colin Buffin	Managing Director	c.buffin@candover.com	+44 207 489 9848
Canterbury Capital Partners	173	PE	Daniel R. Honeker		dhoneker@canterburycp.com	(212) 332-1576
Capital Equipment Leasing	253	LC	Richard C. Walker	President	rwalker@celeasing.com	(858) 551-1214
Capital Investments	116	VC	David Cerf	General Partner	dcerf@capitalinvestments.cc	(972) 896-3164
Capital TempFunds, Inc.	503	AB	James Rothman	Vice President	jrothman@capitaltempfunds.com	(954) 660-7501
CapitalSource Finance LLC	191	CF	Steven Silver		ssilver@capitalsource.com	(866) 876-8723
CapitalWerks, LLC	267	LC	James Raeder	President	jimraeder@capitalwerks.com	(714) 210-7444
Cardinal Capital Partners	320	CF	Robert V. Fitzpatrick, III	Managing Director	bfitzpatrick@cardinalcapital.com	(214) 696-3600
Castanea Partners	550	PE	Marion Schouten	Director	mschouten@castaneapartners.com	(617) 630-2420
Caymus Partners LLC	492	MB	Jeffrey C. Villwock	Managing Partner	jvillwock@caymuspartners.com	(404) 995-8300
CEI Community Ventures	307	VC	Michael H. Gurau	President	mhg@ceicommunityventures.com	(207) 772-5356 x123
Centerfield Capital Partners	346	PE	Matthew Hook	Managing Director	matt@centerfieldcapital.com	(317) 237-2324
Centre Partners Management LLC	399	PE	Bruce Pollack	Managing Partner	bruce.pollack@centrepartners.com	(212) 332-5830
Century Park Capital Partners, LP	207	PE	Charles Roellig	Partner	croellig@cpclp.com	(415) 273-3640
Champlain Capital	530	PE	Dennis Leary	Managing Director	dleary@champlaincapital.com	(415) 281-4181
Charlesbank Capital Partners, LLC	343	PE	Maura M. Turner	Director	mturner@charlesbank.com	(617) 619-5400

Company	Page	Code	Name	Title	Email	Phone
Charlotte Angel Partners	330	VC	Brent Kulman	Vice President	caplic@hotmail.com	(704) 362-4659
Charter One Bank, N.A.	241	BN	Duane K. Bedard	Associate	dbedard@charteronebank.com	(248) 577-4115
Chatham Capital	322	CF	Lin Wang	Principal	lw@chathamcapital.com	(770) 980-0567
CHB Capital Partners	395	PE	Blake Morris	Principal	jbmorris@chbcapital.com	(303) 571-0100
Cherry Tree Investments, Inc.	447	PE	Gordon F. Stofer	Managing Partner	gstofer@cherrytree.com	(952) 893-9012
CID Equity Partners	238	PE	Eric Bruun	Principal	eric@cidequity.com	(317) 269-2350
CIVC Partners	208	PE	Gregg Wilson	General Partner	gregory.w.wilson@civc.com	(312) 828-8021
CL Fund	362	AI	Frank Napoli	Director	fnapoli@clfund.com	(412) 201-2450 x19
Clairvest Group Inc.	239	MB	Michael Wagman	Principal	michaelw@clairvest.com	(416) 925-9270
Code Hennessy & Simmons LLC	384	PE	Steven R. Brown	Partner	sbrown@chsonline.com	(312) 876-9560
Comerica Bank, Technology & Life Sciences Division	350	BN	April Young	Managing Director	april_l_young@comerica.com	(703) 689-3768
Complete Leasing Corporation	465	LC	Jed Fochtman	President	jed@completeleasingcorp.com	(540) 687-8100
Concord Ventures	490	VC	Yaron Rosenboim	General Partner	yaron@concordventures.com	+972 9 9602020
Convergent Capital Partners	249	PE	John Mason	Managing Partner	jmason@cvcap.com	(952) 595-8022
Cornerstone Capital Advisors, Ltd.	283	PE	J. Garvin Warden	Managing Director	gwarden@cstone-ltd.com	(412) 263-2870
Crescent Capital Investments, Inc.	367	PE	Scott Buschmann	Associate	sbuschmann@crescentcapital.com	(404) 920-9000
Crescent State Bank	270	BN	Thomas E. Holder, Jr.	Vice President	tholder@crescentstatebank.com	(919) 460-7685
Cross Atlantic Partners, Inc.	385	VC	John L. Cassis	Managing Partner	jlc@crossatlanticpartners.com	(646) 521-7500
CrossBridge Venture Partners	464	VC	Herman White, Jr.	General Partner	hwhite@crossbridgevp.com	(650) 279-7685
CSG Investments, Inc.	347	CF	Candy Harrison		charrison@csginvestments.com	(469) 467-5900
Davis, Tuttle Venture Partners, LP	323	PE	Philip A. Tuttle	Managing Partner	ptuttle@davistuttle.com	(713) 993-0440
DeltaPoint Capital Management, LLC	403	PE	Andrew P. Trigg	Vice President	atrigg@deltapointcapital.com	(585) 454-6990
Desert Angels	329	AI	Robert Morrison	Managing Director	morrisonr@qwest.net	(520) 490-8137
Deutsche Effecten- und Wechsel-Beteiligungsgesellschaft AG	437	VC	Cornelia Sonntag	Associate	info@dewb-vc.com	0049364165 1000
Diamondhead Ventures	315	VC	David A. Lane	General Partner	david@dhven.com	(650) 233-7526
Dorset Capital Management	423	PE	Jeff Mills	General Partner	jmills@dorsetcapital.com	(415) 398-7101
Drug Royalty Corporation Inc.	128	SI	David MacNaughtan	Vice President	dm@drugroyalty.com	(416) 863-1865
Dubin Clark & Company, Inc.	126	PE	Lisa Wild	Admin	wild@dubinclark.com	(203) 629-2030
Dunedin Capital Partners Limited	404	PE	Ross Marshall	Managing Director	ross.marshall@dunedin.com	+44 131 225 6699
DW Healthcare Partners	454	PE	Andrew Laver	Associate	alaver@dwhp.com	(801) 365-4006
E*Capital Corporation	133	PE	John J. Matise	Vice President	john@e-cap.com	(213) 688-8080
Eastern Technology Fund	440	VC	Wayne D. Kimmel	Managing Director	wayne@easterntechnologyfund.com	(610) 567-2395
Edelson Technology Partners	130	VC	Harry Edelson	Partner	harry@edelsontech.com	(201) 930-9898
Edgeview Partners	436	MB	Susan Moore	Director	moore@edgeviewpartners.com	(704) 602-3900
Edison Venture Fund	107	VC	Elaine Verna	Vice President	elaine@edisonventure.com	(609) 896-1900
Emigrant Capital Corporation	286	PE	John G. Appel	Managing Director	info@emigrantcapital.com	(212) 850-4460

(Continued)

357

Firm	Database ID	Type	Contact	Title	E-mail	Phone
Englefield Capital LLP	254	PE	Dwight Cupit	Vice President	englefield@engcap.com	+44 20 7591 4200
Enterprise Corporation of the Delta	335	CF	Greg Wineland	Managing Partner	capital@ecd.org	(601) 944-1100
EonTech Ventures SA	380	VC	Sandro Grigolli	Managing Director	sandro.grigolli@eontechventures.com	
Essex Woodlands Health Ventures	129	VC	Immanuel Thangaraj	Managing Director	it@essexwoodlands.com	(312) 444-6040
Eureka Growth Capital	269	PE	Christopher G. Hanssens	Partner	chanssens@eurekagrowth.com	(215) 575-2377
Exeter Capital Partners	374	PE	Keith R. Fox	President	contact @exeterfunds.com	(212) 872-1172
FA Technology Ventures	551	VC	John Coccocia	Principal	john@fatechventures.com	(518) 447-8200
Falcon Fund	529	VC	Ed Tuck	Principal	ed@falconfund.com	(626) 966-6235
FdG Associates	361	PE	Howard Romanow	Principal	hlr@fdgassociates.com	(212) 940-6891
First Advisors, Inc.	383	AI	Gary J. Davis	President	gjdavis@firstadvisors-inc.com	(512) 328-8122
FirstFloor Capital	391	PE	Zauqi Abdullah	Principal	mail@firstfloorcapital.com	6032093044
Florida Capital Partners, Inc.	163	PE	David J. Malizia	Managing Director	djm@fcpinvestors.com	(813) 222-8000
Founders Equity Inc.	145	PE	J. Ryan Kelly	Vice President	rkelly@fequity.com	(212) 829-0900 x220
Four J Funding	528	CF	Bette Gandelman	Vice President	bgandelman@raigroup.com	(201) 518-1160
Franklin Street Equity Partners, Inc.	390	PE	Thomas S Ablum	General Partner	tom.ablum@fsequity.com	(877) 372-8529
Friend Capital Funding, LLC	112	AB	Bill Friend	President	bill@friendfunding.com	
Frontier Capital	123	VC	Michael Ramich	Principal	michael@frontierfunds.com	(704) 414-2880
FSN Capital Partners AS	379	PE	Ragnhild Skjaevestad	Fund Manager	rs@fsncapital.no	+47 24 14 73 00
Funk Ventures	171	VC	Submissions		info@funkventures.com	(818) 716-0413
gcp gamma capital partners	386	VC	Nikolaus Spieckermann		n.spieckermann@gamma-capital.com	+431513107 2100
GE Commercial Finance	282	CF	Thomas Murray	Managing Director	tom.murray@ge.com	(212) 880-7196
GE Corporate Financial Services	217	AB	Scott W. Elliotto	Vice President	scott.elliotto@ge.com	(212) 880-7026
Generics Asset Management Ltd	541	VC	Dr Richard Leaver	Fund Manager	richard.leaver@genericsgroup.com	01223 875200
Genesis Campus	547	VC	Roman Kikta	Managing General Partner	rkikta@genesiscampus.com	(972) 991-9942
Geneva Venture Partners	170	VC	Igor Sill	Managing Director	igor@genevavc.com	(415) 433-4646
Giza Venture Capital	366	VC	Ezer Soref	Managing Director	esoref@gizavc.com	9723 6402318
Gladstone Capital Corporation	256	MB	George Stelljes		chip.stelljes@gladstonecapital.com	(703) 286-7000
Gleacher Mezzanine LLC	168	PE	Philip Krall	Managing Director	phillip.krall@gleacher.com	(212) 418-4200
Global Catalyst Partners	467	VC	Mary Denten		many@gc-partners.com	(650) 486-2420
Global Strategy & Capital Group	407	MB	Jose A. Kreidler	General Partner	jose@gscgroup.net	(949) 231-8251
GMB Mezzanine Capital	301	PE	Michael McHugh	Managing Partner	mmchugh@gmbmezz.com	(612) 798-2144
Goense Bounds & Partners	148	MB	Erik Bloom	Director	ewb@goensebounds.com	(847) 735-2000
Golub Associates Incorporated	294	PE	Lawrence E. Golub	President	lgolub@golubassoc.com	(212) 750-6060
Graham Partners, Inc.	182	PE	Robert A. Newbold	Managing Partner	newbold@grahampartners.net	(610) 251-2889
GrandBanks Capital	219	VC	Charles Lax	General Partner	clax@grandbankscapital.com	(617) 928-9314
Great Lakes Angels, Inc.	509	AI	David P. Weaver	President	dweaver@glangels.org	
Greenfield Commercial Credit	188	AB	Donald M Rudnik	Partner	drudnik@greenfieldcredit.com	(773) 298-0595
Gresham Private Equity Limited	524	PE	Roger Casey	Managing Director	gpe@gresham.com.au	+61 2 9221 5133
Grey Mountain Partners, LLC	228	PE	Chris Griffith	Principal	cgriffith@greymountain.com	(212) 588-8845
Greyrock Capital Group	166	PE	Mark French	Principal	french@greyrockcapitalgroup.com	(415) 273-3504

Firm	Type	No.	Contact	Title	Email	Phone
GrowthWorks Capital Ltd.	VC	434	Maya Charles	General Partner	maya.charles@growthworks.ca	(604) 633-1418
Guide Ventures, LLC	VC	176	Russ Aldrich	Managing Director	info@guideventures.com	(206) 447-1350
H. Katz Capital Group	PE	481	Brian Siegel	Managing Director	hkatzgroup@earthlink.net	(215) 364-0400 x2
H.I.G. Capital, LLC	PE	332	Thomas R. Ley	Managing Director	tley@higcapital.com	(415) 4395500
Halyard Capital Fund	PE	119	Robert B. Nolan, Jr	Partner	robert.nolan@bmonb.com	(212) 605-1512
Hamilton Robinson LLC	PE	478	Christian Lund	Partner	cel@hrco.com	(203) 602-0012
Hammond Kennedy Whitney & Co., Inc.	PE	147	Ted Kramer	Vice President	tk@hkwinc.com	(317) 574-6900
Harbert Management Corporation—Mezzanine Capital	PE	299	Charles D. Miller		cmiller@harbert.net	(205) 987-5517
Harbert Management Corporation—Venture Partners	VC	309	Charles D. Miller		cmiller@harbert.net	(205) 987-5517
Harbour Group	PE	491	Clay Hunter	Director	chunter@harbourgroup.com	(314) 727-5550
Hartsko Financial Services, LLC	AB	489	Richard Eitelberg CPA	Vice President	reitelberg@hartsko.com	(516) 906-6682
Hastings Equity Partners	PE	317	Chris Wilmerding	Partner	cwilmerding@hastingsequity.com	(617) 312-8025
HBM BioVentures Ltd.	PE	471	Claudia Capucho		claudia.capucho@hbmpartners.com	+41 41 768 1108
Healthcare Finance Group, Inc.	AB	502	James Craig	Principal	jcraig@hfgusa.com	(212) 785-9220
High Street Capital	PE	475	Joseph R. Katcha	Vice President	jkatcha@highstr.com	(312) 423-2650
Highland Capital Partners	VC	336	Michael Gaiss	President	info@hcp.com	(781) 861-5500
Hilco Capital LP	AB	227	Theodore L. Koenig	Managing Director	tkoenig@hilcocapital.com	(847) 559-9300
HLHZ Investments, LLC	PE	543	Scott Adelson	Associate	sadelson@hlhz.com	(310) 553-8871
Hopewell Ventures	VC	398	Matt McCue	Managing Director	mccue@hopewellventures.com	(312) 357-9600
Horizon Ventures	VC	331	Jack Carsten	Managing Director	jack@horizonvc.com	(650) 917-4100
HSBC Capital	PE	517	James W. Marley	Vice President	james.marley@us.hsbc.com	(212) 525-6455
Hunt Special Situations Group, L.P.	PE	300	Philip Arra	Associate	parra@huntinvestment.com	(214) 978-8104
Huron Capital Partners, LLC	PE	453	Russell L. Owen	Managing Director	rowen@huroncapital.com	(313) 496-1056
Hyde Park Capital Partners, LLC	MB	108	John H. Hill Jr.	General Partner	hill@hydeparkcapital.com	(813) 383-0202
IDG Ventures Europe	VC	169	Chris Smart	Managing Partner	chris@idgve.com	+44 20 72997399
IIG Capital LLC	CF	394	Martin S. Silver	Vice President	client_relations@iigcapital.com	(212) 806-5100
Imperial Capital Corporation	MB	324	Edward Truant	Managing Director	ici@imperialcap.com	(416) 362-3658
Infineon Ventures GmbH	VC	497	Ralf Schnell	Admin.	ralf.schnell@infineon.com	+4989923453380
Infocomm Investments Pte Ltd	PE	520	Brenda Ng	Admin.	brenda_ng@ida.gov.sg	6562110888
InnovationsKapital	VC	371	Gabriella Ohidin	General Partner	go@imkap.se	+46 31 609190
Intersouth Partners	VC	106	Mitch Mumma	Managing Director	info@intersouth.com	(919) 493-6640
Invest Mezzanine Capital Management GmbH	PE	149	Michael Fischer	Managing Partner	m.fischer@investmezzanin.at	
ITF Global Partners	SI	177	Barnett Suskind	President	barnett@itfgp.com	(212) 366-6000
J D Factors	CF	505	Stephen P. Johnson	President	sjohnson@jdfactors.com	(310) 316-7170
J&D Financial Corporation	CF	542	Jonathan Carmel		jon@jfinancial.com	(305) 893-0300

Master List by Firm with Contact Information (*Continued*)

Firm	Database ID	Type	Contact	Title	Email	Phone
Kachi Partners	161	PE	Eric Weissmann	Managing Director	eric@kachipartners.com	(303) 442-1227
Kasten Group, LLC	511	PE	Clinton E. Kasten	Managing Partner	cekasten@kastengroup.com	(618) 632-4097
Key Principal Partners	117	PE	Samir D. Desai	Vice President	sdesai@kppinvest.com	(216) 828-8147
Key Venture Partners	120	VC	Vaibhav Nalwaya	Associate	vn@kppinvest.com	(781) 663-2103
King Trade Capital	508	AB	Edward King	Managing Partner	eking@tradecapital.com	(214) 368-5100
Kirtland Capital Partners	150	PE	Tom Littman	Partner	tlittman@kirtlandcapital.com	(440) 585-9010
Kline Hawkes & Co	450	PE	Cameron Wood	Associate	cwood@klinehawkes.com	(310) 442-4700
KRG Capital Partners	388	PE	Mark King	Managing Director	mking@krgcapital.com	(303) 390-5001
L&L Capital Partners	135	PE	Fernando Acosta-Rua	Partner	far@llcapitalpartners.com	(203) 222-3030
Leo Capital Holdings, LLC	426	VC	Mark Glennon		info@leocapholdings.com	
Lighthouse Venture Partners, LLC	521	VC			hans@lighthouseventurepartners.com	+31 43 3280320
Limburg Ventures BV	414	VC	Casper Bruens	General Partner	casperbruens@limburgventures.com	(617) 695-9400
Lincolnshire Management	164	PE	Thomas W. Janes	Director	tjanes@lincolnshiremgmt.com	(617) 778-0671
Lineage Capital	289	PE	Mark Sullivan	Managing Director	mark@lineagecap.com	(440) 684-1400
Linsalata Capital Partners	279	PE	Eric V. Bacon	General Partner	ebacon@linsalatacapital.com	(770) 818-0335
Linx Partners, LLC	165	PE	Edward A. Leinss	Sr. Managing Director	eleinss@linxpartners.com	+41 22 716 4230
LogiSpring	378	VC	Frans van Schaik	Managing Director	info@logispring.com	(415) 397-5900
Lombard Investments, Inc.	288	PE	Thomas J. Smith	Managing Partner	tsmith@lombardinvestments.com	(248) 591-6000
Long Point Capital, Inc.	451	PE	Gretchen B. Perkins	Vice President	gperkins@longpointcapital.com	(413) 567-3366
Longmeadow Capital, LLC	353	PE	Jonathan Daen	Principal	jdaen@longmeadowcapital.com	(612) 904-8587
M&I Bank	341	BN	Jeff Norton	Vice President	jeff.norton@micorp.com	(724) 743-5650
Main Street Capital Holdings LLC	340	PE	Gerald M. Prado	Principal	prado@mainstcap.com	(713) 350-6009
Main Street Mezzanine Fund, LP	510	PE	David Magdol	Managing Director	dmagdol@mainstreethouston.com	(303) 694-4387
Markwitz Kurtz Investments, LLC	198	PE	Brian Mankiwitz	Partner	brian@mkinvestmentsllc.com	(201) 369-3057
Maple Commercial Finance Group	405	AB	Eugene Braigen	Director	eugeneb@mapleusa.com	(612) 661-3991
Marquette Capital Partners, Inc.	327	PE	Thomas H. Jenkins	President	tom.jenkins@marquette.com	(650) 854-5560
Mayfield	122	VC	Harvey Schloss	Managing Director/COO	hschloss@mayfield.com	(416) 364-8884
McKenna Gale Capital Inc.	460	PE	Craig Ferguson	Vice President	info@mckennagale.com	(216) 514-1840
MCM Capital Partners, L.P.	134	PE	Mark Mansour	Managing Director	mark@mcmcapital.com	(781) 237-6910
MedEquity Capital, LLC	337	PE	Peter R. Gates	Partner	prgates@medequity.com	(215) 736-8882
Mentor Capital Partners Ltd	187	VC	Edward Sager	President	sager@mentorcapitalpartners.com	(610) 992-5681
Merion Investment Partners	178	PE	William M. Means	Managing General Partner	wmeans@merionpartners.com	
Merisel, Inc.	209	PE	Allen D. Chi	Director	ac@km-partners.com	
Merit Capital Partners, LLC	194	PE	Marc J. Walfish	Managing Director	mwalfish@meritcapital.com	(312) 592-6111
Meritage Private Equity Funds	200	PE	Laura Beller		lbeller@meritagefunds.com	(303) 352-2040
Meritum Partners, LLC	303	PE	Franklin Staley	Director	franklin@meritum.com	(415) 616-9803
Meriwether Capital, L.L.C.	433	IN	Robert W. Petit	President	meriwether@rockco.com	(212) 649-5890
Metapoint Partners	408	PE	Erik Dykema	Principal	erik@metapoint.com	(978) 5311-398 x8

Firm	#	Type	Name	Title	Email	Phone
Midwest Mezzanine Funds	287	PE	Jeff DeJesus	Principal	jeff.dejesus@abnamro.com	(312) 992-4580
Milestone Merchant Partners, LLC	121	MB	Murry Gunty	Managing Director	mgunty@milestonecap.com	(202) 367-3008
Mofet Venture Capital Fund	412	VC	David Goldschmidt	Managing Partner	dede@mofet.co.il	97299561290
Mohr Davidow Ventures	243	VC	Pamela Mahoney	Director	pmahoney@mdv.com	(650) 854-7236
Monumental Venture Partners, LLC	462	PE	Jeff Friedman	Managing Director	jfriedman@mvpfunds.com	(703) 821-0400
Morgenthaler	272	PE	Simon Feiglin	Principal	sfeiglin@morgenthaler.com	(216) 416-7500
Mountaineer Capital	397	VC	Eric Nelson	Partner	intern@mhdgp.com	(304) 347-7500
MTI Partners Limited	469	VC	David Ward		dward@mtifirms.com	+44 1923 250244
Murex Investments I, L.P.	444	VC	Tami Fratis	General Partner	tami@murexinvests.com	(215) 951-7200 x3061
Najeti Ventures LLC	501	PE	Thomas W. Hallagan	Managing Director	tom.hallagan@najeti.com	(203) 262-6336
National City Equity Partners, LLC	483	PE	David Sands	Partner	david.sands@ncepi.com	(216) 222-2491
Nautic Partners, LLC	174	PE	Barbara Wheeler		bwheeler@nauticpartners.com	(401) 278-6770
Navigator Equity Partners	357	PE	Bernard B. Markey	Managing Partner	bbmarkey@navigatorequity.com	(908) 273-7733
Navis Capital Partners Limited	410	PE	Richard Foyston	Managing Director	rfoyston@naviscapital.com	+603 20261662
Net Partners	263	VC	Diana Saraceni	Director	saraceni@net-partners.com	
New Mexico Private Investors, Inc	325	PE	George M. Richmond	President	geomrich1@comcast.net	(505) 856-0245
New Mountain Capital	141	PE	Matthew Holt	Associate	mholt@newmountaincapital.com	(212) 720-0355
New York City Investment Fund	365	VC	Janice Cook Roberts	Vice President	proposals@nycif.org	(212) 4937491
NewCastle Partners LLC	240	PE	Jack Lowden	President	jrlowden@newcastle-partners.com	(203) 863-9892
Newhaven Corporate Finance Limited	370	MB	Spencer Wilson	Managing Director	spencer.wilson@newhavencorp.com	
NewWest Mezzanine Fund LP	189	PE	Daniel K. Arenberg	Principal	darenberg@mezzcap.com	(303) 764-9676
Next Step Advisors	482	SI	Dieter Gable	Managing Director	dieter.gable@nextstepadvisors.com	(602) 300-9270
North Atlantic Capital	452	VC	Anja Saloranta	Analyst	asaloranta@northatlanticcapital.com	(207) 772-4470
Northern Illinois Angels LLC	314	AI	Bartley J. Carlson		bart@northernillinoisangels.com	
Northwood Ventures	432	PE	Paul R. Homer	Vice President	phomer@northwoodventures.com	(516) 364-5544
Norvest Capital Partners Inc.	473	PE	Ross Campbell	Managing Director	campbell@norvestcapital.com	(416) 361-5757
Novo A/S	199	VC	Kim L. Dueholm	Partner	kid@novo.dk	+45 4442 7972
Olive Capital LLC	204	MB	Felix Danciu	Managing Director	fdanciu@olivecapital.com	(213) 321-1146
Orix Financial	154	LC	Mark Forsyth	Vice President	mforsyth@orixfin.com	(603) 436-0648
Outlook Ventures	326	VC	Carl Nichols	Managing Director	cnichols@outlookventures.com	
Overseas Private Investment Corporation	295	GOV	Erica Guries		info@opic.gov	(202) 336-8799
Oxford Investment Group	186	PE	Daniel J. Salliotte	Vice President	dsalliotte@oxinvest.com	(248) 988-8792
Pacific Corporate Group LLC	225	PE	Monte Brem	Managing Director	mbrem@pcgfunds.com	(858) 456-6000
Pacific Horizon Ventures	201	VC	Will Robbins	Associate	phv@pacifichorizon.com	(206) 682-1181
Paragon Financial Group, Inc.	214	AB	Jon Anselma	Vice President	jon@paragonfinancial.net	(561) 447-9943
Parthenon Capital	190	PE	Alan Botsford	Managing Director	alanb@parthenoncapital.com	(617) 960-4000
Peachtree Equity Partners	487	PE	Andy Rose	Principal	andy@peachtreeequity.com	(404) 253-6380
Peterson Partners	498	PE	Rick Stratford	General Partner	rick@petersonpartnerslp.com	(801) 359-8880

(Continued)

Master List by Firm with Contact Information (*Continued*)

Firm	Database ID	Type	Contact	Title	Email	Phone
Pfingsten Partners, L.L.C.	488	PE	Thomas M. Turmell	Vice President	tturmell@pfingsten.com	(847) 374-9140
Pine Creek Partners	474	PE	R. Scott Saunders III		scott@pinecreekpartners.com	(202) 251-0499
Platinum Funding Corp	167	AB	Anthony Ventura		anthony@platinumfundingcorp.com	(212) 9442-828 ×16
PNC Business Credit	255	AB	Glenn Burroughs	Vice President	glenn.burroughs@pncbusinesscredit.com	(206) 652-0960
Pouschine Cook Capital Management, LLC	456	PE	Ryan W. Gabel	Associate	rgabel@pouschinecook.com	(212) 784-0620
Primus Venture Partners, Inc.	175	VC	Jonathan Dick	Managing Director	jdick@primusventure.com	(440) 8847900
Prism Mezzanine Fund SBIC, L.P.	522	PE	Blaine Crissman	Partner	blaine@prismfund.com	(312) 464-7906
Private Investors Forum	313	AI	Richard Levin	Managing Director	richl7400@aol.com	
PRIVEQ Capital Partners	234	PE	Kevin Melnyk	General Partner	melnyk@priveq.ca	(416) 447-3330
Prometheus V, LLC	358	PE	Mr. Chris Suh	Principal	csuh@prometheuspartners.com	(770) 395-9091 x2
Prudent Capital	479	PE	Steven J. Schwartz	Fund Manager	sjs@prudentcapital.com	(202) 282-9041
PS Capital Partners, LLC	197	PE	Paul W. Sweeney	Principal	psweeney@pscapitalpartners.com	(414) 831-1804
Quad-C Management	531	PE	Ashish Rughwani	Vice President	abr@qc-inc.com	(212) 3333813
QuestMark Partners	420	VC	Benjamin S. Schapiro	General Partner	bschapiro@questm.com	(410) 895-5800
RAI Group	526	AB	Bette Gandelman	Vice President	bgandelman@raigroup.com	(201) 518-1160
RAI Group—Private Label Credit Cards	527	CF	Bette Gandelman	Vice President	bgandelman@raigroup.com	(201) 518-1160
Research Triangle Ventures	296	VC	Eric Johns		ejohns@rtventures.com	(919) 571-8819
Riordan, Lewis & Haden	485	PE	Rob Zielinski		rzielinski@rhinvestors.com	(213) 229-8500
River Associates Investments, LLC	536	PE	Mark Jones	Partner	mjones@riverassociatesllc.com	(423) 755-0888
River Capital	342	PE	Jerry Wethington	President	jwethington@river-capital.com	(404) 873-2166
River Cities Capital Funds	277	VC	Edward McCarthy	Director	emccarthy@rccf.com	(919) 573-6111
Riverlake Partners	284	PE	Julie Markezich	Admin.	jmarkezich@riverlakepartners.com	(503) 228-7100
Roark Capital Group	512	PE	Dan Lonergan	Partner	danlonergan@roarkcapital.com	(404) 591-3337
Robin Hood Ventures	352	AI	Rob Weber	Managing Partner	info@robinhoodventures.com	(610) 993-9060
Rockland Credit Finance LLC	506	CF	John Fox	President	johnf@rocklandcredit.com	(410) 902-0393
RockWood Equity Partners LLC	151	PE	Brett Keith	Principal	bkeith@rockwoodequity.com	(212) 634-3327
Rocky Mountain Capital Partners	257	PE	Steve Sangalis	General Partner	steve@rockycapital.com	(303) 297-1701
RoundTable Healthcare Partners	431	PE	Len Kuhr	Principal	lkuhr@roundtablehp.com	(847) 739-3200
Royal Bank Asset Based Finance	144	AB	Kevin Lacey	Managing Partner	kevin.lacey@rbc.com	(416) 955-2994
Roynat Capital	470	MB	David Swaine	President	swained@roynat.com	(704) 332-9640
Salem Capital Partners, LP	333	VC	Phillip W Martin	Managing Director	inquiry@salemcapital.com	(336) 768-9343
Salix Ventures	334	VC	Salix Ventures Plans		plans@salixventures.com	(978) 470-2500
Sand Hill Angels, LLC	311	AI	Steve Stephansen	President	sstephansen@sandhillangels.com	
Saw Mill Capital, LLC	216	PE	Douglas Feldman	Vice President	dfeldman@sawmillcapital.com	(914) 741-1300
SBV Venture Partners	435	VC	Graham Burnette	General Partner	info@sbvpartners.com	(650) 522-0085
Scope	411	VC	Jonas Palmquist		info@scope.se	+46 8 50 60 62 00
Scottish Equity Partners	306	VC	Fraser McLatchie	Analyst	enquiries@sep.co.uk	+44 (0) 1412734000

Company			Name	Title	Email	Phone
SCP Private Equity Partners	344	VC	Winston J. Churchill	General Partner	wchurchill@scppartners.com	(610) 995-2900
Seaport Capital	185	PE	Steve McCall	General Partner	smccall@seaportcapital.com	(212) 421-1400
Security Technology Ventures, LLC	138	VC	Peter C. Verbica	Managing Director	peterv@stvc1.com	(408) 288-5100
Siemens Financial Services, Inc.	265	AB	Gregg Simpson	Vice President	gregg.simpson@svc.siemens.com	(704) 423-9992 x2
Siemens Venture Capital GmbH	382	SI	Sabine Zindera	Vice President	businessplan@svc.siemens.com	+49 89 636 33585
Sierra Ventures	369	VC	Mike Scanlin		mscanlin@sierraventures.com	
SilkRoad Equity, Inc.	261	PE	Andrew J.Filipowski	President	flip@silkroadequity.com	(336) 201-5050
SJF Ventures	124	VC	Rick Larson	Managing Director	rlarson@sjfund.com	(919) 530-1177
SOFINNOVA Partners	264	VC	Monique Saulnier	Managing Director	msaulnier@sofinnova.fr	+33 1 53 05 41 00
Southern Appalachian Management Company, LLC	372	VC	Grady Vanderhoofven	Vice President	grady@southapptund.com	(865) 220-2020
SouthPointe Ventures, LLC	273	PE	John Dalton	Partner	john@southpointeventures.com	(404) 249-6000
Southwest Value Acquisitions LLC	533	PE	Stephan Kindt	Managing Partner	stephan@valueacquisitions.com	(480) 236-5134
Sovereign Capital Limited	368	PE	Julie Sieger	Admin.	juliesieger@sovereigncapital.co.uk	020 7828 6944
SpaceVest	355	VC	Roger Widing	Managing Director	rwiding@spacevest.com	(703) 904-9600
Standard Federal Bank	507	AB	Martin Battaglia	Managing Director	martin.battaglia@abnamro.com	(248) 822-5828
STAG Capital Partners	552	AB	Charlie Hipwood	Vice President	chipwood@stagcapital.com	(617) 574-4777
StarVest Partners, L.P.	494	VC	Rachel Masters	Associate	rachel@starvestpartners.com	(212) 863-2500
State Bank	504	AB	Cole Harmonson	Vice President	cole.harmonson@statebanktx.com	(512) 997-2013
Steel Capital Corp.	210	PE	Brian Brillat	Analyst	brian@steelcapital.com	(203) 532-4738
Sterling Venture Partners	441	PE	Jeffrey Moss	Vice President	jmoss@sterlingpartners.us	(443) 703-1700
StoneCreek Capital	285	PE	Bruce Lipian	Managing Director	bruce@stonecreekcapital.com	(949) 752-4580 x22
Summer Street Capital Partners LLC	159	PE	Brian D'Amico	Partner	bdamico@summerstreetcapital.com	(716) 566-2902
Summit Partners	486	PE	Joan Miller	Vice President	jmiller@summitpartners.com	(617) 824-1000
Sustainable Development Fund	537	SI	Rob Sanders	Director	rob.sanders@trfund.com	(215) 574-5800
Synetro Capital—Synetro Capital Partners	143	PE	Pete Georgiadis	Managing Partner	pgeorgiadis@synetrocapital.com	(312) 372-0840
Synetro Capital—Synetro Ventures (early stage)	142	VC	Pete Georgiadis	Managing Partner	pgeorgiadis@synetrocapital.com	(312) 372-0840
Tailwind Capital Partners	213	PE	Larry Sorrel	General Partner	lsorrel@tailwindcapital.com	(212) 271-3800
Talisman Capital Fund I, LLC	248	PE	Michael P. Scott	President	mscott@talcappart.com	(614) 210-5500
Tech Capital Partners Inc.	429	VC	Jacqui Murphy	Associate	jmurphy@techcapital.com	(519) 883-8656
Tech Coast Angels	500	AI	Vern Yates		vern@yatesventures.com	
Tech Strategies	221	MB	Peter Graffman	Managing Director	pgraffman@techstrategies.org	(781) 444-8233
TechStock	446	IN	Simon Ng	Analyst	sn@techstockventure.com	(408) 790-4555
Telos Venture Partners	516	VC	Bruce R. Bourbon	Managing Partner	bourbon@telosvp.com	(650) 251-1850
Terra Firma Capital Partners Ltd	290	PE	Bill Miles		bill.miles@terrafirma.com	020 7521 1270
The Aurora Funds	109	VC	Katie Felix	Admin.	kfelix@aurorafunds.com	(919) 484-0400
The CapStreet Group, LLC	293	PE	Katherine Kohlmeyer	Partner	kkohlmeyer@capstreetgroup.com	(713) 332-2700
The Legacy Equity Group, LLC	136	MB	Gregory R. Ford	Managing Partner	gford@legacyequitygroup.com	(713) 952-4497

(Continued)

Master List by Firm with Contact Information *(Continued)*

Firm	Database ID	Type	Contact	Title	E-mail	Phone
The Oxford Investment Group	246	PE	Brad Lazorka		blazorka@oxinvest.com	(248) 988-8793
The Riverside Company	212	PE	Robert B. Landis	Principal	rbl@riversidecompany.com	(212) 265-6408
The Shansby Group	476	PE	J. Gary Shansby	Managing Director	jgshansby@shansby.com	(415) 217-2300
Thoma Cressey Equity Partners	181	PE	Lee M. Mitchell	Partner	lmitchell@thomacressey.com	(312) 777-4444
Thomas Weisel Healthcare Venture Partners	495	MB	Richard Spalding	Partner	rspalding@tweisel.com	(415) 364-2546
Thomas Weisel Venture Partners	359	VC	Andrew Sessions	Managing Partner	asessions@twp.com	(650) 688-5500
Thomas, McNerney & Partners	463	VC	Susan Haedt	Director	shaedt@tm-partners.com	(612) 465-8660
Thompson Street Capital Partners	202	PE	Peter Villhard	Principal	pvillhard@thompsonstreet.net	(314) 727-2112
Three Arch Partners	276	VC	Barclay Nicholson	Partner	info@threearchpartners.com	(650) 529-8000
Thrive Capital Partners	172	PE	Tom McMakin	Managing Director	tom@thrivecapital.com	(406) 570-5929
Torquest Partners	281	PE	Brent Belzberg	Managing Partner	belzberg@torquest.com	(416) 956-7022
Transcap Trade Finance	113	AB	Paul Schuldiner	Managing Director	pschuldiner@transcaptrade.com	(212) 946-2888
Transpac Capital	424	PE	Will Hoon	General Partner	will.hoon@transpac-capital.com	(65) 6224211
TRF Private Equity	538	PE	Linda DeJure	Fund Manager	linda.dejure@trfund.com	(215) 574-5800
Trident Growth Fund, LP	321	PE	Larry St. Martin	Managing Director	larry@tridentgrowthfund.com	(281) 488-8484
Tri-State Investment Group	312	AI	Stephen Clossick	Admin.	sclossick@mindspring.com	
Tri-State Private Investors Network	439	AI	Ellen Sandles	President	ellen@angelinvestorfunding.com	(212) 677-8739
Triton Pacific Capital Partners, LLC.	406	PE	Larry Simon	Principal	investments@tritonpacific.com	
Triton Ventures	229	VC	Laura J. Kilcrease	Managing Director	laura@tritonventures.com	(512) 795-5820
Trivest Partners, L.P.	192	PE	Derek A. McDowell	Managing Director	dmcdowell@trivest.com	(305) 858-2200
TriWest Capital Management Corp	396	PE	Jeff Belford	Managing Director	jbelford@triwest.ca	(403) 225-1144
Tuckerman Capital	302	PE	Peter Milliken	Partner	peter@tuckermancapital.com	(603) 640-2290
U.S. Bank Business Credit	237	AB	Robert Alexander	Vice President	robert.alexander@usbank.com	(503) 275-8655
United Capital Funding Corp.	484	AB	Mark S. Mandula	Partner	mark@ucfunding.com	(877) 894-8232
Vencon Management Inc.	146	VC	Barbara Burdzy	Analyst	vencon@worldnet.att.net	(212) 581-8787
Venture Capital Solutions, LP	110	PE	Phillip Martin	Managing Director	pmartin@vcslp.com	(336) 768-9343
Ventures West Management Inc.	275	VC	Dr. Robin Louis	President	info@ventureswest.com	(604) 688-9495
Venturis	232	MB	W. van der Hart	Managing Director	info@venturis.nl	+31 (0) 30 2941697
Veronis Suhler Stevenson	230	MB	James P. Rutherfurd	Managing Director	rutherfurdj@vss.com	(212) 935-4990
Vested for Growth	308	SI	John Hamilton	Director	jhamilton@vestedforgrowth.com	(603) 856-0729
W. P. Carey & Co. LLC	513	CF	Gordon F. DuGan	President	gdugan@wpcarey.com	(212) 492-1100
Wafra Partners LLC	179	PE	Eric A. Norfleet	Managing Director	e.norfleet@wafra.com	(212) 759-3700
Wales Fund Managers Limited	419	VC	Richard Harbottle	Managing Director	info@wfml.co.uk	+44 2920 546 250
Walker Ventures	226	VC	Cheryl Ludy	Admin.	plans@walkerventures.com	(301) 854-6850
Warwick Group, Inc.	193	PE	Mark Kozak	President	mkozak@warwickgroup.com	(203) 966-7447
Washington Mutual Equipment Finance	251	BN	Robert Haynes	Vice President	robert.w.haynes@wamu.net	(303) 306-4602
Wells Fargo Business Credit, Inc.	242	AB	Bruce Sim	Managing Director	bruce.sim@wellsfargo.com	(678) 795-8100

Company	No.	Type	Name	Title	Email	Phone
Westar Capital	514	PE	Cindy Cummings	Admin.	ccummings@westarcapital.com	(714) 481-5160
Westgate Financial Corp.	235	AB	Jason Goldberg	Vice President	jgoldberg@westgatefinancial.com	(201) 222-3200
Windjammer Capital Investors	297	PE	Robert Bartholomew	Managing Partner	bob@windjammercapital.com	(949) 721-9944
Wingate Partners	180	PE	Jason Reed		jasonreed@wingatepartners.com	(214) 720-1313
Wisconsin Rural Enterprise Fund, LLC	364	VC	Myron Schuster	General Partner	mschuster@nwrpc.com	(715) 635-2197
Wynnchurch Capital	318	PE	Frank Hayes	Partner	fhayes@wynnchurch.com	(847) 604-6107
Yale Capital, Inc.	111	AB	Lewis Y. Faber	President	lewisfaber@yalecapital.com	(212) 681-9500
Yaletown Venture Partners Inc.	393	VC	Hans Knapp	General Partner	hans@yaletown.com	(604) 688-7807
York Street Capital Partners	158	PE	Rob Golding	Managing Partner	golding@yorkstreetcapital.com	(908) 658-3714
Zenith Capital Partners LLC	211	PE	Dan Mytels	Principal	dmytels@aol.com	(650) 372-9875
Zon Capital Partners LP	518	VC	Valerie Bruder	Admin.	zonadmin@zoncapital.com	(609) 452-1653
ZS Fund L.P.	245	PE	Adam Lehrhoff	Partner	alehrhoff@zsfundlp.com	(212) 398-6200

Master List by Firm with Summary Criteria

($ millions)

Firm	Database ID	Type	Geographic Preference	Minimum Revenue	Typical Deal Size	Minimum Funding	Maximum Funding
@ Ventures	389	VC	USA		5	1	7.5
A. M. Pappas & Associates, LLC	316	VC	USA			0.5	5
Abingworth Management	223	VC	Europe, USA		15	1	20
Access Venture Partners	252	VC	West Coast, Southwest, Midwest		2–5	.5	2
Acorn Campus	131	VC	West Coast, greater China		1.5	.2	3
Advent International	203	VC	USA		8	5	20
Aerostar Capital LLC	373	PE	North America, Europe	50	20	50	250
Agawam Partners LLC	376	MB	USA	5		1	5
Agio Capital Partners I, L.P.	449	PE	Midwest, Southeast	100	5.0	2.5	8
Agrarian Capital, LLC	319	PE	North America		1.5	.5	5
Albion Alliance LLC	231	PE	North America, Europe	10	15	8	30
Allegiance Capital Limited Partnership	415	VC	Mid-Atlantic	10	2	1	3
Alloy Ventures	260	VC	West Coast		4	.5	7.5
Alpine Investors, LP	525	PE	USA	10	5–15		
American Capital	220	PE	North America, Asia, Europe, USA	20		5	60
American Industrial Partners	244	PE	North America, potential global reach	30	100	10	50
Antares Capital Corporation	127	VC	Southeast, Texas	2	1	.5	2
Antares Capital Corporation	258	CF	USA	30	75	15	200
AP Capital Partners	250	PE	Mid-Atlantic, Asia, Southeast, Northeast, USA	10		1	10
Appian Holdings	139	PE	North America	5	20		75
ARCH Development Partners	493	VC	Midwest		.5	.25	2
ArcHelion Capital Partners	345	IN	Northeast, Florida				2.0
Arcturus Capital	455	VC	West Coast				
Argosy Partners	349	PE	Mid-Atlantic, Southeast, Northeast	10	2–4	1	5
Arsenal Capital Partners	292	PE	USA		75–125	10	100
Artisan Capital	156	PE	USA	10	5	10	50
AsiaVest Partners, TCW/YFY	400	PE	Asia, USA		5	5	20
Astorg Partners	224	PE	Europe	40	100	1	60
Austin Capital Partners, L.P.	153	PE	Midwest	8	1–3	.5	4
Autumn Hill Capital Group, LLC	236	PE	Europe, USA	3	5–25	.75	20
Avocet Ventures, LLC	114	PE	West Coast, Midwest, Southeast				
BA Capital Partners Europe	422	PE	Europe		25	15	75
Baird Capital Partners	280	MB	Midwest, Southeast	15	20–60	5	25
Baird Venture Partners	278	VC	Midwest, Southeast	0	5–15	2	5
Bank of the West	472	BN	West Coast		10	2	50
Baring Private Equity Partners	523	PE	Europe			1	15
Baring Private Equity Partners Asia	409	PE	Asia	50	15	10	25

	No.						
Baxter Capital Corporation	125	LC	USA	2.1	1.5	1	5
BayTech Venture Capital	387	VC	Europe			0.5	5
BB&T Capital Partners	132	PE	Mid-Atlantic, Midwest, Southeast, Northeast			2	12
Behrman Capital	425	PE	North America, USA	10	200	25	100
Berkshire Partners LLC	184	PE	North America, Europe, USA	40		30	250
BFI Business Finance, Inc.	363	AB	West Coast	50	2	None	4
Biofrontier Partners USA	459	VC	West Coast, Asia, Northeast		3	5	6
Birchmere Capital LP	268	PE	Mid-Atlantic		1.5–3.0	1	4
Bi-State Investment Group	519	AI	Kansas City region				
Blue Point Capital Partners	266	PE	North America	25	75	10	60
Blue Sage Capital	160	PE	Southwest	5	10	2	12
Boston Millennia Partners	115	PE	USA	1	5	1	30
BP Marsh Private Equity	381	VC	North America, Europe, USA		1	4	5
Bridge Street Capital Partners, LLC	348	PE	Midwest			2.5	7.5
Brook Venture Fund	328	VC	Northeast	.5	2.5	1	4
Brookside Capital Partners	152	PE	USA	20	5	3	7.5
Brookstone Partners	274	PE	Mid-Atlantic, Midwest, Southeast, Northeast	10	5–10	3	15
Business Alliance Capital Corp.	553	AB	USA	2.0	3.0	0.3	7.5
C3 Capital Partners	196	PE	Midwest		4	2	8
Caledonian Private Equity Partners, LLC	375	PE	Europe, USA	10	30	1.5	25
Callidus Capital Corporation	140	AB	Northeast, Canada				
Catius Mezzanine Partners	468	PE	USA	20	10	5	30
Calvert Street Capital Partners	118	PE	USA		30	3	25
Cambridge Capital Partners LLC	233	PE	USA	10	30	5	20
Candover Investments Plc	421	PE	Europe		150	0	500
Canterbury Capital Partners	173	PE	USA	30	15	5	30
Capital Equipment Leasing	253	LC	USA		.25	.01	
Capital Investments	116	VC	Southwest, North America				
Capital TempFunds, Inc.	503	AB	USA	1	1	1	10
CapitalSource Finance LLC	191	CF	USA	10	20–30	5	50
CapitalWerks, LLC	267	LC	USA		0.5–1.0	.025	10
Cardinal Capital Partners	320	CF	Europe, USA		25	2	1,000
Castanea Partners	550	PE	USA, Canada			10.0	20.0+
Caymus Partners LLC	492	MB	USA				
CEI Community Ventures	307	VC	ME, NH, VT, MA		25	5	100
Centerfield Capital Partners	346	PE	Midwest	5	.35	.25	.25
Centre Partners Management LLC	399	PE	North America	50	2–3	1	4
Century Park Capital Partners, LP	207	PE	West Coast	20	150	10	70
Champlain Capital	530	PE	USA		40	5	15
Charlesbank Capital Partners, LLC	343	PE	USA, Canada		50	15	75

(Continued)

Master List by Firm with Summary Criteria (Continued)

($ millions)

Firm	Database ID	Type	Geographic Preference	Minimum Revenue	Typical Deal Size	Minimum Funding	Maximum Funding
Charlotte Angel Partners	330	VC	Carolinas		.4	.2	.5
Charter One Bank, N.A.	241	BN	Midwest, Northeast	5	5	1	25
Chatham Capital	322	CF	USA	10	5	1.5	25
CHB Capital Partners	395	PE	USA	15		3	15
Cherry Tree Investments, Inc.	447	PE	Midwest		1.5	.5	2
CID Equity Partners	238	PE	USA	20	6	2	10
CIVC Partners	208	PE	North America, USA	40	50	15	125
CL Fund	362	AI	Western PA		0.3	0.1	0.5
Clairvest Group Inc.	239	MB	North America	20	15	10	20
Code Hennessy & Simmons LLC	384	PE	USA		200	25	100
Comerica Bank, Technology & Life Sciences Division	350	BN	Mid-Atlantic		3		
Complete Leasing Corporation	465	LC	USA		2.	1	25
Concord Ventures	490	VC	Israel		3	1	10
Convergent Capital Partners	249	PE	USA	10	3.5	1	7
Cornerstone Capital Advisors, Ltd.	283	PE	Midwest, Northeast				
Crescent Capital Investments, Inc.	367	PE	Europe, USA	20	120	30	110
Crescent State Bank	270	BN	Mid-Atlantic				
Cross Atlantic Partners, Inc.	385	VC	USA				
CrossBridge Venture Partners	464	VC	Asia, USA		5.0	3.5	7
CSG Investments, Inc.	347	CF	North America, USA, South America		.5	.1	1
Davis, Tuttle Venture Partners, LP	323	PE	West Coast, Southwest, Midwest		50	5	200
DeltaPoint Capital Management, LLC	403	PE	New York State	5	5–20	1	12
Desert Angels	329	AI	Southwest	0	0.5	0.2	0.7
Deutsche Effecten- und Wechsel- Beteiligungsgesellschaft AG	437	VC	Europe			2	6
Diamondhead Ventures	315	VC	USA			0.5	5.0
Dorset Capital Management	423	PE	USA	20	3.	3	5
Drug Royalty Corporation Inc.	128	SI	North America, Asia, Europe		20	5	10
Dubin Clark & Company, Inc.	126	PE	North America	15	40	5	50
Dunedin Capital Partners Limited	404	PE	UK		15	5	25
DW Healthcare Partners	454	PE	USA		15	6	40
E*Capital Corporation	133	PE	West Coast, USA		5	3	7
Eastern Technology Fund	440	VC	Mid-Atlantic				3
Edelson Technology Partners	130	VC			21		
Edgeview Partners	436	MB	USA		70		
Edison Venture Fund	107	VC	Mid-Atlantic	4.5	3.5	2.5	8
Emigrant Capital Corporation	286	PE	USA	15	20	2	20

Firm	No.	Type		Geographic Focus			
Englefield Capital LLP	254	PE		Europe	50	20	100
Enterprise Corporation of the Delta	335	CF		Southeast	0.2	0.05	1.5
EonTech Ventures SA	380	VC		Europe	1.5	.5	3
Essex Woodlands Health Ventures	129	PE	10	USA	10	5	15
Eureka Growth Capital	269	PE		Mid-Atlantic, Midwest, Southeast, Northeast	5	3	8
Exeter Capital Partners	374	PE		USA	3	.5	5
FA Technology Ventures	551	VC		Northeast	4.0	3.0	8.0
Falcon Fund	529	VC	0	Southwest			
FdG Associates	361	PE		North America	60–100	15	50
First Advisors, Inc.	383	AI	1	Texas	5	.1	1
FirstFloor Capital	391	PE		Asia, Southeast Asia focus	1	.25	2.5
Florida Capital Partners, Inc.	163	PE	10	USA	20	3	15
Founders Equity Inc.	145	PE		USA			
Four J Funding	528	CF	25	USA	2–20	.5	100
Franklin Street Equity Partners, Inc.	390	PE		North America	40	3	25
Friend Capital Funding, LLC	112	AB		USA, global	.150	.01	10
Frontier Capital	123	VC	2	Mid-Atlantic, Southeast	1.5	1	3
FSN Capital Partners AS	379	PE		Europe, Scandinavia			
Funk Ventures	171	VC		West Coast, USA	2.5	1	5
gcp gamma capital partners	386	VC	0	Europe	1.5	.5	3
GE Commercial Finance	282	CF		Europe, USA	35	10	1,000
GE Corporate Financial Services	217	AB		USA		5	30+
Generics Asset Management Ltd	541	VC	10	Europe, USA	1	0.5	5
Genesis Campus	547	VC		USA	2.0	0.5	3.0
Geneva Venture Partners	170	VC		West Coast, Europe	1.5–2.5	1	5
Giza Venture Capital	366	VC		Israel-related	3	3	7
Gladstone Capital Corporation	256	MB	10	North America, Europe, USA	10	3	15
Gleacher Mezzanine LLC	168	PE		North America, Europe, USA	15	5	30
Global Catalyst Partners	467	VC		North America, Europe, USA, South America		3	10
Global Strategy & Capital Group	407	MB		USA			
GMB Mezzanine Capital	301	PE		USA	75	1	10
Goense Bounds & Partners	148	MB		USA	8	10	40
Golub Associates Incorporated	294	PE	20	USA	75	4	25
Graham Partners, Inc.	182	PE		North America, Europe	5	5	30
GrandBanks Capital	219	VC		Mid-Atlantic, Southeast, Northeast, Europe, Canada	.25	1	12
Great Lakes Angels, Inc.	509	AI	1	Midwest		.05	6
Greenfield Commercial Credit	188	AB		USA		.1	6.5
Gresham Private Equity Limited	524	PE	20	Australia, New Zealand	20	A20	A60
Grey Mountain Partners, LLC	228	PE	10	USA	7	5	20
Greyrock Capital Group	166	PE		USA		3	10

(Continued)

Master List by Firm with Summary Criteria (Continued)

($ millions)

Firm	Database ID	Type	Geographic Preference	Minimum Revenue	Typical Deal Size	Minimum Funding	Maximum Funding
GrowthWorks Capital Ltd.	434	VC	Canada	0	3	.5	10
Guide Ventures, LLC	176	VC	West Coast			.5	10
H. Katz Capital Group	481	PE	Europe, USA		1.5	.5	10
H.I.G. Capital, LLC	332	PE	USA	5		5	10
Halyard Capital Fund	119	PE	North America, Europe, USA				
Hamilton Robinson LLC	478	PE	Mid-Atlantic, Midwest, Southeast, Northeast, USA		15–25	5	30
Hammond Kennedy Whitney & Co., Inc.	147	PE	USA	10		2	20
Harbert Management Corporation—Mezzanine Capital	299	PE	USA	20	5	2	10
Harbert Management Corporation—Venture Partners	309	VC	Mid-Atlantic, Southeast	10	2	3	12
Harbour Group	491	PE	North America			10	7.5
Hartsko Financial Services, LLC	489	AB	Asia, Europe, USA	40	125	1	100
Hastings Equity Partners	317	PE	USA		.5	.05	4
HBM BioVentures Ltd.	471	PE	North America, Europe	3	10	2	5
Healthcare Finance Group, Inc.	502	AB	USA		10	5	40
High Street Capital	475	PE	USA	25	25	5	150
Highland Capital Partners	336	VC	Europe, USA	10		1	10
Hilco Capital LP	227	AB	USA			.1	50
HLHZ Investments, LLC	543	PE	North America, Europe		10	4	50
Hopewell Ventures	398	VC	Midwest		25		10
Horizon Ventures	331	VC	CA, AZ		2.5	1	5+
HSBC Capital	517	PE	USA	10	3	1	5
Hunt Special Situations Group, L.P.	300	PE	USA	20		2	15
Huron Capital Partners, LLC	453	PE	North America, USA	5		5	15
Hyde Park Capital Partners, LLC	108	MB	USA		30	4	20
IDG Ventures Europe	169	VC	Europe		25–250		
IIG Capital LLC	394	CF	Europe, USA, worldwide but OECD country risk	6–12	3	1	8
Imperial Capital Corporation	324	MB	North America, USA	50	7–10	2	30
Infineon Ventures GmbH	497	VC			50	10	
Infocomm Investments Pte Ltd	520	PE	Asia, USA		2–3	1	5
InnovationsKapital	371	VC	Europe, Nordic area			0.5	5
Intersouth Partners	106	VC	Mid-Atlantic, Southeast				
Invest Mezzanine Capital Management GmbH	149	PE	Europe	12	0.5–5	2.5	6.3
ITF Global Partners	177	SI	USA		3.3	4+	
J D Factors	505	CF	North America		.1	.005	2
J&D Financial Corporation	542	CF	North America, Europe, USA		.1/mnth	.01/mnth	4/mnth

Firm		Type	Region				
Kachi Partners	161	PE	Southwest, Midwest, Rocky Mountain states			1.5	3.0
Kasten Group, LLC	511	PE	USA	5	10–15	5	25
Key Principal Partners	117	PE	USA	25		3	10
Key Venture Partners	120	VC	USA	3	5	0.05	None
King Trade Capital	508	AB	Other, USA, Canada	25		10	75
Kirtland Capital Partners	150	PE	Mid-Atlantic, Midwest, Southeast, Northeast	5	50	3	15
Kline Hawkes & Co	450	PE	West Coast, Northeast, USA	25		5	
KRG Capital Partners	388	PE	USA			.5	4
L&L Capital Partners	135	PE	North America			.2	2
Leo Capital Holdings, LLC	426	VC	USA	0	1.5	0.25	5
Lighthouse Venture Partners, LLC	521	VC	Southeast	0	2.5	5	2.0
Limburg Ventures BV	414	VC	Europe, Meuse Rhine Euro region		1.0	10	75
Lincolnshire Management	164	PE	North America, USA	30	125	7	40
Lineage Capital	289	PE	North America, USA	20		1	40
Linsalata Capital Partners	279	PE	North America			5	
Linx Partners, LLC	165	PE	Mid-Atlantic, Southeast, Northeast	20		10	10
LogiSpring	378	VC	North America, Europe		5	5	40
Lombard Investments, Inc.	288	PE	North America, Asia	25	25	2	30
Long Point Capital, Inc.	451	PE	USA		75	2	5
Longmeadow Capital, LLC	353	PE	Northeast		2	5	30
M&I Bank	341	BN	Southwest, Midwest	5		1	10
Main Street Capital Holdings LLC	340	PE	Mid-Atlantic, Midwest, Southeast, Northeast	15	10–15	1	15
Main Street Mezzanine Fund, LP	510	PE	USA		5–50	7	500
Mankwitz Kurtz Investments, LLC	198	PE	USA			2	100
Maple Commercial Finance Group	405	AB	North America, Europe, USA, Australia	12	45	10	10
Marquette Capital Partners, Inc.	327	PE	Midwest, USA	10	10–20	.25	10
Mayfield	122	VC	West Coast		2–5	5	75
McKenna Gale Capital Inc.	460	PE	Canada		3.5	2	10
MCM Capital Partners, L.P.	134	PE	USA	20	30	10	50
MedEquity Capital, LLC	337	PE	USA	10	40	.25	1
Mentor Capital Partners Ltd	187	VC	Mid-Atlantic, Northeast		15–20		5
Merion Investment Partners	178	PE	Mid-Atlantic, Southeast, Northeast	10	4–5		50
Merisel, Inc.	209	PE	USA				35
Merit Capital Partners, LLC	194	PE	USA	20	25		10
Meritage Private Equity Funds	200	PE	USA		20		
Meritum Partners, LLC	303	PE	North America		7		
Meriwether Capital, L.L.C.	433	IN	Mid-Atlantic, Northeast	25	6 equity	3 equity	10 equity
Metapoint Partners	408	PE	Mid-Atlantic, Midwest, Southeast, Northeast	8	10	.5	5

(Continued)

Master List by Firm with Summary Criteria (*Continued*)

($ millions)

Firm	Database ID	Type	Geographic Preference	Minimum Revenue	Typical Deal Size	Minimum Funding	Maximum Funding
Midwest Mezzanine Funds	287	PE	USA	20	8	5	15
Milestone Merchant Partners, LLC	121	MB	Mid-Atlantic, Southeast, Northeast, USA	20		1	20
Mofet Venture Capital Fund	412	VC	West Coast, North America, Northeast, USA		5	0.1	2
Mohr Davidow Ventures	243	VC	West Coast, Mid-Atlantic, USA		3–5	.25	10
Monumental Venture Partners, LLC	462	VC	Mid-Atlantic			0.5	3
Morgenthaler	272	PE	North America	25	80	10	85
Mountaineer Capital	397	VC	Mid-Atlantic, Midwest, Southeast, West Virginia	10	1	0.5	2
MTI Partners Limited	469	VC	Europe	0	5	2	15
Murex Investments I, L.P.	444	VC	Mid-Atlantic	.4	.5	.1	1
Najeti Ventures LLC	501	PE	Mid-Atlantic, Midwest, Southeast, Northeast			2	7
National City Equity Partners, LLC	483	PE	North America		10	3	20
Nautic Partners, LLC	174	PE	North America, Europe, USA	50	40	25	75
Navigator Equity Partners	357	PE	Mid-Atlantic, Northeast	10		2	5
Navis Capital Partners Limited	410	PE	Asia	20	15	3	30
Net Partners	263	VC	West Coast, Europe		4	2	
New Mexico Private Investors, Inc	325	PE	Southwest		.5	.1	1
New Mountain Capital	141	PE	North America	50	100	50	200
New York City Investment Fund	365	VC	New York City only		.75–1.0	.25	4
NewCastle Partners LLC	240	PE	USA			21	0
Newhaven Corporate Finance Limited	370	MB	North America	20	25	10	50
NewWest Mezzanine Fund LP	189	PE	Rocky Mountain region	5	2	.5	3
Next Step Advisors	482	SI	West Coast, Southwest	0.1			
North Atlantic Capital	452	VC	Mid-Atlantic, Northeast	3	3	3	10
Northern Illinois Angels LLC	314	AI	Midwest				
Northwood Ventures	432	PE	Europe, USA	0	4	2	5
Norvest Capital Partners Inc.	473	PE	Canada	20	4	2	10
Novo A/S	199	VC	North America, Europe, USA		0.5–10	0.5	10
Olive Capital LLC	204	MB	North America, Europe, USA, Middle East		40		
Orix Financial	154	LC	USA	10	1–2.5	.5	10
Outlook Ventures	326	VC	West Coast		2	0.5	5
Overseas Private Investment Corporation	295	GOV	New and emerging markets			0.1	250
Oxford Investment Group	186	PE	Asia, Europe, USA	10		2	20
Pacific Corporate Group LLC	225	PE	North America	75	50	10	200
Pacific Horizon Ventures	201	VC	West Coast, Pacific Northwest region		.25–10	.25	2.5
Paragon Financial Group, Inc.	214	AB	USA		.25		1
Parthenon Capital	190	PE	North America	75	30–50	20	100
Peachtree Equity Partners	487	PE	Mid-Atlantic, Midwest, Southeast, USA	20	8	5	15
Peterson Partners	498	PE	West Coast, Midwest	8	20	2	10

Pfingsten Partners, L.L.C.	488	PE	Mid-Atlantic, Midwest	25	10	3	15
Pine Creek Partners	474	PE	Mid-Atlantic, Northeast, Eastern U.S.		1–12	.1	15
Platinum Funding Corp	167	AB	USA	1	20	5	25
PNC Business Credit	255	AB	West Coast	20	30	5	15
Pouschine Cook Capital Management, LLC	456	PE	USA	15	10	5	15
Primus Venture Partners, Inc.	175	VC	USA		5	2	8
Prism Mezzanine Fund SBIC, L.P.	522	PE	Midwest	10	.5	.25	1
Private Investors Forum	313	AI	Mid-Atlantic, Northeast				4
PRIVEQ Capital Partners	234	PE	Other, USA, Canada	5	2–3	1	7
Prometheus V, LLC	358	PE	USA		15	3	10
Prudent Capital	479	PE	Mid-Atlantic, Northeast	5	3	1	5
PS Capital Partners, LLC	197	PE	Midwest	5	10		
Quad-C Management	531	PE	Europe, USA		150		
QuestMark Partners	420	VC	USA	4–5	30	5	15+
RAI Group	526	AB	USA		2–5	.5	50
RAI Group—Private Label Credit Cards	527	CF	USA		2–5	2	100
Research Triangle Ventures	296	VC	Southeast		1–3	.2	.6
Riordan, Lewis & Haden	485	PE	West Coast	15		5.0	15
River Associates Investments, LLC	536	PE	North America	10	10–15	1	10
River Capital	342	PE	Southwest, Mid-Atlantic, Midwest, Southeast	10	25	3	10
River Cities Capital Funds	277	VC	Midwest, Southeast	1	3	1	10
Riverlake Partners	284	PE	West Coast, Asia, Midwest, Western Canada			2.5	10
Roark Capital Group	512	PE	USA		50	15	75
Robin Hood Ventures	352	AI	Mid-Atlantic		.25–.5	.25	.5
Rockland Credit Finance LLC	506	CF		1	3	0.1	7
RockWood Equity Partners LLC	151	PE	USA	10	15	1	5
Rocky Mountain Capital Partners	257	PE	USA	10	5	3	10
RoundTable Healthcare Partners	431	PE	North America, Europe, USA		30–50	5	70
Royal Bank Asset Based Finance	144	AB	Mid-Atlantic, Southeast, Canada	5	2–25	1	50
Roynat Capital	470	MB	North America	20	5	2.5	10
Salem Capital Partners, LP	333	VC	Mid-Atlantic, Southeast, Northeast	3	1.5	.750	3
Salix Ventures	334	VC	USA	2	3	2	6
Sand Hill Angels, LLC	311	AI	West Coast			1	5
Saw Mill Capital	216	PE	North America, Europe, USA		.25	10	100
SBV Venture Partners	435	VC	West Coast		2		
Scope	411	VC	Europe			0.5	3
Scottish Equity Partners	306	VC	UK & Ireland			0.9	8.8

(Continued)

Master List by Firm with Summary Criteria (*Continued*)

Firm	Database ID	Type	Geographic Preference	Minimum Revenue	Typical Deal Size	Minimum Funding	Maximum Funding
					($ millions)		
SCP Private Equity Partners	344	VC	USA	7	5–10		
Seaport Capital	185	PE	USA		15	5	40
Security Technology Ventures, LLC	138	VC	USA				
Siemens Financial Services, Inc.	265	AB	USA, Canada			.3	25
Siemens Venture Capital GmbH	382	SI	North America, Europe, Israel			.5 euro	5 euro
Sierra Ventures	369	VC	USA	2	5	3	25
SilkRoad Equity, Inc.	261	PE	North America, Midwest, Southeast, Europe				
SJF Ventures	124	VC	Mid-Atlantic, Midwest, Southeast, Northeast	.5	.75	.5	1.7
SOFINNOVA Partners	264	VC	Europe			.5	15
Southern Appalachian Management Company, LLC	372	VC	Southeast, Southern Appalachia	.1	1	.25	.75
SouthPointe Ventures, LLC	273	PE	Mid-Atlantic, Southeast	5	6	.5	1
Southwest Value Acquisitions LLC	533	PE	West Coast, Southwest	2	5 Rev	.25	5
Sovereign Capital Limited	368	PE	UK only		36.4	9.1	27.3
SpaceVest	355	VC	USA		15	1	6
STAG Capital Partners	552	AB	USA		10	5	25
Standard Federal Bank	507	AB	Midwest, USA	8	3	1	100
StarVest Partners, L.P.	494	VC	North America, USA			2	4
State Bank	504	AB	Southeast			.5	5
Steel Capital Corp.	210	PE	North America, Asia, Europe		1.5	.5	5
Sterling Venture Partners	441	PE	Mid-Atlantic, Midwest, USA		50	3	100
StoneCreek Capital	285	PE	West Coast, USA	10	35	5	15
Summer Street Capital Partners LLC	159	PE	Mid-Atlantic, Midwest, Southeast, Northeast	20	4	5	50
Summit Partners	486	PE	North America, Europe, USA		41	2	10
Sustainable Development Fund	537	SI	Pennsylvania			.1	250
Synetro Capital—Synetro Capital Partners	143	PE	Midwest	8		1	5
Synetro Capital—Synetro Ventures (early stage)	142	VC	Midwest			1	5
Tailwind Capital Partners	213	PE	USA			.1	1
Talisman Capital Fund I, LLC	248	PE	USA	10	50	25	125
Tech Capital Partners Inc.	429	VC	Southwestern Ontario		1.5	.5	4.5
Tech Coast Angels	500	AI	West Coast		.5	.25	1.5
Tech Strategies	221	MB	North America	5	5	1	60
TechStock	446	IN	Asia, USA	0		1	10
Telos Venture Partners	516	VC	West Coast		5	1	3
Terra Firma Capital Partners Ltd	290	PE	Europe		400	150	500
The Aurora Funds	109	VC	Southeast, USA			.05	2
The CapStreet Group, LLC	293	PE	Southwest, Southeast	50	100	15	50
The Legacy Equity Group LLC	136	MB	USA		25–250		

The Oxford Investment Group	246	PE	Midwest, Europe, USA	10	45	7	70
The Riverside Company	212	PE	North America, Europe	20	30–40	20	60
The Shansby Group	476	PE	USA	20	30	10	60
Thoma Cressey Equity Partners	181	PE	North America	25	5–6	3	8
Thomas Weisel Healthcare Venture Partners	495	MB	North America, USA	0		1	15
Thomas Weisel Venture Partners	359	VC	West Coast, Northeast		2–10	22	0
Thomas, McNerney & Partners	463	VC	USA			10	30
Thompson Street Capital Partners	202	PE	North America		50		20
Three Arch Partners	276	VC	USA		51		
Thrive Capital Partners	172	PE	West Coast	6	7	3	12
Torquest Partners	281	PE	North America				
Transcap Trade Finance	113	AB	North America		3	0.5	10
Transpac Capital	424	PE	Asia		81		60
TRF Private Equity	538	PE	Mid-Atlantic	2.5	2.5	1	4
Trident Growth Fund, LP	321	PE	Southwest, Southeast	5	1.5	1	2
Tri-State Investment Group	312	AI	Carolinas and Virginia	0	.25	.150	.35
Tri-State Private Investors Network	439	AI	North America	0	.5–1.0	.25	2
Triton Pacific Capital Partners, LLC	406	PE	USA	5	2–10 equity		
Triton Ventures	229	VC	Southwest				
Trivest Partners, L.P.	192	PE	USA	20	30–250	5	45
TriWest Capital Management Corp	396	PE	West Coast, Midwest, Canada		8	3	25
Tuckerman Capital	302	PE	USA	5	10	5.0	25
U.S. Bank Business Credit	237	AB	North America		15	5	150
United Capital Funding Corp.	484	AB	North America, Europe, USA		.1		2
Vencon Management Inc.	146	VC	Europe, USA, West Asia				
Venture Capital Solutions, LP	110	PE	Southeast	3	1.5	1	2
Ventures West Management Inc.	275	VC	Canada				
Venturis	232	PE	Europe, Netherlands	10			
Veronis Suhler Stevenson	230	MB	North America, Europe, USA		<500M	25	
Vested for Growth	308	SI	NH		.35	.1	.5
W. P. Carey & Co. LLC	513	CF	North America, Europe, USA		50	5	500
Wafra Partners LLC	179	PE	North America, USA, Caribbean		40	5	40
Wales Fund Managers Limited	419	VC	Wales, UK		£.275	£.05	£1
Walker Ventures	226	VC	Mid-Atlantic				
Warwick Group, Inc.	193	PE	USA	10	10–50	2	20
Washington Mutual Equipment Finance	251	BN	USA	10	.75–2.5	.25	15
Wells Fargo Business Credit, Inc.	242	AB	USA	10	<10	2	25

(Continued)

Master List by Firm with Summary Criteria (*Continued*)

($ millions)

Firm	Database ID	Type	Geographic Preference	Minimum Revenue	Typical Deal Size	Minimum Funding	Maximum Funding
Westar Capital	514	PE	North America				
Westgate Financial Corp.	235	AB	North America, USA				
Windjammer Capital Investors	297	PE	North America, USA	50	20	10	60
Wingate Partners	180	PE	USA	40	50	5	20
Wisconsin Rural Enterprise Fund, LLC	364	VC	Midwest		.1	.02	.2
Wynnchurch Capital	318	PE	North America, USA		7.5	4	25
Yale Capital, Inc.	111	AB	NY, NJ, & CT only			.05	5
Yaletown Venture Partners Inc.	393	VC	West Coast		1.0	0.5	2.5
York Street Capital Partners	158	PE	USA		10–20	10	100
Zenith Capital Partners LLC	211	PE	North America, USA	10	50	1	50
Zon Capital Partners LP	518	VC	Mid-Atlantic			12	
ZS Fund L.P.	245	PE	North America				

Corporate Finance Primer

This appendix is a summary of the work from Aswath Damodaran's book *Applied Corporate Finance* (John Wiley & Sons, 1999). Readers who want to expand their understanding of Damodaran's book may want to obtain a copy for reference.

Damodaran starts his text with a confession of a few of his biases. He believes that theory, and the models that flow from it, should provide us with the tools to understand, analyze, and solve problems. The test of a model or theory then should not be based on its elegance, but upon its usefulness in problem solving. Second, in his view, the core principles of corporate finance are common sense ones, and have changed little over time. That should not be surprising. Corporate finance, as a discipline, is only a few decades old, while people have been running businesses for thousands of years. It would be exceedingly presumptuous of us to believe that they were in the dark until corporate theorists came along and told them what to do.

His book tells a story, which essentially summarizes the corporate finance view of the world. It classifies all decisions made by any business into three groups (see Figure A.1)—decisions on where to invest the resources of funds that the business has raised (the investment decision), decisions on where and how to raise funds to finance these investments (the financing decision), and decisions on how much and in what form to return funds back to the owners (the dividend decision). The authors of this handbook are in sync with his views and accordingly have chosen to provide the following as a corporate finance primer.

THE FOUNDATIONS[1]

Every decision that a business makes has financial implications, and any decision which affects the finance of a business is a corporate finance decision.

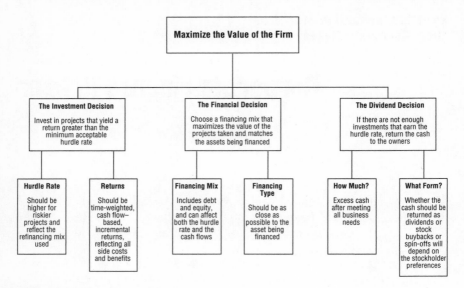

FIGURE A.1 Three Decisions
Source: Aswath Damodaran, *Applied Corporate Finance*, John Wiley & Sons, 1999.

Defined broadly, everything that a business does fits under the rubric of corporate finance. It is, in fact, unfortunate that we even call it corporate finance, since it suggests to many observers a focus on how large corporations make financial decisions, and seems to exclude small and private business from its purview. A more appropriate title might be business finance, since the basic principles remain the same whether one looks at large publicly traded firms or small privately run businesses. All businesses have to invest their resources wisely, find a good mix of financing to make these investments, and return cash to the owners if there are not enough good investments. . . .

The Objective Function of the Firm

No discipline can develop cohesively over time without a unifying objective function. The growth of corporate financial theory can be traced to its choice of a single objective function and its development of models built around this function. *The objective in conventional corporate financial theory is to maximize firm value.* Consequently, any decision (investment, financial, or dividend) that increases firm value is considered a good one, whereas one that reduces firm value is considered a poor one. . . .

Some Fundamental Propositions about Corporate Finance

First, *corporate finance has an internal consistency* that flows from its choice of maximizing firm value as the only objective function and its dependence on a few bedrock principles:

- Risk has to be rewarded.
- Cash flows matter more than accounting income measures.
- Markets are not easily fooled.
- Every decision a firm makes has an effect on its value.

Second, *corporate finance must be viewed as an integrated whole*, rather than as a collection of decisions. Investment decisions generally affect financing decisions, and vice versa; financing decisions generally affect dividend decisions, and vice versa. While there are circumstances under which these decisions may be independent of each other, this is seldom the case. Accordingly, it is unlikely that firms that deal with their problems on a piecemeal basis will ever resolve these problems. For instance, a firm that believes that it has a dividend problem and just cuts dividends may experience consequences for its financing and investment decisions.

Third, *corporate finance matters to everybody*. There is a corporate financial aspect to almost every decision made by a business; while not everyone will find a use for all the components of corporate finance, everyone will find a use for at least some *part* of it.

Fourth, *corporate finance is fun*. This may seem to be the tallest claim of all. After all, most people associate corporate finance with numbers and accounting statements and hardheaded analysis. While corporate finance is quantitative in its focus, there is a significant component of creative thinking involved in coming up with solutions to the financial problems business may encounter. It is no coincidence that financial markets remain the breeding grounds for innovation and change.

Finally, *the best way to learn corporate finance is by applying its models and theories*. While the body of theory that has been developed over the past few decades is impressive, the ultimate test of any theory is in applications. As we show in this book, much, if not all, of the theory can be applied to real companies and not just to abstract examples. . . .

THE CLASSICAL OBJECTIVE FUNCTION[2]

There is general agreement, at least among corporate finance theorists, that the objective of the firm is to maximize value or wealth. There is some disagreement on whether the objective is to maximize the wealth of stockholders or the wealth of the firm, which includes, besides stockholders, the other financial claim holders (debt holders, preferred stockholders, etc.). Furthermore, even among those who argue for stockholder wealth maximization, there is a debate about whether this translates into maximizing the stock price.

These objective functions vary in terms of the assumptions needed to justify them. The least restrictive of the three objectives, in terms of assumptions needed, is to maximize the firm value, and the most restrictive is to maximize the stock price.

Potential Side Costs of Wealth Maximization

If the only objective in decision making is to maximize firm or stockholder wealth, there is a potential for substantial side costs to society that may drown out the benefits from wealth maximization. To the extent that these costs are large relative to the wealth created by the firm, the objective function may have to be modified to allow for these costs. To be fair, however, this is a problem that is likely to persist even if an alternative objective function is used.

The objective of wealth maximization may also face obstacles when there is separation of ownership and management, as there is in most large public corporations. When managers act as agents for the owners (stockholders), there is the potential for a conflict of interest between stockholder and managerial interests, which in turn can lead to decision rules that do not maximize stockholder or firm wealth, but maximize managerial utility.

When the objective function is stated in terms of stockholder wealth, the conflicting interests of stockholders and bondholders have to be reconciled. Since stockholders usually control decision making and bondholders are not completely protected, one way of maximizing stockholder wealth is to take actions that expropriate wealth from the bondholders, even though such actions may reduce the wealth of the firm.

Finally, when the objective function is narrowed further to one of maximizing stock price, inefficiencies in the financial markets may lead to misallocation of resources and bad decisions. For instance, if stock prices do not reflect the long-term consequences of decisions, but respond, as some critics say, to short-term earnings effects, a decision that increases stockholder wealth may reduce the stock price. Conversely, a decision that reduces stockholder wealth, but creates earnings increases in the near term, may increase the stock price. . . .

The Firm and Financial Markets

There is an advantage to maintaining an objective function that focuses on stockholder or firm wealth, rather than stock prices or the market value of the firm, since it does not require any assumptions about the efficiency or otherwise of financial markets. The downside, however, is that stockholder or firm wealth is not easily measurable, making it difficult to establish clear standards for success and failure. . . . Since an essential characteristic of a good objective function is that it comes with a clear and unambiguous measurement mechanism, the advantages of shifting to an objective function that focuses on market prices are obvious. The measure of success or failure is there for all to see. A successful manager raises the firm's stock price, and an unsuccessful one reduces it.

The trouble with market prices, of course, is that they are set by financial markets. To the extent that financial markets are efficient and use the information that is available to make measured and unbiased estimates of future cash flows and risk, market prices will reflect true value. In such markets, both the measurers and the measured will accept the market price as the appropriate mechanism for judging success and failure.

There are two potential barriers to this. The first is that information is the lubricant that enables markets to be efficient. To the extent that this information is hidden, delayed, or misleading, market prices will deviate from true value, even in an otherwise efficient market. The second problem is that there are many, both in academia and in practice, who argue that markets are not efficient, even when information is freely available. In both cases, decisions that maximize stock prices may not be consistent with long-term value maximization.

The Investment Decision

Invest in projects that yield a return greater than the minimum acceptable hurdle rate.

- *Hurdle rate* should be higher for riskier projects and reflect the financing mix used.
- *Returns* should be time-weighted, cash flow–based, incremental returns, reflecting all side costs and benefits.

THE BASICS OF RISK[3]

Risk, in traditional terms, is viewed as a negative. A dictionary definition of risk, for instance, is "exposing to danger or hazard." The Chinese symbols for risk, reproduced in Figure A.2, give a much better description of risk.

FIGURE A.2   Chinese Symbols for Risk

The first symbol is for "danger," while the second symbol is for "opportunity," making risk a mix of danger and opportunity. It illustrates very clearly the trade-off that every investor and business has to make—between the "higher reward" that potentially comes with the opportunity and the "higher risk" that has to be borne as a consequence of the danger. The key test in finance is to ensure that when an investor is exposed to risk, he or she is appropriately rewarded for taking this risk. . . . Another view is that risk is the amount of potential variance from an expected outcome.

Ingredients for a Good Risk and Return Model

. . . It is worth reviewing the five characteristics of a good risk and return model.

1. It should come up with a measure of risk that applies to all assets and is not asset specific.
2. It should clearly delineate what types of risk are rewarded and what are not, and provide a rationale for the delineation.
3. It should come up with standardized risk measures; that is, an investor presented with a risk measure for an individual asset should be able to draw conclusions about whether the asset is above-average or below-average risk.
4. It should translate the measure of risk into a rate of return that the investor should demand as compensation for bearing the risk.
5. It should work well not only at explaining past returns, but also in predicting future expected returns.

Measuring Risk

Investors who buy assets have a return that they expect to make over the time horizon that they will hold the asset. The actual returns that they make over this holding period may be very different from the expected returns, and this is where the risk comes in. . . .

Rewarded and Unrewarded Risk

Risk, as we have defined it in the previous section, arises from the deviation of actual returns from expected returns. This deviation, however, can be caused by any number of reasons, and these reasons can be classified into two categories—those that are specific to the investment being considered (called firm-specific risks) and those that apply across all investments (market risks). . . .

The Components of Risk

The risk that a firm faces when it makes a new investment comes from a number of sources, including the investment itself, competition, shifts in the industry, international considerations, and macroeconomic factors. Some of the risk, however, will be eliminated by the firm itself over the course of multiple investments and some by investors in the firm as they hold diversified portfolios. . . . We think that risk cannot be eliminated but ameliorated.

- *Project risk.* This is risk that affects only the project under consideration and may arise from factors specific to the project or estimation error. . . . It also includes the risk of performance or execution.
- *Competitive risk.* This is the unanticipated effect on the cash flows in a project of competitor actions—these effects can be positive or negative. . . .
- *Industry-specific risk.* These are unanticipated effects on project cash flows of industry-wide shifts in technology, changes in law, or changes in the price of a commodity. . . .
- *International risk.* This is the additional uncertainty created in cash flows of projects by unanticipated changes in exchange rates and by political risk in foreign markets. . . .
- *Market risk.* Market risk refers to the unanticipated changes in project cash flows, created by changes in interest rates, inflation rates, and the economy, that affect all projects and all firms, though to differing degrees. . . .

Why Diversification Reduces or Eliminates Firm-Specific Risk

Diversification reduces, or at the limit, eliminates firm-specific risk for two reasons. The first is that each investment in a diversified portfolio is a much smaller percentage of that portfolio. Thus, any action that increases or reduces the value of only that investment or a small group of investments will have only a small impact in the overall portfolio. The second is that the effects of firm-specific actions on the prices of individual assets in a portfolio can be either positive or negative for each asset for any period. Thus, in large portfolios, it can be reasonably argued that this risk will average out to be zero and thus not impact the overall value of the portfolio.

In contrast, the effects of marketwide movements are likely to be in the same direction for most investments in a portfolio, though some assets may be affected more than others. For instance, other things been equal, an increase in interest rates will lower the value of most assets in a portfolio. Being more diversified does not eliminates the risk, though holding assets in different classes may reduce the impact. . . .

Fidelity Magellan Fund invests in a diversified portfolio of either growth stocks or value stocks. As a reference, note that in February 2004, overall portfolio composition was 95 percent in stocks. The top 10 holdings accounted for 28 percent of total assets, with the highest corporate stock investment at 4.6 percent of total assets. This mutual fund has always been diversified, similarly to the February 2004 investment mix.

Magellan diversification did not preclude the fund from the effects of the stock market downswing between third quarter 2000 and fourth quarter 2002. In this period, the fund unit value dropped from $140 to around $70.

Why Is the Marginal Investor Assumed to Be Diversified?

The argument that diversification reduces an investor's exposure to risk is not contested often, but risk and return models in finance go further. They argue that the marginal investor, who sets prices for investments, is well diversified; thus, the only risk that will be priced is the risk as perceived by the investor. The justification that can be offered is a simple one. The risk in an investment will always be perceived to be higher for an undiversified investor than for a diversified one, since the latter does not consider any firm-specific risks while the former does. If both investors have the same perceptions about future earnings and cash flows on an asset, the diversified investor will be willing to pay a higher price for that asset because of his or her risk perceptions. Consequently, the asset, over time, will end up being held by diversified investors.

While this argument is a powerful one for stocks and other assets, which are traded in small units and are liquid, it is less so for investments which are large and illiquid. Real estate in most countries is still held by investors who are undiversified and have the bulk of their wealth tied up in these investments. The benefits of diversification are strong enough, however, that securities such as real estate investment trusts and mortgage-backed bonds were created to allow investors to invest in real estate and stay diversified at the same time. . . .

Measuring Market Risk

While most risk and return models in use in corporate finance agree on the first two steps of this process (i.e., that risk comes from the distribution of actual returns around the expected return and that risk should be measured from the perspective of a marginal investor who is well diversified), they part ways on how to measure the nondiversifiable or market risk. In this section, we will provide a sense of how each of the four basic models— the capital asset pricing model (CAPM), the arbitrage pricing model (APM), the multifactor model, and the regression model—approaches the issue of measuring market risk.

The Capital Asset Pricing Model The risk and return model which has been in use the longest and is still the standard in most corporate financial analysis is the capital asset pricing model.

Assumptions While diversification has its attractions in terms of reducing the exposure of investors to firm-specific risk, most investors limit their diversification to holding a limited number of assets. Even large mutual funds are reluctant to hold more than a few hundred stocks, and many of them hold as few as 10 to 20 stocks. There are two reasons for this reluctance. The first is that the marginal benefits of diversification become smaller as the portfolio gets more diversified—the twenty-first asset added will generally provide a much smaller reduction in a firm-specific risk than the fifth asset added, and may not cover the marginal costs of diversification, which include transactions and monitoring costs. The second is that many investors (and funds) believe they can find undervalued assets and thus choose not to hold those assets that they believe to be correctly valued or overvalued.

The capital asset pricing model assumes that there are not transactions costs, that all assets are traded, and that investments are infinitely divisible (i.e., you can buy any fraction of a unit of the asset). It also assumes that there is no private information and that investors therefore cannot find under- or overvalued assets in the marketplace. By making these assumptions, it eliminates the factors that cause investors to stop diversifying. With these assumptions in place, the logical end limit of diversification is to hold all traded assets (stocks, bonds, and real assets included) in your portfolio, in proportion to their market value.[4] This portfolio of every traded asset in the marketplace is called the *market portfolio*.

Implications for Investors   If every investor in the market holds the identical market portfolios, how exactly do investors reflect their risk aversion in their investments? In the capital asset pricing model, investors adjust for their risk preferences in their allocation decision, where they decide how much to invest in a riskless asset and how much in the market portfolio, which is a portfolio of all traded risky assets. Investors who are risk averse might choose to put much or even all their wealth in the riskless asset. Investors who want to take more risk will invest the bulk or even all of their wealth in the market portfolio. Those investors who invest all their wealth in the market portfolio and are still desirous of taking on more risk, would do so by borrowing at the riskless rate and investing in the same market portfolio as everyone else.

These results are predicated on two additional assumptions. First, there exists a riskless asset, where expected returns are known with certainty. Second, investors can lend and borrow at the riskless rate to arrive at their optimal allocations. There are variations of the CAPM that allow these assumptions to be relaxed and still arrive at conclusions that are consistent with the model.

The Arbitrage Pricing Model   The restrictive assumptions in the capital asset pricing model and its dependence upon the market portfolio have long been viewed with skepticism by both academics and practitioners. In the late seventies, Ross (1976)[5] suggested an alternative model for measuring risk called the arbitrage pricing model.

Assumptions   The arbitrage pricing model (APM) is built on the simple premise that investors take advantage of arbitrage opportunities. In other words, if two portfolios have the same exposure to risk but offer different expected returns, investors will buy the portfolio that has the higher expected returns and in the process adjust the expected returns to equilibrium.

Like the capital asset pricing model, the arbitrage pricing model begins by breaking risk down into firm-specific and market risk components. The first, firm-specific, covers risk that affects primarily the firm. The second is the market risk that affects all investments, such as unanticipated changes in interest rates, inflation, or other macroeconomic variables. . . .

The Sources of Market Risk While both the capital asset pricing model and the arbitrage pricing model make a distinction between firm-specific and marketwide risk, they part ways when it comes to measuring the market risk. The CAPM assumes that the market risk is captured in the market portfolio, whereas the arbitrage pricing model sticks with economic fundamentals, allowing for multiple sources of marketwide risk, such as unanticipated changes in gross national product, interest rates, and inflation, and measures the sensitivity of investments to these changes with factor betas.[6]

The Effects of Diversification The benefits of diversification have been discussed in our treatment of the capital asset pricing model. The primary point of that discussion was that diversification of investments into portfolio eliminates firm-specific risk. The arbitrage pricing model makes the same point and concludes that the return on a portfolio will not have a firm-specific component of unanticipated returns. . . .

Expected Returns and Betas The fact that the beta of a portfolio is the weighted average of the betas of the assets in the portfolio, in conjunction with the absence of arbitrage, leads to the conclusion that expected returns should be linearly related to the betas. . . .

The APM in Practice The arbitrage pricing model requires estimates of each of the factor betas and factor risk premiums in addition to the riskless rate. In practice, these are usually estimated using historical data on returns on assets and a so-called factor analysis. Intuitively, a factor analysis examines the historical data looking for common patterns that affect broad groups of assets (rather than just one sector or a few assets). . . .

Multifactor Models for Risk and Returns The arbitrage pricing model's failure to identify specifically the factors in the model may be a strength from a statistical standpoint, bur it is a clear weakness from an intuitive standpoint. The solution seems simple: Replace the unidentified statistical factors with specific economic factors, and the resultant model should be intuitive while still retaining much of the strength of the arbitrage pricing model. That is precisely what multifactor models do. . . .

Regression Models   All of the models described so far begin by thinking about market risk in broad intuitive terms and then developing economic models that might best explain this market risk. All of them, however, extract their parameters by looking at historical data. There is a final class of risk and return models that start with the returns and work backwards to a risk and return model by trying to explain differences in returns across long time periods using firm characteristics such as the size of the firm and its price multiples. These models are essentially regression models, and the firm characteristics that best explain differences in returns can be viewed as effective proxies for market risk. . . .

COST OF EQUITY[7]

The *cost of equity* is the rate of return that investors require to make an equity investment in a firm. . . .

The expected return on an equity investment in a firm, given its risk, has strong implications for both equity investors in a firm and the managers of the firm. For equity investors, it is the *rate that they need to make* to be compensated for the market (or nondiversifiable) risk that they have taken on investing in the firm. If after analyzing an investment, they conclude that they cannot make this return, they would not buy this investment; alternatively, if they decide they can make a higher return, they would make the investment.

For managers in the firm, the return that investors need to make to break even on their equity investments becomes the return that they have to try and deliver to keep these investors from becoming restive and rebellious. Thus, it becomes the rate that they have to beat in terms of returns on their equity investments in an individual project. In other words, this is the cost of equity to the firm. . . .

From Cost of Equity to Cost of Capital

While equity is undoubtedly an important and indispensable ingredient of the financing mix for every business, it is but one ingredient. Most businesses finance some or most of their operations using debt or some hybrid of equity and debt. The costs of these sources of financing are generally very different from the cost of equity, and the minimum acceptable hurdle rate for a project will reflect their cost as well, in proportion to their use in the financing mix. Intuitively, the *cost of capital* is the weighted average of the costs of the different components of financing—including debt, equity, and hybrid securities—used by a firm to fund its financial requirements. . . .

Calculating the Cost of Debt

The *cost of debt* measures the current cost to the firm of borrowing funds to finance projects. In general terms, it is determined by the following variables:

The Current Level of Interest Rates As the level of interest rates increases, the cost of debt for firms will also increase.

The Default Risk of the Company As the default risk of a firm increases, the cost of borrowing money will also increase. One way of measuring default risk is to use the bond rating for the firm. Higher ratings lead to lower interest rates, and lower ratings lead to higher interest rates. If bond ratings are not available, as is the case in many markets outside the United States, the rates paid most recently by the firm on its borrowings may provide a measure of the default risk of the firm.

The Tax Advantage Associated with Debt Since interest is tax deductible, the after-tax cost of debt is a function of the tax rate. The tax benefit that accrues from paying interest makes the after-tax cost of debt lower then the pretax cost. Furthermore, this benefit increases as the tax rate increases. . . .

Calculating the Cost of Preferred Stock

Preferred stock shares some of the characteristics of debt (the preferred dividend is prespecified at the time of the issue and is paid out before common dividend) and some of the characteristics of equity (the payments of preferred dividends are not tax deductible). . . .

Calculating the Cost of Other Hybrid Securities

In general terms, *hybrid securities* share some of the characteristics of debt and some of the characteristics of equity. A good example is a convertible bond, which can be viewed as a combination of a straight bond (debt) and a conversion option (equity). Instead of trying to calculate the cost of these hybrid securities directly, they can be broken down into their debt and equity components and treated separately. . . .

MEASURING RETURN ON INVESTMENTS[8]

Basic issues regarding this subject:

- What is a project? In particular, how general is the definition of an investment and what are the different types of investment decisions that firms have to make?
- In measuring the return on a project, should we look at the cash flows generated by the project or at the accounting of earnings?
- If the returns on a project are unevenly spread over time, how do we consider (or should we not consider) differences in returns across time? . . .

What Is a Project?

Investment analysis concerns which projects to accept and which to reject; accordingly, the question of what comprises a project is central to this. . . . The conventional project analyzed in capital budgeting has three criteria: (1) a large up-front cost, (2) cash flows for a specific time period, and (3) a salvage value at the end, which captures the value of the assets of the project when the project ends. While such projects undoubtedly form a significant proportion of investment decisions, especially for manufacturing firms, it would be a mistake to assume that investment decision analysis stops there. If a project is defined more broadly to include any decision that results in using the scarce resources of a business, then everything from strategic decisions and acquisitions to decisions about which air-conditioning system to use in a building would fall within its reach. . . .

Measuring Returns: The Choices

On all of the investment decisions described earlier, we have to choose between alternative approaches to measuring returns on the investment made. We will present our argument for return measurement in three steps. First, we will contrast accounting earnings and cash flows, and argue that cash flows are better measures of true return on an investment. Second, we will note the differences between total cash flows and incremental cash flows and present the case for using incremental cash flows in measuring returns. Finally, we will argue that returns that occur earlier in a project life should be weighted more than returns that occur later in a project life, and that the return on an investment should be measured using time-weighted cash flows.

Accounting Earnings versus Cash Flows The first and most basic choice we have to make when it comes to measuring returns is the one between the accounting measure of income on a project (measured in accounting statements, using accounting principles and standards) and the cash flow generated by a project (measured as the difference between the cash inflows in each period and the cash outflows). . . .

Operating versus Capital Expenditures Accountants draw a distinction between expenditures that yield benefits only in the immediate period or periods (such as labor and material for a manufacturing firm) and those that yield benefits over multiple periods (such as land, buildings, and long-lived plant). The former are called operating expenses and are subtracted from revenues in computing the accounting income, while the latter are capital expenditures and are not subtracted from revenues in the period that they are made. Instead, the expenditure is spread over multiple periods and deducted as an expense in each period—these expenses are called depreciation (if the asset is a tangible asset like a building) or amortization (if the asset is an intangible asset like a patent or a trademark).

While the capital expenditures made at the beginning of a project are often the largest and most prominent, many projects require capital expenditures during their lifetime. These capital expenditures will reduce the cash available in each of these periods.

Noncash Charges The distinction that accountants draw between operating and capital expenses leads to a number of accounting expenses, such as depreciation and amortization, which are not cash expenses. These noncash expenses, while depressing accounting income, do not reduce cash flows. In fact, they can have a significant positive impact on cash flows if they reduce the tax liability of the firm. Some noncash charges reduce the taxable income and the taxes paid by a business. The most important of such charges is depreciation, which, while reducing taxable and net income, does not cause a cash outflow. Consequently, depreciation is added back to net income to arrive at the cash flow on a project. . . .

Accrual versus Cash Revenues and Expenses The accrual system of accounting leads to revenues being recognized when the sale is made, rather than when the customer pays for the good or service. Consequently, accrual revenues may be very different from cash revenues for three reasons. First, some customers who bought their goods and services in prior periods may pay in this period; second, some customers who buy their goods and services in this period (and are therefore shown as part of revenues in this period) may defer payment until future periods. Finally, some customers who buy goods and services may never pay (bad debts). In some cases, customers may even pay in advance for products and services that will not be delivered until future periods.

A similar argument may be made on the expense side. Accrual expenses, relating to payments to third parties, will be different from cash expenses, because of payments made for materials and services acquired in prior periods and because some materials and services acquired in current periods will not be paid for until future periods. Accrual taxes will be different from cash taxes for exactly the same reasons.

When material is used to produce a product or deliver a service, there is an added consideration. Some of the material that is used may have been acquired in previous periods and was brought in as inventory into this period, and some of the material that is acquired in this period may be taken into the next period as inventory.

Accountants define working capital as the difference between current assets (such as inventory and accounts receivable) and current liabilities (such as accounts payable and taxes payable). Differences between accrual earnings and cash earnings, in the absence of noncash charges, can be captured by changes in the net working capital.

Total versus Incremental Cash Flows   The objective in good business analysis is to take investments that make the entire firm or business more valuable. Consequently, we will argue that the cash flows we should look at in investment analysis should be the cash flows that the projects add on to the business (i.e., incremental) and should be after taxes. The total and the incremental cash flows on a project may be different for many reasons. . . .

Sunk Costs   There are some expenses related to a project that might be incurred before the project analysis is done. One example would be expenses associated with a test market done to assess the potential market for a product prior to conducting a full-blown investment analysis. Such expenses are called sunk costs. Since they will not be recovered if the project is rejected, sunk costs are not incremental and therefore should not be considered as part of the investment analysis. This contrasts with their treatment in accounting statements, which do not distinguish between expenses that have already been incurred and expenses that are still to be incurred.

One category of expenses that consistently falls into the sunk cost column in project analysis is research and development, which occurs well before a product is even considered for introduction. Firms that spend large amounts on research and development . . . have struggled to come to terms with the fact that the analysis of these expenses generally occurs after the fact, when little can be done about them. . . .

Allocated Costs An accounting device created to ensure that every part of a business bears its fair share of costs is *allocation*, whereby costs that are not directly traceable to revenues generated by individual products or divisions are allocated across the units, based on revenues, profits, or assets. While the purposes of such allocations may be rational, their effects on investment analysis have to be viewed in terms of whether they create incremental cash flows. An allocated cost that will exist with or without the project being analyzed does not belong in the investment analysis.

Any increase in administrative or staff costs that can be traced to the project is an incremental cost and belongs in the analysis. One way to estimate the incremental component of these costs is to break them down on the basis of whether they are fixed or variable, and if they are variable, what they are a function of. Thus, a portion of administrative costs may be related to revenue, and the revenue projections of a new project can be used to estimate the administrative costs to be assigned to it.

Product Cannibalization *Product cannibalization* refers to the phenomenon whereby a new product introduced by a firm competes with and reduces sales of the firm's existing products. On one level, it can be argued that this is a negative incremental effect of the new product, and the lost cash flow or profits from the existing products should be treated as costs in analyzing whether to introduce the product. Doing so introduces the possibility that the new product will be rejected, however. If this happens, and a competitor now exploits the opening to introduce a new product that fills the niche that the new product would have filled and consequently erodes the sales of the firm's existing products, the worst of all scenarios is created—the firm loses sales to a competitor rather than to itself.

Thus, the decision whether to build in the lost sales created by the product cannibalization will depend on the potential for a competitor to introduce a close substitute to the new product being considered. . . .

The Argument for Incremental Cash Flows When analyzing investments it is easy to get tunnel vision and focus on the project or investment at hand, and to act as if the objective of the exercise is to maximize the value of the individual investment. There is also the tendency, with perfect hindsight, to require projects to cover all costs that they have generated for the firm, even if such costs will not be recovered by rejecting the project. The objective in investment analysis is to maximize the value of the business or firm taking the investment. Consequently, it is the cash flows that an investment will add on in the future to the business (i.e., the incremental cash flows) that we should focus on. . . .

Time-Weighted versus Nominal Cash Flows   Very few projects with long lifetimes generate earnings or cash flows evenly over their life. In sectors with huge investments in infrastructure, such as telecommunications, the earnings and cash flows might be negative for an extended period before they turn positive. In other sectors, the earnings may occur earlier in time. Whatever the reason for the unevenness of cash flows, a basic question that has to be addressed when measuring returns is whether they should reflect the timing of the earnings or cash flows. We will argue that they should, with earlier earnings and cash flows being weighted more than earnings and cash flows later in the project life.

Why Cash Flows across Time Are Not Comparable

There are three reasons why cash flows across time are not comparable, and a cash flow in the future is worth less than a similar cash flow today:

1. Individuals *prefer present consumption to future consumption*. People would have to be offered more in the future to give up present consumption—this is called the *real rate of return*. The greater the real rate of return, the greater will be the difference in value between a cash flow today and an equal cash flow in the future.
2. When there is *monetary inflation*, the value of the currency decreases over time. The greater the inflation, the greater the difference in value between a cash flow today and a cash flow in the future.
3. Any *uncertainty (risk)* associated with the cash flow in the future reduces the value of the cash flow. The greater the uncertainty associated with the cash flow, the greater will be the difference between receiving the cash flow today and receiving an equal amount in the future.

The process by which future cash flows are adjusted to reflect these factors is called *discounting*, and the magnitude of these factors is reflected in the *discount rate*. . . .

The Case for Time-Weighted Returns

If we accept the arguments that cash flows measure returns more accurately than earnings, and that the incremental cash flows more precisely estimate returns than total cash flows, we should logically follow up by using discounted cash flows (i.e., time-weighted returns) rather than nominal cash flows for two reasons:

1. Nominal cash flows at different points in time are not comparable and cannot be aggregated to arrive at returns. Discounted cash flows, on

the other hand, convert all cash flows on a project to today's terms and allow us to compute returns more consistently.

2. If the objective in investment analysis is to maximize the value of the business taking the investments, we should be weighting cash flows that occur early more than cash flows that occur later, because investors in the business will also do so.

INVESTMENT DECISION RULES

Accounting Income–Based Decision Rules

Many of the oldest and most established investment decision rules have been drawn from the accounting statements and, in particular, from accounting measures of income. Some of these rules are based on income to equity investors (i.e., net income) while others are based on predebt operating income.

Return on Capital   The expected *return on capital* on a project is a function of both the total investment required on the project and its capacity to generate operating income. . . .

Cash Flow–Based Decision Rules

Payback   The payback on a project is a measure of how quickly the cash flows generated by the project cover the initial investment. . . .

As with other measures, the payback can be estimated either for all investors in the project or just for the equity investors. To estimate the payback for the entire firm, the free cash flows to the firm are cumulated until they cover the total initial investment. To estimate payback just for the equity investors, the free cash flows to equity are cumulated until they cover the initial equity investment in the project. . . .

Discounted Cash Flow Measures   Investment decision rules not only replace accounting income with cash flows, but explicitly factor in the time value of money. The two most widely used discounted cash flows rules are *net present value* and the *internal rate of return*. . . .

Net Present Value (NPV)   The net present value of a project is the sum of the present values of the expected cash flows on the project, net of the initial investment. . . .

Internal Rate of Return (IRR)   The internal rate of return is based on discounted cash flows. Unlike the net present value rule, however, it is a percentage rate of return. It is the discounted cash flow analog to the accounting rates of return. In general terms, the internal rate of return is that discount rate that makes the net present value of a project equal to zero. . . .

One advantage of the internal rate of return according to its proponents is that it can be used in cases where the discount rate is unknown. While this is true for the calculation of the IRR, it is *not true* when the decision maker has to use the IRR to decide whether to take a project. At that stage in the process, the internal rate of return has to be compared to the discount rate—if the IRR is greater than the discount rate, the project is a good one; alternatively, the project should be rejected. . . .

The Role of Acquisitions

As firms mature and increase in size, they are often confronted with a quandary. Instead of being cash poor and project rich, they find that their existing products generate far more cash than they have available projects in which to invest. This can be attributed partly to size and partly to competition. As they face up to their new status as cash-rich companies, with limited investment opportunities, acquiring other firms with a ready supply of high-return projects looks like an attractive option. . . .

A GENERAL FRAMEWORK FOR ANALYZING OPPORTUNITY COSTS[9]

The general framework for analyzing opportunity costs begins by asking the question "Is there any other use for this resource right now?" For many resources, there will be an alternative use if the project being analyzed is not taken. For instance,

- The resource may be rented out, in which case the rental revenue is the opportunity lost by taking the project. For example, if the project is considering the use of a vacant building owned by the business already, the potential revenue from renting out this building to an outsider will be the opportunity cost.
- The resource could be sold, in which case the sales price, net of any tax liability and lost depreciation tax benefits, would be the opportunity cost from taking this project.
- The resource might be used elsewhere in the firm, in which case the cost of replacing the resource is considered the opportunity cost. Thus,

the transfer of experienced employees from established divisions to a new project creates a cost to these divisions, which has to be factored into the decision making.

Sometimes, decision makers have to decide whether the opportunity cost will be estimated based on the lost rental revenue, the forgone sales price, or the cost of replacing the resource. When such a choice has to be made, it is the highest of the costs—that is, the best alternative forgone—that should be considered as an opportunity cost. . . .

The Financing Decision

Choose a financing mix that maximizes the value of the projects taken and matches the assets being financed.

- *Financing mix.* Includes debt and equity, and can affect both the hurdle rate and the cash flows.
- *Financing type.* Should be as close as possible to the asset being financed.

THE CONTINUUM BETWEEN DEBT AND EQUITY[10]

While the distinction between debt and equity is often made in terms of bonds and stocks, its roots lie in the nature of the cash flow claims of each type of financing. The first distinction is that a *debt claim* entitles the holder to a contracted set of cash flows (usually interest and principal payments), whereas an *equity claim* entitles the holder to any residual cash flows left over after meeting all other promised claims. While this remains the fundamental difference, other distinctions have arisen, partly as a result of the tax code and partly as a consequence of legal developments.

The second distinction, which is a logical outgrowth of the nature of cash flow claims (contractual versus residual), is that debt has a prior claim on both cash flows on a period-to-period basis (for interest and principal payments) and on the assets of the firm (in the case of liquidation). Third, the tax laws have generally treated interest expenses, which accrue to debt holders, very differently and often much more advantageously than dividends or other cash flows that accrue to equity. In the United States, for instance, interest expenses are deductible, and thus create tax savings, whereas dividend payments have to be made out of after-tax cash flows. Fourth, usually debt has a fixed maturity date, at which point the principal is due, while equity generally has an infinite life. Finally, equity investors, by virtue of their claim on the residual cash flows of the firm, are generally given the bulk of or all the control of the management of the firm. Debt investors, on the other hand, play a much more passive role in management, exercising, at most, veto power[11] over significant financial decisions. . . .

How Firms Choose Their Capital Structures

While the theory suggests that firms should pick the mix of debt and equity that maximizes firm value, the most common approach is to set leverage close to that of the peer group to which the firm belongs. If firms in the peer group are similar on the fundamental characteristics (tax rate and cash flow variability) and tend to be right, at least on average, it can be argued that this approach provides a shortcut to arriving at the optimal. It is likely to fail, however, when firms differ on these characteristics. . . .

A Financing Hierarchy

It can be argued that firms follow a financing hierarchy: Retained earnings are the most preferred choice for financing, followed by debt; new equity, common and preferred, is the least preferred choice. The argument is supported as follows. First, managers value flexibility and control. To the extent that external financing reduces flexibility for future financing (especially if it is debt) and control (bonds have covenants; new equity attracts new stockholders into the company and may reduce inside holdings as a percentage of total holding), managers prefer retained earnings as a source of capital. Second, while it costs nothing in terms of flotation costs to use retained earnings, it costs more to use external debt and even more to use external equity. . . .

COST OF CAPITAL APPROACH[12]

. . . We defined the cost of capital to be the weighted average of the costs of the different components of financing—including debt, equity, and hybrid securities—used by a firm to fund its financial requirements. By altering the weights of the different components, firms might be able to change their cost of capital.[13] . . .

Definition of the Weighted Average of Cost of Capital

The weighted average cost of capital (WAAC) is defined as the weighted average of the costs of the different components of financing used by a firm. . . .

Role of Cost of Capital in Investment Analysis and Valuation

The value of a firm is . . . a function of its cash flows and its cost of capital. In the specific case where the cash flows to the firm are unaffected by the debt/equity mix, and the cost of capital is reduced, the value of the firm will increase. If the objective in choosing the financing mix for the firm is the maximization of firm value, this can be accomplished, in this case, *by minimizing the cost of capital*. In the more general case where the cash flows to the firm are a function of the debt/equity mix, the optimal financing mix is the one that maximizes firm value.[14]

A FRAMEWORK FOR CAPITAL STRUCTURE CHANGES[15]

A firm whose actual debt ratio is very different from its optimal has several choices to make. First, it has to decide whether to move toward the optimal or preserve the status quo. Second, once it decides to move toward the optimal, the firm has to choose between changing its leverage quickly or moving more deliberately. This decision may also be governed by pressure from external sources, such as impatient stockholders or bond ratings agency concerns. Third, if the firm decides to move gradually to the optimal, it has to decide whether to use new financing to take new projects, or to shift its financing mix on existing projects. . . .

Immediate or Gradual Change

When firms are significantly underlevered or overlevered, they have to decide whether to adjust their leverage quickly or gradually over time. The advantage of a prompt movement to the optimal is that the firm immediately receives the benefits of the optimal leverage, which includes a lower cost of capital and a higher value. The disadvantage of a sudden change in leverage is that it changes both the way and the environment in which managers make decisions within the firm. If the optimal debt ratio has been misestimated, a sudden change may also increase the risk that the firm may have to backtrack and reverse its financing decisions. . . .

Underlevered Firms

For underlevered firms, the decision to increase the debt ratio to the optimal quickly or gradually is determined by a number of factors:

Degree of Confidence in the Optimal Leverage Estimate The greater the noise in the estimate of optimal leverage, the more likely the firm will choose to move gradually to the optimal.

Comparability to Peer Group   When the optimal debt ratio for a firm is very different from that of its peer group, the firm is much less likely to move to the optimal quickly because analysts and ratings agencies might not look favorably on the change.

Likelihood of a Takeover   Empirical studies of the characteristics of target firms in acquisitions have noted that underleveraged firms are more likely to be acquired than are overleveraged firms.[16] Often, the acquisition is financed at least partially by the target firm's unused debt capacity. Consequently, firms with excess debt capacity which delay increasing debt run the risk of being taken over; the greater this risk, the more likely the firm will choose to take on additional debt quickly. . . .

Need for Financing Slack   On occasion, firms may require financial slack to meet unanticipated needs for funds, either to keep existing projects going, or to take on new ones. Firms that need and value financial slack will be less likely to move quickly to their optimal debt ratios and use up their excess debt capacity. . . .

The Dividend Decision

If there are not enough investments that earn the hurdle rate, return the cash to the owners.

- *How much?* Excess cash after meeting all business needs.
- *What form?* Whether the cash should be returned as dividend or stock buybacks or spin-offs will depend on the stockholder preferences.

WAYS OF RETURNING CASH TO STOCKHOLDERS[17]

While dividends have traditionally been considered the primary approach for publicly traded firms to return cash or assets to their stockholders, they comprise only one of many ways available to the firm to accomplish this objective. In particular, firms can return cash to stockholders through *equity repurchases*, where the cash is used to buy back outstanding stock in the firm and reduce the number of shares outstanding, or through *forward contracts*, where the firm commits to buying back its own stock in future periods at a fixed price. In addition, firms can return some of their assets to their stockholders in the form of spin-offs and split-offs.

THE HISTORICAL EVIDENCE ON DIVIDENDS

Several interesting findings emerge from an examination of the dividend policies practiced by firms in the United States in the past 50 years. First, dividends tend to lag behind earnings; that is, increases in earnings are followed by increases in dividends, and decreases in earnings by dividend cuts. Second, firms are typically reluctant to change dividends; this hesitancy is magnified when it comes to cutting dividends, making for "sticky" dividend policies. Third, dividends tend to follow a much smoother path than do earnings. Finally, there are distinct differences in dividend policy over the life cycle of a firm, driven by changes in growth rates, cash flows, and project availability. . . .

Stockholders, Managers, and Dividends

In examining debt policy, we noted that one reason for taking on more debt was to induce managers to be more disciplined in their project choice. Implicit in this free cash flow argument is the assumption that cash accumulations, if left to the discretion of the managers of the firm, would be wasted on poor projects. If this is true, we can argue that forcing a firm to make a commitment to pay dividends reduces cash available to managers. This, in turn, forces managers to be disciplined in project choice.

If this is the reason stockholders want managers to commit to paying larger dividends, firms in which there is a clear separation between ownership and management should pay larger dividends than should firms with substantial insider ownership and involvement in managerial decisions. . . .

Stock Dividends and Stock Splits

A stock dividend involves issuing to existing stockholders additional shares in the company at no cost. Thus, in a 5 percent stock dividend, every existing stockholder in the firm receives new shares equivalent to 5 percent of the numbers of shares currently owned. Many firms use stock dividends to supplement cash dividends; others view them as an alternative. A stock split, in some ways, is just a large stock dividend, since it too increases the number of shares outstanding, but it does so by a much larger factor. Thus, a firm may have a two-for-one stock split, whereby the number of shares in the firm is doubled. . . .

Divestitures, Spin-offs, Split-ups, and Split-offs

Divestitures, spin-offs, split-ups, and split-offs are other options for returning noncash assets to stockholders. Consider a firm with operations in multiple business lines, some of which are being systematically undervalued; the whole firm is therefore worth less than its parts. This firm has four options:

1. *Divest the undervalued business and pay a liquidating dividend.* One way in which this firm can deal with its predicament is through divestiture, which involves selling those parts that are being undervalued by the market for their true market value and then paying out the cash to stockholders in the form of either equity repurchases or dividends.
2. *Spin off the undervalued businesses.* An alternative is to spin off or create a new class of shares in the undervalued business line and to distribute these shares to the existing stockholders. Since the shares are distributed in proportion to the existing share ownership, it does not alter the proportional ownership in the firm.
3. *Split up the entire firm.* In a split-up, the firm splits itself off into different business lines, distributes these shares to the original stockholders in proportion to their original ownership in the firm, and then ceases to exist.
4. *Split off the undervalued business.* A split-off is similar to a spin-off, insofar as it creates new shores in the undervalued business line. In this case, however, the existing stockholders are given the option to exchange their parent company stock for these new shares, which changes the proportional ownership in the new structure. . . .

A Framework for Analyzing Dividend Policy

In applying a rational framework for analyzing dividend policy, a firm will attempt to answer two questions:

1. How much cash is available to be paid out as dividends, after meeting capital expenditure and working capital needs to sustain future growth, and how much of this cash is actually paid out to stockholders?
2. How good are the projects that are available to the firm?

In general, firms that have good projects will have much more leeway on dividend policy, since stockholders will expect that the cash accumulated in the firm will be invested in these projects and eventually earn high returns. By contrast, firms that do not have good projects will find themselves under pressure to pay out all or most of the cash that is available as dividends. . . .

Institutional Investors

The large stock holdings by institutional investors in the United States, including mutual funds, play a role in corporate dividend policies.[18] These large investors are not infinite investors in the firms. They mostly seek capital appreciation, with significant portfolio asset turnarounds. Dividend payments are not the primary consideration in their investment decisions.

Consequently, firms can keep dividend payments low if their overall business performance and stock market value are good enough for institutional investors holding large quantities of their stocks.

Financial Statements

There are three basic financial statements—the income statement that measures the revenues and expenses of the firm, the balance sheet that reports on the assets and liabilities of the firm, and the statement of cash flows that examines the sources and the uses of cash.

INCOME STATEMENT

An income statement provides information about a firm's operating activities over a specific time period. The net income of a company is equal to the revenues minus expenses, where revenues arise from selling goods or services, and expenses measure the costs associated with generating these revenues.

Classification—A Typical Income Statement

Since income can be generated from a number of different sources, generally accepted accounting principles (GAAP) require that income statements be classified into four sections—income from continuing operations, income from discontinued operations, extraordinary gains or losses, and adjustments for changes in accounting principles. A typical income statement starts with revenues, and adjusts for the cost of the goods sold, depreciation on assets used to produce the revenues, and any selling or administrative expenses to arrive at an operating profit. The operating profit, when reduced by interest expenses, yields the taxable income, which when reduced by taxes yields net income.

Accrual versus Cash Basis—Income Statements

Firms often expend resources to acquire materials or manufacture goods in one period, but do not sell them until the following period. Alternatively, they often provide product or services in one period but do not get paid until the following period. In accrual-based accounting, the revenue from selling a good or service is recognized in the period in which the good is sold or the service is performed (in whole or substantially). A corresponding effort is made on the expense side to match[1] expenses to revenues. Under a cash-based system of accounting, revenues are recognized when payment is received, while expenses are recorded when paid. Since there is no matching of revenues and expenses, GAAP requires that firms use accrual-based accounting in income statements.

Income Statement

Revenues
- Cost of goods sold
- Depreciation
- Selling expenses
- Administrative expenses
= Earnings before interest and taxes (EBIT)
- Interest expenses
= Earnings before taxes
- Taxes
= Net income before extraordinary items
+ Gains (or losses) from discontinued operations
+ Extraordinary gains (or losses)
+ Net income changes caused by changes in accounting methods
= Net income after extraordinary items
- Preferred dividends
= Profit to common stockholders

GAAP—Recognizing Income

Generally accepted accounting principles require the recognition of revenues when the good or service for which the firm is getting paid has been performed in full or substantially, and the firm has received in return either cash or a receivable that is both observable and measurable. For expenses that are directly linked to the production of revenues (like labor and materials), expenses are recognized in the same period in which revenues are recognized. Any expenses that are not directly linked to the production of revenues are recognized in the period in which the firm consumes the services.

While accrual accounting is straightforward in firms which produce goods and sell them, there are special cases where accrual accounting can be complicated by the nature of the product or service being offered.

Long-Term Contracts Long-term contracts span several accounting periods, and customers often make periodic payments as the contract progresses (example: a new home or commercial building). When a long-term contractor has a contract with a buyer with an agreed-upon price, revenue during the period of construction is recognized on the basis of the percentage of the contract that is completed. As the revenue is recognized on a percentage of completion basis, a corresponding proportion of the expense is also recognized. An alternative is to wait until the contract is completed, and recognize the total revenue and expense on completion. Since this delays the payment of income taxes, it is not permitted under the Internal Revenue Code for tax purposes.

Uncertainty about Cash Collections When there is considerable uncertainty about the capacity of the buyer of a good or service to pay for a service, the firm providing the good or service may recognize the income only when it collects portions of the selling price under the installment method. While this is similar to revenue recognition in the cash method, the expenses under the installment method are recognized only when the cash is collected, even though payment may be made in the period of the initial sale. An alternative to this approach is the cost-recovery-first method, where cash receipts and expenses are matched dollar for dollar (thus generating no profits) until all the expenses are covered, after which any additional revenues are reported as profits.

BALANCE SHEET

Unlike the income statement, which measures flows over a period of time, the balance sheet provides a summary of what the firm owns in terms of assets and what it owes to both its lenders and its equity investors on a specific date. The balance sheet is built around the equality:

$$\text{Assets} = \text{Liabilities} + \text{Shareholders' Equity}$$

Assets and liabilities can be further broken down into current and non-current portions.

Assets	Liabilities and Equity
Current assets:	Current liabilities:
Cash and marketable securities	Accounts payable
Accounts receivable	Short-term borrowing
Inventories	Other current liabilities
Other current assets	Long-term debt
Investments	Other noncurrent liabilities
Property, plant, and equipment	Stockholders' equity:
(fixed assets)	Preferred stock
Intangible assets	Common stock
	Retained earnings
	Treasury stock

Assets

An asset is any resource that has the potential to either generate future cash inflows or reduce future cash outflows. For a resource to be an asset, therefore, a firm has to have acquired it in a prior transaction and be able to quantify future benefits with reasonable precision. Assets can be classified on several bases—fixed and current assets, monetary assets (like cash and notes receivable), and nonmonetary assets—and the GAAP principles on valuation vary from asset to asset.

Fixed Assets Generally accepted accounting principles in almost all countries require the valuation of fixed assets at historical costs, adjusted for any depreciation charges on these assets. The rationale that is often provided for this practice is that:

- Book value is easier to obtain than market value for most assets, since an active secondary market does not exist for most assets.
- Book value can be more objectively valued than market value, and is less likely to be manipulated by firms to suit their purposes.
- Book value is a more conservative estimate of true value than market value.

All these arguments are open to challenge, and it is quite clear that the book value of many fixed assets bears little resemblance to the market value.

Since fixed assets are valued at book value, and are adjusted for depreciation provisions, the value of a fixed asset is strongly influenced by both its depreciable life and the depreciation method used. Since firms estimate the depreciable life, and lengthening the depreciable life can increase[2] reported earnings, it provides an opportunity for firms to manage reported earnings. Firms are also offered an opportunity to manage earnings through the choice of a depreciation method, since GAAP allows firms to use either straight-line depreciation (where depreciation is spread evenly over the life of the asset) or accelerated depreciation methods (where more depreciation is taken in the initial years, and less later on). Most U.S. firms use straight-line depreciation for financial reporting, while they use accelerated depreciation for tax purposes, since firms can report better earnings with the former, at least in the years right after the asset is acquired. In contrast, Japanese and German firms often use accelerated depreciation for both tax and financial reporting purposes, leading to income which is understated relative to their U.S. counterparts.

Inventory   There are three basic approaches to valuing inventory that are allowed by GAAP:

1. *First in, first out (FIFO)*. Under FIFO, the cost of goods sold is based on the cost of material bought earliest in the period, while the cost of inventory is based on the cost of material bought later in the year. This results in inventory being valued close to current replacement cost. During periods of inflation, the use of FIFO will result in the lowest estimate of cost of goods sold among the three approaches, and the highest net income.
2. *Last in, first out (LIFO)*. Under LIFO, the cost of goods sold is based on the cost of material bought toward the end of the period, resulting in costs that closely approximate current costs. The inventory, however, is valued on the basis of the cost of material bought earlier in the year. During periods of inflation, the use of LIFO will result in the highest estimate of cost of goods sold among the three approaches, and the lowest net income.
3. *Weighted average*. Under the weighted average approach, both inventory and the cost of goods sold are based upon the average cost of all units bought during the period.

Firms often adopt the LIFO approach for tax benefits during periods of high inflation, and studies indicate that firms with the following characteristics are more likely to adopt LIFO—rising prices for raw materials and labor, more variable inventory growth, an absence of other tax loss carry-forwards, and large size. When firms switch from FIFO to LIFO in valuing inventory, there is likely to be a drop in net income and a concurrent increase in cash flows (because of the tax savings). The reverse will apply when firms switch from LIFO to FIFO.

Given the income and cash flow effects of inventory valuation methods, it is often difficult to compare the earnings of firms which use different methods. There is, however, one way of adjusting for these differences. Firms that choose to use the LIFO approach to value inventories have to specify in a footnote the difference in inventory valuation between FIFO and LIFO, and this difference is termed the LIFO reserve. This can be used to adjust the beginning and ending inventories, and consequently the cost of goods sold, and to restate income based on FIFO valuation.

Intangible Assets   Intangible assets include a wide array of assets that do not have a physical presence, ranging from patents and trademarks to goodwill. GAAP requires that intangible assets be accounted for in the following way:

- The costs incurred in developing the intangible asset are expensed in that period, even though the asset might have a life of several accounting periods. Thus, the research and development expenditure that creates the patent (the intangible asset) is nevertheless expensed in the period it is incurred.
- When an intangible asset is acquired from an external party, the expenditure is treated as an asset, in contrast to the treatment of expenditures incurred in internally developing the same asset.
- Intangible assets have to be amortized over their expected lives, depending on their nature. The standard practice is to use straight-line amortization. For tax purposes, however, firms are not allowed to amortize goodwill and other intangible assets with no specific lifetime.

Intangible assets are often by-products of acquisitions. When a firm acquires another firm, the purchase price is first allocated over tangible assets, and the excess price is then allocated to any intangible assets such as patents or trade names. Any residual amount becomes goodwill. While accounting principles suggest that goodwill captures the value of any intangibles that are not specifically identifiable, it is really a reflection of the difference between the book value of assets and their market value.

Liabilities

For an obligation to be recognized as a liability, it must meet three requirements—it must be expected to lead to a future cash outflow or the loss of a future cash inflow at some specified or determinable date, the firm cannot avoid the obligation, and the transaction giving rise to the obligation has happened.

Degree of Certitude   Liabilities vary in the degree to which they create a future obligation. At one extreme, a straight bond creates an obligation to make fixed payments on fixed dates and results in a very specific and certain obligation. At the other extreme, an option contract entered into by the firm creates a contingent obligation, where the amount and the timing of the obligation are unclear. Along the continuum, GAAP recognizes as accounting liabilities those obligations that create future payments that can be both quantified and timed, even if the amount and the timing have to be estimated by the firm. It does not recognize purchase or employment commitments or contingent contracts as accounting liabilities.

As firms enter into more and more complex arrangements to manage their financial and operating risk, a number of gray areas are emerging, where generally accepted accounting principles do not provide sufficient guidance on the right path to take. One example is the use of hybrid securities by firms, possessing some of the properties of debt and some of equity, making a classification into liabilities and stockholders' equity very difficult. Another is the use of off-balance-sheet financing by firms, where a liability is created but not recognized. The evolving attitude toward this phenomenon is that firms must disclose information[3] about the off-balance-sheet risk of any financial instruments or agreements that they have entered into.

Dealing with Leases   Firms often choose to lease long-term assets rather than buy them for a variety of reasons—the tax benefits are greater to the lessor than the lessee, and leases offer more flexibility in terms of adjusting to changes in technology and capacity needs. Lease payments create the same kind of obligation that interest payments on debt create, and have to be viewed in a similar light. If a firm is allowed to lease a significant portion of its assets and keep it off its financial statements, a perusal of the statements will give a very misleading view of the company's financial strength. Consequently, accounting rules have been devised to force firms to reveal the extent of their lease obligations on their books.

There are two ways of accounting for leases. In an operating lease, the lessor (or owner) transfers only the right to use the property to the lessee. At the end of the lease period, the lessee returns the property to the lessor. Since the lessee does not assume the risk of ownership, the lease expense is treated as an operating expense in the income statement and the lease does not affect the balance sheet. In a capital lease, the lessee assumes some of the risks of ownership and enjoys some of the benefits. Consequently, the lease, when signed, is recognized both as an asset and as a liability (for the lease payments) on the balance sheet. The firm gets to claim depreciation each year on the asset and also deducts the interest expense component of the lease payment each year. In general, capital leases recognize expenses sooner than equivalent operating leases.

Since firms prefer to keep leases off the books, and sometimes prefer to defer expenses, there is a strong incentive on the part of firms to report all leases as operating leases. Consequently the Financial Accounting Standards Board has ruled that a lease should be treated as a capital lease if it meets any one of the following four conditions:

1. If the lease life exceeds 75 percent of the life of the asset.
2. If there is a transfer of ownership to the lessee at the end of the lease term.
3. If there is an option to purchase the asset at a bargain price at the end of the lease term.
4. If the present value of the lease payments, discounted at an appropriate discount rate, exceeds 90 percent of the fair market value of the asset.

The lessor uses the same criteria for determining whether the lease is a capital or operating lease and accounts for it accordingly. If it is a capital lease, the lessor records the present value of future cash flows as revenue and recognizes expenses. The lease receivable is also shown as an asset on the balance sheet, and the interest revenue is recognized over the term of the lease as paid.

From a tax standpoint, the lessor can claim the tax benefits (such as depreciation) of the leased asset only if it is an operating lease, though the tax code uses slightly different criteria[4] for determining whether the lease is an operating lease.

Employee Benefits Employers provide pension and health care benefits to their employees. In many cases, the obligations created by these benefits are extensive, and a failure by the firm to adequately fund these obligations needs to be revealed in financial statements.

Pension Plans In a pension plan, the firm agrees to provide certain benefits to its employees, either by specifying a defined contribution (where a fixed contribution is made to the plan each year by the employer, without any promises on the benefits which will be delivered in the plan) or a defined benefit (where the employer promises to pay a certain benefit to the employee). Under the latter, the employer has to put sufficient money into the plan each period, such that the amounts with reinvestment are sufficient to meet the defined benefits.

Under a defined contribution plan, the firm meets its obligation once it has made the prespecified contribution to the plan. Under a defined benefit plan, the firm's obligations are much more difficult to estimate, since they will be determined by a number of variables, including (1) the benefits that employees are entitled to, which will change as their salaries and employment status change; (2) the prior contributions made by the employer and the returns they have earned; and (3) the rate of return that the employer expects to make on current contributions. As these variables change, the value of the pension fund assets can be greater than, less than, or equal to pension fund liabilities (which include the present value of promised benefits). A pension fund whose assets exceed its liabilities is an overfunded plan, whereas one whose assets are less than its liabilities is an underfunded plan, and disclosures to that effect have to be included in financial statements, generally in the footnotes.

When a pension fund is overfunded, the firm has several options—it can withdraw the excess assets from the fund, it can discontinue contributions to the plan, or it can continue to make contributions on the assumption that the overfunding is a transitory phenomenon that could well disappear by the next period. When a fund is underfunded, the firm has a liability, though the FASB rule requires that firms reveal only the excess of accumulated[5] pension fund liabilities over pension fund assets on the balance sheet.

Health Care Benefits A firm can provide health care benefits in one of two ways—by making a fixed contribution to a health care plan, without promising specific benefits (analogous to a defined contribution plan), or by promising specific health benefits, and setting aside the funds to provide these benefits (analogous to a defined benefit plan). The accounting for health care benefits is very similar to the accounting for pension obligations. The key difference between the two is that firms do not have to report[6] the excess of their health care obligations over the health care fund assets as a liability on the balance sheet, though a footnote to that effect has to be added to the financial statement.

Income Taxes Firms often use different methods of accounting for tax and financial reporting purposes, leading to a question of how tax liabilities should be reported. Since the use of accelerated depreciation and favorable inventory valuation methods for tax accounting purposes leads to a deferral of taxes, the taxes on the income reported in the financial statements will be much greater than the actual tax paid. The same principles of matching expenses to income that underlie accrual accounting suggest that the deferred income tax be recognized in the financial statements. Thus a company that pays $55,000 on its taxable income based on its tax accounting, and that would have paid $75,000 on the income reported in its financial statements, will be forced to recognize the difference ($20,000) as deferred taxes. Since the deferred taxes will be paid in later years, they will be recognized as paid.

The question of whether the deferred tax liability is really a liability is an interesting one. Firms do not owe the amount categorized as deferred taxes to any entity, and treating it as a liability makes the firm look more risky than it really is.

Reserves in Financial Statements   Reserves can appear in financial statements as a deduction from an asset, as a liability, or as a reduction of stockholders' equity. While reserves have to be for specific purposes in the United States, firms in Germany and Japan are allowed to create general reserves to equalize income across time periods. Reserve accounts are created for at least two reasons:

1. *To match expenses with benefits.* A firm can create a reserve for an expense that is expected to arise from an activity from the current period, and reduce the income in the current period by the expense. When the expense actually occurs, the reserve is reduced by the amount and the net income in the future period is not affected by the expense. Thus, a bank which expects 1 percent of its loans to go uncollected may create a reserve for bad debts in the period the loan is made, and charge income in that period with a charge transferring funds to the reserve. Any subsequent loan defaults will be charged to the reserve.
2. *To keep expenses out of income statements.* Firms can keep some expenses out of the income statement, by directly reducing the stockholders' equity by a reserve created to meet the expense. While the net effect on stockholders' equity is the same as if the expense had been shown in the income statement, it results in an overstatement of net income for that period.

The varied uses to which reserves are put, and the wide diversity of accounting standards relating to reserves in different countries, suggest that analysts should be careful about how they factor in reserves when comparing the profitability of companies in different countries using different accounting standards.

STATEMENT OF CASH FLOWS

The statement of cash flows is based on a reformulation of the basic equation relating assets to liabilities:

$$\text{Assets} = \text{Liabilities} + \text{Stockholders' Equity}$$

If each of these variables is measured in terms of changes (Δ), this equation can be rewritten as follows:

$$\Delta \text{ Assets} = \Delta \text{ Liabilities} + \Delta \text{ Stockholders' Equity}$$

If assets are broken out on the basis of whether they are cash assets or noncash assets, this works out to:

$$\Delta \text{ Cash} + \Delta \text{ Noncash Assets} = \Delta \text{ Liabilities} + \Delta \text{ Stockholders' Equity}$$

Rearranging terms:

$$\Delta \text{ Cash} = \Delta \text{ Liabilities} + \Delta \text{ Stockholders' Equity} - \Delta \text{ Noncash Assets}$$

Changes in cash flows can be traced to the following reasons:

- An increase in noncash assets will decrease cash flows; increases in both current assets (such as inventory and accounts receivable), financial assets (through the purchase of securities), and fixed assets (through capital expenditures) will result in a drain on cash flows.
- Net profit will increase cash flows; this cash flow will be further increased if there are any noncash charges (such as depreciation and amortization).
- Any payment of dividends or stock repurchases will decrease cash flows, as will the principal payment on debt; an issue of stock or debt will increase cash flows.

A statement of changes in cash flows classifies all changes into one of three categories—operating, investing, or financing activities. The final step in preparing a statement of changes in cash flows is to classify changes in liabilities, stockholders' equity, and noncash assets into one of these three categories, though some items will not fit easily into one or another of the categories. Once categorized, the statement of cash flows provides a breakdown of the changes in the cash balance over the period.

Discount Rates

This appendix[1] relates to the valuation of emerging growth and lower-middle-market privately held companies using a discount rate derived from use of the adjusted capital asset pricing model (ACAPM). A discount rate is defined as the rate of return an investor would require to be induced to invest in the cash flow stream being discounted. The discount rates are affected by the market, vary with time, depend on what is being discounted, must be risk adjusted, are based on yields available on alternate investments, and are inflation adjusted.

If the model is applied to after-tax earnings, you are most likely valuing the equity portion of the company, whereas if the model is applied to cash flow preinterest, you are valuing the enterprise, which, as we described previously, consists of equity and the interest-bearing debt of the company. Our preferred method is valuation of cash flow without regard to financing. This eliminates the issue of determining the weighted average cost of capital (WACC) and specifics of the financing and focuses on the actual firm value.

The CAPM formula modified for the target companies is:[2]

$$r = rf + B_i(M_{rh} - rf) + (SCM_{rh} - M_{rh}) + SCR$$

where r = discount rate to be used with the associated growth rate for valuing the firm

rf = current intermediate-term Treasury note rate

M_{rh} = historical expected return in the market for the S&P 500 (11 to 14%)

SCM_{rh} = historical return in the market for micro-cap stocks, average market cap determined by the Ibbotson small stock premium. The $SCM_{rh} - M_{rh}$ term is the premium required by the market for micro-cap stocks over the S&P 500 normal returns.

TABLE C.1 Typical Ranges of Specific Company Risks

Target Company Net Worth	Target Company Sales	Specific Company Risk (SCR)
<$500,000	<$2 million	10–15%
$500,000–$2 million	$2–10 million	2–10%
$2–5 million	$10–50 million	1–6%
>$5 million	>$50 million	–3 to 2%

B_i = beta of the industry for the target company

SCR = specific company risks of the target in comparison to micro-cap firms (added risk above comparable micro-cap company risks), which may include:

- Key person
- Management depth
- Concentration of customers, products, market, and location
- Adverse historical performance: absolute size and industry condition

SCR typical ranges are presented in Table C.1.

This model accounts for the operational and financial risks of a small private company by modifying the CAPM. Also to be considered is whether the valuation is for a minority interest or a controlling interest. The CAPM is often for minority interests in public companies, though many valuation practitioners consider it to be a controlling interest if control adjustments are made to the projected income statements. There is a premium to be considered when valuing a company for a controlling buyer.

How Fast Can Your
Company Afford to Grow?

Everyone knows that starting a business requires cash, and growing a business requires even more—for working capital, facilities and equipment, and operating expenses. But few people understand that a profitable company that tries to grow too fast can run out of cash—even if its products are great successes. A key challenge for managers of any growing concern, then, is to strike the proper balance between consuming cash and generating it. Fail to strike that balance, and even a thriving company can soon find itself out of business—a victim of its own success.

Fortunately, there's a straightforward way to calculate the growth rate a company's current operations can sustain and, conversely, the point at which it would need to adjust operations or find new funding to support its growth. In this article, we will lay out a framework for managing growth that takes into account three critical factors:

- A company's operating cash cycle—the amount of time the company's money is tied up in inventory and other current assets before the company is paid for the goods and services it produces.

Neil C. Churchill is a visiting professor at the Anderson School at UCLA and a professor emeritus of entrepreneurship at INSEAD in Fontainebleau, France. John W. Mullins is an associate professor of marketing at the Daniels College of Business at the University of Denver and a visiting associate professor of entrepreneurship at London Business School.

- The amount of cash needed to finance each dollar of sales, including working capital and operating expenses.
- The amount of cash generated by each dollar of sales.

Together, these three factors determine what we call the *self-financeable growth* (SFG) *rate*—that is, the rate at which a company can sustain its growth through the revenues it generates without going hat in hand to financiers.

The usefulness of this framework goes beyond the calculation of a sustainable growth rate. It can also give managers practical insights into how efficiently their operations are running, how profit margins affect their ability to fuel faster growth, which of their product lines and customer segments hold the greatest growth potential, and what kinds of businesses might be attractive investment targets.

THREE LEVERS FOR GROWTH

To begin, we'll show how the SFG rate is calculated in a simplified example for a hypothetical company we'll call Chullins Distributors. Then we'll demonstrate how the three factors work as levers that can be manipulated to enhance Chullins's ability to grow from internally generated funds. To determine the SFG rate, we must first calculate each of the three factors that compose it.

The Operating Cash Cycle

Every business has an *operating cash cycle* (OCC), essentially the length of time a company's cash is tied up in working capital before that money is finally returned when customers pay for the products sold or services rendered. Companies that require little inventory and are paid by their customers immediately in cash, like many service firms, have a relatively short OCC. But companies that must tie up funds in components and inventory at one end and then wait to collect accounts receivable at the other have a fairly long OCC. All other things being equal, the shorter the cycle, the faster a company can redeploy its cash and grow from internal sources (see Figure D.1).

To calculate Chullins's OCC, take a look at its most recent income statement and balance sheet, shown in Figure D.2. At the right side of the balance sheet, we see that customers pay their invoices in 70 days and that inventory is held for an average of 80 days before it's sold. So the cash that

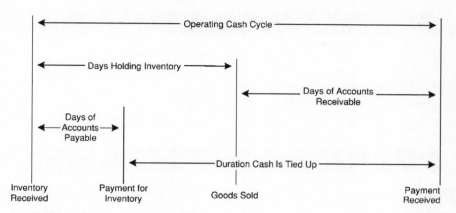

FIGURE D.1 Components of an Operating Cash Cycle
Reprinted by permission of *Harvard Business Review*, "How Fast Can Your Company Afford to Grow?" by Neil C. Churchill and John W. Mullins, May 2001. Copyright © 2001 Harvard Business School Publishing Corporation, all rights reserved.

Chullins invests in working capital is tied up for a total of 150 days. That's Chullins's operating cash cycle.

Fortunately, Chullins's cash isn't really tied up for the entire OCC. We need to take into account the delay between the time Chullins receives supplies and the time it pays for them. As the exhibit shows, the company is on 30-day credit terms with its suppliers, so cash is not actually expended for inventory the moment it arrives but, rather, 30 days afterward, when the supplier is paid. This shortens the time the cash is tied up for inventory and accounts receivable (ultimately, therefore, for cost of sales) to only 120 days, or 80 percent of the 150-day cycle.

Of course, in addition to working capital, we must also account for the cash needed for everyday operating expenses—payroll, marketing and selling costs, utilities, and the like. These expenses are paid from time to time throughout the cycle, and the cash for them may be tied up anywhere from 150 days (for bills paid on the first day of the cycle) to zero days (for invoices paid on the same day the company receives its cash from customers). We shall assume, though, that bills are paid more or less uniformly throughout the cycle and so are outstanding, on average, for half the period, or 75 days. A summary of the duration Chullins's cash is tied up for cost of sales and operating expenses appears in Figure D.3; to simplify this first example, we've included income taxes within operating expenses and ignored depreciation.

Income Statement (in 000's)		
Sales	$2,000	100.0%
Cost of sales	1,200	60.0
Gross profit	800	40.0
Operating expenses	700	35.0
Net profit after tax	$ 100	5.0%

Balance Sheet (in 000's)			
Cash	$ 10		
Accounts receivable	384		70 days*
Inventory	263		80 days
Total current assets		$657	
Plant and equipment	$ 25		
Total assets		$682	
Accounts payable	$ 99		30 days
Bank loan payable	50		
Total current liabilities		$149	
Contributed capital	$350		
Retained earnings	183		
Total owners' equity		$533	
Total equities		$682	

FIGURE D.2   Chullins Distributors' Financial Statements

*Calculate the number of days as follows. For accounts receivable, divide the dollar amount ($384) by the daily *sales* ($2,000 ÷ 365). For inventory and accounts payable, divide the dollar amounts ($263 and $99) by the daily *cost of sales* ($1,200 ÷ 365).

Reprinted by permission of *Harvard Business Review*, "How Fast Can Your Company Afford to Grow?" by Neil C. Churchill and John W. Mullins, May 2001. Copyright © 2001 Harvard Business School Publishing Corporation, all rights reserved.

	Base Case
Duration Cash Is Tied Up (in days)	
Accounts receivable	70
Inventory	80
OCC	**150**
Accounts payable	30
Cost of sales	120
Operating expenses	75
Income Statement	
Sales	$1.000
Cost of sales	0.600
Operating expenses	0.350
Total costs	$0.950
Profit (cash)	$0.050
Amount of Cash Tied Up per Sales Dollar	
Cost of sales	$0.600 × (120/150) = $0.480
Operations	$0.350 × (75/150) = $0.175
Cash required for each OCC	$0.655
Cash Generated per Sales Dollar	$0.050
SFG Rate Calculations	
OCC SFG rate	$0.050/$0.655 = **7.63%**
OCCs per year	365/150 = **2.433**
Annual SFG rate	7.63% × 2.433 = **18.58%**
Compounded annual SFG rate	$(1 + 0.0763)^{2.433} - 1 =$ **19.60%**

FIGURE D.3 Chullins Distributors' Operating Cash Cycle
Reprinted by permission of *Harvard Business Review*, "How Fast Can Your Company Afford to Grow?" by Neil C. Churchill and John W. Mullins, May 2001. Copyright © 2001 Harvard Business School Publishing Corporation, all rights reserved.

The Amount of Cash Tied Up per Cycle

Now that we know how long Chullins's cash will be tied up, we next calculate how much cash is involved. The income statement shows that to produce one dollar of sales, Chullins incurs 60 cents in cost of sales, money that Chullins must invest in working capital, which we've already determined is tied up for 80 percent of the 150-day cycle. The average amount of cash needed for cost of sales over the entire cycle is thus 80 percent of 60 cents, or 48 cents per dollar of sales.

The income statement also shows that Chullins must invest 35 cents per dollar of sales to pay its operating expenses throughout the cycle. Since we've calculated that this cash is tied up, on average, for half the cycle, or 75 days, the average amount of cash needed for operating expenses over the entire cycle is 17.5 cents per dollar of sales. So all in all, Chullins must invest a total of 65.5 cents per dollar of sales over each operating cash cycle.

The Amount of Cash Coming In per Cycle

Happily, Chullins is a thriving, profitable business: After using 60 cents of each sales dollar for working capital to support cost of sales and another 35 cents for operating expenses, it reaps a full dollar at the end of the cycle. To finance another trip around the cycle at the same level of sales, it will need to reinvest 95 cents of that dollar, 60 cents for cost of sales and 35 cents for operating expenses. The extra 5 cents that each dollar of sales produces can be invested in additional working capital and operating expenses to generate more revenue in the next cycle. How much more revenue? A simple calculation will lead us to that number—the SFG rate—for each cycle.

THE MAXIMUM SFG RATE

Suppose Chullins decides to invest the entire 5 cents in working capital and operating expenses to finance additional sales volume. Assuming the company has the productive capacity and marketing capability to generate additional sales, adding the 5 cents to the 65.5 cents already invested would increase its investment by 7.63 percent each cycle,[1] which directly translates into a 7.63 percent increase in sales volume in the next cycle.

If Chullins can grow 7.63 percent every 150 days, how much can it grow annually? Since there are 2.433 cycles of 150 days in a 365-day year, the company can afford to finance an annual growth rate of 2.433 times

7.63 percent, or 18.58 percent, on the money it generates from its own sales. Its SFG rate, in other words, is 18.58 percent.

Of course, in each subsequent cycle, Chullins is earning more and more, and this calculation has not taken into account the compounding effect. If it did, the SFG would come out to 19.60 percent.[2] As a practical matter, though, unless your operating cash cycle is very short—less than about 100 days—the simpler straight-multiplication calculation is sufficient. That's because our framework assumes a company's past performance is an accurate predictor of its future performance, which most managers know is a tenuous assumption at best. So using the more conservative SFG figure offers some measure of protection from unanticipated slips in performance.

What does that 18.58 percent figure tell us? If Chullins grows more slowly than 18.58 percent (assuming all variables remain constant), it will produce more cash than it needs to support its growth. But if it attempts to grow faster than 18.58 percent per year, it must either free up more cash from its operations or find additional funding. Otherwise, it could unexpectedly find itself strapped for cash.

PULLING THE LEVERS

Chullins may see a market opportunity to grow faster than 18.58 percent and, for any number of reasons, may want to fund it by internal, not external, financing. The company could afford to grow faster by manipulating any of the three levers that determine its SFG rate. Our framework shows how each of these decisions will change the maximum growth rate Chullins can afford to finance by itself.

Lever 1: Speeding Cash Flow

Suppose Chullins's accounts receivable manager can get customers to pay faster, shrinking collection time from 70 days to 66. Let's also suppose that management can improve the rate at which it turns its inventory, perhaps through better forecasting, thereby reducing the time its cash is tied up from 80 days to 74. These changes reduce the OCC from 150 to 140 days. The company is still paying the same 60 cents for every dollar of inventory, and it's still on 30-day terms.

Now that the 60 cents is tied up for only 110 out of 140 days, the cash needed for inventory over the entire cycle is reduced from 48 cents to 47.1 cents (see Figure D.4 regarding Lever 1, calculated in the same way as in Figure D.3). Operating expenses remain at 35 cents and are still tied

	Lever 1: Speeding Cash Flow	Lever 2: Reducing Costs	Lever 3: Raising Prices		Pulling Multiple Levers
	66	70	70		66
Inventory	74	80	80		74
OCC	**140**	**150**	**150**		**140**
	30	30	30		30
Cost of sales	110	120	120		110
	70	75	75		70
			Unadjusted	Adjusted	
Sales	$1.000	$1.000	$1.015	$1.0000	$1.000
	0.600	0.590	0.600	0.5911	0.590
	0.350	0.345	0.350	0.3448	0.345
Total costs	$0.950	$0.935	$0.950	$0.9360	$0.935
Profit (cash)	$0.050	$0.065	$0.065	$0.0640	$0.065
Amount of Cash Tied Up per Sales Dollar					
	$0.471	$0.4720	$0.4729		$0.4636
Operations	$0.175	$0.1725	$0.1724		$0.1725
	$0.646	$0.6445	$0.6453		$0.6361
	$0.050	$0.065	$0.064		$0.065
	7.73%	**10.09%**	**9.92%**		**10.22%**
OCCs per year	2.607	2.433	2.433		2.607
Annual SFG rate	**20.17%**	**24.54%**	**24.15%**		**26.64%**
	21.44%	**26.34%**	**25.89%**		**28.87%**

FIGURE D.4 Pulling the Three Levers to Manage Cash for Growth
Reprinted by permission of *Harvard Business Review*, "How Fast Can Your Company Afford to Grow?" by Neil C. Churchill and John W. Mullins, May 2001. Copyright © 2001 Harvard Business School Publishing Corporation, all rights reserved.

up for half the OCC, so 17.5 cents is still needed each cycle for operating expenses. Thus, the company needs 64.6 cents cash to generate one dollar of sales in each cycle. It still generates 5 cents profit, so the extra 5 cents will generate 7.73 percent more sales (5 divided by 64.6 cents) for each cycle. There are now more cycles per year (2.607 rather than 2.433), so that slight increase in growth per cycle works out to an annual SFG rate of 20.17 percent. The framework clearly shows the effect of better asset management by modestly decreasing the amount of time for inventory turnover (7.5 percent) and for collecting receivables (5.7 percent); Chullins increases the amount it can afford to grow by slightly more than 1.5 percentage points.

Many entrepreneurs understand in a general way the importance of effectively managing cash flow. Using the tools presented in this article, they can calculate the real impact of any proposed changes in their working capital on the rate at which they can grow.

Lever 2: Reducing Costs

Instead of speeding up cash flow, management could seek to decrease the amount of cash it needs to invest. Suppose Chullins's managers can negotiate better prices from key suppliers, thereby reducing the cost of sales from 60 percent to 59 percent. Suppose they can trim operating expenses by half a percentage point as well, dropping from 35 percent to 34.5 percent of sales. That would reduce the cash required to finance the next cycle from 65.5 cents to 64.45 cents, a savings of 1.05 cents per dollar of sales. If Chullins passed on these savings to its customers to hold its profit margin at 5 percent, the savings would have little impact on its ability to finance further growth, as its SFG rate would increase infinitesimally from 18.58 percent to 18.88 percent.

But if prices were held constant, the extra cash generated in each cycle would rise from 5 cents per dollar of sales to 6.5 cents. Now, needing only 64.45 cents to generate each dollar of sales in each cycle and generating 6.5 cents profit on each dollar, Chullins can generate 10.09 percent more sales in the next cycle, for an annualized SFG rate of 24.54 percent. (See the figures for Lever 2 in the exhibit.)

Look at the power of the profit margin. An increase of 1.5 percentage points in the net margin led to an increase of six percentage points from the original 18.58 percent in the rate at which Chullins can grow—that's an increase of 32 percent in its SFG rate. Companies with huge gross margins, such as many software companies (which can produce CDs for only a few dollars and sell them for hundreds), are able to grow so fast because they need to tie up relatively little cash for inventory and because their high profit margins generate lots of cash for growth.

Lever 3: Raising Prices

Rather than reduce costs, Chullins could achieve essentially the same result by raising prices (assuming the market would bear it). Suppose management thinks it can raise prices 1.5 percent without dampening demand. That too raises profit margins from 5 cents to 6.5 cents. If all costs remain the same, the higher prices would, in effect, lower the cost of sales and operating expenses. The result is that Chullins would be able to sustain a growth rate of 24.15 percent, slightly lower than it could afford if it instead reduced costs while keeping its price steady, since in that case, slightly more cash is invested during the cycle. (See the figures for Lever 3 in the exhibit.)

Pulling Multiple Levers

There is, of course, nothing to prevent management from using more than one lever at a time. If Chullins could manage to both speed its cash flow and reduce costs, it would be able to sustain an annual growth rate of 26.64 percent—43 percent more than its original growth rate—without going to external sources of capital. (See the figures in the exhibit for using multiple levers.)

ADDING COMPLEXITY TO THE FRAMEWORK

So far, we've considered a simplified situation: The operating cash cycle encompasses all the cash flows involved in generating sales, and there are no noncash expenses, so profit equals cash at the end of each cycle. We've included income taxes in operating expenses and ignored depreciation. In reality, however, the effects of taxes and depreciation are more complex than this, and we can account for them within the framework.

Income Taxes

Two complications arise regarding income taxes for most companies: Taxes are not paid uniformly over a company's OCC (in the United States, for example, taxes are paid quarterly), and their calculation includes noncash expenses such as depreciation.

Let's assume that 40 percent of pretax profits are paid quarterly in income taxes. As we did with operating expenses, we'll treat income taxes as if we paid them uniformly throughout the 90-day quarter such that cash for taxes will be tied up for 45 days and will accrue for 45 days. To make the example comparable, we must adjust the figures so that Chullins generates 5 percent profit from operations after taxes rather than before (which we do by raising pretax profits from sales to 8.3 percent). Cash for cost of sales and operating expenses remains the same, but we must now include cash for income taxes (3.3 percent for 105 of the cycle's 150 days, since we subtract the 45 days when taxes will not have been paid). Chullins's ability to grow according to this more precise treatment, 18.39 percent, is barely less than the 18.58 percent in our original example. That's because cash tied up for income taxes is very small relative to the amount needed for cost of sales and operating expenses.

Depreciation and Asset Replacement

In most companies, depreciation expenses are offset wholly or mostly by real cash used to maintain their asset bases. Equipment must be replaced, facilities updated, and so on, just to maintain a company's current rate of sales. To include these costs, we will use the depreciation figure (1 percent of sales) that Chullins historically shows on its income statement, together with our assumptions about the company's asset replacement history.

If Chullins doesn't need to invest cash to upgrade assets (which may be true in the short term), its SFG rate rises to 19.94 percent. That's because the depreciation allowance saves on taxes, yielding more cash from operations (5.4 percent of sales rather than 5 percent). But if we assume that the company spends all of its depreciation allowance on asset replacement to maintain its current sales level, the SFG rate falls to 16.25 percent. This makes sense, because the cash being invested in asset replacement exceeds the cash generated from the tax break.

Making adjustments for taxes, depreciation, and asset replacement can be tedious, and as their impact on the SFG rate is generally extremely small, we suggest that for preliminary, back-of-the-envelope planning, managers should omit them. In a spreadsheet analysis, the calculations are relatively easier, and we include them in our remaining comparisons to be more precise.

INVESTING OVER MANY CYCLES

So far, we've assumed that Chullins Distributors has enough capacity to accommodate an increase in sales without increasing fixed assets; we've also assumed that all marketing and R&D expenditures could remain at their historical levels as a percentage of sales.

At some point for almost all companies, however, these assumptions fail to hold. Plants are working around the clock, perhaps. Maybe Chullins's warehouse is bursting at the seams. Or the company needs to embark on a major promotion or costly R&D effort. In such cases, a portion of the cash generated in each operating cash cycle must be set aside to fund expenses that span a number of cycles.

Investing in Additional Fixed Assets

The period over which a company finances its fixed assets has a marked effect on its ability to grow, perhaps more than many managers would expect. Let's say that Chullins needs $400,000 to expand its facilities in a year in which its annual sales volume is $10 million. It must therefore set aside 4 cents of each annual sales dollar for expansion (i.e., 4 cents in cash for each sales dollar in Chullins's 150-day cycle). Deducting this amount and the 1 cent for asset replacement from its 5.4 percent profit leaves 0.4 cents to fund growth in subsequent cycles, and the SFG rate drops to a mere 1.48 percent. Chullins, therefore, may be unable to serve potential new customers just before expansion, although it could resume a faster rate of growth after the facilities are in place.

But what if the company decides to take two years to set aside that $400,000? Then each annual sales dollar would provide cash for growth of 2.4 cents per dollar of sales, because only 2 cents per sales dollar must be set aside for expansion during each 150-day cycle. Chullins's patience would permit a faster SFG rate, 8.86 percent, during the funding period.

After making the investment in new capacity, Chullins could resume its previous full SFG rate, assuming that its levels of operating and working capital remain unchanged. If, however, the new investment reduces the cost of sales or operating expenses, as it might, Chullins's growth rate would increase. Of course, the company could, perhaps, lease its additional facilities, to avoid the initial cash outlay entirely. Doing so would avoid depressing its SFG rate for a year or two, as in the examples above, but would add costs over the life of the lease. Projecting the extra costs and comparing them to any additional cash the new facilities would generate would enable the company to calculate its SFG rate for this scenario.

Investing in R&D and Marketing

Suppose the company invests a hefty $400,000 in R&D or marketing, paid out evenly over the year. How that expense is accounted for has a major effect on Chullins's ability to finance future growth. If the investment is treated as a capital expenditure, it becomes the equivalent of purchasing a fixed asset, and the SFG drops to the same 1.48 percent. But how about expensing the investment in the current year for tax purposes? That will reduce Chullins's taxable income from 7.3 percent to 3.3 percent. The resulting tax savings means that cash from operations falls 2.4 percentage points rather than 4 points. For working capital, Chullins now needs 66.8 cents instead of 65.9 cents for each cycle to fund the higher level of operating expenses. Thus, allowing for tax savings, Chullins would now be generating cash at the rate of 2 cents per sales dollar, for an SFG rate of 7.29 percent during the period in which the additional 4 percent expense in R&D or marketing takes place.

Different Product Lines within a Business

Different product lines, different customers, different business units, and so on often exhibit different cash and operating characteristics. Some customers, for example, may need extended terms, thereby requiring greater investments in working capital. Others may demand volume discounts. Let's give Chullins two product lines to illustrate how to use the framework to make decisions about their growth potential.

Product A is its original line, which has a net profit margin of 4 percent. At 7 percent, Product B is a higher-margin line of customized items sold to a few large customers who require extended terms. When we calculate the SFG rate for each in the usual way, we find that even though Product A carries lower margins, the duration of its cash cycle is so much shorter (92 days versus 271 days) that its SFG rate comes to 27.08 percent, nearly twice Product B's 13.65 percent. If we assume that the prospects for growth are equal for the two product lines, Chullins will grow faster in the long run by pursuing the lower-margin Product A. Since its annual SFG rate is twice as high, a dollar of cash invested in efforts to grow Product A will bring slightly more net profit (4 percent profit on 27.08 percent additional sales will yield 1.08 percent more net profit) than that same dollar would reap if invested in Product B (7 percent net profit on 13.65 percent additional sales will yield 0.96 percent more net profit). As sales growth compounds, the advantage of Product A over Product B can only grow. Counterintuitively, perhaps, serving large new customers with their equally large demands—even at higher margins—is not always the most attractive route to growth.

BRINGING TOGETHER OPERATIONS AND ASSET MANAGEMENT

Operating management decisions (which usually focus on the income statement) and asset management decisions (which typically focus on the balance sheet) are often made by different groups of managers within an organization. Our framework provides a way to bring together these discrete kinds of decisions and managerial perspectives for a common discussion of the merits of various operating and financial strategies and their impacts on the ability of a company to finance its own growth.

This collaboration need not be restricted to company-wide decisions. SFG rates can be calculated for companies of any size, for business units, or for market segments. They can be calculated from historical financial data or extrapolated from planned future performance assumptions to facilitate what-if planning. As such, the SFG framework can be the source of a new, more complete, and more powerful understanding of the consequences of managerial decisions.

WHERE IS THE MOST GROWTH POTENTIAL?

For simplicity's sake, we've used a distribution company for our hypothetical example. But different kinds of businesses differ in their ability to grow from internally generated funds. Our framework can demonstrate how.

Manufacturing Companies

Rather than being a distributor, what if Chullins were a retailer or a manufacturer? The variables work in essentially the same way for retailers, and they're almost the same for manufacturers. But rather than figuring in operating expenses throughout the operating cash cycle, manufacturers factor in labor costs, the duration of which is slightly shorter, leading to a small difference in the SFG rate. If we keep all variables comparable and now include labor costs, Chullins Manufacturing could sustain a self-financed growth rate of 16.35 percent, practically identical to Chullins Distributors' 16.25 percent (accounting for taxes, depreciation, and asset replacement). The greater capital intensity of the manufacturing business has virtually no effect, given our assumption that all depreciation allowance is used to fund asset replacement. But to the extent that fixed assets must be added to grow, the SFG rate would be reduced. In fact, unless gross margins are extraordinary, as they are for software companies, SFG rates for manufacturers are not likely to be very high relative to other kinds of businesses because of the ongoing need to add capacity to support sales growth.

Direct Marketers and Importers

For companies like these, working capital can be tied up in more arenas than inventory and accounts receivable. Importers, for example, must typically post letters of credit before merchandise will be shipped, essentially paying for goods some 30 or 45 days before they are received. Direct marketers often mail catalogs or buy media time for infomercials long before sales are made, and neither postal services nor television stations are likely to offer trade credit. In such cases, the OCC increases dramatically. But that doesn't necessarily depress a company's ability to finance growth, as we can demonstrate if we reconfigure Chullins Manufacturing into Chullins Imports.

Let's say the company decides to begin importing all of its inventory from Asia instead of buying domestically. Its suppliers require letters of credit, backed by Chullins's cash, before the merchandise is sent on its 40-day trip across the Pacific, through customs, and on to Chullins's domestic warehouse. This requirement increases the company's operating cash cycle from 150 to 190 days. And since it has no trade credit from suppliers anymore, its cash for cost of sales is now tied up for that entire 190-day period instead of Chullins Distributors' 120 days. Those changes alone would dramatically depress Chullins's SFG rate.

But we must factor in the reason for switching suppliers, which is, typically, to reduce overall merchandise costs. So let's assume that, despite the added transportation costs, overall costs drop by 10 percentage points, lowering cost of sales from 60 percent to 50 percent. If Chullins's operating expenses remain at 31.7 percent of sales, the pretax profit margin rises 10 percentage points over that in the manufacturing example, to 17.3 percent, resulting in a dramatic rise—to 28.09 percent per year—in its ability to finance growth.

So even though Chullins Imports had to tie up its cash for inventory 58 percent longer (from 120 days to 190 days), the power of the profit margin pays big dividends in its ability to grow. It's no wonder we see so much movement of manufacturing activities to lower-cost locations.

Now, let's say that Chullins Imports decides to become a direct marketer, changes its name to Chullins Gadgets, and begins selling its products with late-night and weekend infomercials on television. We'll assume that, as a direct marketer, the company has focused its product line very well so that its inventory now turns over in a mere 35 days instead of 80. Its accounts receivable drop to five days, since customers are paying by credit card, but it must prepay its advertising 90 days in advance to get the best time slots on the best stations. The OCC for Chullins Gadgets stretches from the time it pays for advertising to the time it gets the credit card revenue, or just 95 days, radically shorter than Chullins Imports' 190 days.

Let's assume that expenses equaling 15 percent of sales move from operating expenses to media expenses, reflecting the change from retailing or distributing to direct marketing. This shift keeps Chullins Gadgets' profit margin equal to that of Chullins Imports. Leaving all other data the same, the rate at which Chullins Gadgets can grow is 57.84 percent, more than double its rate as an importer.

Why can Chullins Gadgets grow so fast? Eliminating most of its accounts receivable time shortens the operating cash cycle dramatically at one end. And because 80 of the 95 days it ties up its cash in advertising media are concurrent with its inventory and letter of credit investments, the cycle does not lengthen at the other end. A 95-day OCC enables the company to recycle its cash much faster, paying dramatic dividends in the direct marketer's ability to finance a higher rate of growth.

Service Companies

From an SFG perspective, service companies—except for capital-intensive businesses such as hotels and telecommunications companies—are blessed. They have little inventory, and some—such as hair salons—are paid when the service is delivered. Others, such as airlines, are even paid well in advance of service delivery. But let's assume that our service company, Chullins Facilities Management, still has to wait 70 days to get paid by its customers. Let's also say that it pays its employees, on average, 10 days after the service is delivered and that it carries essentially no inventory. This shortens its OCC to only the time it waits to get paid, or 70 days, which allows it to finance a growth rate of 33.59 percent, not quite the rate of Chullins Gadgets because it can't match the direct marketer's higher profit margin.

To take the service business one step further, let's now put Chullins into the trendy hairstyling business. Chullins Salons gets paid in cash (or by credit card or check) when its services are delivered, so receivables are now outstanding only five days (to take the cash to the bank and clear the checks and credit charges). If the employees are paid, as before, 10 days after the delivery of the service, Chullins Salons can use the customers' cash to make payroll and pay operating expenses and taxes, so the cash it needs to tie up in an OCC is actually negative: Each cycle actually generates cash for working capital and operations. The salons still generate the original cash from operations of 5.4 cents, which can be used for growth, and now its operations contribute an additional 67.6 cents in excess cash in each five-day cycle. That means there's theoretically no limit to Chullins's ability to finance its own growth, other than the limits imposed by a need to invest in additional fixed assets, like new salons or large-scale marketing efforts.

It's not surprising, then, that many of today's fastest-growing businesses are service providers. Limits to their growth are imposed by their productive capacity, their ability to attract and train service providers, and their market presence, not their cash.

Notes about Start-Ups

Here we present some observations and practical suggestions about start-ups, particularly ones that are bootstrapped or ones that do not have institutional investors who tend to impose certain disciplines.

CASH FLOW

A typical issue with first-time start-up entrepreneurs is the failure to understand the cash flow cycle of the business. Cash revenues usually trail cash expenses. In most cases, cash expenses start from the beginning. Usually new businesses are not able to obtain credit terms immediately from suppliers. In many instances they use their credit cards to buy materials and services, but their credit card limits are low, in comparison to their business requirements. In most cases, cash revenues ramp up over a period of time until reaching their high-level potentials in a few months or few years, in the best cases. The cash outflow could be higher if there is a need to buy production equipment and computers. The cash revenue realization is sometimes further compounded for the time required to develop a product or service and test it to ensure the commercial quality that will make it sellable.

The cash flow cycle is as follows: (1) out, in short-term expenses, payroll payments to employees, and purchases of equipment; (2) in, after collecting credit sales, 30 to 45 days after shipping the products or delivering the services. The shortfall gap of cash outflow over cash inflow, prevailing in most cases, determines the working capital the business requires to operate in an orderly manner.

ALLURE AND FALLACY (AN ACTUAL CASE SCENARIO)

There is an overall allure when investors are invited to participate in ventures where the business legal structure represents that the moneys at risk are limited to the amounts invested in the C or S corporations or the limited partnerships. (See *business structures* in the Glossary.)

It happens frequently with successful professionals, and with groups of friends or family members investing in a start-up venture. The common denominator is that these individuals have large disposable income from their professional practices or trades, sums of inherited money, or easy access to family loans. The feeling of the small risk involved is particularly present when the investing group is composed of several individuals. The dollar amount to be invested by each one is small in relation to their personal net worth.

The business venture could be the same or similar to their trades or business backgrounds, or could be high tech or modern dot-com companies, or any other business unfamiliar to the investors. Regardless, the investors do not actively participate in the day-to-day running of operations. They are busy with their professional business or trade business. They believe it is only a matter of investing some money in a deal that a promoter indicates is a potential big winner. In many instances management is assigned to the venture's promoter. In other cases management is assigned to a rather inexperienced manager who is hired as an employee at a low pay scale. It is hands-off from the beginning.

Most of these investors do not have business experience and fail to request an evaluation of cash flow projections beforehand. They read some documents and charts with business plans ranging from short and rather flimsy narratives to various degrees of sophisticated presentations.

In many instances, the venture starts operations and (even in those cases in which revenue is generated from the beginning) sooner or a little later the undercapitalization of the company comes into play. The venture always requires a level of working capital and equipment.

As an example: Ten professional individuals are asked to invest $30,000 each—not a significant personal risk given their level of disposable income. They are told that the legal structure of the company ensures that only the $30,000 investment of each is at risk; this is true as the company is a C or S corporation or a limited partnership.

The venture starts with $300,000 in its bank account. After a few months, the start-up's negative cash flow begins to have an impact and it becomes apparent that the business does not have enough working capital. The business manager goes to a commercial bank and requests a loan. The balance sheet is weak; the original $300,000 has been mostly consumed by cash expenses exceeding cash revenues. The bank officer indicates that the bank will grant a line of credit provided the shareholders or partners (investors) sign off personal guarantees supported by their homes and personal assets as collateral for the bank loan. The same happens when the manager approaches a leasing company to acquire equipment and computers. The leasing company requires the shareholders or partners to put up their homes and personal assets as collateral.

The allure of the limited monetary risk becomes a fallacy once the investors put their personal assets as collateral in support of the venture's bank loans and equipment leases.

And, without fully realizing it, the limited risk situation becomes an open-ended risk where homes, bank accounts, and investments in the investors' names are in jeopardy if the business venture goes sideways. The venture's losses could force the company into bankruptcy but the Chapter 11 protection would be related only to small unsecured liabilities. The major liabilities would be represented by the collateralized bank loan and leases. The investors in cases like this will find that they not only lose their original $30,000 but some other high dollars they have to come up with to satisfy their share of the payments to the bank and the leasing company, as the company has no cash or assets to speak of.

A WISER ALTERNATIVE

A better alternative for hands-off investors in start-ups is to obtain reliable cash flow projections and a reasonable determination of the capital required to fund, at least, the working capital for the entire start-up phase, including the payroll expenses of an experienced manager. It is much easier to confront the need in advance and make the investment with a complete understanding of the risk.

Maybe the original investment request should have been $80,000 each. These investors might have decided "no-go" at the $80,000 level. But if they decided "go," they probably would have put some mechanism of controls in place, eventually improving the chances of success for the venture.

INCOME TAXATION

For business structures where the ventures' profits flow through as earnings for the investors annually, the successful venture can pose a dilemma for the investors. The company's success does not necessarily mean that there is cash available to be paid out to investors as they share in the company's profits. The company is growing, and all cash is needed to support its expansion.

The investors receive large profit distributions on paper (Form K-1), which increase their taxable income and their income tax payouts to the IRS and to their state revenue department. The investors have no choice but to cover the additional income tax amounts out of their own resources, or from borrowings. To this extent the investors are increasing their investment in the company, which enjoys the benefit of not paying income taxes. The company has more cash available and the investors have less cash available.

The investors could decide to take cash out of the company to cover the amounts of their income taxes. The trade-off is that the company curtails its expansion plans or obtains additional outside capital to support its growth.

Monitoring the company legal structure is advisable. An S corporation or a partnership could have been the best alternative in the early stages of a business, but at a given success level, it could be wise to change the legal structure to a C corporation. Always consult your counsel and accountant for this decision.

EARLY SUCCESS PERILS

There are perils with early venture successes, especially in bootstrapped operations and companies that do not have the external discipline imposed by institutional investors. Entrepreneurs keep a tight rein on expenses and cash flow in the early stages. Sometimes when the venture makes the transition from early struggling to a solid good performance and positive cash flow the entrepreneur changes his or her modus operandi from frugality to freewheeling.

There is no assurance that early successes are permanent. Competition and general economic conditions can halt the early progress of a company or turn performance into a tailspin at various degrees of intensity. Entrepreneurs who fail to maintain discipline and focus in managing and growing the company will inevitably "hit the wall."

It is advisable to avoid management decisions leading into luxury car leases, leasing expensive premises (or building fancy new offices), purchasing the highest-priced furniture, and approving exorbitant off-site meetings and first-class travel. A certain degree of temperance should be maintained and a close watch on performance and expenses is needed until early success is consolidated during a reasonable period of time. As early success becomes apparent, management should ensure that expenses and capital expenditures are committed to projects that will contribute to improved performance and increasing company value.

Glossary

Herein is a glossary of terms used in corporate finance and business.* We have attempted to provide a comprehensive listing of terms generally used, as well as those we have referenced in previous sections. A searchable version is available online at www.HandbookOfFinancingGrowth.com for your use. You will need the reader code "HOFG_Reader" to access the site.

A round　A financing event whereby venture capitalists become involved in a fast-growth company that was previously financed by founders and/or angels.

accelerated depreciation　A depreciation method that yields higher depreciation in the early years and less in the later years.[1]

accounts payable　See **payables.**

accounts receivable　See **receivables.**

accredited investor　A person or legal entity, such as a company or trust fund, that meets certain net worth and income qualifications and is considered to be sufficiently sophisticated to make investment decisions in complex situations. Regulation D of the Securities Act of 1933 exempts accredited investors from protection under the Securities Act. Typical qualifications for a person are: $1 million net worth and the two most recent years of annual income equal to or exceeding $200,000 individually or $300,000 with a spouse, and the expectation of the same level of income for the current year; $5 million in assets for an entity.

advisory board　See **board of advisers.**

alternative asset class　A class of investments that includes private equity, real estate, and oil and gas, but excludes publicly traded securities. Pension plans, college endowments, and other relatively large institutional investors typically allocate a certain percentage of their investments to alternative assets with an objective to diversify their portfolios.

AMEX　Stock exchange with the third highest volume of trading in the United States. Located at 86 Trinity Place in downtown Manhattan. The bulk of

---

*Much of the content of this glossary was developed and written in 2003 by Professors Colin Blaydon and Fred Wainwright, Tuck School of Business at Dartmouth. The authors gratefully acknowledge the support of the Tuck Center for Private Equity and Entrepreneurship. Copyright © Trustees of Dartmouth College. All rights reserved.

437

trading on AMEX consists of index options (computer technology index, institutional index, major market index), and shares of small to medium-size companies are predominant. Recently merged with Nasdaq.[2]

angel   A person who invests in companies in relatively early stages of development. Usually angels invest less than $1 million per start-up. The typical angel-financed start-up is in concept or product development phase.

antidilution   A contract clause that protects an investor from issuances of securities at a price below that paid by the investor; upon a sale at a lower price, the clause applies a formula to the investor's investment that increases the number of shares issuable to the investor. There are two basic antidilution provisions—weighted average and ratchet.

arbitrage   An investment opportunity that requires zero investment, has no risk, and still yields a positive return is called an arbitrage opportunity.[3] This can be accomplished by taking advantage of a price imbalance of two or more markets.

asset-based lending (ABL)   The traditional definition of asset-based financing refers to a loan extended to a borrower in the form of a revolving credit facility or term loan. An asset-based loan in the form of a revolving credit facility focuses on the level of current assets of a company. A loan amount is negotiated up front, and the amount of the loan that a lender funds will be a function of the levels of assets generated or held by the borrower. Typical revolving credit facilities apply a negotiated percentage to the level of accounts receivable and the level of inventory in order to determine the variable levels of borrowing capacity available to a borrower during the life of a loan.

B round   A financing event whereby professional investors such as venture capitalists are sufficiently interested in a company to provide additional funds after the A round of financing. Subsequent rounds are called C, D, and so on.

bankruptcy   Bankruptcy law provides for the development of a plan that allows a debtor who is unable to pay his or her creditors to resolve the debts through the division of his or her assets among creditors. This supervised division also allows the interests of all creditors to be treated with some measure of equality. Certain bankruptcy proceedings allow a debtor to stay in business and use revenue generated to resolve his or her debts. An additional purpose of bankruptcy law is to allow certain debtors to free themselves (to be discharged) of the financial obligations they have accumulated, after their assets are distributed, even if their debts have not been paid in full. There are two basic types of bankruptcy proceedings. A filing under Chapter 7 is called liquidation. It is the most common type of bankruptcy proceeding. Liquidation involves the appointment of a trustee who collects the nonexempt property of the debtor, sells it, and distributes the proceeds to the creditors. Bankruptcy proceedings under Chapter 11, 12, and 13 involve the rehabilitation of the debtor to allow him or her to use future earnings to pay off creditors.[4]

barter   To trade goods or services without the exchange of money.[5]

best efforts offering   A commitment by a syndicate of investment banks to use best efforts to ensure the sale to investors of a company's offering of securities. In a best efforts offering, the syndicate avoids any firm commitment for a specific number of shares or bonds.

beta   A product that is being tested by potential customers prior to being formally launched into the marketplace.

blue-sky law   State regulations governing the sale of securities. These regulations provide investors with full and complete disclosures regarding contemplated investment opportunities.

blue-sky stock   Stocks that have values based on promises of performance in the future with little or no real prospect of success.

blowout round   A financing event in which new investors with substantial capital are able to demand and receive contractual terms that effectively cause the issuance of sufficient new shares by the start-up company to significantly reduce (dilute) the ownership percentage of previous investors.

board of advisers   A group of individuals, typically composed of technical and industry experts, who provide guidance and feedback to the company's managers and board of directors. The board of advisers does not have a fiduciary responsibility and is usually established by the senior management and the board of directors.

board of directors   A group of individuals, typically composed of managers, investors, and experts, which have a fiduciary responsibility for the well-being and proper guidance of a corporation. The board is elected by the shareholders.

boat anchor   In business, a person, project, or activity that hinders the growth of a company.

bond covenants   Covenants are restrictions built into contractual agreements. Covenants may be affirmative or negative in nature, reflecting actions required of or restrictions placed on a company.

book   See **private placement memorandum (PPM)**.

book-to-market ratio   The ratio of the book value of equity to the market value of equity.[6]

bootstrapping   The actions of a start-up to minimize expenses and build cash flow, thereby reducing or eliminating the need for outside investors. See the discussion within the body of this handbook in Chapter 5.

breakeven   The level of revenue in a business in which sales minus variable costs minus fixed costs equals zero.

breakup fee   Amount paid by a selling company to a potential buyer when the seller terminates an agreement in favor of a higher bid for the selling company.

bridge financing   Temporary funding that will eventually be replaced by permanent capital from equity investors or debt lenders. In venture capital, a bridge is usually a short-term note (6 to 12 months) that converts to preferred stock; in addition to receiving interest, a bridge lender receives warrant coverage to compensate the investor for taking an early risk in the company. Typically, the bridge lender has the right to convert the note to preferred stock at a price equal to the price of the preferred stock in the next financing round that meets minimum specified levels of funding. See **Hamburger Helper bridge; wipeout bridge.**

broad-based weighted average ratchet A type of antidilution mechanism. A weighted average ratchet adjusts downward the price per share of the preferred stock of investor A due to the issuance of options, warrants, convertible securities, or shares to new investor B at a price lower than the price investor A originally paid. Investor A's preferred stock is repriced to a weighted average of investor A's price and investor B's price. A broad-based weighted average antidilution formula uses all common stock outstanding on a fully diluted basis (including all convertible securities, warrants, and options) in the denominator of the formula for determining the new weighted average price. See **narrow-based weighted average antidilution.**

burn rate The rate at which a company with little or no revenue uses cash savings to cover expenses, usually expressed on a monthly or weekly basis. The term is typically used in reference to start-ups.

business cycle Repetitive cycle of economic expansion and contraction. The official peaks and troughs of the U.S. cycle are determined by the National Bureau of Economic Research in Cambridge, Massachusetts.[7]

business plan A document that describes the concept for a business opportunity. A business plan typically includes the following sections: executive summary, market need, solution, technology, competition, marketing, management, operations, and financials.

business structures[8] Legal alternatives of business ownership.

- **corporation** An ownership structure that allows a number of individuals or companies to own shares of the capital investment in a business. A corporation is a stand-alone legal entity, so it offers risk protection to its owners, managers, and investors from liability resulting from its actions, including bankruptcy. The invested moneys are at risk.
- **C corporation** A designation for tax purposes but not relevant for structural purposes; with respect to taxation, there is no limit to number of shareholders. Profit and loss remains in the C corporation books. Ownership is represented by the possession of common or preferred stock. The C corporation pays income taxes. Earnings are distributed to shareholders in the form of dividends. Dividends are taxable to the recipients when received. Income taxes on profits are paid twice: once by the corporation each fiscal year and a second time by the shareholders receiving distributions from the corporation.
- **S corporation** A tax designation that is not relevant for structural purposes; with respect to taxation, an ownership structure that limits its number of shareholders to 75. An S corporation does not pay income taxes; rather its owners pay income taxes on their proportion of the corporation's profits allocated to them on their K-1 tax form for each fiscal year. Taxes are paid on income allocated to shareholders whether or

not the income is actually distributed to them. Losses are also passed to shareholders as reported on Form K-1. Losses can be deducted from shareholder taxable income under certain IRS rules. S corporation earnings are taxed only one time because earnings pass through to the investors.

- **partnership** Relationship between two or more persons who join to carry on a trade or business, with each person contributing money, property, labor, or skill and each expecting to share in the profits and losses of the business as reported in Form K-1 for each partnership fiscal year. Earnings are taxed only once. Related glossary terms follow:
- **general partner (GP)** A class of partner in a partnership. Each general partner retains liability for the actions of the partnership and is personally liable for partnership debts. In the private equity world, the GP is the fund manager while the limited partners (LPs) are the institutional and high net worth investors in the partnership. The GP earns a management fee and, after limited partners receive a return of their capital, a percentage of profits (see **carried interest**) typically based on an 80/20 split, where 80 percent is distributed to the limited partners.
- **limited partner (LP)** An investor in a limited partnership. The general partner is liable for the actions of the partnership while the limited partners are generally protected from legal actions and any losses beyond their original investment.
- **limited partnership** A legal entity formed under a state limited partnership law and composed of at least one general partner and one or more limited partners. The general partner manages the business or trade and is liable for the actions of the partnership while the limited partners are generally protected from legal actions and any losses beyond their investment. The general partner receives a management fee and a percentage of profits (see **carried interest**), while the limited partners receive income, capital gains, and tax benefits.
- **limited liability partnership (LLP)** A legal entity formed under a state limited partnership law for professionals. Generally, a partner in an LLP is responsible for the partner's own actions, but not personally liable for the debts of the LLP or any other partner, nor is a partner liable for the acts or omissions of any other partner, solely by reason of being a partner.
- **limited liability company (LLC)** An ownership entity formed under state law and designed to limit the founders' and investors' losses to the amount of their investment. An LLC does not pay taxes; rather its owners pay taxes on their proportion of the LLC profits at their individual tax rates. An LLC may be classified for federal income tax purposes as either a partnership or an entity disregarded as an entity separate from its owner by applying the IRS regulations, and as determined on IRS Form 8832, Entity Classification Election. LLCs may elect to be taxed as corporations.

- **sole proprietor (SP)**　Unincorporated business owned and controlled by one person under his or her name, or doing business as (DBA) a name other than the owner's. Many successful SPs start as garage operations and are subsequently converted into entities such as corporations or LLCs.

buyout firm　An entity in the private equity industry that purchases a controlling interest in a company (as in a leveraged buyout), in many cases accompanied by a management team (as in a management buyout).

buy-sell agreement　A contract that sets forth the conditions under which a shareholder must first offer his or her shares for sale to the other shareholders before being allowed to sell to entities outside the company.

C corporation　See **business structures.**

capital asset pricing model (CAPM)　Used to determine the required rate of return for stocks.

capital call　When a general partner requests that an investor in a partnership or LLC provide additional capital. Usually an investor will agree to a maximum investment amount and the general partner will make a series of capital calls over time to the investor as opportunities arise to finance the capital requirements of targeted companies.

capital charge　The product of the cost of capital times the amount of capital used by a particular company or business unit. Typically referred to in the calculation of economic profits versus operating profits.

capital efficiency (leverage alliances)　Refers to the concept of efficient deployment of capital by venture capitalists. Best practices include offshore development and understanding the sales and distribution model for a start-up business before ramping operations; hire two to four people to experiment and test the market, then ramp.

capital expenditure　Also referred to as capex; this is the investment of funds in fixed or capital assets of a company. Among other things, this can include software, office equipment, buildings, land, factory, and equipment.

capital gains (losses)　A tax classification of investment earnings (losses) resulting from the purchase and sale of assets. Typically, an investor prefers that investment earnings be classified as long-term capital gains (held for a year or longer), which are taxed at a lower rate than ordinary income.

capitalization table　A table showing the owners of a company's shares and their ownership percentages. It also lists the forms of ownership, such as common stock, preferred stock, warrants, and options.

capital stock　Stock authorized by a company's charter and having par value, stated value, or no par value. Capital stock includes common stock and preferred stock.[9]

capped participating preferred　Preferred stock whose participating feature is limited so that an investor cannot receive more than a specified amount without converting to common stock. See **participating preferred stock.**

carried interest　A share in the profits of a private equity fund. Typically, a fund must return the capital given to it by limited partners before the general partner can share in the profits of the fund. The general partner will then receive a

20 percent carried interest, although some successful firms receive 25 percent to 30 percent. Also known as carry or promote.

cash cow   One of the four categories (quadrants) in the Boston Consulting Group's growth-share matrix. The cash cows fund their own growth, pay the corporate dividend, pay the corporate overhead, pay the corporate interest charges, supply the funds for R&D, and supply the investment resources for other products. They justify the debt capacity for the whole company, so protect them. By definition, a cash cow has a return on assets that exceeds the growth rate. Only if that is true will it generate more cash than it uses. This requires high return and slow growth if the cash generation is to be high. Almost invariably the cash cow has a high market share relative to the next two or three competitors.[10]

cash flow   The amount of cash generated from operations. This amount may be negative. Generally considered the amount of cash available to stockholders and long-term lenders of the corporation. There are several calculations that serve as a proxy for cash flow: net operating profit less adjust taxes (NOPLAT), earnings before interest and taxes (EBIT), or earnings before interest, taxes, depreciation, and amortization (EBITDA).

catch-up   A clause in the agreement between the general partner and the limited partners of a private equity fund. Once the limited partners have received a certain portion of their expected return, the general partner can then receive a majority of profits until the previously agreed-upon profit split is reached.

change of control bonus   A bonus of cash or stock given to members of a management group upon successful completion of the sale of a company.

clawback   A clause in the agreement between the general partner and the limited partners of a private equity fund. The clawback gives limited partners the right to reclaim a portion of disbursements to a general partner early in the life of a limited partnership for profitable investments when there are significant losses from later investments in a portfolio.

closing   The conclusion of a transaction whereby all necessary legal documents are signed.

collateral   Hard assets of the borrower, such as real estate or equipment, for which a lender has an equitable interest until a loan obligation is fully paid off.

commercial bank   Widely known as a source of debt financing for businesses, commercial banks generally provide lines of credit, term loans, and revolving loans. Traditionally, commercial banks are cash flow lenders and view collateral as a secondary source of repayment; from experience, bankers' actions do not always evidence this thinking. Focus is placed on lending to borrowers that have durability and predictability of cash flows. To assure liquidity and stability for the public, banks are highly regulated by states, the Federal Deposit Insurance Corporation (FDIC), and by the operating cash cycle (OCC).

commercial paper   An unsecured, short-term loan issued by a corporation, typically for financing accounts receivable and inventories. It is usually issued at a discount reflecting prevailing market interest rates. Maturities on commercial paper rarely are any longer than 270 days.[11]

commitment An obligation, typically the maximum amount that an investor or lender agrees to invest in a fund or to loan to a company.

common stock A type of security representing ownership rights in a company. Usually, company founders, management, and employees own common stock while investors own preferred stock. In the event of a liquidation of the company, the claims of secured and unsecured creditors, bondholders, and preferred stockholders take precedence over common stockholders. See **preferred stock.**

comparable A publicly traded company with similar characteristics to a private company that is being valued. For example, a telecommunications equipment manufacturer whose market value is two times revenues can be used to estimate the value of a similar and relatively new company with a new product in the same industry. See **liquidity discount.**

consolidation See **rollup.**

contingent value rights (CVR) Provides the holder with the right to sell a share of stock in the underlying company at a fixed price during the life of the right.[12]

contribution margin Selling price minus variable cost. For a business operating above breakeven, the contribution margin from incremental sales becomes operating profit.

control The authority of an individual or entity that owns more than 50 percent of equity in a company or owns the largest block of shares compared to other shareholders.

conversion The right of an investor or lender to force a company to replace the investor's preferred shares or the lender's debt with common shares at a preset conversion ratio. A conversion feature was first used in railroad bonds in the 1800s.

convertible debt A loan that allows the lender to exchange the debt for common shares in a company at a preset conversion ratio.

convertible preferred stock A type of stock that gives an owner the right to convert to common shares of stock. Preferred stock is granted certain rights not normally granted to the holders of common stock, such as decision-making management control, a guaranteed return on investment, or senior priority in receiving proceeds from a sale or liquidation of the company. Convertible preferred is the most common tool for private equity funds to invest in companies.

convertible security A security that gives its owner the right to exchange the security for common shares in a company at a preset conversion ratio. The security is typically preferred stock or debt.

corporate charter The document prepared when a corporation is formed. The charter sets forth the objectives and goals of the corporation, as well as a general statement of what the corporation can and cannot do while pursuing these goals.[13]

corporate resolution A document stating that the corporation's board of directors has taken a specified action, such as authorizing management to act on behalf of the corporation.[14]

corporate venturing Venture capital provided by in-house investment funds of large corporations to further their own strategic interests.[15]

corporation   See **business structures.**

cost of capital   Actual or implied interest rate for the use of money or assets of a company.

cost of goods sold (COGS)   Same as **cost of sales.**

cost of revenue   Same as cost of goods sold, though the term usually refers to costs incurred to generate service revenues versus those of product revenues. Cost of revenue and cost of goods sold are usually comprised of direct and indirect costs. Direct costs are those that are attributed directly and proportionally to creating the product or service (i.e., materials and labor). Indirect costs are those expenses that are attributed to creating the product or service but are general in nature and not easily allocated on a per unit basis (i.e., engineering support costs and facilities costs related to producing the product or service).

cost of sales (COS)   The burdened expenses incurred to generate the revenue of a company; includes direct and indirect costs.

covenant   A legal promise to do or not do a certain thing. For example, in a financing arrangement, company management may agree to a negative covenant whereby it promises not to incur additional debt. The penalties for violation of a covenant may vary from repairing the mistake to losing control of the company.

cram-down round   See **blowout round.**

cumulative dividends   The owner of preferred stock with cumulative dividends has the right to receive accrued (previously unpaid) dividends in full before dividends are paid to any other classes of stock.

current ratio   The ratio of current assets to current liabilities. Less than 1 indicates negative working capital. The current ratio is used to measure liquidity.

data room   Central location for due diligence materials provided by a company to all potential purchasers or investors in connection with an acquisition or investment.

days sales outstanding (DSO)   The average period in days in which a company's accounts receivable remain due from the customer.

deal flow   A measure of the number of potential investments that a fund reviews in any given period.

debt-for-equity swaps   A voluntary exchange of outstanding debt for equity of equal market value.[16]

debt service   The ratio of a loan payment amount to available cash flow earned during a specific period. Typically lenders insist that a company maintain a certain debt service ratio or else risk penalties such as having to pay off the loan immediately.

debt-to-equity (D/E) ratio   Total liabilities divided by total equity of the entity as shown in its balance sheet. The D/E measures the entity's leverage level. A debt-to-equity ratio of 1 indicates that the entity's total liabilities equal the equity dollar amount.

default   A company's failure to comply with the terms and conditions of a financing arrangement.

definitive agreement   The final, fully negotiated agreement between parties, containing all material terms, conditions, and agreements relating to the subject matter of the transaction in question.

demand right   A type of registration right. Demand rights give an investor the right to force a company to register its shares with the SEC.

dilution   The reduction in the ownership percentage of current investors, founders, and employees caused by the issuance of new shares to new investors.

dilution protection   See **antidilution; ratchet**.

direct costs   See **cost of revenue**.

disbursement   An investment by a fund in a company.

discount rate   The interest rate used to determine the present value of a series of future cash flows.

discounted cash flow (DCF)   Calculation of the present value of a stream of forecasted cash flow discounted using an interest rate appropriate to the risk of the venture creating the cash flow.

discounted free cash flow (DFCF)   Equity valuation method in which a discount percentage is applied to a stream of forecasted free cash flows, where free cash flow is defined as net operating cash flow increased by net debt issuances and decreased by net investment.

distribution   The transfer of cash or securities to a limited partner resulting from the sale, liquidation, or IPO of one or more portfolio companies in which a general partner chose to invest.

dividends   Payments made by a company to the owners of its securities out of earnings of the company based solely on the amount of securities owned.

dividend yield   The dollar dividend per share divided by the current price per share.[17]

domain expertise   Intelligence of an investor, partner, or potential employee in the specific business or industry occupied by a company.

double taxation   Refers to the same income being taxed twice, once at the entity level and once at the individual level. Thus, dividends, which are paid out of after-tax corporate profits, are double taxed when individuals have to pay taxes on them as well.[18]

down round   A round of financing whereby the valuation of the company is lower than the value determined by investors in an earlier round.

drag-along rights   The contractual right of an investor in a company to force all other investors to agree to a specific action, such as the sale of the company.

drive-by VC   A venture capitalist who appears only during board meetings of a portfolio company and rarely offers advice to management.

due diligence   The investigatory process performed by individuals or entities considering transactions with a third party to evaluate the business and finances of a company.

early stage   The stage of a company after the seed (formation) stage but before middle stage (generating revenues). Typically, a company in early stage will have a core management team and a proven concept or product, but no positive cash flow.

earnings before interest and taxes (EBIT)   A measurement of the operating profit of a company. One possible valuation methodology is based on a comparison of private and public companies' value as a multiple of EBIT.

earnings before interest, taxes, depreciation, and amortization (EBITDA)   A measurement of the cash flow of a company. One possible valuation methodology is based on a comparison of private and public companies' value as a multiple of EBITDA less funded debt.

economic profit The difference between the amount received in connection with the sale of a good or service and the cost of goods or services sold analyzed on the basis of their opportunity cost. Also defined as EBIT minus a charge for the cost of capital deployed to generate the EBIT.

elevator pitch A concise presentation, lasting only a few minutes (an elevator ride), by an entrepreneur to a potential investor about an investment opportunity.

employee stock ownership program (ESOP) An equity plan established by a company that permits the grant of options on stock of the company for long-term incentive compensation for employees.

equity The ownership structure of a company represented by common shares, preferred shares, or unit interests. Equity = Assets − Liabilities.

escrow Documents, real estate, money, or securities deposited with a neutral third party (the escrow agent) to be delivered upon fulfillment of certain conditions, as established in a written agreement.

evergreen fund A fund that reinvests its profits in order to ensure the availability of capital for future investments.

exit strategy The plan for generating profits for owners and investors of a company. Typically, exit strategies include mergers and acquisitions, recapitalizations, and initial public offerings (IPOs).

expansion stage The stage of a company characterized by a complete management team and a substantial increase in revenues.

factor analysis A statistical technique where past data is analyzed with the intent of extracting common factors that might have affected the data.[19]

factoring The selling of a company's accounts receivable, at a discount, to a third party who either then assumes the credit risk of the account debtors, known as nonrecourse factoring, or assumes no credit risk, known as recourse factoring, and receives cash as the company's customers pay their accounts.

fairness hearing The hearing conducted by a state agency in connection with a proposed business combination, merger, or acquisition that results in the issuer of securities receiving a transactional exemption from registration of the securities, and the target shareholders, other than affiliates of the resulting company, receiving freely tradable shares.

fairness opinion A letter issued by an investment bank to assess the fairness of a transaction such as the negotiated price for a merger or an acquisition.

Financial Accounting Standards Board (FASB) The private-sector organization empowered to establish financial accounting and reporting standards. Although this function legally resides with the Securities and Exchange Commission for public companies, the SEC has traditionally provided the private sector with the opportunity for self-regulation. Since 1973, the SEC has relied on the FASB for standard setting. The FASB operates under the oversight of the Financial Accounting Foundation, which is responsible for funding the activities of both the FASB and its counterpart for state and local government, the Governmental Accounting Standards Board. The Financial Accounting Foundation also is responsible for selecting the members of both accounting standards boards and their respective advisory councils. Eleven members of the board of trustees of the Financial Accounting Foundation are nominated by eight organizations and approved by the trustees. The nominating organizations are:

1. American Accounting Association.
2. American Institute of Certified Public Accountants.
3. Association for Investment Management and Research.
4. Financial Executives International.
5. Government Finance Officers Association.
6. Institute of Management Accountants
7. National Association of State Auditors, Comptrollers and Treasurers.
8. Securities Industry Association.

Five additional trustees serve as at-large members and are selected by the board of trustees. The Foundation is incorporated to operate exclusively for charitable, educational, scientific, and literary purposes within the meaning of Section 501(c)(3) of the Internal Revenue Code.[20]

financial engineering   Refers to the financial structuring of a company or particular transaction.

financial intermediaries   Institutions that provide the market function of matching borrowers and lenders or traders.[21]

financial investor   An investor interested solely in achieving a financial return from an investment, rather than a return coupled with a strategic benefit associated with the investment.

financing slack   The difference between the debt that a firm chooses to carry and the optimal debt that it could carry, when the former is less than the latter.[22]

financing statement   Document filed with a lender detailing personal property taken as collateral from a borrower. The financing statement, a standard document under the Uniform Commercial Code, is filed with the secretary of state or other designated public official. The document is time stamped, the filing date is noted, and a file number is assigned, placing the public on notice to the lender's claim to the specified collateral.[23]

fire sale   A sale of merchandise and other assets after a fire at very low prices. It is also used figuratively when merchandise and other assets of companies are sold at very low prices to ensure a fast disposal of surplus items.

firm commitment   A commitment by a syndicate of investment banks to purchase all the shares available for sale in a public offering of a company. The shares will then be resold to investors by the syndicate.

flipping   The act of selling shares immediately after an initial public offering. Investment banks that underwrite new stock issues attempt to allocate shares to new investors who indicate they will retain the shares for several months.

Form S-1   Registration statement under the Securities Act of 1933. This form is typically used in conjunction with a company's initial public offering of securities.

Form U7   Short form registration statement, also called Small Company Offering Registration (SCOR) form, used in connection with Rule 504 offerings or Regulation A offerings where the aggregate amount of securities offered is $1 million or less.

forward contract   An agreement to buy or sell the underlying asset at a fixed price at a future point in time.[24]

founder   person who participates in the creation of a company. Typically, founders manage the company until it has enough capital to hire professional managers.

free cash flow   The amount of cash a company has after expenses, debt service, capital expenditures, and dividends. Free cash flow measures the financial comfort level of the company as a going concern.

friends and family financing   Capital provided by the friends and family of founders of an early stage company. Founders should be careful not to create an ownership structure that may hinder the participation of professional investors once the company begins to achieve success.

full ratchet   An antidilution protection mechanism whereby the price per share of the preferred stock of investor A is adjusted downward due to the issuance of options, warrants, or securities to new investor B at a price lower than the price investor A originally received. Investor A's preferred stock is repriced to match the price of investor B's option, warrant, or securities. See **broad-based weighted average ratchet; narrow-based weighted average antidilution**.

fully diluted basis   A methodology for calculating any per share ratios whereby the denominator is the total number of shares issued by the company on the assumption that all warrants and options are exercised and that all convertible securities have been converted.

fund of funds   A fund created to invest in private equity funds to minimize portfolio management efforts.

GAAP   See **generally accepted accounting principles (GAAP)**.

garage operation   Figurative denomination applied to a start-up business venture with very little resources; a reference to businesses that actually started from an individual's garage at home where the individual or small group sets up an office, a lab, or a light manufacturing operation.

general partner (GP)   See **business structures**.

generally accepted accounting principles (GAAP)   A voluminous set of standards, interpretations, opinions, and bulletins developed by the Financial Accounting Standards Board.

general partner (GP)   See **business structures**.

going-concern value   The value of a company to another company or individual in terms of an operating business. The difference between a company's going-concern value and its asset or liquidation value is deemed goodwill and plays a major role in mergers and acquisitions.[25]

golden parachute   A contractual clause in a management contract that allows the manager to be paid a specified sum of money in the event the control of the firm changes.[26]

GP   See **business structures**.

graduated payment   Repayment terms calling for gradual increases in the payments on a closed-end obligation. A graduated payment loan usually involves negative amortization.[27]

greenmail   The purchase of a potential hostile acquirer's stake in a business at a premium over the current fair market value of the stock.[28]

grossing up   An adjustment of an option pool for management and employees of a company that increases the number of shares available over time. This usually occurs after a financing round whereby one or more investors receive a relatively large percentage of the company.

gross margin   Revenue associated with the sale of a product or service less the direct costs of providing the product or service.

growth stage   The stage of a company when it has received one or more rounds of financing and is generating revenue from its product or service. Same as **middle stage.**

haircut   Reduction in value taken by one party in order to compensate another party or facilitate a transaction.

Hamburger Helper bridge   A colorful label for a traditional bridge loan that includes the right of the bridge lender to convert the note to preferred stock at a price that is a 20 percent discount from the price of the preferred stock in the next financing round.

Hart-Scott-Rodino Act   A law permitting the Federal Trade Commission and the U.S. Department of Justice to examine potential investments and acquisitions and to deny permission to the companies to consummate the proposed transaction where the transaction has the potential for reducing competition in an industry or business segment.

harvest   To generate cash or stock from the sale or IPO of companies in a private equity portfolio of investments.

hedge   A transaction that reduces the risk of an investment.[29]

hockey stick   The general shape and form of a chart showing revenue, customers, cash, or some other financial or operational measure that increases dramatically at some point in the future. Entrepreneurs often develop business plans with hockey stick charts to impress potential investors.

holding period   Length of time an asset (property) is held by its owner. The holding period for short-term capital gains and losses is one year or less. The holding period for long-term capital gains and losses is more than one year. To figure the holding period, begin counting on the day after you receive the property and include the day you disposed of it.

hot issue   Stock in an initial public offering that is in high demand.

hurdle rate   A minimum rate of return required before an investor will make an investment.

incubator   A company or facility designed to host start-up companies. Incubators help start-ups grow while controlling costs by offering networks of contacts and shared back-office resources.

indicative offer   Short form term sheet in which a potential investor, partner, or acquirer provides a target with an informal description of the material terms and conditions of an offer.

information asymmetry   Imbalance that arises anytime one party to a transaction or agreement has more or better information than others.[30]

initial public offering (IPO)   The first offering of stock by a company to the public. New public offerings must be registered with the Securities and Exchange Commission.

inside round A round of financing in which the investors are the same investors as the previous round.

insider information Material information about a company that has not yet been made public. It is illegal for holders of this information to make trades based on it, however received.[31]

insiders Directors and senior officers of a corporation—in effect, those who have access to inside information about a company. An insider also is someone who owns more than 10 percent of the voting shares of a company.[32]

insolvency risk The risk that a firm will be unable to satisfy its debts. Also known as bankruptcy risk.[33]

insolvent Unable to pay debts (e.g., a firm's liabilities exceed its assets).[34]

institutional investors Organizations that invest, including insurance companies, depository institutions, pension funds, investment companies, mutual funds, and endowment funds.[35]

interest The price paid for borrowing money. It is expressed as a percentage rate over a period of time and reflects the rate of exchange of present consumption for future consumption. Also, a share or title in property.[36]

interest coverage ratio Earnings before interest and taxes divided by the interest expense. The interest coverage ratio is a measure of the firm's capacity to service its interest payments, with higher coverage ratios representing more safety.[37]

interest coverage test A debt limitation that prohibits the issuance of additional long-term debt if the issuer's interest coverage would, as a result of the issue, fall below some specified minimum.[38]

interest deduction An interest expense, such as interest on a margin account, that is allowed as a deduction for tax purposes.[39]

interest expense The money the corporation or individual pays out in interest on loans.[40]

interest in arrears Interest that is due only at the maturity date rather than periodically over the life of the loan.[41]

interest-only loan A loan in which payment of principal is deferred and interest payments are the only current obligation.[42]

interest tax shield The reduction in income taxes that results from the tax-deductibility of interest payments.[43]

interim statement A financial statement that reflects only a limited period of a company's financial statement, not the entire fiscal year.[44]

internal finance Finance generated within a firm by retained earnings and depreciation.[45]

internal growth rate Maximum rate a firm can expand without outside sources of funding. Growth generated by cash flows retained by the company.[46]

internal rate of return (IRR) Interest rate that is applied to a stream of cash outflows and inflows that causes the sum of the outflows and inflows to equal zero.

intrinsic value of a firm The present value of a firm's expected future net cash flows discounted by the required rate of return.[47]

inventory turnover A measure of how often the company sells and replaces its inventory. It is the ratio of annual cost of sales to the latest inventory. One can also interpret the ratio as the time for which inventory is held. For example, a ratio of 26 implies that inventory is held, on average, for two weeks. It is best to use this ratio to compare companies within an industry (high turnover is a good sign) because there are huge differences in this ratio across industries.[48]

invested capital   Total assets minus non-interest-bearing liabilities. This term is used in the calculation of return on invested capital (ROIC).

investment banking   Financial intermediaries who perform a variety of services, including aiding in the sale of securities, facilitating mergers and other corporate reorganizations, acting as brokers to both individual and institutional clients, and trading for their own accounts.[49]

investment grade bond   A bond with a rating better than BBB. Some institutional investors, such as pension funds, are constrained from holding bonds with lower ratings.[50]

investment tax credit   Tax credit provided by some states for investments made into qualified investments.

investment thesis/investment philosophy   The fundamental ideas that determine the types of investments that an investment fund will choose in order to achieve its financial goals.

IPO   See **initial public offering (IPO)**.

IRR   See **internal rate of return (IRR)**.

issuer   A company that sells its debt or equity securities.

junior debt   A loan that has a lower priority than a senior loan in case of a liquidation of the asset or borrowing company. Same as **subordinated debt**.

junk bond   A bond with a speculative credit rating of BB (S&P) or BA (Moody's) or lower. Junk or high-yield bonds offer investors higher yields than bonds of financially sound companies. Two agencies, Standard & Poor's and Moody's Investors Service, provide the rating systems for companies' credit.[51]

Keogh plan   A type of pension account in which taxes are deferred. Available to those who are self-employed.[52]

kicker   An additional feature of a debt obligation that increases its marketability and attractiveness to investors.[53]

later stage   The stage of a company that has proven its concept, achieved significant revenues compared to its competition, and is approaching cash flow breakeven or positive net income. The rate of return for venture capitalists that invest in later stage, less risky ventures is lower than in earlier stage ventures.

LBO   See **leveraged buyout (LBO)**.

lead investor   The venture capital investor that makes the largest investment in a financing round and manages the documentation and closing of that round. The lead investor sets the price per share of the financing round, thereby determining the valuation of the company.

letter of intent   A document confirming the intent of an investor to participate in a round of financing for a company. By signing this document, the subject company agrees to begin the legal and due diligence process prior to the closing of the transaction. Same as **term sheet**.

leverage   The use of debt to acquire assets, build operations, and increase revenues. By using debt, a company is attempting to achieve results faster than if it used only its cash available from preleverage operations.

leveraged buyout (LBO)   The purchase of a company or a business unit of a company by an outside investor using mostly borrowed capital.

leveraged recapitalization   Transaction in which a firm borrows money and either buys back stock or pays a dividend, thus increasing its debt ratio substantially.[54]

LIBOR   See **London Interbank Offered Rate (LIBOR)**.

limited liability company (LLC)   See **business structures**.

limited liability partnership (LLP)   See **business structures**.

limited partner (LP)   See **business structures**.

limited partnership   See **business structures**.

line of credit   An informal loan arrangement between a bank and a customer allowing the customer to borrow up to a prespecified amount.[55] Also called credit line.

liquid yield option note (LYON)   Notes whose holders have the right either to put them back to the firm under specified circumstances or to convert them into equity.[56]

liquidation   The selling off of all assets of a company prior to the complete cessation of operations. Corporations electing formal insolvency proceedings to liquidate declare Chapter 7 bankruptcy. In a liquidation, the claims of secured and unsecured creditors, bondholders, and preferred stockholders take precedence over common stockholders.

liquidation analysis   Consideration of the market factors that influence the values of assets to be liquidated in connection with the cessation of a going concern's operations.

liquidation balance sheet   A company's balance sheet adjusted to reflect reductions in the value of assets that are normally experienced when the assets of a going concern are sold off after the entity stops conducting business. See **liquidation value**.

liquidation preference   The contractual right of an investor to priority in receiving the proceeds from the liquidation of a company. For example, a venture capital investor with a "2× liquidation preference" has the right to receive two times its original investment upon liquidation.

liquidation value   The estimated amount of money that an asset or company could quickly be sold for, such as if it were to go out of business.

liquidity discount   A decrease in the value of a private company compared to the value of a similar but publicly traded company. Since an investor in a private company cannot readily sell his or her investment, the shares in the private company are normally valued less than a comparable public company.

liquidity event   A transaction whereby owners of a significant portion of the shares of a private company sell their shares in exchange for cash or shares in another, usually larger company. For example, an IPO is a liquidity event.

lockup agreement   Investors, management, and employees often agree not to sell their shares for a specific time period after an IPO, usually 6 to 12 months.

London Interbank Offered Rate (LIBOR)   A short-term interest rate often quoted as a one-, three-, or six-month rate for U.S. dollars.[57]

LP   See **business structures.**

LYON   See **liquid yield option note (LYON).**

management buyout (MBO)   A leveraged buyout controlled by the members of the management team of a company or a division.

management fee   A fee charged to the limited partners in a fund by the general partner. Management fees in a private equity fund typically range from 0.75 percent to 3 percent of capital under management, depending on the type and size of fund.

management presentation   A program presented by the officers or directors of a company in connection with a potential equity or debt transaction, or strategic or collaborative partnering agreement.

management rights   The rights often required by a venture capitalist as part of the agreement to invest in a company. The venture capitalist has the right to consult with management on key operational issues, attend board meetings, and review information about the company's financial situation.

marginal cost   An increase or a decrease in the total costs of a business firm as the result of one more or one less unit of output. Also called incremental cost or differential cost. A firm is operating at optimum output when marginal cost coincides with average total unit cost. Thus, at less than optimum output, an increase in the rate of production will result in a marginal unit cost lower than average total unit cost; production in excess of the optimum point will result in marginal cost higher than average total unit cost.

market capitalization   The value of a publicly traded company as determined by multiplying the number of shares outstanding by the current price per share.

MBO   See **management buyout (MBO).**

merchant banking   A merchant bank invests its own capital in leveraged buyouts, corporate acquisitions, and other structured finance transactions. Merchant banking is a fee-based business, where the bank assumes market risk but no long-term credit risk. The Gramm-Leach-Bliley Act allows financial holding companies, a type of bank holding company created by the Act, to engage in merchant banking activities.[58]

mezzanine   A layer of financing that has intermediate priority (seniority) in the capital structure of a company. For example, mezzanine debt has lower priority than senior debt but higher priority than equity. Mezzanine debt usually has a higher interest rate than senior debt and often includes warrants. In venture capital, a mezzanine round is generally the round of financing that is designed to fund the operations of a company to a liquidity event such as an IPO.

middle-market   Companies with revenues up to $500 million.

middle stage   The stage of a company when it has received one or more rounds of financing and is generating revenue from its product or service. Same as **growth stage.**

monetary assets and liabilities   Assets and liabilities in which the amounts are fixed in currency units. If the value of the currency unit changes, it is still settled with the same number of units.[59]

multiple   A valuation methodology that compares public and private companies in terms of a ratio of value to an operations figure such as revenue or net income. For example, if several publicly traded computer hardware companies are valued at approximately 2 times revenues, then it is reasonable to assume that a start-up computer hardware company that is growing fast has the potential to achieve a valuation of 2 times its revenues. Before the start-up issues its IPO, it will likely be valued at less than 2 times revenue because of the lack of liquidity of its shares. See **liquidity discount.**

narrow-based weighted average antidilution   A type of antidilution mechanism that adjusts downward the price per share of the preferred stock of investor A due to the issuance of options, warrants, or securities to new investor B at a price lower than the price investor A originally paid. Investor A's preferred stock is repriced to a weighted average of investor A's price and investor B's price. A narrow-based weighted average antidilution formula uses only common stock outstanding in the denominator for determining the new weighted average price.

Nasdaq   Formerly an acronym for the National Association of Securities Dealers Automated Quotation system. An electronic quotation system that provides price quotations to market participants about the more actively traded common stock issues in the over-the-counter market. About 4,000 common stock issues are included in the Nasdaq system.[60]

NDA   See **nondisclosure agreement (NDA).**

net capital expenditure   The difference between capital expenditures and depreciation. It is a measure of the financing needed, from internal or external sources, to meet investment needs.[61]

net operating income (or loss)   See **operating profit (or loss).**

net operating profit less adjusted taxes (NOPLAT)   Represents the after-tax operating profits of a company after adjusting the taxes to a cash basis.[62]

net present value (NPV)   The sum of the discounted present values of the expected cash flows of the investment.[63]

net present value (NPV) profile   This measures the sensitivity of the net present value to changes in the discount rate.[64]

New York Stock Exchange (NYSE)   The oldest and largest stock exchange in the United States. Also known as the Big Board or the Exchange.[65]

noncompete   An agreement often signed by employees and management whereby they agree not to work for competitor companies or form a new competitor company for a certain time period after termination of employment.

noncumulative dividends   Dividends that are payable to owners of preferred stock at a specific point in time only if there is sufficient cash flow available after all company expenses have been paid.

nondisclosure agreement (NDA)   An agreement issued by entrepreneurs to protect the privacy of their ideas when disclosing those ideas to third parties.

noninterference   An agreement often signed by employees and management whereby they agree not to interfere with the company's relationships with employees, clients, suppliers, and subcontractors for a certain time period after termination of employment.

nonrecourse   Term referring to the absence of any legal claim against a seller or prior endorser. The seller (or the endorser of a check or other negotiable document) is not liable or otherwise responsible for payment to the holder.[66]

nonsolicitation   An agreement often signed by employees and management whereby they agree not to solicit other employees of the company regarding job opportunities.

NOPLAT   See **net operating profit less adjusted taxes (NOPLAT)**.

NYSE   See **New York Stock Exchange (NYSE)**.

offering memorandum   A legal document that provides details of an investment to potential investors. See **private placement memorandum (PPM)**.

OID   See **original issue discount (OID)**.

operating profit (or loss)   Earnings before interest and taxes or operating income.

opportunity cost   The cost assigned to a project resource that is already owned by the firm. It is based on the next best alternative use.[67]

optics   The way a concept is presented. Sometimes entrepreneurs' presentations are strong on optics but weak in content.

options   See **stock option**.

option pool   A group of options set aside for long-term, phased compensation to management and employees.

original issue discount (OID)   A discount from par value of a bond or debtlike instrument. In structuring a private equity transaction, the use of a preferred stock with liquidation preference or other clauses that guarantee a fixed payment in the future can potentially create adverse tax consequences. The IRS views this cash flow stream as, in essence, a zero coupon bond upon which tax payments are due yearly based on so-called phantom income imputed from the difference between the original investment and guaranteed eventual payout.

origination fee   A fee charged by a lender or investor to formally process a loan or conduct due diligence. Generally expressed as a percentage of the amount to be lent or invested.

orphan   A start-up company that does not have a venture capitalist as an investor.

outstanding shares   The total amount of common shares of a company, not including treasury stock, convertible preferred stock, warrants, and options.

oversubscription   When demand exceeds supply for shares of an IPO or a private placement.

over-the-counter (OTC)   A decentralized market (as opposed to an exchange market) where geographically dispersed dealers are linked by telephones and computer screens. The market is for securities not listed on a stock or bond exchange. The Nasdaq market is an OTC market for U.S. stocks. Antithesis of listed.[68]

par   Equal to the nominal or face value of a security.[69]

pari passu   A legal term referring to the equal treatment of two or more parties in an agreement. For example, a venture capitalist may agree to have registration rights that are pari passu with the other investors in a financing round.

participating dividends The right of holders of certain preferred stock to receive dividends and participate in additional distributions of cash, stock, or other assets.

participating preferred stock A unit of ownership that repays an investor the face amount of the original investment, plus an amount equal to the investor's pro rata ownership of a company.

partnership See **business structures.**

pay to play A clause in a financing agreement whereby any investor that does not participate in a future round agrees to suffer significant dilution compared to other investors. The most onerous version of pay to play is automatic conversion to common shares, which in essence ends any preferential rights of an investor, such as the right to influence key management decisions.

payables Accounts payable resulting from purchases of materials and services from vendors and other creditors on credit terms.

payback The length of time it will take for nominal cash flows from a project to cover the initial investment.[70]

P/E ratio See **price-earnings (P/E) ratio.**

piggyback rights Rights of an investor to have shares included in a registration filed with the SEC.

pink sheets Refers to over-the-counter trading. Daily publication of the National Quotation Bureau that reports the bid and ask prices of thousands of OTC stocks, as well as the market makers who trade each stock.[71]

PIPE See **private investment in public equities (PIPE).**

placement agent A company that specializes in finding institutional investors that are willing and able to invest in a transaction. Management typically hires a placement agent so the managers can focus on operating their company rather than on raising capital.

poison pill A security or a provision that is triggered by the hostile acquisition of a company, resulting in a large cost to the acquirer.[72]

portfolio company A company that has received an investment from an investment fund.

postmoney valuation The valuation of a company including the capital provided by the current round of financing. For example, a venture capitalist may invest $5 million in a company valued at $2 million premoney (before the investment was made). As a result, the start-up will have a postmoney valuation of $7 million.

PPM See **private placement memorandum (PPM).**

preference Seniority, usually with respect to dividends and proceeds from a sale or dissolution of a company.

preferred stock A type of stock that has certain rights that common stock does not have. These special rights may include dividends, participation, liquidity preference, antidilution protection, and veto provisions, among others. Private equity investors usually purchase preferred stock when they make investments in companies.

premoney valuation The valuation of a company prior to the current round of financing. For example, a venture capitalist may invest $5 million in a company valued at $2 million premoney. As a result, the start-up will have a postmoney valuation of $7 million.

price-earnings (P/E) ratio The ratio of a public company's price per share and its net income after taxes on a per share basis.

private equity Equity investments in nonpublic companies.

private investment in public equities (PIPE) Private investments in a publicly traded company.

private placement The sale of a security directly to a limited number of institutional and qualified individual investors. If structured correctly, a private placement avoids registration with the Securities and Exchange Commission.

private placement memorandum (PPM) A document explaining the details of an investment to potential investors. For example, a private equity fund will issue a PPM when it is raising capital from institutional investors. Also, a start-up may issue a PPM when it needs growth capital. Same as **offering memorandum.**

private securities Securities that are not registered with the Securities and Exchange Commission and do not trade on any exchanges. The price per share is negotiated between the buyer and the seller (the issuer).

probit A statistical technique that allows the probability of an event to be estimated as a function of the observable characteristics.[73]

promote See **carried interest.**

pro rata Shared or divided according to a ratio or in proportion to participation.[74]

prospectus Formal written document to sell securities that describes the plan for a proposed business enterprise, or the facts concerning an existing one, that an investor needs to make an informed decision. Prospectuses are used by mutual funds to describe fund objectives, risks, and other essential information.[75] Also called offering circular or circular.

protective puts (in bonds) A protective put in a bond allows a bondholder to return the bonds to the issuer before maturity and receive the face value, under a series of conditions that are enumerated in the bond covenants. For instance, the put may be triggered by an increase in the leverage.[76]

Prudent Man Rule A fundamental principle for professional money management, which serves as a basis for the Prudent Investor Act. The principle is based on a statement by Judge Samuel Putnum in 1830: "Those with the responsibility to invest money for others should act with prudence, discretion, intelligence and regard for the safety of capital as well as income."

public and private information Public information refers to any information that is available to the investing public, whereas private information is information that is restricted to only insiders or a few investors in the firm.[77]

purchase order (PO) financing Credit obtained from a third party based on advancing a portion of the proceeds of the company's potential sale in connection with the promise by a customer that products or services will be purchased in specific quantities.

puts   The right to sell an underlying asset at a price that is fixed at the time the right is issued and during a specified time period.[78]

qualified business venture (QBV)   In the State of North Carolina, this is a business organized to engage primarily in manufacturing, processing, warehousing, wholesaling, research and development, or a service-related industry. To be eligible for registration as a QBV, the business must have been organized in the same year as the year in which it applies for registration, or it must not have generated more than $5 million in gross revenues as of its last fiscal year. Furthermore, it cannot engage to any substantial degree in the following: providing professional services, contracting or construction, selling or leasing at retail, investing, entertainment or recreation, or managing or operating real estate.

qualified IPO   A public offering of securities valued at or above a total amount specified in a financing agreement. This amount is usually specified to be sufficiently large to force a conversion of preferred stock to common stock in connection with an IPO.

qualified opinion   An auditor's opinion expressing certain limitations of an audit.[79] Opposite of unqualified opinion.

quartile   One-fourth of the data points in a data set. Often, private equity investors are measured by the results of their investments during a particular period of time. Institutional investors often prefer to invest in private equity funds that demonstrate consistent results over time, placing in the upper quartile of the investment results for all funds.

quiet period   Refers to the period of time during which a company makes no public comments, and approximates the period of time during which a company has a registration statement filed with the SEC. Same as **waiting period.**

raider   Individual or corporate investor who intends to take control of a company (often ostensibly for greenmail) by buying a controlling interest in its stock and installing new management. Raiders who accumulate 5 percent or more of the outstanding shares in the target company must report their purchases to the SEC, the exchange of listing, and the target itself.[80]

ratchet   A mechanism to prevent dilution. An antidilution clause is a contract clause that protects an investor from a reduction in percentage ownership in a company due to the future issuance by the company of additional shares to other entities. A ratchet protects an investor by reducing the effective purchase price paid by the investor to the lowest price paid by a subsequent investor for options, warrants, or securities.

real estate investment trust (REIT)   An entity that owns real estate and is allowed to pass through its earnings to its investors without being taxed. In return, it is restricted to just real estate investments, and it has to pay 95 percent of its earnings as dividends.[81]

realization ratio   The ratio of cumulative distributions to paid-in capital. The realization ratio is used as a measure of the distributions from investment results of a private equity partnership compared to the capital under management.

recapitalization   The reorganization of a company's capital structure.

receivables   Accounts receivable resulting from sales of products or services to customers on credit terms.

recourse   Term describing a type of loan. If a loan is with recourse, the lender has the ability to fall back to the guarantor of the loan if the borrower fails to pay. For example, Bank A has a loan with Company X. Bank A sells the loan to Bank B with recourse. If Company X defaults, Bank B can demand Bank A fulfill the loan obligation.[82]

red herring   A preliminary prospectus filed with the Securities and Exchange Commission and containing the details of an IPO offering. The name refers to the disclosure warning printed in red on the cover of each preliminary prospectus.

redeemable preferred   Preferred stock that can be purchased by a company in exchange for a specific sum of money, or preferred stock than an investor can force a company to repurchase.

redemption or call   Right of the issuer to force holders on a certain date to redeem their convertibles for cash. The objective usually is to force holders to convert into common prior to the redemption deadline. Typically, an issue is not called away unless the conversion price is 15 to 25 percent below the current level of the common. An exception might occur when an issuer's tax rate is high, and the issuer could replace it with debt securities at a lower after-tax cost.[83]

redemption rights   The right of an investor to force a company to buy back the shares issued as a result of the investment. In effect, the investor has the right to take back his/her investment.

registration   The process whereby shares of a company are registered with the Securities and Exchange Commission under the Securities Act of 1933 in preparation for a sale of the shares to the public.

registration rights   The rights of investors to have their shares included in a registration. Demand rights are granted to investors to permit the investors to force management to register the investors' shares for a public offering. Piggyback rights are granted to investors to permit the investors to add their shares to a registration statement filed by the company on behalf of the company or on behalf of other investors.

Regulation D (Reg D)   An SEC regulation that provides a safe harbor from the registration requirements of the Securities Act of 1933. An unlimited number of accredited investors may participate, but only 35 nonaccredited investors can participate.

Regulation S (Reg S)   An SEC regulation that governs offers and sales of securities made outside the United States without registration under the Securities Act of 1933.

REIT   See **real estate investment trust (REIT)**.

reserve   (1) In asset-based lending, the difference between the value of the collateral and the amount lent. From the point of view of financial statements, reserves are provided as an estimate of liabilities that have a good probability of arising, such as bad debt reserve attempts to estimate what percentage of the firm's debtors will not pay (based on previous records and practical experience). Reserves are always a subjective estimate (since they reflect contingent liabilities). (2) An accounting entry that properly reflects contingent liabilities.[84]

restricted stock Shares that cannot be traded in the public markets. In some instances these shares are subject to transfer restrictions in the private market.

restructure Transaction or series of transactions associated with rearranging the debt or equity structure of a company, and typically associated with poor financial performance of the company.

return on assets (ROA) Indicator of profitability. Determined by dividing net income for the past 12 months by total average assets. Result is shown as a percentage. ROA can be decomposed into return on sales (net income/sales) multiplied by asset utilization (sales/assets).[85]

return on equity (ROE) Indicator of profitability. Determined by dividing net income for the past 12 months by common stockholder equity (adjusted for stock splits). Result is shown as a percentage. Investors use ROE as a measure of how a company is using its money. ROE may be decomposed into return on assets (ROA) multiplied by financial leverage (total assets/total equity).[86]

return on invested capital (ROIC) NOPLAT divided by invested capital. Invested capital is calculated by subtracting non-interest-bearing liabilities from total assets.

return on investment (ROI) The proceeds from an investment, during a specific time period, calculated as a percentage of the original investment.

return on sales (ROS) A measurement of operational efficiency equaling net pretax profits divided by net sales expressed as a percentage.[87]

reverse split A proportionate decrease in the number of shares, but not the total value of shares of stock held by shareholders. Shareholders maintain the same percentage of equity as before the split. For example, a 1-for-3 split would result in stockholders owning one share for every three shares owned before the split. After the reverse split, the firm's stock price is, in this example, three times the prereverse split price. A firm generally institutes a reverse split to boost its stock's market price. Some think this supposedly attracts investors.[88]

revolving loan Loan with a stated maximum loan amount, but variable amounts that can actually be drawn down by a borrower that are determined periodically by reference to certain levels of borrower assets. Assets used to determine a borrower's available loan amount normally include accounts receivable and inventory. Also called revolver or revolving credit facility.

right of co-sale with founders A clause in venture capital investment agreements that allows the VC fund to sell shares at the same time that the founders of a start-up choose to sell.

right of first refusal A contractual right to participate in a transaction. For example, a venture capitalist may participate in a first round of investment in a start-up and request a right of first refusal in any following rounds of investment.

rights offering An offering of stock to current shareholders that entitles them to purchase the new issue.

road show Presentations made in several cities to potential investors and other interested parties. For example, a company will often conduct a road show to generate interest among institutional investors prior to its IPO.

ROI   See **return on investment (ROI)**.

rollup   The purchase of relatively smaller companies in a sector by a rapidly growing company in the same sector. The strategy is to create economies of scale.

round   A financing event usually involving several private equity investors.

Rule 144   A rule of the Securities and Exchange Commission that specifies the conditions under which the holder of shares acquired in a private transaction may sell those shares without registration.

S corporation   See **business structures**.

salvage value   The estimated liquidation value of the assets invested in the project at the end of the project's life.[89]

Sarbanes-Oxley   Corporate regulations resulting from the Sarbanes-Oxley Act of 2002. The Act creates a set of disclosure obligations intended to restore confidence in the financial information provided by publicly traded companies to the investing public. The Act creates a five-member Public Company Accounting Oversight Board (PCAOB), which has the authority to set and enforce auditing, attestation, quality control, and ethics (including independence) standards for auditors of public companies. It also is empowered to inspect the auditing operations of public accounting firms that audit public companies as well as impose disciplinary and remedial sanctions for violations of the board's rules, securities laws, and professional auditing and accounting standards.[90]

scalability   A characteristic of a new business concept that entails the growth of sales and revenues with a much slower growth of organizational complexity and expenses. Venture capitalists look for scalability in the start-ups they select to finance.

scale-up   The process of a company growing quickly while maintaining operational and financial controls in place.

Schedule K-1   IRS form sent by legal entities that pay no income taxes to each owner of the entity, indicating the recipient's share of income or loss for the fiscal year.

SEC   See **Securities and Exchange Commission (SEC)**.

secondary market   A market for the sale of partnership interests in private equity funds. Sometimes limited partners choose to sell their interest in a partnership, typically to raise cash or because they cannot meet their obligation to invest more capital according to the takedown schedule. Certain investment companies specialize in buying these partnership interests at a discount.

Securities and Exchange Commission (SEC)   The regulatory body that enforces federal securities laws such as the Securities Act of 1933 and the Securities Exchange Act of 1934, as amended over the years.

security   A document that represents an interest in a company. Shares of stock, notes, and bonds are examples of securities.

seed capital   Investment provided by angels, friends, and family to the founders of a start-up in its seed stage.

seed stage   The stage of a company when it has just been incorporated and its founders are developing their product or service.

senior debt   A loan that has a higher priority in case of liquidation of the assets of a company.

seniority   Higher priority.

series A preferred stock   Preferred stock issued by a company in exchange for capital from investors in the A round of financing. The preferred stock has priority over common stock for dividends and the proceeds of any liquidation or sale of a company.

shell   Usually refers to a company with little or no assets with more than 300 shareholders that is formed for the purpose of becoming a de facto public entity. This shell company is used to acquire or merge with a privately held company as a vehicle for the private company to become public without an initial public offering.

SIC   A four-digit industry code used by most services in the United States to classify firms. For a broader aggregation, the classification is often done using the first two digits of the code.[91]

Small Business Administration (SBA)   An agency of the United States government that focuses on aiding, counseling, assisting, and protecting the interests of small businesses. As it relates to financing growth companies, the SBA sometimes provides loans directly and through commercial banks for small businesses.

Small Business Investment Company (SBIC)   A company licensed by the Small Business Administration to receive government loans in order to raise capital to use in venture investing.

sole proprietor (SP)   See **business structures.**

spin-off   A company can create an independent company from an existing part of the company by selling or distributing new shares in the so-called spin-off.[70]

spin-out   A division of an established company that becomes an independent entity.

stalking horse   Third party bidder in the investment or acquisition process that is used by a company to obtain a higher share or acquisition price.

sticky dividends   Term refers to the reluctance on the part of firms to change dividends from period to period.[92]

stock   A share of ownership in a corporation.

stock grant   Determination by the board of directors of a company to issue stock to an employee or third party in connection with the provision of services to a company or the extension of debt or equity to a company.

stock option   A right to purchase or sell a share of stock at a specific price within a specific period of time. Stock purchase options are commonly used as long-term incentive compensation for employees and management of fast-growth companies.

strategic investor   A third party that agrees to invest in a company in order to have access to a proprietary technology, product, or service. By having this access, the third party can potentially achieve its strategic goals.

structured overadvance   A loan in excess of the agreed-upon borrowing base. Repayment is typically scheduled within 12 to 24 months.[93]

subordinated debt   A loan that has a lower priority than a senior loan in case of a liquidation of the asset or company. Also known as junior debt.

sweat equity   Ownership of shares in a company resulting from work rather than investment of capital.

sweetener   A feature of a security that makes it more attractive to potential purchasers.[94] An example is a warrant.

syndicate   A group of investors who agree to participate in a round of funding for a company. Alternatively, a syndicate can refer to a group of investment banks that agree to participate in the sale of stock to the public as part of an IPO.

syndication   The process of arranging a syndicate.

synergy   The additional value created by bringing together two entities and pooling their strengths. In the context of a merger, synergy is the difference between the values of the merged firm and the sum of the values of the firms operating independently.[95]

tag-along rights   The right of an investor to receive the same rights as owners of a majority of the shares of a company. For example, if a majority shareholder wants to sell his or her interest in a company, an investor with minority ownership and tag-along rights would be able to sell his or her interest as well.

takedown   A schedule of the transfer of capital in phases in order to complete a commitment of funds. Typically, a takedown is used by a general partner to secure capital from an entity's limited partners to fund the entity's investments.

takeover   The transfer of control of a company.

ten bagger   An investment that returns 10 times the initial capital.

term loan   A fixed amount of money advanced by a lender to a borrower where the borrower is expected to repay the loan amount plus interest over a specified period of time. The repayment terms are negotiated based on the ability of the borrower to repay the loan based on financial projections provided by the borrower and agreed to by the lender. A term loan may be repaid in a lump sum at the end of a fixed period or amortized and paid in specified periodic payments during the term of the loan.

term sheet   A document confirming the intent of an investor to participate in a round of financing for a company. By signing this document, the subject company agrees to begin the legal and due diligence process prior to the closing of the transaction. Same as **letter of intent.**

tranche   The piece, portion, or slice of a deal or structured financing. The so-called A to Z securities of a collateralized mortgage obligation (CMO) offering of a partitioned mortgage-backed securities (MBS) portfolio. It can also refer to segments that are offered domestically and internationally. Tranches have distinctive features that for economic or legal purposes must be financially engineered or structured in order to conform to prevailing requirements.[96]

treasury stock   Common stock that has been repurchased by the company and held in the company's treasury.[97]

turnaround   A process resulting in a substantial increase in a company's revenues, profits, and reputation.

2×   A statement referring to twice the original amount. For example, a preferred stock may have a 2× liquidation preference, so in case of liquidation of the company, the preferred stock investor would receive twice his or her original investment.

underwriter An investment bank that chooses to be responsible for the process of selling new securities to the public. An underwriter usually chooses to work with a syndicate of investment banks in order to maximize the distribution of the securities.

unrestricted stock Freely tradable shares.

value of equity The value of the equity stake in a business; in the context of a publicly traded firm, it is the value of the common stock in the firm.[98]

value of firm The value of all investors who have claims on the firm; thus, it includes lenders and debt holders (who have fixed claims) and equity investors (who have residual claims).[99]

variance in returns A measure of the squared difference between the actual returns and the expected returns of an investment.[100]

venture capital A segment of the private equity industry that focuses on investing in companies with high growth rates.

venture capital method A valuation method whereby an estimate of the future value of a company is discounted by a certain interest rate and adjusted for future anticipated dilution in order to determine the current value. Usually, discount rates for the venture capital method are considerably higher than public stock return rates, representing the fact that venture capitalists must achieve significant returns on investment in order to compensate for the risks they take in funding unproven companies.

vintage The year that a private equity fund stops accepting new investors and begins to make investments on behalf of those investors.

voting rights The rights of holders of preferred and common stock in a company to vote on certain acts affecting the company. These matters may include payment of dividends, issuance of a new class of stock, merger, or liquidation.

waiting period See **quiet period.**

walk-away point A predetermined amount at which either the buyer will not pay a higher price or the seller will not accept a lower price.

warrant A security that gives the holder the right to purchase shares in a company at a predetermined price. A warrant is a long-term option, usually valid for several years. Typically, warrants are issued concurrently with debt instruments in order to increase the appeal of the debt instrument to potential investors.

washout round A financing round whereby previous investors, the founders, and management suffer significant dilution. Usually as a result of a washout round, the new investor gains majority ownership and control of the company.

weighted average antidilution An antidilution protection mechanism whereby the conversion rate of preferred stock is adjusted in order to reflect the issuance of options, warrants, or securities at a price less than the conversion rate of the existing preferred stock.

weighted average cost of capital (WACC) A calculation of the cost of capital by adding the products of relative amounts of equity, debt, and preferred stock investments multiplied by their respective rates of return:

$$r_{WACC} = r_E[E/(E + D + P)] + r_D[D/(E + D + P)] + r_P[P/(E + D + P)]$$

white space   Refers to market opportunities not being pursued within a company's plan; new opportunity areas.

wipeout bridge   A short-term financing that has onerous features whereby if the company does not secure additional long-term financing within a certain time frame, the bridge investor gains ownership control of the company. See **bridge financing.**

wipeout round   See **washout round.**

write-down   A decrease in the reported value of an asset or a company.

write-off   A decrease in the reported value of an asset or a company to zero.

write-up   An increase in the reported value of an asset or a company.

yield   The percentage return paid on a stock in the form of dividends, or the effective rate of interest paid on a bond or note.[101]

zero coupon bond   A bond that pays no interest during the life of the bond and pays the face value of the bond at maturity. It has a duration equal to its maturity.[102]

zombie   A company that has received capital from investors but has only generated sufficient revenues and cash flow to maintain its operations without significant growth. Typically, a venture capitalist has to make a difficult decision as to whether to kill off a zombie or continue to invest funds in the hopes that the zombie will become a winner.

Notes

Preface

1. Presentation by Adam Reinebach, Thomson Venture Economics, "Private Equity State of the Market 2004," M&A Conference and Private Equity Forum, Association of Corporate Growth, May 27, 2004, McLean, Virginia.
2. Aswath Damodaran, *Applied Corporate Finance* (New York: John Wiley & Sons, 1999).

CHAPTER 2   Business Performance and Strategy

1. Michael E. Porter, *On Competition* (Boston: Harvard Business Review Books, 1998).
2. Neil C. Churchill & Virginia L. Lewis, "The Five Stages of Small Business Growth," *Harvard Business Review*, May–June 1983, page 7.
3. Adapted from *Mission Critical: The 7 Strategic Traps That Derail Even the Smartest Companies*, by Joseph C. Picken and Gregory G. Dess, Burr Ridge, IL: Irwin Professional Publishing, 1997.

CHAPTER 3   Valuation

1. Advanced Business Valuation, Essential Software Corporation, Version 4, 1995, p. 5-4.
2. Loraine MacDonald, "Valuation of Private vs. Public Firms," www.entrepreneur.com/article/0,4621,290784,00.html, July 3, 2001.

CHAPTER 4   Capital Structure

1. "Re-thinking the Capital Structure Decision" by Roy L. Simerly, Professor of Management at East Carolina University, and Mingfang Li, Professor of Management at California State University, Northridge (*Business Quest: A Journal of Applied Topics in Business and Economics*, 2002).
2. Ibid.
3. Ibid.
4. ROIC = (NOPLAT/Invested Capital), where NOPLAT is defined as net operating profit less adjusted taxes and invested capital is defined as total assets minus non-interest-bearing liabilities.

467

5. "Re-thinking the Capital Structure Decision" by Simerly and Li.
6. www.bizstats.com, 2003.
7. The liquidation balance sheet approach is only an example. We suggest that management and shareholders seek legal and accounting counsel if actually using this technique to assure completeness and thoroughness of the analysis based on the specific company and situation being analyzed.

CHAPTER 5   Sources of Capital and What to Expect

1. Verne Harnish, "Finding Money You Didn't Know You Had," *Fortune Small Business*, June 11, 2002.
2. http://beginnersinvest.about.com/cs/investinglessons/l/blles3negwrk.htm.
3. Zenas Block and Ian C. MacMillan, *Corporate Venturing* (Boston: *Harvard Business School Press*, 1995).
4. Neil C. Churchill and John W. Mullins, "How Fast Can Your Company Afford to Grow?" *Harvard Business Review*, May 2001.
5. Ibid.
6. Interview with Thomas E. Holder Jr., senior vice president, Crescent State Bank, June 22, 2004.
7. Interview with Andrew G. Burch, president, Carolina Securities, September 3, 2004.
8. Ibid.
9. Ibid.
10 Interview with Thomas E. Holder Jr.
11. Ibid.
12. Interview with Andrew G. Burch.
13. Ibid.
14. www.cfa.com /what-is ABL/what is abl.htm.
15. Ibid.
16. The last five definitions are from www.greenfieldcredit.com/Prod_Fact.asp.
17. Interview with Donald M. Rudnik, regional manager, Greenfield Commercial Credit, August 26, 2004.
18. www.hartsko.com/advantages.htm.
19. Ibid.
20. www.greenfieldcredit.com/Prod_PO.asp.
21. IIG Capital LLC, 2004.
22. Interview with Ira Edelson, president, Transcap Trade Finance LLC, August 26, 2004.
23. IIG Capital LLC, 2004.
24. Ibid.
25. Henry Frommer, "Intellectual Property Leasing and Its Implications for the Leasing Industry," Wells Fargo Leasing, Inc., 2002, p. 21.
26. www.chooseleasing.org/Basics/.

27. www.orixfin.com/ofs/3_020102.asp?bgid={C5C9F5AD-8A78-11D5-826C-0050DA5A2392}&prodid={C5C9F65B-8A78-11D5-826C-0050DA5A2392}.
28. www.pcgfunds.com/research.html#pe.
29. www.altassets.com/knowledgebank/learningcurve/2002/nz3100.php.
30. "The Venture Capital Industry: An Overview," www.nvca.org/.
31. Henry Sender and Dennis K. Berman, "For Sale: Again and Again and . . . ," *Wall Street Journal*, September 4, 2004, p. C1.
32. The MoneyTree Survey by PricewaterhouseCoopers, Thomson Venture Economics, and the National Venture Capital Association, www.pwcmoneytree.com/moneytree/index.jsp.
33. Robert S. Winter, "Venture Funding Process and Valuation," 1997, Slide 4.
34. Winter, Slide 6.
35. Frederick J. Beste III, "The Twelve (Almost) Sure-Fire Secrets to Entrepreneurial Success," Mid-Atlantic Venture Funds, LP.
36. Ibid.
37. Winter, Slide 7.
38. Winter, Slide 8.
39. Winter, Slide 11.
40. Winter, Slide 17.
41. Winter, Slide 18.
42. Interview with Andrew G. Burch.
43. PricewaterhouseCoopers/Thomson Venture Economics/National Venture Capital Association MoneyTree Survey.
44. Ernst & Young Corporate Venture Capital Report, Fall 2002, p. 9.
45. Ibid., p. 4.
46. Written interview with Bruce Kasson, CEO, eXOS, Inc., 2004.
47. Ernst & Young, p. 8.
48. Interview with James Rutherfurd, executive vice president and managing director, Veronis Suhler Stevenson, August 26, 2004.
49. Based partially on information provided by the Nidus Center for Scientific Enterprise, St. Louis, Missouri, www.niduscenter.com.
50. www.communitycapital.org/community_development/index.html, Beth Community Capital 215.320.4315.
51. www.cdvca.org/fund.html.
52. Ibid.
53. This example is from the article "Royalty Financing" in *Entrepreneur* magazine, June 14, 2002. http://www.entrepreneur.com/article/0,4621,300801,00.html.
54. www.drugroyalty.com/index_flash.html.
55. www.entrepreneur.com/article/0,4621,300801,00.html.
56. Ellyn E. Spragins, "A New Deal," *Inc.* magazine, January 1991.
57. Ibid.
58. Bruce Berman, *From Ideas to Assets* (John Wiley & Sons, 2002), pp. 424–425.
59. Michael R. Cartwright, CMA, ASA, RPG, "Understanding and Using Royalty Based Financing," 1995, www.minval.com/royltyfin_mineral.html.

CHAPTER 7   Expert Support—The Players and Their Roles

1. Robert Lenzner, "Big Kid on the Block," *Forbes*, September 20, 2004, p. 82.
2. www.morebusiness.com/running_your_business/financing/inv-bank.brc, Stephen Graham and Andrew Hamilton.
3. Interview with Mark Larson, partner, Grant Thornton LLP, Raleigh, North Carolina, September 1, 2004.
4. www.pcaobus.org/pcaob_registration.asp.
5. Interview with Mark Larson.
6. Interview with Ian D. Cookson, corporate finance director, Grant Thornton LLP, August 10, 2004.

APPENDIX A   Corporate Finance Primer

1. Aswath Damodaran, *Applied Corporate Finance* (John Wiley & Sons, 1999), Chapter 1. Reprinted with permission of John Wiley & Sons, Inc.
2. Damodaran, Chapter 2.
3. Damodaran, Chapter 3.
4. If investments are not held in proportion to their market value, investors are still losing some diversification benefits. Since there is no gain from overweighting some sectors and underweighting others in a marketplace where the odds are random of finding undervalued and overvalued assets, investors will not do so.
5. Stephen A. Ross, 1976, "The Arbitrage Theory of Capital Asset Pricing," *Journal of Economic Theory*, Vol. 13(3), pp. 341–360.
6. The beta of any investment in the CAPM is a standardized measure of the risk that it adds to the market portfolio.
7. Damodaran, Chapter 4.
8. Damodaran, Chapter 5.
9. Damodaran, Chapter 6.
10. Damodaran, Chapter 7.
11. The veto power is usually exercised through covenants in bond agreements.
12. Damodaran, Chapter 8.
13. If capital structure is irrelevant, the cost of capital will be unchanged as the capital structured is altered.
14. In other words, the value of the firm might not be maximized at the point that cost of capital is minimized, if firm cash flows are much lower at that level.
15. Damodaran, Chapter 9.
16. Palepu (1986) notes that one of the variables that seems to predict a takeover is a low debt ratio, in conjunction with poor operating performance. Krishna G. Palepu, 1986, "Predicting Takeover Targets: A Methodology and Empirical Analysis," *Journal of Accounting and Economics*, Vol. 8(1), pp. 3–35.
17. Damodaran, Chapter 10.
18. Holdings of corporate equities in the United States, 9/30/2000. Total equity held by U.S. institutions: 50.8 percent. Largest holdings: mutual funds 19 per-

cent, private pension funds 13 percent, state and local pension funds 10 percent, and life insurance companies 5 percent. *Source:* Federal Reserve Board, "Flow of Funds" (www.federalreserve.gov).

APPENDIX B   Financial Statements

1. If a cost (such as an administrative cost) cannot be easily linked with a particular revenue, it is usually recognized as an expense in the period in which it is consumed.
2. It has the opposite effect on cash flows, since lengthening the depreciable life reduces depreciation and increases both taxable income and taxes.
3. FASB 105 requires that the following be disclosed—the face value or notional principal amount, the terms of the instrument and the credit and market risk involved, and the accounting loss that the firm would incur if any party to the agreement did not perform.
4. The requirements for an operating lease in the Internal Revenue Code are as follows: (1) The property can be used by someone other than the lessee at the end of the lease term, (2) the lessee cannot buy the asset using a bargain purchase option, (3) the lessor has at least 20 percent of its capital at risk, (4) the lessor has a positive cash flow from the lease independent of tax benefits, and (5) the lessee does not have an investment in the lease.
5. The accumulated pension fund liability does not take into account the projected benefit obligation, where actuarial estimates of future benefits are made. Consequently, it is much smaller than the total pension liabilities.
6. While companies might not have to report the excess of their health care obligations over assets as a liability, some firms choose to do so anyway. Boeing, in 1993, for instance, reported an accrued retiree health care obligation of $2.158 billion as a liability.

APPENDIX C   Discount Rates

1. Z. Christopher Mercer, ASA, CFA, *Valuing Enterprise and Shareholder Cash-flows: The Integrated Theory of Business Valuation* (Memphis, TN: Peabody Publishing, LP, 2004), pp. 203–249. www.integratedtheory.com.
2. This discount rate applies to net income or net cash flow.

APPENDIX D   How Fast Can Your Company Afford to Grow?

1. Calculation discrepancies are due to Excel spreadsheet rounding anomalies; calculations in the spreadsheets use more precise figures.
2. To account for compounding, we must raise the multiple for each subsequent cycle (1.0763, in our case) to the nth power, where n is the number of cycles in a year (2.433 here), and then subtract 1 to get the SFG rate as a percentage. In this example, 1.0763 to the 2.433 power = 1.1960 − 1 = 19.60%.

Glossary

1. Aswath Damodaran, *Applied Corporate Finance (ACF)* (John Wiley & Sons, 1999), p. 149. Reprinted with permission of John Wiley & Sons, Inc.
2. Campbell R. Harvey's Hypertextual Finance Glossary (crh), http://www.duke .edu/~charvey/, Copyright 2004.
3. *ACF*, p. 49.
4. Legal Information Institute, Cornell Law School, http://www.law.cornell.edu /topics/bankruptcy.html.
5. www.dictionary.com.
6. *ACF*, p. 52.
7. crh.
8. IRS Package X, Volume 2 of 2, 2002, p. 92.
9. John Downes and Jordan Elliot Goodman, *Dictionary of Finance and Investment Terms*, Sixth Edition, Barron's Educational Series, 2003, p. 54.
10. *Anatomy of the Cash Cow*, Bruce D. Henderson, Boston Consulting Group, 1976.
11. Investopedia.com.
12. *ACF*, p. 320.
13. From www.VCExperts.com. Written permission requested and granted specifically for this publication.
14. From www.VCExperts.com. Written permission requested and granted specifically for this publication.
15. From www.VCExperts.com. Written permission requested and granted specifically for this publication.
16. *ACF*, p. 309.
17. *ACF*, p. 353.
18. *ACF*, p. 224.
19. *ACF*, p. 84.
20. www.FASB.com.
21. crh.
22. *ACF*, p. 307.
23. Thomas Fitch, *Dictionary of Banking Terms*, Fourth Edition, *Barron's Educational Series*, 2000, p. 252.
24. crh.
25. crh.
26. *ACF*, p. 320.
27. crh.
28. *ACF*, p. 16.
29. crh.
30. *ACF*, p. 333.
31. crh.
32. crh.
33. crh.
34. crh.
35. crh.

36. crh.
37. *ACF*, p. 264.
38. crh.
39. crh.
40. crh.
41. crh.
42. crh.
43. crh.
44. crh.
45. crh.
46. crh.
47. crh.
48. crh.
49. crh.
50. *ACF*, p. 273.
51. crh.
52. crh.
53. crh.
54. *ACF*, p. 229.
55. crh.
56. *ACF*, p. 334.
57. crh.
58. Fitch, p. 381.
59. Floyd A. Beams, John A. Brozovsky, and Craig D. Shoulders, *Advanced Accounting*, Seventh Edition, Prentice Hall, 2000, p. 887.
60. crh.
61. *ACF*, p. 402.
62. Tom Copeland, Tim Koller, and Jack Murrin, *Valuation* (John Wiley & Sons, 1995), p. 155.
63. *ACF*, p. 159.
64. *ACF*, p. 168.
65. crh.
66. Fitch, p. 319.
67. *ACF*, p. 189.
68. crh.
69. crh.
70. *ACF*, p. 157.
71. crh.
72. *ACF*, p. 16.
73. *ACF*, p. 287.
74. crh.
75. crh.
76. *ACF*, p. 234.
77. *ACF*, p. 20.
78. *ACF*, p. 320.

79. crh.
80. crh.
81. *ACF*, p. 227.
82. crh.
83. crh.
84. crh.
85. crh.
86. crh.
87. crh.
88. crh.
89. *ACF*, p. 123.
90. www.aicpa.org, American Institute of Certified Public Accountants.
91. *ACF*, p. 293.
92. *ACF*, p. 352.
93. www.wellsfargo.com.
94. crh.
95. *ACF*, p. 17.
96. Barkley's Comprehensive Financial Glossary (www.oasismanagement.com).
97. crh.
98. *ACF*, p. 440.
99. *ACF*, p. 440.
100. *ACF*, p. 37.
101. crh.
102. *ACF*, p. 330.

Absolute control, 43
Accountants:
  accounting firm selection, 274–275
  consulting groups, 276
  functions of, 264, 272–274, 392, 436
  relationship management, 275
Accounts payable, 55–56
Accounts receivable, 9, 28, 42, 49, 55–56,
  75–78, 81, 172, 203–205, 392
Accredited investor, 58
Accrual accounting method, 391–392,
  404–405
Acheson, Rees, 326
Acquisitions, see Leveraged buyouts (LBOs)
  case studies, 305–316
  characterized, 92–93, 115, 179–180, 234,
  396
Ade-Drakes, Najah, 323
Adkins, Dinah, 139
Administrative costs/expenses, 393, 404
Advance rate, 79, 82
Advisers:
  accountants, 264, 272–276
  board of directors, 264–266
  consultants, 276–277
  counsel, 202, 262–263, 275, 282, 284
  importance of, 262, 277–278, 282, 284
  investment bankers, 267–272
Affirmative covenants, 238, 250
Agency costs, 24
Alliances, 21, 52
Allocated costs, 393
Amortization, 28–29, 132
Andrews, Fred, 141
Angel financing, developments in, 66–67.
  See also Angel investors
Angel investors:
  benefits of, 68–69
  business plan evaluation, 65–66
  case study, 297–299

characterized, 58–67, 107
defined, 58
groups of, 61–64, 68
presentation for, 63–64
referrals, 59, 68
relationship with, 68
sample questionnaire, 62–63
source directory, 330, 332
term sheet clauses, types of, 64
types of, 59, 61
valuations, 66
venture capitalists distinguished from,
  60–61
Antidilution protection, 231–233, 237, 241
Applied Intelligent Systems Inc. (AISI), 157
Arbitrage pricing model (APM), 386–387
Asset(s), types of, 287, 407–409. See also
  specific types of assets
Asset-based lenders (ABLs):
  accounts receivable financing, 75–78
  assignment for benefit of creditors case
  study, 292–297
  benefits of, 74–75
  capital expense (capex) line of credit, 83
  case studies, 289–297, 302
  characterized, 70, 74
  debtor-in-possession financing, 84
  factoring, 78–82
  high-risk case study, 289–291
  import financing, 84
  inventory financing, 81–82
  purchase order (PO) financing, 82–83
  sales-leaseback arrangements, 84
  source directory, 330, 333
  term sheet, 76–77
  trade tranche, 84–85
  Transactional Equity, 85
  venture banking, 84–85
  warehouse financing, 85–86
Asset management, 429–430

Assignment, 72, 197, 292–297
Attorney, functions of, 202, 262–263, 275, 282, 284
Avanir Pharmaceuticals (AVN), 300–301

Balance sheet, 9–10, 16, 30, 40–41, 189, 406–413
Band of Angels, 67, 297
Banking relationship, significance of, 73–74
Bank loans, 174, 202, 208. *See also specific types of banks*
Bankruptcy, 22, 435
Barnette, Meg, 325
Barter arrangements, 50
Benchmarking, 18
Benson, Tedd, 326
Beta, 387, 416
Big Four accounting firms, 272
Biotechnology industry, 39, 159–160
BizMiner, 33
BizStats, 33
Board of directors, 68, 117–119, 231, 236–237, 246, 264–266
Book value, 16, 407–408
Bootstrapping:
  accounts receivable, discounting, 49
  alternate revenue, 48
  barter arrangements, 50
  characterized, 46–47, 56–57, 131
  customer prepayments, 49
  deferred employee compensation, 53–54
  downside to, 47
  investments, customer and
    supplier/vendor, 51–53
  loans, from friends and family, 48
  operating profit, 56
  outsourcing, 54–55
  revenue and pricing, 50–51
  supplier/vendor financing, 49–50
  working capital management, 55–56
Borrower requirements:
  financial statements, 178–179
  operations, 180–181
  organization structure, 177–178
Borrowing base, 172
Bortech, Inc., 326–327
Bridge loans, 215
Broker-dealers, 254, 267
Brookside Capital Partners, 304–305
"Bulge bracket" investment firms, 267

Business life cycle, 10, 13, 25
Business performance:
  case illustrations, 10–14
  components of, 6–10
Business plan:
  components of, 220–222
  evaluation of, 65–66
  executive summary, 220, 280
  importance of, 53, 144, 185, 190, 214, 253, 277
  venture funding process, 104
Business strategy, 11–14
Buttolph, David D., 305
Buyout funds, 128–135

Call, Chuck, 297
Capital, generally:
  availability of, 20
  expenditures, 391
  investment analysis, 399
  least expensive, 27
  sources of, *see* Capital sources
  structure, *see* Capital structure
Capital asset pricing model (CAPM), 17, 385–386, 415–416
Capital expense (capex) line of credit, 83
Capital issuance selling, 15
Capitalization, leveraged buyouts, 132–133
Capital lease, 89–90, 410–411
Capital sources:
  angel investors, 58–67
  asset-based lenders, 70, 74–86
  best practices, 67–68
  bootstrapping, 46–57
  buyout funds, 128–135
  characterized, 44
  commercial banks, 69–74
  commercial finance companies, 86–87
  community development initiators, 138–145
  corporate venture capital, 135–137
  government agencies, 145–153
  individual investors, 57–58
  leasing companies, 87–92
  merchant banks, 137–138
  mezzanine funds, 124–128
  micro-cap public entities, 153–155
  private equity, 92–94
  royalty financing, 155–160
  by stage, 46

types of, 44–45
venture capital, 94–124
Capital structure:
  agency costs, 24
  analysis of, *see* Capital structure analysis
  changes, 399–400
  company stages, 24–25
  development of, 22
  liability limits, development of, 40–43
  private companies, 20
  risk management, 22–23
  short-term goals and, 23–24
  significance of, 5
Capital structure analysis:
  base assumptions, overview, 26–29
  company characteristics, 30–31
  company stages, 30
  industry dynamics, 31–33
  industry norms, 33
  industry trends, 33–39
  shareholder objectives, 27, 39–40
  use of funds, 29–30
CAPLines, 152–153
Carve-outs, 184, 199
Case studies, *see specific types of funding*
Cash basis accounting method, 404–406
Cash collections, 406
Cash flow, 9, 17–18, 20, 31, 56, 66, 77,
  185–186, 391–397, 415, 425
Cash flow–based financings, 205–207
Cash sweep, 133
Certificate of incorporation:
  characteristics of, 242–243
  conversion rights, 246–248
  dividends, 244
  liquidation preferences, 245
  redemption provisions, 248
  voting rights, 245–246
Certified Development Company (CDC),
  SBA funding, 147–148
Certified public accountants (CPAs), 272
Change implementation, 13–14
Chief executive officers (CEOs), 14, 111,
  123, 262–266
Churchill, Neil C., 12, 56
Closing process:
  due diligence, 283–284
  market testing, 280
  negotiations, 284–285
  relationship management, 285–286

team participants, 279–281
team preparation, 282
timing, significance of, 282–283
Co-investments, 87, 135, 138
Collateral, 40, 42, 70, 77, 82, 124, 150,
  197–198
Collateralized mortgage obligations, 205
Commercial banks:
  characteristics of, 69–74
  loans from, 174, 202, 208
  source directory, 330, 332
Commercial finance companies:
  case study, 302–304
  characterized, 86–87
  source directory, 330, 334
Commitment fees, 173
Commitment letter, 166–169, 285
Common stock, 162, 218
Communications, venture capital
  investments, 118, 123
Community Adjustment and Investment
  Program (CAIP), 151–152
Community bank loans, 174, 202, 208
Community development financial
  institutions (CDFIs), 144–145
Community development financing, case
  study, 322–326
Community development initiators, 138–145
Community development loan funds,
  144
Community Development Venture Capital
  Alliance (CDVCA), 322, 325
Community development venture capital
  (CDVC) funds, 144
Company-specific risk, 416
Company stages, 24–25, 30
Comparables, 17–18
Compensation, 9, 53–54, 268
Competitive advantage, 12, 21, 66
Competitive risk, 383
Competitive strategy, 11
Construction and development loans,
  174–176
Consultants, functions of, 276–277,
  284
Contribution margin, 50–51
Control, loss of, 42–43
Controlling interest, 93, 416
Conversion rights, 246–248
Core processes, 13

Corporate finance, fundamental
propositions, 379. *See also* Corporate
finance primer
Corporate finance primer:
  capital structure changes, 399–400
  cost of capital, 398–399
  cost of equity, 388–389
  debt and equity continuum, 397–398
  dividends, 401–403
  foundations, 377–379
  investment decision rules, 395–396
  objective function, 379–381
  opportunity cost analysis, 396–397
  returning cash to stockholders, 400
  return on investments, 390–395
  risk, 381–388
Corporate venture capital, 109, 135–137
Cost of capital, 20, 22, 389, 398–399
Cost of debt, calculation of, 389
Cost of equity, 388–389
Cost of goods sold, 408
Cost of sales, 427
Cost-recovery-first collection, 406
Counsel, *see* Attorney
Cram-down financing, 229–230
Credibility, significance of, xv, 10, 47, 276,
  278, 286
Credit, 3 C's of, 69–70
Credit agreement, 170
Credit facilities, 171–176
Credit insurance, 81
Creditors, 24
Credit rating, 175, 217–218
Credit reporting agencies, 217–218
Credit unions, community development, 144
Creditworthiness, 82–83, 89, 202
Cross-collateralization, 42

Damodaran, Aswath, xvi, 377
Debt/debt financing, 5, 9, 20, 22, 31,
  162–164, 209–211, 214–215, 326–328,
  389, 397–398
Debt investors, 398
Debtor in possession (DIP), 84, 217
Debt-to-equity (D/E) ratio:
  defined, 33
  implications of, 33, 72, 89
  by industry, 34–38
  liability limitations, 42
Decision-making process, 378

Default, 22, 80, 189–192
Default risk, 389
Defense Economic Transition Assistance
  (DETA) SBA loan program, 151
Defined benefit plans/defined contribution
  plans, 411–412
Demand registration rights, 234, 248–249
Department of Housing and Urban
  Development (HUD), 217
Depreciation, 404, 407–408, 411,
  427
Development agreement, 238–239
Direct marketers, growth potential, 430–432
Disclosure requirements, 91
Discounted cash flow (DCF), 17–18, 394–395
Discounting, 394
Discount rate, 79, 394, 411
Dispute resolution, 251
Distressed companies, 229, 294
Distribution agreement, 52
Diversification, 12, 384–385, 387
Divestitures, 402
Dividends, 8, 226, 244, 400–403
Documentation, *see specific types of*
  documents
Drag-along right, 251
Drug Royalty, 300–301
Due diligence, 239–240, 243, 283–284
Dun & Bradstreet, 9, 33, 218
Dunn Paper, Inc., 307
Dwyer Group, Inc., 312–316
Dwyer-Owens, Dina, 315

Early stage companies, 24, 42, 217,
  280
Earnings before interest, taxes, depreciation,
  and amortization (EBITDA), 17–18, 20,
  115, 188–189, 207, 212–213
Economic conditions, impact of, 20
EDGAR database, 9
Eldorado Stone, 306
Elpis Group, 323
Emerging growth companies, 18, 20, 29, 30,
  42, 46, 57, 71, 267, 279, 285
Employee benefits, 411–412
Employee compensation, deferred, 53–54
Enterprise value, 20
Entity value, 15–16, 20
Entrepreneurial angels, 59
Environmental dynamism, 31–32

Equity/equity investment:
  characteristics of, 163
  co-investments, 87, 135, 138
  debt distinguished from, 126, 163
  defined, 33, 162
  instruments, types of, 218–220
  investment documentation, *see* Equity
    investment documentation
  preparation for, 220–222
  securities regulations, 164
Equity investment documentation:
  certificate of incorporation, 243–248
  components of, 222–223
  investors' rights agreement, 248–250
  shareholders' agreement, 251
  stock purchase provisions, 239–243
  term sheet, *see* Equity investment term sheet
Equity investment term sheet:
  antidilution provisions, 231–233
  board composition, 236–237
  employee stock options, 237
  founder share vesting, 237–238
  liquidation preference, 226–230
  miscellaneous provisions, 238–239
  protective provisions, 231
  redemption, 233–234
  registration rights, 234–236
  valuation, premoney and postmoney,
    223–225
  voting rights, 230–231
Equity investors, 397–398
Equity ownership, 111, 225
Equity repurchases, 400
ERISA, 181
Ethics, 275–276
Executive summary, 220, 280
Exit strategies, 134, 233, 268
Expectations, 5, 8, 15
Expected returns, 387
Export financing, 302
Export Working Capital Program (EWCP),
  SBA funding, 148–149

Factor analysis, 387
Factoring, 78–82, 204, 302
Failure rates, 112
Fair market value (FMV) appraisal, 83
Fairness hearings, 259
Federal Communications Commission
  (FCC), 196–197

Fee letter, 169–170
Fees, types of, 71, 77, 82, 127–128, 132,
  135, 173, 202, 263, 271
Financial Accounting Standards Board
  (FASB), 90, 411–412
Financial position, 4–5, 9–10
Financial slack, 400
Financial statements:
  analysis of, 9–10
  balance sheet, 9–10, 16, 30, 40–41, 189,
    406–413
  forecasted, 42
  implications of, 8, 178–179, 238, 241–242
  income statement, 10, 404–406, 420, 422
  sample, 420
  statement of cash flows, 10, 414
Financing mix, 397
Financing process:
  business performance and strategy, 3, 6–14
  capital, sources of, *see* Capital sources
  capital structure, 3, 22–43
  closing the deal, 279–286
  flow chart, 4
  managerial roles in, 5
  overview of, 3–5
  valuation, 3, 15–21
Financing sources:
  angel investors, 330, 332
  asset-based lenders (ABLs), 330, 333
  commercial banks, 330, 332
  commercial finance, 330, 334
  directory, 329–376
  firm list with contact information,
    355–365
  firm list with location, 344–355
  firm list with summary criteria, 366–376
  government agency, 330, 343
  individual investors, 330, 332
  industry investor, 330, 343
  leasing company, 330, 334
  merchant bank, 330, 343
  private equity fund, 330, 338–342
  strategic investor, 330, 343
  venture capital fund, 330, 335–337
Firm-specific risk, 384–385, 387
First in, first out (FIFO), 408–409
First Law of Entrepreneurial Gravity, xi
First right of refusal, 250
First round funding, 107
504 Loan Program, 147–148, 151–152

Fixed assets, 30, 407, 428
Fixed costs, 393
Follow-on funding, 107
Forecasting, 17–18, 26, 112–113
Forward contracts, 400
Foster, Jay, 140
4(2) exemption, 252
Full recourse factoring, 78–79
Funded debt, 33
Funding sources, use of funds matched with, 27–30. *See also* Financing sources

Generally accepted accounting principles (GAAP), 9, 179, 186, 242, 250, 273, 404–410
Glass-Steagall Act, 269
Goal-setting, 13
Godshall, Ned, 297–298
Going public, *see* Initial public offerings (IPOs)
Goodwill, 16
Google, 44
Government agencies:
  as funding source, 145–153
  source directory, 330, 343
Graham Partners, 305–306
Greenfield Commercial Credit (GCC), 289–296
Growth companies, 23, 52–53
Growth management:
  asset replacement, 427
  case illustration, 417–432
  cash management strategies, 423–426
  cost reduction, 425–426
  depreciation, 427
  direct marketers, 430–432
  importance of, 417
  importers, 430–432
  income taxes, 426–427
  manufacturing companies, 430
  maximum self-financeable growth rate, 422–423
  operating cash cycle (OCC), 417–422
  raising prices, 426
  service companies, 432
Guarantees, 31, 200–202
Guardian angels, 59

Hands-off angels, 61
Hanley Wood, LLC, 317–318

Health care benefits, 412
High yield debt, 209–211
High yield loans, 176, 193
High yield offerings, 257–258
Holding period, 8
HUD, *see* Department of Housing and Urban Development (HUD)
Hurdle rate, 381
Hybrid business model, 48
Hybrid securities, cost calculation, 389

IE, 298–299
IIG Capital LLC, 302
Importers, growth potential, 430–432
Import financing, 28, 84, 302
Inactive public company (IPC), 154–155
Incentive plans, 15
Incidental registration rights, 234–236, 248–249
Income statement, 10, 404–406, 420, 422
Income taxes, 16, 412–413, 426–427
Incremental cash flows, 393
Incremental revenue, 50–51
Incubators:
  client profile, 140
  functions of, 138–141
  selection factors, 142–143
  services agreement, 143
  terms and conditions of, 143–144
  types of, 141–142
Individual investors:
  as funding source, 57–58
  source directory, 330, 332
  types of, 57–58
Industrial revenue bonds, 216–217
Industry dynamics, 31–33
Industry investor, source directory, 330, 343
Industry margins, 21
Industry norms, 33
Industry-specific risk, 383
Industry standards, 21
Industry trends, 33, 39
Inflation, 384, 387, 394, 408
Information resources, 9, 33. *See also* Source directory
Initial public offerings (IPOs), 19, 115, 120, 153–155, 234–236, 246, 249, 267–270
Insolvency, 248
Institutional investors, 257, 403
Intangible assets, 409

Intellectual property, 56, 158–159, 242, 251
Intercreditor agreement, 197–200
Interest expenses, 397
Interest rate(s), 132, 173–176, 213, 384, 387, 389
Internal rate of return (IRR), 213, 395–396
Internal Revenue Code, 217, 406
Internal Revenue Service, 436
International risk, 383
International trade loans, 150
Internet bubble, xv
Intrinsic market valuation, 115
Inventory:
    implications of, 42, 55–56, 172, 392
    valuation methods, 408–409
Inventory financing, 28, 81–82, 303
Investment banks/bankers:
    boutique investment bank, 270–271
    functions of, 267–270, 272
    selection factors, 270
Investment decision, 381
Investment decision rules, 395–396
Investor confidence, 123
Investor-owners, 68
Investor relationship, 285–286
Investors' rights agreement:
    covenants, 250–251
    information rights, 250
    preemptive rights, 250
    registration rights, 248–250
IRS Form K-1, 435
Ison, Lisa, 140

Johnston Textiles, 310–311
Joint marketing initiatives, 52
Joint ventures, 52
Junior debt, 87, 132–133, 176
Junior secured loans, 193, 207–208
Junk bonds, 133

Landis, Robert B., 316
Larson, Rick, 323, 325
Last in, first out (LIFO), 408–409
Leadership, significance of, 13, 47
Lease(s), 28, 89–90, 143, 410–411
Leasing companies:
    characterized, 87–92
    source directory, 330, 334
Lemming, angel investors, 61
Lender relationship, 285–286

Letters of credit, 83, 173, 431
Leverage, 9, 22, 399
Leveraged buyouts (LBOs):
    buyout firm structure/organization, 134–135
    characteristics of, 92–94
    current state of, 129–130
    defined, 128
    historical perspective, 129–131
    revenue generation, 134–135
    terms of, 132–134
    theory of, 131–132
Leverage ratios, 187–189
Lewis, Virginia, 12
Li, Mingfang, 31
Liabilities:
    defined, 409–410
    degree or certitude, 410
    employee benefits, 411–412
    income taxes, 412–413
    leases, 410–411
    limitations, *see* Liability limits
    reserves in financial statements, 413
Liability limits, development of, 40–43
Liens, 72
Limited liability company (LLC), 68
Line of credit (LOC), 27–30, 42, 72, 75, 82–83
Liquidation, generally:
    balance sheet, 40–41
    preference, 226–230, 245
Liquidity, 5, 268
Liquidity ratios, 187
Litigation, 15
Loan(s), *see specific types of loans*
    components of, 164–170
    credit qualification, 217–218
    documentation, *see* Loan documentation
    from friends and family, 48
    specialized, 216–217
    types of, 202–203
Loan covenants:
    affirmative, 181–183, 238, 250
    financial, 185–187
    implications of, 187–189
    negative, 181–184, 231, 251
    prepayment, 182, 184–185
Loan documentation:
    credit agreement, 170
    credit facilities, 171–176
    default events, 189–192

Loan documentation (*Continued*)
   guarantees, 200–202
   intercreditor agreement, 197–200
   loan covenants, 181–189
   promissory note, 192–194
   representations, 177–181
   security agreement, 194–196
   types of, 170
   warranties, 177–181
Loan-to-value ratio, 83
Lockbox, 79–80
Lockup agreements, 236, 249–250
London Interbank Offered Rate (LIBOR),
   171–173, 176
Low-income housing finance, 217
Lyons, Adele, 140

MacNaughtan, David, 301
Macroeconomics, 39, 73, 387
Management quality, 8, 10, 12–13, 21, 24,
   30–31, 47, 71, 103–104, 282, 286
Manufacturing companies, growth
   potential, 430
Market approach to valuation, 17
Marketing expenses, 428–429
Market portfolio, 386
Market risk:
   defined, 383
   measurement of, 385–388
   sources of, 387
Market value, 15–16
Maximum leverage ratio, 206–207
Merchant banks:
   buy-and-build strategy implementation
      case study, 316–319
   characterized, 137–138
   source directory, 330, 343
Mergers, 15, 234
Meriturn Partners, 307–309
Meso Fuel, Inc. (MFI), 297–299
Mezzanine funds:
   borrowing profile, 124
   case study, 304–305
   characteristics of, 107, 112, 124–125,
      211–214, 124, 128
   equity debt *vs.,* 126
   interest rates, 176
   loan size and structure, 126–127
   price of, 127–128
   repayment in LBO, 132–133

Micro-cap public entities, 153–155
Microenterprise development loan funds, 145
Microloan Program, SBA funding, 138, 148
Middle-market companies, 12, 18, 20,
   29–30, 39, 46, 57, 71, 170, 193, 267,
   274, 279, 283
Milestone financing, 67
Miller, Merton, 22
Minimum debt service coverage ratio,
   206–207
Minority interest/shareholders, 251, 416
Minority investments, 43, 93
Minority-owned business enterprises, 39
Modigliani, Franco, 22
MontaVista Software, Inc., 320–321
Moody's Investors Service, 175–176, 217
Mortgages, 29, 87, 205
Mullins, John W., 56
Multifactor models, market risk analysis, 388
Multiyear investments, 27

Nanotechnology industry, 39
National Business Incubation Association
   (NBIA), 139
Negative covenants, 231, 251
Negotiations, 16, 18, 49, 72, 200, 202, 214,
   235, 238–239, 246, 263, 284–285
Net assets, 16–17
Net operating losses (NOLs), 273
Net present value (NPV), 395
Networking, importance of, 141
New Hampshire Community Loan Fund
   (NHCLF), 326–327
New Markets Venture Capital (NMVC)
   Program, SBA, 146
New Mexico Private Investors, Inc. (NMPI),
   297
New product development, 53, 393
Nominal cash flow, 394
Noncompetition agreements, 239–240, 250
Nondisclosure agreement, 238
Nonoperating assets, 16
Nonrecourse factoring, 78–79
Nonsolicitation agreements, 239–240, 250
Notification, in factoring process, 79

Objective function, 379–381
Off-balance-sheet assets, 16
Off-balance-sheet financing, 89, 410
Offering memorandum, 253, 280

Operating assets, 16
Operating cash cycle (OCC), 417–422
Operating expenses, 391, 419, 423
Operating income, 9
Operating leases, 89–90, 411
Operating management, 429–430
Operating performance, 15
Operating profit, 56
Operating ratios, 187
Operational angels, 59
Operational effectiveness (OE), 11–12
Opportunity cost analysis, 396–397
Option to purchase, 250
Outsourcing, 39, 54–55, 94
Overleveraged companies, 31
Owner compensation, 9

Partnerships, 21, 437
Patents, 66
Pay-in-kind (PIK):
    dividends, 133, 226
    payments, 213–214, 244
Payback, 395
Peer group comparables, 400
Pension plans, 411–412
Personal guarantees, 71–73, 148, 150
Piggyback registration rights, 234–236,
    248–249
Political risk, 383
Pollution Control Loans, SBA funding, 152
Porter, Michael, 11–12
Portfolio management, 12
Postmoney valuation, 111, 115, 223–226
Postseed investing, 112
Preemptive right, 250
Preferred interest, 133
Preferred stock:
    characteristics of, 43, 162, 218–219
    convertible, 214–215, 219, 226–227, 245
    cost calculation, 389
    death spiral, 247–248
    liquidation preference, 226–229, 245
    participating, 219–220, 228, 245
    redeemable, 42
    voting rights, 218, 230–231, 245–246
Premoney valuation, 111, 223–226
Prepayment, 49, 128, 171, 182, 184–185
Preseed investments, 107
Present value, 17
Price-earnings (P/E) ratios, 20

Pricing strategies, 50–51, 426
Private companies, 9, 19–20, 24
Private equity firms, 133
Private equity funding:
    acquisition to exit case study, 305–306
    acquisition with management
        participation case study, 309–312
    characterized, 92–94
    public-to-private acquisition case study,
        312–316
    restructuring case study, 307–309
    source directory, 330, 338–342
Private investment in public equities (PIPE),
    247, 256–257
Private placement, 57–58, 240, 252–254, 258
Proactive mode, 27, 39
Product cannibalization, 393
Product line development, 429
Profitability ratios, 187
Project risk, 383
Promissory note, 192–194
Prospectus, 254
Prototyping, 53
Public companies, 9
Public company multiples, 18–20
Publicly traded companies, capital structure,
    24
Public offerings, 205, 254–255. *See also*
    Initial public offerings (IPOs)
Purchase order (PO) financing, 28, 82–83, 204

Qualified business venture (QBV), 273

Raad, Valérie, 304
Rally Capital Services, LLC, 294–295
Ratchet-based antidilution, 231–233
Rates of return, 44–45, 213, 295–296, 394
Real property loans, 204–205
Real rate of return, 394
Recapitalizations, 234
Receivables financing, 302. *See also*
    Accounts receivable
Recordkeeping guidelines, 10
Redemption provisions, 248
Refinancing case study, 289–291
Regression models, market risk analysis, 388
Regulation D:
    components of, 252–253
    Rule 501, 240
    Rule 506, 252–254, 256, 259

Relationship management, 285–286
Remedies, default events, 191–192
Rent, 29
Repayment, mezzanine debt, 213
Reporting requirements, 82
Representations, 177–181, 239–241
Research and development (R&D), 10, 51, 273, 392, 428–429
Reseller agreement, 52
Reserves, 413
Restart financing, 229
Restructuring case study, 307–309
Return on capital, 395
Return on invested capital (ROIC), 27
Return on investment (ROI), 44, 381, 390–395. *See also* Return on investment (ROI) measurement
Return on investment (ROI) measurement:
  accounting earnings *vs.* cash flow, 391–392
  project analysis, 44, 390
  total *vs.* incremental cash flow, 392–394
Revenue, 48, 50–51, 115
Reverse acquisition, 154
Reverse triangular merger, 258–259
Revolving credit, 138, 198, 203
Revolving loans, 172–173
Richmond, George M., 299
Ridgeway, Blake, 298
Right of first offer, 250
Risk, *see specific types of risk*
  cash flow and, 394
  Chinese symbols for, 382
  components of, 383
  defined, 381
  diversification and, 384–385, 387
  management strategies, 5, 8, 20–22
  measurement of, 382–383, 385
  minimization strategies, 72
  mitigation, 112
  reduction strategies, 384–385
  rewarded, 383
  risk-return model, 382–383
  unrewarded, 383
Risk Management Association (RMA), 9, 33
Riverside Company, 312–316
Road show, 255
Royalty financing:
  case illustrations/case studies, 156–158, 300–301

characteristics of, 155
  intellectual property, 158–159
  life science applications, 159–160
  for mining, 159
Rudnik, Donald M., 291, 297
Russo, Vito, 311–312
Rutherfurd, James P., 319
Ryla Teleservices, 323–325

Sale-leaseback arrangements, 84, 91–92
Sale of company, 15
Sarbanes-Oxley rules, 257, 264, 269, 274
SBA, *see* U.S. Small Business Administration (SBA)
S corporation, 436
SEC forms:
  S-1, 235
  S-3, 249, 255
  S-4, 255, 259
  S-8, 255
  SB-1/SB-2, 253
SEC rules:
  Rule 144, 235, 259
  Rule 144A, 211, 257
  Rule 145, 249
  Rule 415, 260
Second round funding, 107
Secured loans, 193, 203–208. *See also* Collateral
Securities Act (1933), 252, 259
Securities and Exchange Act of 1934, 257
Securities and Exchange Commission (SEC), 9, 252, 256, 259, 270, 273. *See also* SEC forms; SEC rules
Securities regulation:
  deal structures, 255–261
  importance of, 164, 251–252
  private placement, 252–254
  public offerings, 254–255
  specialized offerings, 255–261
Security agreement, 194–196
Seed financing, 114
Seed investments, 107
Self-financeable growth (SFG) rate, 418–428
Self-funding, 56
Senior debt, 87, 132
Senior lenders, 124
Senior management, functions of, 5
Senior secured loans, 193
Sensitivity analysis, 11, 42

Series A/Series B/Series C financing, 114–115
Service companies, growth potential, 432
7(a) Loan Guarantee Program, 146–147,
    151–152
Shareholder(s), 24, 27, 33–34, 400. *See also*
    Shareholder objectives
Shareholder objectives:
    achievement of, 27
    and preferences, 39–40
Shareholders' agreement, equity
    investments, 251
Shareholders' rights agreement, 118
Shelf registration, 260–261
Shell corporations, 154, 258–259
Shinn, Michael, 48
Short-form offering, 255
Short-form registration rights, 234–235, 248
Short sales, 247
Siemens Venture Capital GmbH (SVC),
    319–322
Silver, Martin, 304
Simerly, Roy L., 31
SJF Ventures, 322–325
Small Business Investment Company (SBIC),
    146
Source directory, firm list(s):
    with contact information, 355–365
    with location, 344–355
    with summary criteria, 366–376
Specified purpose acquisition company
    (SPAC), 154–155
Spin-offs, 400, 402
Split-offs, 400, 402
Split-ups, 402
Sponsorships, 50–51
Stakeholders, 31–32
Staley, Franklin, 309
Stand-alone businesses, 19
Standard & Poor's, 175–176, 217
Start-up capital, 107
Start-up companies, 12, 30, 46, 48, 52, 65,
    112, 139–140, 217, 279–280, 285,
    433–436
Statement of cash flow, 10, 414
Stock options, 90, 144
Stock purchase agreements:
    basic investment transaction, 239
    closing conditions, 243
    company operations, 242–243
    corporate organization, 241

    financial statement presentation, 241–242
    representations and warranties, 239–240
Stock splits, 401
Strategic investment, case study, 319–322
Strategic investor(s), source directory, 330, 343
Strategic planning, 12–13, 104, 279. *See
    also* Business strategy
Strategic positioning, 12
Subordinated debt, 124–125
Subordination agreement, 199–200
Sunk costs, 392
Supplier(s), financing from, 28, 49–53, 78
Sweat equity, 48
SWOT (strengths, weaknesses, opportunities,
    and threats) analysis, 10–12
Syndicated loans, 170, 184

Takeovers, 400
Taxation, 16, 40, 217, 273, 412–413,
    426–427
Teaming agreement, 52
Telecom industry, 39
Tenex Greenhouse, 67
Term debt, 28–29
Term equity, 29
Term loan, 83, 87–88, 171–172
Term sheet, *see* Equity investment term sheet
Thomas H. Lee Company, 130
Ticking fees, 169–170
Time horizon, 6
Time-weighted returns, 394–395
Total cost, 78, 81
Trade financing, case study, 302–304
Trade tranche, 84–85
Transactional equity, 85, 303

Uncertainty, 394, 406
Underlevered firms, 399–400
Undervalued businesses, 402
Underwriters/underwriting, 169, 173, 270
Uniform Commercial Code, 164, 196
U.S. Small Business Administration (SBA):
    bonding programs, 146
    CAPLines, 152–153
    Community Adjustment and Investment
        Program (CAIP), 151–152
    Defense Economic Transition Assistance
        (DETA) program, 151
    Export Working Capital Program
        (EWCP), 148–149

U.S. Small Business Administration (SBA)
(*Continued*)
  504 Loan Program, 147–148, 151–152
  functions of, 83, 145
  international trade loans, 150
  investment programs, 146
  loan prequalification, 148
  loan programs, generally, 145–146, 216
  Microloan Program, 148
  Pollution Control Loans, 152
  7(a) Loan Guarantee Program, 146–147,
    151–152
U.S. Treasuries, 175
Unsecured loans:
  bridge loans, 215
  characteristics of, 126, 165, 208–210,
    257
  convertible debt/convertible preferred
    stock, 214–215
  high yield debt, 209–211
  mezzanine financing, 211–214
  pricing of, 209

Valuation:
  angel financing process, 66
  approaches to, 16–18
  discounts, 19–20
  equity investments, 223–226
  increasing value, 20–21
  inventory, 408–409
  premiums, 19–20
  of private companies, influential factors, 20
  process, overview of, 18–19
  purpose of, 15–16
  raising capital and, 39
  unrealistic expectations, 15
  venture capital funding, 110–117
Van Ert, Eric, 318
Variable costs, 393
Venture banking, 84–85
Venture capital/venture capital funding:
  board management, 119–123
  business model, 110
  characteristics of, 52, 94–124
  community development, 144
  company performance monitoring, 118–119
  conversion rights and, 246
  corporate, 109, 135–137
  by development stage, 98
  exit strategies, 108

  by financing sequence, 98
  funding process, 103–105
  industry overview, 95–97
  key criteria for, 104–105
  partner interaction with portfolio
    companies, 117–118
  preparation for, 105–106
  by region, 101
  rejections, 106
  source directory, 330, 335–337
  trends in, 123–124
  valuation process, 110–117
  value-added investors, 100–102
Venture capitalists:
  angel investors distinguished from, 60–61
  crisis management, 102
  functions of, 56, 102
  initial public offerings (IPOs) and, 268
  management considerations, 119–123
  meetings with, 106–108
  most active list, 99–100
  referrals to, 68
  selection factors, 108–109
Venture Investment Management Company
    LLC (VIMAC), 67
Venture leasing, 90–91
Veronis Suhler Stevenson (VSS), 316–319
Vested for Growth (VfG), 326–328
Vesting, 237–238
Vision, importance of, 279, 286
Voting control, 43
Voting rights, 218, 230–231, 245–246
VSS Fund Management LLC, 317

Warehouse financing, 85–86, 303
Warner, Dave, 322
Warranties, 177–181, 239–241
Warrants, 90–91, 154–155, 212
Wealth maximization, 380
Weighted average, 408
Weighted average–based antidilution,
    231–232
Weighted average cost of capital (WACC),
    22–23, 398, 415
Wilson, Mark and Evelyn, 323–325
Women-owned business enterprises, 39
Working capital, 8, 28–29, 42, 50, 55–56,
    78, 125, 149, 392, 419, 430, 435

Zindera, Sabine, 322